AFRO-AMERICAN HISTORY: PRIMARY SOURCES

Edited by **THOMAS R. FRAZIER**

The Bernard M. Baruch College of The City University of New York

Under the General Editorship of

John Morton Blum

Yale University

Harcourt, Brace & World, Inc.

New York / Chicago / San Francisco / Atlanta

TO

WILLIS B. GLOVER

teacher and friend

LIBRARY OF CONGRESS CATALOG CARD NUMBER: 74-110339

PRINTED IN THE UNITED STATES OF AMERICA

AFRO-AMERICAN HISTORY: PRIMARY SOURCES

PREFACE

fro-American history has been studied and taught for many years in black colleges, and since the founding of the Association for the Study of Negro Life and History by Carter G. Woodson in 1915, it has been promoted by this organization. Only recently, however, have courses in black history been offered in predominantly white universities, and only recently has the general reading public become aware of this field. The systematic, though not always deliberate, denial of a significant past to the black American community has tended to distort the self-image of Americans, white and black. Much of the writing and teaching of American history, when it has considered the black man at all, has considered him as a slave up to 1863 and as a problem after that. Today, however, the position of Afro-American history as an important segment of American history is rapidly becoming established. More and more, it is recognized that our history is that of many Americas and not just one.

This book is intended to serve as an introduction to the history of Afro-Americans through the use of historical documents that originated in the black community. Although the number of documents that could be used was of course limited, a careful attempt has been made to represent the wide range of black life and thought that has contributed to the development of black America.

The material is arranged chronologically in fourteen sections, covering the entire range of American history, from the colonial period to the present. Each section has a brief historical introduction and contains from three to five documents. Each document, in turn, is introduced by a short note giving its specific historical context. The documents were selected on the basis of vividness and pertinence. They are presented in their entirety, or, if abridged, they are complete enough to enable the reader to grasp the range of thought and the frame of reference of their authors. Included are descriptions of black life, statements of black leaders, and position papers of black organizations.

Each section of the book concludes with an extensive annotated bibliography to guide readers in further study, and a general bibliography appears at the end of the book. In all bibliographies, titles available in paperback are marked with an asterisk.

We gratefully acknowledge the help of James M. McPherson of Princeton University, who read the manuscript and made many useful suggestions. The following libraries provided much appreciated assistance: the Harvard College Library, the Massachusetts Historical Society Library, the Boston Public Library, the Boston Athenæum Library, the New York Historical Society Library, the New York Public Library (including the Schomburg Collection), the Columbia University Library, the Union Theological Seminary Library, and the University of Michigan Library.

THOMAS R. FRAZIER

CONTENTS

2

THE AFRO-AMERICAN BEFORE 1800

3

SLAVERY IN THE NINETEENTH CENTURY

AFRO-AMERICAN HISTORY: PRIMARY SOURCES

1 AFRICA AND THE SLAVE TRADE

Although Moslem traders from north of the Sahara had carried on an extensive trade with the states of West Africa during the Middle Ages, Africa remained the "dark continent" to the light-skinned Christians of the North until the time of the discovery and exploitation of the Americas by the Europeans. Then, as the demand from the New World for cheap labor grew, the Europeans turned to Africa, and the West African coast from the Senegal River south to the mouth of the Congo began to swarm with ships intent on capitalizing on the trade in human beings.

Estimates of the number of Africans taken into slavery in the Americas run from fifteen million to fifty million, with the true figure probably close to the former. However, this figure does not include all the blacks uprooted from their homes. Millions died fighting in the wars to capture slaves, making the arduous trek to the coast where the slave ships waited, or undergoing the devastating passage across the Atlantic.

As the control of the Atlantic slave trade passed successively through the hands of the Portuguese, the Dutch, the French, and the English (including the American colonists), the typical European cared little and knew less about the land from which the blacks were being taken. Until recent years, with the exception of a few studies of the trade itself, Europeans gave no serious thought to the history of West Africa prior to and during the trade.

Most of coastal Africa—the area with which the slavers dealt—was organized into states rather than into tribes or simple societies. Between the tenth and sixteenth centuries, in the interior, centered around the bend of the Niger River, the empires of Ghana, Mali, and Songhai flourished. These interior kingdoms had no direct contact with the Atlantic slave trade. The states of the West African coast were so strong and well fortified that the European traders were not able to penetrate the interior in order to capture slaves; instead, they had to depend on the coastal kings for their booty. These African political leaders competed for the monopoly on slaves with the various European traders. The blacks who were sold into slavery usually came from the area just behind the coast, and most were either captured in wars waged for the trade or collected by the coastal rulers as tribute from weaker states.

There is much controversy today about the effect of the slave trade on the coastal states. It is unclear whether the states benefited from the trade in terms of the improved standard of living that resulted from the increased commerce or whether the buying and selling of millions of men only brought about moral degeneration, which eventually led to the decline and virtual disappearance of the coastal kingdoms. The same questions might be asked, of course, of the individual traders and the countries involved in the trade. What is clear is that competition between the African states, fostered by the use of guns as trade goods by the European slavers, led to ruinous wars that weakened the states to the point that they could be taken over during the period of European colonization in the late nineteenth century.

Two of the main reasons Africans were so successfully used as slaves had to do with their physical resistance to European diseases and the high level of commercial organization they had achieved in West Africa. The American Indian population that had been enslaved by the Spanish in the New World was dying out at a startling rate because of the diseases introduced by the Europeans. The same diseases seem to have existed widely enough in Africa to allow the Africans to develop a certain immunity to them. Thus they were able to endure the conditions of slavery in the New World.

The African states' previous experience in commerce enabled them to adapt easily to dealing in human beings—the commodity then in demand—instead of in gold or salt. And the old trade routes into the interior began to yield the new trade item. Indeed, a high degree of commercial organization was needed to supply up to 100,000 men a year for the trade.

By the seventeenth century, most of the slave trade was carried on in standard commercial patterns. A ship would arrive off the coast of a trading station; depending on the particular arrangement, African businessmen would come aboard the ship to bargain or the ship's captain would go ashore. Customarily, there would be some haggling over the terms of the trade. European money had no value in Africa, so the blacks were usually bought with rolls of tobacco, rum, guns, or bars of useful metal, such as iron, copper, and brass. From time to time, cowrie shells, widely used in Africa as a medium of exchange, were introduced. After the deal was made, it was necessary to examine the goods. Only the best physical specimens were acceptable. Those who proved fit were branded with the mark of the trader, lest a substitution be made between the examination and the sailing.

When the time came to sail, the slaves were chained together and loaded into the ships. At this point there were many violent struggles. Sometimes the blacks would capture the ship; sometimes they would break away and dive overboard, preferring to face drowning rather than go as slaves to an unknown fate. The traders considered loading the ship the most dangerous part of the transaction.

Once under way, the traders would relax somewhat and begin the infamous "middle passage," so called because it was the second leg of the triangular pattern characteristic of the Atlantic trade during this period—from Europe or New England to Africa, from Africa to the West Indies, from the West Indies to Europe or New England. Once the ship was at sea, speed was of the essence. The shorter the voyage, the fewer the slaves who would die on board. It has been estimated that one of every eight slaves died during this part of the trade. The quickest time between Africa and the New World was three weeks, but when winds were contrary or there was no wind at all, the voyage sometimes lasted over three months.

If weather permitted, the captives were kept on deck during the day and forced to exercise and eat. But when the weather was bad, they were kept chained for most of the voyage in incredibly cramped and poorly ventilated quarters below.

Upon arriving at its destination, the ship would disgorge its contents at a local slave mart, where the entire lot would be bid for on the basis of an average price. The purchaser was usually a slave dealer, who would either resell the slaves on the spot to individuals who had been unable to participate in the initial bidding or transport the slaves elsewhere for resale.

The slave trade was so extensive that by 1850 one-third of the people in the world with African ancestry lived outside Africa, most of them in the Americas. This forced migration, one of the largest movements of people in the history of the world, had an incalculable effect on both Africa and the New World.

TAKEN FROM THE GUINEA COAST AS A CHILD

Venture Smith / A Narrative of the Life and Adventures of Venture

When this narrative was composed, Venture Smith was an old man, living in East Haddam, Connecticut. He had taken his surname from Colonel Oliver Smith, his last owner, who had permitted him to work evenings in order to buy his freedom. After freeing himself, he had bought his wife and children from their master and settled in Connecticut.

The events Smith describes here took place in Africa, the home that he left at the age of six. Though he surely did not have total recall of his life in Africa, his general description is probably quite accurate. Perhaps the most important aspect of this narrative is its depiction of the warfare between the states of the coast and those of the interior, where Smith was born. This commercial warfare, waged for the slave trade, brought about great changes in the political life of Africa.

I was born at Dukandarra, in Guinea, about the year 1729. My father's name was Saungm Furro, Prince of the tribe of Dukandarra. My father had three wives. Polygamy was not uncommon in that country, especially among the rich, as every man was allowed to keep as many wives as he could maintain. By his first wife he had three children. The eldest of them was myself, named by my father, Broteer. The other two were named Cundazo and Soozaduka. My father had two children by his second wife, and one by his third. I descended from a very large, tall and stout race of beings, much larger than the generality of people in other parts of the globe, being commonly considerable above six feet in height, and every way well proportioned.

The first thing worthy of notice which I remember was, a contention between my father and mother, on account of my father marrying his third wife without the consent of his first and eldest, which was contrary to the custom generally observed among my countrymen. In consequence of this rupture, my mother left her husband and country, and travelled away with her three children to the eastward. I was then five years old. She took not the least sustenance along with her, to support either herself or children. I was able to travel along by her side; the other two of her offspring she carried one on her back, and the other being a sucking child, in her arms. When we became hungry, our mother used to set us down on the ground,

FROM Venture Smith, *A Narrative of the Life and Adventures of Venture, A Native of Africa but Resident about Sixty Years in the United States of America* (New London, 1798). Reprinted A.D. 1835 and published by a descendant of Venture, pp. 3–9.

and gather some of the fruits which grew spontaneously in that climate. These served us for food on the way. At night we all lay down together in the most secure place we could find, and reposed ourselves until morning. Though there were many noxious animals there; yet so kind was our Almighty protector, that none of them were ever permitted to hurt or molest us. Thus we went on our journey until the second day after our departure from Dukandarra, when we came to the entrance of a great desert. During our travel in that we were often affrighted with the doleful howlings and yellings of wolves, lions, and other animals. After five days travel we came to the end of this desert, and immediately entered into a beautiful and extensive interval country. Here my mother was pleased to stop and seek a refuge for me. She left me at the house of a very rich farmer. I was then, as I should judge, not less than one hundred and forty miles from my native place, separated from all my relations and acquaintance. At this place my mother took her farewell of me, and set out for my own country. My new guardian, as I shall call the man with whom I was left, put me into the business of tending sheep, immediately after I was left with him. The flock which I kept with the assistance of a boy, consisted of about forty. We drove them every morning between two and three miles to pasture, into the wide and delightful plains. When night drew on, we drove them home and secured them in the cote. In this round I continued during my stay here. One incident which befel me when I was driving my flock from pasture, was so dreadful to me in that age, and is to this time so fresh in my memory, that I cannot help noticing it in this place. Two large dogs sallied out of a certain house and set upon me. One of them took me by the arm, and the other by the thigh, and before their master could come and relieve me, they lacerated my flesh to such a degree, that the scars are very visible to the present day. My master was immediately sent for. He came and carried me home, as I was unable to go myself on account of my wounds. Nothing remarkable happened afterwards until my father sent for me to return home.

Before I dismiss this country, I must just inform my reader what I remember concerning this place. A large river runs through this country in a westerly course. The land for a great way on each side is flat and level, hedged in by a considerable rise in the country at a great distance from it. It scarce ever rains there, yet the land is fertile; great dews fall in the night which refresh the soil. About the latter end of June or first of July, the river begins to rise, and gradually increases until it has inundated the country for a great distance, to the height of seven or eight feet. This brings on a slime which enriches the land surprisingly. When the river has subsided, the natives begin to sow and plant, and the vegetation is exceeding rapid. Near this rich river my guardian's land lay. He possessed, I cannot exactly tell how much, yet this I am certain of respecting it, that he owned an immense tract. He possessed likewise a great many cattle and goats. During my stay with him I was kindly used, and with as much tenderness, for what I saw, as his only son, although I was an entire stranger to him, remote from friends and relations. The principal occupations of the inhabitants there, were the cultivation of the soil and the care of their flocks. They were a people pretty similar in every respect to that of mine, except in their persons, which were not so tall and stout. They appeared to be very kind and friendly. I will now return to my departure from that place.

My father sent a man and horse after me. After settling with my guardian for keeping me, he took me away and went for home. It was then about one year since my mother brought me here. Nothing remarkable occurred to us on our journey until we arrived safe home.

I found then that the difference between my parents had been made up previous to their sending for me. On my return, I was received both by my father and mother with great joy and affection, and was once more restored to my paternal dwelling in peace and happiness. I was then about six years old.

Not more than six weeks had passed after my return, before a message was brought by an inhabitant of the place where I lived the preceding year to my father, that the place had been invaded by a numerous army, from a nation not far distant, furnished with musical instruments, and all kinds of arms then in use; that they were instigated by some white nation who equipped and sent them to subdue and possess the country; that his nation had made no preparation for war, having been for a long time in profound peace; that they could not defend themselves against such a formidable train of invaders, and must therefore necessarily evacuate their lands to the fierce enemy, and fly to the protection of some chief; and that if he would permit them they would come under his rule and protection when they had to retreat from their own possessions. He was a kind and merciful prince, and therefore consented to these proposals.

He had scarcely returned to his nation with the message, before the whole of his people were obliged to retreat from their country, and come to my father's dominions.

He gave them every privilege and all the protection his government could afford. But they had not been there longer than four days before news came to them that the invaders had laid waste their country, and were coming speedily to destroy them in my father's territories. This affrighted them, and therefore they immediately pushed off to the southward, into the unknown countries there, and were never more heard of.

Two days after their retreat, the report turned out to be but too true. A detachment from the enemy came to my father and informed him, that the whole army was encamped not far out of his dominions, and would invade the territory and deprive his people of their liberties and rights, if he did not comply with the following terms. These were to pay them a large sum of money, three hundred fat cattle, and a great number of goats, sheep, asses, &c.

My father told the messenger he would comply rather than that his subjects should be deprived of their rights and privileges, which he was not then in circumstances to defend from so sudden an invasion. Upon turning out those articles, the enemy pledged their faith and honor that they would not attack him. On these he relied and therefore thought it unnecessary to be on his guard against the enemy. But their pledges of faith and honor proved no better than those of other unprincipled hostile nations; for a few days after a certain relation of the king came and informed him, that the enemy who sent terms of accommodation to him and received tribute to their satisfaction, yet meditated an attack upon his subjects by surprise, and that probably they would commence their attack in less than one day, and concluded with advising him, as he was not prepared for war, to order a speedy retreat of his family and subjects. He complied with this advice.

The same night which was fixed upon to retreat, my father and his family set off about the break of day. The king and his two younger wives went in one company, and my mother and her children in another. We left our dwellings in succession, and my father's company went on first. We directed our course for a large shrub plain, some distance off, where we intended to conceal ourselves from the approaching enemy, until we could refresh ourselves a little. But we presently found that our retreat was not secure. For having struck up a little fire for the purpose of cooking victuals, the enemy who happened to be encamped a little distance off, had sent out a scouting party who discovered us by the smoke of the fire, just as we were extinguishing it, and about to eat. As soon as we had finished eating, my father discovered the party, and immediately began to discharge arrows at them. This was what I first saw, and it alarmed both me and the women, who being unable to make any resistance, immediately betook ourselves to the tall thick reeds not far off, and left the old king to fight alone. For some time I beheld him from the reeds defending himself with great courage and firmness, till at last he was obliged to surrender himself into their hands.

They then came to us in the reeds, and the very first salute I had from them was a violent blow on the back part of the head with the fore part of a gun, and at the same time a grasp round the neck. I then had a rope put about my neck, as had all the women in the thicket with me, and was immediately led to my father, who was likewise pinioned and haltered for leading. In this condition we were all led to the camp. The women and myself being pretty submissive, had tolerable treatment from the enemy, while my father was closely interrogated respecting his money which they knew he must have. But as he gave them no account of it, he was instantly cut and pounded on his body with great inhumanity, that he might be induced by the torture he suffered to make the discovery. All this availed not in the least to make him give up his money, but he despised all the tortures which they inflicted, until the continued exercise and increase of torment, obliged him to sink and expire. He thus died without informing his enemies where his money lay. I saw him while he was thus tortured to death. The shocking scene is to this day fresh in my mind, and I have often been overcome while thinking on it. He was a man of remarkable stature. I should judge as much as six feet and six or seven inches high, two feet across his shoulders, and every way well proportioned. He was a man of remarkable strength and resolution, affable, kind and gentle, ruling with equity and moderation.

The army of the enemy was large, I should suppose consisting of about six thousand men. Their leader was called Baukurre. After destroying the old prince, they decamped and immediately marched towards the sea, lying to the west, taking with them myself and the women prisoners. In the march a scouting party was detached from the main army. To the leader of this party I was made waiter, having to carry his gun, &c. As we were a-scouting we came across a herd of fat cattle, consisting of about thirty in number. These we set upon, and immediately wrested from their keepers, and afterwards converted them into food for the army. The enemy had remarkable success in destroying the country wherever they went. For as far as they had penetrated, they laid the habitations waste and captured the people. The distance they had now brought me was about four hundred miles. All the march I had very hard tasks imposed on me, which I must perform on pain of punishment. I was obliged to carry on my head a large flat stone used for grinding our corn, weighing as I should suppose, as much as twenty-five pounds; besides victuals, mat and cooking utensils. Though I was pretty large and stout of my age, yet these burdens were very grievous to me, being only six years and a half old.

We were then come to a place called Malagasco. When we entered the place we could not see the least appearance of either houses or inhabitants, but upon stricter search found, that instead of houses above ground they had dens in the sides of hillocks, contiguous to ponds and streams of water. In these we perceived they had all hid themselves, as I suppose they usually did on such occasions. In order to compel them to surrender, the enemy contrived to smoke them out with faggots. These they put to the entrance of the caves and set them on fire. While they were engaged in this business, to their great surprise some of them were desperately wounded with arrows which fell from above on them. This mystery they soon found out. They perceived that the enemy discharged these arrows through holes on the top of the dens directly into the air. Their weight brought them back, point downwards on their enemies heads, whilst they were smoking the inhabitants out. The points of their arrows were poisoned, but their enemy had an antidote for it, which they instantly applied to the wounded part. The smoke at last obliged the people to give themselves up. They came out of their caves, first spatting the palms of their hands together, and immediately after extended their arms, crossed at their wrists, ready to be bound and pinioned. I should judge that the dens above mentioned were extended about eight feet horizontally into the earth, six feet in height and as many wide. They were arched over head and lined with earth, which was of the clay kind, and made the surface of their walls firm and smooth.

The invaders then pinioned the prisoners of all ages and sexes indiscriminately, took their flocks and all their effects, and moved on their way towards the sea. On the march the prisoners were treated with clemency, on account of their being submissive and humble. Having come to the next tribe, the enemy laid siege and immediately took men, women, children, flocks, and all their valuable effects. They then went on to the next district which was contiguous to the sea, called in Africa, Anamaboo. The enemies' provisions were then almost spent, as well as their strength. The inhabitants knowing what conduct they had pursued, and what were their present intentions, improved the favorable opportunity, attacked them, and took enemy, prisoners, flocks and all their effects. I was then taken a second time. All of us were then put into the castle, and kept for market. On a certain time I and other prisoners were put on board a canoe, under our master, and rowed away to a vessel belonging to Rhode Island, commanded by Captain Collingwood, and the mate Thomas Mumford. While we were going to the vessel, our master told us all to appear to the best possible advantage for sale. I was bought on board by one Robertson Mumford, steward of said vessel, for four gallons of rum, and a piece of calico, and called VENTURE, on account of his having purchased me with his own private venture. Thus I came by my name. All the slaves that were bought for that vessel's cargo, were two hundred and sixty.

AN AFRICAN PRINCE SOLD INTO SLAVERY BY A RIVAL KING

Ukawsaw Gronniosaw / A Narrative of the Most Remarkable Particulars in the Life of James Albert Ukawsaw Gronniosaw

The highly emotional and introspective autobiography was one of the most popular forms of literature during the Great Awakening in the eighteenth century. Several of these were composed by Africans, both slave and free. The passage that follows is a portion of one of these spiritual outpourings—a narration by a former slave, Ukawsaw Gronniosaw, who was given his freedom when his master died. After serving as a sailor in the French and Indian War, Gronniosaw left New York, where he had settled when he gained his freedom, and went to England. There he and his family fell into bad times, and one purpose of the narrative he composed was to raise money to help him out of debt.

Gronniosaw was sold into slavery when he was about fifteen, so his memory of African life may be more trustworthy than that of Venture Smith. At any rate, his narrative is very colorful and gives one a strong feeling of the intrigue and the culture shock produced in West Africa by the slave trade. Of particular interest is Gronniosaw's description of spiritual insights, the memory of which was undoubtedly enhanced by his later conversion to Christianity.

I was born in the city of *Bournou;* my mother was the eldest daughter of the reigning King there. I was the youngest of six children, and particularly loved by my mother, and my grandfather almost doted on me.

I had, from my infancy, a curious turn of mind; was more grave and reserved, in my disposition, than either of my brothers and sisters, I often teazed them with questions they could not answer; for which reason they disliked me, as they supposed that I was either foolish or insane. 'Twas certain that I was, at times, very unhappy in myself: It being strongly impressed on my mind that there was some GREAT MAN of power, which resided above the sun, moon and stars, the objects of our worship.—My dear indulgent mother would bear more with me than any of my friends beside.—I often raised my hands to heaven, and asked her who lived there? Was much dissatisfied when she told me the sun, moon and stars, being persuaded, in my own mind, that there must be some SUPERIOR POWER.—I was frequently lost in wonder at the works of the creation: Was afraid, and uneasy, and restless, but could not tell for what. I wanted to be informed of things that no person could tell me; and was always dissatisfied.—These wonderful impressions began in my childhood, and followed me continually till I left my parents, which affords me matter of admiration and thankfulness.

To this moment I grew more and more uneasy every day, insomuch that one Saturday (which is the day on which we keep our sabbath) I labored under anxieties and fears that cannot be expressed; and, what is more extraordinary, I could not give a reason for it.—I rose, as our custom is, about three o'clock (as we are obliged to be at our place of worship an hour before the sunrise:) we say nothing in our worship, but continue on our knees with our hands held up, observing a strict silence till the sun is at a certain height, which I suppose to be about 10 or 11 o'clock in *England:* When, at a certain sign made by the Priest, we get up (our duty being over) and disperse to our different houses.—Our place of meeting is under a large palm tree; we divide ourselves into many congregations; as it is impossible for the same tree to cover the inhabitants of the whole city, though they are extremely large, high and majestic; the beauty and usefulness of

FROM Ukawsaw Gronniosaw, *A Narrative of the Most Remarkable Particulars in the Life of James Albert Ukawsaw Gronniosaw, An African Prince* (Bath, 1780?), pp. 7–17.

them are not to be described; they supply the inhabitants of the country with meat, drink, and clothes;[1] the body of the palm tree is very large; at a certain season of the year they tap it, and bring vessels to receive the wine, of which they draw great quantities, the quality of which is very delicious: The leaves of this tree are of a silky nature; they are large and soft: when they are dried and pulled to pieces, it has much the same appearance as the English flax, and the inhabitants of *Bournou* manufacture it for clothing, &c. This tree likewise produces a plant, or substance, which has the appearance of a cabbage, and very like it, in taste almost the same: it grows between the branches. Also the palm tree produces a nut, something like a cocoa, which contains a kernel, in which is a large quantity of milk, very pleasant to the taste: The shell is of a hard substance, and of a very beautiful appearance, and serves for basons, bowls, &c.

I hope this digression will be forgiven.—I was going to observe, that after the duty of our sabbath was over (on the day in which I was more distressed and afflicted than ever) we were all on our way home as usual, when a remarkable black cloud arose and covered the sun; then followed very heavy rain and thunder, more dreadful than ever I had heard: The heavens roared, and the earth trembled at it: I was highly affected and cast down; insomuch that I wept sadly, and could not follow my relations & friends home.—I was obliged to stop, and felt as if my legs were tied, they seemed to shake under me: So I stood still, being in great fear of the MAN OF POWER, that I was persuaded, in myself, lived above. One of my young companions (who entertained a particular friendship for me, and I for him) came back to see for me: He asked me why I stood still in such very hard rain? I only said to him that my legs were weak, and I could not come faster: He was much affected to see me cry, and took me by the hand, and said he would lead me home, which he did. My mother was greatly alarmed at my tarrying out in such terrible weather; she asked me many questions, such as what I did so for? And if I was well? My dear mother, says I, pray tell me who is the GREAT MAN OF POWER that makes the thunder? She said, there was no power but the sun, moon, and stars; that they made all our country.—I then inquired how all our people came? She answered me, from one another; and so carried me to many generations back.—Then says I, who made the *first man*? And who made the first cow, and the first lion, and where does the fly come from, as no one can make him? My mother seemed in great trouble; she was apprehensive that my senses were impaired, or that I was foolish. My father came in, and seeing her in grief asked the cause, but when she related our conversation to him he was exceedingly angry with me, and told me he would punish me severely if ever I was so troublesome again; so that I resolved never to say any thing more to him. But I grew very unhappy in

---

[1] It is a general received opinion, in *England*, that the natives of *Africa* go entirely unclothed; but this supposition is very unjust: They have a kind of dress so as to appear decent, though it is very slight and thin.

myself; my relations and acquaintance endeavoured, by all the means they could think on, to divert me, by taking me to ride on goats (which is much the custom of our country) and to shoot with a bow and arrow; but I experienced no satisfaction at all in any of these things; nor could I be easy by any means whatever: My parents were very unhappy to see me so dejected and melancholy.

About this time there came a merchant from the *Gold Coast* (the third city in GUINEA) he traded with the inhabitants of our country in ivory, &c. he took great notice of my unhappy situation, and inquired into the cause; he expressed vast concern for me, and said, if my parents would part with me for a little while, and let him take me home with him, it would be of more service to me than any thing they could do for me.—He told me that if I would go with him, I should see houses with wings to them walk upon the water, and should also see the white folks; and that he had many sons of my age, which should be my companions; and he added to all this that he would bring me safe back again soon.—I was highly pleased with the account of this strange place, and was very desirous of going.—I seemed sensible of a secret impulse upon my mind, which I could not resist, that seemed to tell me I must go. When my dear mother saw that I was willing to leave them, she spoke to my father and grandfather and the rest of my relations, who all agreed that I should accompany the merchant to the Gold Coast. I was the more willing as my brothers and sisters despised me, and looked on me with contempt on the account of my unhappy disposition; and even my servants slighted me, and disregarded all I said to them. I had one sister who was always exceeding fond of me, and I loved her entirely; her name was LOGWY, she was quite white, and fair, with fine light hair, though my father and mother were black.—I was truly concerned to leave my beloved sister, and she cry'd most sadly to part with me, wringing her hands, and discovered every sign of grief that can be imagined. Indeed if I could have known when I left my friends and country, that I should never return to them again my misery on that occasion would have been inexpressible. All my relations were sorry to part with me; my dear mother came with me upon a camel more than three hundred miles, the first of our journey lay chiefly through woods: At night we secured ourselves from the wild beasts by making fires all around us; we and our camels kept within the circle, or we must have been torn to pieces by the lions, and other wild creatures, that roared terribly as soon as night came on, and continued to do so till morning.—There can be little said in favor of the country through which we passed; only a valley of marble that we came through, which is unspeakably beautiful.—On each side of this valley are exceedingly high and almost inaccessible mountains.— Some of these pieces of marble are of a prodigious length and breadth but of different sizes and colour, and shaped in a variety of forms, in a wonderful manner.—It is most of it veined with gold mixed with striking and beautiful colours; so that when the sun darts upon it, it is as pleasing a sight as can be imagined. The merchant that brought me from BOURNOU was in partnership with another gentleman who accompanied us; he was very unwilling that he should take me from home, as, he said, he foresaw many difficulties that would attend my going with them.—He endeavoured to prevail on the merchant to throw me into a very deep pit that was in the valley, but he refused to listen to him, and said, he was resolved to take care of me: But the other was greatly dissatisfied; and when we came to a river, which we were obliged to pass through, he purposed throwing me in and drowning me; but the merchant would not consent to it, so that I was preserved.

We travel'd till about four o'clock every day, and then began to make preparations for night, by cutting down large quantities of wood, to make fires to preserve us from the wild beasts.—I had a very unhappy and discontented journey, being in continual fear that the people I was with would murder me. I often reflected with extreme regret on the kind friends I had left, and the idea of my dear mother frequently drew tears from my eyes. I cannot recollect how long we were in going from *Bournou* to the *Gold Coast;* but as there is no shipping nearer to *Bournou* than that city, it was tedious in travelling so far by land, being upwards of a thousand miles.—I was heartily rejoiced when we arrived at the end of our journey: I now vainly imagined that all my troubles and inquietudes would terminate here; but could I have looked into futurity, I should have perceived that I had much more to suffer than I had before experienced, and that they had as yet but barely commenced.

I was now more than a thousand miles from home, without a friend or means to procure one. Soon after I came to the merchant's house I heard the drums beat remarkably loud, and the trumpets blow—the persons accustom'd to this employ, are oblig'd to go upon a very high structure appointed for that purpose, that the sound might be heard at a great distance: They are higher than the steeples are in *England*. I was mightily pleased with sounds so entirely new to me, and was very inquisitive to know the cause of this rejoicing, and asked many questions concerning it; I was answered that it was meant as a compliment to me, because I was grandson to the King of *Bournou*.

This account gave me a secret pleasure; but I was not suffered long to enjoy this satisfaction, for, in the evening of the same day, two of the merchant's sons (boys about my own age) came running to me, and told me, that the next day I was to die, for the King intended to behead me.—I reply'd that I was sure it could not be true, for that I came there to play with them, and to see houses walk upon the water with wings to them, and the white folks; but I was soon informed that their King imagined I was sent by my father as a spy, and would make such discoveries, at my return home, that would enable them to make war with greater advantage to ourselves; and for these reasons he had resolved I should never return to my native country.— When I heard this, I suffered misery that cannot be described.—I wished, a thousand times, that I had never left my friends and country.—But still the Almighty was pleased to work miracles for me.

The morning I was to die, I was washed and all my gold ornaments made bright and shining, and then carried to the palace, where the King was to behead me himself (as is the custom of the place).—He was seated upon a throne at the top of an exceeding large yard, or court, which you must go through to enter the palace, it is as wide and spacious as a large field in *England*. I had a lane of life-guards to go through,—I guessed it to be about three hundred paces.

I was conducted by my friend, the merchant, about half way up; then he durst proceed no farther: I went up to the king alone—I went with an undaunted courage, and it pleased God to melt the heart of the King, who sat with his scymitar in his hand ready to behead me; yet, being himself so affected, he dropped it out of his hand, and took me upon his knee and wept over me. I put my right hand round his neck, and prest him to my heart. He set me down and blest me; and added, that he would not kill me, and that I should not go home, but be sold for a slave, so then I was conducted back again to the merchant's house.

The next day he took me on board a French brig; the captain did not choose to buy me: He said I was too small; so the merchant took me home with him again.

The partner, whom I have spoken of as my enemy, was very angry to see me return, and again purposed putting an end to my life; for he represented to the other, that I should bring them into troubles and difficulties, and that I was so little that no person would buy me.

The merchant's resolution began to waver, and I was indeed afraid that I should be put to death: but however he said he would try me once more.

A few days after a *Dutch* ship came into the harbour, and they carried me on board, in hopes that the captain would purchase me.—As they went, I heard them agree, that, if they could not sell me *then*, they would throw me overboard.—I was in extreme agonies when I heard this; and as soon as ever I saw the *Dutch* Captain, I ran to him, and put my arms round him, and said, "Father save me;" (for I knew that if he did not buy me, I should be treated very ill, or, possibly murdered.) And though he did not understand my language, yet it pleased the Almighty to influence him in my behalf, and he bought me *for two yards of check*, which is of more value *there*, than in England.

When I left my dear mother I had a large quantity of gold about me, as is the custom of our country, it was made into rings, and they were linked into one another, and formed into a kind of chain, and so put round my neck, and arms and legs, and a large piece hanging at one ear almost in the shape of a pear. I found all this troublesome, and was glad when my new master took it from me.—I was now washed & clothed in the *Dutch* or *English* manner.—My master grew very fond of me, and I loved him exceedingly. I watched every look, was always ready when he wanted me, and endeavoured to convince him, by every action, that my only pleasure was to serve him well.—I have since thought that he must have been a serious man. His actions corresponded very well with such a character.—He used to read prayers in public to the ship's crew every sabbath day; and when first I saw him read, I was never so surprised in my whole life as when I saw the book talk to my master; for I thought it did, as I observed him to look upon it, and move his lips.—I wished it would do so to me.—As soon as my master had done reading I follow'd him to the place where he put the book, being mightily delighted with it, and when nobody saw me, I open'd it and put my ear down close upon it, in great hope that it would say something to me; but was very sorry and greatly disappointed when I found it would not speak, this thought immediately presented itself to me, that every body and every thing despised me because I was black.

THE HORRORS OF THE MIDDLE PASSAGE

Olaudah Equiano   /   The Interesting Narrative of the Life of
Olaudah Equiano

Olaudah Equiano, the author of this selection, was from the Ibo country around Benin in what is now Nigeria. He was sold into slavery in 1756 to the British, who brought him to the New World. In 1766, he bought his freedom and went to England, where he worked as a barber and as a personal servant. He became actively involved in the anti-slavery movement in England and was interested in colonizing freed blacks in Sierra Leone. His autobiography, written in 1789, is one of the most informative of all such narratives by former slaves.

The portion of Equiano's narrative included here describes his experience of the "middle passage" from Africa to the West Indies. He recalled it as a horrifying example of man's inhumanity to his brothers. Included is a reference to the widespread fear among the captured Africans that they were to be eaten by the white men.

The first object which saluted my eyes when I arrived on the coast was the sea, and a slave ship, which was then riding at anchor, and waiting for its cargo. These filled me with astonishment, which was soon converted into

FROM Olaudah Equiano, *The Interesting Narrative of the Life of Olaudah Equiano or Gustavus Vasa, The African*, Vol. I (New York, 1791), pp. 49–62.

terror, when I was carried on board I was immediately handled, and tossed up, to see if I were sound, by some of the crew; and I was now persuaded that I had got into a world of bad spirits, and that they were going to kill me. Their complexions too differing so much from ours, their long hair, and the language they spoke (which was very different from any I had ever heard) united to confirm me in this belief. Indeed such were the horrors of my views and fears at the moment, that, if ten thousand worlds had been my own, I would have freely parted with them all to have exchanged my condition with that of the meanest slave in my own country. When I looked round the ship too and saw a large furnace or copper boiling, and a multitude of black people of every description chained together, every one of their countenances expressing dejection and sorrow, I no longer doubted of my fate; and, quite overpowered with horror and anguish, I fell motionless on the deck and fainted. When I recovered a little I found some black people about me, who I believed were some of those who had brought me on board, and had been receiving their pay; they talked to me in order to cheer me, but all in vain. I asked them if we were not to be eaten by those white men with horrible looks, red faces, and long hair. They told me I was not; and one of the crew brought me a small portion of spirituous liquor in a wine-glass; but being afraid of him, I would not take it out of his hand. One of the blacks therefore took it from him and gave it to me, and I took a little down my palate, which, instead of reviving me, as they thought it would, threw me into the greatest consternation at the strange feeling it produced, having never tasted any such liquor before. Soon after this the blacks who brought me on board went off, and left me abandoned to despair. I now saw myself deprived of all chance of returning to my native country, or even the least glimpse of hope of gaining the shore, which I now considered as friendly; and I even wished for my former slavery in preference to my present situation, which was filled with horrors of every kind, still heightened by my ignorance of what I was to undergo. I was not long suffered to indulge my grief; I was soon put down under the decks, and there I received such a salutation in my nostrils as I had never experienced in my life: so that with the loathsomeness of the stench, and crying together, I became so sick and low that I was not able to eat, nor had I the least desire to taste any thing. I now wished for the last friend, death, to relieve me; but soon, to my grief, two of the white men offered me eatables; and, on my refusing to eat, one of them held me fast by the hands, and laid me across, I think the windlass, and tied my feet, while the other flogged me severely. I had never experienced any thing of this kind before: and, although not being used to the water, I naturally feared that element the first time I saw it, yet, nevertheless, could I have got over the nettings, I would have jumped over the side, but I could not; and, besides, the crew used to watch us very closely who were not chained down to the decks, lest we should leap into the water: and I have seen some of these poor African prisoners most severely cut for attempting to do so, and hourly whipped for not eating. This indeed was often the case with myself. In a little time after, amongst the poor chained men, I found some of my own nation, which in a small degree gave ease to my mind. I inquired of these what was to be done with us? they gave me to understand we were to be carried to these white people's country to work for them. I then was a little revived, and thought, if it were no worse than working, my situation was not so desperate: but still I feared I should be put to death, the white people looked and acted, as I thought, in so savage a manner; for I had never seen among any people such instances of brutal cruelty; and this not only shown towards us blacks, but also to some of the whites themselves. One white man in particular I saw, when we were permitted to be on deck, flogged so unmercifully with a large rope near the foremast, that he died in consequence of it; and they tossed him over the side as they would have done a brute. This made me fear these people the more; and I expected nothing less than to be treated in the same manner. I could not help expressing my fears and apprehensions to some of my countrymen: I asked them if these people had no country, but lived in this hollow place (the ship)? they told me they did not, but came from a distant one, "Then," said I, "how comes it in all our country we never heard of them!" They told me, because they lived so very far off. I then asked where were their women? had they any like themselves? I was told they had: "And why," said I, "do we not see them?" they answered, because they were left behind. I asked how the vessel could go? they told me they could not tell; but that there were cloth put upon the masts by the help of the ropes I saw, and then the vessel went on; and the white men had some spell or magic they put in the water when they liked in order to stop the vessel, I was exceedingly amazed at this account, and really thought they were spirits. I therefore wished much to be from amongst them, for I expected they would sacrifice me: but my wishes were vain; for we were so quartered that it was impossible for any of us to make our escape. While we stayed on the coast I was mostly on deck; and one day, to my great astonishment, I saw one of these vessels coming in with the sails up. As soon as the whites saw it, they gave a great shout, at which we were amazed: and the more so as the vessel appeared larger by approaching nearer. At last she came to an anchor in my sight, and when the anchor was let go I and my countrymen who saw it were lost in astonishment to observe the vesssel stop; and were now convinced it was done by magic. Soon after this the other ship got her boats out, and they came on board of us, and the people of both ships seemed very glad to see each other. Several of the strangers also shook hands with us black people, and made motions with their hands, signifying I suppose, we were to go to their country; but we did not understand them. At last, when the ship we were in, had got in all her cargo, they made ready with many fearful noises, and we were all put under deck, so that we could not see how they managed the vessel. But this disappointment was the least of my sorrow. The stench of the hold while we were on the coast was so intolerably loathsome, that it was dangerous to remain there for any time, and some of us had been permitted to stay on the deck for the fresh air; but now that the whole ship's cargo were confined together, it became absolutely pestilential. The closeness of the place, and the heat of the climate, added to the number in the ship, which was so crowded that each had scarcely room to turn himself, almost suffocated us. This produced copious perspirations, so that the air soon became unfit for respiration, from a variety of loathsome smells, and brought on a sickness amongst the slaves, of which many died, thus falling victims to the improvident avarice, as I may call it, of their purchasers. This wretched situation was again aggravated by the galling of the chains, now become insupportable; and the filth of the necessary tubs, into which the children often fell, and were almost suffocated. The shrieks of the women, and the groans of the dying, rendered the whole a scene of horror almost inconceivable. Happily perhaps for myself I was soon reduced so low here that it was thought necessary to keep me almost always on deck; and from my extreme youth I was not put in fetters. In this situation I expected every hour to share the fate of my companions, some of whom were almost daily brought upon deck at the point of death, which I began to hope would soon put an end to my miseries. Often did I think many of the inhabitants of the deep much more happy than myself, I envied them the freedom they enjoyed, and as often wished I could change my condition for theirs. Every circumstance I met with served only to render my state more painful, and heightened my apprehensions and my opinion of the cruelty of the whites. One day they had taken a number of fishes; and when they had killed and satisfied themselves with as many as they thought fit, to our astonishment who were on the deck, rather than give any of them to us to eat, as we expected, they tossed the remaining fish into the sea again, although we begged and prayed for some as well as we could, but in vain; and some of my countrymen, being pressed by hunger, took an opportunity, when they thought no one saw them, of trying to get a little privately; but they were discovered, and the attempt procured them some very severe floggings. One day, when we had a smooth sea and moderate wind, two of my wearied countrymen who were chained together (I was near them at the time), preferring death to such a life of misery, somehow made through the nettings and jumped into the sea: immediately another quite dejected fellow, who on account of his illness, was suffered to be out of irons, also followed their example; and I believe many more would very soon have done the same if they had not been prevented by the ship's crew who were instantly alarmed. Those of us that were the most active were in a moment put down under the deck, and there was such a noise and confusion amongst the people of the ship as I never heard before, to stop her, and get the boat out to go after the slaves. However two of the wretches were drowned, but they got the other, and afterwards flogged him unmercifully for thus attempting to prefer death to slavery. In this manner we continued to undergo more hardships than I can now relate, hardships which are inseparable from this accursed trade. Many a time we were near suffocation from the want of fresh air, which we were often without for whole days together. This, and the stench of the necessary tubs, carried off many. During our passage I first saw flying fishes, which surprised me very much: they used frequently to fly across the ship, and many of them fell on the deck. I also now first saw the use of the quadrant; I had often with astonishment seen the mariners make observations with it, and I could not think what it meant. They at last took notice of my surprise: and one of them, willing to increase it, as well as to gratify my curiosity, made me one day look through it. The clouds appeared to me to be land, which disappeared as they passed along. This heightened my wonder; and I was now more persuaded than ever that I was in another world, and that every thing about me was magic. At last we came in sight of the island of Barbadoes, at which the whites on board gave a great shout, and made many signs of joy to us. We did not know what to think of this; but as the vessel drew nearer, we plainly saw the harbour, and other ships of different kinds and sizes; and we soon anchored amongst them off Bridge-Town. Many merchants and planters now came on board, though it was in the evening. They put us in separate parcels, and examined us attentively. They also made us jump, and pointed to the land, signifying we were to go there. We thought by this we should be eaten by these ugly men, as they appeared to us; and, when soon after we were all put down under the deck again, there was much dread and trembling among us, and nothing but bitter cries to be heard all the night from these apprehensions, insomuch that at last the white people got some old slaves from the land to pacify us. They told us we were not to be eaten, but to work, and were soon to go on land, where we should see many of our country people. This report eased us much; and sure enough, soon after we landed, there came to us Africans of all languages. We were conducted immediately to the merchant's yard, where we were all pent up together like so many sheep in a fold, without regard to sex or age. As every object was new to me, every thing I saw filled me with surprise. What struck me first was that the houses were built with bricks and stories, and in every other respect different from those I had seen in Africa: but I was still more astonished on seeing people on horseback. I did not know what this could mean; and indeed I thought these people were full of nothing but magical arts. While I was in this astonishment one of my fellow prisoners spoke to a countryman of his about the horses, who said they were the same kind they had in their country. I understood them, though they were from a distant part of Africa, and I thought it odd I had not seen any horses there; but afterwards when I came to converse with different Africans, I found they had many horses amongst them, and much larger than those I then saw. We were not many days in the merchant's custody before we were sold after their usual manner, which is this:—On a signal given, (as the beat of a drum) the buyers rush at once into the yard where the slaves are confined, and make choice of that parcel they like best. The noise and clamour with which this is attended, and the eagerness visible in the countenances of the buyers, serve not a little to increase the apprehension of terrified Africans, who may well be supposed to consider them as the ministers of that destruction to which they think themselves devoted. In this manner, without scruple, are relations and friends separated, most of them never to see each other again. I remember in the vessel in which I was brought over, in the men's apartment, there were several brothers, who, in the sale were sold in different lots; and it was very moving on this occasion to see and hear their cries at parting. O, ye nominal Christians! might not an African ask you, learned you this from your God, who says unto you, Do unto all men as you would men should do unto you? Is it not enough that we are torn from our country and friends, to toil for your luxury and lust of gain? Must every tender feeling be likewise sacrificed to your avarice? Are the dearest friends and relations, now rendered more dear by their separation from their kindred, still to be parted from each other, and thus prevented from cheering the gloom of slavery with the small comfort of being together, and mingling their sufferings and sorrows? Why are parents to lose their children, brothers their sisters, or husbands their wives? Surely this is a new refinement in cruelty, which, while it has no advantage to atone for it, thus aggravates distress, and adds fresh horrors even to the wretchedness of slavery.

A DEVOUT MOSLEM SOLD TO THE INFIDELS

Omar ibn Seid / Autobiography

By the year 1100 the states of West Africa had come under the influence of Islam, and the rulers of Mali and Songhai were devout Moslems. It comes as no surprise, then, that many slaves brought to America were Moslem and spoke Arabic.

Omar ibn Seid, the author of the following sketch, was a member of the Fula tribe from what is now called Senegal. He was born about 1770. After being trained in Arabic and mathematics by his uncle, he became a merchant dealing primarily in cotton cloth. Subsequently, he was captured and sold into slavery in Charleston, South Carolina, by the infidels—in this case, the Christians.

He ran away from his master in South Carolina and was arrested in Fayetteville, North Carolina. While in jail, he began writing on the walls of his cell in Arabic, a feat that brought him to the attention of General James Owen, who purchased him. Although Omar was still a devout Moslem when bought by General Owen, he later converted to Christianity.

This brief autobiography is translated from the Arabic and begins with scattered selections from the Koran that Omar considered relevant to the story he had to tell.

In the name of God, the merciful the gracious.—God grant his blessing upon our Prophet Mohammed. Blessed be He in whose hands is the kingdom and who is Almighty; who created death and life that he might test you; for he is exalted; he is the forgiver (of sins), who created seven heavens one above the other. Do you discern anything trifling in creation? Bring back your thoughts. Do you see anything worthless? Recall your vision in earnest. Turn your eye inward for it is diseased. God has adorned the heavens and the world with lamps, and has made us missiles for the devils, and given us for them a grievous punishment, and to those who have disbelieved their Lord, the punishment of hell and pains of body. Whoever associates with them shall hear a boiling caldron, and what is cast therein may fitly represent those who suffer under the anger of God.—Ask them if a prophet has not been sent unto them. They say, "Yes, a prophet has come to us, but we have lied to him." We said, "God has not sent us down anything, and you are in grievous error." They say, "If we had listened and been wise we should not now have been suffering the punishment of the Omniscient." So they have sinned in destroying the followers of the Omniscient. Those who fear their Lord and profess his name, they receive pardon and great honor. Guard your words, (ye wicked), make it known that God is all-wise in all his manifestations. Do you not know from the creation that God is full of skill? that He has made for you the way of error, and you have walked therein, and have chosen to live upon what your god Nasûr has furnished you? Believe on Him who dwells in heaven, who has fitted the earth to be your support and it shall give you food. Believe on Him who dwells in Heaven, who has sent you a prophet, and you shall understand what a teacher (He has sent you). Those that were before them deceived them (in regard to their prophet). And how came they to reject him? Did they not see in the heavens above them, how the fowls of the air receive with pleasure that which is sent them? God looks after all. Believe ye: it is He who supplies your wants, that you may take his gifts and enjoy them, and take great pleasure in them. And now will you go on in error, or walk in the path of righteousness. Say to them, "He who regards you with care, and who has

FROM "Autobiography of Omar ibn Seid, Slave in North Carolina, 1831," *American Historical Review*, Vol. XXX (July 1925), pp. 791–95.

made for you the heavens and the earth and gives you prosperity, Him you think little of. This is He that planted you in the earth, and to whom you are soon to be gathered." But they say, "If you are men of truth, tell us when shall this promise be fulfilled?" Say to them, "Does not God know? and am not I an evident Prophet?" When those who disbelieve shall see the things draw near before their faces, it shall then be told them, "These are the things about which you made inquiry." Have you seen that God has destroyed me or those with me? or rather that He has shewn us mercy? And who will defend the unbeliever from a miserable punishment? Say, "Knowledge is from God." Say, "Have you not seen that your water has become impure? Who will bring you fresh water from the fountain?"

O Sheikh Hunter, I cannot write my life because I have forgotten much of my own language, as well as of the Arabic. Do not be hard upon me, my brother.—To God let many thanks be paid for his great mercy and goodness.

In the name of God, the Gracious, the Merciful.—Thanks be to God, supreme in goodness and kindness and grace, and who is worthy of all honor, who created all things for his service, even man's power of action and of speech.

FROM OMAR TO SHEIKH HUNTER

You asked me to write my life. I am not able to do this because I have much forgotten my own, as well as the Arabic language. Neither can I write very grammatically or according to the true idiom. And so, my brother, I beg you, in God's name, not to blame me, for I am a man of weak eyes, and of a weak body.

My name is Omar ibn Seid. My birthplace was Fut Tûr, between the two rivers. I sought knowledge under the instruction of a Sheikh called Mohammed Seid, my own brother, and Sheikh Soleiman Kembeh, and Sheikh Gabriel Abdal. I continued my studies twenty-five years, and then returned to my home where I remained six years. Then there came to our place a large army, who killed many men, and took me, and brought me to the great sea, and sold me into the hands of the Christians, who bound me and sent me on board a great ship and we sailed upon the great sea a month and a half, when we came to a place called Charleston in the Christian language. There they sold me to a small, weak, and wicked man, called Johnson, a complete infidel, who had no fear of God at all. Now I am a small man, and unable to do hard work so I fled from the hand of Johnson and after a month came to a place called Fayd-il [Fayetteville]. There I saw some great houses (churches). On the new moon I went into a church to pray. A lad saw me and rode off to the place of his father and informed him that he had seen a black man in the church. A man named Handah (Hunter?) and another man with him on horseback, came attended by a troop of dogs. They took me and made me go with them twelve miles to a place called Fayd-il, where they put me into a great house from which I could not go out. I continued in the great house (which, in the Christian language, they called *jail*) sixteen days and nights. One Friday the jailor came and opened the door of the house and I saw a great many men, all Christians, some of whom called out to me, "What is your name? Is it Omar or Seid?" I did not understand their Christian language. A man called Bob Mumford took me and led me out of the jail, and I was very well pleased to go with them to their place. I stayed at Mumford's four days and nights, and then a man named Jim Owen, son-in-law of Mumford, having married his daughter Betsey, asked me if I was willing to go to a place called Bladen. I said, Yes, I was willing. I went with them and have remained in the place of Jim Owen until now.

Before [after?] I came into the hand of Gen. Owen a man by the name of Mitchell came to buy me. He asked me if I were willing to go to Charleston City. I said "*No, no, no, no, no, no, no*, I not willing to go to Charleston. I stay in the hand of Jim Owen."

O ye people of North Carolina, O ye people of S. Carolina, O ye people of America all of you; have you among you any two such men as Jim Owen and John Owen? These men are good men. What food they eat they give to me to eat. As they clothe themselves they clothe me. They permit me to read the gospel of God, our Lord, and Saviour, and King; who regulates all our circumstances, our health and wealth, and who bestows his mercies willingly, not by constraint. According to power I open my heart, as to a great light, to receive the true way, the way of the Lord Jesus the Messiah.

Before I came to the Christian country, my religion was the religion of "Mohammed, the Apostle of God—may God have mercy upon him and give him peace." I walked to the mosque before day-break, washed my face and head and hands and feet. I prayed at noon, prayed in the afternoon, prayed at sunset, prayed in the evening. I gave alms every year, gold, silver, seeds, cattle, sheep, goats, rice, wheat, and barley. I gave tithes of all the above-named things. I went every year to the holy war against the infidels. I went on pilgrimage to Mecca, as all did who were able.—My father had six sons and five daughters, and my mother had three sons and one daughter. When I left my country I was thirty-seven years old; I have been in the country of the Christians twenty-four years.—Written A.D. 1831.

O ye people of North Carolina, O ye people of South Carolina, O all ye people of America—

The first son of Jim Owen is called Thomas, and his sister is called Masajein (Martha Jane?). This is an excellent family.

Tom Owen and Nell Owen have two sons and a daughter. The first son is called Jim and the second John. The daughter is named Melissa.

Seid Jim Owen and his wife Betsey have two sons and five daughters. Their names are Tom, and John, and Mercy, Miriam, Sophia, Margaret and Eliza. This family is a very nice family. The wife of John Owen is called

Lucy and an excellent wife she is. She had five children. Three of them died and two are still living.

O ye Americans, ye people of North Carolina—have you, have you, have you, have you, have you among you a family like this family, having so much love to God as they?

Formerly I, Omar, loved to read the book of the Koran the famous. General Jim Owen and his wife used to read the gospel, and they read it to me very much,—the gospel of God, our Lord, our Creator, our King, He that orders all our circumstances, health and wealth, willingly, not constrainedly, according to his power.—Open thou my heart to the gospel, to the way of uprightness.—Thanks to the Lord of all worlds, thanks in abundance. He is plenteous in mercy and abundant in goodness.

For the law was given by Moses but grace and truth were by Jesus the Messiah.

When I was a Mohammedan I prayed thus: "Thanks be to God, Lord of all worlds, the merciful the gracious, Lord of the day of Judgment, thee we serve, on thee we call for help. Direct us in the right way, the way of those on whom thou hast had mercy, with whom thou hast not been angry and who walk not in error. Amen."—But now I pray "Our Father", etc., in the words of our Lord Jesus the Messiah.

I reside in this our country by reason of great necessity. Wicked men took me by violence and sold me to the Christians. We sailed a month and a half on the great sea to the place called Charleston in the Christian land. I fell into the hands of a small, weak and wicked man, who feared not God at all, nor did he read (the gospel) at all nor pray. I was afraid to remain with a man so depraved and who committed so many crimes and I ran away. After a month our Lord God brought me forward to the hand of a good man, who fears God, and loves to do good, and whose name is Jim Owen and whose brother is called Col. John Owen. These are two excellent men.—I am residing in Bladen County.

I continue in the hand of Jim Owen who never beats me, nor scolds me. I neither go hungry nor naked, and I have no hard work to do. I am not able to do hard work for I am a small man and feeble. During the last twenty years I have known no want in the hand of Jim Owen.

1 SUGGESTIONS FOR FURTHER READING

A good place to begin a study of African history is with Robert O. Collins (ed.), *Problems in African History** (Prentice-Hall, 1967), or the two volumes of radio talks edited by Roland Oliver: *The Dawn of African History** (Oxford University Press, 1961) and *The Middle Age of African History** (Oxford University Press, 1967). Two works treating the background of the area from which most New World blacks came are J. D. Fage, *An Introduction to the History of West Africa** (Cambridge, 1962), and Basil Davidson, *A History of West Africa to the Nineteenth Century** (Longmans, Green, 1965). Documents illustrative of African history are collected in Philip Curtin (ed.), *Africa Remembered: Narratives by West Africans from the Era of the Slave Trade** (University of Wisconsin Press, 1967); Basil Davidson (ed.), *The African Past: Chronicles from Antiquity to Modern Times** (Little, Brown, 1964); and Roland Oliver and Caroline Oliver (eds.), *Africa in the Days of Exploration** (Prentice-Hall, 1965). Melville Herskovits, in *The Myth of the Negro Past** (Harper, 1941), describes the culture of West Africa, and Basil Davidson, in *The Lost Cities of Africa** (Little, Brown, 1959), gives a description of the civilization of medieval African cities.

The prime source for information about the Atlantic slave trade is Elizabeth Donnan (ed.), *Documents Illustrative of the History of the Slave Trade to America*, 4 vols. (Carnegie Institution of Washington, 1930-35). Two good secondary works are Basil Davidson, *Black Mother: The Years of the African Slave Trade* (Little, Brown, 1961), published in paperback under the title *The African Slave Trade**, and D. P. Mannix and Malcolm Cowley, *Black Cargoes: The Story of the Atlantic Slave Trade, 1518-1865** (Viking, 1962). An important new study of the extent of the trade is Philip D. Curtin, *The Atlantic Slave Trade* (University of Wisconsin Press, 1969). Douglas Grant, in *The Fortunate Slave* (Oxford University Press, 1968), views the trade by telling the story of a slave who was returned to his African homeland. In *Capitalism and Slavery** (University of North Carolina Press, 1944), Eric Williams explores the economics of the establishment of slavery in the New World. The basic study of attempts to end the slave trade is W. E. B. Du Bois' Harvard dissertation, *The Suppression of the African Slave Trade to the United States, 1638-1870** (Longmans, Green, 1896).

2 THE AFRO-AMERICAN BEFORE 1800

In 1619, the year before the *Mayflower* crossing, twenty blacks were brought to Jamestown, Virginia, by a Dutch man-of-war. It appears that the Africans had been pirated from a Spanish slave vessel bound for the Caribbean. The blacks were sold by the master of the ship into indentured servitude, thus becoming the first black inhabitants of the English colonies.

In the beginning, it seems that no clear-cut distinction was made between black and white indentured servants, but by 1640 a clear difference in treatment had emerged. In 1641, Massachusetts became the first colony to legally recognize slavery. After the middle of the century, all blacks—and only blacks—entering the colonies came under the slave laws. One of the controversial historiographical questions of the first half of the seventeenth century is whether slavery led to racial prejudice or racial prejudice led to slavery.

Not all Africans in the English colonies were slaves: the original twenty, their descendants, and others who gained their freedom in various ways lived in all parts of the colonies. By the middle of the century, several of these free blacks had become prosperous enough to import white indentured servants to work on their lands.

Black slavery grew slowly in the South until the end of the century, when the rapid growth of plantation agriculture and the opening up of the slave trade on a non-monopoly basis led to a large increase in the number of Africans imported to the English colonies. This increase in the number of slaves led to the adoption of legal codes designed to limit the activity of the slaves and, hopefully, prevent insurrection and rebellion. These codes generally prohibited the slaves from owning property, carrying weapons, and traveling without a pass. After several abortive insurrections in New York City and in the Southern colonies, the laws became even more repressive.

The slaves were never an important part of the economy of the Northern colonies. Blacks, both slave and free, worked in a variety of capacities in the cities, primarily as domestic servants, artisans, and unskilled laborers. It was customary for a slave to hire himself out and then pay his master the wages he received. Sometimes the owner allowed the slave to work out his freedom in this way.

In several Northern cities, white artisans found themselves competing regularly with blacks for the available work. On more than one occasion the blacks provided such a threat that attempts were made to have them legally barred from doing certain kinds of skilled labor.

As the agitation for self-government grew in the colonies, so the agitation for liberty grew on the part of the slaves, particularly in Massachusetts. In that colony, several slaves sued for their freedom in the courts and won, but each case was separate, and no general ruling was made. Many slaves gained their freedom by fighting in the War for American Independence. Although blacks for the most part had been prohibited from serving in the military, a shortage of troops in 1777 led to a relaxation of the laws, and blacks entered the service of the Continental Army.

As slavery began to be abolished in the North about the time of the War, the racist ideology of the English colonists was threatened by the emergence of the "natural rights" ideas expressed in the Declaration of Independence. But the Constitutional Convention of 1787 got back down to practical matters, and the Great Compromise, which stated that five slaves were to be considered the equivalent of three free men in determining representation in the lower house of Congress, gave slavery a clear legal basis. As an institution, it was now backed up by the federal Constitution and the strength of federal authority. The retrogressive Constitution, coupled with new technological developments in Southern agriculture, led to a rapid increase in the slave trade, both external and internal. The number of slaves in the United States increased from 697,624 in 1790 to 3,953,760 in 1860—an average increase per decade of 28.2 per cent.

Because of widespread racial prejudice, even the free blacks in the North suffered from the indifference and the outright hostility of white society. The extent of this prejudice can be seen, for example, in the development of black religion. When the Africans were first brought to this country, Protestant Christians were reluctant to allow them to be exposed to the teachings of Christianity for fear that they would be converted and thereby gain a claim to freedom. This particular problem was solved when the Virginia legislature ruled in 1677 that becoming a Christian did not alter the status of the convert in this world. No great rush to convert the slaves was made, however, and very few blacks, slave or free, became even nominal Christians during the colonial period.

Only with the growth of Methodist and Baptist churches after the War for American Independence did large numbers of blacks become Christian. Even within these churches, however, they met with so much discrimination that before the end of the century several separate black religious societies had been founded.

The free blacks began to realize that individually they were power-less. Only when they began to organize themselves would they have any force in society. Beginning in the 1770's, groups of free blacks began appealing for redress of their grievances to such groups as the Boston Town Selectmen and the Massachusetts legislature. Though their petitions were not always granted, their efforts had a positive effect: the records of those official bodies reflect an attitude of greater respect than before toward the black population. Such groups as the African Society and the African Lodge in Boston and the Free African Society in Philadelphia gave black men a voice in the public arena that was not easily ignored. Societies like these also provided blacks with financial protection in the form of insurance, a training ground for leadership, and a place where group solidarity could be affirmed.

Though many blacks, both slave and free, had learned to read and write in informal ways before the War, progress in black education was slow in coming. By the end of the eighteenth century, several private schools for blacks had been founded—through white benevolence as well as black initiative. But no public schools for black children were established in the eighteenth century, and the few black children who attended white schools did not remain long because of the discrimination they met there.

Organization of free blacks for self-help and self-protection grew apace after the War for American Independence and continued until the Civil War, when the victory of the North led the black population to assume it would be able to move more freely than before within the structure of white institutions, both political and religious.

BLACKS SERVE THE CITY IN A TIME OF CRISIS

Absalom Jones and Richard Allen / A Narrative of the Proceedings of the Black People During the Late Awful Calamity in Philadelphia

---

In 1793, an epidemic of yellow fever broke out in Philadelphia. Since an eminent physician of that city, Benjamin Rush, believed that blacks were immune to its ravages, the Free African Society was asked by the mayor to supply nurses and men for burial duty. Hundreds of blacks responded, and—contrary to current medical supposition—hundreds of blacks contracted the disease and died.

At the conclusion of the epidemic, a pamphlet entitled **A Short Account of the Malignant Fever, lately prevalent in Philadelphia . . .** appeared. The author, Matthew Carey, accused some blacks of having looted the possessions of the dead and charged exorbitantly for their services. Although they themselves were specifically exempted from the accusation, Absalom Jones and Richard Allen, who had founded the Free African Society in 1787, replied to the charges in detail.

Their pamphlet of reply, reprinted in the following pages, gives a vivid idea of the terror that struck the city along with the disease. As the black leaders point out, profiteering certainly took place during the epidemic, but there was no color line in the matter.

In consequence of a partial representation of the conduct of the people who were employed to nurse the sick, in the late calamitous state of the city of Philadelphia, we are solicited, by a number of those who feel themselves injured thereby, and by the advice of several respectable citizens, to step forward and declare facts as they really were; seeing that from our situation, on account of the charge we took upon us, we had it more fully and generally in our power, to know and observe the conduct and behavior of those that were so employed.

Early in September, a solicitation appeared in the public papers, to the people of colour to come forward and assist the distressed, perishing, and neglected sick; with a kind of assurance, that people of our colour were not liable to take the infection. Upon which we and a few others met and consulted how to act on so truly alarming and melancholy an occasion. After some conversation, we found a freedom to go forth, confiding in him who

---

FROM A. J. and R. A. (Absalom Jones and Richard Allen), *A Narrative of the Proceedings of the Black People During the Late Awful Calamity in Philadelphia in the Year 1793 . . .* (Philadelphia, 1794).

can preserve in the midst of a burning fiery furnace, sensible that it was our duty to do all the good we could to our suffering fellow mortals. We set out to see where we could be useful. The first we visited was a man in Emsley's alley, who was dying, and his wife lay dead at the time in the house, there were none to assist but two poor helpless children. We administered what relief we could, and applied to the overseers of the poor to have the woman buried. We visited upwards of twenty families that day— they were scenes of woe indeed! The Lord was pleased to strengthen us, and remove all fear from us, and disposed our hearts to be as useful as possible.

In order the better to regulate our conduct, we called on the mayor next day, to consult with him how to proceed, so as to be most useful. The first object he recommended was a strict attention to the sick, and the procuring of nurses. This was attended to by Absalom Jones and William Gray; and, in order that the distressed might know where to apply, the mayor advertised the public that upon application to them they would be supplied. Soon after, the mortality increasing, the difficulty of getting a corpse taken away, was such, that few were willing to do it, when offered great rewards. The black people were looked to. We then offered our services in the public papers, by advertising that we would remove the dead and procure nurses. Our services were the production of real sensibility;—we sought not fee nor reward, until the increase of the disorder rendered our labour so arduous that we were not adequate to the service we had assumed. The mortality increasing rapidly, obliged us to call in the assistance of five[1] hired men, in the awful discharge of interring the dead. They, with great reluctance, were prevailed upon to join us. It was very uncommon, at this time, to find any one that would go near, much more, handle, a sick or dead person.

Mr. Carey, in page 106 of his third edition, has observed, that, "for the honor of human nature, it ought to be recorded, that some of the convicts in the gaol, a part of the term of whose confinement had been remitted as a reward for their peaceable, orderly behavior, voluntarily offered themselves as nurses to attend the sick at Bush-hill; and have, in that capacity, conducted themselves with great fidelity, &c." Here it ought to be remarked, (although Mr. Carey hath not done it) that two thirds of the persons, who rendered these essential services, were people of colour, who, on the application of the elders of the African church, (who met to consider what they could do for the help of the sick) were liberated, on condition of their doing the duty of nurses at the hospital at Bush-hill; which they as voluntarily accepted to do, as they did faithfully discharge, this severe and disagreeable duty.—May the Lord reward them, both temporally and spiritually.

When the sickness became general, and several of the physicians died, and most of the survivors were exhausted by sickness or fatigue; that good

---

[1] Two of whom were Richard Allen's brothers.

man, Doctor Rush, called us more immediately to attend upon the sick, knowing we could both bleed; he told us we could increase our utility, by attending to his instructions, and accordingly directed us where to procure medicine duly prepared, with proper directions how to administer them, and at what stages of the disorder to bleed; and when we found ourselves incapable of judging what was proper to be done, to apply to him, and he would, if able, attend them himself, or send Edward Fisher, his pupil, which he often did; and Mr. Fisher manifested his humanity, by an affectionate attention for their relief.—This has been no small satisfaction to us; for, we think, that when a physician was not attainable, we have been the instruments in the hand of God, for saving the lives of some hundreds of our suffering fellow mortals.

We feel ourselves sensibly aggrieved by the censorious epithets of many, who did not render the least assistance in the time of necessity, yet are liberal of their censure of us, for the prices paid for our services, when no one knew how to make a proposal to any one they wanted to assist them. At first we made no charge, but left it to those we served in removing their dead, to give what they thought fit—we set no price, until the reward was fixed by those we had served. After paying the people we had to assist us, our compensation is much less than many will believe.

We do assure the public, that *all* the money we have received, for burying, and for coffins which we ourselves purchased and procured, has not defrayed the expence of wages which we had to pay to those whom we employed to assist us. The following statement is accurately made:

CASH RECEIVED

The whole amount of Cash we received for burying the
dead, and for burying beds, is, - - - - - - - - - - - - - £233 10 4

CASH PAID

For coffins, for which we have received
nothing, - - - - - - - - - - - - - - - - -   £33 0 0

For the hire of five men, 3 of them 70 days
each, and the other two, 63 days each,
at 22/6 per day, - - - - - - - - - - - -   378 0 0
                                                        411 0 0

Debts due us, for which we expect but
little,- - - - - - - - - - - - - - - - - -   £110 0 0

From this statement, for the truth of which we solemnly
vouch, it is evident, and we sensibly feel the operation
of the fact, that we are out of pocket, - - - - - - - - -   £177 9 8

Besides the costs of hearses, the maintenance of our families for 70 days, (being the period of our labours) and the support of the five hired men, during the respective times of their being employed; which expences, together with sundry gifts we occasionally made to poor families, might reasonably and properly be introduced, to show our actual situation with regard to profit—but it is enough to exhibit to the public, from the above specified items, of *Cash paid and Cash received*, without taking into view the other expences, that, by the employment we were engaged in, we lost £ 177 9 8. But, if the other expenses, which we have actually paid, are added to that sum, how much then may we not say we have suffered! We leave the public to judge.

It may possibly appear strange to some who know how constantly we were employed, that we should have received no more Cash than £ 233 10 4. But we repeat our assurance, that this is the fact, and we add another, which will serve the better to explain it: We have buried *several hundreds* of poor persons and strangers, for which service we have never received, nor never asked any compensation.

We feel ourselves hurt most by a partial, censorious paragraph, in Mr. Carey's second edition, of his account of the sickness, &c. in Philadelphia; pages 76 and 77, where he asperses the blacks alone, for having taken the advantage of the distressed situation of the people. That some extravagant prices were paid, we admit; but how came they to be demanded? the reason is plain. It was with difficulty persons could be had to supply the wants of the sick, as nurses;—applications became more and more numerous, the consequence was, when we procured them at six dollars per week, and called upon them to go where they were wanted, we found they were gone elsewhere; here was a disappointment; upon enquiring the cause, we found, they had been allured away by others who offered greater wages, until they got from two to four dollars per day. We had no restraint upon the people. It was natural for people in low circumstances to accept a voluntary, bounteous reward; especially under the loathsomeness of many of the sick, when nature shuddered at the thoughts of the infection, and the task assigned was aggravated by lunacy, and being left much alone with them. Had Mr. Carey been solicited to such an undertaking, for hire, *Query*, "what would *he* have demanded?" but Mr. Carey, although chosen a member of that band of worthies who have so eminently distinguished themselves by their labours, for the relief of the sick and helpless—yet, quickly after his election, left them to struggle with their arduous and hazardous task, by leaving the city. 'Tis true Mr. Carey was no hireling, and had a right to flee, and upon his return, to plead the cause of those who fled; yet, we think, he was wrong in giving so partial and injurious an account of the black nurses; if they have taken advantage of the public distress, is it any more than he hath done of its desire for information? We believe he has made more money by the sale of his "scraps" than a dozen of the greatest extortioners among the black nurses. The great prices paid did not escape the observation of that worthy and vigilant magistrate, Mathew Clarkson, mayor of the city, and president of the committee—he sent for us, and requested we would use our influence, to lessen the wages of the nurses, but on informing him the cause, i.e. that of the people overbidding one another, it was concluded unnecessary to attempt any thing on that head; therefore it was left to the people concerned. That there were some few black people guilty of plundering the distressed, we acknowledge; but in that they only are pointed out, and made mention of, we esteem partial and injurious; we know as many whites who were guilty of it; but this is looked over, while the blacks are held up to censure.—Is it a greater crime for a black to pilfer, than for a white to privateer?

We wish not to offend, but when an unprovoked attempt is made, to make us blacker than we are, it becomes less necessary to be over cautious on that account; therefore we shall take the liberty to tell of the conduct of some of the whites.

We know six pounds was demanded by, and paid, to a white woman, for putting a corpse into a coffin; and forty dollars was demanded, and paid, to four white men, for bringing it down the stairs.

Mr. and Mrs. Taylor both died in one night; a white woman had the care of them; after they were dead she called on Jacob Servoss, esq. for her pay, demanding six pounds for laying them out; upon seeing a bundle with her, he suspected she had pilfered; on searching her, Mr. Taylor's buckles were found in her pocket, with other things.

An elderly lady, Mrs. Malony, was given into the care of a white woman, she died, we were called to remove the corpse, when we came the woman was laying so drunk that she did not know what we were doing, but we know she had one of Mrs. Malony's rings on her finger, and another in her pocket.

Mr. Carey tells us, Bush-hill exhibited as wrtched a picture of human misery, as ever existed. A profligate abandoned set of nurses and attendants (hardly any of good character could at that time be procured,) rioted on the provisions and comforts, prepared for the sick, who (unless at the hours when the doctors attended) were left almost entirely destitute of every assistance. The dying and dead were indiscriminately mingled together. The ordure and other evacuations of the sick, were allowed to remain in the most offensive state imaginable. Not the smallest appearance of order or regularity existed. It was in fact a great human slaughter house, where numerous victims were immolated at the altar of intemperance.

It is unpleasant to point out the bad and unfeeling conduct of any colour, yet the defence we have undertaken obliges us to remark, that although "hardly any of good character at that time could be procured" yet only two black women were at this time in the hospital, and they were retained and the others discharged, when it was reduced to order and good government.

The bad consequences many of our colour apprehend from a partial relation of our conduct are, that it will prejudice the minds of the people in general against us—because it is impossible that one individual, can have knowledge of all, therefore at some future day, when some of the most virtuous, that were upon most praise-worthy motives, induced to serve the sick, may fall into the service of a family that are strangers to him, or her, and it is discovered that it is one of those stigmatised wretches, what may we suppose will be the consequence? Is it not reasonable to think the person will be abhored, despised, and perhaps dismissed from employment, to their great disadvantage, would not this be hard? and have we not therefore sufficient reason to seek for redress? We can with certainty assure the public that we have seen more humanity, more real sensibility from the poor blacks, than from the poor whites. When many of the former, of their own accord rendered services where extreme necessity called for it, the general part of the poor white people were so dismayed, that instead of attempting to be useful, they in a manner hid themselves —— a remarkable instance of this —— A poor afflicted dying man, stood at his chamber window, praying and beseeching every one that passed by, to help him to a drink of water; a number of white people passed, and instead of being moved by the poor man's distress, they hurried as fast as they could out of the sound of his cries—until at length a gentleman, who seemed to be a foreigner came up, he could not pass by, but had not resolution enough to go into the house, he held eight dollars in his hand, and offered it to several as a reward for giving the poor man a drink of water, but was refused by every one, until a poor black man came up, the gentleman offered the eight dollars to him, if he would relieve the poor man with a little water, "Master" replied the good natured fellow, "I will supply the gentleman with water, but surely I will not take your money for it" nor could he be prevailed upon to accept his bounty: he went in, supplied the poor object with water, and rendered him every service he could.

A poor black man, named Sampson, went constantly from house to house where distress was, and no assistance without fee or reward; he was smote with the disorder, and died, after his death his family were neglected by those he had served.

Sarah Bass, a poor black widow, gave all the assistance she could, in several families, for which she did not receive any thing; and when any thing was offered her, she left it to the option of those she served.

A woman of our colour, nursed Richard Mason and son, when they died, Richard's widow considering the risk the poor woman had run, and from observing the fears that sometimes rested on her mind, expected she would have demanded something considerable, but upon asking what she demanded, her reply was half a dollar per day. Mrs. Mason, intimated it was not sufficient for her attendance, she replied it was enough for what she had done, and would take no more. Mrs. Mason's feelings were such, that she settled an annuity of six pounds a year, on her, for life. Her name is Mary Scott.

An elderly black woman nursed —— with great diligence and attention;

when recovered he asked what he must give for her services —— she replied "a dinner master on a cold winter's day," and thus she went from place to place rendering every service in her power without an eye to reward.

A young black woman, was requested to attend one night upon a white man and his wife, who were very ill, no other person could be had;—great wages were offered her—she replied, I will not go for money, if I go for money God will see it, and may be make me take the disorder and die, but if I go, and take no money, he may spare my life. She went about nine o'clock, and found them both on the floor; she could procure no candle or other light, but staid with them about two hours, and then left them. They both died that night. She was afterward very ill with the fever—her life was spared.

Cæsar Cranchal, a black man, offered his services to attend the sick, and said, I will not take your money, I will not sell my life for money. It is said he died with the flux.

A black lad, at the Widow Gilpin's, was intrusted with his young Master's keys, on his leaving the city, and transacted his business, with the greatest honesty, and dispatch, having unloaded a vessel for him in the time, and loaded it again.

A woman, that nursed David Bacon, charged with exemplary moderation, and said she would not have any more.

It may be said, in vindication of the conduct of those, who discovered ignorance or incapacity in nursing, that it is, in itself, a considerable art, derived from experience, as well as the exercise of the finer feelings of humanity—this experience, nine tenths of those employed, it is probable were wholly strangers to.

We do not recollect such acts of humanity from the poor white people, in all the round we have been engaged in. We could mention many other instances of the like nature, but think it needless.

It is unpleasant for us to make these remarks, but justice to our colour, demands it. Mr. Carey pays William Gray and us a compliment; he says, our services and others of their colour, have been very great &c. By naming us, he leaves these others, in the hazardous state of being classed with those who are called the "vilest." The few that were discovered to merit public censure, were brought to justice, which ought to have sufficed, without being canvassed over in his "Trifle" of a pamphlet—which causes us to be more particular, and endeavour to recall the esteem of the public for our friends, and the people of colour, as far as they may be found worthy; for we conceive, and experience proves it, that an ill name is easier given than taken away. We have many unprovoked enemies, who begrudge us the liberty we enjoy, and are glad to hear of any complaint against our colour, be it just or unjust; in consequence of which we are more earnestly endeavouring all in our power, to warn, rebuke, and exhort our African friends, to keep a conscience void of offence towards God and man; and, at the same time, would not be backward to interfere, when stigmas or oppression appear pointed at, or attempted against them, unjustly; and, we are confident, we shall stand justified in the sight of the candid and judicious, for such conduct.

Mr. Carey's first, second, and third editions, are gone forth into the world, and in all probability, have been read by thousands that will never read his fourth—consequently, any alteration he may hereafter make, in the paragraph alluded to, cannot have the desired effect, or atone for the past; therefore we apprehend it necessary to publish our thoughts on the occasion. Had Mr. Carey said, a number of white and black Wretches eagerly seized on the opportunity to extort from the distressed, and some few of both were detected in plundering the sick, it might extenuate, in a great degree, the having made mention of the blacks.

We can assure the public, there were as many white as black people, detected in pilfering, although the number of the latter, employed as nurses, was twenty times as great as the former, and that there is, in our opinion, as great a proportion of white, as of black, inclined to such practices. It is rather to be admired, that so few instances of pilfering and robbery happened, considering the great opportunities there were for such things: we do not know of more than five black people, suspected of any thing clandestine, out of the great number employed; the people were glad to get any person to assist them—a black was preferred, because it was supposed, they were not so likely to take the disorder, the most worthless were acceptable, so that it would have been no cause of wonder, if twenty causes of complaint occurred, for one that hath. It has been alledged, that many of the sick, were neglected by the nurses; we do not wonder at it, considering their situation, in many instances, up night and day, without any one to relieve them, worn down with fatigue, and want of sleep, they could not in many cases, render that assistance, which was needful: where we visited, the causes of complaint on this score, were not numerous. The case of the nurses, in many instances, were deserving of commiseration, the patient raging and frightful to behold; it has frequently required two persons, to hold them from running away, others have made attempts to jump out of a window, in many chambers they were nailed down, and the door was kept locked, to prevent them from running away, or breaking their necks, others lay vomiting blood, and screaming enough to chill them with horror. Thus were many of the nurses circumstanced, alone, until the patient died, then called away to another scene of distress, and thus have been for a week or ten days left to do the best they could without any sufficient rest, many of them having some of their dearest connections sick at the time, and suffering for want, while their husband, wife, father, mother, &c. have been engaged in the service of the white people. We mention this to shew the difference between this and nursing in common cases, we have suffered equally with the whites, our distress hath been very great, but much unknown to the white people.

Few have been the whites that paid attention to us while the black were engaged in the other's service. We can assure the public we have taken four and five black people in a day to be buried. In several instances when they have been seized with the sickness while nursing, they have been turned out of the house, and wandering and destitute until taking shelter wherever they could (as many of them would not be admitted to their former homes) they have languished alone and we know of one who even died in a stable. Others acted with more tenderness, when their nurses were taken sick they had proper care taken of them at their houses. We know of two instances of this.

It is even to this day a generally received opinion in this city, that our colour was not so liable to the sickness as the whites. We hope our friends will pardon us for setting this matter in its true state.

The public were informed that in the West-Indies and other places where this terrible malady had been, it was observed the blacks were not affected with it. Happy would it have been for you, and much more so for us, if this observation had been verified by our experience.

When the people of colour had the sickness and died, we were imposed upon and told it was not with the prevailing sickness, until it became too notorious to be denied, then we were told some few died but not many. Thus were our services extorted *at the peril of our lives,* yet you accuse us of extorting *a little money from you.*

The bill of mortality for the year 1793, published by Matthew White-head, and John Ormrod, clerks, and Joseph Dolby, sexton, will convince any reasonable man that will examine it, that as many coloured people died in proportion as others. In 1792, there were 67 of our colour buried, and in 1793 it amounted to 305; thus the burials among us have increased more than fourfold, was not this in a great degree the effects of the services of the unjustly vilified black people?

Perhaps it may be acceptable to the reader to know how we found the sick affected by the sickness; our opportunities of hearing and seeing them have been very great. They were taken with a chill, a headach, a sick stomach, with pains in their limbs and back, this was the way the sickness in general began, but all were not affected alike, some appeared but slightly affected with some of these symptoms, what confirmed us in the opinion of a person being smitten was the colour of their eyes. In some it raged more furiously than in others—some have languished for seven and ten days, and appeared to get better the day, or some hours before they died, while others were cut off in one, two, or three days, but their complaints were similar. Some lost their reason and raged with all the fury madness could produce, and died in strong convulsions. Others retained their reason to the last, and seemed rather to fall asleep than die. We could not help remarking that the former were of strong passions, and the latter of a mild temper. Numbers died in a kind of dejection, they concluded they must go, (so the phrase for dying was) and therefore in a kind of fixed determined state of mind went off.

It struck our minds with awe, to have application made by those in health, to take charge of them in their sickness, and of their funeral. Such applications have been made to us; many appeared as though they thought they must die, and not live; some have lain on the floor, to be measured for their coffin and grave. A gentleman called one evening, to request a good nurse might be got for him, when he was sick, and to superintend his funeral, and gave particular directions how he would have it conducted, it seemed a surprising circumstance, for the man appeared at the time, to be in perfect health, but calling two or three days after to see him, found a woman dead in the house, and the man so far gone, that to adminster any thing for his recovery, was needless—he died that evening. We mention this, as an instance of the dejection and despondence, that took hold on the minds of thousands, and are of opinion, it aggravated the case of many, while others who bore up chearfully, got up again, that probably would otherwise have died.

When the mortality came to its greatest stage, it was impossible to procure sufficient assistance, therefore many whose friends, and relations had left them, died unseen, and unassisted. We have found them in various situations, some laying on the floor, as bloody as if they had been dipt in it, without any appearance of their having had, even a drink of water for their relief; others laying on a bed with their clothes on, as if they had came in fatigued, and lain down to rest; some appeared, as if they had fallen dead on the floor, from the position we found them in.

Truly our task was hard, yet through mercy, we were enabled to go on.

One thing we observed in several instances—when we were called, on the first appearance of the disorder to bleed, the person frequently, on the opening a vein before the operation was near over, felt a change for the better, and expressed a relief in their chief complaints; and we made it a practice to take more blood from them, than is usual in other cases; these in a general way recovered; those who did omit bleeding any considerable time, after being taken by the sickness, rarely expressed any change they felt in the operation.

We feel a great satisfaction in believing, that we have been useful to the sick, and thus publicly thank Doctor Rush, for enabling us to be so. We have bled upwards of eight hundred people, and do declare, we have not received to the value of a dollar and a half, therefor: we were willing to imitate the Doctor's benevolence, who sick or well, kept his house open day and night, to give what assistance he could in this time of trouble.

Several affecting instances occurred, when we were engaged in burying the dead. We have been called to bury some, who when we came, we found alive; at other places we found a parent dead, and none but little innocent babes to be seen, whose ignorance led them to think their parent was asleep; on account of their situation, and their little prattle, we have been so wounded and our feelings so hurt, that we almost concluded to withdraw from our undertaking, but seeing others so backward, we still went on.

An affecting instance.—A woman died, we were sent for to bury her, on our going into the house and taking the coffin in, a dear little innocent accosted us, with, mamma is asleep, don't wake her; but when she saw us put her in the coffin, the distress of the child was so great, that it almost overcame us; when she demanded why we put her mamma in the box? We did not know how to answer her, but committed her to the care of a neighbour, and left her with heavy hearts. In other places where we have been to take the corpse of a parent, and have found a group of little ones alone, some of them in a measure capable of knowing their situation, their cries and the innocent confusion of the little ones, seemed almost too much for human nature to bear. We have picked up little children that were wandering they knew not where, (whose parents were cut off) and taken them to the orphan house, for at this time the dread that prevailed over people's minds was so general, that it was a rare instance to see one neighbour visit another, and even friends when they met in the streets were afraid of each other, much less would they admit into their houses the distressed orphan that had been where the sickness was; this extreme seemed in some instances to have the appearance of barbarity; with reluctance we call to mind the many opportunities there were in the power of individuals to be useful to their fellow-men, yet through the terror of the times was omitted. A black man riding through the street, saw a man push a woman out of the house, the woman staggered and fell on her face in the gutter, and was not able to turn herself, the black man thought she was drunk, but observing she was in danger of suffocation alighted, and taking the woman up found her perfectly sober, but so far gone with the disorder that she was not able to help herself; the hard hearted man that threw her down, shut the door and left her—in such a situation, she might have perished in a few minutes; we heard of it, and took her to Bush-hill. Many of the white people, that ought to be patterns for us to follow after, have acted in a manner that would make humanity shudder. We remember an instance of cruelty, which we trust, no black man would be guilty of: two sisters orderly, decent, white women were sick with the fever, one of them recovered so as to come to the door; a neighbouring white man saw her, and in an angry tone asked her if her sister was dead or not? She answered no, upon which he replied, damn her, if she don't die before morning, I will make her die. The poor woman shocked at such an expression, from this monster of a man, made a modest reply, upon which he snatched up a tub of water, and would have dashed it over her, if he had not been prevented by a black man; he then went and took a couple of fowls out of a coop, (which had been given them for nourishment) and threw them into an open alley; he had his wish, the poor woman that he would make die, died that night. A white man threatened to shoot us, if we passed by his house with a corpse: we buried him three days after.

We have been pained to see the widows come to us, crying and wringing their hands, and in very great distress, on account of their husbands' death; having nobody to help them, they were obliged to come to get their husbands buried, their neighbours were afraid to go to their help or to condole with them; we ascribe such unfriendly conduct to the frailty of human nature, and not to wilful unkindness, or hardness of heart.

Notwithstanding the compliment Mr. Carey hath paid us, we have found reports spread, of our taking between one, and two hundred beds, from houses where people died; such slanderers as these, who propagate such wilful lies are dangerous, although unworthy notice. We wish if any person hath the least suspicion of us, they would endeavour to bring us to the punishment which such atrocious conduct must deserve; and by this means, the innocent will be cleared from reproach, and the guilty known.

We shall now conclude with the following old proverb, which we think applicable to those of our colour who exposed their lives in the late afflicting dispensation:—

> God and a soldier, all men do adore,
> In time of war, and not before;
> When the war is over, and all things righted,
> God is forgotten, and the soldier slighted.

BLACK PEOPLE ORGANIZE FOR SELF-PROTECTION

The Rules of the African Society

In 1693, the Puritan leader Cotton Mather printed what he called "Rules for a Society of Negroes." These rules were designed to guide the blacks in becoming docile, obedient, loyal, sober Christians. They showed little understanding of the black man's need for freedom and self-expression. Although Mather was a zealous advocate of education for blacks, his recommendations seemed to be primarily in the interests of white society.

When blacks began to organize themselves, it became clear that their interests were a good deal less abstract than Mather's. True, they were interested in moral uplift; but their major concern was economic protection—protection of themselves and of their families. Hence most of the early African societies stressed the need for life (actually death) insurance and for legal protection of heirs, lest they be sold into slavery on one pretext or another.

The document that follows is a simple and straightforward list of the rules of the African Society of Boston, formed in 1796. In 1802, when this list was published in pamphlet form, the Society had forty-four members.

1st. We, the African Members, form ourselves into a Society, under the above name, for the mutual benefit of each other, which may from time to time offer; behaving ourselves at the same time as true and faithful Citizens of the Commonwealth in which we live; and that we take no one into the Society, who shall commit any injustice or outrage against the laws of their country.

2d. That before any person can become a Member of the Society, he must be presented by three of the Members of the same; and the person, or persons, wishing to become Members, must make application one month at least beforehand, and that at one of the monthly, or three monthly meetings. Person, or persons if approved of shall be received into the Society. And, that before the admittance of any person into the Society, he shall be obliged to read the rules, or cause the same to be read to him; and not be admitted as a member unless he approves them.

3d. That each Member on admittance, shall pay one quarter of a Dollar to the Treasurer; and be credited for the same, in the books of the Society; and his name added to the list of the Members.

4th. That each Member shall pay one quarter of a Dollar per month to the Treasurer, and be credited for the same on the book; but no benefit can be tendered to any Member, until he has belonged to the Society one year.

5th. That any Member, or Members, not able to attend the regular meetings of the Society, may pay their part by appointing one of their brothers to pay the same for him: So any travelling, at a distance by sea, or land, may, by appointing any person to pay their subscription, will be, though absent for any length of time, or on their return, will pay up the same, shall still be considered as brothers, and belonging to the Society.

6th. That no money shall be returned to any one, that shall leave the Society; but if the Society should see fit to dismiss any one from their community, it shall then be put to a vote, whether the one, thus dismissed shall have his money again, if he should have any left, when the expences he may have been to the Society are deducted.

7th. That any Member, absenting himself from the Society, for the space of one year, shall be considered as separating himself from the same; but, if he should return at the end of that time, and pay up his subscription, he shall in six months be re-established in all the benefits of a Societain: But after that time he shall be considered as a new Member.

8th. That a committee, consisting of three, or five persons, shall be

FROM *Laws of the African Society, Instituted at Boston, Anno Domini, 1796* (Boston, 1802). Reprinted by permission from a pamphlet in the Library of the Boston Athenæum.

chosen by the members every three months; and that their chief care shall be, to attend to the sick, and see that they want nothing that the Society can give, and inform the Society, at their next meeting of those who stand in need of assistance of the Society, and of what was done during the time of their committeement. The committee shall likewise be empowered to call the Society together as often as may be necessary.

9th. That all monies, paid into the Society, shall be credited to the payers; and all going out, shall be debted to whom, or what for; and a regular account kept by one, chosen by the Society for that purpose.

10th. When any Member, or Members of the Society is sick, and not able to supply themselves with necessaries, suitable to their situations, the committee shall then tender to them and their family whatever the Society have, or may think fit for them. And should any Member die, and not leave wherewith to pay the expences of his funeral, the Society shall then see that any, so situated, be decently buried. But it must be remembered, that any Member, bringing on himself any sickness, or disorder, by intemperance, shall not be considered, as entitled to any benefits, or assistance from the Society.

11th. Should any Member die, and leave a lawful widow and children, the Society shall consider themselves bound to relieve her necessities, so long as she behaves herself decently, and remains a widow; and that the Society do the best in their power to place the children so that they may in time be capable of getting an honest living.

12th. Should the Society, with the blessing of Heaven, acquire a sum, suitable to bear interest, they will then take into consideration the best method they can, of making it useful.

13th. The Members will watch over each other in their Spiritual concerns; and by advice, exhortation, and prayer excite each other to grow in Grace, and in the knowledge of our Lord and Saviour Jesus Christ, and to live soberly, righteously and Godly, in this present world, that we may all be accepted of the Redeemer, and live together with him in Glory hereafter.

14th. That each Member traveling for any length of time, by Sea or Land, shall leave a Will with the Society, or being married, with his wife, all other Members to leave a Will with the Society, for to enable them to recover their effects, if they should not return, but on their return, this Will is to be returned to the one that gave it, but if he should not return, and leave a lawful heir, the property is to be delivered to him; otherwise deemed to the Society.

☞ The African Society have a Charity Lecture quarterly, on the second Tuesday in every third month.

BLACK PEOPLE MUST SUPPORT ONE ANOTHER IN THEIR OPPRESSION

Prince Hall   /   A Charge

Prince Hall was one of the most important black men in Massachusetts in the last quarter of the eighteenth century. Born in Barbados in 1748, he came to Massachusetts in 1765. In 1775, he was initiated into a Masonic lodge connected with the British army. After the War for American Independence, during which he served in the colonial army, he became a Methodist minister in Cambridge, Massachusetts, and applied to the American Masons for a charter to establish a black lodge. He was refused by the American organization, but in 1784 he made the same request to the British Masons, and the Grand Lodge of England granted him a charter immediately. In 1787, the African Lodge, No. 459, was organized in Boston with Hall as its Master. Hall delivered the address that follows to the members of the African Lodge in 1797.

The unquestioned political leader of Boston's blacks, Hall was the organizer of several petition campaigns for civil rights. His political acumen is clear from the brief pamphlet reprinted here, in which he advocates submission to the proper authorities along with insistence on the rights due all men as children of God.

Beloved Brethren of the African Lodge,

'Tis now five years since I deliver'd a Charge to you on some parts and points of Masonry. As one branch or superstructure on the foundation; when I endeavoured to shew you the duty of a Mason to a Mason, and charity or love to all mankind, as the mark and image of the great God, and the Father of the human race.

I shall now attempt to shew you, that it is our duty to sympathise with our fellow men under their troubles: the families of our brethren who are gone: we hope to the Grand Lodge above, here to return no more. But the cheerfulness that you have ever had to relieve them, and ease their burdens, under their sorrows, will never be forgotten by them; and in this manner you will never be weary in doing good.

But my brethren, although we are to begin here, we must not end here; for only look around you and you will see and hear of numbers of our fellow men crying out with holy Job, Have pity on me, O my friends, for the hand of the Lord hath touched me. And this is not to be confined to

---

FROM Prince Hall, *A Charge Delivered to the African Lodge, June 24, 1797 at Menotomy* (1797).

parties or colours; not to towns or states; not to a kingdom, but to the kingdoms of the whole earth, over whom Christ the king is head and grand master.

Among these numerous sons and daughters of distress, I shall begin with our friends and brethren; and first, let us see them dragg'd from their native country, by the iron hand of tyranny and oppression, from their dear friends and connections, with weeping eyes and aching hearts, to a strange land and strange people, whose tender mercies are cruel; and there to bear the iron yoke of slavery & cruelty till death as a friend shall relieve them. And must not the unhappy condition of these our fellow men draw forth our hearty prayer and wishes for their deliverance from these merchants and traders, whose characters you have in the xviii chap. of the Revelations, 11, 12, & 13 verses, and who knows but these same sort of traders may in a short time, in the like manner, bewail the loss of the African traffick, to their shame and confusion: and if I mistake not, it now begins to dawn in some of the West-India islands; which puts me in mind of a nation (that I have somewhere read of) called Ethiopeans, that cannot change their skin: But God can and will change their conditions, and their hearts too; and let Boston and the world know, that He hath no respect of persons; and that that bulwark of envy, pride, scorn and contempt; which is so visible to be seen in some and felt, shall fall, to rise no more.

When we hear of the bloody wars which are now in the world, and thousands of our fellow men slain; fathers and mothers bewailing the loss of their sons; wives for the loss of their husbands; towns and cities burnt and destroy'd; what must be the heart-felt sorrow and distress of these poor and unhappy people! Though we cannot help them, the distance being so great, yet we may sympathize with them in their troubles, and mingle a tear of sorrow with them, and do as we are exhorted to—weep with those that weep.

Thus my brethren we see what a chequered world we live in. Sometimes happy in having our wives and children like olive-branches about our tables; receiving the bounties of our great Benefactor. The next year, or month, or week, we may be deprived of some of them, and we go mourning about the streets: so in societies; we are this day to celebrate this Feast of St. John's, and the next week we might be called upon to attend a funeral of some one here, as we have experienced since our last in this Lodge. So in the common affairs of life we sometimes enjoy health and prosperity; at another time sickness and adversity, crosses and disappointments.

So in states and kingdoms; sometimes in tranquility; then wars and tumults; rich today, and poor to-morrow; which shews that there is not an independent mortal on earth; but dependent one upon the other, from the king to the beggar.

The great law-giver, Moses, who instructed by his father-in-law, Jethro, an Ethiopean, how to regulate his courts of justice, and what sort of men to choose for the different offices; hear now my words, said he, I will give you counsel, and God shall be with you; be thou for the people to Godward, that thou mayest bring the causes unto God, and thou shall teach them ordinances and laws, and shall shew the way wherein they must walk; and the work that they must do: moreover thou shall provide out of all the people, able men, such as fear God, men of truth, hating covetousness, and place such over them, to be rulers of thousands, of hundreds and of tens.

So Moses hearkened to the voice of his father-in-law, and did all that he said.—Exodus xviii. 22–24.

This is the first and grandest lecture that Moses ever received from the mouth of man; for Jethro understood geometry as well as laws, *that* a Mason may plainly see: so a little captive servant maid by whose advice Nomen, the great general of Syria's army was healed of his leprosy; and by a servant his proud spirit was brought down: 2 Kings, v, 3–14. The feelings of this little captive, for this great man, her captor, was so great, that she forgot her state of captivity, and felt for the distress of her enemy. Would to God (said she to her mistress) my lord were with the prophets in Samaria, he should be healed of his leprosy: So after he went to the prophet, his proud host was so haughty that he not only disdain'd the prophet's direction, but derided the good old prophet; and had it not been for his servant, he would have gone to his grave, with a double leprosy, the outward and the inward, in the heart, which is the worst of leprosies; a black heart is worse than a white leprosy.

How unlike was this great general's behaviour to that of as grand a character, and as well beloved by his prince as he was; I mean Obadiah, to a like prophet. See for this 1st Kings, xviii. from 7 to the 16th.

And as Obadiah was in the way, behold Elijah met him, and he knew him, and fell on his face, and said, Art not thou, my Lord, Elijah, and he told him, Yea, go and tell thy Lord, behold Elijah is here: and so on to the 16th verse. Thus we see, that great and good men have, and always will have, a respect for ministers and servants of God. Another instance of this is in Acts viii. 27 to 31, of the European Eunuch, a man of great authority, to Philip, the apostle: here is mutual love and friendship between them. This minister of Jesus Christ did not think himself too good to receive the hand, and ride in a chariot with a black man in the face of day; neither did this great monarch (for so he was) think it beneath him to take a poor servant of the Lord by the hand, and invite him into his carriage, though but with a staff, one coat and no money in his pocket. So our Grand Master, Solomon, was not asham'd to take the Queen of Sheba by the hand, and lead her into his court, at the hour of high twelve, and there converse with her on points of masonry (for if ever there was a female mason in the world she was one) and other curious matters; and gratified her, by shewing her all his riches and curious pieces of architecture in the temple, and in his house: After some time staying with her, he loaded her with much rich presents: he gave her the right hand of affection and parted in love.

I hope that no one will dare openly (tho' in fact the behaviour of some implies as much) to say, as our Lord said on another occasion. Behold a greater than Solomon is here. But yet let them consider that our Grand Master Solomon did not divide the living child, whatever he might do with the dead one, neither did he pretend to make a law, to forbid the parties from having free intercourse with one another without the fear of censure, or be turned out of the synagogue.

Now my brethren, as we see and experience, that all things here are frail and changeable and nothing here to be depended upon: Let us seek those things which are above, which are sure and stedfast, and unchangeable, and at the same time let us pray to Almighty God, while we remain in the tabernacle, that he would give us the grace of patience and strength to bear up under all our troubles, which at this day God knows we have our share. Patience I say, for were we not possess'd of a great measure of it you could not bear up under the daily insults you meet with in the streets of Boston; much more on public days of recreation, how are you shamefully abus'd, and that at such a degree, that you may truly be said to carry your lives in your hands; and the arrows of death are flying about your heads; helpless old women have their clothes torn off their backs, even to the exposing of their nakedness; and by whom are these disgraceful and abusive actions committed, not by the men born and bred in Boston, for they are better bred; but by a mob or horde of shameless, low-lived, envious, spiteful persons, some of them not long since, servants in gentlemen's kitchings, scouring knives, tending horses, and driving chaise. 'Twas said by a gentleman who saw that filthy behaviour in the common, that in all the places he had been in, he never saw so cruel behaviour in all his life, and that a slave in the West-Indies, on Sunday or holidays enjoys himself and friends without any molestation. Not only this man, but many in town who hath seen their behaviour to you, and that without any provocations, twenty or thirty cowards fall upon one man, have wonder'd at the patience of the Blacks: 'tis not for want of courage in you, for they know that they dare not face you man for man, but in a mob, which we despise, and had rather suffer wrong than to do wrong, to the disturbance of the community and the disgrace of our reputation: for every good citizen doth honor to the laws of the State where he resides.

My brethren, let us not be cast down under these and many other abuses we at present labour under: for the darkest is before the break of day: My brethren, let us remember what a dark day it was with our African brethren six years ago, in the French West-Indies. Nothing but the snap of the whip was heard from morning to evening; hanging, broken on the wheel, burning, and all manner of tortures inflicted on those unhappy people, for nothing else but to gratify their masters pride, wantonness and cruelty: but blessed be God, the scene is changed; they now confess that God hath no respect of persons, and therefore receive them as their friends, and treat them as brothers. Thus doth Ethiopia begin to stretch forth her hand, from a sink of slavery to freedom and equality.

Although you are deprived of the means of education; yet you are not deprived of the means of meditation; by which I mean thinking, hearing and weighing matters, men and things in your own mind, and making that judgment of them as you think reasonable to satisfy your minds and give an answer to those who may ask you a question. This nature hath furnished you with, without letter learning; and some have made great progress therein, some of those I have heard repeat psalms and hymns, and a great part of a sermon, only by hearing it read or preached and why not in other things in nature: how many of this class of our brethren that follow the seas; can foretell a storm some days before it comes; whether it will be a heavy or light, a long or short one; foretell a hurricane whether it will be destructive or moderate; without any other means than observation and consideration.

So in the observation of the heavenly bodies, this same class without a tellescope or other apparatus have through a smoak'd glass observed the eclipse of the sun: One being ask'd what he saw through his smoak'd glass? said, Saw, saw, de clipsey, or de clipseys;—and what do you think of it?— stop, dere be two;—right, and what do they look like?—Look like, why if I tell you, they look like two ships sailing one bigger than tother; so they sail by one another, and make no noise. As simple as the answers are they have a meaning, and shew, that God can out of the mouth of babes and Africans shew forth his glory; let us then love and adore him as the God who defends us and supports us and will support us under our pressures, let them be ever so heavy and pressing. Let us by the blessing of God, in whatsoever state we are, or may be in, to be content; for clouds and darkness are about him; but justice and truth is his habitation; who hath said, Vengeance is mine and I will repay it, therefore let us kiss the rod and be still, and see the works of the Lord.

Another thing I would warn you against, is the slavish fear of man, which bringest a snare, saith Solomon. This passion of fear, like pride and envy, hath slain its thousands.—What but this makes so many perjure themselves; for fear of offending them at home they are a little depending on, for some trifles: A man that is under a panic of fear, is afraid to be alone; you cannot hear of a robbery or house broke open or set on fire, but he hath an accomplice with him, who must share the spoil with him; whereas if he was truly bold, and void of fear, he would keep the whole plunder to himself: so when either of them is detected and not the other, he may be call'd to oath to keep it secret, but through fear, (and that passion is so strong) he will not confess, till the fatal cord is put on his neck; then death will deliver him from the fear of man, and he will confess the truth when it will not be of any good to himself or the community: nor is this passion of fear only to be found in this class of men, but among the great.

What was the reason that our African kings and princes have plung'd themselves and their peaceable kingdoms into bloody wars, to the destroying of towns and kingdoms, but the fear of the report of a great gun or the glittering of arms and swords, which struck these kings near the seaports with such a panic of fear, as not only to destroy the peace and happiness of their inland brethren, but plung'd millions of their fellow countrymen into slavery and cruel bondage.

So in other countries; see Felix trembling on his throne. How many Emperors and kings have left their kingdoms and best friends, at the sight of a handful of men in arms: how many have we seen that have left their estates and their friends and ran over to the stronger side as they thought: all through the fear of men; who is but a worm, and hath no more power to hurt his fellow worm, without the permission of God, than a real worm.

Thus we see my brethren, what a miserable condition it is to be under the slavish fear of men; it is of such a destructive nature to mankind, that the scriptures every where from Genesis to the Revelations warns us against it; and even our blessed Saviour himself forbids us from this slavish fear of man, in his sermon on the mount; and the only way to avoid it is to be in the fear of God: let a man consider the greatness of his power, as the maker and upholder of all things here below, and that in Him we live, and move, and have our being, the giver of the mercies we enjoy here from day to day, and that our lives are in his hands, and that he made the heavens, the sun, moon and stars to move in their various orders; let us thus view the greatness of God, and then turn our eyes on mortal man, a worm, a shade, a wafer, and see whether he is an object of fear or not; on the contrary, you will think him in his best estate, to be but vanity, feeble and a dependent mortal, and stands in need of your help, and cannot do without your assistance, in some way or other; and yet some of these poor mortals will try to make you believe they are Gods, but worship them not. My brethren let us pay all due respect to all whom God hath put in places of honor over us: do justly and be faithful to them that hire you, and treat them with that respect they may deserve; but worship no man. Worship God, this much is your duty as christians and as masons.

We see then how becoming and necessary it is to have a fellow feeling for our distress'd brethren of the human race, in their troubles, both spiritual and temporal—How refreshing it is to a sick man, to see his sympathising friends around his bed, ready to administer all the relief in their power; although they can't relieve his bodily pain yet they may ease his mind by good instructions and cheer his heart by their company.

How doth it cheer up the heart of a man when his house is on fire, to see a number of friends coming to his relief; he is so transported that he almost forgets his loss and his danger, and fills him with love and gratitude: and their joys and sorrows are mutual.

So a man wreck'd at sea, how must it revive his drooping heart to see a ship bearing down for his relief.

How doth it rejoice the heart of a stranger in a strange land to see the people cheerful and pleasant and are ready to help him.

How did it, think you, cheer the heart of those our poor unhappy

African brethren, to see a ship commissioned from God, and from a nation that without flattery saith, that all men are free and are brethren; I say to see them in an instant deliver such a number from their cruel bolts and galling chains, and to be fed like men, and treated like brethren. Where is the man that has the least spark of humanity, that will not rejoice with them; and bless a righteous God who knows how and when to relieve the oppressed, as we see he did in the deliverance of the captives among the Algerines; how sudden were they delivered by the sympathising members of the Congress of the United States, who now enjoy the free air of peace and liberty, to their great joy and surprize, to them and their friends. Here we see the hand of God in various ways, bringing about his own glory for the good of mankind, by the mutual help of their fellow men; which ought to teach us in all our straits, be they what they may, to put our trust in Him, firmly believing, that he is able and will deliver us and defend us against all our enemies; and that no weapon form'd against us shall prosper; only let us be steady and uniform in our walks, speech and behaviour; always doing to all men as we wish and desire they would do to us in the like cases and circumstances.

Live and act as Masons, that you may die as Masons; let those despisers see, altho' many of us cannot read, yet by our searches and researches into men and things, we have supplied that defect, and if they will let us we shall call ourselves a charter'd lodge, of just and lawful Masons; be always ready to give an answer to those that ask you a question; give the right hand of affection and fellowship to whom it justly belongs let their colour and complexion be what it will: let their nation be what it may, for they are your brethren, and it is your indispensible duty so to do; let them as Masons deny this, and we & the world know what to think of them be they ever so grand: for we know this was Solomon's creed, Solomon's creed did I say, it is the decree of the Almighty, and all Masons have learnt it: plain market language and plain and true facts need no apologies.

I shall now conclude with an old poem which I found among some papers: —

> Let blind admirers handsome faces praise,
> And graceful features to great honor raise,
> The glories of the red and white express,
> I know no beauty but in holiness;
> If God of beauty be the uncreate
> Perfect idea, in this lower state,
> The greatest beauties of an human mould
> Who most resemble Him we justly hold;
> Whom we resemble not in flesh and blood,
> But being pure and holy, just and good:
> May such a beauty fall but to my share,
> For curious shape or face I'll never care.

A PLEA FOR FEDERAL PROTECTION FOR MANUMITTED SLAVES IN THE SOUTH

Petition of Four Free Blacks to the
United States House of Representatives, 1797

Toward the close of the eighteenth century, the Southern states were beginning to fear the large number of free blacks living in their midst. As a result, they passed laws severely restricting the freeing, or manumission, of slaves. In 1775, North Carolina passed a law forbidding manumission not previously approved by a county court. Certain whites, however, continued to free their slaves; so, in 1778, North Carolina passed another law, providing a reward for the capture and resale of illegally freed blacks.

Needless to say, all free blacks were soon threatened by roving bands of whites intent on collecting the rewards. Many blacks left the state and settled in the North. In 1797, four of these "fugitive" free men filed a petition in the House of Representatives seeking federal protection for themselves and freedom for their relatives who had been freed and then sold again into slavery. The petition is reprinted here in its entirety.

After some debate, the House voted not to accept the petition, and the fate of black men was left to the discretion of the individual states.

To the President, Senate, and House of Representatives.

The Petition and Representation of the under-named Freemen, respectfully showeth: —

That, being of African descent, late inhabitants and natives of North Carolina, to you only, under God, can we apply with any hope of effect, for redress of our grievances, having been compelled to leave the State wherein we had a right of residence, as freemen liberated under the hand and seal of humane and conscientious masters, the validity of which act of justice, in restoring us to our native right of freedom, was confirmed by judgment of the Superior Court of North Carolina, wherein it was brought to trial; yet, not long after this decision, a law of that State was enacted, under which men of cruel disposition, and void of just principle, received countenance and authority in violently seizing, imprisoning, and selling into slavery, such as had been so emancipated; whereby we were reduced to the necessity of separating from some of our nearest and most tender connexions,

FROM *Annals of the Congress of the United States*, 4th Congress, 2nd Session (1796–97), pp. 2015–18.

and of seeking refuge in such parts of the Union where more regard is paid to the public declaration in favor of liberty and the common right of man, several hundreds, under our circumstances, having in consequence of the said law, been hunted day and night, like beasts of the forest, by armed men with dogs, and made a prey of as free and lawful plunder. Among others thus exposed, I, Jupiter Nicholson, of Perquimans county, North Carolina, after being set free by my master, Thomas Nicholson, and having been about two years employed as a seaman in the service of Zachary Nickson, on coming on shore, was pursued by men with dogs and arms; but was favored to escape by night to Virginia, with my wife, who was manumitted by Gabriel Cosand, where I resided about four years in the town of Portsmouth, chiefly employed in sawing boards and scantling; from thence I removed with my wife to Philadelphia, where I have been employed, at times, by water, working along shore, or sawing wood. I left behind me a father and mother, who were manumitted by Thomas Nicholson and Zachary Nickson; they have since been taken up, with a beloved brother, and sold into cruel bondage.

I, Jacob Nicholson, also of North Carolina, being set free by my master, Joseph Nicholson, but continuing to live with him till, being pursued night and day, I was obliged to leave my abode, sleep in the woods, and stacks in the fields, &c, to escape the hands of violent men who, induced by the profit afforded them by law, followed this course as a business; at length, by night, I made my escape, leaving a mother, one child, and two brothers, to see whom I dare not return.

I, Job Albert, manumitted by Benjamin Albertson, who was my careful guardian to protect me from being afterwards taken and sold, providing me with a house to accommodate me and my wife, who was liberated by William Robertson; but we were night and day hunted by men armed with guns, swords, and pistols, accompanied with mastiff dogs; from whose violence, being one night apprehensive of immediate danger, I left my dwelling, locked and barred, and fastened with a chain, being at some distance from it, while my wife was by my kind master locked up under his roof. I heard them break into my house, where, not finding their prey, they got but a small booty, a handkerchief of about a dollar value, and some provisions; but, not long after, I was discovered and seized by Alexander Stafford, William Stafford, and Thomas Creesy, who were armed with guns and clubs. After binding me with my hands behind me, and a rope around my arms and body, they took me about four miles to Hartford prison, where I lay four weeks, suffering much from want of provision; from thence, with the assistance of a fellow-prisoner, (a white man,) I made my escape and for three dollars was conveyed, with my wife, by a humane person, in a covered wagon by night, to Virginia, where, in the neighborhood of Portsmouth, I continued unmolested about four years, being chiefly engaged in sawing boards and plank. On being advised to move Northward, I came with my wife to Philadelphia, where I have labored for a livelihood upwards of two years, in Summer mostly, along shore in vessels and stores, and sawing wood in the Winter. My mother was set free by Phineas Nickson, my sister by John Trueblood, and both taken up and sold into slavery, myself deprived of the consolation of seeing them, without being exposed to the like grievous oppression.

I, Thomas Pritchet, was set free by my master Thomas Pritchet, who furnished me with land to raise provisions for my use, where I built myself a house, cleared a sufficient spot of woodland to produce ten bushels of corn; the second year about fifteen, and the third, had as much planted as I suppose would have produced thirty bushels; this I was obliged to leave about one month before it was fit for gathering, being threatened by Holland Lockwood, who married my said master's widow, that if I would not come and serve him, he would apprehend me, and send me to the West Indies; Enoch Ralph also threatening to send me to jail, and sell me for the good of the country; being thus in jeopardy, I left my little farm, with my small stock and utensils, and my corn standing, and escaped by night into Virginia, where shipping myself for Boston, I was, through stress of weather landed in New York, where I served as a waiter for seventeen months; but my mind being distressed on account of the situation of my wife and children, I returned to Norfolk in Virginia, with a hope of at least seeing them, if I could not obtain their freedom; but finding I was advertised in the newspaper, twenty dollars the reward for apprehending me, my dangerous situation obliged me to leave Virginia, disappointed of seeing my wife and children, coming to Philadelphia, where I resided in the employment of a waiter upward of two years.

In addition to the hardship of our own case, as above set forth, we believe ourselves warranted, on the present occasion, in offering to your consideration the singular case of a fellow-black now confined in the jail of this city, under sanction of the act of General Government, called the Fugitive Law, as it appears to us a flagrant proof how far human beings, merely on account of color and complexion, are, through prevailing prejudice, outlawed and excluded from common justice and common humanity, by the operation of such partial laws in support of habits and customs cruelly oppressive. This man, having been many years past manumitted by his master in North Carolina, was under the authority of the aforementioned law of that State, sold again into slavery, and, after serving his purchaser upwards of six years, made his escape to Philadelphia, where he has resided eleven years, having a wife and [f]our children; and, by an agent of the Carolina claimer, has been lately apprehended and committed to prison, his said claimer, soon after the man's escaping from him, having advertised him, offering a reward of ten silver dollars to any person that would bring him back, or five times that sum to any person that would make due proof of his being killed, and no questions asked by whom.

We beseech your impartial attention to our hard condition, not only with respect to our personal sufferings, as freemen, but as a class of that people who, distinguished by color, are therefore with a degrading partiality, considered by many, even of those in eminent stations, as unentitled to that public justice and protection which is the great object of Government. We indulge not a hope, or presume to ask for the interposition of your honorable body, beyond the extent of your constitutional power or influence, yet are willing to believe your serious, disinterested, and candid consideration of the premises, under the benign impressions of equity and mercy, producing upright exertion of what is in your power, may not be without some salutary effect, both for our relief as a people, and toward the removal of obstructions to public order and well-being.

If, notwithstanding all that has been publicly avowed as essential principles respecting the extent of human right to freedom; notwithstanding we have had that right restored to us, so far as was in the power of those by whom we were held as slaves, we cannot claim the privilege of representation in your councils, yet we trust we may address you as fellow-men, who, under God, the sovereign Ruler of the Universe, are intrusted with the distribution of justice, for the terror of evil-doers, the encouragement and protection of the innocent, not doubting that you are men of liberal minds, susceptible of benevolent feelings and clear conception of rectitude to a catholic extent, who can admit that black people (servile as their condition generally is throughout this Continent) have natural affections, social and domestic attachments and sensibilities; and that, therefore, we may hope for a share in your sympathetic attention while we represent that the unconstitutional bondage in which multitudes of our fellows in complexion are held, is to us a subject sorrowfully affecting; for we cannot conceive this condition (more especially those who have been emancipated and tasted the sweets of liberty, and again reduced to slavery by kidnappers and man-stealers) to be less afflicting or deplorable than the situation of citizens of the United States, captured and enslaved through the unrighteous policy prevalent in Algiers. We are far from considering all those who retain slaves as wilful oppressors, being well assured that numbers in the State from whence we are exiles, hold their slaves in bondage, not of choice, but possessing them by inheritance, feel their minds burdened under the slavish restraint of legal impediments to doing justice which they are convinced is due to fellow-rationals. May we not be allowed to consider this stretch of power, morally and politically, a Governmental defect, if not a direct violation of the declared fundamental principles of the Constitution; and finally, is not some remedy for an evil of such magnitude highly worthy of the deep inquiry and unfeigned zeal of the supreme Legislative body of a free and enlightened people? Submitting our cause to God, and humbly craving your best aid and influence, as you may be favored and directed by that wisdom which is from above, wherewith that you may be eminently dignified and rendered conspicuously, in the view of nations, a blessing to the people you represent, is the sincere prayer of your petitioners.

JACOB NICHOLSON,
JUPITER NICHOLSON, his mark,
JOB ALBERT, his mark,
THOMAS PRITCHET, his mark.

Philadelphia, January 23, 1787.

2

SUGGESTIONS FOR FURTHER READING

Only a few good books dealing with the black man in colonial America are available. Lorenzo J. Greene, *The Negro in Colonial New England** (Columbia University Press, 1942), and Thad Tate, Jr., *The Negro in Eighteenth Century Williamsburg** (University of Virginia Press, 1965), are among these. The relevant chapters of Marcus Jernegan, *Laboring and Dependent Classses in Colonial America, 1607–1783* (University of Chicago Press, 1931), are excellent.

There are several good books that treat the beginnings of the institution of slavery in the New World. These concern themselves primarily with the white community's attitudes toward blacks and the development of legal structures to support the slave system. Two recent prize-winning studies are Winthrop Jordan, *White Over Black: American Attitudes Toward the Negro, 1550–1812** (University of North Carolina Press, 1968), and David B. Davis, *The Problem of Slavery in Western Culture** (Cornell University Press, 1966). E. J. McManus, *A History of Negro Slavery in New York* (Syracuse University Press, 1966), is a study based largely on legal documents. A work dealing with early anti-slavery ideas is Thomas Drake, *Quakers and Slavery in America* (Yale University Press, 1950).

Several books now available offer a comparison of the development of the institution of slavery in North America and South America. The most recent of these are Herbert Klein, *Slavery in the Americas: A Comparative Study of Virginia and Cuba* (University of Chicago Press, 1967), and Marvin Harris, *Patterns of Race in the Americas** (Walker, 1964). These two studies correct some of the mistaken emphases of earlier works such as Frank Tannenbaum, *Slave and Citizen: The Negro in the Americas** (Knopf, 1946), and Gilberto Freyre, *The Masters and the Slaves** (Knopf, 1946).

Other studies of special interest are Benjamin Quarles, *The Negro in the American Revolution** (University of North Carolina Press, 1961), and Arthur Zilversmit, *The First Emancipation: The Abolition of Slavery in the North* (University of Chicago Press, 1967). A successful slave revolt in the Caribbean that had a great effect on nineteenth-century American slavery is treated by C. L. R. James in *Black Jacobins: Toussaint L'Ouverture and the San Domingo Revolution** (Dial, 1938).

3 SLAVERY IN THE NINETEENTH CENTURY

Slavery was virtually eliminated in the North, except in New York and New Jersey, before the end of the eighteenth century. It had proved to be economically unviable, and under pressure from free labor, abolitionists, and the blacks themselves, the new state constitutions and the various legislatures had ruled the enslavement of human beings illegal. It is sometimes suggested that slavery was on its way out in the South at the same time. Although this view has been discredited, there is no doubt that slavery in the South changed character and dimension radically in the nineteenth century.

The invention of the cotton gin in 1793, which made it possible to separate the seeds from the fiber of cotton quickly and on a large scale, and the purchase of the Louisiana Territory in 1803, which freed the Gulf Coast and the Mississippi River for the transportation of cotton bales, made short-staple cotton king in the Deep South. By the early nineteenth century, cotton had become the basic crop of Georgia and the Carolina foothills. In 1811, two-thirds of all the cotton grown in the United States came from this region. The cultivation of cotton rapidly spread farther south, however, and as it became clear that the rich soil of the Deep South provided ideal conditions for the growing of cotton, the center of production shifted. By 1860, the states of the Deep South and the Southwest as far as Texas were producing three-fourths of the cotton grown in the United States.

Many yeoman farmers found that cotton could be a money crop even on a small farm, but the plantation system came to be the most profitable one for cotton production. The backbone of the plantation system was, of course, the field slave. As cotton production moved south into the coastal and delta lands, plantations that were often quite large were set up there, and large numbers of slaves were called for. There were two obvious ways to procure the needed slaves—through the external and the internal slave trades. Although the external trade was declared illegal by the federal government in 1808, only token attempts were made to enforce this legislation, and it is estimated that from 250,000 to 300,000 African slaves were brought into the South between 1808 and 1860. More important, however, was the internal trade.

As the slave system became less viable in the Southeast because of the havoc wrought with the soil through intensive tobacco farming, the surplus of slaves could be sold to the new cotton-producing areas at great profit. Soon, then, the Southeast found itself literally breeding slaves for the market. The selling of slaves became a major item in Virginia's economy, and the sight of a hundred or more slaves chained together, walking from the upper to the lower South, was not uncommon.

Even though cotton was king, just under half the slaves in the South were engaged in cotton production. The rest were engaged in other kinds of agricultural work or—in the case of the 400,000 who lived in towns or cities—were involved in various trades, both skilled and unskilled.

When considering the creative role played in American history by black men, one must note first of all that most slaves were merely victims. There were, however, many who found ways of seeking deliverance from the system that denied them even the most fundamental of human rights. It was in this search for freedom and self-expression that the slave made his most important contributions to our heritage.

The first and most obvious way of seeking deliverance was through organized rebellion or insurrection. There is much controversy over the number of slave rebellions that actually occurred in the South. Many of the so-called uprisings undoubtedly took place only in the minds of an increasingly fearful white slave-owning population. But the threat of insurrection was real, and the slave-owners' fear was historically justified, for groups of slaves had been rebelling ever since the Africans arrived in the New World. In the Caribbean and in Brazil, for instance, large numbers of slaves had fought for freedom from their masters and had succeeded in setting up independent states. And Southern whites were well informed about the role played by the slaves in establishing Haiti as a free black state and thus destroying Napoleon's dream of a Western empire.

The three most widely publicized slave conspiracies in the United States were those led by Gabriel Prosser in Richmond, Virginia, in 1800; by Denmark Vesey in Charleston, South Carolina, in 1822; and by Nat Turner near Southampton, Virginia, in 1831. As a result of these conspiracies, the laws restricting the freedom of slaves and free blacks in the South were made even more oppressive. The very heavy-handedness of the measures taken to suppress the slaves indicates that the slave masters lived in great fear of black rebellion—a fact that belies the pious utterings of those who have sought to defend slavery on the grounds that the slaves themselves were content.

A second form of revolt for the slave was simply running away. From the beginning of slavery in the colonies, large numbers of slaves won their freedom in this way. Some of them joined Indian tribes; others formed bands that terrorized white settlers in Virginia, the Carolinas, and Alabama. Many of the runaways must have died in the forest, forgotten but free. It is estimated that by 1855 as many as 60,000 slaves had fled toward the North, sometimes leaving behind dead or wounded masters. By that time, the Underground Railroad, conducted primarily by blacks, was in operation, aiding fugitives as they sought to escape not only the South but also the enforcement of the federal Fugitive Slave Laws in the free states.

A third way of seeking deliverance was through non-cooperation with the system. Slaves soon earned a reputation for being lazy, refusing to work hard; clumsy, breaking tools and other equipment; and dishonest, stealing food and valuables of all kinds. These characteristics were often cited as evidence of the inferiority of the slave. Indeed, much of the writing that has been done about the uncivilized nature of the black man is based on such testimony from former slave-owners. Needless to say, this behavior can be interpreted another way. By such deliberate gestures, the slave was able to indicate his hostility to the system.

The Christian religion provided the slave with his ultimate means of deliverance. As the spiritual says of the promise of heaven, "Free at last, free at last, / I thank God I'm free at last."

REBELLION

The Confessions of Nat Turner

Whites who were reluctant to allow slaves to hear about Christianity had a good sense of the danger inherent in the gospel of liberation: several of the leaders of slave insurrections considered themselves called by God to free their people. The most famous of these was Nat Turner, who led a rebellion of slaves in Virginia in 1831. Approximately seventy slaves were involved in the uprising, and some fifty-five whites were killed. The rebellion was finally put down with the use of local militia, and many prisoners were taken. About twenty were tried and executed for their part in the disturbance, and at least a hundred innocent blacks were murdered in the weeks that followed by vigilante bands of whites that roamed the Virginia countryside. Nat Turner himself was tried, found guilty, and hanged. Subsequently, the work of black ministers in the South was severely circumscribed, and whites tried to extend their control over the religious life of the slaves.

The text that follows is the entire confession of Nat Turner as taken down by a white lawyer immediately before the trial.

Agreeable to his own appointment, on the evening he was committed to prison, with permission of the jailor, I visited NAT on Tuesday the 1st November, when, without being questioned at all, he commenced his narrative in the following words:—

Sir,—You have asked me to give a history of the motives which induced me to undertake the late insurrection, as you call it—To do so I must go back to the days of my infancy, and even before I was born. I was thirty-one years of age the 2d of October last, and born the property of Benj. Turner, of this county. In my childhood a circumstance occurred which made an indelible impression on my mind, and laid the ground work of that enthusiasm, which has terminated so fatally to many, both white and black, and for which I am about to atone at the gallows. It is here necessary to relate this circumstance—trifling as it may seem, it was the commencement of that belief which has grown with time, and even now, sir, in this dungeon, helpless and forsaken as I am, I cannot divest myself of. Being at play with other children, when three or four years old, I was telling them something, which my mother overhearing, said it had happened before I was born—I stuck to my story, however, and related some things which went, in her

---

FROM *The Confessions of Nat Turner, the leader of the late insurrection in Southampton, Va. As fully and voluntarily made to Thomas R. Gray* . . . (Baltimore, 1831).

opinion, to confirm it—others being called on were greatly astonished, knowing that these things had happened, and caused them to say in my hearing, I surely would be a prophet, as the Lord had shewn me things that had happened before my birth. And my father and mother strengthened me in this my first impression, saying in my presence, I was intended for some great purpose, which they had always thought from certain marks on my head and breast—[a parcel of excrescences which I believe are not at all uncommon, particularly among negroes, as I have seen several with the same. In this case he has either cut them off or they have nearly disappeared]—My grand mother, who was very religious, and to whom I was much attached—my master, who belonged to the church, and other religious persons who visited the house, and whom I often saw at prayers, noticing the singularity of my manners, I suppose, and my uncommon intelligence for a child, remarked I had too much sense to be raised, and if I was, I would never be of any service to any one as a slave—To a mind like mine, restless, inquisitive and observant of every thing that was passing, it is easy to suppose that religion was the subject to which it would be directed, and although this subject principally occupied my thoughts—there was nothing that I saw or heard of to which my attention was not directed—The manner in which I learned to read and write, not only had great influence on my own mind, as I acquired it with the most perfect ease, so much so, that I have no recollection whatever of learning the alphabet—but to the astonishment of the family, one day, when a book was shewn me to keep me from crying, I began spelling the names of different objects—this was a source of wonder to all in the neighborhood, particularly the blacks—and this learning was constantly improved at all opportunities—when I got large enough to go to work, while employed, I was reflecting on many things that would present themselves to my imagination, and whenever an opportunity occurred of looking at a book, when the school children were getting their lessons, I would find many things that the fertility of my own imagination had depicted to me before; all my time, not devoted to my master's service, was spent either in prayer, or in making experiments in casting different things in moulds made of earth, in attempting to make paper, gun-powder, and many other experiments, that although I could not perfect, yet convinced me of its practicability if I had the means.[1] I was not addicted to stealing in my youth, nor have ever been—Yet such was the confidence of the negroes in the neighborhood, even at this early period of my life, in my superior judgment, that they would often carry me with them when they were going on any roguery, to plan for them. Growing up among them, with this confidence in my superior judgment, and when this, in their opinions, was perfected by Divine inspiration, from the circumstances already alluded to in

---

[1] When questioned as to the manner of manufacturing those different articles, he was found well informed on the subject.

my infancy, and which belief was ever afterwards zealously inculcated by the austerity of my life and manners, which became the subject of remark by white and black.—Having soon discovered to be great, I must appear so, and therefore studiously avoided mixing in society, and wrapped myself in mystery, devoting my time to fasting and prayer—By this time, having arrived to man's estate, and hearing the scriptures commented on at meetings, I was struck with that particular passage which says: "Seek ye the kingdom of Heaven and all things shall be added unto you." I reflected much on this passage, and prayed daily for light on this subject—As I was praying one day at my plough, the spirit spoke to me, saying "Seek ye the kingdom of Heaven and all things shall be added unto you." *Question*—what do you mean by the Spirit. *Ans.* The Spirit that spoke to the prophets in former days— and I was greatly astonished, and for two years prayed continually, whenever my duty would permit—and then again I had the same revelation, which fully confirmed me in the impression that I was ordained for some great purpose in the hands of the Almighty. Several years rolled round, in which many events occurred to strengthen me in this my belief. At this time I reverted in my mind to the remarks made of me in my childhood, and the things that had been shewn me—and as it had been said of me in my childhood by those by whom I had been taught to pray, both white and black, and in whom I had the greatest confidence, that I had too much sense to be raised, and if I was, I would never be of any use to any one as a slave. Now finding I had arrived to man's estate, and was a slave, and these revelations being made known to me, I began to direct my attention to this great object, to fulfil the purpose for which, by this time, I felt assured I was intended. Knowing the influence I had obtained over the minds of my fellow servants, (not by the means of conjuring and such like tricks—for to them I always spoke of such things with contempt) but by the communion of the Spirit whose revelations I often communicated to them, and they believed and said my wisdom came from God. I now began to prepare them for my purpose, by telling them something was about to happen that would terminate in fulfilling the great promise that had been made to me—About this time I was placed under an overseer, from whom I ran away—and after remaining in the woods thirty days, I returned, to the astonishment of the negroes on the plantation, who thought I had made my escape to some other part of the country, as my father had done before. But the reason of my return was, that the Spirit appeared to me and said I had my wishes directed to the things of this world, and not to the kingdom of Heaven, and that I should return to the service of my earthly master—"For he who knoweth his Master's will, and doeth it not, shall be beaten with many stripes, and thus have I chastened you." And the negroes found fault, and murmured against me, saying that if they had my sense they would not serve any master in the world. And about this time I had a vision—and I saw white spirits and black spirits engaged in battle, and the sun was darkened—the thunder rolled in the Heavens, and blood flowed in streams—and I heard a voice saying, "Such is your luck, such you are called to see, and let it come rough or smooth, you must surely bear it." I now withdrew myself as much as my situation would permit, from the intercourse of my fellow servants, for the avowed purpose of serving the Spirit more fully—and it appeared to me, and reminded me of the things it had already shown me, and that it would then reveal to me the knowledge of the elements, the revolution of the planets, the operation of tides, and changes of the seasons. After this revelation in the year 1825, and the knowledge of the elements being made known to me, I sought more than ever to obtain true holiness before the great day of judgment should appear, and then I began to receive the true knowledge of faith. And from the first steps of righteousness until the last, was I made perfect; and the Holy Ghost was with me, and said, "Behold me as I stand in the Heavens"—and I looked and saw the forms of men in different attitudes—and there were lights in the sky to which the children of darkness gave other names than what they really were—for they were the lights of the Saviour's hands, stretched forth from east to west, even as they were extended on the cross on Calvary for the redemption of sinners. And I wondered greatly at these miracles, and prayed to be informed of a certainty of the meaning thereof—and shortly afterwards, while laboring in the field, I discovered drops of blood on the corn as though it were dew from heaven —and I communicated it to many, both white and black, in the neighborhood—and I then found on the leaves in the woods hieroglyphic characters, and numbers, with the forms of men in different attitudes, portrayed in blood, and representing the figures I had seen before in the heavens. And now the Holy Ghost had revealed itself to me, and made plain the miracles it had shown me—For as the blood of Christ had been shed on this earth, and had ascended to heaven for the salvation of sinners, and was now returning to earth again in the form of dew—and as the leaves on the trees bore the impression of the figures I had seen in the heavens, it was plain to me that the Saviour was about to lay down the yoke he had borne for the sins of men, and the great day of judgment was at hand. About this time I told these things to a white man, (Etheldred T. Brantley) on whom it had a wonderful effect—and he ceased from his wickedness, and was attacked immediately with a cutaneous eruption, and blood oozed from the pores of his skin, and after praying and fasting nine days, he was healed, and the Spirit appeared to me again, and said, as the Saviour had been baptised so should we be also—and when the white people would not let us be baptised by the church, we went down into the water together, in the sight of many who reviled us, and were baptised by the Spirit—After this I rejoiced greatly, and gave thanks to God. And on the 12th of May, 1828, I heard a loud noise in the heavens, and the Spirit instantly appeared to me and said the Serpent was loosened, and Christ had laid down the yoke he had borne for the sins of men, and that I should take it on and fight against the Serpent, for the time was fast approaching when the first should be last and the last should be first. *Ques.* Do you not find yourself mistaken now? *Ans.* Was not Christ crucified. And by signs in the heavens that it would make known to me when I should commence the great work—and until the first sign appeared, I should conceal it from the knowledge of men—And on the appearance of the sign, (the eclipse of the sun last February) I should arise and prepare myself, and slay my enemies with their own weapons. And immediately on the sign appearing in the heavens, the seal was removed from my lips, and I communicated the great work laid out for me to do, to four in whom I had the greatest confidence, (Henry, Hark, Nelson, and Sam)—It was intended by us to have begun the work of death on the 4th July last—Many were the plans formed and rejected by us, and it affected my mind to such a degree, that I fell sick, and the time passed without our coming to any determination how to commence —Still forming new schemes and rejecting them, when the sign appeared again, which determined me not to wait longer.

Since the commencement of 1830, I had been living with Mr. Joseph Travis, who was to me a kind master, and placed the greatest confidence in me; in fact, I had no cause to complain of his treatment to me. On Saturday evening, the 20th of August, it was agreed between Henry, Hark and myself, to prepare a dinner the next day for the men we expected, and then to concert a plan, as we had not yet determined on any. Hark, on the following morning, brought a pig, and Henry brandy, and being joined by Sam, Nelson, Will and Jack, they prepared in the woods a dinner, where, about three o'clock, I joined them.

Q. Why were you so backward in joining them.

A. The same reason that had caused me not to mix with them for years before.

I saluted them on coming up, and asked Will how came he there, he answered, his life was worth no more than others, and his liberty as dear to him. I asked him if he thought to obtain it? He said he would, or loose his life. This was enough to put him in full confidence. Jack, I knew, was only a tool in the hands of Hark, it was quickly agreed we should commence at home (Mr. J. Travis') on that night, and until we had armed and equipped ourselves, and gathered sufficient force, neither age nor sex was to be spared, (which was invariably adhered to.) We remained at the feast, until about two hours in the night, when we went to the house and found Austin; they all went to the cider press and drank, except myself. On returning to the house, Hark went to the door with an axe, for the purpose of breaking it open, as we knew we were strong enough to murder the family, if they were awakened by the noise; but reflecting that it might create an alarm in the neighborhood, we determined to enter the house secretly, and murder them whilst sleeping. Hark got a ladder and set it against the chimney, on which I ascended, and hoisting a window, entered and came down stairs, unbarred the door, and removed the guns from their places. It was then observed that I must spill the first blood. On which, armed with a hatchet, and accompanied by Will, I entered my master's chamber, it being dark, I could not give a death blow, the hatchet glanced from his head, he sprang from the bed and called his wife, it was his last word, Will laid him dead, with a blow of his axe, and Mrs. Travis shared the same fate, as she lay in bed. The murder of this family, five in number, was the work of a moment, not one of them awoke; there was a little infant sleeping in a cradle, that was forgotten, until we had left the house and gone some distance, when Henry and Will returned and killed it; we got here, four guns that would shoot, and several old muskets, with a pound or two of powder. We remained some time at the barn, where we paraded; I formed them in a line as soldiers, and after carrying them through all the manœuvres I was master of, marched them off to Mr. Salathul Francis', about six hundred yards distant. Sam and Will went to the door and knocked. Mr. Francis asked who was there, Sam replied it was him, and he had a letter for him, on which he got up and came to the door; they immediately seized him, and dragging him out a little from the door, he was dispatched by repeated blows on the head; there was no other white person in the family. We started from there for Mrs. Reese's, maintaining the most perfect silence on our march, where finding the door unlocked, we entered, and murdered Mrs. Reese in her bed, while sleeping; her son awoke, but it was only to sleep the sleep of death, he had only time to say who is that, and he was no more. From Mrs. Reese's we went to Mrs. Turner's, a mile distant, which we reached about sunrise, on Monday morning. Henry, Austin, and Sam, went to the still, where, finding Mr. Peebles, Austin shot him, and the rest of us went to the house; as we approached, the family discovered us, and shut the door. Vain hope! Will, with one stroke of his axe, opened it, and we entered and found Mrs. Turner and Mrs. Newsome in the middle of a room, almost frightened to death. Will immediately killed Mrs. Turner, with one blow of his axe. I took Mrs. Newsome by the hand, and with the sword I had when I was apprehended, I struck her several blows over the head, but not being able to kill her, as the sword was dull. Will turning around and discovering it, despatched her also. A general destruction of property and search for money and ammunition, always succeeded the murders. By this time my company amounted to fifteen, and nine men mounted, who started for Mrs. Whitehead's, (the other six were to go through a byway to Mr. Bryant's, and rejoin us at Mrs. Whitehead's,) as we approached the house we discovered Mr. Richard Whitehead standing in the cotton patch, near the lane fence; we called him over into the lane, and Will, the executioner, was near at hand, with his fatal axe, to send him to an untimely grave. As we pushed on to the house, I discovered some one run round the garden, and thinking it was some of the white family, I pursued them, but finding it was a servant girl belonging to the house, I returned to commence the work of death, but they whom I left, had not been idle; all the family were already murdered, but Mrs. Whitehead and her daughter

Margaret. As I came round to the door I saw Will pulling Mrs. Whitehead out of the house, and at the step he nearly severed her head from her body, with his broad axe. Miss Margaret, when I discovered her, had concealed herself in the corner, formed by the projection of the cellar cap from the house; on my approach she fled, but was soon overtaken, and after repeated blows with a sword, I killed her by a blow on the head, with a fence rail. By this time, the six who had gone by Mr. Bryant's, rejoined us, and informed me they had done the work of death assigned them. We again divided, part going to Mr. Richard Porter's, and from thence to Nathaniel Francis', the others to Mr. Howell Harris', and Mr. T. Doyles. On my reaching Mr. Porter's, he had escaped with his family. I understood there, that the alarm had already spread, and I immediately returned to bring up those sent to Mr. Doyles, and Mr. Howell Harris'; the party I left going on to Mr. Francis', having told them I would join them in that neighborhood. I met these sent to Mr. Doyles' and Mr. Harris' returning, having met Mr. Doyle on the road and killed him; and learning from some who joined them, that Mr. Harris was from home, I immediately pursued the course taken by the party gone on before; but knowing they would complete the work of death and pillage, at Mr. Francis' before I could get there, I went to Mr. Peter Edwards', expecting to find them there, but they had been here also. I then went to Mr. John T. Barrow's, they had been here and murdered him. I pursued on their track to Capt. Newit Harris', where I found the greater part mounted, and ready to start; the men now amounting to about forty, shouted and hurraed as I rode up, some were in the yard, loading their guns, others drinking. They said Captain Harris and his family had escaped, the property in the house they destroyed, robbing him of money and other valuables. I ordered them to mount and march instantly, this was about nine or ten o'clock, Monday morning. I proceeded to Mr. Levi Waller's, two or three miles distant. I took my station in the rear, and as it 'twas my object to carry terror and devastation wherever we went, I placed fifteen or twenty of the best armed and most to be relied on, in front, who generally approached the house as fast as their horses could run; this was for two purposes, to prevent their escape and strike terror to the inhabitants—on this account I never got to the houses, after leaving Mrs. Whitehead's, until the murders were committed, except in one case. I sometimes got in sight in time to see the work of death completed, viewed the mangled bodies as they lay, in silent satisfaction, and immediately started in quest of other victims—Having murdered Mrs. Waller and ten children, we started for Mr. William Williams'—having killed him and two little boys that were there; while engaged in this, Mrs. Williams fled and got some distance from the house, but she was pursued, overtaken, and compelled to get up behind one of the company, who brought her back, and after showing her the mangled body of her lifeless husband, she was told to get down and lay by his side, where she was shot dead. I then started for Mr. Jacob Williams, where the family were murdered—Here we found a young man named Drury, who had come on business with Mr. Williams—he was pursued, overtaken and shot. Mrs. Vaughan was the next place we visited—and after murdering the family here, I determined on starting for Jerusalem—Our number amounted now to fifty or sixty, all mounted and armed with guns, axes, swords and clubs—On reaching Mr. James W. Parkers' gate, immediately on the road leading to Jerusalem, and about three miles distant, it was proposed to me to call there, but I objected, as I knew he was gone to Jerusalem, and my object was to reach there as soon as possible; but some of the men having relations at Mr. Parker's it was agreed that they might call and get his people. I remained at the gate on the road, with seven or eight; the others going across the field to the house, about half a mile off. After waiting some time for them, I became impatient, and started to the house for them, and on our return we were met by a party of white men, who had pursued our blood-stained track, and who had fired on those at the gate, and dispersed them, which I knew nothing of, not having been at that time rejoined by any of them—immediately on discovering the whites, I ordered my men to halt and form, as they appeared to be alarmed—The white men, eighteen in number, approached us in about one hundred yards, when one of them fired, (this was against the positive orders of Captain Alexander P. Peete, who commanded, and who had directed the men to reserve their fire until within thirty paces) And I discovered about half of them retreating, I then ordered my men to fire and rush on them; the few remaining stood their ground until we approached within fifty yards, when they fired and retreated. We pursued and overtook some of them who we thought we left dead; (they were not killed) after pursuing them about two hundred yards, and rising a little hill, I discovered they were met by another party, and had halted, and were re-loading their guns, (this was a small party from Jerusalem who knew the negroes were in the field, and had just tied their horses to await their return to the road, knowing that Mr. Parker and family were in Jerusalem, but knew nothing of the party that had gone in with Captain Peete; on hearing the firing they immediately rushed to the spot and arrived just in time to arrest the progress of these barbarous villains, and save the lives of their friends and fellow citizens.) Thinking that those who retreated first, and the party who fired on us at fifty or sixty yards distant, had all only fallen back to meet others with ammunition. As I saw them re-loading their guns, and more coming up than I saw at first, and several of my bravest men being wounded, the others became panick struck and squandered over the field; the white men pursued and fired on us several times. Hark had his horse shot under him, and I caught another for him as it was running by me; five or six of my men were wounded, but none left on the field; finding myself defeated here I instantly determined to go through a private way, and cross the Nottoway river at the Cypress Bridge, three miles below Jerusalem, and attack that place in the rear, as I expected they would look for me on the other road, and I had a great desire to get there to procure arms and ammunition. After going a short distance in this private way, accompanied by about twenty men, I overtook two or three who told me the others were dispersed in every direction. After trying in vain to collect a sufficient force to proceed to Jerusalem, I determined to return, as I was sure they would make back to their old neighborhood, where they would rejoin me, make new recruits, and come down again. On my way back, I called at Mrs. Thomas's, Mrs. Spencer's, and several other places, the white families having fled, we found no more victims to gratify our thirst for blood, we stopped at Maj. Ridley's quarter for the night, and being joined by four of his men, with the recruits made since my defeat, we mustered now about forty strong. After placing out sentinels, I laid down to sleep, but was quickly roused by a great racket; starting up, I found some mounted, and others in great confusion; one of the sentinels having given the alarm that we were about to be attacked, I ordered some to ride round and reconnoitre, and on their return the others being more alarmed, not knowing who they were, fled in different ways, so that I was reduced to about twenty again; with this I determined to attempt to recruit, and proceed on to rally in the neighborhood, I had left. Dr. Blunt's was the nearest house, which we reached just before day; on riding up the yard, Hark fired a gun. We expected Dr. Blunt and his family were at Maj. Ridley's, as I knew there was a company of men there; the gun was fired to ascertain if any of the family were at home; we were immediately fired upon and retreated, leaving several of my men. I do not know what became of them, as I never saw them afterwards. Pursuing our course back and coming in sight of Captain Harris', where we had been the day before, we discovered a party of white men at the house, on which all deserted me but two, (Jacob and Nat,) we concealed ourselves in the woods until near night, when I sent them in search of Henry, Sam, Nelson, and Hark, and directed them to rally all they could, at the place we had had our dinner the Sunday before, where they would find me, and I accordingly returned there as soon as it was dark and remained until Wednesday evening, when discovering white men riding around the place as though they were looking for some one, and none of my men joining me, I concluded Jacob and Nat had been taken, and compelled to betray me. On this I gave up all hope for the present; and on Thursday night after having supplied myself with provisions from Mr. Travis's, I scratched a hole under a pile of fence rails in a field, where I concealed myself for six weeks, never leaving my hiding place but for a few minutes in the dead of night to get water which was very near; thinking by this time I could venture out, I began to go about in the night and eaves drop the houses in the neighborhood; pursuing this course for about a fortnight and gathering little or no intelligence, afraid of speaking to any human being, and returning every morning to my cave before the dawn of day. I know not how long I might have led this life, if accident had not betrayed me, a dog in the neighborhood passing by my hiding place one night while I was out, was attracted by some meat I had in my cave, and crawled in and stole it, and was coming out just as I returned. A few nights after, two negroes having started to go hunting with the same dog, and passed that way, the dog came again to the place, and having just gone out to walk about, discovered me and barked, on which thinking myself discovered, I spoke to them to beg concealment. On making myself known they fled from me. Knowing then they would betray me, I immediately left my hiding place, and was pursued almost incessantly until I was taken a fortnight afterwards by Mr. Benjamin Phipps, in a little hole I had dug out with my sword, for the purpose of concealment, under the top of a fallen tree. On Mr. Phipps' discovering the place of my concealment, he cocked his gun and aimed at me. I requested him not to shoot and I would give up, upon which he demanded my sword. I delivered it to him, and he brought me to prison. During the time I was pursued, I had many hair breadth escapes, which your time will not permit you to relate. I am here loaded with chains, and willing to suffer the fate that awaits me.

I here proceeded to make some inquiries of him, after assuring him of the certain death that awaited him, and that concealment would only bring destruction on the innocent as well as guilty, of his own color, if he knew of any extensive or concerted plan. His answer was, I do not. When I questioned him as to the insurrection in North Carolina happening about the same time, he denied any knowledge of it; and when I looked him in the face as though I would search his inmost thoughts, he replied, "I see sir, you doubt my word; but can you not think the same ideas, and strange appearances about this time in the heaven's might prompt others, as well as myself, to this undertaking." I now had much conversation with and asked him many questions, having forborne to do so previously, except in the cases noted in parenthesis; but during his statement, I had, unnoticed by him, taken notes as to some particular circumstances, and having the advantage of his statement before me in writing, on the evening of the third day that I had been with him, I began a cross examination, and found his statement corroborated by every circumstance coming within my own knowledge or the confessions of others who had been either killed or executed, and whom he had not seen nor had any knowledge since 22d of August last, he expressed himself fully satisfied as to the impracticability of his attempt. It has been said he was ignorant and cowardly, and that his object was to murder and rob for the purpose of obtaining money to make his escape. It is notorious, that he was never known to have a dollar in his life; to swear an oath, or drink a drop of spirits. As to his ignorance, he certainly never had the advantages of education, but he can read and write, (it was taught him by his parents,) and for natural intelligence and quickness of apprehension, is surpassed by few men I have ever seen. As to his being a coward, his reason as given for not resisting Mr. Phipps, shews the decision of his character.

When he saw Mr. Phipps present his gun, he said he knew it was impossible for him to escape as the woods were full of men; he therefore thought it was better to surrender, and trust to fortune for his escape. He is a complete fanatic, or plays his part most admirably. On other subjects he possesses an uncommon share of intelligence, with a mind capable of attaining any thing; but warped and perverted by the influence of early impressions. He is below the ordinary stature, though strong and active, having the true negro face, every feature of which is strongly marked. I shall not attempt to describe the effect of his narrative, as told and commented on by himself, in the condemned hole of the prison. The calm, deliberate composure with which he spoke of his late deeds and intentions, the expression of his fiend-like face when excited by enthusiasm, still bearing the stains of the blood of helpless innocence about him; clothed with rags and covered with chains; yet daring to raise his manacled hands to heaven, with a spirit soaring above the attributes of man; I looked on him and my blood curdled in my veins.

I will not shock the feelings of humanity, nor wound afresh the bosoms of the disconsolate sufferers in this unparalleled and inhuman massacre, by detailing the deeds of their fiend-like barbarity. There were two or three who were in the power of these wretches, had they known it, and who escaped in the most providential manner. There were two whom they thought they left dead on the field at Mr. Parker's, but who were only stunned by the blows of their guns, as they did not take time to re-load when they charged on them. The escape of a little girl who went to school at Mr. Waller's, and where the children were collecting for that purpose, excited general sympathy. As their teacher had not arrived, they were at play in the yard, and seeing the negroes approach, she ran up on a dirt chimney, (such as are common to log houses,) and remained there unnoticed during the massacre of the eleven that were killed at this place. She remained on her hiding place till just before the arrival of a party, who were in pursuit of the murderers, when she came down and fled to a swamp, where, a mere child as she was, with the horrors of the late scene before her, she lay concealed until the next day, when seeing a party go up to the house, she came up, and on being asked how she escaped, replied with the utmost simplicity, "The Lord helped her." She was taken up behind a gentleman of the party, and returned to the arms of her weeping mother. Miss Whitehead concealed herself between the bed and the mat that supported it, while they murdered her sister in the same room, without discovering her. She was afterwards carried off, and concealed for protection by a slave of the family, who gave evidence against several of them on their trial. Mrs. Nathaniel Francis, while concealed in a closet heard their blows, and the shrieks of the victims of these ruthless savages; they then entered the closet where she was concealed, and went out without discovering her. While in this hiding place, she heard two of her women in a quarrel about the division of her clothes. Mr. John T. Baron, discovering them approaching his house, told his wife to make her escape, and scorning to fly, fell fighting on his own threshold.

After firing his rifle, he discharged his gun at them, and then broke it over the villain who first approached him, but he was overpowered, and slain. His bravery, however, saved from the hands of these monsters, his lovely and amiable wife, who will long lament a husband so deserving of her love. As directed by him, she attempted to escape through the garden, when she was caught and held by one of her servant girls, but another coming to her rescue, she fled to the woods, and concealed herself. Few indeed, were those who escaped their work of death. But fortunate for society, the hand of retributive justice has overtaken them; and not one that was known to be concerned has escaped.

LIFE AS A SLAVE

Mary Reynolds   /   A Narrative

During the Great Depression of the 1930's, the Federal Writers' Project, one of the New Deal programs, recorded the reminiscences of a large number of former slaves who were still living. Over ten thousand manuscript pages were collected in this fashion. A selection from them was published in 1945 in a book entitled **Lay My Burden Down: A Folk History of Slavery.** An exceedingly rich source of folk recollection about slavery, the book includes folk-tales, stories about plantation life, and memories of the freedom that the Civil War brought.

Reprinted here is the reminiscence of Mary Reynolds, of Dallas, Texas, who was almost a hundred years old at the time of her interview. She had been a slave on a big cotton plantation in Louisiana, and the wit and vigor with which she describes her life there make this narrative one of the liveliest documents of its kind.

My paw's name was Tom Vaughn, and he was from the North, born free man and lived and died free to the end of his days. He wasn't no educated man, but he was what he calls himself a piano man. He told me once he lived in New York and Chicago and he built the insides of pianos and knew how to make them play in tune. He said some white folks from the

FROM B. A. Botkin (ed.), *Lay My Burden Down: A Folk History of Slavery* (Chicago, 1945), pp. 119–25. Copyright 1945 by The University of Chicago. All rights reserved. Published 1945. Fourth Impression 1958.

South told he if he'd come with them to the South he'd find a lot of work to do with pianos in them parts, and he come off with them.

He saw my maw on the place and her man was dead. He told my massa he'd buy my maw and her three children with all the money he had, iffen he'd sell her. But Massa was never one to sell any but the old niggers who was past working in the fields and past their breeding times. So my paw married my maw and works the fields, same as any other nigger. They had six gals: Martha and Panela and Josephine and Ellen and Katherine and me.

I was born same time as Miss Dora. Massa's first wife and my maw come to their time right together. Miss Dora's maw died, and they brung Miss Dora to suck with me. It's a thing we ain't never forgot. My maw's name was Sallie and Miss Dora always looked with kindness on my maw. We sucked till we was a fair size and played together, which wasn't no common thing. None the other little niggers played with the white children. But Miss Dora loved me so good.

I was just 'bout big 'nough to start playing with a broom to go 'bout sweeping up and not even half doing it when Massa sold me. They was a old white man in Trinity, and his wife died and he didn't have chick or child or slave or nothing. Massa sold me cheap, 'cause he didn't want Miss Dora to play with no nigger young-un. That old man bought me a big doll and went off and left me all day, with the door open. I just sot on the floor and played with that doll. I used to cry. He'd come home and give me something to eat and then go to bed, and I slept on the foot of the bed with him. I was scared all the time in the dark. He never did close the door.

Miss Dora pined and sickened. Massa done what he could, but they wasn't no pertness in her. She got sicker and sicker, and Massa brung 'nother doctor. He say, "You little gal is grieving the life out her body, and she sure gwine die iffen you don't do something 'bout it." Miss Dora says over and over, "I wants Mary." Massa say to the doctor, "That a little nigger young-un I done sold." The doctor tells him he better git me back iffen he wants to save the life of his child. Massa has to give a big plenty more to git me back than what he sold me for, but Miss Dora plumps up right off and grows into fine health.

Then Massa marries a rich lady from Mississippi, and they has children for company to Miss Dora and seem like for a time she forgits me.

Massa wasn't no piddling man. He was a man of plenty. He had a big house with no more style to it than a crib, but it could room plenty people. He was a medicine doctor, and they was rooms in the second story for sick folks what come to lay in. It would take two days to go all over the land he owned. He had cattle and stock and sheep and more'n a hundred slaves and more besides. He bought the best of niggers near every time the speculators come that way. He'd make a swap of the old ones and give money for young ones what could work.

He raised corn and cotton and cane and 'taters and goobers, 'sides the peas and other feeding for the niggers. I 'member I held a hoe handle mighty unsteady when they put a old woman to larn me and some other children to scrape the fields. That old woman would be in a frantic. She'd show me and then turn 'bout to show some other little nigger, and I'd have the young corn cut clean as the grass. She say, "For the love of God, you better larn it right, or Solomon will beat the breath out you body." Old Man Solomon was the nigger driver.

Slavery was the worst days was ever seed in the world. They was things past telling, but I got the scars on my old body to show to this day. I seed worse than what happened to me. I seed them put the men and women in the stock with they hands screwed down through holes in the board and they feets tied together and they naked behinds to the world. Solomon the overseer beat them with a big whip and Massa look on. The niggers better not stop in the fields when they hear them yelling. They cut the flesh 'most to the bones, and some they was when they taken them out of stock and put them on the beds, they never got up again.

When a nigger died, they let his folks come out the fields to see him afore he died. They buried him the same day, take a big plank and bust it with a ax in the middle 'nough to bend it back, and put the dead nigger in betwixt it. They'd cart them down to the graveyard on the place and not bury them deep 'nough that buzzards wouldn't come circling round. Niggers mourns now, but in them days they wasn't no time for mourning.

The conch shell blowed afore daylight, and all hands better git out for roll call, or Solomon bust the door down and git them out. It was work hard, git beatings, and half-fed. They brung the victuals and water to the fields on a slide pulled by a old mule. Plenty times they was only a half barrel water and it stale and hot, for all us niggers on the hottest days. Mostly we ate pickled pork and corn bread and peas and beans and 'taters. They never was as much as we needed.

The times I hated most was picking cotton when the frost was on the bolls. My hands git sore and crack open and bleed. We'd have a little fire in the fields, and iffen the ones with tender hands couldn't stand it no longer, we'd run and warm our hands a little bit. When I could steal a 'tater, I used to slip it in the ashes, and when I'd run to the fire I'd take it out and eat it on the sly.

In the cabins it was nice and warm. They was built of pine boarding, and they was one long row of them up the hill back of the big house. Near one side of the cabins was a fireplace. They'd bring in two-three big logs and put on the fire, and they'd last near a week. The beds was made out of puncheons fitted in holes bored in the wall, and planks laid 'cross them poles. We had ticking mattresses filled with corn shucks. Sometimes the men build chairs at night. We didn't know much 'bout having nothing, though.

Sometimes Massa let niggers have a little patch. They'd raise 'taters or goobers. They liked to have them to help fill out on the victuals. 'Taters roasted in the ashes was the best-tasting eating I ever had. I could die better satisfied to have just one more 'tater roasted in hot ashes. The niggers had to work the patches at night and dig the 'taters and goobers at night. Then if they wanted to sell any in town, they'd have to git a pass to go. They had to go at night, 'cause they couldn't ever spare a hand from the fields.

Once in a while they'd give us a little piece of Saturday evening to wash out clothes in the branch. We hanged them on the ground in the woods to dry. They was a place to wash clothes from the well, but they was so many niggers all couldn't git round to it on Sundays. When they'd git through with the clothes on Saturday evenings, the niggers which sold they goobers and 'taters brung fiddles and guitars and come out and play. The others clap they hands and stomp they feet and we young-uns cut a step round. I was plenty biggity and liked to cut a step.

We was scared of Solomon and his whip, though, and he didn't like frol-icking. He didn't like for us niggers to pray, either. We never heared of no church, but us have praying in the cabins. We'd set on the floor and pray with our heads down low and sing low, but if Solomon heared he'd come and beat on the wall with the stock of his whip. He'd say, "I'll come in there and tear the hide off you backs." But some the old niggers tell us we got to pray to God that He don't think different of the blacks and the whites. I know that Solomon is burning in hell today, and it pleasures me to know it.

Once my maw and paw taken me and Katherine after night to slip to 'nother place to a praying and singing. A nigger man with white beard told us a day am coming when niggers only be slaves of God. We prays for the end of tribulation and the end of beatings and for shoes that fit our feet. We prayed that us niggers could have all we wanted to eat and special for fresh meat. Some the old ones say we have to bear all, 'cause that all we can do. Some say they was glad to the time they's dead, 'cause they'd rather rot in the ground than have the beatings. What I hated most was when they'd beat me and I didn't know what they beat me for, and I hated them stripping me naked as the day I was born.

When we's coming back from that praying, I thunk I heared the nigger dogs and somebody on horseback. I say, "Maw, it's them nigger hounds and they'll eat us up." You could hear them old hounds and sluts a-baying. Maw listens and say, "Sure 'nough, them dogs am running and God help us!" Then she and Paw talk and they take us to a fence corner and stands us up 'gainst the rails and say don't move and if anyone comes near, don't breathe loud. They went to the woods, so the hounds chase them and not git us. Me and Katherine stand there, holding hands, shaking so we can hardly stand. We hears the hounds come nearer, but we don't move. They goes after Paw and Maw, but they circles round to the cabins and gits in. Maw say it the power of God.

In them days I weared shirts, like all the young-uns. They had collars and come below the knees and was split up the sides. That's all we weared in hot weather. The men weared jeans and the women gingham. Shoes was the worstest trouble. We weared rough russets when it got cold, and it seem powerful strange they'd never git them to fit. Once when I was a young gal, they got me a new pair and all brass studs in the toes. They was too little for me, but I had to wear them. The brass trimmings cut into my ankles and them places got miserable bad. I rubs tallow in them sore places and wrops rags round them and my sores got worser and worser. The scars are there to this day.

I wasn't sick much, though. Some the niggers had chills and fever a lot, but they hadn't discovered so many diseases then as now. Massa give sick niggers ipecac and asafetida and oil and turpentine and black fever pills.

They was a cabin called the spinning-house and two looms and two spinning wheels going all the time, and two nigger women sewing all the time. It took plenty sewing to make all the things for a place so big. Once Massa goes to Baton Rouge and brung back a yaller gal dressed in fine style. She was a seamster nigger. He builds her a house 'way from the quarters, and she done fine sewing for the whites. Us niggers knowed the doctor took a black woman quick as he did a white and took any on his place he wanted, and he took them often. But mostly the children born on the place looked like niggers. Aunt Cheyney always say four of hers was Massa's, but he didn't give them no mind. But this yaller gal breeds so fast and gits a mess of white young-uns. She larnt them fine manners and combs out they hair.

Oncet two of them goes down the hill to the dollhouse, where the Missy's children am playing. They wants to go in the dollhouse and one the Missy's boys say, "That's for white children." They say, "We ain't no niggers, 'cause we got the same daddy you has, and he comes to see us near every day and fotches us clothes and things from town." They is fussing, and Missy is listening out her chamber window. She heard them white niggers say, "He is our daddy and we call him daddy when he comes to our house to see our mama."

When Massa come home that evening, his wife hardly say nothing to him, and he ask her what the matter, and she tells him, "Since you asks me, I'm studying in my mind 'bout them white young-uns of that yaller nigger wench from Baton Rouge." He say, "Now, honey, I fotches that gal just for you, 'cause she a fine seamster." She say, "It look kind of funny they got the same kind of hair and eyes as my children, and they got a nose look like yours." He say, "Honey, you just paying 'tention to talk of little children that ain't got no mind to what they say." She say, "Over in Mississippi I got a home and plenty with my daddy, and I got that in my mind."

Well, she didn't never leave, and Massa bought her a fine, new span of surrey hosses. But she don't never have no more children, and she ain't so cordial with the Massa. That yaller gal has more white young-uns, but they don't never go down the hill no more to the big house.

Aunt Cheyney was just out of bed with a suckling baby one time, and she run away. Some say that was 'nother baby of Massa's breeding. She don't come to the house to nurse her baby, so they misses her and Old Solomon gits the nigger hounds and takes her trail. They gits near her and she grabs a limb and tries to hist herself in a tree, but them dogs grab her and pull her down. The men hollers them onto her, and the dogs tore her naked and et the breasts plumb off her body. She got well and lived to be a old woman, but 'nother woman has to suck her baby, and she ain't got no sign of breasts no more.

They give all the niggers fresh meat on Christmas and a plug tobacco all round. The highest cotton-picker gits a suit of clothes, and all the women what had twins that year gits a outfitting of clothes for the twins and a double, warm blanket.

Seems like after I got bigger, I 'member more and more niggers run away. They's 'most always cotched. Massa used to hire out his niggers for wage hands. One time he hired me and a nigger boy, Turner, to work for some ornery white trash, name of Kidd. One day Turner goes off and don't come back. Old Man Kidd say I knowed 'bout it, and he tied my wrists together and stripped me. He hanged me by the wrists from a limb on a tree and spraddled my legs round the trunk and tied my feet together. Then he beat me. He beat me worser than I ever been beat before, and I faints dead away. When I come to I'm in bed. I didn't care so much iffen I died.

I didn't know 'bout the passing of time, but Miss Dora come to me. Some white folks done git word to her. Mr. Kidd tries to talk hisself out of it, but Miss Dora fotches me home when I'm well 'nough to move. She took me in a cart and my maw takes care of me. Massa looks me over good and says I'll git well, but I'm ruint for breeding children.

After while I taken a notion to marry and Massa and Missy marries us same as all the niggers. They stands inside the house with a broom held crosswise of the door and we stands outside. Missy puts a little wreath on my head they kept there, and we steps over the broom into the house. Now, that's all they was to the marrying. After freedom I gits married and has it put in the book by a preacher.

One day we was working in the fields and hears the conch shell blow, so we all goes to the back gate of the big house. Massa am there. He say, "Call the roll for every nigger big 'nough to walk, and I wants them to go to the river and wait there. They's gwine be a show and I wants you to see it." They was a big boat down there, done built up on the sides with boards and holes in the boards and a big gun barrel sticking through every hole. We ain't never seed nothing like that. Massa goes up the plank onto the boat and comes out on the boat porch. He say, "This am a Yankee boat." He goes inside and the water wheels starts moving and that boat goes moving up the river, and they says it goes to Natchez.

The boat wasn't more'n out of sight when a big drove of soldiers comes into town. They say they's Federals. More'n half the niggers goes off with them soldiers, but I goes on back home 'cause of my old mammy.

Next day them Yankees is swarming the place. Some the niggers wants to show them something. I follows to the woods. The niggers shows them soldiers a big pit in the ground, bigger'n a big house. It is got wooden doors that lifts up, but the top am sodded and grass growing on it, so you couldn't tell it. In that pit is stock, hosses and cows and mules and money and china-ware and silver and a mess of stuff them soldiers takes.

We just sot on the place doing nothing till the white folks comes home. Miss Dora come out to the cabin and say she wants to read a letter to my mammy. It come from Louis, which is brother to my mammy, and he done follow the Federals to Galveston. A white man down there write the letter for him. It am tored in half and Massa done that. The letter say Louis am working in Galveston and wants Mammy to come with us, and he'll pay our way. Miss Dora say Massa swear, "Damn Louis. I ain't gwine tell Sallie nothing," and he starts to tear the letter up. But she won't let him, and she reads it to Mammy.

After a time Massa takes all his niggers what wants to Texas with him and Mammy gits to Galveston and dies there. I goes with Massa to the Tennessee Colony and then to Navasota. Miss Dora marries and goes to El Paso. She wrote and told me to come to her, and I always meant to go.

My husband and me farmed round for times, and then I done housework and cooking for many years. I come to Dallas and cooked for seven year for one white family. My husband died years ago. I guess Miss Dora been dead these long years. I always kept my years by Miss Dora's years, 'count we is born so close.

I been blind and 'most helpless for five year. I'm gitting mighty enfee-bling, and I ain't walked outside the door for a long time back. I sets and 'members the times in the world. I 'members now clear as yesterday things I forgot for a long time. I 'members 'bout the days of slavery, and I don't 'lieve they ever gwine have slaves no more on this earth. I think God done took that burden offen his black children, and I'm aiming to praise Him for it to His face in the days of glory what ain't so far off.

THE ESCAPE OF A FUGITIVE SLAVE

James W. C. Pennington   /   The Fugitive Blacksmith

So many individual slaves ran away from their masters during the first half of the nineteenth century that a certain Dr. Samuel Cart-wright of the University of Louisiana declared the blacks suffered from a peculiar disease that he called "Drapetomania, or the Disease Causing Negroes to Run Away." The story of the runaways and those who aided them in both North and South is one of the most exciting chapters of American history.

James W. C. Pennington, the author of the autobiography from which the following passage is taken, was a slave on a plantation in Maryland. In 1828, he fled alone into the woods. Miraculously, he succeeded in reaching the Pennsylvania border, where he was directed to two white Quaker men who were known to have aided fugitives in the past. They hid him until it was safe for him to proceed to New York. Once settled in the North, Pennington became the pastor of a Presbyterian church and one of the leaders of the anti-slavery and convention movements in the years before the Civil War. He eventually purchased his freedom, for only in that way could he be sure of escaping prosecution under the federal Fugitive Slave Laws.

THE FLIGHT

It was the Sabbath: the holy day which God in his infinite wisdom gave for the rest of both man and beast. In the state of Maryland, the slaves generally have the Sabbath, except in those districts where the evil weed, tobacco, is cultivated; and then, when it is the season for setting the plant, they are liable to be robbed of this only rest.

It was in the month of November, somewhat past the middle of the month. It was a bright day, and all was quiet. Most of the slaves were resting about their quarters; others had leave to visit their friends on other plantations, and were absent. The evening previous I had arranged my little bundle of clothing, and had secreted it at some distance from the house. I had spent most of the forenoon in my workshop, engaged in deep and solemn thought.

It is impossible for me now to recollect all the perplexing thoughts that passed through my mind during that forenoon; it was a day of heartaching to me. But I distinctly remember the two great difficulties that stood in the way of my flight: I had a father and mother whom I dearly loved,—I had also six sisters and four brothers on the plantation. The question was, shall I hide my purpose from them? moreover, how will my flight affect them when I am gone? Will they not be suspected? Will not the whole family be sold off as a disaffected family, as is generally the case when one of its members flies? But a still more trying question was, how can I expect to succeed, I have no knowledge of distance or direction. I know that Pennsylvania is a free state, but I know not where its soil begins, or where that of Maryland ends? Indeed, at this time there was no safety in Pennsylvania, New Jersey,

FROM James W. C. Pennington, *The Fugitive Blacksmith; or, Events in the History of James W. C. Pennington, Pastor of a Presbyterian Church, New York, Formerly a slave in the State of Maryland, United States* (London, 1849), pp. 12–29.

or New York, for a fugitive, except in lurking-places, or under the care of judicious friends, who could be entrusted not only with liberty, but also with life itself.

With such difficulties before my mind, the day had rapidly worn away; and it was just past noon. One of my perplexing questions I had settled—I had resolved to let no one into my secret; but the other difficulty was now to be met. It was to be met without the least knowledge of its magnitude, except by imagination. Yet of one thing there could be no mistake, that the consequences of a failure would be most serious. Within my recollection no one had attempted to escape from my master; but I had many cases in my mind's eye, of slaves of other planters who had failed, and who had been made examples of the most cruel treatment, by flogging and selling to the far South, where they were never to see their friends more. I was not without serious apprehension that such would be my fate. The bare possibility was impressively solemn; but the hour was now come, and the man must act and be free, or remain a slave for ever. How the impression came to be upon my mind I cannot tell; but there was a strange and horrifying belief, that if I did not meet the crisis that day, I should be self-doomed—that my ear would be nailed to the door-post for ever. The emotions of that moment I cannot fully depict. Hope, fear, dread, terror, love, sorrow, and deep melancholy were mingled in my mind together; my mental state was one of most painful distraction. When I looked at my numerous family—a beloved father and mother, eleven brothers and sisters, &c.; but when I looked at slavery as such; when I looked at it in its mildest form, with all its annoyances; and above all, when I remembered that one of the chief annoyances of slavery, in the most mild form, is the liability of being at any moment sold into the worst form; it seemed that no consideration, not even that of life itself, could tempt me to give up the thought of flight. And then when I considered the difficulties of the way—the reward that would be offered—the human blood-hounds that would be set upon my track—the weariness—the hunger—the gloomy thought, of not only losing all one's friends in one day, but of having to seek and to make new friends in a strange world. But, as I have said, the hour was come, and the man must act, or for ever be a slave.

It was now two o'clock. I stepped into the quarter; there was a strange and melancholy silence mingled with the destitution that was apparent in every part of the house. The only morsel I could see in the shape of food, was a piece of Indian flour bread, it might be half-a-pound in weight. This I placed in my pocket, and giving a last look at the aspect of the house, and at a few small children who were playing at the door, I sallied forth thoughtfully and melancholy, and after crossing the barn-yard, a few moments' walk brought me to a small cave, near the mouth of which lay a pile of stones, and into which I had deposited my clothes. From this, my course lay through thick and heavy woods and back lands to —— town, where my brother lived. This town was six miles distance. It was now near three o'clock, but my object was neither to be seen on the road, or to approach the town by daylight, as I was well-known there, and as any intelligence of my having been seen there would at once put the pursuers on my track. This first six miles of my flight, I not only travelled very slowly, therefore, so as to avoid carrying any daylight to this town; but during this walk another very perplexing question was agitating my mind. Shall I call on my brother as I pass through, and shew him what I am about? My brother was older than I, we were much attached; I had been in the habit of looking to him for counsel.

I entered the town about dark, resolved, all things in view, *not* to shew myself to my brother. Having passed through the town without being recognised, I now found myself under cover of night, a solitary wanderer from home and friends; my only guide was the *north star*, by this I knew my general course northward, but at what point I should strike Penn, or when and where I should find a friend, I knew not. Another feeling now occupied my mind,—I felt like a mariner who has gotten his ship outside of the harbour and has spread his sails to the breeze. The cargo is on board— the ship is cleared—and the voyage I must make; besides, this being my first night, almost every thing will depend upon my clearing the coast before the day dawns. In order to do this my flight must be rapid. I therefore set forth in sorrowful earnest, only now and then I was cheered by the *wild* hope, that I should somewhere and at sometime be free.

The night was fine for the season, and passed on with little interruption for want of strength, until, about three o'clock in the morning, I began to feel the chilling effects of the dew.

At this moment, gloom and melancholy again spread through my whole soul. The prospect of utter destitution which threatened me was more than I could bear, and my heart began to melt. What substance is there in a piece of dry Indian bread; what nourishment is there in it to warm the nerves of one already chilled to the heart? Will this afford a sufficient sustenance after the toil of the night? But while these thoughts were agitating my mind, the day dawned upon me, in the midst of an open extent of country, where the only shelter I could find, without risking my travel by daylight, was a corn shock, but a few hundred yards from the road, and here I must pass my first day out. The day was an unhappy one; my hiding-place was extremely precarious. I had to sit in a squatting position the whole day, without the least chance to rest. But, besides this, my scanty pittance did not afford me that nourishment which my hard night's travel needed. Night came again to my relief, and I sallied forth to pursue my journey. By this time, not a crumb of my crust remained, and I was hungry and began to feel the desperation of distress.

As I travelled I felt my strength failing and my spirits wavered; my mind was in a deep and melancholy dream. It was cloudy; I could not see my star, and had serious misgivings about my course.

In this way the night passed away, and just at the dawn of day I found a few sour apples, and took my shelter under the arch of a small bridge that crossed the road. Here I passed the second day in ambush.

This day would have been more pleasant than the previous, but the sour apples, and a draught of cold water, had produced anything but a favourable effect; indeed, I suffered most of the day with severe symptoms of cramp. The day passed away again without any further incident, and as I set out at nightfall, I felt quite satisfied that I could not pass another twenty-four hours without nourishment. I made but little progress during the night, and often sat down, and slept frequently fifteen or twenty minutes. At the dawn of the third day I continued my travel. As I had found my way to a public turnpike road during the night, I came very early in the morning to a tollgate, where the only person I saw, was a lad about twelve years of age. I inquired of him where the road led to. He informed me it led to Baltimore. I asked him the distance, he said it was eighteen miles.

This intelligence was perfectly astounding to me. My master lived eighty miles from Baltimore. I was now sixty-two miles from home. That distance in the right direction, would have placed me several miles across Mason and Dixon's line, but I was evidently yet in the state of Maryland.

I ventured to ask the lad at the gate another question—Which is the best way to Philadelphia? Said he, you can take a road which turns off about half-a-mile below this, and goes to Getsburgh, or you can go on to Baltimore and take the packet.

I made no reply, but my thought was, that I was as near Baltimore and Baltimore-packets as would answer my purpose.

In a few moments I came to the road to which the lad had referred, and felt some relief when I had gotten out of that great public highway, "The National Turnpike," which I found it to be.

When I had walked a mile on this road, and when it had now gotten to be about nine o'clock, I met a young man with a load of hay. He drew up his horses, and addressed me in a very kind tone, when the following dialogue took place between us.

"Are you travelling any distance, my friend?"

"I am on my way to Philadelphia."

"Are you free?"

"Yes, sir."

"I suppose, then, you are provided with free papers?"

"No, sir. I have no papers."

"Well, my friend, you should not travel on this road: you will be taken up before you have gone three miles. There are men living on this road who are constantly on the look-out for your people; and it is seldom that one escapes them who attempts to pass by day."

He then very kindly gave me advice where to turn off the road at a certain point, and how to find my way to a certain house, where I would meet with an old gentleman who would further advise me whether I had better remain till night, or go on.

I left this interesting young man; and such was my surprise and chagrin at the thought of having so widely missed my way, and my alarm at being in such a dangerous position, that in ten minutes I had so far forgotten his directions as to deem it unwise to attempt to follow them, lest I should miss my way, and get into evil hands.

I, however, left the road, and went into a small piece of wood, but not finding a sufficient hiding-place, and it being a busy part of the day, when persons were at work about the fields, I thought I should excite less suspicion by keeping in the road, so I returned to the road; but the events of the next few moments proved that I committed a serious mistake.

I went about a mile, making in all two miles from the spot where I met my young friend, and about five miles from the toll-gate to which I have referred, and I found myself at the twenty-four miles' stone from Baltimore. It was now about ten o'clock in the forenoon; my strength was greatly exhausted by reason of the want of suitable food; but the excitement that was then going on in my mind, left me little time to think of my *need* of food. Under ordinary circumstances as a traveller, I should have been glad to see the "Tavern," which was near the mile-stone; but as the case stood with me, I deemed it a dangerous place to pass, much less to stop at. I was therefore passing it as quietly and as rapidly as possible, when from the lot just opposite the house, or sign-post, I heard a coarse stern voice cry, "Halloo!"

I turned my face to the left, the direction from which the voice came, and observed that it proceeded from a man who was digging potatoes. I answered him politely; when the following occurred:—

"Who do *you* belong to?"

"I am free, sir."

"Have you got papers?"

"No, sir."

"Well, you must stop here."

By this time he had got astride the fence, making his way into the road. I said,

"My business is onward, sir, and I do not wish to stop."

"I will see then if you don't stop, you black rascal."

He was now in the middle of the road, making after me in a brisk walk.

I saw that a crisis was at hand; I had no weapons of any kind, not even a pocket-knife; but I asked myself, shall I surrender without a struggle. The instinctive answer was "No." What will you do? continue to walk; if he runs after you, run; get him as far from the house as you can, then turn suddenly and smite him on the knee with a stone; that will render him, at least, unable to pursue you.

This was a desperate scheme, but I could think of no other, and my habits as a blacksmith had given my eye and hand such mechanical skill, that I felt quite sure that if I could only get a stone in my hand, and have time to wield it, I should not miss his knee-pan.

He began to breathe short. He was evidently vexed because I did not halt, and I felt more and more provoked at the idea of being thus pursued by a man to whom I had not done the least injury. I had just began to glance my eye about for a stone to grasp, when he made a tiger-like leap at me. This of course brought us to running. At this moment he yelled out "Jake Shouster!" and at the next moment the door of a small house standing to the left was opened, and out jumped a shoemaker girded up in his leather apron, with his knife in hand. He sprang forward and seized me by the collar, while the other seized my arms behind. I was now in the grasp of two men, either of whom were larger bodied than myself, and one of whom was armed with a dangerous weapon.

Standing in the door of the shoemaker's shop, was a third man; and in the potatoe lot I had passed, was still a fourth man. Thus surrounded by superior physical force, the fortune of the day it seemed to me was gone.

My heart melted away, I sunk resistlessly into the hands of my captors, who dragged me immediately into the tavern which was near. I ask my reader to go in with me, and see how the case goes.

GREAT MORAL DILEMMA

A few moments after I was taken into the bar-room, the news having gone as by electricity, the house and yard were crowded with gossippers, who had left their business to come and see "the runaway nigger." This hastily assembled congregation consisted of men, women, and children, each one had a look to give at, and a word to say about, the "nigger."

But among the whole, there stood one whose name I have never known, but who evidently wore the garb of a man whose profession bound him to speak for the dumb, but he, standing head and shoulders above all that were round about, spoke the first hard sentence against me. Said he, "That fellow is a runaway I know; put him in jail a few days, and you will soon hear where he came from." And then fixing a fiend-like gaze upon me, he continued, "if I lived on this road, *you* fellows would not find such clear running as you do, I'd trap more of you."

But now comes the pinch of the case, the case of conscience to me even at this moment. Emboldened by the cruel speech just recited, my captors enclosed me, and said, "Come now, this matter may easily be settled without you going to jail; who do you belong to, and where did you come from?"

The facts here demanded were in my breast. I knew according to the law of slavery, who I belonged to and where I came from, and I must now do one of three things—I must refuse to speak at all, or I must communicate the fact, or I must tell an untruth. How would an untutored slave, who had never heard of such a writer as Archdeacon Paley, be likely to act in such a dilemma? The first point decided, was, the facts in this case are my private property. These men have no more right to them than a highway robber has to my purse. What will be the consequence if I put them in possession of the facts. In forty-eight hours, I shall have received perhaps one hundred lashes, and be on my way to the Louisiana cotton fields. Of what service will it be to them. They will get a paltry sum of two hundred dollars. Is not my liberty worth more to me than two hundred dollars are to them?

I resolved therefore, to insist that I was free. This not being satisfactory without other evidence, they tied my hands and set out, and went to a magistrate who lived about half a mile distant. It so happened, that when we arrived at his house he was not at home. This was to them a disappointment, but to me it was a relief; but I soon learned by their conversation, that there was still another magistrate in the neighbourhood, and that they would go to him. In about twenty minutes, and after climbing fences and jumping ditches, we, captors and captive, stood before his door, but it was after the same manner as before—he was not at home. By this time the day had worn away to one or two o'clock, and my captors evidently began to feel somewhat impatient of the loss of time. We were about a mile and a quarter from the tavern. As we set out on our return, they began to parley. Finding it was difficult for me to get over fences with my hands tied, they untied me, and said, "Now John," that being the name they had given me, "if you have run away from any one, it would be much better for you to tell us!" but I continued to affirm that I was free. I knew, however, that my situation was very critical, owing to the shortness of the distance I must be from home: my advertisement might overtake me at any moment.

On our way back to the tavern, we passed through a small skirt of wood, where I resolved to make an effort to escape again. One of my captors was walking on either side of me; I made a sudden turn, with my left arm sweeping the legs of one of my captors from under him; I left him nearly standing on his head, and took to my heels. As soon as they could recover they both took after me. We had to mount a fence. This I did most successfully, and making across an open field towards another wood; one of my captors being a long-legged man, was in advance of the other, and consequently nearing me. We had a hill to rise, and during the ascent he gained on me. Once more I thought of self-defence. I am trying to escape peaceably, but this man is determined that I shall not.

My case was now desperate; and I took this desperate thought: "I will run him a little farther from his coadjutor; I will then suddenly catch a stone, and wound him in the breast." This was my fixed purpose, and I had arrived near the point on the top of the hill, where I expected to do the act, when to my surprise and dismay, I saw the other side of the hill was not only all ploughed up, but we came suddenly upon a man ploughing, who as suddenly left his plough and cut off my flight, by seizing me by the collar, when at the same moment my pursuer seized my arms behind. Here I was again in a sad fix. By this time the other pursuer had come up; I was most savagely thrown down on the ploughed ground with my face downward, the ploughman placed his knee upon my shoulders, one of my captors put his upon my legs, while the other tied my arms behind me. I was then dragged up, and marched off with kicks, punches and imprecations.

We got to the tavern at three o'clock. Here they again cooled down, and made an appeal to me to make a disclosure. I saw that my attempt to escape strengthened their belief that I was a fugitive. I said to them, "If you will not put me in jail, I will now tell you where I am from." They promised. "Well," said I, "a few weeks ago, I was sold from the eastern shore to a slave-trader, who had a large gang, and set out for Georgia, but when he got to a town in Virginia, he was taken sick, and died with the small-pox. Several of his gang also died with it, so that the people in the town became alarmed, and did not wish the gang to remain among them. No one claimed us, or wished to have anything to do with us; I left the rest, and thought I would go somewhere and get work."

When I said this, it was evidently believed by those who were present, and notwithstanding the unkind feeling that had existed, there was a murmur of approbation. At the same time I perceived that a panic began to seize some, at the idea that I was one of a small-pox gang. Several who had clustered near me, moved off to a respectful distance. One or two left the bar-room, and murmured, "better let the small-pox nigger go."

I was then asked what was the name of the slave-trader. Without pre-meditation, I said, "John Henderson."

"John Henderson!" said one of my captors, "I knew him; I took up a yaller boy for him about two years ago, and got fifty dollars. He passed out with a gang about that time, and the boy ran away from him at Fredericks-town. What kind of a man was he?"

At a venture, I gave a description of him. "Yes," said he, "that is the man." By this time, all the gossippers had cleared the coast; our friend, "Jake Shouster," had also gone back to his bench to finish his custom work, after having "lost nearly the whole day, trotting about with a nigger tied," as I heard his wife say as she called him home to his dinner. I was now left alone with the man who first called to me in the morning. In a sober manner, he made this proposal to me: "John, I have a brother living in Risterstown, four miles off, who keeps a tavern; I think you had better go and live with him, till we see what will turn up. He wants an ostler." I at once assented to this. "Well," said he, "take something to eat, and I will go with you."

Although I had so completely frustrated their designs for the moment, I knew that it would by no means answer for me to go into that town, where there were prisons, handbills, newspapers, and travellers. My intention was, to start with him, but not to enter the town alive.

I sat down to eat; it was Wednesday, four o'clock, and this was the first regular meal I had since Sunday morning. This over, we set out, and to my surprise, he proposed to walk. We had gone about a mile and a-half, and were approaching a wood through which the road passed with a bend. I fixed upon that as the spot where I would either free myself from this man, or die in his arms. I had resolved upon a plan of operation—it was this: to stop short, face about, and commence action; and neither ask or give quarters, until I was free or dead!

We had got within six rods of the spot, when a gentleman turned the corner, meeting us on horseback. He came up, and entered into conversation with my captor, both of them speaking in Dutch, so that I knew not what they said. After a few moments, this gentleman addressed himself to me in English, and I then learned that he was one of the magistrates on whom we had called in the morning; I felt that another crisis was at hand. Using his saddle as his bench, he put on an extremely stern and magisterial-like face, holding up his horse not unlike a field-marshal in the act of reviewing troops, and carried me through a most rigid examination in reference to the statement I had made. I repeated carefully all I had said; at the close, he said, "Well, you had better stay among us a few months, until we see what is to be done with you." It was then agreed that we should go back to the tavern, and there settle upon some further plan. When we arived at the tavern, the magistrate alighted from his horse, and went into the bar-room. He took another close glance at me, and went over some points of the former examination. He seemed quite satisfied of the correctness of my statement, and made the following proposition: that I should go and live with him for a short time, stating that he had a few acres of corn and potatoes to get in, and that he would give me twenty-five cents per day. I most cheerfully assented to this proposal. It was also agreed that I should remain at the tavern with my captor that night, and that he would accompany me in the morning. This part of the arrangement I did not like, but of course I could not say so. Things being thus arranged, the magistrate mounted his horse, and went on his way home.

It had been cloudy and rainy during the afternoon, but the western sky having partially cleared at this moment, I perceived that it was near the setting of the sun.

My captor had left his hired man most of the day to dig potatoes alone; but the waggon being now loaded, it being time to convey the potatoes into the barn, and the horses being all ready for that purpose, he was obliged to go into the potatoe field and give assistance.

I should say here, that his wife had been driven away by the small-pox panic about three o'clock, and had not yet returned; this left no one in the house, but a boy, about nine years of age.

As he went out, he spoke to the boy in Dutch, which I supposed, from the little fellow's conduct, to be instructions to watch me closely, which he certainly did.

The potatoe lot was across the public road, directly in front of the house; at the back of the house, and about 300 yards distant, there was a thick wood. The circumstances of the case would not allow me to think for one moment of remaining there for the night—the time had come for another effort—but there were two serious difficulties. One was, that I must either deceive or dispatch this boy who is watching me with intense vigilance. I am glad to say, that the latter did not for a moment seriously enter my mind. To deceive him effectually, I left my coat and went to the back door, from which my course would be direct to the wood. When I got to the door, I found that the barn, to which the waggon must soon come, lay just to the right, and over-looking the path I must take to the wood. In front of me lay a garden surrounded by a picket fence, to the left of me was a small gate, and that by passing through that gate would throw me into an open field, and give me clear running to the wood; but on looking through the gate, I saw that my captor, being with the team, would see me if I attempted to start before he moved from the position he then occupied. To add to my difficulty the horses had baulked; while waiting for the decisive moment, the boy came to the door and asked me why I did not come in. I told him I felt unwell, and wished him to be so kind as to hand me a glass of water; expecting while he was gone to get it, the team would clear, so that I could start. While he was gone, another attempt was made to start the team but failed; he came with the water and I quickly used it up by gargling my throat and by drinking a part. I asked him to serve me by giving me another glass: he gave me a look of close scrutiny, but went in for the water. I heard him fill the glass, and start to return with it; when the hind end of the waggon cleared the corner of the house, which stood in a range with the fence along which I was to pass in getting to the wood. As I passed out the gate, I "squared my main yard," and laid my course up the line of fence, I cast a last glance over my right shoulder, and saw the boy just perch his head above the garden picket to look after me; I heard at the same time great confusion with the team, the rain having made the ground slippery, and the horses having to cross the road with a slant and rise to get into the barn, it required great effort after they started to prevent their baulking. I felt some assurance that although the boy might give the alarm, my captor could not leave the team until it was in the barn. I heard the horses' feet on the barn-floor, just as I leaped the fence, and darted into the wood.

LET MY PEOPLE GO: SPIRITUALS

Little attempt was made to convert the Southern slaves to Christianity until the period of the Second Great Awakening early in the nineteenth century, when Baptist and Methodist churches made great headway among blacks. Although it is impossible to know how many slaves adopted the religion of the slave masters, it is clear that in becoming Christian, the blacks made the religion their own. They saw in the Old Testament story of a captive chosen people many elements that were analogous to their own condition, and they drew hope from the gospel of freedom and deliverance preached in the New Testament, finding in it the promise that a righteous God would intervene in this world and establish justice.

Most of our knowledge of slave religion comes from the surviving Spirituals, religious folk songs that originated among the slaves of the South. These songs richly reflect the attitudes of the slaves toward this world and their condition in it. Running through the whole literature of the slave songs are three major themes: dissatisfaction with the conditions of slavery, faith in ultimate deliverance by a righteous God, and anticipation of a better world "over there." "Over there" often refers at the same time to freedom in this world and freedom in the next. As they sang "Ev'rybody talkin' 'bout heab'n ain't goin' dere," the slaves who had adopted Christianity made it clear that they had little doubt about who the true Christians were—the slaves themselves or the slave masters.

Go Down, Moses

Go down, Moses,
'Way down in Egypt land,
Tell ole Pharaoh,
To let my people go.

Go down, Moses,
'Way down in Egypt land,
Tell ole Pharaoh,
To let my people go.

When Israel was in Egypt land,
Let my people go,
Oppressed so hard they could not stand,
Let my people go,
Thus spoke the Lord, bold Moses said,
Let my people go,
If not I'll smite your first-born dead,
Let my people go.

Go down, Moses,
'Way down in Egypt land,
Tell ole Pharaoh,
To let my people go.

All God's Chillun Got Wings

I got a robe, you got a robe,
All o' God's chillun got a robe.
When I get to heab'n, goin' to put on my robe,
I'm goin' to shout all ovah God's heab'n,
Heab'n, heab'n,
Ev'rybody talkin' 'bout heab'n ain't goin' dere;
Heab'n, heab'n,
I'm goin' to shout all ovah God's heab'n.

I got-a wings, you got-a wings,
All o' God's chillun got-a wings.
When I get to heab'n, goin' to put on my wings,
I'm goin' to fly all ovah God's heab'n,
Heab'n, heab'n,
Ev'rybody talkin' 'bout heab'n ain't goin' dere;
Heab'n, heab'n,
I'm goin' to fly all ovah God's heab'n.

I got a harp, you got a harp,
All o' God's chillun got a harp.
When I get to heab'n, goin' to play on my harp,
I'm goin' to play all ovah God's heab'n,
Heab'n, heab'n,
Ev'rybody talkin' 'bout heab'n ain't goin' dere;
Heab'n, heab'n,
I'm goin' to play all ovah God's heab'n.

I got-a shoes, you got-a shoes,
All o' God's chillun got-a shoes.
When I get to heab'n, goin' to put on my shoes,
I'm goin' to walk all ovah God's heab'n,
Heab'n, heab'n,
Ev'rybody talkin' 'bout heab'n ain't goin' dere;
Heab'n, heab'n,
I'm goin' to walk all ovah God's heab'n.

Steal Away to Jesus

Steal away, steal away, steal away to Jesus!
Steal away, steal away home,
I ain't got long to stay here.

My Lord, He calls me, He calls me by the thunder,
The trumpet sounds within-a my soul,
I ain't got long to stay here.

Steal away, steal away, steal away to Jesus!
Steal away, steal away home,
I ain't got long to stay here.

Green trees a-bending, po' sinner stand a-trembling,
The trumpet sounds within-a my soul,
I ain't got long to stay here.

Steal away, steal away, steal away to Jesus!
Steal away, steal away home,
I ain't got long to stay here.

Didn't My Lord Deliver Daniel

Didn't my Lord deliver Daniel,
   deliver Daniel, deliver Daniel,
Didn't my Lord deliver Daniel,
An' why not every man.

He delivered Daniel from the lion's den,
Jonah from the belly of the whale,
An' the Hebrew chillun from the fiery furnace,
An' why not every man.

Didn't my Lord deliver Daniel,
   deliver Daniel, deliver Daniel,
Didn't my Lord deliver Daniel,
An' why not every man.

The moon run down in a purple stream,
The sun forbear to shine,
An' every star disappear,
King Jesus shall-a be mine.

The win' blows eas' an' the win' blows wes',
It blows like the judg-a-ment day,
An' ev'ry po' soul that never did pray'll
Be glad to pray that day.

Didn't my Lord deliver Daniel,
  deliver Daniel, deliver Daniel,
Didn't my Lord deliver Daniel,
An' why not every man.

I Thank God I'm Free at Last

Free at last, free at last,
I thank God I'm free at last.
Free at last, free at last,
I thank God I'm free at last.

Way down yonder in the graveyard walk,
I thank God I'm free at last,
Me and my Jesus gonna meet an' talk,
I thank God I'm free at last.

On-a my knees when the light pass by,
I thank God I'm free at last,
Thought my soul would rise an' fly,
I thank God I'm free at last.

One o' these mornin's bright an' fair,
I thank God I'm free at last,
Gonna meet my Jesus in the middle o' the air,
I thank God I'm free at last.

Free at last, free at last,
I thank God I'm free at last,
Free at last, free at last,
I thank God I'm free at last.

3 SUGGESTIONS FOR FURTHER READING

The basic secondary work on slavery is Kenneth Stampp, *The Peculiar Institution: Slavery in the Ante-Bellum South** (Knopf, 1956). Useful as supplements are two works by U. B. Phillips: *American Negro Slavery** (Appleton, 1918) and *Life and Labor in the Old South** (Little, Brown, 1929). Although these works are tinged with Phillips' racist attitudes, they nevertheless contain much valuable information. An extremely helpful collection of essays and excerpts from recent works on slavery is Allen Weinstein and Frank O. Gatell (eds.), *American Negro Slavery: A Modern Reader** (Oxford, 1968).

Stanley M. Elkins, *Slavery: A Problem in American Institutional and Intellectual Life** (University of Chicago Press, 1959), a work that stressed and sought to explain the docility of the black slave in the South, aroused a controversy that led to a resurgence of emphasis on slave rebelliousness. *American Negro Slave Revolts** (Columbia University Press, 1943) and *Nat Turner's Slave Rebellion** (Humanities Press, 1966), two studies by Herbert Aptheker, are basic secondary works on slave rebelliousness. Individual conspiracies are treated in John Lofton, *Insurrection in South Carolina, The Turbulent World of Denmark Vesey* (Antioch College Press, 1964), and Arna Bontemps, *Black Thunder** (Macmillan, 1936), an excellent novel about the conspiracy of Gabriel Prosser in 1800. William Styron's novel about the Turner rebellion, *The Confessions of Nat Turner** (Random House, 1967), raised a storm of controversy and elicited a response from the black community in John Henrik Clarke (ed.), *William Styron's Nat Turner: Ten Black Writers Respond** (Beacon Press, 1968).

There have been many studies of slavery in the various Southern states. The best of these are Charles S. Sydnor, *Slavery in Mississippi** (American Historical Association, 1933), and James B. Sellers, *Slavery in Alabama* (University of Alabama Press, 1950).

The question of the economics of slavery is explored in an excellent group of essays edited by Harold Woodman, *Slavery and the Southern Economy** (Harcourt, Brace & World, 1966), and in Eugene Genovese, *The Political Economy of Slavery** (Pantheon, 1965). Frederick Bancroft, in *Slave Trading in the Old South* (Furst, 1931), presents a view of the internal slave trade. The special quality of urban slavery is discussed in Richard C. Wade, *Slavery in the Cities: The South, 1820–1860** (Oxford University Press, 1964).

Two ante-bellum works that may be of interest are Frederick L. Olmsted, *The Cotton Kingdom*, 2 vols. (Mason, 1861), published in paperback in an abridged form under the title *Slave States Before the Civil War**, and Theodore D. Weld, *American Slavery as It Is: Testimony of a Thousand Witnesses* (American Anti-Slavery Society, 1839).

The slaves themselves left three kinds of literature that are invaluable to a study of slavery in the nineteenth century: Spirituals, folk-tales, and the slave narratives (autobiographical descriptions of life as a slave written by ex-slaves in the period before the Civil War). The most complete collection of Spirituals is that edited by James Weldon Johnson and J. Rosamond Johnson, *The Books of American Negro Spirituals** (Viking, 1925, 1926). Harold Courlander, *Negro Folk Music, U.S.A.* (Columbia University Press, 1963), is the most complete essay on the subject of the black folk songs. Folk-tales are collected in Richard Dorson (ed.), *American Negro Folktales** (Fawcett, 1967), and J. Mason Brewer (ed.), *American Negro Folklore* (Quadrangle, 1968).

The most valuable slave narratives are Frederick Douglass, *A Narrative of the Life of Frederick Douglass, an American Slave, Written by Himself** (Anti-Slavery Office, 1845); William Wells Brown, *The Narrative of William W. Brown, a Fugitive Slave** (Anti-Slavery Office, 1847); Lunsford Lane, *The Narrative of Lunsford Lane* (published by the author, 1842); Josiah Henson, *An Autobiography of the Reverend Josiah Henson** (Schuyler, Smith, 1881); Austin Steward, *Twenty-two Years a Slave, and Forty Years a Freeman** (William Alling, 1856); Solomon Northrup, *Twelve Years a Slave** (Derby and Miller, 1853); Sojourner Truth, *Narrative of Sojourner Truth* (privately printed, 1850); and Benjamin Drew, *The Refugee: A North-side View of Slavery** (Jewett, 1855).

4 THE FREE BLACK COMMUNITY, 1800-1860

When the first federal census was taken in 1799, there were 59,557 free persons of African descent in the United States. By 1860, the number had risen to 488,070. At this time, the free black population was concentrated in the upper South and the Middle Atlantic States, and about half the total number of free blacks lived in the South. The increase in the number of free blacks was due primarily to the process of manumission, the freeing of slaves through private or public action. In the early decades of the new nation, manumission had proceeded apace in both North and South. But as sectional antagonism increased and the threat of slave insurrection grew, most Southern states prohibited or severely restricted private manumission.

In the South in 1850, mulattoes—persons of mixed white and black parentage—constituted 37 per cent of the free black population but only 8 per cent of the slave population. Many of the free mulattoes were children slave women bore to their white masters. The masters regularly freed the children born of these illicit unions. In several Southern cities, there were organizations of free mulattoes that denied membership to blacks of unmixed ancestry.

In both North and South, the free blacks who lived in the cities were usually in a better position economically than those who lived in rural areas. It has been suggested that Southern cities held better economic opportunities for free blacks than did Northern ones, for in the South certain occupations were open to blacks almost exclusively, whereas in the North they had to compete with a growing white immigrant population. Though it may be true that the blacks in Southern cities had certain economic advantages, they were suppressed in many other ways and were not allowed even the small amount of personal freedom that the Northern states offered free blacks. With the exception of New Orleans, Southern cities allowed the blacks virtually no public voice until 1865.

In the Northern cities, on the other hand, the free blacks were able to speak out about their condition with some degree of freedom. Beginning with *Freedom's Journal*, first published in New York City in 1827, several newspapers edited by blacks appeared. The primary purpose of these papers was to give voice to the feelings and the needs of the black people. Despite these printed cries, however, the black people found themselves less and less able to influence public affairs, for throughout the first half of the nineteenth century the political activity of blacks was increasingly restricted by legislation. By the 1840's, all Northern states except Maine, Massachusetts, New Hampshire, Rhode Island, and Vermont had either severely limited or completely abolished the right of the black people to vote.

The Northern black was also seriously restricted in the job market. Craft and trade unions would not accept him, so he was generally limited to jobs in unskilled or domestic labor. Toward the end of the ante-bellum period, even those positions became elusive because of the massive influx of unskilled white immigrants, particularly the Irish. Several severe clashes between blacks and whites resulted from this development, culminating in the bloody Draft Riots of 1863, when mobs of Irish hoodlums roamed the streets of New York City, beating and burning black people and destroying their homes.

Deprived of the ballot, deprived of economic mobility, deprived for the most part of public schooling, the blacks developed a variety of responses to their condition—responses that in many cases have continued to this day. Although these responses are sometimes placed on a continuum from accommodation to protest, they must all be considered as protests of some kind. What varies from one to the other is merely the public expression of the rage within.

As has been the case during the entire history of the Afro-American, most of the black people who lived in the nineteenth century led lives of quiet desperation. To them, the avenues of public protest seemed either closed (as in the South) or futile (as in the North). They had only to struggle through their lives in silent anonymity.

Others were not so quiet in their desperation. Rejecting the notion that protest was useless, they together and singly called out for God's justice. Here and there appeared lonely prophets like David Walker, whose impassioned demand that the slaves rise up and throw off their oppression brought him the enmity of both North and South—and probably hastened his death. More commonly, those who wished to make themselves heard joined together. In the nineteenth century, more and more societies for the self-help and self-protection of black people were organized.

The message of the Christian gospel had given the black man an ideology of freedom and justice. Many of the leaders of black protest in the nineteenth century were clergymen, and many others used the imagery of the Bible as they called for a world in which men were truly equal—equal before one another as well as before God. Although some of these leaders—Frederick Douglass, for example—rejected the idea of separate religious organizations for blacks, the establishment of all-black churches continued throughout the period.

The black church spawned one of the most important movements of organized protest among black people—the convention movement. The first convention was held in 1830 to protest the suggestion of the white colonizers that free blacks move to Africa in order to eliminate the race problem in the North. Conventions were held from time to time during the rest of the century.

Most of the conventions of the ante-bellum years emphasized the necessity of alleviating the oppression of free blacks and dealt with problems related to education, suffrage, and job training. Often, however, resolutions of support for the enslaved blacks of the South were passed at the convention meetings. Needless to say, resolutions were not enough, and blacks in the North, many of whom were active in the Underground Railroad, began to form vigilance committees to help protect fugitive slaves from recapture and to find them jobs and housing. Northern blacks were also involved in the work of the many abolitionist organizations.

Although most black men had rejected emigration as a way to put an end to their difficulties, there was a revival of emigrationist sentiment within the black community toward the middle of the century. Such men as Martin Delany proposed that blacks look elsewhere for the future denied them in the United States. Originally, Delany suggested that Central America become the home of American blacks; later, he advocated a return to Africa and even went so far as to take a lease on some land on the Niger River for resettlement purposes. In the 1850's, several black emigrationist societies were organized. With the outbreak of the Civil War, however, new hope for domestic freedom was aroused in the hearts of the black people.

THE WHITE CHURCH'S OPPRESSION OF THE BLACK MAN

David Walker / Our Wretchedness in Consequence of the Preachers of
the Religion of Jesus Christ

David Walker's **Appeal** burst like a bomb on the scene of American
race relations in 1829. The author's bitter call for slave rebellion
frightened the South into taking extraordinary pains to suppress
the circulation of the document.

Walker was born in the South in 1785, the son of a free black
woman. Since a child assumed the status of his mother under
Southern law, he was born free. During his youth he traveled
widely, finally setting up an old-clothes shop in Boston in the
1820's. In 1827, he began writing and lecturing on the abolition
of slavery. After the publication of his **Appeal,** there were rumors
that a reward was being offered for his head. He died mysteriously
on a Boston street in 1830, probably from poison.

The section of the **Appeal** that follows is an attack on the white
Christians who sent missionaries to convert the heathen abroad
but denied the American black man the right to worship in the
Christian church. Walker firmly believed that because God was
just, America was doomed for its treatment of the African.

R eligion, my brethren, is a substance of deep consideration among all
nations of earth. The Pagans have a kind, as well as the Mahometans,
the Jews and the Christians. But pure and undefiled religion, such as was
preached by Jesus Christ and his apostles, is hard to be found in all the earth.
God, through his instrument, Moses, handed a dispensation of his Divine
will, to the children of Israel after they had left Egypt for the land of Canaan
or of Promise, who through hypocrisy, oppression and unbelief, departed
from the faith.—He then, by his apostles, handed a dispensation of his, together with the will of Jesus Christ, to the Europeans in Europe, who, in
open violation of which, have made *merchandise* of us, and it does appear
as though they take this very dispensation to aid them in their *infernal* depredations upon us. Indeed, the way in which religion was and is conducted by
the Europeans and their descendants, one might believe it was a plan fabricated by themselves and the *devils* to oppress us. But hark! My master has
taught me better than to believe it—he has taught me that his gospel as it was
preached by himself and his apostles remains the same, notwithstanding
Europe has tried to mingle blood and oppression with it.

It is well known to the Christian world, that Bartholomew Las Casas,

---

FROM David Walker, "Article III" of *David Walker's Appeal, in Four Articles* . . .
(Boston, 1829).

that very very notoriously avaricious Catholic priest or preacher, and adventurer with Columbus in his second voyage, proposed to his countrymen, the Spaniards in Hispaniola to import the Africans from the Portuguese settlement in Africa, to dig up gold and silver, and work their plantations for them, to effect which, he made a voyage thence to Spain, and opened the subject to his master, Ferdinand then in declining health, who listened to the plan: but who died soon after, and left it in the hand of his successor, Charles V.[1] This wretch, ("Las Casas, the Preacher,") succeeded so well in his plans of oppression, that in 1503, the first blacks had been imported into the new world. Elated with this success, and stimulated by sordid avarice only, he importuned Charles V in 1511, to grant permission to a French merchant, to import 4000 blacks at one time.[2] Thus we see, through the instrumentality of a pretended preacher of the gospel of Jesus Christ our common master, our wretchedness first commenced in America—where it has been continued from 1503, to this day, 1829. A period of three hundred and twenty-six years. But two hundred and nine, from 1620—when twenty of our fathers were brought into Jamestown, Virginia, by a Dutch man of war, and sold off like brutes to the highest bidders; and there is not a doubt in my mind, but that tyrants are in hope to perpetuate our miseries under them and their children until the final consummation of all things.—But if they do not get dreadfully deceived, it will be because God has forgotten them.

The Pagans, Jews and Mahometans try to make proselytes to their religions, and whatever human beings adopt their religions they extend to them their protection. But Christian Americans, not only hinder their fellow creatures, the Africans, but thousands of them *will absolutely beat a coloured person nearly to death, if they catch him on his knees, supplicating the throne of grace.* This barbarous cruelty was by all the heathen nations of antiquity, and is by the Pagans, Jews and Mahometans of the present day, left entirely to Christian Americans to inflict on the Africans and their descendants, that their cup which is nearly full may be completed. I have known tyrants or usurpers of human liberty in different parts of this country to take their

---

[1] See Butler's History of the United States, vol. 1, page 24.—See also, page 25.

[2] It is not unworthy of remark, that the Portuguese and Spaniards, were among, if not the very first Nations upon Earth, about three hundred and fifty or sixty years ago— But see what those *Christians* have come to now in consequence of afflicting our fathers and us, who have never molested, or disturbed them or any other of the white *Christians*, but have they received one quarter of what the Lord will yet bring upon them, for the murders they have inflicted upon us?—They have had, and in some degree have now, sweet times on our blood and groans, the time however, of bitterness have sometime since commenced with them.—There is a God the Maker and preserver of all things, who will as sure as the world exists, give all his creatures their just recompense of reward in this and in the world to come,—we may fool or deceive, and keep each other in the most profound ignorance, beat, murder and keep each other out of what is our lawful rights, or the rights of man, yet it is impossible for us to deceive or escape the Lord Almighty.

fellow creatures, the coloured people, and beat them until they would scarcely leave life in them; what for? Why they say "The black devils had the audacity to be found *making prayers and supplications to the God who made them!!!!*" Yes, I have known small collections of coloured people to have convened together, for no other purpose than to worship God Almighty, in spirit and in truth, to the best of their knowledge; when tyrants, calling themselves *patrols,* would also convene and wait almost in breathless silence for the poor coloured people to commence singing and praying to the Lord our God, as soon as they had commenced, the wretches would burst in upon them and drag them out and commence beating them as they would rattle-snakes—many of whom, they would beat so unmercifully, that they would hardly be able to crawl for weeks and sometimes for months. Yet the American ministers send out missionaries to convert the heathen, while they keep us and our children sunk at their feet in the most abject ignorance and wretchedness that ever a people was afflicted with since the world began. Will the Lord suffer this people to proceed much longer? Will he not stop them in their career? Does he regard the heathens abroad, more than the heathens among the Americans? Surely the Americans must believe that God is partial, notwithstanding his Apostle Peter, declared before Cornelius and others that he has no respect to persons, but in every nation he that feareth God and worketh righteousness is accepted with him. —"The word," said he, "which God sent unto the children of Israel, preaching peace, by Jesus Christ, (he is Lord of all.")[3]) Have not the Americans the Bible in their hands? Do they believe it? Surely they do not. See how they treat us in open violation of the Bible!! They no doubt will be greatly offended with me, but if God does not awaken them, it will be, because they are superior to other men, as they have represented themselves to be. Our divine Lord and Master said, "all things whatsoever ye would that men should do unto you, do ye even so unto them." But an American minister, with the Bible in his hand, holds us and our children in the most abject slavery and wretchedness. Now I ask them, would they like for us to hold them and their children in abject slavery and wretchedness? No, says one, that never can be done—you are too abject and ignorant to do it—you are not men—you were made to be slaves to us, to dig up gold and silver for us and our children. Know this, my dear sirs, that although you treat us and our children now, as you do your domestic beast—yet the final result of all future events are known but to God Almighty alone, who rules in the armies of heaven and among the inhabitants of the earth, and who dethrones one earthly king and sets up another, as it seemeth good in his holy sight. We may attribute these vicissitudes to what we please, but the God of armies and of justice rules in heaven and in earth, and the whole American people shall see and know it yet, to their satisfaction. I have known pre-

---

[3] See Acts of the Apostles, chap. x. v.—25–27.

tended preachers of the gospel of my Master, who not only held us as their natural inheritance, but treated us with as much rigor as any Infidel or Deist in the world—just as though they were intent only on taking our blood and groans to glorify the Lord Jesus Christ. The wicked and ungodly, seeing their preachers treat us with so much cruelty, they say: our preachers, who must be right, if any body are, treat them like brutes, and why cannot we?— They think it is no harm to keep them in slavery and put the whip to them, and why cannot we do the same!—They being preachers of the gospel of Jesus Christ, if it were any harm, they would surely preach against their oppression and do their utmost to erase it from the country; not only in one or two cities, but one continual cry would be raised in all parts of this confederacy, and would cease only with the complete overthrow of the system of slavery, in every part of the country. But how far the American preachers are from preaching against slavery and oppression, which have carried their country to the brink of a precipice; to save them from plunging down the side of which, will hardly be affected, will appear in the sequel of this paragraph, which I shall narrate just as it transpired. I remember a Camp Meeting in South Carolina, for which I embarked in a Steam Boat at Charleston, and having been five or six hours on the water, we at last arrived at the place of hearing, where was a very great concourse of people, who were no doubt, collected together to hear the word of God, (that some had collected barely as spectators to the scene, I will not here pretend to doubt, however, that is left to themselves and their God.) Myself and boat companions, having been there a little while, we were all called up to hear; I among the rest went up and took my seat—being seated, I fixed myself in a complete position to hear the word of my Saviour and to receive such as I thought was authenticated by the Holy Scriptures; but to my no ordinary astonishment, our Reverend gentleman got up and told us (coloured people) that slaves must be obedient to their masters—must do their duty to their masters or be whipped—the whip was made for the backs of fools, &c. Here I pause for a moment, to give the world time to consider what was my surprise, to hear such preaching from a minister of my Master, whose very gospel is that of peace and not of blood and whips, as this pretended preacher tried to make us believe. What the American preachers can think of us, I aver this day before my God, I have never been able to define. They have newspapers and monthly periodicals, which they receive in continual succession, but on the pages of which, you will scarcely ever find a paragraph respecting slavery, which is ten thousand times more injurious to this country than all the other evils put together; and which will be the final overthrow of its government, unless something is very speedily done; for their cup is nearly full.—Perhaps they will laugh at or make light of this; but I tell you Americans! that unless you speedily alter your course, *you* and your *Country are gone!!!!!!* For God Almighty will tear up the very face of the earth!!! Will not that very remarkable passage of Scripture be fulfilled on Christian Americans? Hear it

Americans!! "He that is unjust, let him be unjust still:—and he which is filthy, let him be filthy still: and he that is righteous, let him be righteous still: and he that is holy, let him be holy still."[4] I hope that the Americans may hear, but I am afraid that they have done us so much injury, and are so firm in the belief that our Creator made us to be an inheritance to them for ever, that their hearts will be hardened, so that their destruction may be sure. This language, perhaps is too harsh for the American's delicate ears. But Oh Americans! Americans!! I warn you in the name of the Lord, (whether you will hear, or forbear,) to repent and reform, or you are ruined!!! Do you think that our blood is hidden from the Lord, because you can hide it from the rest of the world, by sending out missionaries, and by your charitable deeds to the Greeks, Irish, &c.? Will he not publish your secret crimes on the house top? Even here in Boston, pride and prejudice have got to such a pitch, that in the very houses erected to the Lord, they have built little places for the reception of coloured people, where they must sit during meeting, or keep away from the house of God, and the preachers say nothing about it—much less go into the hedges and highways seeking the lost sheep of the house of Israel, and try to bring them in to their Lord and Master. There are not a more wretched, ignorant, miserable, and abject set of beings in all the world, than the blacks in the Southern and Western sections of this country, under tyrants and devils. The preachers of America cannot see them, but they can send out missionaries to convert the heathens, notwithstanding. Americans! unless you speedily alter your course of proceeding, if God Almighty does not stop, I say it in his name, that you may go on and do as you please for ever, both in time and eternity—never fear any evil at all!!!!!!!!

☞ ADDITION.—The preachers and people of the United States form societies against Free Masonry and Intemperance, and write against Sabbath breaking, Sabbath mails, Infidelity, &c. &c. But the fountain head,[5] compared with which, all those other evils are comparatively nothing, and from the bloody and murderous head of which, they receive no trifling support, is hardly noticed by the Americans. This is a fair illustration of the state of society in this country—it shows what a bearing *avarice* has upon a people, when they are nearly given up by the Lord to a hard heart and a reprobate mind, in consequence of afflicting their fellow creatures. God suffers some to go on until they are ruined for ever!!!!! Will it be the case with the whites of the United States of America?—We hope not—we would not wish to see them destroyed notwithstanding, they have and do now treat us more cruel than any people have treated another, on this earth since it came from the hands of its Creator (with the exceptions of the French and the Dutch, they treat us nearly as bad as the Americans of the United States.) The will of God must however, in spite of us, *be done*.

---

[4] See Revelation, chap. xxii. 11.
[5] Slavery and oppression.

The English are the best friends the coloured people have upon earth. Though they have oppressed us a little and have colonies now in the West Indies, which oppress us *sorely*.—Yet notwithstanding they (the English) have done one hundred times more for the melioration of our condition, than all the other nations of the earth put together. The blacks cannot but respect the English as a nation, notwithstanding they have treated us a little cruel.

There is no intelligent *black man* who knows any thing, but esteems a real Englishman, let him see him in what part of the world he will—for they are the greatest benefactors we have upon earth. We have here and there, in other nations, good friends. But as a nation, the English are our friends. ☞

How can the preachers and people of America believe the Bible? Does it teach them any distinction on account of a man's colour? Hearken, Americans! to the injunctions of our Lord and Master, to his humble followers.

[6]"And Jesus came and spake unto them, saying, all power is given unto me in Heaven and in earth.

"Go ye, therefore, and teach all nations, baptizing them in the name of the Father, and of the Son, and of the Holy Ghost.

"Teaching them to observe all things whatsoever I have commanded you; and lo, I am with you alway, even unto the end of the world. Amen."

I declare, that the very face of these injunctions appear to be of God and not of man. They do not show the slightest degree of distinction. "Go ye therefore," (says my divine Master) "and teach all nations," (or in other words, all people) "baptizing them in the name of the Father, and of the Son, and of the Holy Ghost." Do you understand the above, Americans? We are a people, notwithstanding many of you doubt it. You have the Bible in your hands, with this very injunction.—Have you been to Africa, teaching the inhabitants thereof the words of the Lord Jesus? "Baptizing them in the name of the Father, and of the Son and of the Holy Ghost." Have you not, on the contrary, entered among us, and learnt us the art of throat-cutting, by setting us to fight, one against another, to take each other as prisoners of war, and sell to you for small bits of calicoes, old swords, knives, &c. to make slaves for you and your children? This being done, have you not brought us among you, in chains and hand-cuffs, like brutes, and treated us with all the cruelties and rigour your ingenuity could invent, consistent with the laws of your country, which (for the blacks) are tyrannical enough? Can the American preachers appeal unto God, the Maker and Searcher of hearts, and tell him, with the Bible in their hands, that they make no distinction on account of men's colour? Can they say, O God! thou knowest all things—thou knowest that we make no distinction between thy creatures, to whom we have to preach thy Word? Let them answer the Lord; and if they cannot do it in the affirmative, have they not departed from the Lord Jesus Christ, their master? But some may say, that they never had, or were in possession of reli-

---

[6] See St. Matthew's Gospel, chap. xxviii. 18, 19, 20. After Jesus was risen from the dead.

gion, which made no distinction, and of course they could not have departed from it. I ask you then, in the name of the Lord, of what kind can your religion be? Can it be that which was preached by our Lord Jesus Christ from Heaven? I believe you cannot be so wicked as to tell him that his Gospel was that of *distinction*. What can the American preachers and people take God to be? Do they believe his words? If they do, do they believe that he will be mocked? Or do they believe, because they are whites and we blacks, that God will have respect to them? Did not God make us all as it seemed best to himself? What right, then, has one of us, to despise another, and to treat him cruel, on account of his colour, which none, but the God who made it can alter? Can there be a greater absurdity in nature, and particularly in a free republican country? But the Americans, having introduced slavery among them, their hearts have become almost seared, as with an hot iron, and God has nearly given them up to believe a lie in preference to the truth!!! And I am awfully afraid that pride, prejudice, avarice and blood, will, before long prove the final ruin of this happy republic, or land of *liberty!!!!* Can any thing be a greater mockery of religion than the way in which it is conducted by the Americans? It appears as though they are bent only on daring God Almighty to do his best—they chain and handcuff us and our children and drive us around the country like brutes, and go into the house of the God of justice to return him thanks for having aided them in their infernal cruelties inflicted upon us. Will the Lord suffer this people to go on much longer, taking his holy name in vain? Will he not stop them, PREACHERS and all? O Americans! Americans!! I call God—I call angels—I call men, to witness, that your DESTRUCTION *is at hand*, and will be speedily consummated unless you REPENT.

DISCRIMINATION IN THE FREE STATES

Charles L. Remond / Address to a Legislative Committee in the Massachusetts House of Representatives, 1842

Many thoughtful black men were active in the various abolitionist societies, giving speeches and writing articles about the evils of slavery. But they were also concerned about the discrimination free blacks met in the North. Among the most effective of the black spokesmen was Charles Lenox Remond of Massachusetts, who was employed by the American Anti-Slavery Society and became one of the most prominent black abolitionists. He attended the London World Anti-Slavery Conference in 1840, then lectured on abolition in the British Isles for two years before returning home. Upon his return, he met with segregation on the railroads and determined to have it abolished.

The following address was made by Remond in 1842 to a legislative committee in the Massachusetts House of Representatives that was studying the problem of segregation. In the address, he emphasized the contrast between the nondiscriminatory treatment he received while abroad and the segregation he was forced into at home. A year later, the Massachusetts legislature abolished segregation.

Mr. Chairman, and Gentlemen of the Committee:

In rising at this time, and on this occasion, being the first person of color who has ever addressed either of the bodies assembling in this building, I should, perhaps, in the first place, observe that, in consequence of the many misconstructions of the principles and measures of which I am the humble advocate, I may in like manner be subject to similar misconceptions from the moment I open my lips in behalf of the prayer of the petitioners for whom I appear, and therefore feel I have the right at least to ask, at the hands of this intelligent Committee, an impartial hearing; and that whatever prejudices they may have imbibed, be eradicated from their minds, if such exist. I have, however, too much confidence in their intelligence, and too much faith in their determination to do their duty as the representatives of this Commonwealth, to presume they can be actuated by partial motives. Trusting, as I do, that the day is not distant, when, on all questions touching the rights of the citizens of this State, men shall be considered *great* only as they are *good*— and not that it shall be told, and painfully experienced, that, in this country, this State, ay, this city, the Athens of America, the rights, privileges and immunities of its citizens are measured by complexion, or any other physical peculiarity or conformation, especially such as over which no man has any control. Complexion can in no sense be construed into crime, much less be rightfully made the criterion of rights. Should the people of color, through a revolution of Providence, become a majority, to the last I would oppose it upon the same principle; for, in either case, it would be equally reprehensible and unjustifiable—alike to be condemned and repudiated. It is JUSTICE I stand here to claim, and not FAVOR for either complexion.

And now, sir, I shall endeavor to confine my remarks to the same subject which has occupied the attention of the Committee thus far, and to stand upon the same principle which has been so ably and so eloquently maintained and established by my esteemed friend, Mr. Phillips.

FROM Charles L. Remond, "Before the Legislative Committee in the House of Representatives [Mass.] respecting the rights of colored citizens in travelling, etc.," *Liberator* (February 25, 1842).

Our right to citizenship in this State has been acknowledged and secured by the allowance of the elective franchise and consequent taxation; and I know of no good reason, if admitted in this instance, why it should be denied in any other.

With reference to the wrongs inflicted and injuries received on rail-roads, by persons of color, I need not say they do not end with the termination of the route, but, in effect, tend to discourage, disparage and depress this class of citizens. All hope of reward for upright conduct is cut off. Vice in them becomes a virtue. No distinction is made by the community in which we live. The most vicious is treated as well as the most respectable, both in public and private.

But it is said we all look alike. If this is true, it is not true that we all behave alike. There is a marked difference; and we claim a recognition of this difference.

In the present state of things, they find God's provisions interfered with in such a way, by these and kindred regulations, that virtue may not claim her divinely appointed rewards. Color is made to obscure the brightest endowments, to degrade the fairest character, and to check the highest and most praiseworthy aspirations. If the colored man is vicious, it makes but little difference; if besotted, it matters not; if vulgar, it is quite as well; and he finds himself as well treated, and received as readily into society, as those of an opposite character. Nay, the higher our aspirations, the loftier our purposes and pursuits, does this iniquitous principle of prejudice fasten upon us, and especial pains are taken to irritate, obstruct and injure. No reward of merit, no remuneration for services, no equivalent is rendered the deserving. And I submit, whether this unkind and unchristian policy is not well calculated to make every man disregardful of his conduct, and every woman unmindful of her reputation.

The grievances of which we complain, be assured, sir, are not imaginary, but real—not local, but universal—not occasional, but continual—every day matter of fact things—and have become, to the disgrace of our common country, matter of history.

Mr. Chairman, the treatment to which colored Americans are exposed in their own country, finds a counterpart in no other; and I am free to declare, that, in the course of nineteen months' traveling in England, Ireland, and Scotland, I was received, treated and recognised, in public and private society, without any regard to my complexion. From the moment I left the American packet ship in Liverpool, up to the moment I came in contact with it again, I was never reminded of my complexion; and all that know anything of my usage in the American ship, will testify that it was unfit for a brute, and none but one could inflict it. But how unlike that afforded in the British steamer Columbia! Owing to my limited resources, I took a steerage passage. On the first day out, the second officer came to inquire after my health; and finding me the only passenger in that part of the ship, ordered the steward to give me berth in the second cabin; and from that hour until my stepping on shore at Boston, every politeness was shown me by the officers, and every kindness and attention by the stewards; and I feel under deep and lasting obligations to them, individually and collectively.

In no instance was I insulted or treated in any way distinct or dissimilar from other passengers or travelers, either in coaches, rail-roads, steampackets, or hotels; and if the feeling was entertained, in no case did I discover its existence.

I may with propriety here relate an accident, illustrative of the subject now under consideration. I took a passage ticket at the steam packet office in Glasgow, for Dublin; and on going into the cabin to retire, I found the berth I had engaged occupied by an Irish gentleman and merchant. I enquired if he had not mistaken the number of his berth. He thought not. On comparing tickets, we saw that the clerk had given two tickets of the same number; and it appeared I had received mine first. The gentleman at once offered to vacate the berth, against which I remonstrated, and took my berth in an opposite state room. Here, sir, we discover treatment just, impartial, reasonable; and we ask nothing beside.

There is a marked difference between social and civil rights. It has been well and justly remarked, by my friend Mr. Phillips, that we all claim the privilege of selecting our society and associations; but, in civil rights, one man has not the prerogative to define rights for another. For instance, sir, in public conveyances, for the rich man to usurp the privileges to himself, to the injury of the poor man, would be submitted to in no well regulated society. And such is the position suffered by persons of color. On my arrival home from England, I went to the rail way station, to go to Salem, being anxious to see my parents and sisters as soon as possible—asked for a ticket—paid 50 cents for it, and was pointed to the American designation car. Having previously received information of the regulations, I took my seat peaceably, believing it better to suffer wrong than do wrong. I felt then, as I felt on many occasions prior to leaving home, unwilling to descend so low as to bandy words with the superintendents, or contest my rights with conductors, or any others in the capacity of servants of any stage or steamboat company, or rail-road corporation; although I never, by any means, gave evidence that, by my submission, I intended to sanction usages which would derogate from uncivilized, much less long and loud professing and high pretending America.

Bear with me while I relate an additional occurrence. On the morning after my return home, I was obliged to go to Boston again, and on going to the Salem station I met two friends, who enquired if I had any objection to their taking seats with me. I answered, I should be most happy. They took their seats accordingly, and soon afterwards one of them remarked to me— 'Charles, I don't know if they will allow us to ride with you.' It was some time before I could understand what they meant, and; on doing so, I laughed —feeling it to be a climax to every absurdity I had heard attributed to

Americans. To say nothing of the wrong done those friends, and the insult and indignity offered me by the appearance of the conductor, who ordered the friends from the car in a somewhat harsh manner—they immediately left the carriage.

On returning to Salem some few evenings afterwards, Mr. Chase, the superintendent on this road, made himself known to me, by recalling by-gone days and scenes, and then enquired if I was not glad to get home after so long an absence in Europe. I told him I was glad to see my parents and family again, and this the only object I could have, unless he thought I should be glad to take a hermit's life in the great pasture; inasmuch as I never felt to loathe my American name so much as since my arrival. He wished to know my reasons for the remark. I immediately gave them, and wished to know of him, if, in the event of his having a brother with red hair, he should find himself separated while travelling because of this difference, he should deem it just. He could make no reply. I then wished to know if the principle was not the same; and if so, there was an insult implied by his question. In conclusion, I challenged him as the instrument inflicting the manifold injuries upon all not colored like himself, to the presentation of an instance in any other Christian or unchristian country, tolerating usages at once so disgraceful, unjust and inhuman. What if some few of the West or East India planters and merchants should visit our liberty-loving country, with their colored wives—how would he manage? Or, if R. M. Johnson, the gentleman who has been elevated to the second office in the gift of the people, should be travelling from Boston to Salem, if he was prepared to separate him from his wife or daughters (involuntary burst of applause, instantly restrained.)

Sir, it happens to be my lot to have a sister a few shades lighter than myself; and who knows, if this state of things is encouraged, whether I may not on some future occasion be mobbed in Washington-street, on the supposition of walking with a white young lady! (Suppressed indications of sympathy and applause.)

Gentlemen of the Committee, these distinctions react in all their wickedness—to say nothing of their concocted and systematized odiousness and absurdity—upon those who instituted them; and particularly so upon those who are illiberal and mean enough to practise them.

Mr. Chairman, if colored people have abused any rights granted them, or failed to exhibit due appreciation of favors bestowed, or shrunk from dangers or responsibility, let it be made to appear. Or if our country contains a population to compare with them in loyalty and patriotism, circumstances duly considered, I have it yet to learn. The history of our country must ever testify in their behalf. In view of these and many additional considerations, I unhesitatingly assert their claim, on the naked principle of merit, to every advantage set forth in the Constitution of this Commonwealth.

Finally, Mr. Chairman, there is in this and other States a large and growing colored population, whose residence in your midst has not been from choice, (let this be understood and reflected upon,) but by the force of circumstances over which they never had control. Upon the heads of their oppressors and calumniators be the censure and responsibility. If to ask at your hands redress for injuries, and protection in our rights and immunities, as citizens, is reasonable, and dictated alike by justice, humanity and religion, you will not reject, I trust, the prayer of your petitioners.

Before sitting down, I owe it to myself to remark, that I was not appraised of the wish of my friends to appear here until passing through Boston, a day or two since; and having been occupied with other matters, I have had no opportunity for preparation on this occasion. I feel much obliged to the Committee for their kind, patient, and attentive hearing. (Applause.)

THE SLAVE MUST THROW OFF THE SLAVEHOLDER

Henry Highland Garnet   /   Address to a Convention in Buffalo, 1843

In the 1840's the convention movement provided a major outlet for black abolitionist thought. Although many leading blacks were active in the predominantly white anti-slavery organizations, it was widely felt that there were some things black people should deal with among themselves. When Henry Highland Garnet made an address to the convention in Buffalo in 1843 calling for a violent overthrow of the slave masters by the slaves, the development of the movement reached a decided turning point. Although the assembled delegates rejected a resolution supporting the address by one vote, subsequent conventions treated the question of violence with much more sympathy. By 1854, in fact, violence was being openly advocated.

Garnet was the minister of a white Presbyterian congregation in Troy, New York, and he took his militant posture seriously enough to wear a pistol. As the middle of the century drew near, Garnet's hope for an ultimate solution to America's color problem faded, and he became and remained a staunch supporter of emigrationism.

Garnet's address, reprinted in the following pages, was bound together with David Walker's **Appeal** in a special edition in 1848. The words of these two prophets were finally translated into action in 1859 by John Brown, who raided the federal arsenal at Harpers Ferry, West Virginia, in order to incite an uprising of the slaves.

Brethren and Fellow Citizens:

Your brethren of the North, East, and West have been accustomed to meet together in National Conventions, to sympathize with each other, and to weep over your unhappy condition. In these meetings we have addressed all classes of the free, but we have never, until this time, sent a word of consolation and advice to you. We have been contented in sitting still and mourning over your sorrows, earnestly hoping that before this day your sacred liberty would have been restored. But, we have hoped in vain. Years have rolled on, and tens of thousands have been borne on streams of blood and tears, to the shores of eternity. While you have been oppressed, we have also been partakers with you; nor can we be free while you are enslaved. We, therefore, write to you as being bound with you.

Many of you are bound to us, not only by the ties of a common humanity, but we are connected by the more tender relations of parents, wives, husbands, children, brothers, and sisters, and friends. As such we most affectionately address you.

Slavery has fixed a deep gulf between you and us, and while it shuts out from you the relief and consolation which your friends would willingly render, it affects and persecutes you with a fierceness which we might not expect to see in the fiends of hell. But still the Almighty Father of mercies has left to us a glimmering ray of hope, which shines out like a lone star in a cloudy sky. Mankind are becoming wiser, and better—the oppressor's power is fading, and you, every day, are becoming better informed, and more numerous. Your grievances, brethren, are many. We shall not attempt, in this short address, to present to the world all the dark catalogue of this nation's sins, which have been committed upon an innocent people. Nor is it indeed necessary, for you feel them from day to day, and all the civilized world look upon them with amazement.

Two hundred and twenty-seven years ago the first of our injured race were brought to the shores of America. They came not with glad spirits to select their homes in the New World. They came not with their own consent, to find an unmolested enjoyment of the blessings of this fruitful soil. The first dealings they had with men calling themselves Christians, exhibited to them the worst features of corrupt and sordid hearts; and convinced them that no cruelty is too great, no villainy and no robbery too abhorrent for even enlightened men to perform, when influenced by avarice and lust. Neither did they come flying upon the wings of Liberty, to a land of freedom. But they came with broken hearts, from their beloved native land, and were doomed to unrequited toil and deep degradation. Nor did the evil of their bondage end at their emancipation by death. Succeeding generations inherited their chains, and millions have come from eternity into

FROM Henry Highland Garnet, "An Address to the Slaves of the United States of America" (1843).

time, and have returned again to the world of spirits, cursed and ruined by American slavery.

The propagators of the system, or their immediate ancestors, very soon discovered its growing evil, and its tremendous wickedness, and secret promises were made to destroy it. The gross inconsistency of a people holding slaves, who had themselves "ferried o'er the wave" for freedom's sake, was too apparent to be entirely overlooked. The voice of Freedom cried, "Emancipate yourselves." Humanity supplicated with tears for the deliverance of the children of Africa. Wisdom urged her solemn plea. The bleeding captive plead his innocence, and pointed to Christianity who stood weeping at the cross. Jehovah frowned upon the nefarious institution, and thunderbolts, red with vengeance, struggled to leap forth to blast the guilty wretches who maintained it. But all was in vain. Slavery had stretched its dark wings of death over the land, the Church stood silently by—the priests prophesied falsely, and the people loved to have it so. Its throne is established, and now it reigns triumphant.

Nearly three millions of your fellow-citizens are prohibited by law and public opinion, (which in this country is stronger than law,) from reading the Book of Life. Your intellect has been destroyed as much as possible, and every ray of light they have attempted to shut out from your minds. The oppressors themselves have become involved in the ruin. They have become weak, sensual, and rapacious—they have cursed you—they have cursed themselves—they have cursed the earth which they have trod.

The colonists threw the blame upon England. They said that the mother country entailed the evil upon them, and that they would rid themselves of it if they could. The world thought they were sincere, and the philanthropic pitied them. But time soon tested their sincerity.

In a few years the colonists grew strong, and severed themselves from the British Government. Their independence was declared, and they took their station among the sovereign powers of the earth. The declaration was a glorious document. Sages admired it, and the patriotic of every nation reverenced the God-like sentiments which it contained. When the power of Government returned to their hands, did they emancipate the slaves? No; they rather added new links to our chains. Were they ignorant of the principles of Liberty? Certainly they were not. The sentiments of their revolutionary orators fell in burning eloquence upon their hearts, and with one voice they cried, Liberty or Death. Oh what a sentence was that! It ran from soul to soul like electric fire, and nerved the arm of thousands to fight in the holy cause of Freedom. Among the diversity of opinions that are entertained in regard to physical resistance, there are but a few found to gainsay that stern declaration. We are among those who do not. Slavery! How much misery is comprehended in that single word. What mind is there that does not shrink from its direful effects? Unless the image of God be obliterated from the soul, all men cherish the love of Liberty. The nice discerning political economist does not regard the sacred right more than the untutored African who roams in the wilds of Congo. Nor has the one more right to the full enjoyment of his freedom than the other. In every man's mind the good seeds of liberty are planted, and he who brings his fellow down so low, as to make him contented with a condition of slavery, commits the highest crime against God and man. Brethren, your oppressors aim to do this. They endeavor to make you as much like brutes as possible. When they have blinded the eyes of your mind—when they have embittered the sweet waters of life—then, and not till then, has American slavery done its perfect work.

To such degradation it is sinful in the extreme for you to make voluntary submission. The divine commandments you are in duty bound to reverence and obey. If you do not obey them, you will surely meet with the displeasure of the Almighty. He requires you to love him supremely, and your neïghbor as yourself—to keep the Sabbath day holy—to search the Scriptures—and bring up your children with respect for his laws, and to worship no other God but him. But slavery sets all these at nought, and hurls defiance in the face of Jehovah. The forlorn condition in which you are placed, does not destroy your moral obligation to God. You are not certain of heaven, because you suffer yourselves to remain in a state of slavery, where you cannot obey the commandments of the Sovereign of the universe. If the ignorance of slavery is a passport to heaven, then it is a blessing, and no curse, and you should rather desire its perpetuity than its abolition. God will not receive slavery, nor ignorance, nor any other state of mind, for love and obedience to him. Your condition does not absolve you from your moral obligation. The diabolical injustice by which your liberties are cloven down, NEITHER GOD, NOR ANGELS, OR JUST MEN, COMMAND YOU TO SUFFER FOR A SINGLE MOMENT. THEREFORE IT IS YOUR SOLEMN AND IMPERATIVE DUTY TO USE EVERY MEANS, BOTH MORAL, INTELLECTUAL, AND PHYSICAL THAT PROMISES SUCCESS. If a band of heathen men should attempt to enslave a race of Christians, and to place their children under the influence of some false religion, surely Heaven would frown upon the men who would not resist such aggression, even to death. If, on the other hand, a band of Christians should attempt to enslave a race of heathen men, and to entail slavery upon them, and to keep them in heathenism in the midst of Christianity, the God of heaven would smile upon every effort which the injured might make to disenthral themselves.

Brethren, it is as wrong for your lordly oppressors to keep you in slavery, as it was for the man thief to steal our ancestors from the coast of Africa. You should therefore now use the same manner of resistance, as would have been just in our ancestors when the bloody foot-prints of the first remorseless soul-thief was placed upon the shores of our fatherland. The humblest peasant is as free in the sight of God as the proudest monarch that ever swayed a sceptre. Liberty is a spirit sent out from God, and like its great Author, is no respecter of persons.

Brethren, the time has come when you must act for yourselves. It is an old and true saying that, "if hereditary bondmen would be free, they must themselves strike the blow." You can plead your own cause, and do the work of emancipation better than any others. The nations of the world are moving in the great cause of universal freedom, and some of them at least will, ere long, do you justice. The combined powers of Europe have placed their broad seal of disapprobation upon the African slave-trade. But in the slave-holding parts of the United States, the trade is as brisk as ever. They buy and sell you as though you were brute beasts. The North has done much—her opinion of slavery in the abstract is known. But in regard to the South, we adopt the opinion of the *New York Evangelist*—We have advanced so far, that the cause apparently waits for a more effectual door to be thrown open than has been yet. We are about to point out that more effectual door. Look around you, and behold the bosoms of your loving wives heaving with untold agonies! Hear the cries of your poor children! Remember the stripes your fathers bore. Think of the torture and disgrace of your noble mothers. Think of your wretched sisters, loving virtue and purity, as they are driven into concubinage and are exposed to the unbridled lusts of incarnate devils. Think of the undying glory that hangs around the ancient name of Africa—and forget not that you are native born American citizens, and as such, you are justly entitled to all the rights that are granted to the freest. Think how many tears you have poured out upon the soil which you have cultivated with unrequited toil and enriched with your blood; and then go to your lordly enslavers and tell them plainly, that you *are determined to be free*. Appeal to their sense of justice, and tell them that they have no more right to oppress you, than you have to enslave them. Entreat them to remove the grievous burdens which they have imposed upon you, and to remunerate you for your labor. Promise them renewed diligence in the cultivation of the soil, if they will render to you an equivalent for your services. Point them to the increase of happiness and prosperity in the British West Indies since the Act of Emancipation.

Tell them in language which they cannot misunderstand, of the exceeding sinfulness of slavery, and of a future judgment, and of the righteous retributions of an indignant God. Inform them that all you desire is FREE-DOM, and that nothing else will suffice. Do this, and for ever after cease to toil for the heartless tyrants, who give you no other reward but stripes and abuse. If they then commence the work of death, they, and not you, will be responsible for the consequences. You had better all die—*die immediately*, than live slaves and entail your wretchedness upon your posterity. If you would be free in this generation, here is your only hope. However much you and all of us may desire it, there is not much hope of redemption without the shedding of blood. If you must bleed, let it all come at once—rather *die freemen, than live to be slaves*. It is impossible like the children of Israel, to make a grand exodus from the land of bondage. The Pharaohs are on both sides of the blood-red waters! You cannot move *en masse*, to the dominions of the British Queen—nor can you pass through Florida and overrun Texas, and at last find peace in Mexico. The propagators of American slavery are spending their blood and treasure, that they may plant the black flag in the heart of Mexico and riot in the halls of the Montezeumas. In the language of the Rev. Robert Hall, when addressing the volunteers of Bristol, who were rushing forth to repel the invasion of Napoleon, who threatened to lay waste the fair homes of England, "Religion is too much interested in your behalf, not to shed over you her most gracious influences."

You will not be compelled to spend much time in order to become inured to hardships. From the first moment that you breathed the air of heaven, you have been accustomed to nothing else but hardships. The heroes of the American Revolution were never put upon harder fare than a peck of corn and a few herrings per week. You have not become enervated by the luxuries of life. Your sternest energies have been beaten out upon the anvil of severe trial. Slavery has done this, to make you subservient, to its own purposes; but it has done more than this, it has prepared you for any emergency. If you receive good treatment, it is what you could hardly expect; if you meet with pain, sorrow, and even death, these are the common lot of slaves.

Fellow men! Patient sufferers! behold your dearest rights crushed to the earth! See your sons murdered, and your wives, mothers and sisters doomed to prostitution. In the name of the merciful God, and by all that life is worth, let it no longer be a debatable question whether it is better to choose *Liberty or death.*

In 1822, Denmark Veazie, of South Carolina, formed a plan for the liberation of his fellow men. In the whole history of human efforts to overthrow slavery, a more complicated and tremendous plan was never formed. He was betrayed by the treachery of his own people, and died a martyr to freedom. Many a brave hero fell, but history, faithful to her high trust, will transcribe his name on the same monument with Moses, Hampden, Tell, Bruce and Wallace, Toussaint L'Ouverture, Lafayette and Washington. That tremendous movement shook the whole empire of slavery. The guilty soul-thieves were overwhelmed with fear. It is a matter of fact, that at that time, and in consequence of the threatened revolution, the slave States talked strongly of emancipation. But they blew but one blast of the trumpet of freedom and then laid it aside. As these men became quiet, the slaveholders ceased to talk about emancipation; and now behold your condition today! Angels sigh over it, and humanity has long since exhausted her tears in weeping on your account!

The patriotic Nathaniel Turner followed Denmark Veazie. He was goaded to desperation by wrong and injustice. By despotism, his name has been recorded on the list of infamy, and future generations will remember him among the noble and brave.

Next arose the immortal Joseph Cinque, the hero of the *Amistad*. He was a native African, and by the help of God he emancipated a whole ship-load of his fellow men on the high seas. And he now sings of liberty on the sunny hills of Africa and beneath his native palm-trees, where he hears the lion roar and feels himself as free as that king of the forest.

Next arose Madison Washington that bright star of freedom, and took his station in the constellation of true heroism. He was a slave on board the brig *Creole*, of Richmond, bound to New Orleans, that great slave mart, with a hundred and four others. Nineteen struck for liberty or death. But one life was taken, and the whole were emancipated, and the vessel was carried into Nassau, New Providence.

Noble men! Those who have fallen in freedom's conflict, their memories will be cherished by the true-hearted and the God-fearing in all future generations; those who are living, their names are surrounded by a halo of glory.

Brethren, arise, arise! Strike for your lives and liberties. Now is the day and the hour. Let every slave throughout the land do this, and the days of slavery are numbered. You cannot be more oppressed than you have been— you cannot suffer greater cruelties than you have already. *Rather die free-men than live to be slaves.* Remember that you are FOUR MILLIONS!

It is in your power so to torment the God-cursed slaveholders that they will be glad to let you go free. If the scale was turned, and black men were the masters and white men the slaves, every destructive agent and element would be employed to lay the oppressor low. Danger and death would hang over their heads day and night. Yes, the tyrants would meet with plagues more terrible than those of Pharaoh. But you are a patient people. You act as though, you were made for the special use of these devils. You act as though your daughters were born to pamper the lusts of your masters and overseers. And worse than all, you tamely submit while your lords tear your wives from your embraces and defile them before your eyes. In the name of God, we ask, are you men? Where is the blood of your fathers? Has it all run out of your veins? Awake, awake; millions of voices are calling you! Your dead fathers speak to you from their graves. Heaven, as with a voice of thunder, calls on you to arise from the dust.

Let your motto be resistance! *resistance!* RESISTANCE! No oppressed people have ever secured their liberty without resistance. What kind of resistance you had better make, you must decide by the circumstances that surround you, and according to the suggestion of expediency. Brethren, adieu! Trust in the living God. Labor for the peace of the human race, and remember that you are FOUR MILLIONS.

BLACK PRIDE

John S. Rock / Address to a Meeting in Boston, 1858

In March 1858, a meeting was held in Faneuil Hall, Boston, commemorating the anniversary of the Boston Massacre of 1770 and, particularly, the death of Crispus Attucks, a fugitive slave who was killed by the British in that encounter. Among the speakers on the occasion were white abolitionists Theodore Parker and Wendell Phillips. The most controversial address was made by a Boston black man, Dr. John Rock.

Rock, who was thirty-three years old when he made the following remarks, was perhaps the most highly educated black man of his day. During his lifetime, he taught school, practiced as a dentist and a physician, and became a lawyer. In 1865, he was admitted to plead before the Supreme Court of the United States —the first black person to be accorded this privilege. Rock's address of 1858 is brilliant in its historical understanding and analysis of the phenomenon of racism. Many of its points are as relevant today as they were upon their presentation a hundred years ago.

Ladies and Gentlemen:

You will not expect a lengthened speech from me to-night. My health is too poor to allow me to indulge much in speech-making. But I have not been able to resist the temptation to unite with you in this demonstration of respect for some of my noble but misguided ancestors.

White Americans have taken great pains to try to prove that we are cowards. We are often insulted with the assertion, that if we had had the courage of the Indians or the white man, we would never have submitted to be slaves. I ask if Indians and white men have never been slaves? The white man tested the Indian's courage here when he had his organized armies, his battle-grounds, his places of retreat, with everything to hope for and everything to lose. The position of the African slave has been very different. Seized a prisoner of war, unarmed, bound hand and foot, and conveyed to a distant country among what to him were worse than cannibals; brutally beaten, half-starved, closely watched by armed men, with no means of knowing their own strength or the strength of their enemies, with no weapons, and without a probability of success. But if the white man will take the trouble to fight the black man in Africa or in Hayti, and fight him as fair as the black man will fight him there—if the black man does not come off

FROM John S. Rock, *Liberator* (March 12, 1858).

victor, I am deceived in his prowess. But, take a man, armed or unarmed, from his home, his country, or his friends, and place him among savages, and who is he that would not make good his retreat? 'Discretion is the better part of valor,' but for a man to resist where he knows it will destroy him, shows more fool-hardiness than courage. There have been many Anglo-Saxons and Anglo-Americans enslaved in Africa, but I have never heard that they successfully resisted any government. They always resort to running indispensables.

The courage of the Anglo-Saxon is best illustrated in his treatment of the negro. A score or two of them can pounce upon a poor negro, tie and beat him, and then call him a coward because he submits. Many of their most brilliant victories have been achieved in the same manner. But the greatest battles which they have fought have been upon paper. We can easily account for this; their trumpeter is dead. He died when they used to be exposed for sale in the Roman market, about the time that Cicero cautioned his friend Atticus not to buy them, on account of their stupidity. A little more than half a century ago, this race, in connection with their Celtic neighbors, who have long been considered (by themselves, of course,) the bravest soldiers in the world, so far forgot themselves, as to attack a few cowardly, stupid negro slaves, who, according to their accounts, had not sense enough to go to bed. And what was the result? Why, sir, the negroes drove them out from the island like so many sheep, and they have never dared to show their faces, except with hat in hand.

Our true and tried friend, Rev. Theodore Parker, said, in his speech at the State House, a few weeks since, that 'the stroke of the axe would have settled the question long ago, but the black man would not strike.' Mr. Parker makes a very low estimate of the courage of his race, if he means that one, two or three millions of these ignorant and cowardly black slaves could, without means, have brought to their knees five, ten, or twenty millions of intelligent, brave white men, backed up by a rich oligarchy. But I know of no one who is more familiar with the true character of the Anglo-Saxon race than Mr. Parker. I will not dispute this point with him, but I will thank him or any one else to tell us how it could have been done. His remark calls to my mind the day which is to come, when one shall chase a thousand, and two put ten thousand to flight. But when he says that 'the black man *would not* strike,' I am prepared to say that he does us great injustice. The black man is not a coward. The history of the bloody struggles for freedom in Hayti, in which the blacks whipped the French and the English, and gained their independence, in spite of the perfidy of that villainous First Consul, will be a lasting refutation of the malicious aspersions of our enemies. The history of the struggles for the liberty of the U.S. ought to silence every American calumniator. I have learned that even so late as the Texan war, a number of black men were silly enough to offer themselves as living sacrifices for our country's shame. A gentleman who delivered a lecture before the New York

Legislature, a few years since, whose name I do not now remember, but whose language I give with some precision, said, 'In the Revolution, colored soldiers fought side by side with you in your struggles for liberty, and there is not a battle-field from Maine to Georgia that has not been crimsoned with their blood, and whitened with their bones.' In 1814, a bill passed the Legislature of New York, accepting the services of 2000 colored volunteers. Many black men served under Com. McDonough when he conquered on lake Champlain. Many were in the battles of Plattsburgh and Sackett's Harbor, and General Jackson called out colored troops from Louisiana and Alabama, and in a solemn proclamation attested to their fidelity and courage.

The white man contradicts himself who says, that if he were in our situation, he would throw off the yoke. Thirty millions of white men of this proud Caucasian race are at this moment held as slaves, and bought and sold with horses and cattle. The iron heel of oppression grinds the masses of all European races to the dust. They suffer every kind of oppression, and no one dares to open his mouth to protest against it. Even in the Southern portion of this boasted land of liberty, no white man dares advocate so much of the Declaration of Independence as declares that 'all men are created free and equal, and have an inalienable right to life, liberty,' &c.

White men have no room to taunt us with tamely submitting. If they were black men, they would work wonders; but, as white men, they can do nothing. 'O, Consistency, thou art a jewel!'

Now, it would not be surprising if the brutal treatment which we have received for the past two centuries should have crushed our spirits. But this is not the case. Nothing but a superior force keeps us down. And when I see the slaves rising up by hundreds annually, in the majesty of human nature, bidding defiance to every slave code and its penalties, making the issue Canada or death, and that too while they are closely watched by paid men armed with pistols, clubs and bowie-knives, with the army and navy of this great Model Republic arrayed against them, I am disposed to ask if the charge of cowardice does not come with ill-grace.

But some men are so steeped in folly and imbecility; so lost to all feelings of their own littleness; so destitute of principle, and so regardless of humanity, that they dare attempt to destroy everything which exists in opposition to their interests or opinions which their narrow comprehensions cannot grasp.

We ought not to come here simply to honor those brave men who shed their blood for freedom, or to protest against the Dred Scott decision, but to take counsel of each other, and to enter into new vows of duty. Our fathers fought nobly for freedom, but they were not victorious. They fought for liberty, but they got slavery. The white man was benefitted, but the black man was injured. I do not envy the white American the little liberty which he enjoys. It is his right, and he ought to have it. I wish him success, though I do not think he deserves it. But I would have all men free. We have had much sad experience in this country, and it would be strange indeed if we do not profit by some of the lessons which we have so dearly paid for. Sooner or later, the clashing of arms will be heard in this country, and the black man's services will be needed: 150,000 freemen capable of bearing arms, and not all cowards and fools, and three quarters of a million slaves, wild with the enthusiasm caused by the dawn of the glorious opportunity of being able to strike a genuine blow for freedom, will be a power which white men will be "bound to respect." Will the blacks fight? Of course they will. The black man will never be neutral. He could not if he would, and he would not if he could. Will he fight for this country, right or wrong? This the common sense of every one answers; and when the time comes, and come it will, the black man will give an intelligent answer. Judge Taney may outlaw us; Caleb Cushing may show the depravity of his heart by abusing us; and this wicked government may oppress us; but the black man will live when Judge Taney, Caleb Cushing and this wicked government are no more. White man may despise, ridicule, slander and abuse us; they may seek as they always have done to divide us, and make us feel degraded; but no man shall cause me to turn my back upon my race. With it I will sink or swim.

The prejudice which some white men have, or affected to have, against my color gives me no pain. If any man does not fancy my color, that is his business, and I shall not meddle with it. I shall give myself no trouble because he lacks good taste. If he judges my intellectual capacity by my color, he certainly cannot expect much profundity, for it is only skin deep, and is really of no very great importance to any one but myself. I will not deny that I admire the talents and noble characters of many white men. But I cannot say that I am particularly pleased with their physical appearance. If old mother nature had held out as well as she commenced, we should, probably, have had fewer varieties in the races. When I contrast the fine tough muscular system, the beautiful, rich color, the full broad features, and the gracefully frizzled hair of the Negro, with the delicate physical organization, wan color, sharp features and lank hair of the Caucasian, I am inclined to believe that when the white man was created, nature was pretty well exhausted—but determined to keep up appearances, she pinched up his features, and did the best she could under the circumstances. (Great laughter.)

I would have you understand, that I not only love my race, but am pleased with my color; and while many colored persons may feel degraded by being called negroes, and wish to be classed among other races more favored, I shall feel it my duty, my pleasure and my pride, to concentrate my feeble efforts in elevating to a fair position a race to which I am especially identified by feelings and by blood.

My friends, we can never become elevated until we are true to ourselves. We can come here and make brilliant speeches, but our field of duty is elsewhere. Let us go to work—each man in his place, determined to do what he can for himself and his race. Let us try to carry out some of the resolutions which we have made, and are so fond of making. If we do this, friends will spring up in every quarter, and where we least expect them. But we must not rely on them. They cannot elevate us. Whenever the colored man is elevated, it will be by his own exertions. Our friends can do what many of them are nobly doing, assist us to remove the obstacles which prevent our elevation, and stimulate the worthy to persevere. The colored man who, by dint of perseverance and industry, educates and elevates himself, prepares the way for others, gives character to the race, and hastens the day of general emancipation. While the negro who hangs around the corners of the streets, or lives in the grog-shops or by gambling, or who has no higher ambition than to serve, is by his vocation forging fetters for the slave, and is 'to all intents and purposes' a curse to his race. It is true, considering the circumstances under which we have been placed by our white neighbors, we have a right to ask them not only to cease to oppress us, but to give us that encouragement which our talents and industry may merit. When this is done, they will see our minds expand, and our pockets filled with rocks. How very few colored men are encouraged in their trades or business! Our young men see this, and become disheartened. In this country, where money is the great sympathetic nerve which ramifies society, and has a ganglia in every man's pocket, a man is respected in proportion to his success in business. When the avenues to wealth are opened to us, we will then become educated and wealthy, and then the roughest looking colored man that you ever saw, or ever will see, will be pleasanter than the harmonies of Orpheus, and black will be a very pretty color. It will make our jargon, wit—our words, oracles; flattery will then take the place of slander, and you will find no prejudice in the Yankee whatever. We do not expect to occupy a much better position than we now do, until we shall have our educated and wealthy men, who can wield a power that cannot be misunderstood. Then, and not till then, will the tongue of slander be silenced, and the lip of prejudice sealed. Then, and not till then, will we be able to enjoy true equality, which can exist only among peers.

4.
SUGGESTIONS FOR FURTHER READING

For a general study of the free Northern black, see Leon F. Litwack, *North of Slavery: The Negro in the Free States, 1790–1860** (University of Chicago Press, 1961). No general work on the free Southern black exists, but a helpful specific study is John Hope Franklin, *The Free Negro in North Carolina, 1790–1860* (University of North Carolina Press, 1943). Carter G. Woodson, in *The Education of the Negro Prior to 1861* (Putnam's, 1915), deals primarily with the education of free blacks in both North and South. The work that marked the beginning of E. Franklin Frazier's studies of the black family is *The Free Negro Family* (Fisk University Press, 1932).

The role of the free black in the anti-slavery movement is examined in Benjamin Quarles, *The Black Abolitionists* (Oxford University Press, 1969). Frederick Douglass, in his last autobiography, *The Life and Times of Frederick Douglass** (Park, 1882), deals with his own career as an abolitionist and his later life. In Philip S. Foner (ed.), *Life and Writings of Frederick Douglass**, 4 vols. (International, 1950–55), Douglass' most important incidental writings and speeches are collected. The best biography of Douglass is Benjamin Quarles, *Frederick Douglass** (Associated Publishers, 1948).

William Still, *The Underground Railroad* (Porter and Coates, 1872), presents the reminiscences of a black participant in the Railroad, and *The Liberty Line: The Legend of the Underground Railroad** (University of Kentucky Press, 1961), by Larry Gara, provides a critical view of several myths that have developed about the escape procedure. Henrietta Buckmaster tells the story of the Railroad in *Let My People Go** (Harper, 1941). The social experiments of some of the fugitive slaves are described by William N. Pease and Jane Pease in *Black Utopia: Negro Communal Experiments in America* (State Historical Society of Wisconsin, 1963).

Philip J. Staudenraus, in *The African Colonization Movement, 1816–1865* (Columbia University Press, 1961), surveys both the attempts of whites to remove black people from America and the attempts of blacks to remove themselves. Black emigrationist ideas are presented in two works by Martin R. Delany, *The Condition, Elevation, Emigration and Destiny of the Colored People in the United States* (published by the author, 1852) and *Official Report of the Niger Valley Exploring Party* (Hamilton, 1861), and in Robert Campbell, *A Pilgrimage to My Motherland* (Hamilton, 1861). The last two works are published together in paperback under the title *Search for a Place: Black Separatism and Africa, 1860** (University of Michigan Press, 1969).

5 THE CIVIL WAR AND RECONSTRUCTION

When the Civil War began, the black man had two major goals—to get into the fight and to see to it that all black men were free. Blacks had fought in all previous wars of the United States, and they felt that in this war above all they had a place. The day after Lincoln's call for troops went out, groups of black men all over the North offered themselves for military service. Everywhere they were turned down. The War Department had no intention of using black troops. This attitude might be accounted for in several ways. There was a general feeling among whites that blacks lacked courage; thus the military leaders may have thought their presence in the ranks would do more harm than good. But there was also an idea among whites that blacks had fiery, impulsive natures. This may have led to the reasoning that if the black men got guns, they would use them to insist on their own equality.

As the war drew on, however, and there was a need for more and more soldiers, certain field commanders began using runaway slaves, or "contraband," as they were called, in the battle lines. In July 1862, Congress passed a bill authorizing the use of black troops, and open recruiting began shortly thereafter. Before the end of the war, about 180,000 black soldiers served in the Union army, making up about 10 per cent of the total federal troops, and nearly 29,000 served in the navy, making up about 25 per cent of the Union sailors. Some historians feel that the decision to allow blacks to fight was a crucial factor in ultimate Union victory.

Although Lincoln and his cabinet insisted that slavery was not the issue at the heart of the war, the slave question overshadowed all others. Lincoln himself was opposed to slavery in principle, but he was opposed to notions of social or political equality as well. If he had had his way, he would have eliminated the race problem through a program of gradual, compensated emancipation and colonization. When his colonization schemes were made public in 1862, black people throughout the Union held meetings of protest.

One reason Lincoln was urging migration was that he had decided to issue a proclamation of emancipation for the slaves in the rebel territories, and he felt that it would be easier for whites to accept the situation if the freed blacks were to leave the country. When Lincoln issued the Emancipation Proclamation, to take effect on January 1, 1863, it had little but symbolic effect. It took the Thirteenth Amendment, ratified in December 1865, to free the remaining slaves. But the Proclamation did stimulate the enlistment of black troops in the Union army and encourage the runaway slaves.

Black women participated in the war effort also. Many worked in hospitals or in military camps. A group of black women in Washington helped the "contraband" find jobs and homes. School teachers moved into liberated areas of the South in order to set up schools and help the freedmen develop the tools of citizenship.

Even though Union victory was to ensure the legal freedom of the former slaves, many questions about the future of all black men in America remained unanswered. Blacks were disfranchised in both North and South. Competition for jobs was becoming more and more a source of violent confrontation in Northern cities. What would happen to the freedman who had agricultural skills but no land on which to exercise them?

There was a clear division between the educated blacks of the North and the rural freedmen of the South. The former were interested primarily in obtaining political and civil rights. Most of them had some degree of economic security because of their training and experience; now they sought freedom to participate more actively in the general life of the society. The freedmen, on the other hand, knew little but the farm, and their future was tied up with getting the land necessary to allow them a measure of economic independence. All other rights depended on that one.

Several proposals were made for providing each freedman with "forty acres and a mule" so that he might make a start toward real freedom. As different parts of the South became liberated. however, various plans put into operation by federal authority effectively prevented the freedmen from procuring the needed land. Before the assassination of Lincoln, there was a possibility that land would be confiscated from plantation owners who had supported the Southern war effort and distributed among the former slaves. But, for the most part, the land policy of the Union—even before the end of the war—seemed but another form of slavery. Instead of being given land of their own, the freedmen were required to sign labor contracts with Northern adventurers to whom the former plantations had been leased in order to provide support for federal troops. Many of these lessees were more interested in making money than in aiding the freedmen, and the former slaves often worked as hard as they had in the past at ridiculously low wages.

With the accession of Andrew Johnson to the presidency, the rural freedmen lost all hope. Johnson's policy was to restore as many plantations as possible to their former owners. He felt that this was the way to provide for the South's return to the Union with a minimum of residual hostility. Unfortunately, it was the black man who paid the price of this policy. Most rural freedmen ended up as sharecroppers in a system that drove them deeper and deeper into debt. By the end of the century, they had fallen into a condition that approached serfdom.

During Reconstruction, many blacks in the South participated in elective politics for the first time in American history. There were sixteen black men in Congress during this period, including two in the Senate; of the sixteen, thirteen were former slaves. Even more important, perhaps, were the black members of the various state constitutional conventions and legislatures. Under their influence, the new state constitutions called for an extension of the franchise, free public education, and significant reforms in such areas as state penal and judicial systems. Ironically, although blacks formed a majority in only one Southern state legislature (the lower house in South Carolina), the reforms enacted under their leadership contributed in a major way to the renaissance of the white South.

FREE THE SLAVES, THEN LEAVE THEM ALONE

Frederick Douglass / Address to the Emancipation League in
Boston, 1862

Frederick Douglass was unquestionably the most impressive black man in nineteenth-century America. Born a slave, he escaped the South in 1838. Almost the day he arrived in the North, he began working to improve the lot of American blacks. His initial appearance as a speaker at an anti-slavery rally in 1841 was so electrifying that he soon became the most sought-after black speaker in the movement. While lecturing in England in 1845, he was persuaded by his English supporters to allow them to buy his freedom. In 1847, he started the first of several newspapers he was to edit, in Rochester, New York.

Douglass was a militant crusader for the abolition of slavery, the right of blacks to serve in the Civil War, the securing of political and civil rights for freedmen, and virtually every other cause involving the liberation of blacks. The capstone of his career was his appointment in 1889 as United States Minister to Haiti.

Douglass made the following address before the Emancipation League in Boston in 1862. This organization, which had been founded the year before by prominent white abolitionists, sought the immediate emancipation of the slaves as the only way to bring peace to the nation. The speech contains many of the ideas that Douglass so brilliantly advocated in the course of his distinguished career, including the need to solve the color problem in America without recourse to black emigration.

Ladies and Gentlemen:

The progress of the present tremendous war has developed great qualities of mind and heart among the loyal people, and none more conspicuously than patience. We have seen our sons, brothers, and fathers led to the battle field by untried and unskillful generals, and have held our breath; we have seen them repeatedly marched in thousands upon concealed batteries of the enemy, to be swept down by storms of iron and fire, and have scarcely murmured: we have seen the wealth of the land poured out at the frightful rate of a million a day without complaint; we have seen our Capital surrounded, hemmed in, blockaded in the presence of a fettered but chafing loyal army of a quarter of a million on the Potomac during seven long months, and still we have cried patience and forbearance. We have seen able and earnest

---

FROM Frederick Douglass, "The Future of the Negro People of the Slave States," *Douglass' Monthly* (March 1862).

men displaced from high and important positions to make room for men who have yet to win our confidence, and still have believed in the Government. This is all right, all proper. Our Government however defective is still our Government. It is all we have to shield us from the fury and vengeance of treason, rebellion, and anarchy.

If I were asked to describe the most painful and mortifying feature presented in the prosecution and management of the present war on the part of the United States Government, against the slaveholding rebels now marshalled against it, I should not point to Ball's Bluff, Big Bethel, Bull Run, or any of the many blunders and disaster on flood or field; but I should point to the vacillation, doubt, uncertainty and hesitation, which have thus far distinguished our government in regard to the true method of dealing with the vital cause of the rebellion. We are without any declared and settled policy—and our policy seems to be, to have no policy.

The winds and currents are ever changing, and after beating about for almost a whole year on the perilous coast of a wildering ocean unable to find our bearings, we at last discover that we are in the same latitude as when we set sail, as far from the desired port as ever and with much less heart, health and provisions for pursuing the voyage than on the morning we weighed anchor.

If it be true that he that doubteth is condemned already, there is certainly but little chance for this Republic.

At the opening session of the present Congress there was a marked, decided, and emphatic expression against slavery as the great motive power of the present slaveholding war. Many petitions, numerously and influentially signed, were duly sent in and presented to that body, praying, first, for the entire abolition of slavery in all the slaveholding States; secondly, that a just award be made by Congress to loyal slaveholders; and thirdly, that the slaves of rebels be wholly confiscated. The vigor, earnestness, and power with which these objects were advocated, as war measures, by Messrs. Stevens, Bingham, Elliott, Gurley, Lovejoy and others, inspired the loyal friends of Freedom all over the North with renewed confidence and hope, both for the country and for the slave. The conviction was general that at last the country was to have a policy, and that that policy would bring freedom and safety to the Republic.

Thus far, however, this hope, this confidence, this conviction has not been justified. The country is without a known policy. The enemies of the Abolition cause, taking alarm from these early efforts, have earnestly set themselves to the work of producing a reaction in favor of slavery, and have succeeded beyond what they themselves must have expected at the first.

Among other old, and threadbare, and worn out objections which they have raised against the Emancipation policy, is the question as to what shall be done with the four million slaves of the South, if they are emancipated? or in other words, what shall be the future of the four million slaves?

I am sensible, deeply sensible, of the importance of this subject, and of the many difficulties which are supposed to surround it.

If there is any one great, pressing, and all-commanding problem for this nation to solve, and to solve without delay, that problem is slavery. Its claims are urgent, palpable, and powerful. The issue involves the whole question of life and death to the nation.

Some who speak on this subject are already sure as to how this question will finally be decided. I am not, but one thing I know:—If we are a wise, liberty-loving, a just and courageous nation—knowing what is right and daring to do it—we shall solve this problem, and solve it speedily, in accordance with national safety, national unity, national prosperity, national glory, and shall win for ourselves the admiration of an onlooking world and the grateful applause of after-coming generations. If on the other hand, we are a cunning, cowardly, and selfish nation given over—as other nations have been before us—to hardness of heart and blindness of mind, it needs no prophet to foretell our doom.

Before proceeding to discuss the future of the colored people of the slave States, you will allow me to make a few remarks, personal and general, respecting the tremendous crisis through which we are passing. In the first place I have not the vanity to suppose—and I say it without affectation—that I can add any thing to the powerful arguments of the able men who have preceded me in this course of lectures. I take the stand tonight more as an humble witness than as an advocate. I have studied slavery and studied freedom on both sides of Mason and Dixon's line. Nearly twenty-two years of my life were spent in Slavery, and more than twenty-three have been spent in freedom. I am of age in both conditions, and there seems an eminent fitness in allowing me to speak for myself and my race. If I take my stand tonight as I shall do, with the down-trodden and enslaved, and view the facts of the hour more as a bondman than as a freeman, it is not because I feel no interest in the general welfare of the country. Far from it.

I am an American citizen. In birth, in sentiment, in ideas, in hopes, in aspirations, and responsibilities, I am an American citizen. According to Judge Kent there are but two classes of people in America: they are citizens and aliens, natives and foreigners.—Natives are citizens—foreigners are aliens until naturalized.

But I am not only a citizen by birth and lineage, I am such by choice.

I once had a very tempting offer of citizenship in another country; but declined it because I preferred the hardships and duties of my mission here. I have never regretted that decision, although my pathway has been anything than a smooth one; and to-night, I allow no man to exceed me in the desire for the safety and welfare of this country. And just here do allow me to boast a little. There is nothing in the circumstances of the present hour, nothing in the behavior of the colored people, either North or South, which requires apology at my hands. Though everywhere spoken against, the most malignant and unscrupulous of all our slanderers have not, in this dark and terrible hour of the nation's trial dared to accuse us of a want of patriotism or loyalty. Though ignored by our friends and repelled by our enemies, the colored people, both north and south, have evinced the most ardent desire to serve the cause of the country, as against the rebels and traitors who are endeavoring to break it down and destroy it. That they are not largely represented in the loyal army, is the fault of the Government, and a very grievous fault it is. Mark here our nation's degeneracy. Colored men were good enough to fight under Washington. They are not good enough to fight under McClellan.—They were good enough to fight under Andrew Jackson. They are not good enough to fight under Gen. Halleck. They were good enough to help win American independence but they are not good enough to help preserve that independence against treason and rebellion. They were good enough to defend New Orleans but not good enough to defend our poor beleaguered Capital. I am not arguing against, not condemning those in power, but simply stating facts in vindication of my people; and as these facts stand, I do say that I am proud to be recognized here as an humble representative of that rejected race. Whether in peace or in war, whether in safety or in peril, whether in evil report or good report, at home or abroad, my mission is to stand up for the down-trodden, to open my mouth for the dumb, to remember those in bonds as bound with them.

Happily, however, in standing up in their cause I do, and you do, but stand in defense of the cause of the whole country. The circumstances of this eventful hour make the cause of the slaves and the cause of the country identical. They must fall or flourish together. A blow struck for the freedom of the slave, is equally a blow struck for the safety and welfare of the country. As Liberty and Union have become identical, so slavery and treason have become one and inseparable. I shall not argue this point. It has already been most ably argued. All eyes see it, all hearts begin to feel it; and all that is needed is the wisdom and the manhood to perform the solemn duty pointed out by the stern logic of our situation. It is now or never with us.

The field is ripe for the harvest. God forbid that when the smoke and thunder of this slaveholding war shall have rolled from the troubled face of our country it shall be said that the harvest is past, the summer is ended and we are not saved.

There are two classes of men who are endeavoring to put down this strange and most unnatural rebellion. About patriotism and loyalty, they talk alike; but the difference between them is heaven wide—and if we fail to suppress the rebels and restore the country to a condition of permanent safety it will be chargeable less to the skill and power of the rebels themselves, than to this division and conflict among ourselves. Never could it be said more truly and sadly than now, that our enemies are those of our own household.—The traitors of the South are open, bold, decided. We know just where to find them.—They are on the battle field, with arms in their hands and bullets in their pockets. It is easy to deal with them, but it is not so easy to deal with the so-called Union men in Maryland, Western Virginia, and Kentucky, and those who sympathize with them in the Northern States.

One class is for putting down the rebellion if that can be done by force and force alone, and without abolishing slavery, and the other is for putting down the rebellion by putting down slavery upon every rod of earth which shall be made sacred by the footprints of a single loyal soldier. One class would strike down the effect, the other would strike at the cause. Can any man doubt for a moment that the latter is the wisest and best course? Is it not as plain as the sun in the heavens, that slavery is the life, the soul, the inspiration, and power of the rebellion? Is it not equally plain that any peace which may be secured which shall leave slavery still existing at the South, will prove a hollow and worthless peace, a mere suspension of hostilities, to be renewed again at the first favorable opportunity?—Does any man think that the slaveholders would relinquish all hope of Southern independence in the future because defeated in the present contest? Would they not come out of the war with a deadlier hate and a firmer purpose to renew the struggle hereafter, with larger knowledge and better means of success? He who thinks or flatters himself that they would not, has read history and studied human nature to little purpose.

But why, O why should we not abolish slavery now? All admit that it must be abolished at some time. What better time than now can be assigned for that great work?—Why should it longer live? What good thing has it done that it should be given further lease of life? What evil thing has it left undone? Behold its dreadful history! Saying nothing of the rivers of tears and streams of blood poured out by its 4,000,000 victims—saying nothing of the leprous poison it has diffused through the life blood of our morals and our religion—saying nothing of the many humiliating concessions already made to it—saying nothing of the deep and scandalous reproach it has brought upon our national good name—saying nothing of all this, and more the simple fact that this monster Slavery has eaten up and devoured the patriotism of the whole South, kindled the lurid flames of a bloody rebellion in our midst, invited the armies of hostile nations to desolate our soil, and break down our Government, is good and all-sufficient cause of smiting it as with a bolt from heaven. If it is possible for any system of barbarism to sing its own death warrant, Slavery, by its own natural working, is that system. All the arguments of conscience, sound expediency, national honor and safety unite in the fiat—let it die the death of its own election.

One feature of the passing hour is notable in showing how narrow and limited may be the channel through which a great reformatory movement can run for long and weary years, without once overflowing its banks and enriching the surrounding country through which it passes.

Notwithstanding all our books, pamphlets, newspapers, our great conventions, addresses, and resolutions, tens of thousands of the American people are now taking their *first* lessons as to the character and influence of slavery and slaveholders. Tongues that used to bless Slavery now curse it, and men who formerly found paragons of the race only among slave mongers and their abettors, are but now having the scales torn from their eyes by slave-holding treason and rebellion. They are just coming to believe what we have all along been trying to tell them, that is: that he who breaks faith with God may not be expected to keep faith with man. I gladly welcome this great change in the public sentiment of the country. And yet I do not rely very confidently upon it. I am not deceived either in regard to its origin or its quality.— I know that national self-preservation, national safety, rather than any regard to the bondman as a man and a brother, is at the bottom of much that now meets us in the shape of opposition to slavery. The little finger of him who denounced slavery from a high moral conviction of its enormity is more than the loins of him that merely denounces it for the peril into which it has brought the country. Nevertheless, I rejoice in this change, the result will be nearly the same to the slave, if from motives of necessity or any other motives the nation shall be led to the extinction of slavery. Every consideration of expediency and justice may be consistently brought to bear against that sum of all villanies.

A WORD AS TO THE COURSE OF THE ABOLITIONISTS

Upon the first outburst of the now raging rebellion, awakening the nation as from a sleep of death, the Abolitionists of the country very generally dropped their distinctive character, and were fused with the mass of their fellow-citizens. Patriotism for the moment took the place of philanthropy, and those who had for long years given their best energies to save the slave, were not behind any other class of citizens in their efforts to save the country. They suspended their agencies, postponed their fire the Northern heart to the great contest to which it was summoned in the name of an imperiled country. In this, however, we may have been more patriotic than wise. Every day bears witness that Slavery is not only the cause of the rebellion, but that it is and has been from the beginning, the only real obstacle to crushing out the rebellion; and that all efforts to save the country are utterly vain, unless guided by the principles which the Abolitionists know best how to teach.

I rejoice therefore in the formation of the Emancipation league. May its work be quick, certain and complete. I perceive that it has not entered upon its career unobserved. The guardians of slavery in Boston, for there are such guardians, have honored it by very lengthened and very bitter denunciations.—No better reception could have been expected, even if deserved, than that given it by the *Boston Courier*. A like denunciation came from the Tory press of England when the anti-corn law League was formed. Nevertheless that grand League put down the Corn monopoly in seven years, gave bread to the starving millions, broke down the tory party beyond the hope of regaining power, changed the policy of the British nation, transferred the power of the landed aristocracy to the people and gave us the Brights, the Cobdens, the Wilsons, and the Thompsons, and the William Edward Forsters, the men who represent the middle classes of England and who are now in our days of trouble as in our days of peace and prosperity, America's best and truest friends. Humanity is proud of the triumphs of that League. It will not be otherwise of this League.

But I come now to the more immediate subject of my lecture, namely: What shall be done with the four millions of slaves if they are emancipated? This singular question comes from the same two very different and very opposite classes of the American people, who are endeavoring to put down the rebels. The first have no moral, religious, or political objection to Slavery, and, so far as they are concerned, Slavery might live and flourish to the end of time. They are the men who have an abiding affection for rebels, and at the beginning marched to the tune of "No Coercion—No subjugation." They have now dropped these unpopular "Noes," and have taken up another set, equally treacherous. Their tune now is, No Emancipation. No Confiscation of slave property, No Arming of the Negroes. They were driven from the first set of "Noes" by the gleaming of a half million bayonets, and I predict that they will be driven from the last set, though I cannot promise that they will not find another set.

The second class of persons are those who may be called young converts, newly awakened persons, who are convinced of the great evil and danger of Slavery, and would be glad to see some wise and unobjectionable plan of emancipation devised and adopted by the Government. They hate Slavery and love Freedom, but they are yet too much trammeled by the popular habit of thought respecting the Negro to trust the operation of their own principles. Like the man in the Scriptures, they see men only as trees walking. They differ from the first class only in motive and purpose, and not in premise and argument, and hence the answer to Pro-Slavery objections will answer those raised by our new anti-Slavery men. When some of the most potent, grave and reverend defenders of Slavery in England urged Wilberforce for a statement of his plan of Emancipation, his simple response was quit stealing.

My answer to the question, What shall be done with the four million slaves if emancipated? shall be alike short and simple: Do nothing with them, but leave them like you have left other men, to do with and for themselves. We would be entirely respectful to those who raise the inquiry, and yet it is hard not to say to them just what they would say to us, if we manifested a like concern for them, and that is; please to mind your business, and leave us to mind ours. If we cannot stand up, then let us fall down.—We ask nothing at the hands of the American people but simple justice, and an equal chance to live; and if we cannot live and flourish on such terms, our case should be referred to the Author of our existence. Injustice, oppression, and Slavery with their manifold concomitants have been tried with us during a period of more than two hundred years. Under the whole heavens you will find no parallel to the wrongs we have endured. We have worked without wages; we have lived without hope, wept without sympathy, and bled without mercy. Now, in the name of common humanity, and according to the laws of the Living God, we simply ask the right to bear the responsibility of our own existence.

Let us alone. Do nothing with us, for us, or by us as a particular class. What you have done with us thus far has only worked to our disadvantage. We now simply ask to be allowed to do for ourselves. I submit that there is nothing unreasonable or unnatural in all this request. The black man is said to be unfortunate. He is so. But I affirm that the broadest and bitterest of the black man's misfortunes is the fact that he is everywhere regarded and treated as an exception to the principles and maxims which apply to other men, and that nothing short of the extension of those principles to him can satisfy any honest advocate of his claims.

Even those who are sincerely desirous to serve us and to help us out of our difficulties, stand in doubt of us and fear that we could not stand the application of the rules which they freely apply to all other people.

Now, whence comes this doubt and fear? I will tell you. There is no difficulty whatever in giving ample and satisfactory explanation of the source of this estimate of the black man's capacity.

What have been his condition and circumstances for more than two centuries? These will explain all.

Take any race you please, French, English, Irish, or Scotch, subject them to slavery for ages—regard and treat them everywhere, every way, as property, as having no rights which other men are required to respect.—Let them be loaded with chains, scarred with the whip, branded with hot irons, sold in the market, kept in ignorance, by force of law and by common usage, and I venture to say that the same doubt would spring up concerning either of them, which now confronts the Negro. The common talk of the streets on this subject shows great ignorance. It assumes that no other race has ever been enslaved or could be held in slavery, and the fact that the black man submits to that condition is often cited as a proof of original and permanent inferiority, and of the fitness of the black man only for that condition. Just this is the argument of the Confederate States; the argument of Stephens in defense of S. C. But what are the facts? I believe it will not be denied that the Anglo-Saxons are a fine race of men, and have done something for the civilization of mankind, yet who does not know that this now grand and leading race was in bondage and abject slavery for ages upon their own native soil. They were not stolen away from their own country in small numbers, where they could make no resistance to their enslavers, but were enslaved in their own country.

Turn to the pages of the history of the Norman Conquest, by Monsieur Thierry, and you will find this statement fully attested.—He says: Foreigners visiting England, even so late as the sixteenth century, were astonished at the great number of serfs they beheld, and the excessive harshness of their servitude. The word bondage, in the Norman tongue, expressed at the time all that was most wretched in the condition of humanity. He again says: About the year 1381, all who were called bonds in English or in Anglo-Norman—that is, all the cultivators of land—were serfs in body and goods, obliged to pay heavy aids for the small portions of land which served them to feed their families, and were not at liberty to give up that portion of land without the consent of the Lords for whom they were obliged to do gratuitously their tillage, their gardening, and their carriage of all kinds. The Lords could sell them, together with their horses, their oxen, and their implements of husbandry—their children and their posterity—which in the English deeds was expressed in the following manner: Know that I have sold ——, my knave, and all his offspring, born or to be born.

Sir Walter Scott, after describing very minutely the dress of a Saxon serf, says: One part of the dress only remains, but it is too remarkable to be suppressed. It was a brass ring resembling a dog's collar, but without any opening, and soldered fast around the neck, so loose as to form no impediment to breathing, and yet so tight as to be incapable of being removed excepting by the use of the file. On this singular gorget was engraved, in Saxon letters, an inscription of the following purport; Gurth, the son of Beowulph, is the born thrall of Cedric Rotherwood.

As an evidence of the contempt and degradation in which the Saxons were held, Monsieur Thierry says that after the conquest the Bishop of Lincoln reckoned only two languages in England—Latin for men of letters and French for the ignorant, in which language he himself wrote pious books for the use of the French, making no account of the English language and those who spoke it.

The poets of the same period, even those of English birth, composed all their verses in French when they wished to derive from them either profit or honor. Such is a brief view of the social condition occupied for ages by a people now the mightiest on the globe. The Saxon was of no account then; the Negro is of no account now. May not history one day carry the analogy a step further? In the case of the Saxon, we have a people held in abject slavery, upon their own native soil by strangers and foreigners. Their very language made no account of, and themselves wearing brass collars on their necks like dogs, bearing the names of their masters. They were bought and sold like the beast of the field, and their offspring born and to be born doomed to the same wretched condition. No doubt that the people of this now proud and grand race in their then abject condition were compelled to listen to disparagement and insults from their Norman oppressors, as galling as those which meet the black man here. No doubt that these disparagements hung about their necks like a mountain weight to keep them down, and no doubt there were men of shallow brain and selfish hearts to tell them that Slavery was their normal condition.

The misfortunes of my own race in this respect are not singular. They have happened to all nations, when under the heel of oppression. Whenever and wherever any particular variety of the human family has been enslaved by another, their slavers and oppressors, in every such instance, have found their best apology for their own base conduct in the bad character of their victims. The cunning, the deceit, the indolence, and the manifold vices and crimes, which naturally grow out of the condition of Slavery, are generally charged as inherent characteristics of the oppressed and enslaved race. The Jews, the Indians, the Saxons and the ancient Britons, have all had a taste of this bitter experience.

When the United States coveted a part of Mexico, and sought to wrest from that sister Republic her coveted domain, some of you remember how our press teemed from day to day with charges of Mexican inferiority— How they were assailed as a worn-out race; how they were denounced as a weak, worthless, indolent, and turbulent nation, given up to the sway of animal passions, totally incapable of self-government, and how excellent a thing we were told it would be for civilization if the strong beneficent arms of the Anglo-Saxon could be extended over them; and how, with our usual blending of piety with plunder, we justified our avarice by appeals to the hand-writing of Divine Providence. All this, I say, you remember, for the facts are but little more than a dozen years old.

As between us and unfortunate Mexico, so it was with Russia and the Ottoman Empire. In the eyes of Nicholas, the Turk was the sick man of Europe—just as the Negro is now the sick man of America.

So, too, in former years, it was with England and Ireland. When any new burden was sought to be imposed upon that ill-fated country, or when any improvement in the condition of its people was suggested, and pressed by philanthropic and liberal statesmen, the occasion never failed to call forth the most angry and disparaging arguments and assaults upon the Irish race.

Necessity is said to be the plea of tyrants. The alleged inferiority of the oppressed is also the plea of tyrants. The effect upon these against whom it is directed is to smite them as with the hand of death. Under its paralyzing touch all manly aspirations and self-reliance die out and the smitten race comes almost to assent to the justice of their own degradation.

No wonder, therefore, that the colored people in America appear stupid, helpless and degraded. The wonder is rather that they evince so much spirit and manhood as they do. What have they not suffered and endured? They have been weighed, measured, marked and prized—in detail and in the aggregate. Their estimated value a little while ago was twenty hundred millions. Those twenty hundred millions of dollars have all the effect of twenty hundred millions of arguments against the Negro as a man and a brother. Here we have a mountain of gold, depending upon the continuance of our enslavement and degradation. No wonder that it has been able to bribe the press against us.—No wonder that it has been able to employ learning and eloquence against us. No wonder that it has bought up the American pulpit and obtained the sanction of religion against us. No wonder that it has turned every department of the Government into engines of oppression and tyranny toward us.—No nation, however gifted by nature, could hope to bear up under such oppressive weights.

But to return. What shall be done with the four million slaves, if emancipated. I answer, deal justly with them; pay them honest wages for honest work; dispense with the biting lash, and pay them the ready cash; awaken a new class of motives in them; remove those old motives of shriveling fear of punishment which benumb and degrade the soul, and supplant them by the higher and better motives of hope, of self-respect, of honor, and of personal responsibility. Reverse the whole current of feeling in regard to them. They have been compelled hitherto to regard the white man as a cruel, selfish, and remorseless tyrant, thirsting for wealth, greedy of gain, and caring nothing as to the means by which he obtains it. Now, let him see that the white man has a nobler and better side to his character, and he will love, honor, esteem the white man.

But it is said that the black man is naturally indolent, and that he will not work without a master. I know that this is a part of his bad reputation; but I also know that he is indebted for this bad reputation to the most indolent and lazy of all the American people, the slaveholders—men who live in absolute idleness, and eat their daily bread in the briny sweat of other men's faces. That the black man in Slavery shirks labor—aims to do as little as he can, and to do that little in the most slovenly manner—only proves that he is a man. Thackery says that all men are about as lazy as they can afford to be —and I do not claim that the Negro is an exception to this rule. He loves ease and abundance just as other people love ease and abundance. If this is a crime, then all men are criminals, and the Negro no more than the rest.

Again, it is affirmed that the Negro, if emancipated, could not take care of himself. My answer to this is, let him have a fair chance to try it. For 200 years he has taken care of himself and his master in the bargain. I see no reason to believe that he could not take care, and very excellent care, of himself when having only himself to support. The case of the freed slaves in the British West Indies has already been dwelt upon in the course of these lectures, and facts, arguments, and statistics have been presented demonstrating beyond all controversy that the black man not only has the ability and the disposition to work, but knows well how to take care of his earnings. The country over which he has toiled as a slave is rapidly becoming his property —that freedom has made him both a better producer and a better consumer.

LIBERTY AN EXPERIMENT

It is one of the strangest and most humiliating triumphs of human selfishness and prejudice over human reason, that it leads men to look upon emancipation as an experiment, instead of being, as it is, the natural order of human relations. Slavery, and not Freedom, is the experiment; and to witness its horrible failure we have to open our eyes, not merely upon the blasted soil of Virginia and other Slave States, but upon a whole land brought to the verge of ruin.

We are asked if we would turn the slaves all loose. I answer, Yes. Why not? They are not wolves nor tigers, but men. They are endowed with reason—can decide upon questions of right and wrong, good and evil, benefits and injuries—and are therefore subjects of government precisely as other men are.

But would you have them stay here? Why should they not? What better is here than there? What class of people can show a better title to the land on which they live than the colored people of the South? They have watered the soil with their tears and enriched it with their blood, and tilled it with their hard hands during two centuries; they have leveled its forests, raked out the obstructions to the plow and hoe, reclaimed the swamps, and produced whatever has made it a goodly land to dwell in, and it would be a shame and a crime little inferior in enormity to Slavery itself if these natural owners of the Southern and Gulf States should be driven away from their country to make room for others—even if others could be obtained to fill their places.

But unjust and revolting to every right-minded and humane man as is this talk of the expatriation of the slaves, the offense is not more shocking than it is unwise. For a nation to drive away its laboring population is to commit political suicide. It is like cutting off one's right hand in order to work the better and to produce the more. To say that Negroes shall not live in the Southern States is like saying that the lands of the South shall be no longer cultivated. The cry has all along been, We must have Negroes to work in the South, for white men cannot stand the hot sun and the fell diseases of the rice swamp and the sugar plantation. Even the leaders of the rebellion made it one of their grievances that they could not get more Negroes, though from motives of policy they have now dropped this plank from their platform. No one doubts that the Gulf States mean to have more slaves from Africa just so soon as they shall get well settled in their independence. Again, why not allow the colored people of the South remain where they are? Will they occupy more room in freedom than slavery? If you could bear them as objects of your injustice, can they be more offensive as objects of your justice and your humanity? Why send them away? Who wants to take their places in the cotton field, in the rice swamp, and sugar fields, which they have tilled for ages? The whole scheme of colonization would be too absurd for discussion, but that the madness of the moment has drowned the voice of common sense as well as common justice.

There is a measure now before Congress duly reported from one of its

Committees proposing, first, to make the Negroes leave the land of their birth, and secondly to pay the expense of their enforced removal. If such a measure can become a law, the nation is more deeply wicked than any Abolitionist has hitherto ventured to believe. It is a most mischievous and scandalous proposition, unworthy of any man not dead to the claims of every sentiment of honor and humanity. I predict that if it passes it will become like the Fugitive Slave law—it will die dead upon the statute book—having no other effect than to alarm the freed men of the South and disgrace the Congress by which it is passed.

Once free the slaves, and at once the motives which now require their expatriation will become too weak to breathe. In the single little State of Maryland, with climate and soil which invite the white laborer to its borders, there are at this moment nearly one hundred thousand free colored people. Now, notwithstanding that Maryland is a Slave State, and thus possesses a strong motive for getting rid of their free colored people, the better to hold her slaves—and notwithstanding the circumstances of climate and soil—that Slave State only a year or two ago voted down by a large majority of their people the inhuman and barbarous proposition concerning her free colored population.

The number of colored people now on this continent and in the adjacent islands cannot fall far below twenty millions. An attempt to remove them would be as vain as to bail out the ocean. The whole naval power of the United States could not remove the natural increase of our part of this population. Every fact in our circumstances here marks us as a permanent element of the American people. Mark the readiness with which we adapt ourselves to your civilization. You can take no step in any direction where the black man is not at your back or side.—Go to California and dig gold: the black man is there. Go to war with Mexico, and let your armies penetrate the very heart of the country, and the black man is there. Go down into the coast of North and South Carolina, and the black man is there, and there as your friend, to give you more important and more trustworthy information than you can find among all the loyal poor white trash you can scare up in that region. The Negro is sometimes compared with the Indian, and it is predicted that, like the Indian, he will die out before the onward progress of the Anglo-Saxon race. I have not the least apprehension at this point. In features and complexion, the Negro is more unlike the European than is his Mongolian brother. But the interior resemblance is greater than the exterior difference. The Indian wraps himself in gloom, and proudly glories in isolation—he retreats before the onward march of civilization. The humming of the honey bee warns him away from his hunting grounds. He sees the plowshare of civilization tossing up the bones of his venerated fathers, and he dies of a broken heart. Not so with the Negro. There is a vitality about him that seems alike invincible to hardship and cruelty. Work him, whip him, sell him, torment him, and he still lives, and clings to American civilization—an Uncle

Tom in the Church, and an Uncle Ben on the Southern coast, to guide our Burnside expeditions.

My friends, the destiny of the colored American, however this mighty war shall terminate, is the destiny of America. We shall never leave you. The allotments of Providence seem to make the black man of America the open book out of which the American people are to learn lessons of wisdom, power, and goodness—more sublime and glorious than any yet attained by the nations of the old or the new world. Over the bleeding back of the American bondman we shall learn mercy. In the very extreme difference of color and features of the Negro and the Anglo-Saxon, shall be learned the highest ideas of the sacredness of man and the fullness and perfection of human brotherhood.

> *Throughout the delivery of his address, Mr. Douglass was interrupted with most hearty and enthusiastic applause.*

EDUCATING THE FREEDMEN OF THE SEA ISLANDS

Charlotte Forten / Life on the Sea Islands

When Northern troops, anxious to blockade the harbor at Charleston, South Carolina, captured Port Royal in the Sea Islands late in 1861, the first major attempt of the war to aid the freedmen got under way. There were about ten thousand "contraband" in the area, and their previous isolation made them perhaps the most un-Americanized of all the slaves in the South. For several years, a serious effort was made to "civilize" the former slaves New agricultural methods were introduced, schools were established, and troops were recruited. The famous First South Carolina Volunteers, who fought under the leadership of Thomas Wentworth Higginson, a white Boston abolitionist, were from Port Royal.

Charlotte Forten was the granddaughter and daughter of wealthy free blacks from Philadelphia. She lived for a time with the family of the fiery Charles L. Remond in Salem, Massachusetts. When the call for teachers at Port Royal went out, Miss Forten volunteered. She reached the island late in 1862, determined to prove that the blacks were as capable of self-improvement as were whites. The selection that follows is taken from two articles compiled from letters written by Miss Forten to the poet John Greenleaf Whittier, her good friend, who sent them to the **Atlantic Monthly** for publication.

The next morning L. and I were awakened by the cheerful voices of men and women, children and chickens, in the yard below. We ran to the window, and looked out. Women in bright-colored handkerchiefs, some carrying pails on their heads, were crossing the yard, busy with their morning work; children were playing and tumbling around them. On every face there was a look of serenity and cheerfulness. My heart gave a great throb of happiness as I looked at them, and thought, "They are free! so long downtrodden, so long crushed to the earth, but now in their old homes, forever free!" And I thanked God that I had lived to see this day.

After breakfast Miss T. drove us to Oaklands, our future home. The road leading to the house was nearly choked with weeds. The house itself was in a dilapidated condition, and the yard and garden had a sadly neglected look. But there were roses in bloom; we plucked handfuls of feathery, fragrant acacia-blossoms; ivy crept along the ground and under the house. The freed people on the place seemed glad to see us. After talking with them, and giving some directions for cleaning the house, we drove to the school, in which I was to teach. It is kept in the Baptist Church,—a brick building, beautifully situated in a grove of live-oaks. These trees are the first objects that attract one's attention here: not that they are finer than our Northern oaks, but because of the singular gray moss with which every branch is heavily draped. This hanging moss grows on nearly all the trees, but on none so luxuriantly as on the live-oak. The pendants are often four or five feet long, very graceful and beautiful, but giving the trees a solemn, almost funereal look. The school was opened in September. Many of the children had, however, received instruction during the summer. It was evident that they had made very rapid improvement, and we noticed with pleasure how bright and eager to learn many of them seemed. They sang in rich, sweet tones, and with a peculiar swaying motion of the body, which made their singing the more effective. They sang "Marching Along," with great spirit, and then one of their own hymns, the air of which is beautiful and touching:—

"My sister, you want to git religion,
 Go down in de Lonesome Valley;
My brudder, you want to git religion,
 Go down in de Lonesome Valley.

CHORUS
"Go down in de Lonesome Valley,
 Go down in de Lonesome Valley, my Lord,
 Go down in de Lonesome Valley,
  To meet my Jesus dere!

Oh, feed on milk and honey, my Lord,
 Oh, feed on milk and honey,

FROM Charlotte Forten, "Life on the Sea Islands," *Atlantic Monthly*, Vol. XIII (May and June 1864), pp. 588–89, 591–94, 666–67.

"Oh, feed on milk and honey,
        To meet my Jesus dere!

Oh, John he brought a letter,
Oh, John he brought a letter, my Lord,
Oh, Mary and Marta read 'em,
        Meet my Jesus dere!

CHORUS
"Go down in de Lonesome Valley," etc.

They repeat their hymns several times, and while singing keep perfect time with their hands and feet.

. . . .

The Sunday after our arrival we attended service at the Baptist Church. The people came in slowly; for they have no way of knowing the hour, except by the sun. By eleven they had all assembled, and the church was well filled. They were neatly dressed in their Sunday attire, the women mostly wearing clean, dark frocks, with white aprons and bright-colored head-handkerchiefs. Some had attained to the dignity of straw hats with gay feathers, but these were not nearly as becoming nor as picturesque as the handkerchiefs. The day was warm, and the windows were thrown open as if it were summer, although it was the second day of November. It was very pleasant to listen to the beautiful hymns, and look from the crowd of dark, earnest faces within, upon the grove of noble oaks without. The people sang, "Roll, Jordan, roll," the grandest of all their hymns. There is a great, rolling wave of sound through it all.

"Mr. Fuller settin' on de Tree ob Life,
  Fur to hear de ven Jordan roll.
  Oh, roll, Jordan! roll, Jordan! roll, Jordan, roll!

CHORUS
"Oh, roll, Jordan, roll! oh, roll, Jordan, roll!
  My soul arise in heab'n, Lord,
  Fur to hear de ven Jordan roll!

"Little chil'en, learn to fear de Lord,
  And let your days be long.
  Oh, roll, Jordan! roll, Jordan! roll, Jordan, roll!

CHORUS
"Oh, march, de angel, march! oh, march, de angel, march!
  My soul arise in heab'n, Lord,
  Fur to hear de ven Jordan roll!"

The "Mr. Fuller" referred to was their former minister, to whom they seem to have been much attached. He is a Southerner, but loyal, and is now, I believe, living in Baltimore. After the sermon the minister called upon one of the elders, a gray-headed old man, to pray. His manner was very fervent and impressive, but his language was so broken that to our unaccustomed ears it was quite unintelligible. After the services the people gathered in groups outside, talking among themselves, and exchanging kindly greetings with the superintendents and teachers. In their bright handkerchiefs and white aprons they made a striking picture under the gray-mossed trees. We drove afterward a mile farther, to the Episcopal Church, in which the aristocracy of the island used to worship. It is a small white building, situated in a fine grove of live-oaks, at the junction of several roads. On one of the tombstones in the yard is the touching inscription in memory of two children,—"Blessed little lambs, and *art thou* gathered into the fold of the only true shepherd? Sweet *lillies* of the valley, and *art thou* removed to a more congenial soil?" The floor of the church is of stone, the pews of polished oak. It has an organ, which is not so entirely out of tune as are the pianos on the island. One of the ladies played, while the gentlemen sang,—old-fashioned New-England church-music, which it was pleasant to hear, but it did not thrill us as the singing of the people had done.

. . . .

The first day at school was rather trying. Most of my children were very small, and consequently restless. Some were too young to learn the alphabet. These little ones were brought to school because the older children —in whose care their parents leave them while at work—could not come without them. We were therefore willing to have them come, although they seemed to have discovered the secret of perpetual motion, and tried one's patience sadly. But after some days of positive, though not severe treatment, order was brought out of chaos, and I found but little difficulty in managing and quieting the tiniest and most restless spirits. I never before saw children so eager to learn, although I had had several years' experience in New-England schools. Coming to school is a constant delight and recreation to them. They come here as other children go to play. The older ones, during the summer, work in the fields from early morning until eleven or twelve o'clock, and then come into school, after their hard toil in the hot sun, as bright and as anxious to learn as ever.

Of course there are some stupid ones, but these are the minority. The majority learn with wonderful rapidity. Many of the grown people are desirous of learning to read. It is wonderful how a people who have been so long crushed to the earth, so imbruted as these have been,—and they are said to be among the most degraded negroes of the South,—can have so great a desire for knowledge, and such a capability for attaining it. One cannot believe that the haughty Anglo-Saxon race, after centuries of such an experience as these people have had, would be very much superior to them. And one's indignation increases against those who, North as well as South, taunt the colored race with inferiority while they themselves use every means in their power to crush and degrade them, denying them every right and privilege, closing against them every avenue of elevation and improvement. Were they, under such circumstances, intellectual and refined, they would certainly be vastly superior to any other race that ever existed.

After the lessons, we used to talk freely to the children, often giving them slight sketches of some of the great and good men. Before teaching them the "John Brown" song, which they learned to sing with great spirit, Miss T. told them the story of the brave old man who had died for them. I told them about Toussaint, thinking it well they should know what one of their own color had done for his race. They listened attentively, and seemed to understand. We found it rather hard to keep their attention in school. It is not strange, as they have been so entirely unused to intellectual concentration. It is necessary to interest them every moment, in order to keep their thoughts from wandering. Teaching here is consequently far more fatiguing than at the North. In the church, we had of course but one room in which to hear all the children; and to make one's self heard, when there were often as many as a hundred and forty reciting at once, it was necessary to tax the lungs very severely.

My walk to school, of about a mile, was part of the way through a road lined with trees,—on one side stately pines, on the other noble live-oaks, hung with moss and canopied with vines. The ground was carpeted with brown, fragrant pine-leaves; and as I passed through in the morning, the woods were enlivened by the delicious songs of mocking-birds, which abound here, making one realize the truthful felicity of the description in "Evangeline,"—

> "The mocking-bird, wildest of singers,
> Shook from his little throat such floods of delirious music
> That the whole air and the woods and the waves seemed silent to listen."

The hedges were all aglow with the brilliant scarlet berries of the cassena, and on some of the oaks we observed the mistletoe, laden with its pure white, pearl-like berries. Out of the woods the roads are generally bad, and we found it hard work plodding through the deep sand.

. . . .

Harry, the foreman on the plantation, a man of a good deal of natural intelligence, was most desirous of learning to read. He came in at night to be taught, and learned very rapidly. I never saw any one more determined to learn. We enjoyed hearing him talk about the "gun-shoot,"—so the people call the capture of Bay Point and Hilton Head. They never weary of telling you "how Massa run when he hear de fust gun."

"Why did n't you go with him, Harry?" I asked.

"Oh, Miss, 't was n't 'cause Massa did n't try to 'suade me. He tell we dat de Yankees would shoot we, or would sell we to Cuba, an' do all de wust tings to we, when dey come, 'Berry well, Sar,' says I. 'If I go wid you, I be good as dead. If I stay here, I can't be no wust; so if I got to dead, I might's well dead here as anywhere. So I'll stay here an' wait for de "dam Yankees." ' Lor', Miss, I knowed he was n't tellin' de truth all de time."

"But why did n't you believe him, Harry?"

"Dunno, Miss; somehow we hear de Yankees was our friends, an' dat we 'd be free when dey come, an' 'pears like we believe *dat*."

I found this to be true of nearly all the people I talked with, and I thought it strange they should have had so much faith in the Northerners. Truly, for years past, they had had but little cause to think them very friendly. Cupid told us that his master was so daring as to come back, after he had fled from the island, at the risk of being taken prisoner by our soldiers; and that he ordered the people to get all the furniture together and take it to a plantation on the opposite side of the creek, and to stay on that side themselves. "So," said Cupid, "dey could jus' sweep us all up in a heap, an' put us in de boat. An' he telled me to take Patience—dat's my wife—an' de chil'en down to a certain pint, an' den I could come back, if I choose. Jus' as if I was gwine to be sich a goat!" added he, with a look and gesture of ineffable contempt. He and the rest of the people, instead of obeying their master, left the place and hid themselves in the woods; and when he came to look for them, not one of all his "faithful servants" was to be found. A few, principally house-servants, had previously been carried away.

In the evenings, the children frequently came in to sing and shout for us. These "shouts" are very strange,—in truth, almost indescribable. It is necessary to hear and see in order to have any clear idea of them. The children form a ring, and move around in a kind of shuffling dance, singing all the time. Four or five stand apart, and sing very energetically, clapping their hands, stamping their feet, and rocking their bodies to and fro. These are the musicians, to whose performance the shouters keep perfect time. The grown people on this plantation did not shout, but they do on some of the other plantations. It is very comical to see little children, not more than three or four years old, entering into the performance with all their might. But the shouting of the grown people is rather solemn and impressive otherwise. We cannot determine whether it has a religious character or not. Some of the people tell us that it has, others that it has not. But as the shouts of the grown people are always in connection with their religious meetings, it is probable that they are the barbarous expression of religion, handed down to them from their African ancestors, and destined to pass away under the influence of Christian teachings. The people on this island have no songs. They sing only hymns, and most of these are sad. Prince, a large black boy from a neighboring plantation, was the principal shouter among the children. It seemed impossible for him to keep still for a moment. His performances were most amusing specimens of Ethiopian gymnastics. Amaretta the younger, a cunning, kittenish little creature of only six years old, had a remarkably sweet voice. Her favorite hymn, which we used to hear her singing to herself as she walked through the yard, is one of the oddest we have heard:—

> "What makes ole Satan follow me so?
> Satan got nuttin' 't all fur to do wid me.
>
> CHORUS
> "Tiddy Rosa, hold your light!
> Brudder Tony, hold your light!
> All de member, hold bright light
>   On Canaan's shore!"

This is one of the most spirited shouting-tunes. "Tiddy" is their word for sister.

A very queer-looking old man came into the store one day. He was dressed in a complete suit of brilliant Brussels carpeting. Probably it had been taken from his master's house after the "gun-shoot"; but he looked so very dignified that we did not like to question him about it. The people called him Doctor Crofts,—which was, I believe, his master's name, his own being Scipio. He was very jubilant over the new state of things, and said to Mr. H.,—"Don't hab me feelins hurt now. Used to hab me feelins hurt all de time. But don't hab 'em hurt now no more." Poor old soul! We rejoiced with him that he and his brethren no longer have their "feelins" hurt, as in the old time.

.   .   .   .

A few days before Christmas, we were delighted at receiving a beautiful Christmas Hymn from Whittier, written by request, especially for our children. They learned it very easily, and enjoyed singing it. We showed them the writer's picture, and told them he was a very good friend of theirs, who felt the deepest interest in them, and had written this hymn expressly for them to sing,—which made them very proud and happy. Early Christmas morning, we were wakened by the people knocking at the doors and windows, and shouting, "Merry Christmas!" After distributing some little presents among them, we went to the church, which had been decorated with holly, pine, cassena, mistletoe, and the hanging moss, and had a very Christmas-like look. The children of our school assembled there, and we gave them the nice, comfortable clothing, and the picture-books, which had been kindly sent by some Philadelphia ladies. There were at least a hundred and fifty children present. It was very pleasant to see their happy, expectant little faces. To them, it was a wonderful Christmas-Day,—such as they had never dreamed of before. There was cheerful sunshine without, lighting up the beautiful moss-drapery of the oaks, and looking in joyously through the open widows; and there were bright faces and glad hearts within. The long, dark night of the Past, with all its sorrows and its fears, was forgotten; and for the Future,—the eyes of these freed children see no clouds in it. It is full of sunlight, they think, and they trust in it, perfectly.

After the distribution of the gifts, the children were addressed by some of the gentlemen present. They then sang Whittier's Hymn, the "John Brown" song, and several of their own hymns, among them a very singular one, commencing,—

> "I wonder where my mudder gone;
>   Sing, O graveyard!
> Graveyard ought to know me;
>   Ring, Jerusalem!
> Grass grow in de graveyard;
>   Sing, O graveyard!
> Graveyard ought to know me;
>   Ring, Jerusalem!"

They improvise many more words as they sing. It is one of the strangest, most mournful things I ever heard. It is impossible to give any idea of the deep pathos of the refrain,—

> "Sing, O graveyard!"

In this, and many other hymns, the words seem to have but little meaning; but the tones,—a whole lifetime of despairing sadness is concentrated in them. They sing, also, "Jehovyah, Hallelujah," which we like particularly:—

> "De foxes hab holes,
> An' de birdies hab nes',
> But de Son ob Man he hab not where
> To lay de weary head.
>
> CHORUS
> "Jehovyah, Hallelujah! De Lord He will purvide!
> Jehovyah, Hallelujah! De Lord He will purvide!"

They repeat the words many times. "De foxes hab holes," and the succeeding lines, are sung in the most touching, mournful tones; and then the chorus—"Jehovyah, Hallelujah"—swells forth triumphantly, in glad contrast.

Christmas night, the children came in and had several grand shouts. They were too happy to keep still.

"Oh, Miss, all I want to do is to sing and shout!" said our little pet, Amaretta. And sing and shout she did, to her heart's content.

She read nicely, and was very fond of books. The tiniest children are delighted to get a book in their hands. Many of them already know their letters. The parents are eager to have them learn. They sometimes said to me,—

"Do, Miss, let de chil'en learn everyting dey can. *We* nebber hab no chance to learn nuttin', but we wants de chil'en to learn."

They are willing to make many sacrifices that their children may attend school. One old woman, who had a large family of children and grandchildren, came regularly to school in the winter, and took her seat among the little ones. She was at least sixty years old. Another woman—who had one of the best faces I ever saw—came daily, and brought her baby in her arms. It happened to be one of the best babies in the world, a perfect little "model of deportment," and allowed its mother to pursue her studies without interruption.

DEBATE ON COMPULSORY FREE PUBLIC EDUCATION FOR ALL

A Record of Proceedings at the Constitutional Convention of South Carolina, 1868

Historians have often misconstrued Reconstruction as an era in which illiterate black men, aided by white carpetbaggers, rode roughshod over the rights of the native white population of the South. Recently, however, it has become clear that black men played the same kinds of roles in Reconstruction politics as did whites—some good and some, unfortunately, bad.

Seventy-four black men, a majority of the total delegates, participated in the South Carolina Constitutional Convention of 1868. Fourteen of these were from the North; sixty were from the South, and of these, thirty-eight were former slaves. The constitution they wrote was the most progressive to date in the South.

The following is a transcription of a debate that took place during the convention over whether school attendance should be compulsory. It aptly illustrates many of the concerns of Southern blacks of the time—formerly free or formerly slave. Of the participants in the portion of the debate reprinted here, Leslie, Duncan, and Holmes were white; all others were black. The chairman of the education committee that drew up the proposal under discussion was F. L. Cardozo, a free black educated at Glasgow and London who had returned to the South to teach school.

As can be seen from the following passages, the split on the issue was not along racial lines. Both blacks and whites opposed the idea, but for different reasons. Ultimately, the South Carolina Constitution did include a provision for compulsory, non-segregated schools. Neither aspect of this provision, however, was put into effect by the political authorities of the state.

MR. R. C. DE LARGE.   Although laboring under great inconvenience, I shall attempt to defend the amendment proposing to strike out the word "compulsory." In the first place, we have a report which is to become a portion of the Constitution, and that Constitution emphatically declares, in terms that cannot be misunderstood, that "no distinction shall be made on account of race, color, or previous condition." It has been remarked this morning that in the Constitution of Massachusetts, and other Northern States, the same proviso exists. But any one who reflects for a moment upon the condition of the people of Massachusetts, and those of South Carolina, will fully appreciate the great difference between them. As already stated, I object to the word "compulsory," because it is contrary to the spirit and principles of republicanism. Where is the necessity for placing in the Constitution a proviso that can never be enforced. It is just as impossible to put such a section in practical operation, as it would be for a man to fly to the moon. No one will deny that an attempt to enforce it would entail the greatest trouble and expense. Who, I ask, do we propose to set up as a censor of learning? Perhaps the opponents of the measure will say the School Commissioner. I deny that he can do it. He may be the father of half a dozen children. I, too, am the father of children; but will any body tell me that, as a free citizen of South Carolina, I have not the right to choose whether I shall send those children to school or not. Will any one say I shall not teach my child myself? It may be said, such a right is not denied me. Whether it be so or not, I plant myself upon the broad principle of the equality of all men as the basis of true republicanism; and to compel any man to do what this section provides is contrary to this principle.

Again, this clause will lead to difficulties of a serious character, to which neither you nor myself can blind our eyes. In Massachusetts there is a population cradled in the arms of freedom and liberty, free of all prejudice and devoid of passion, to a great extent. In South Carolina we have an entirely different set of people. We are about to inaugurate great changes, which it is our desire shall be successful.

MR. C. P. LESLIE.   Do I understand you to say that the people of Massachusetts have no prejudices of race?

MR. F. L. CARDOZO.   I would also like to ask the gentleman where he gets his authority for saying that the people of Massachusetts are cradled in the

FROM *Proceedings of the Constitutional Convention of South Carolina* (Charleston, 1868), pp. 686–94, 705–08.

principles of freedom and liberty. Is it so provided in the Constitution of Massachusetts?

MR. R. C. DE LARGE. I am not well acquainted with all the clauses in the Constitution of Massachusetts, and speak only from my historic knowledge of that people. This section proposes to open these schools to all persons, irrespective of color, to open every seminary of learning to all. Heartily do I endorse the object, but the manner in which it is to be enforced meets my most earnest disapproval. I do not propose to enact in this report a section that may be used by our enemies to appeal to the worst passions of a class of people in this State. The schools may be opened to all, under proper provisions in the Constitution, but to declare that parents "shall" send their children to them whether they are willing or not is, in my judgment, going a step beyond the bounds of prudence. Is there any logic or reason in inserting in the Constitution a provision which cannot be enforced? What do we intend to give the Legislature power to do? In one breath you propose to protect minor children, and in the next to punish their parents by fine and imprisonment if they do not send their children to school. For these reasons I am opposed to the section, and urge that the word "compulsory" shall be stricken out.

MR. A. J. RANSIER. I am sorry to differ with my colleague from Charleston on this question. I contend that in proportion to the education of the people so is their progress in civilization. Believing this, I believe that the Committee have properly provided for the compulsory education of all the children in this State between the ages named in the section.

I recognize the importance of this measure. There is a seeming objection to the word "compulsory," but I do not think it of grave importance. My friend does not like it, because he says it is contrary to the spirit of republicanism. To be free, however, is not to enjoy unlimited license, or my friend himself might desire to enslave again his fellow men.

Now I propose to support this section fully, and believe that the more it is considered in all its bearings upon the welfare of our people, the greater will be the desire that every parent shall, by some means, be compelled to educate his children and fit them for the responsibilities of life. As to the particular mode of enforcing attendance at school, we leave that an open question. At present we are only asserting the general principle, and the Legislature will provide for its application.

Upon the success of republicanism depends the progress which our people are destined to make. If parents are disposed to clog this progress by neglecting the education of their children, for one, I will not aid and abet them. Hence, this, in my opinion, is an exceedingly wise provision, and I am content to trust to the Legislature to carry out the measures to which it necessarily leads.

Vice and degradation go hand in hand with ignorance. Civilization and enlightenment follow fast upon the footsteps of the schoolmaster; and if education must be enforced to secure these grand results. I say let the compulsory process go on.

MR. R. C. DE LARGE. Can the gentleman demonstrate how the Legislature is to enforce the education of children without punishment of their parents by fine or imprisonment.

MR. A. J. RANSIER. When that question arises in the Legislature, I hope we shall have the benefit of my friend's counsel, and he himself may possibly answer that question. If there is any one thing to which we may attribute the sufferings endured by this people, it is the gross ignorance of the masses. While we propose to avoid all difficulties which may be fraught with evil to the community, we shall, nevertheless, insist upon our right to provide for the exercise of the great moral agencies which education always brings to bear upon public opinion. Had there been such a provision as this in the Constitution of South Carolina heretofore, there is no doubt that many of the evils which at present exist would have been avoided, and the people would have been advanced to a higher stage of civilization and morals, and we would not have been called upon to mourn the loss of the flower of the youth of our country. In conclusion, I favor this section as it stands. I do not think it will militate against the cause of republicanism, but, on the contrary, be of benefit both to it and to the people whom we represent. Feeling that everything depends on the education of the rising generation. I shall give this measure my vote, and use all my exertions to secure its adoption into this Constitution.

MR. B. F. RANDOLPH. In favoring, as I do, compulsory attendance at school, I cannot for the life of me see in what manner republicanism is at stake. It seems to have been the fashion on this floor to question a man's republicanism because he chooses to differ with others on general principles. Now this is a question which does not concern republicanism at all. It is simply a matter of justice which is due to a people, and it might be just as consistently urged that it is contrary to republican principles to organize the militia, to force every man to enroll his name, and to arm and equip them, as to urge that this provision is anti-republican because it compels parents to see to the education of their children.

MR. B. O. DUNCAN. Does the gentleman propose to educate children at the point of the bayonet, through the militia?

MR. B. F. RANDOLPH. If necessary we may call out the militia to enforce the law. Now, the gentlemen on the other side have given no reasons why the word "compulsory" should be stricken out.

MR. R. C. DE LARGE. Can you name any State where the provision exists in its Constitution?

MR. B. F. RANDOLPH. It exists in Massachusetts.

MR. R. C. DE LARGE. That is not so.

MR. F. L. CARDOZO. This system has been tested in Germany, and I defy the gentleman from Charleston to deny the fact. It has also been tested in several States of the Union, and I defy the gentleman to show that it has not been a success. It becomes the duty of the opposition if they want this section stricken from the report, to show that where it has been applied it has failed to produce the result desired.

MR. J. J. WRIGHT. Will you inform us what State in the Union compels parents to send their children to school?

MR. B. F. RANDOLPH. The State of New Hampshire is one. It may be asked what is the object of law? It is not only for the purpose of restraining men from doing wrong, but for the protection of all the citizens of a State, and the promotion of the general welfare. Blackstone lays it down as one of the objects, the furthering, as far as it can consistently be done, of the general welfare of the people. It is one of the objects of law, as far as practicable, not to restrain wrong by punishing man for violating the right, but also one of its grand objects to build up civilization, and this is the grand object of this provision in the report of the Committee on Education. It proposes to further civilization, and I look upon it as one of the most important results which will follow the defeat of the rebel armies, the establishment among the people who have long been deprived of the privilege of education, a law which will compel parents to send their children to school.

MR. R. B. ELLIOTT. Is it not regulated by general statutes in the State of Massachusetts, that parents shall be compelled to send their children to school?

MR. B. F. RANDOLPH. We propose to do that here. I consider this one of the most important measures which has yet come before this body. I think I can read it in the eyes of the members of this Convention to favor this measure. I feel that every one here believes it to be his duty to the people he represents. I believe every one here is zealous in doing all he can to further civilization, in building up educational institutions in the State, and doing all that is calculated to diffuse intelligence among the people generally. I had the honor of being principal of a free school two years; and, in the midst of one of the most intelligent systems of schools, the most trying thing which teachers had to contend with was the want of regular attendance on the part of the children. The most intelligent parents would sometimes neglect to send their children to school. The teachers had to adopt rules closing their doors to whose who were irregular in their attendance. This law will assist the teachers and assist our school system. It will prove beneficial to the State not only for the reasons I have given, but for various other reasons. I hope you will all vote for it. I shall vote for it with all my heart, because I believe it to be something beneficial to the welfare of the people of the State.

MR. A. C. RICHMOND. I desire to say but a few words on this subject. I shall speak principally in reference to our common schools and public funds. We expect to have a public school fund, although it may not be very large. We expect our parishes to be divided into school districts of convenient size. We can erect only a limited number of school houses each year, and it may be five or ten years before school houses are erected in all the districts, and the fund becomes large enough to assist in the education of all the people. If the word "compulsory" remains, it will be impossible to enforce the law for sometime to come. We say the public schools shall be opened to all. Every school district will have its school houses and its teachers. There is to be a particular school fund, school districts, and school houses. It is supposed by legislators and others that it is an excellent thing to have the children to go to school. It opens up a vast field for discussion, and affords a beautiful opportunity for making buncombe speeches. It is admitted by all legislators in every State of the Union, that cheap education is the best defense of the State. There must be schools to which colored children can go; but we wish to look into the propriety of compelling parents to send their children to school. I believe the efforts of the teachers, preachers, and all those interested in the welfare of the State, and the efforts of all those interested in the welfare of the colored people, will bring out nearly all the colored children. I believe nearly all the colored children of the State will go to school. We have societies that will help to furnish the books; we have preachers who are much interested; we have missionaries, all of whom are interested in this class of our people, and who will see to it that the colored children are educated, so that settles that point. The next point is, how are the white children going to school? By means of moral suasion nearly all the colored children will be brought to school; and by means of white schools, nearly all the white children will go to school and be educated. It will regulate itself. The word "compulsory" is used to compel the attendance of children in one or the other class of schools.

MR. R. C. DE LARGE.   What does the tenth section of that report say?

MR. A. C. RICHMOND.   I believe it is the meaning, that if families of white people are not able to send their children to private schools, they shall be obliged to send their children to the public schools, in which all white and colored shall be educated.

MR. F. L. CARDOZO.   We only compel parents to send their children to some school, not that they shall send them with the colored children; we simply give those colored children who desire to go to white schools, the privilege to do so.

MR. A. C. RICHMOND.   By means of moral suasion, I believe nearly all the colored people, as well as a large number of the children of white parents will go to school; such schools as their parents may select. If parents are too proud to take advantage of the means of education afforded, why then I say let their children grow up in ignorance.

MR. J. A. CHESTNUT.   So far as I have been able to see and judge, this report of the Committee is a sensible one, and ought to be adopted as it stands. How it can affect the rights of the people, or interfere with the spirit of republicanism, I am at a loss to discover. On the contrary, from all the experience I have had among the people, I unhesitatingly declare that no measure adopted by this Convention will be more in consonance with their wishes than this, or more productive of material blessings to all classes. Sir, you cannot by any persuasive and reasonable means establish civilization among an ignorant and degraded community, such as we have in our country. Force is necessary, and, for one, I say let force be used. Republicanism has given us freedom, equal rights, and equal laws. Republicanism must also give us education and wisdom.

It seems that the great difficulty in this section is in the fact that difficulty may arise between the two races in the same school, or that the whites will not send their children to the same schools with the colored children. What of that? Has not this Convention a right to establish a free school system for the benefit of the poorer classes? Undoubtedly. Then if there be a hostile disposition among the whites, an unwillingness to send their children to school, the fault is their own, not ours. Look at the idle youths around us. Is the sight not enough to invigorate every man with a desire to do something to remove this vast weight of ignorance that presses the masses down? I have no desire to curtail the privileges of freemen, but when we look at the opportunities neglected, even by the whites of South Carolina, I must confess that I am more than ever disposed to compel parents, especially of my own race, to send their children to school. If the whites object to it, let it be so. The consequences will rest with themselves.

I hope, therefore, that the motion to strike out the word "compulsory" will be laid upon the table.

MR. R. H. CAIN. It seems to me that we are spending a great deal of unnecessary time in the discussion of this subject. It is true, the question is one of great interest, and there are few who are not anxious that provisions shall be made by this Convention for the education of all classes in the State. But I am confident that it will not be necessary to use compulsion to effect this object. Hence, I am opposed to the insertion of the obnoxious word. I see no necessity for it. You cannot compel parents to send their children to school; and if you could, it would be unwise, impolitic, and injudicious. Massachusetts is fifty years ahead of South Carolina, and, under the circumstances which exist in that State, I might, if a resident, insist upon a compulsory education; but in South Carolina the case is different. There is a class of persons here whose situation, interests and necessities are varied, and controlled by surroundings which do not exist at the North. And justice is demanded for them. To do justice in this matter of education, compulsion is not required. I am willing to trust the people. They have good sense, and experience itself will be better than all the force you can employ to instill the idea of duty to their children.

Now, as a compromise with the other side, I propose the following amendment, namely that "the General Assembly may require the attendance at either public or private schools," &c.

This is a question that should be left to the Legislature. If the circumstances demand it, compulsion may be used to secure the attendance of pupils; but I do not believe such a contingency ever will occur.

As to the idea that both classes of children will be compelled to go to school together, I do not think it is comprehended in the subject at all. I remember that in my younger days I stumped the State of Iowa for the purpose of having stricken from the Constitution a clause which created distinction of color in the public schools. This was prior to the assembling of the Constitutional Convention. All we claimed was that they should make provision for the education of all the youth. We succeeded, and such a clause was engrafted in the Constitution, and that instrument was ratified by a majority of ten thousand. We said nothing about color. We simply said "youth."

I say to you, therefore, leave this question open. Leave it to the Legislature. I have great faith in humanity. We are in a stage of progress, such as our country never has seen, and while the wheels are rolling on, depend upon it, there are few persons in this country who will not seek to enjoy it by sending their children to school. White or black, all will desire to have their children educated. Let us then make this platform broad enough for all to stand upon without prejudice or objection. The matter will regulate itself, and to the Legislature may safely be confided the task of providing for any emergency which may arise.

MR. R. G. HOLMES. If there is anything we want in this State, it is some measure to compel the attendance of children between the ages of six and sixteen at some school. If it is left to parents, I believe the great majority will lock up their children at home. I hope, therefore, we shall have a law compelling the attendance of all children at school. It is the statute law in Massachusetts, and I hope we will have the provision inserted in our Constitution. The idea that it is not republican to educate children is supremely ridiculous. Republicanism, as has been well said, is not license. No man has the right, as a republican, to put his hand in my pocket, or steal money from it, because he wishes to do it. I can conceive of a way in which my child may be robbed by that system of republicanism which some members have undertaken to defend. My child may be left an orphan, poor and dependent on the kindness of neighbors or friends. They may think it to the best interest of that child to bind it out as an apprentice to some person. My child may be robbed of an education, because the person to whom it was bound does not think it advisable to send that child to school, as there may happen to be some objectionable children in the school. I have seen white children sitting by the side of colored children in school, and observed that there could not have been better friends. I do not want this privilege of attending schools confined to any exclusive class. We want no laws made here to prevent children from attending school. If any one chooses to educate their children in a private school, this law does not debar them that privilege.

But there are some who oppose all education. I remember the case of an individual who refused to have his children educated because, as he said, he himself had got along well enough without it, and he guessed his children could do the same. There is too much of that spirit in our State, and we want to contrive something to counteract it. In the case to which I have alluded, that individual some fifteen years afterwards, when his children had grown up, regretted his action, and was very much mortified because his children had no education. I hope we will engraft something into the Constitution, making it obligatory upon parents to send their children to school, and with that view, I hope the section will pass as it is.

. . . .

MR. F. L. CARDOZO. Before I resume my remarks this morning, I would ask the favor of the Convention, and especially the opposition, to give me their close attention, and I think I can settle this matter perfectly satisfactory to every one in the house.

It was argued by some yesterday, with some considerable weight, that we should do everything in our power to incorporate into the Constitution all possible measures that will conciliate those opposed to us.

No one would go farther in conciliating others than I would. But those whom we desire to conciliate consist of three different classes, and we should be careful, therefore, what we do to conciliate.

In the first place there is an element which is opposed to us, no matter what we do will never be conciliated. It is not that they are opposed so much to the Constitution we may frame, but they are opposed to us sitting in Convention. Their objection is of such a fundamental and radical nature, that any attempt to frame a Constitution to please them would be utterly abortive.

In the next place, there are those who are doubtful, and gentlemen here say if we frame a Constitution to suit these parties they will come over with us. They are only waiting, and I will say these parties do not particularly care what kind of a Constitution you frame, they only want to see whether it is going to be successful, and if it is, they will come any way.

Then there is a third class who honestly question our capacity to frame a Constitution. I respect that class, and believe if we do justice to them, laying our corner stone on the sure foundation of republican government and liberal principles, the intelligence of that class will be conciliated, and they are worthy of conciliation.

Before I proceed to discuss the question, I want to divest it of all false issues, of the imaginary consequences that some gentlemen have illogically thought will result from the adoption of this section with the word compulsory. They affirm that it compels the attendance of both white and colored children in the same schools. There is nothing of the kind in the section. It means nothing of the kind, and no such construction can be legitimately placed upon it. It simply says all the children shall be educated; but how is left with the parents to decide. It is left to the parent to say whether the child shall be sent to a public or private school. The eleventh section has been referred to as bearing upon this section. I will ask attention to this fact. The eleventh section does not say, nor does the report in any part say there shall not be separate schools. There can be separate schools for white and colored. It is simply left so that if any colored child wishes to go to a white school, it shall have the privilege to do so. I have no doubt, in most localities, colored people would prefer separate schools, particularly until some of the present prejudice against their race is removed.

We have not provided that there shall be separate schools; but I do not consider these issues as properly belonging to the question. I shall, therefore, confine myself to the more important matter connected with this subject.

My friend yesterday referred to Prussia and Massachusetts as examples that we should imitate, and I was much surprised to hear some of the members who have spoken, ridicule that argument. It was equivalent to saying we do not want the teachings of history, or the examples of any of those countries foremost in civilization.

It was said that the condition of affairs in Prussia and Massachusetts was entirely different. But they are highly civilized countries, with liberty-loving, industrious citizens, and the highest social order exists there. I want South Carolina to imitate those countries, which require the compulsory attendance of all children of certain ages for fixed periods, at some school. If you deem a certain end worthy of being attained, it must be accompanied by precisely the same means those countries have attained it.

Prussia, in her late victories over Austria, reaped the fruits of the superiority of her school system and the intelligence of her people, and in every conflict with the powers of darkness and error we should imitate just such a country as Prussia. To ignore the example of a country because far from us, would be to ignore all philosophy and history.

It was also remarked that there was no other State that compelled the attendance of their children at schools. Arkansas does it in her Constitution, and notwithstanding assertions to the contrary, I would say that Massachusetts does it in her statutes.

Another argument was that this matter had better be left to the Legislature. I have been charged with appealing to the prejudices and feelings of the colored delegates to this Convention. It is true to a certain extent. I do direct their attention to matters concerning their peculiar interests but if it is meant to charge me with appealing to their passions or against the white people, I respectfully deny the charge, and stamp the assertion as gratuitous. But I do desire we shall use the opportunities we now have to our best advantage, as we may not ever have a more propitious time. We know when the old aristocracy and ruling power of this State get into power, as they undoubtedly will, because intelligence and wealth will win in the long run, they will never pass such a law as this. Why? Because their power is built on and sustained by ignorance. They will take precious good care that the colored people shall never be enlightened.

Again, it has been argued that it was anti-republican, and an infringement of individual rights to pass such a law. Men living in a savage, uncivilized state are perfectly free, and should be untrammeled. But the first thing, when a man goes into society, is to concede certain individual rights necessary for the protection and preservation of society. If you deny this great principle, there can be no law, for every law you propose is an infringement of my individual right. If you tax me for the education of the poor people of the State, I simply say that it shall not be exclusively for the rich to build up their power, but that it is for all the people, the poor as well as the rich.

I hope every gentleman will see that the argument against it is anti-republican and utterly groundless. Some may think that we go too far, and take away too many individual rights. I maintain that in this instance it is only for the benefit of the State, as well as for the benefit of society.

The question is, will you pay the poll tax to educate your children in schools, or support them in penitentiaries? No intelligent person will prefer to support them as criminals.

Some ask how it is to be enforced, and say it is impossible. I will simply say what has been done elsewhere can be done here. Our Legislature will at first, of course, make the penalties very light, will consider all the circumstances by which we are surrounded, and will not make the law onerous. Every law should be considered in a two-fold aspect—in its moral effect and its penalties. The moral power of a law almost always compels obedience. Ninety-nine out of one hundred men who may be indifferent to their children, when they know there is a law compelling them to send their children to school, will make sacrifices in order not to violate that law.

I have had several years experience as a teacher, and I know exactly its effects. I can best satisfy the house by simply describing one out of the one hundred cases that have come under my own observation.

In my school I have the highest class of boys who were kept under my own special care and tuition. Among these boys was one highly gifted, universally loved, and talented. He was not only superior in regard to intellectual qualities, but also in regard to moral qualities. He was a noble boy, truly loveable and talented. I had watched the development of that boy's mind, and took the highest pleasure in assisting that development. I spent much time in assisting the development of that boy's mind, and watched his career with much interest and jealousy. At the commencement of our last session, he came to me with tears in his eyes, and bid me good bye. I asked him, "are you really going to leave school?" "Yes," he answered, "I must go; my parents are going to take me away." "Tell them," I said, "that I will consult with them." The mother, with tears, said she did not want the child to leave, but the father insisted upon it. I talked with him, but with no effect. He was a low, degraded, besotted drunkard. I endeavored by every argument in my power, by praising his boy as he deserved, and by offering to adopt him and take him North to one of the best institutions in the country, to effect my object in giving that boy a thorough education. What do you think was the reply? "No," he said, "I cannot spare him. In the morning he chops the wood, gets the water, and I want him to run on errands." Those errands, I learned, were running to the corner to buy beer and brandy for his father. If by a law of the State we could have taken that boy from his drunken father, and educated him, he would have been an ornament to us and an honor to the State. As I meet him in the street now, he slinks away from me to go, perhaps, to the corner to get liquor for his father. He told me from the time his father takes a glass in the morning till night he is never sober, and he wished his father was dead.

I am anxious to reconcile all differences on this question, and I move a reconsideration of the previous question, in order to offer an amendment, to the following effect:

> *Provided,* That no law to that effect shall be passed until a system of public schools has been thoroughly and completely organized, and facilities afforded to all the inhabitants of the State for the free education of their children.

The motion to reconsider was agreed to, and the question being taken on the adoption of this amendment, it was agreed to, and the fourth section passed to its third reading.

DISCRIMINATION IN MISSISSIPPI ELECTIONS

Blanche K. Bruce / Address to the United States Senate, 1876

Two black men served in the Senate during the Reconstruction period—both, oddly enough, from Mississippi. The first, Hiram Revels, was a free black born in North Carolina. He left the South to study at Knox College in Illinois, then worked in Missouri as an educator and a minister of the African Methodist Episcopal Church. Finally, he settled in Natchez, Mississippi, where he was persuaded to enter politics. In 1870 he was chosen to fill the seat vacated by Jefferson Davis in 1861, when Mississippi seceded from the Union.

The second, Blanche K. Bruce, was an exceedingly skillful politician and the only Mississippi black ever elected to a full term in the Senate. Born a slave in Virginia, he was chosen by his master—who may have been also his father—to be educated by a private tutor. When freed at the end of the Civil War, Bruce organized the first school for blacks in Missouri. Later, he moved to Mississippi and, after making a fortune as a planter, entered politics. In 1874, he was elected to the United States Senate, where he served with distinction. After completing his term in the Senate, he filled various appointive positions in Washington until his death.

Bruce made the following speech to the Senate in 1876. In it, he gives some of the details of the discrimination suffered by Mississippi freedmen in the elections of 1875 and offers some suggestions for the solution of the race problem in Mississippi.

MR. BRUCE. Mr. President, I had hoped that no occasion would arise to make it necessary for me again to claim the attention of the Senate until at least I had acquired a larger acquaintance with its methods of business and a fuller experience in public affairs; but silence at this time would be infidelity to my senatorial trust and unjust to both the people and the State I have the honor in part to represent.

The conduct of the late election in Mississippi affected not merely the fortunes of partisans—as the same were necessarily involved in the defeat or success of the respective parties to the contest—but put in question and jeopardy the sacred rights of the citizens; and the investigation contemplated in the pending resolution has for its object not the determination of the question whether the offices shall be held and the public affairs of that State be administered by democrats or republicans, but the higher and more important end, the protection in all their purity and significance of the political right of the people and the free institutions of the country. I believe the action sought is within the legitimate province of the Senate; but I shall waive a discussion of that phase of the question, and address myself to the consideration of the importance of the proposed investigation.

The demand of the substitute of the Senator from Michigan proceeds upon the allegation that fraud and intimidation were practiced by the opposition in the late State election, so as not only to deprive many citizens of their political rights, but so far as practically to have defeated a fair expression of the will of a majority of the legal voters of the State of Mississippi, resulting in placing in power many men who do not represent the popular will.

The truth of the allegations relative to fraud and violence is strongly suggested by the very success claimed by the democracy. In 1872 the republicans carried the State by 20,000 majority; in November last the opposition claimed to have carried it by 30,000; thus a democratic gain of more than 50,000. Now, by what miraculous or extraordinary interposition was this brought about? I can conceive that a large State like New York, where free speech and free press operate upon intelligent masses—a State full of railroads, telegraphs, and newspapers—on the occasion of a great national contest,

FROM Blanche K. Bruce, *Congressional Record*, 44th Congress, 1st Session (March 31, 1876), pp. 2101–04.

might furnish an illustration of such a thorough and general change in the political views of the people; but such a change of front is unnatural and highly improbable in a State like my own, with few railroads, and a widely scattered and sparse population. Under the most active and friendly canvass the voting masses could not have been so rapidly and thoroughly reached as to have rendered this result probable.

There was nothing in the character of the issues nor in the method of the canvass that would produce such an overwhelming revolution in the sentiments of the colored voters of the State as implied in this pretended democratic success. The republicans—nineteen-twentieths of whom are colored—were not brought, through the press or public discussions, in contact with democratic influences to such an extent as would operate a change in their political convictions, and there was nothing in democratic sentiments nor in the proscriptive and violent temper of their leaders to justify such a change of political relations.

The evil practices so naturally suggested by this view of the question as probable will be found in many instances by the proposed investigation to have been actual. Not desiring to anticipate the work of the committee nor to weary Senators with details, I instance the single county of Yazoo as illustrative of the effects of the outrages of which we complain. This county gave in 1873 a republican majority of nearly two thousand. It was cursed with riot and bloodshed prior to the late election, and gave but seven votes for the republican ticket, and some of these, I am credibly informed, were cast in derision by the democrats, who declared that republicans must have some votes in the county.

To illustrate the spirit that prevailed in that section, I read from the Yazoo Democrat, an influential paper published at its county seat:

> Let unanimity of sentiment pervade the minds of men. Let invincible determination be depicted on every countenance. Send forth from our deliberative assembly of the eighteenth the soul-stirring announcement that Mississippians shall rule Mississippi though the heavens fall. Then will woe, irretrievable woe, betide the radical tatterdemalions. Hit them hip and thigh, everywhere and at all times.
> Carry the election peaceably if we can, forcibly if we must.

Again:

> There is no radical ticket in the field, and it is more than likely there will be none; for the leaders are not in this city, and dare not press their claims in this county.

Speaking of the troubles in Madison County, the Yazoo City Democrat for the 26th of October says:

> Try the rope on such characters. It acts finely on such characters here.

The evidence in hand and accessible will show beyond peradventure that in many parts of the State corrupt and violent influences were brought to bear upon the registrars of voters, thus materially affecting the character of the voting or poll lists; upon the inspectors of election, prejudicially and unfairly thereby changing the number of votes cast; and, finally, threats and violence were practiced directly upon the masses of voters in such measure and strength as to produce grave apprehensions for their personal safety, and as to deter them from the exercise of their political franchises.

Lawless outbreaks have not been confined to any particular section of the country, but have prevailed in nearly every State at some period in its history. But the violence complained of and exhibited in Mississippi and other Southern States, pending a political canvass, is exceptional and peculiar. It is not the blow that the beggared miner strikes that he may give bread to his children, nor the stroke of the bondsman that he may win liberty for himself, nor the mad turbulence of the ignorant masses when their passions have been stirred by the appeals of the demogogue; but it is an attack by an aggressive, intelligent, white political organization upon inoffensive, law-abiding fellow-citizens; a violent method for political supremacy, that seeks not the protection of the rights of the aggressors, but the destruction of the rights of the party assailed. Violence so unprovoked, inspired by such motives, and looking to such ends, is a spectacle not only discreditable to the country, but dangerous to the integrity of our free institutions.

I beg Senators to believe that I refer to this painful and reproachful condition of affairs in my own State not in resentment, but with sentiments of profound regret and humiliation.

If honorable Senators ask why such flagrant wrongs were allowed to go unpunished by a republican State government, and unresented by a race claiming 20,000 majority of the voters, the answer is at hand. The civil officers of the State were unequal to meet and suppress the murderous violence that frequently broke out in different parts of the State, and the State executive found himself thrown for support upon a militia partially organized and poorly armed. When he attempted to perfect and call out this force and to use the very small appropriation that had been made for their equipment, he was met by the courts with an injunction against the use of the money, and by the proscriptive element of the opposition with such fierce outcry and show of counter-force, that he became convinced a civil strife, a war of races, would be precipitated unless he staid his hand. As a last resort, the protection provided in the national Constitution for a State threatened with domestic violence was sought; but the national Executive—from perhaps a scrupulous desire to avoid the appearance of interference by the Federal authority with the internal affairs of that State—declined to accede to the request made for Federal troops.

It will not accord with the laws of nature or history to brand the colored people as a race of cowards. On more than one historic field, beginning in 1776 and coming down to this centennial year of the Republic, they have attested in blood their courage as well as love of liberty. I ask Senators to believe that no consideration of fear or personal danger has kept us quiet and forbearing under the provocations and wrongs that have so sorely tried our souls. But feeling kindly toward our white fellow-citizens, appreciating the good purposes and offices of the better classes, and, above all, abhorring a war of races, we determined to wait until such time as an appeal to the good sense and justice of the American people could be made.

A notable feature of the outrages alleged is that they have referred almost exclusively to the colored citizens of the State. Why is the colored voter to be proscribed? Why direct the attack upon him? While the methods of violence, resorted to for political purposes in the South, are foreign to the genius of our institutions as applied to citizens generally—and so much is conceded by even the opposition—yet they seem to think we are an exceptional class and citizens, rather by sufferance than right; and when pressed to account for their bitterness and proscription toward us they, with more or less boldness, allege incompetent and bad government as their justification before the public opinion of the country. Now, I declare that neither political incapacity nor venality are qualities of the masses of colored citizens. The emancipation of the colored race during the late civil strife was an expression alike of the magnanimity and needs of the nation; and the subsequent and early subtraction of millions of industrial values from the resources of the insurrectionary States and the presence of many thousand additional brave hearts and strong hands around the flag of the country vindicated the justice and wisdom of the measure.

The close of the war found four millions of freedmen, without homes or property, charged with the duty of self-support and with the oversight of their personal freedom, yet without civil and political rights! The problem presented by this condition of things was one of the gravest that has ever been submitted to the American people. Shall these liberated millions of a separate race, while retaining personal liberty, be deprived of political rights? The practical sense of the American people definitely settled this delicate and difficult question, and the demand for a more pronounced loyal element in the work of reconstruction in the lately rebellious States furnished an opportunity for the recognition of the political rights of the race, both in the interest of justice and good government.

The history of my race since enfranchisement, considered in connection with the difficulties that have environed us, will exhibit hopeful progress and attest that we have been neither ungrateful for the civil and political privileges received nor wanting in appreciation of the correspondingly weighty obligations imposed upon us.

. . . .

Again, we began our political career under the disadvantages of the inexperience in public affairs that generations of enforced bondage had entailed upon our race. We suffered also from the vicious leadership of some of the men whom our necessities forced us temporarily to accept. Consider further that the States of the South, where we were supposed to control by our majorities, were in an impoverished and semi-revolutionary condition— society demoralized, the industries of the country prostrated, the people sore, morbid, and sometimes turbulent, and no healthy controlling public opinion either existent or possible—consider all these conditions, and it will be seen that we began our political novitiate and formed the organic and statutory laws under great embarrassments.

Despite the difficulties and drawbacks suggested, the constitutions formed under colored majorities, whatever their defects may be, were improvements on the instruments they were designed to supersede; and the statutes framed, though necessarily defective because of the crude and varying social and in- dustrial conditions upon which they were based, were more in harmony with the spirit of the age and the genius of our free institutions than the obsolete laws that they supplanted. Nor is there just or any sufficient grounds upon which to charge an oppressive administration of the laws.

The State debt proper is less than a half million dollars and the State taxes are light. Nor can complaint be reasonably made of the judiciary. The records of the supreme judicial tribunal of the State will show, in 1859-'60, 266 decisions in cases of appeal from the lower courts, of which 169 were affirmed and 97 reversed. In 1872-'73 the records show 328 decisions ren- dered in cases of appeal from below, of which 221 were affirmed and 107 reversed; in 1876, of appeals from chancellors, appointed by Governor Ames, up to date, 41 decisions have been rendered, of which 33 were affirmed and 8 reversed. This exhibit, whether of legislation or administration, shows there has been no adequate provocation to revolution and no justification for violence in Mississippi. That we should have made mistakes, under the circumstances, in measures of both legislation and administration, was natural, and that we have had any success is both creditable and hopeful.

But if it can be shown that we have used the ballot either to abridge the rights of our fellow-citizens or to oppress them; if it shall appear that we have ever used our newly acquired power as a sword of attack and not as a shield of defense, then we may with some show of propriety be charged with incapacity, dishonesty, or tyranny. But, even then, I submit that the corrective is in the hands of the people, and not of a favored class, and the remedy is in the honest exercise of the ballot, and not in fraud and violence.

Mr. President, do not misunderstand me; I do not hold that all the white people of the State of Mississippi aided and abetted the white-league organ- izations. There is in Mississippi a large and respectable element among the opposition who are not only honest in their recognition of the political rights of the colored citizen and deprecate the fraud and violence through which those rights have been assailed, but who would be glad to see the color line in politics abandoned and good-will obtain and govern among all classes of her people. But the fact is to be regretted that this better class of citizens in many parts of the State is dominated by a turbulent and violent element of the opposition, known as the White League—a ferocious minority —and has thus far proved powerless to prevent the recurrence of the outrages it deprecates and deplores.

The uses of this investigation are various. It will be important in suggesting such action as may be found necessary not only to correct and repair the wrongs perpetrated, but to prevent their recurrence. But I will venture to assert that the investigation will be most beneficial in this, that it will largely contribute to the formation of a public sentiment that, while it restrains the vicious in their attacks upon the rights of the loyal, law-abiding voters of the South, will so energize the laws as to secure condign punishment to wrong-doers, and give a security to all classes, which will effectively and abundantly produce the mutual good-will and confidence that constitute the foundations of the public prosperity.

We want peace and good order at the South; but it can only come by the fullest recognition of the rights of all classes. The opposition must concede the necessity of change, not only in the temper but in the philosophy of their party organization and management. The sober American judgment must obtain in the South as elsewhere in the Republic, that the only distinctions upon which parties can be safely organized and in harmony with our institutions are differences of opinions relative to principles and policy of government, and that differences of religion, nationality, or race can neither with safety nor propriety be permitted for a moment to enter into the party contests of the day. The unanimity with which the colored voters act with a party is not referable to any race prejudice on their part. On the contrary, they invite the political co-operation of their white brethren, and vote as a unit because proscribed as such. They deprecate the establishment of the color line by the opposition, not only because the act is unwise and wrong in principle, but because it isolates them from the white men of the South, and forces them, in sheer self-protection and against their inclination, to act seemingly upon the basis of a race prejudice that they neither respect nor entertain. As a class they are free from prejudices, and have no uncharitable suspicions against their white fellow-citizens, whether native born or settlers from the Northern States. They not only recognize the equality of citizenship and the right of every man to hold, without proscription, any position of honor and trust to which the confidence of the people may elevate him; but owing nothing to race, birth, or surroundings, they, above all other classes in the community, are interested to see prejudices drop out of both politics and the business of the country, and success in life proceed only upon the integrity and merit of the man who seeks it. They are also appreciative—feeling and exhibiting the liveliest gratitude for counsel and help in their new career, whether they come from the men of the North or of the South. But withal, as they progress in intelligence and appreciation of the dignity of their prerogatives as citizens, they, as an evidence of growth, begin to realize the significance of the proverb, "When thou doest well for thyself, men shall praise thee;" and are disposed to exact the same protection and concession of rights that are conferred upon other citizens by the Constitution, and that, too, without the humiliation involved in the enforced abandonment of their political convictions.

We simply demand the practical recognition of the rights given us in the Constitution and laws, and ask from our white fellow-citizens only the consideration and fairness that we so willingly extend to them. Let them generally realize and concede that citizenship imports to us what it does to them, no more and no less, and impress the colored people that a party defeat does not imperil their political franchise. Let them cease their attempts to coerce our political co-operation, and invite and secure it by a policy so fair and just as to commend itself to our judgment, and resort to no motive or measure to control us that self-respect would preclude their applying to themselves. When we can entertain opinions and select party affiliations without proscription, and cast our ballots as other citizens and without jeopardy to person or privilege, we can safely afford to be governed by the considerations that ordinarily determine the political action of American citizens. But we must be guaranteed in the unproscribed exercise of our honest convictions and be absolutely, from within or without, protected in the use of our ballot before we can either wisely or safely divide our vote. In union, not division, is strength, so long as White League proscription renders division of our vote impracticable by making a difference of opinion opprobrious and an antagonism in politics a crime. On the other hand, if we should, from considerations of fear, yield to the shot-gun policy of our opponents, the White League might win a temporary success, but the ultimate result would be disastrous to both races, for they would first become aggressively turbulent, and we, as a class, would become servile, unreliable, and worthless.

It has been suggested, as the popular sentiment of the country, that the colored citizens must no longer expect special legislation for their benefit, nor exceptional interference by the National Government for their protection. If this is true, if such is the judgment relative to our demands and needs, I venture to offset the suggestion, so far as it may be used as a reason for a denial of the protection we seek, by the statement of another and more prevalent popular conviction. Back of this, and underlying the foundations of the Republic itself, there lies deep in the breasts of the patriotic millions of the country the conviction that the laws must be enforced, and life, liberty, and property must, alike to all and for all, be protected. But I allege that we do not seek special action in our behalf, except to meet special danger, and only then such as all classes of citizens are entitled to receive under the Constitution. We do not ask the enactment of new laws, but only the enforcement of those that already exist.

The vicious and exceptional political action had by the White League in Mississippi has been repeated in other contests and in other States of the South, and the colored voters have been subjected therein to outrages upon their rights similar to those perpetrated in my own State at the recent election. Because violence has become so general a quality in the political canvasses of the South and my people the common sufferers in each instance, I have considered this subject more in detail than would, under other circumstances, have been either appropriate or necessary. As the proscription and violence toward the colored voters are special and almost exclusive, and seem to proceed upon the assumption that there is something exceptionally offensive and unworthy in them, I have felt, as the only representative of my race in the Senate of the United States, that I was placed, in some sort, upon the defensive, and I have consequently endeavored to show how aggravated and inexcusable were the wrongs worked upon us, and have sought to vindicate our title to both the respect and good-will of the just people of the nation. The gravity of the issues involved has demanded great plainness of speech from me. But I have endeavored to present my views to the Senate with the moderation and deference inspired by the recollection that both my race and myself were once bondsmen, and are to-day debtors largely to the love and justice of a great people for the enjoyment of our personal and political liberty. While my antecedents and surroundings suggest modesty, there are some considerations that justify frankness, and even boldness of speech.

Mr. President, I represent, in an important sense, the interest of nearly a million of voters, constituting a new, hopeful, permanent, and influential political element, and large enough to affect in critical periods the fortunes of this great Republic; and the public safety and common weal alike demand that the integrity of this element should be preserved and its character improved. They number more than a million of producers, who, since their emancipation and outside of their contributions to the production of sugar, rice, tobacco, cereals, and the mechanical industries of the country, have furnished nearly forty million bales of cotton, which, at the ruling prices of the world's market, have yielded $2,000,000,000, a sum nearly equal to the national debt; producers who, at the accepted ratio that an able-bodied laborer earns, on an average $800 per year, annually bring to the aggregate of the nation's great bulk of values more than $800,000,000.

I have confidence, not only in my country and her institutions, but in the endurance, capacity, and destiny of my people. We will, as opportunity offers and ability serves, seek our places, sometimes in the field of letters, arts, sciences, and the professions. More frequently mechanical pursuits will attract and elicit our efforts; more still of my people will find employment and livelihood as the cultivators of the soil. The bulk of this people—by surroundings, habits, adaptation, and choice—will continue to find their homes in the South, and constitute the masses of its yeomanry. We will there probably, of our own volition and more abundantly than in the past, produce the great staples that will contribute to the basis of foreign exchange, aid in giving the nation a balance of trade, and minister to the wants and comfort and build up the prosperity of the whole land. Whatever our ultimate position in the composite civilization of the Republic and whatever varying fortunes attend our career, we will not forget our instincts for freedom nor our love of country. Guided and guarded by a beneficent Providence, and living under the genial influence of liberal institutions, we have no apprehensions that we shall fail from the land from attrition with other races, or ignobly disappear from either the politics or industries of the country.

Mr. President, allow me here to say that, although many of us are uneducated in the schools, we are informed and advised as to our duties to the Government, our State, and ourselves. Without class prejudice or animosities, with obedience to authority as the lesson and love of peace and order as the passion of our lives, with scrupulous respect for the rights of others, and with the hopefulness of political youth, we are determined that the great Government that gave us liberty, and rendered its gift valuable by giving us the ballot, shall not find us wanting in a sufficient response to any demand that humanity or patriotism may make upon us; and we ask such action as will not only protect us in the enjoyment of our constitutional rights, but will preserve the integrity of our republican institutions.

5

SUGGESTIONS FOR FURTHER READING

The story of the black man during the era of the Civil War is most interestingly told in the collection of primary source material imaginatively edited by James McPherson, *The Negro's Civil War** (Pantheon, 1965). Secondary works on black troops in the war are Dudley T. Cornish, *The Sable Arm: Negro Troops in the Union Army** (Longmans, Green, 1956), and Benjamin Quarles, *The Negro in the Civil War* (Little, Brown, 1953). Willie Lee Rose, in *Rehearsal for Reconstruction: The Port Royal Experiment** (Bobbs-Merrill, 1964), tells what happened to the black people of Port Royal, in the Sea Islands—the first freedmen in the United States. *Army Life in a Black Regiment** (Fields, Osgood, 1870), by Thomas Wentworth Higginson, is the story of the black troops recruited at Port Royal, as told by their white abolitionist commander. *The Journal of Charlotte Forten** (Dryden, 1953), edited by Ray A. Billington, describes Miss Forten's work at Port Royal as well as her earlier experiences as a free Northern black. The effect of the war itself on Southern blacks is discussed by Bell Irwin Wiley in *Southern Negroes, 1861–1865** (Yale University Press, 1938).

Lincoln's proclamation freeing the slaves of the Confederacy is discussed in John Hope Franklin, *The Emancipation Proclamation** (Doubleday, 1963), and James McPherson, in *The Struggle for Equality: Abolitionists and the Negro in the Civil War and Reconstruction** (Princeton University Press, 1964), reports on the efforts of friends of the black man to secure for him real freedom. James McCague, in *The Second Rebellion: The Story of the New York City Draft Riots* (Dial, 1968), gives an example of the kind of violence black people regularly met at the hands of whites, even in the North.

*Black Reconstruction in America** (Harcourt, Brace & World, 1935), by W. E. B. Du Bois, was the work that began the revision of Reconstruction history still in progress. Some of the more recent revisionist works are Kenneth Stampp, *The Era of Reconstruction, 1865–1877** (Knopf, 1966), and John Hope Franklin, *Reconstruction After the Civil War** (University of Chicago Press, 1961). Two recent works dealing specifically with black people are Lerone Bennett, Jr., *Black Power: The Human Side of Reconstruction** (Johnson. 1967), and Robert Cruden, *The Negro in Reconstruction** (Prentice-Hall, 1969).

The best studies of black people in the individual states during Reconstruction are Joel Williamson, *After Slavery: The Negro in South Carolina During Reconstruction, 1861–1877** (University of North Carolina Press, 1965), and Vernon Lane Wharton, *The Negro in Mississippi, 1865–1890** (University of North Carolina Press, 1947).

6 THE LEGAL SEGREGATION OF FREE PEOPLE

The years from 1877 to 1900 were a period of renewed victimization for the black population of the United States, both North and South. The Republican Party, which had served as a guarantor of black political freedom, withdrew its support in 1877 under President Rutherford B. Hayes and gave the white South the freedom to deal with the black population as it saw fit. Abandoned by the federal government and bereft of Northern support, the blacks of the South were driven rapidly into political impotence, or—what was often worse —they were forced to support political policies that were clearly contrary to their own interests.

Extralegal disfranchisement of the blacks, effected through intimidation and outright violence, was gradually supplanted in the South by legal exclusion from the political process. Mississippi, in 1890, was the first state to apply the new suffrage restrictions in constitutional fashion. The key provision was that each applicant for the vote be able to interpret a portion of the state constitution to the satisfaction of a state-appointed registrar. Although on the face of it the new provision did not call for racial discrimination, it was clearly intended and used to eliminate black people from the voting lists.

In the process of disfranchisement, other states added a "good conduct" clause to their constitutions, requiring each registrant to have a recommendation from a responsible (that is, white) citizen; a "grandfather" clause, stating that if one's grandfather had voted in 1860, it was not necessary to meet the usual voting requirements; and a ruling that only whites could participate in primary elections, which effectively eliminated the black vote in the one-party South. Some of these restrictions were removed only with the federal Voting Act of 1965.

Along with legal disfranchisement came legal segregation. Many Southerners, black as well as white, were willing to live with the separation of the races that characterized much of Reconstruction life. But fear of a possible breakdown in racial customs led whites to impose legal restrictions on the activities of black people. The first segregation laws applied in the field of public education. By 1878, most Southern states operated a dual educational system, with blacks receiving a much smaller per capita expenditure than whites. Transportation segregation came next, and though the laws developed at different rates in different places, by the turn of the century most Southern states enforced segregation on streetcars and railroads. When the First World War broke out, segregation was legally maintained in almost every area of social contact.

While his political and social rights were being restricted, the black man in Southern cities was losing the economic position he had enjoyed earlier. An influx of white labor, skilled and unskilled, began to edge the black man out of even the jobs that had traditionally been his. When the Civil War ended, five of every six artisans in the South were black; by 1900, only one of every twenty was black.

The condition of the black man in the rural South has already been mentioned (see pages 128–29). Since land was not made available to them, most black farmers were dependent on the white plantation owners for work. The work consisted of sharecropping, a system in which the cropper existed on credit extended by the landowner. Inevitably, at the end of the year the cropper remained in debt and was required to sign labor contracts that virtually tied him to the soil. Equally discriminatory in effect was the convict-lease system, whereby blacks arrested on minor charges were rented to plantation owners by law-enforcement authorities.

As might have been expected, these conditions led many rural blacks to seek ways to migrate to more promising lands. Some suggested that the Indian Territory (now a part of Oklahoma) be made into an all-black state, and in anticipation of such an event, several all-black towns were founded in the area beginning in 1891. Some of the towns, still all-black, exist to this day. The most notable migration of the period, however, occurred in 1879, when over 7,000 poor blacks, under the leadership of an ex-slave, "Pop" Singleton, arrived in Kansas to begin a new life. Unfortunately, there was nothing there for them except a severe winter and white hostility. Many died, and many of those who survived the winter returned home or went elsewhere.

When Reconstruction ended, the hostility of local white authorities caused black people to look to the federal government for legal aid. At that time, the Civil Rights Act of 1875, which provided for protection against segregation in transportation and public accommodations, was in effect, and the blacks had every reason to expect federal support. The Supreme Court, however, struck the struggle for equal rights several near-fatal blows. The first came in 1883, when the Court declared the Civil Rights Act of 1875 unconstitutional on the grounds that the Fourteenth Amendment did not prohibit discrimination by individuals.

Later, in 1896, in the *Plessy v. Ferguson* decision, the Court ruled that "separate but equal" facilities were permissible and that states could use police power to enforce segregation law. Shortly thereafter it ruled that states could limit the franchise in any way that was not explicitly based on race, color, or previous condition of servitude. The federal government's betrayal of the black man was complete.

There were two short-lived signs of hope during the last quarter of the nineteenth century—one in the area of jobs and the other in politics. The first was the emergence of the Knights of Labor, a group that sought to organize skilled and unskilled industrial workers on an interracial basis. During the 1870's and the 1880's, the Knights worked hard to enlist black members in both North and South, and it has been estimated that in 1886 blacks formed from 9 to 11 percent of the total membership of 700,000. A reputation for radicalism and violence cost the Knights their power after the 1880's, however, and they were supplanted by the American Federation of Labor (AFL). Although originally opposed to racial discrimination, by the close of the century the AFL adopted a policy of permitting—even sometimes encouraging—the exclusion of blacks from union locals.

The Populist Movement was the second sign of hope. For a time it looked as though poor white and poor black farmers would be able to cooperate in order to bring about an improvement in the condition of both groups. In many states, black men ran for office on a Populist or fusion ticket. Opportunistic white politicians, however, revived the residual fear of and hostility to the blacks, and in an attempt to maintain political power the Populist leaders shifted emphasis from interracial cooperation to virulent race hatred. By early in the twentieth century, the racial attitudes of white Populist leaders could hardly be distinguished from those of Southern Democrats; if anything, the former were the more intensely discriminatory.

THE AREAS OF RACIAL DISCRIMINATION

Report of the Committee on Grievances at the State Convention of Colored Men of Texas, 1883

The convention movement among blacks did not cease with emancipation. On the contrary, since its primary concern before the Civil War was the status and the treatment of free blacks, it had even more reason for being after the remaining slaves were freed. When federal support was removed from Southern blacks at the end of Reconstruction and power reverted to the former ruling class, conventions were called to deal with the problem of growing segregation and the raising of new caste barriers.

In 1883, a national convention was scheduled to be held in Louisville, Kentucky; preliminary to that meeting, various state conventions met to elect delegates and draw up recommendations. The document reprinted here is the report made at the Texas convention by its grievance committee. From it one can get a clear idea of some of the ways in which legal segregation was beginning to take shape. It is interesting to note that the committee of black Texans was prepared to accept separate facilities if they were truly equal.

Mr. Chairman and Gentlemen:

We, your Committee on Grievances, beg leave to make the following report: We find that the denial to the colored people of the free exercise of many of the rights of citizenship, is due to the fact of there being such great prejudice against them as a race. This prejudice was engendered from the belief which underlay the institution of slavery, and which kept that institution alive, and built it to the enormous proportions which it has attained; that is, the belief that the Negro was intended by the Divine Creator as servants and menials for the more favored races; hence, was not to be accorded the rights and privileges exercised by other races. Very naturally, then, was it thought fitting and proper, and in keeping with Divine intention, to keep the Negro bowed down in slavery. The sudden change from a status wherein we were slaves to one in which we were made freemen; and then, further, to that in which we became citizens equal before the law, was so unexpected and contrary, both to the training and teaching of our former owners, that they have never fully accepted said changes, though

---

FROM *Proceedings of the State Convention of Colored Men of Texas, Held at the City of Austin, July 10–12, 1883* (Houston, 1883), pp. 12–17. Reprinted by permission from a pamphlet in the Library of the University of Michigan, Ann Arbor.

they have affected to accept them, because their acceptance was made the only condition upon which they could regain their former position in the Union. We submit, that it is contrary to the natural order of things for them to have surrendered their belief in the matter simply because they were physically overpowered. And, not only is the belief in the Negro's inferiority and creation for servants, deeply rooted in the minds of its advocates, but it has culminated in what seems to be a bitter hatred and fixed prejudice. This culmination was brought about by the Negro being taken from the position of a slave and forcibly placed equal to his former master; also, by his being subsequently utilized in carrying on the war against the unfortunates of the lost cause after the battle had been transferred from the field to the ballot box; and in doing this he adhered to a political party which he kept up by his support, and which was nearly identical with the triumphant party which had caused their former owners' defeat on the bloody field of battle. This is the outcome of a train of circumstances naturally liable to produce just such a result. The reason given by our debasers, when attempting to justify themselves in regarding us socially so grossly inferior is, that it always has been their policy to do so, and hence it will always be. This remark refers to the fact that they regarded us thus during slavery as a ground upon which they justified slavery, and as they have experienced no change of mind they will continue thus to regard us. Your committee arrived at this conclusion: that if our former owners deny our social equality, they cannot be expected to be swift in respecting our legal equality or equality before the law; for it is the social regard one has for another as a member of society, which impels him to protect and accord unto such a one his legal rights. Hence, if there be a class who socially regard us less favorably than they do other races, to an extent that they are prejudiced, such a class certainly are indifferent as to whether we obtain our legal rights or not. Accordingly, social disregard may well imply absolute indifference as to another's legal rights, but never that *mutual* regard which is supposed to possess citizens of a common country. It is a true rule that the degree to which any right is enjoyed as a citizen, is measured by the willingness of the whole body of citizens to protect such a right; if there is lack of regard there is, therefore, lack of the will to protect. We find, therefore, that this social disregard is the sole cause of all the infringements upon our rights as a race, as we shall specify:

MISCEGENATION LAW

Prominent among the enactments in furtherance of this social disregard, is a law of this State punishing as felons all persons who intermarry when one is a descendant of the Negro race and the other is not. The same series of laws impose an insignificant fine only for the same persons to live together in unlawful wedlock, or have carnal intercourse with each other without being married. In most cases, say ninety-nine cases in one hundred, parties of the two races thus unlawfully cohabiting are not even reported, or if reported not punished. And, sad to remark, in many cases officers of the law are disqualified to try such cases; in many others, those who would in good faith testify against offenders of this class, would do so at the risk of their lives. The result of this series of crimes, tolerated and encouraged by our Criminal Code, which makes pretensions to preserving public morals, common decency and chastity, is to increase immorality in the lower classes of both races to an alarming extent. The law should never imply that a thing otherwise lawful is a felony, and that a thing of the same nature unlawful in itself is less than a felony. Colored females, victims of this well-laid plan, called a law to protect public morals, and common decency and chastity, are severely censured, and our whole race indiscriminately described as a race without morals. A careful consideration of the operation of the law convinces all fair-minded persons, that the law was intended to gratify the basest passions of certain classes of men who do not seek such gratification by means of lawful wedlock. We are pained to announce that the law bears its evil fruits. The committee dismiss the consideration of this dark subject with the recommendation that the Convention urge upon our next Legislature the necessity of an amendment to this law that will punish as rigidly for all carnal intercourse between the two races, unlawfully carried on, as it punishes them for intermarrying. If the Legislature do this, they will show a willingness to stop the tide of immorality that now makes such inroads upon the morals of some of our most promising females.

FREE SCHOOLS

The Constitution, and laws made in pursuance thereof, make provision for the education of the youth of the State, without regard to race or previous condition. Further, they make provision that cities may assume the control of school affairs within their limits, on condition that they make a special taxation upon their property in order to lengthen the school term to ten months. What we complain of is, that notwithstanding the Constitution, laws, courts, and the Board of Education have decided that provision for each race must be equal and impartial, many cities make shameful discrimination because the colored people do not own as much property on which to pay taxes as the white people do, in proportion to the number of children in each race. They utterly refuse to give colored schools the same provision as to character of buildings, furniture, number and grade of teachers as required by law. The result of this discrimination is, that the white schools of such cities show good fruit, while the colored show poor fruit or none at all. We here say that this charge of discrimination is not made against all cities, but against only such as really discriminate. And again, there are many colored teachers appointed mainly on account of their personal relation with the individuals composing the Boards, and not with reference to the peculiar needs of the pupils to be benefitted, neither the fitness of the teacher nor the wishes of patrons.

We are glad to say, however, that many school boards, exclusively white, do their full duty towards colored schools. Still we deem it proper and just, in recognition of our rights, to assist in supervising and controlling, to have some colored man or men appointed on school boards in cities where there is a large number of colored pupils and patrons—especially where suitable men can be found. We make no complaint against the provision made by the Legislature of our State for the education of our children, but against the partial manner in which those provisions are executed by some of the local authorities.

TREATMENT OF CONVICTS

Another sore grievance that calls for the consideration of this Convention is the treatment of convicts, a large proportion of whom are colored. It is inhuman and cruel in the extreme. We do not refer to those that are kept within the walls. They are under the immediate care and supervision of the management, and we believe considerately treated. But most of the convicts are scattered over the State on farms, having no one to administer to their physical, moral or spiritual needs but a host of inhuman, brutal convict guards. When a fresh convict is carried to the farms, he is taken down by the other convicts and beaten, at the command of the guard, and that, too, with a large piece of cowhide. The guard takes this method of taming the newcomer. Of course this lays him up, but in a few days he is hauled out of his sick quarters and put to work, whether he is physically able to do it or not. The law provides that a convict physically unable to work shall not be required to do so, such inability to be ascertained by the examination of the penitentiary physician. But, convicts on farms, who are mostly colored, have no physician to determine such inability, and even when sick and dying have none, unless the hiring planter, who has no particular interest in saving his life, sees fit to employ one. In many cases sick convicts are made to toil until they drop dead in their tracks. Many again, driven to desperation by inhuman treatment, seek to relieve themselves by attempting to escape when the chances are against them, thus inducing the guards to shoot them, which they are ready to do on the slightest pretext. Others are maltreated by being placed in the pillory or stocks until they are dead or nearly so. When convicts are brutally murdered, nothing is done with their slayers unless the indignant citizens are prompt in insisting upon their punishment. In nine cases out of ten, parties sent to investigate these occurrences report the killing justifiable, because guards and their friends find it convenient to make it appear so. When legislative committees visit one of these convict camps, they always find the convicts ready to report that they are well treated, because all of them, both white and black, are previously warned by their guards to report thus or accept the consequences which will surely follow. Again we will state, although the law justifies the killing of a convict escaping from the penitentiary, when his escape can be prevented in no other way, still we fail to see wherein it can be justified when the convict is carried on a farm, away from the penitentiary, and given a chance to escape only to be deliberately shot down in attempting to do so. We believe such to be deliberate murder, and should be punished as such. Believing that most of the evils can be remedied by the appointment of a colored inspector who is a humane man, having power to investigate the affairs of convict camps and the management of convict labor on private farms, therefore, we recommend to the Governor and Board such an appointment at the earliest possible moment. We recommend also, that as most of the State convicts are colored, that there be appointed at least one colored commissioner of penitentiaries. Though our men and youths are sent to the penitentiary to be reformed, in most cases they are made worse by the inhumanities and immoral habits of their guards, who, in many cases, are worse morally than the convicts themselves. We think that this Convention should pass a resolution condemning, in strongest terms, the practice of yoking or chaining male and female convicts together. This is an act of officials, done only for the purpose of further demoralizing those persons, especially so where they are only county convicts.

RAILWAYS, INNS AND TAVERNS

The criticisms and censures of many, that colored persons in demanding admission to first class cars are forcing social intercourse, are unjust and unwarranted. For those who censure know that if the companies were to furnish accommodations for colored passengers holding first class tickets, equal to the accommodations furnished white passengers holding the same, though such accommodations be in separate cars, no complaint will be made. But selling two classes of passengers the same kind of tickets, at the same time and price, certainly sell to them the same accommodations and privileges. The colored people, like any other class of citizens, will contend for the right in this matter as long as our Constitution reads, "all men when they form a social compact have equal rights," and even longer.

We would also state that we do not contend for the privilege of riding in the car with whites, but for the right of riding in cars equally as good, and for the mutual right of riding in their car if they have a separate one, whenever they are permitted to ride in ours if we have a separate one. We believe the State laws to be adequate to protect us in every right, and that there is no necessity of appealing to a law of Congress unless the laws and government of our own State refuse to recognize and protect these rights.

As for accommodations at public inns, taverns and hotels, we have the same right as other races to be accommodated on equal terms and conditions, though we cannot compel them to accommodate us in the same room, at the same table or even in the same building, but the proprietor can be compelled to make provision as good. We recognize the fact that our State law is as adequate to protect a colored man in the exercise of his rights as it is to protect a white man. While not encouraging the contention for our rights at hotels when we can make other provision, we recommend our people to invoke the aid of the courts when their rights with reference to railroads are violated, and ask that they assert our rights thereon by such damages as are sufficient to assert them.

JURIES

The prevailing practice among sheriffs and jury commissioners of summoning jurors exclusively white or nearly so, is in direct violation of the laws of this State, for no person is disqualified as a juror on account of his color. If the sheriff and commissioners exclude any one by practice on account of color, it is such an exclusion as is not contemplated by law, for the parties summoning cannot excuse themselves by saying they knew of none who could read and write, for that is a qualification they are to assume and let the court test jurors' qualifications after they are summoned. A juror who sits in judgment on a case involving the rights of a man whom he regards with less consideration than he does members of his own class, is in law an incompetent juror, and should by law be excluded on evidence of such lack of regard. We deem it to be the duty of all judges to, at all times, specially instruct sheriffs and commisioners with reference to correcting these abuses, so as to secure to every individual, white or black, a fair and impartial trial by a jury composed of men acknowledging themselves to be his peers.

In furtherance of a desire to effectually and legitimately prescribe a remedy for the evils and wrongs complained of, we recommend the formation of an organization to be known and called "The Colored People's Progressive Union." It shall have for its object the protection of the rights of the colored people of Texas, by giving aid and direction in the prosecution of suits in the support of every right guaranteed to colored people as citizens. We recommend that our delegates to the National Convention be instructed to urge upon said Convention the necessity of organizing a national convention of the same name and for the same object, under which, if organized, this State Association shall act as a branch.

All of which is respectfully submitted.

MACK HENSON, Chairman
A. R. NORRIS,
J. N. JOHNSON,
J. Q. A. POTTS.

ATTACK ON THE SUPREME COURT

Henry M. Turner / The Outrage of the Supreme Court:
A Letter from Henry M. Turner

The Supreme Court's failure to support the fight for equal rights during the last quarter of the nineteenth century came as a severe blow to the black man. No one expressed the rage and the dismay of the nation's blacks better than Henry M. Turner. Educated in the North to be a clergyman in the African Methodist Episcopal Church, Turner was appointed chaplain to black troops by Lincoln in 1863. After the war, he moved to Georgia, where he became active in Radical Republican politics. In 1868 he was elected to the Georgia state legislature, but because of a Democratic majority he and twenty-six other black legislators were barred from their seats at the opening session. A massive protest to Washington succeeded in gaining them admittance to the second session of the legislature.

Throughout his political career, Turner served as a minister in Atlanta. When violent attacks on the Supreme Court decisions of 1883 and 1896 came to no avail, he gave up in disgust and joined the emigrationists in advocating a return to Africa for American blacks.

The following document was written in response to a question about Turner's attack on the 1883 decision of the Court declaring the Civil Rights Act of 1875 unconstitutional. Turner's reply makes clear his anger at the Court's decision to leave Southern blacks at the mercy of Southern society.

Editor of the New York Voice:

A midst multitudinous duties I find, calling my attention, your note of recent date, asking me to briefly refer to the "Civil Rights Decisions," which, since their delivery has drawn from me expressions which many are pleased to call severe adverse strictures upon the highest court in this country, and upon all of its judges save one, Mr. Justice Harlan. It is to me a matter of that kind of surprise called wonder suddenly excited to find a single, solitary individual who belongs in the United States, or who has been here for any considerable time, unacquainted with those famous FIVE DEATH DEALING DECISIONS. Indeed, sir, those decisions have had, since the 15th day of October, A.D. 1883, the day of their pronouncement, more of my study than any other civil subject. I incline to the opinion that I have an argument which, taken

FROM Henry M. Turner, "Civil Rights: The Outrage of the Supreme Court of the United States upon the Black Man" (Atlanta, 1889).

as a concomitant of the learned dissenting sentiments of that eminent jurist, Mr. Justice Harlan, would to a rational mind make the judgment of Justice Bradley and his associates a deliquescence—a bubble on the wave of equity— a legal nothing. You bid me in my reply to observe brevity. Shortness and conciseness seem to be the ever present rule when the Negro and his case is under treatment. However, I am satisfied that in saying this, I do not convey your reason for commanding me to condense, "boil down." The more I ponder the non-agreeing words of that member of our chief assize, who had the moral courage to bid defiance to race prejudice, the more certain am I that no words of mine, condemnatory of that decision, have been sufficiently harsh.

March 1st, 1875, Congress passed an act entitled "An act for the prevention of discrimination on the ground of race, color or previous condition of servitude," said act being generally known as the Civil Rights Bill, introduced during the lifetime of the Negro's champion, the immortal Charles Sumner. The act provided:

"SECTION 1. That all persons within the jurisdiction of the United States shall be entitled to the full and equal enjoyment of the accommodations, advantages, facilities, and privileges of inns, public conveyances on land or water, theaters, and other places of public amusements—subject only to the conditions and limitations established by law and applicable alike to citizens of every color and race, regardless of any previous condition of servitude.

"SEC. 2. That any person who shall violate the foregoing section by denying to any citizen, except for reasons by law applicable to citizens of every race and color, and regardless of any previous condition of servitude, the full enjoyment of any of the accommodations, advantages, facilities or privileges in said section enumerated, or by aiding or inciting such denial, shall for every such offence forfeit and pay the sum of five hundred dollars to the person aggrieved thereby, to be recovered in an action of debt, with full costs; and shall also, for every such offence, be deemed guilty of a misdemeanor, and, upon conviction thereof, shall be fined not less than five hundred, nor more than one thousand, dollars, or shall be imprisoned not less than thirty days nor more than one year. Provided, that all persons may elect to sue for the penalty aforesaid, or to proceed under their rights at common law and by State statutes; and having so elected to proceed in the one mode on the other, their right to proceed in the other jurisdiction shall be barred. But this provision shall not apply to criminal proceedings, either under this act or the criminal law of any State. And provided further, that a judgment for the penalty in favor of the party aggrieved, or a judgment upon an indictment, shall be a bar to either prosecution respectively."

Here we have the exact language of the law:

First, what is forbidden; second, the penalty; third, the mode for gaining redress; and fourth, the defendant's security against excessive punishment. The questions that come forward and will not down are: Was this law just?

Did this law violate the principle which should be foremost in every hall of legislation—hurt no one, give unto every man his just due? Should the color of one's skin deny him privileges any more than the color of one's hair, seeing that the individual had nothing to do with the cause for the one or for the other? Before attempting to answer the above questions, which must and will suggest themselves to every *compos mentis*, we state the constitutional amendments upon which the act under consideration was founded and upheld. We cannot see how one so learned in the law as Mr. Justice Bradley is presumed to be, by reason of his exalted position, can see only the Fourteenth Amendment, as the part of the Constitution, relied on. It is undeniably patent to all that the Thirteenth Amendment more nearly expresses the foundation for the "act." The language of the Thirteenth Amendment says:

SECTION 1. "Neither slavery nor involuntary servitude, except as a punishment for a crime, whereof the party shall have duly been convicted, shall exist within the United States, or any place subject to their jurisdiction." This amendment in its second section, declares that "Congress shall have the power to enforce this article by appropriate legislation." Under this article, alone, I am satisfied that our National Legislature had full warrant and authority to enact the law now abrogated. The Fourteenth Amendment to the Constitution provides that "All persons born or naturalized in the United States, and subject to the jurisdiction thereof, are citizens of the United States, and of the State wherein they reside. No State shall make or enforce any law which shall abridge the privileges or immunities of the citizens of the United States; nor shall any State deprive any person of life, liberty or property without due process of law, nor deny to any person in its jurisdiction the equal protection of the laws." Upon these two amendments, say these wise judges, depends the constitutionality of the act or law under discussion.

In October, 1882, five cases were filed or submitted: United States *vs.* Stanley, from Kansas; United States *vs.* Ryan, from California; United States *vs.* Nichols, from Missouri; United States *vs.* Singleton, from New York; and Robinson and wife *vs.* Memphis and Charleston Railroad Company, from Tennessee. Our learned (?) judges occupied a year in considering what their dicta should be. October 15, 1883, found Justice Bradley in his place, on the bench, prepared to voice the opinion of the court as to the rights of more than seven millions of human beings. Mr. Solicitor-General Phillips, had delivered his argument for the life of the law to be maintained. The argument of the Solicitor-General had been supplemented by the eloquent efforts of Mr. William M. Randolph, on behalf of Robinson and wife. Numerous authorities were cited to show that where the Constitution guarantees a right, Congress is empowered to pass the legislation appropriate to give effect to that right. It was also maintained and established by judicial precedents, that the constitutionality of the act was not harmed by the nice distinction of "guaranteed rights," instead of "created rights." Justice Bradley consumes seventeen pages, to do what in his conscientious (?) opinion he believes to be right. Justice Harlan, in opposing the position taken by Mr. Bradley, occupies thirty-seven pages. After reciting the law countenancing the actions instituted by the sorely aggrieved persons, the first question which propounded itself to the member reading the opinion was, "Are these sections constitutional?" After taking space and time to tell what it is not the essence of the law to do, the Honorable Judge in *obiter dictum* language says: "But the responsibility of an independent judgment is now thrown upon this court; and we are bound to exercise it according to the best lights we have."

Why this apologetic language? Are we not acquainted with the functions and duties of our court of last resort? Do we not know that the judges thereof are appointed for life, subject only to their good behavior? This deciding judge says: "The power is sought, first in the Fourteenth Amendment: and the views and arguments of distinguished senators, advanced whilst the law was under consideration, claiming authority to pass it by virtue of that amendment, are the principal arguments adduced in favor of the power. We have carefully considered those arguments, as was due to the eminent ability of those who put them forward, and have felt, in all its force, the weight of authority which always invests a law that Congress deems itself competent to pass." It is not said that arguments opposed to the passage of the act were noticed. It is not said that this Honorable Judge, long before this question of law was brought before him, had predetermined its non-constitutionality.

It is not hinted that this Republican Supreme Court had caused it to be noised abroad what their "finding" would be if the "law" was inquired into. The court, it is said, could see, and only see, negroes in Kansas and Missouri intermingling with white persons in hotels and inns; negroes in California and New York associating on equal terms with Caucasians in theaters; and negroes in the presence of those free from the taint of African blood in the parlor-cars of Tennessee. These sights completely blinded the eyes of the, at other times, learned judges, and one of their number, not too full of indignation for utterance, proclaimed aloud, these things may not be; these pictures shall not in future be produced; the law is unconstitutional; and all of the other members, save one, said, amen. Negroes may come as servants into all of the hotels, inns, theaters and parlor-cars, but they shall never be received as equals—as are other persons. A negro woman with a white baby in her arms may go to the table in the finest and most aristocratic hotel, and there, as a servant, be permitted to associate with all present, of whatever nationality. The same woman, unaccompanied by said baby, or coming without the distinguished rank of servant, is given to understand that she can not enter. And what is more, by the Bradley infamous decision, may be by force of arms prevented from entering. A negro, whose father is a white man, and whose mother's father was white, if marked sufficiently to tell that he is somewhat negro is denied admission into certain places; the same resorts or places of entertainment being readily granted to the inky dark negro who is accompanying an invalid white man. The gambler, cut-throat, thief, despoiler of happy homes and the cowardly assassin need only to have white faces in order to be accommodated with more celerity and respect than are our lawyers, doctors, teachers and humble preachers. Talk about the "Dred Scott" decision; why it was only a mole-hill in comparison with this obstructing Rocky Mountain to the freedom of citizenship. I am charged by your Pennsylvania correspondent with saying that, "By the decision of the Republican Supreme Court colored people may be turned out of hotels, cheated, abused and insulted on steamboats and railroads without legal redress." I am of the opinion that the reporter on your paper who published the above quotation as coming from me, made no mistake unless it was that of making it more mild than I intended. When I use the term, "cheated," I mean that colored persons are required to pay first-class fare and in payment there for are given no-class treatment, or at least the kind which no other human being, paying first-class fare, is served. Some conveyances excepted, I must say to their credit. Bohemians, Scandinavians, Greasers, Italians and Mongolians all precede negroes. When Mr. Justice Harlan shall have retired from the bench by reason of age and infirmity, I pray him to accept, take and carry with him into his retirement the boiled-down essence of the love of more than eight million negroes, who delight to honor an individual whose vertebræ is strong enough to stem the tide of race prejudice. His decision dissenting in favor of equal and exact justice to all men will last always, will never be forgotten as long as there is a descendant of the American negro on the earth: I have no doubt that the feeling of Justice Harlan when seeking rest upon his soft couch on the night of that fateful day in October, was different to the emotions present with Judge Bradley. The latter had doomed seven million human beings and their posterity to "stalls" and "nooks," denoting inferiority: the other had attempted to protect them from American barbarism and vandalism. Seven million persons, many of whom are not only related to Justice Bradley's race by affinity, but by consanguinity, cannot move the bowels of his compassion to the extent of framing or constructing even one sentence in all of that notorious decision which fairly can be interpreted as a friendly regard for the rights of those struggling souls who cried to God, while carrying the burden of bondage for more than two hundred and forty years. God will some day raise up another Lincoln, another Thad. Stevens and another Charles Sumner. In my opinion, if Jesus was on earth, he would say, when speaking of eight members of the Supreme Court and the decision which worked such acerb and cruel wrong upon my people, "Father, forgive them; they know not what they do."

Mr. Justice Harlan, in his protesting language, says many things which stand non-controvertible and may some day be remembered only to be thought about when it is too late. He says: "The opinion in these cases proceeds, it seems to me, upon grounds entirely too narrow and artificial. I cannot resist the conclusion that the substance and spirit of the recent amendments of the Constitution, have been sacrificed by a subtle and ingenious verbal criticism." He then quotes an authority which is so old and well established that the memory of man goeth not to the contrary, which says:

"It is not the words of the law, but the internal sense of it that makes the law; the letter of the law is the body; the sense and reason of the law is the soul." Continuing, he says: "Constitutional provisions, adopted in the interest of liberty, and for the purpose of securing, through national legislation, if need be, rights inhering in a state of freedom, and belonging to American citizenship, have been so construed as to defeat the ends the people desired to accomplish, which they attempted to accomplish, and which they thought they had accomplished by changes in their fundamental law. By this, I do not mean that the determination of these cases should have been materially controlled by considerations of mere expediency or policy. I mean only, in this form, to express an earnest conviction that the court has departed from the familiar rule requiring, in the interpretation of constitutional provisions, that full effect be given to the intent with which they were adopted. The court adjudges, I think, erroneously, that Congress is without power, under either the Thirteenth or Fourteenth Amendment, to establish such regulations, and that the first and second sections of the statute are, in all their parts, unconstitutional and void."

Then follows a great number of authorities maintaining his position. No sane man can read the record, law and authorities relating to these cases, without forming a conclusion that cannot be brushed away, that the bench of judges were narrow even to wicked ingeniousness, superinduced by color-phobeism. Sane men know that the gentlemen in Congress who voted for this act of 1875 understood full well the condition of our country, as did the powers amending the Constitution abolishing slavery. The intention was to entirely free, not to partly liberate. The desire was to remove the once slave so far from his place of bondage, that he would not even remember it, if such a thing were possible. Congress stepped in and said, he shall vote, he shall serve on juries, he shall testify in court, he shall enter the professions, he shall hold offices, he shall be treated like other men, in all places the conduct of which is regulated by law, he shall in no way be reminded by partial treatment, by discrimination, that he was once a "chattel," a "thing." Certainly Congress had a right to do this. The power that made the slave a man instead of a "thing" had the right to fix his status. The height of absurdity, the chief point in idiocy, the brand of total imbecility, is to say that the Negro shall vote a privilege into existence which one citizen may enjoy for pay, to the exclusion of another, coming in the same way, but clothed in the vesture covering the earth when God first looked upon it. Are colored men to vote grants to railroads upon which they cannot receive equal accommodation? When we ask redress, we are told that the State must first pass a law prohibiting us from enjoying certain privileges and rights, and that after such laws have been passed by the State, we can apply to the United States courts to have such laws declared null and void by *quo warranto* proceedings. The Supreme Court, when applied to, will say to the State, you must not place such laws on your statute book. You can continue your discrimination on account of color. You can continue to place the badge of slavery on persons having more than one-eighth part of Negro blood in their veins, and so long as your State legislatures do not license you so to do, you are safe. For if they (the Negroes) come to us for redress, we will talk about the autonomy of the State must be held inviolate, referring them back to you for satisfaction.

Do you know of anything more degrading to our country, more damnable? The year after this decision the Republican party met with defeat, because it acquiesced by its silence in that abominable decision, nor did it lift a hand to strike down that diabolical sham of judicial monstrosity, neither in Congress nor the great national convention which nominated Blaine and Logan. God, however, has placed them in power again, using the voters and our manner of electing electors as instruments in his hands. God would have men do right, harm no one, and to render to every man his just due. Mr. Justice Harlan rightly says that the Thirteenth Amendment intended that the white race should have no privilege whatsoever pertaining to citizenship and freedom, that was not alike extended and to be enjoyed by those persons who, though the greater part of them were slaves, were invited by an act of Congress to aid in saving from overthrow a government which, theretofore by all of its departments, had treated them as an inferior race, with no legal rights or privileges except such as the white race might choose to grant. It is an indisputable fact that the amendment last mentioned may be exerted by legislation of a direct and primary character for the eradication, not simply of the institution of slavery, but of its badges and incidents indicating that the individual was once a slave. The Supreme Court must decide the interstate commerce law to be unconstitutional on account of interference with the State's autonomy, for it must be remembered that Mrs. Robinson, a citizen of Mississippi, bought a ticket from Grand Junction, Tennessee, to Lynchburg, Virginia, and when praying for satisfaction for rough and contumacious treatment, received at the hands of the company's agent, she was informed by the court, that the court was without power to act. Congress had constitutional power to pursue a runaway slave into all the States by legislation, to punish the man that would dare to conceal the slave. Congress could find the poor fellow seeking God's best blessing to man, liberty, and return him to his master, but Congress cannot, so say our honorable court, give aid sufficient to the poor black man, to prove beyond all doubt to him that he is as free as any other citizen. Mr. Justice Harlan says: "The difficulty has been to compel a recognition of the legal right of the black race to take the rank of citizens, and to secure the enjoyment of privileges belonging under the law to them as a component part of the people for whose welfare government is ordained. At every step in this direction, the Nation has been confronted with class tyranny, which is of all tyrannies the most intolerable, for it is ubiquitous in its operation, and weighs perhaps most heavily on those whose obscurity or distance would draw them from the notice of a single despot. To-day it is the colored race which is denied by corporations and individuals wielding public authority, rights fundamental in their freedom and citizenship. AT SOME FUTURE TIME IT MAY BE THAT SOME OTHER RACE WILL FALL UNDER THE BAN OF RACE DISCRIMINATION." This last preceding sentence sounds like prophecy from on high. Will the day come when Justice Bradley will want to hide from his decree of the 15th day of October, 1883, and say *non est factum?* I conclude with great reluctance these brief lines, assuring you that the subject is just opened and if desired by you, I will be glad to give it elaborate attention. I ask no rights and privileges for my race in this country, which I would not contend for on behalf of the white people were the conditions changed, or were I to find proscribed white men in Africa where black rules.

A word more and I am done, as you wish brevity. God may forgive this corps of unjust judges, but I never can, their very memories will also be detested by my children's children, nor am I alone in this detestation. The eight millions of my race and their posterity will stand horror-frozen at the very mention of their names. The scenes that have passed under my eyes upon the public highways, the brutal treatment of helpless women which I have witnessed, since that decision was proclaimed, is enough to move heaven to tears and raise a loud acclaim in hell over the conquest of wrong. But we will wait and pray, and look for a better day, for God still lives and the LORD OF HOSTS REIGNS.

I am, sir, yours, for the Fatherhood of God, and the Brotherhood of man.

H. M. TURNER.

Atlanta, Georgia, January 4, 1889

PEONAGE IN THE SOUTH

The Life Story of a Negro Peon

Peonage is the system in which a debtor must work out what he owes in compulsory service to his creditor. In the South, this was the condition of the sharecropper, who went deeper and deeper into debt to the planter on whose farm he worked. Since the planter furnished the goods the cropper needed and kept the account books himself, it was virtually impossible for the black cropper to free himself from debt and thus escape the system.

The selection that follows was obtained from an interview with a black peon. It is of particular interest because it describes not only peonage but also the convict-lease system, whereby black people were arrested for minor offenses then leased to white farmers by the state for a fee. Needless to say, the number of arrests made rose with the need for labor on farms.

I am a Negro and was born sometime during the war in Elbert County, Ga., and I reckon by this time I must be a little over forty years old. My mother was not married when I was born, and I never knew who my father was or anything about him. Shortly after the war my mother died, and I was left to the care of my uncle. All this happened before I was eight years old, and so I can't remember very much about it. When I was about ten years old my uncle hired me out to Captain ——. I had already learned how to plow, and was also a good hand at picking cotton. I was told that the Captain wanted me for his houseboy, and that later on he was going to train me to be his coachman. To be a coachman in those days was considered a post of honor, and young as I was, I was glad of the chance.

But I had not been at the Captain's a month before I was put to work on the farm, with some twenty or thirty other Negroes—men, women and children. From the beginning the boys had the same tasks as the men and women. There was no difference. We all worked hard during the week, and would frolic on Saturday nights and often on Sundays. And everybody was happy. The men got $3 a week and the women $2. I don't know what the children got. Every week my uncle collected my money for me, but it was very little of it that I ever saw. My uncle fed and clothed me, gave me a place to sleep, and allowed me ten or fifteen cents a week for "spending change," as he called it.

I must have been seventeen or eighteen years old before I got tired of that arrangement, and felt that I was man enough to be working for myself and handling my own wages. The other boys about my age and size were "drawing" their own pay, and they used to laugh at me and call me "Baby," because my old uncle was always on hand to "draw" my pay. Worked up by these things, I made a break for liberty. Unknown to my uncle or the Captain I went off to a neighboring plantation and hired myself out to another man. The new landlord agreed to give me forty cents a day and

FROM "The Life Story of a Negro Peon," in *The Life Stories of Undistinguished Americans as Told by Themselves*, ed. by Hamilton Holt (New York, 1906), pp. 183–99.

furnish me one meal. I thought that was doing fine. Bright and early one Monday morning I started for work, still not letting the others know anything about it. But they found it out before sundown. The Captain came over to the new place and brought some kind of officer of the law. The officer pulled out a long piece of paper from his pocket and read it to my employer. When this was done I heard my new boss say:

"I beg your pardon, Captain. I didn't know this Negro was bound out to you, or I wouldn't have hired him."

"He certainly is bound out to me," said the Captain. "He belongs to me until he is twenty-one, and I'm going to make him know his place."

So I was carried back to the Captain's. That night he made me strip off my clothing down to my waist, ordered his foreman to give me thirty lashes with a buggy whip across my bare back, and stood by until it was done. After that experience the Captain made me stay on his place night and day—but my uncle still continued to "draw" my money.

I was a man nearly grown before I knew how to count from one to one hundred. I was a man nearly grown before I ever saw a colored teacher. I never went to school a day in my life. Today I can't write my own name, though I can read a little. I was a man nearly grown before I ever rode on a railroad train, and then I went on an excursion from Elberton to Athens. What was true of me was true of hundreds of other Negroes around me— 'way off there in the country, fifteen or twenty miles from the nearest town.

When I reached twenty-one the Captain told me I was a free man, but he urged me to stay with him. He said he would treat me right, and pay me as much as anybody else would. The Captain's son and I were about the same age, and the Captain said that, as he had owned my mother and uncle during slavery, and as his son didn't want me to leave them (since I had been with them so long), he wanted me to stay with the old family. And I stayed. I signed a contract—that is, I made my mark—for one year. The Captain was to give me $3.50 a week, and furnish me a little house on the plantation—a one-room log cabin similar to those used by his other laborers.

During that year I married Mandy. For several years Mandy had been the house-servant for the Captain, his wife, his son and his three daughters, and they all seemed to think a good deal of her. As an evidence of their regard they gave us a suit of furniture, which cost about $25, and we set up housekeeping in one of the Captain's two-room shanties. I thought I was the biggest man in Georgia. Mandy still kept her place in the "Big House" after our marriage. We did so well for the first year that I renewed my contract for the second year, and for the third, fourth and fifth year I did the same thing. Before the end of the fifth year the Captain had died, and his son, who had married some two or three years before, took charge of the plantation. Also, for two or three years, this son had been serving at Atlanta in some big office to which he had been elected. I think it was in the Legislature or something of that sort—anyhow, all the people called him Senator.

At the end of the fifth year the Senator suggested that I sign up a contract for ten years; then, he said, we wouldn't have to fix up papers every year. I asked my wife about it; she consented; and so I made a ten-year contract.

Not long afterward the Senator had a long, low shanty built on his place. A great big chimney, with a wide, open fireplace, was built at one end of it and on each side of the house, running lengthwise, there was a row of frames or stalls just large enough to hold a single mattress. The places for these mattresses were fixed one above the other; so that there was a double row of these stalls or pens on each side. They looked for all the world like stalls for horses. Since then I have seen cabooses similarly arranged as sleeping quarters for railroad laborers.

Nobody seemed to know what the Senator was fixing for. All doubts were put aside one bright day in April when about forty able-bodied Negroes, bound in iron chains, and some of them handcuffed, were brought out to the Senator's farm in three big wagons. They were quartered in the long, low shanty, and it was afterward called the stockade. This was the beginning of the Senator's convict camp. These men were prisoners who had been leased by the Senator from the State of Georgia at about $200 each per year, the State agreeing to pay for guards and physicians, for necessary inspection, for inquests, all rewards for escaped convicts, the cost of litigation and all other incidental expenses.

When I saw these men in shackles, and the guards with their guns, I was scared nearly to death. I felt like running away, but I didn't know where to go. And if there had been any place to go to, I would have had to leave my wife and child behind. We free laborers held a meeting. We all wanted to quit. We sent a man to tell the Senator about it. Word came back that we were all under contract for ten years and that the Senator would hold us to the letter of the contract, or put us in chains and lock us up—the same as the other prisoners. It was made plain to us by some white people we talked to that in the contracts we had signed we had all agreed to be locked up in a stockade at night or at any other time that our employer saw fit; further, we learned that we could not lawfully break our contract for any reason and go and hire ourselves to somebody else without the consent of our employer; and, more than that, if we got mad and ran away, we could be run down by bloodhounds, arrested without process of law, and be returned to our employer, who, according to the contract, might beat us brutally or administer any kind of punishment that he thought proper. In other words, we had sold ourselves into slavery—and what could we do about it? The white folks had all the courts, all the guns, all the hounds, all the railroads, all the telegraph wires, all the newspapers, all the money, and nearly all the land—and we had only our ignorance, our poverty and our empty hands. We decided that the best thing to do was to shut our mouths, say nothing, and go back to work. And most of us worked side by side with those convicts during the remainder of the ten years.

But this first batch of convicts was only the beginning. Within six months another stockade was built, and twenty or thirty other convicts were brought to the plantation, among them six or eight women! The Senator had bought an additional thousand acres of land, and to his already large cotton plantation he added two great big sawmills and went into the lumber business. Within two years the Senator had in all 200 Negroes working on his plantation—about half of them free laborers, so called, and about half of them convicts. The only difference between the free laborers and the others was that the free laborers could come and go as they pleased, at night —that is, they were not locked up at night, and were not, as a general thing, whipped for slight offenses.

The troubles of the free laborers began at the close of the ten-year period. To a man they all refused to sign new contracts—even for one year, not to say anything of ten years. And just when we thought that our bondage was at an end we found that it had really just begun. Two or three years before, or about a year and a half after the Senator had started his camp, he had established a large store, which was called the commissary. All of us free laborers were compelled to buy our supplies—food, clothing, etc.—from that store. We never used any money in our dealings with the commissary, only tickets or orders, and we had a general settlement once each year, in October. In this store we were charged all sorts of high prices for goods, because every year we would come out in debt to our employer. If not that, we seldom had more than $5 or $10 coming to us—and that for a whole year's work. Well, at the close of the tenth year, when we kicked and meant to leave the Senator, he said to some of us with a smile (and I never will forget that smile—I can see it now):

"Boys, I'm sorry you're going to leave me. I hope you will do well in your new places—so well that you will be able to pay me the little balances which most of you owe me."

Word was sent out for all of us to meet him at the commissary at 2 o'clock. There he told us that, after we had signed what he called a written acknowledgement of our debts, we might go and look for new places. The storekeeper took us one by one and read to us statements of our accounts. According to the books there was no man of us who owed the Senator less than $100; some of us were put down for as much as $200. I owed $165, according to the bookkeeper. These debts were not accumulated during one year, but ran back for three and four years, so we were told—in spite of the fact that we understood that we had had a full settlement at the end of each year. But no one of us would have dared to dispute a white man's word— oh, no; not in those days. Besides, we fellows didn't care anything about the amounts—we were after getting away; and we had been told that we might too, if we signed the acknowledgment. We would have signed anything, just to get away. So we stepped up, we did, and made our marks. That same night we were rounded up by a constable and ten or twelve white men, who aided him, and we were locked up, every one of us, in one of the Senator's stockades. The next morning it was explained to us by the two guards appointed to watch us that, in the papers we had signed the day before, we had not only made acknowledgement of our indebtedness, but that we had also agreed to work for the Senator until the debts were paid by hard labor. And from that day forward we were treated just like convicts. Really we had made ourselves lifetime slaves, or peons, as the laws called us. But call it slavery, peonage, or what not, the truth is we lived in a hell on earth what time we spent in the Senator's peon camp.

I lived in that camp, as a peon, for nearly three years. My wife fared better than I did, as did the wives of some of the other Negroes, because the white men about the camp used these unfortunate creatures as their mistresses. When I was first put in the stockade my wife was still kept for a while in the "Big House," but my little boy, who was only nine years old, was given away to a Negro family across the river in South Carolina, and I never saw or heard of him after that. When I left the camp my wife had had two children by some one of the white bosses, and she was living in a fairly good shape in a little house off to herself. But the poor Negro women who were not in the class with my wife fared about as bad as the helpless Negro men. Most of the time the women who were peons or convicts were compelled to wear men's clothes. Sometimes, when I have seen them dressed like men, and plowing or hoeing or hauling logs or working at the blacksmith's trade, just the same as men, my heart would bleed and my blood would boil, but I was powerless to raise a hand. It would have meant death on the spot to have said a word. Of the first six women brought to the camp, two of them gave birth to children after they had been there more than twelve months—and the babies had white men for their fathers!

The stockades in which we slept, were, I believe, the filthiest places in the world. They were cesspools of nastiness. During the thirteen years that I was there I am willing to swear that a mattress was never moved after it had been brought there, except to turn it over once or twice a month. No sheets were used, only dark-colored blankets. Most of the men slept every night in the clothing that they had worked in all day. Some of the worst characters were made to sleep in chairs. The doors were locked and barred, each night, and tallow-candles were the only lights allowed. Really the stockades were but little more than cow sheds, horse stables, or hog pens. Strange to say, not a great number of these people died while I was there, though a great many came away maimed and bruised and, in some cases, disabled for life. As far as I can remember only about ten died during the last ten years that I was there, two of these being killed outright by the guards for trivial offenses.

It was a hard school that peon camp was, but I learned more there in a few short months by contact with those poor fellows from the outside world than ever I had known before. Most of what I learned was evil, and I now know that I should have been better off without the knowledge, but much of what I learned was helpful to me. Barring two or three severe and brutal whippings which I received, I got along very well, all things considered; but the system is damnable. A favorite way of whipping a man was to strap him down to a log, flat on his back, and spank him fifty or sixty times on his bare feet with a shingle or a huge piece of plank. When the man would get up with sore and blistered feet and an aching body, if he could not then keep up with the other men at work he would be strapped to the log again, this time face downward, and would be lashed with a buggy trace on his bare back. When a woman had to be whipped it was usually done in private, though they would be compelled to fall down across a barrel or something of the kind and receive the licks on their backsides.

The working day on a peon farm begins with sunrise and ends when the sun goes down; or, in other words, the average peon works from ten to twelve hours each day, with one hour (from 12 o'clock to 1 o'clock) for dinner. Hot or cold, sun or rain, this is the rule. As to their meals, the laborers are divided up into squads or companies, just the same as soldiers in a great military camp would be. Two or three men in each stockade are appointed as cooks. From thirty to forty men report to each cook. In the warm months (or eight or nine months out of the year) the cooking is done on the outside, just behind the stockades; in the cold months the cooking is done inside the stockades. Each peon is provided with a great big tin cup, a flat tin pan and two big tin spoons. No knives or forks are ever seen, except those used by the cooks. At meal time the peons pass in single file before the cooks, and hold out their pans and cups to receive their allowances. Cow peas (red or white, which when boiled turn black), fat bacon and old-fashioned Georgia cornbread, baked in pones from one to two and three inches thick, made up the chief articles of food. Black coffee, black molasses and brown sugar are also used abundantly. Once in a great while, on Sundays, biscuits would be made, but they would always be made from the kind of flour called "shorts." As a rule, breakfast consisted of coffee, fried bacon, cornbread, and some-times molasses—and one "helping" of each was all that was allowed. Peas, boiled with huge hunks of fat bacon, and a hoe-cake, as big as a man's hand, usually answered for dinner. Sometimes this dinner bill of fare gave place to bacon and greens (collard or turnip) and pot liquor. Though we raised corn, potatoes and other vegetables, we never got a chance at such things unless we could steal them and cook them secretly. Supper consisted of coffee, fried bacon and molasses. But, although the food was limited to cer-tain things, I am sure we all got a plenty of the things allowed. As coarse as these things were, we kept, as a rule, fat and sleek and as strong as mules. And that, too, in spite of the fact that we had no special arrangements for taking regular baths, and no very great effort was made to keep us regularly in clean clothes. No tables were used or allowed. In summer we would sit down on the ground and eat our meals, and in winter we would sit around inside the filthy stockades. Each man was his own dishwasher—that is to say, each man was responsible for the care of his pan and cup and spoons. My dishes got washed about once a week!

Today, I am told, there are six or seven of these private camps in Georgia —that is to say, camps where most of the convicts are leased from the State of Georgia. But there are hundreds and hundreds of farms all over the State where Negroes, and in some cases poor white folks, are held in bondage on the ground that they are working out debts, or where the contracts which they have made hold them in a kind of perpetual bondage, because, under those contracts they may not quit one employer and hire out to another except by and with the knowledge and consent of the former employer.

One of the usual ways to secure laborers for a large peonage camp is for the proprietor to send out an agent to the little courts in the towns and villages, and where a man charged with some petty offense has no friends or money the agent will urge him to plead guilty, with the understanding that the agent will pay his fine, and in that way save him from the disgrace of being sent to jail or the chain-gang! For this high favor the man must sign beforehand a paper signifying his willingness to go to the farm and work out the amount of the fine imposed. When he reaches the farm he has to be fed and clothed, to be sure, and these things are charged up to his account. By the time he has worked out his first debt another is hanging over his head, and so on and so on, by a sort of endless chain, for an indefinite period, as in every case the indebtedness is arbitrarily arranged by the employer. In many cases it is very evident that the court officials are in collusion with the proprietors or agents, and that they divide the "graft" among themselves. As an example of this dickering among the whites, every year many convicts were brought to the Senator's camp from a certain county in South Georgia, 'way down in the turpentine district. The majority of these men were charged with adultery, which is an offense against the laws of the great and sovereign State of Georgia! Upon inquiry I learned that down in that county a number of Negro lewd women were employed by certain white men to entice Negro men into their houses; and then, on a certain night, at a given signal, when all was in readiness, raids would be made by the officers upon these houses, and the men would be arrested and charged with living in adultery. Nine out of ten of these men, so arrested and so charged, would find their way ultimately to some convict camp, and, as I said, many of them found their way every year to the Senator's camp while I was there. The low-down women were never punished in any way. On the contrary, I was told that they always seemed to stand in high favor with the sheriffs, constables and other officers. There can be no room to doubt that they assisted very materially in furnishing laborers for the prison pens of Georgia, and the belief was general among the men that they were regularly paid for their work. I could tell more, but I've said enough to make anybody's heart sick. This great and terrible iniquity is, I know, widespread throughout Georgia and many other Southern States.

But I didn't tell you how I got out. I didn't get out—they put me out. When I had served as a peon for nearly three years—and you remember that they claimed I owed them only $165—when I had served for nearly three years one of the bosses came to me and said that my time was up. He happened to be the one who was said to be living with my wife. He gave me a new suit of overalls, which cost about seventy-five cents, took me in a buggy and carried me across the Broad River into South Carolina, set me down and told me to "git." I didn't have a cent of money, and I wasn't feeling well, but somehow I managed to get a move on me. I begged my way to Columbia. In two or three days I ran across a man looking for laborers to carry to Birmingham, and I joined his gang. I have been here in the Birmingham district since they released me, and I reckon I'll die either in a coal mine or an iron furnace. It don't make much difference which. Either is better than a Georgia peon camp. And a Georgia peon camp is hell itself!

VALEDICTORY ADDRESS OF THE LAST BLACK
SOUTHERN CONGRESSMAN

George H. White / Address to the United States House of Representatives, 1901

The Populist Movement provided a temporary rapprochement of whites and blacks in the South and the Midwest. Large numbers of black farmers joined the Populist Colored Alliance, which tried unsuccessfully to mount a cotton-pickers' strike against the white planters in the South in 1891. Later in the 1890's, blacks were selected as delegates to Populist party conventions in various states and served in policy-making roles in these bodies. In the Southern states, the party platforms of the Populists attacked lynching and the convict-lease system and supported black suffrage.

In the North Carolina election of 1896, a fusion of Populists and black Republicans resulted in the election of a black man, George H. White, to the United States House of Representatives. White was reelected in 1898, but the fusion then fell apart, and the Democrats, through fraud, intimidation, and violence, regained control of the state. In fact, White was the last Southern black man to serve in either house of the United States Congress.

The address reprinted here was White's swan song in Congress. In it, he gave the details of his defeat by fraud the previous fall and declared—prophetically—that black men would return.

want to enter a plea for the colored man, the colored woman, the colored boy, and the colored girl of this country. I would not thus digress from the question at issue and detain the House in a discussion of the interests of this particular people at this time but for the constant and the persistent efforts of certain gentlemen upon this floor to mold and rivet public sentiment against us as a people and to lose no opportunity to hold up the unfortunate few who commit crimes and depredations and lead lives of infamy and shame, as other races do, as fair specimens of representatives of the entire colored race. And at no time, perhaps, during the Fifty-sixth Congress were these charges and countercharges, containing, as they do, slanderous statements, more persistently magnified and pressed upon the attention of the nation than during the consideration of the recent reapportionment bill, which is now a law. As stated some days ago on this floor by me, I then sought diligently to obtain an opportunity to answer some of the statements made by gentlemen from different States, but the privilege was denied me; and I therefore must embrace this opportunity to say, out of season, perhaps, that which I was not permitted to say in season.

In the catalogue of members of Congress in this House perhaps none have been more persistent in their determination to bring the black man into disrepute and, with a labored effort, to show that he was unworthy of the right of citizenship than my colleague from North Carolina, Mr. Kitchin. During the first session of this Congress, while the Constitutional amendment was pending in North Carolina, he labored long and hard to show that the white race was at all times and under all circumstances superior to the negro by inheritance if not otherwise, and the excuse for his party supporting that amendment, which has since been adopted, was that an illiterate negro was unfit to participate in making the laws of a sovereign State and the administration and execution of them; but an illiterate white man living by his side, with no more or perhaps not as much property, with no more exalted character, no higher thoughts of civilization, no more knowledge of the handicraft of government, had by birth, because he was white, inherited some peculiar qualification, clear, I presume, only in the mind of the gentleman who endeavored to impress it upon others, that entitled him to vote, though he knew nothing whatever of letters. It is true, in my opinion, that men brood over things at times which they would have exist until they fool themselves and actually, sometimes honestly, believe that such things do exist.

I would like to call the gentleman's attention to the fact that the Constitution of the United States forbids the granting of any title of nobility to any citizen thereof, and while it does not in letters forbid the inheritance of this superior caste, I believe in the fertile imagination of the gentleman promulgating it, his position is at least in conflict with the spirit of that organic

---

FROM George H. White, *Congressional Record*, 56th Congress, 2nd Session (January 29, 1901), pp. 1634–38.

law of the land. He insists and, I believe, has introduced a resolution in this House for the repeal of the fifteenth amendment to the Constitution. As an excuse for his peculiar notions about the exercise of the right of franchise by citizens of the United States of different nationality, perhaps it would not be amiss to call the attention of this House to a few facts and figures surrounding his birth and rearing. To begin with, he was born in one of the counties in my district, Halifax, a rather significant name.

I might state as a further general fact that the Democrats of North Carolina got possession of the State and local government since my last election in 1898, and that I bid adieu to these historic walls on the 4th day of next March, and that the brother of Mr. Kitchin will succeed me. Comment is unnecessary. In the town where this young gentleman was born, at the general election last August for the adoption of the constitutional amendment, and the general election for State and county officers, Scotland Neck had a registered white vote of 395, most of whom of course were Democrats, and a registered colored vote of 534, virtually if not all of whom were Republicans, and so voted. When the count was announced, however, there were 831 Democrats to 75 Republicans; but in the town of Halifax, same county, the result was much more pronounced.

In that town the registered Republican vote was 345, and the total registered vote of the township was 539, but when the count was announced it stood 990 Democrats to 41 Republicans, or 492 more Democratic votes counted than were registered votes in the township. Comment here is unnecessary, nor do I think it necessary for anyone to wonder at the peculiar notion my colleague has with reference to the manner of voting and the method of counting those votes, nor is it to be a wonder that he is a member of this Congress, having been brought up and educated in such wonderful notions of dealing out fair-handed justice to his fellow-man.

It would be unfair, however, for me to leave the inference upon the minds of those who hear me that all of the white people of the State of North Carolina hold views with Mr. Kitchin and think as he does. Thank God there are many noble exceptions to the example he sets, that, too, in the Democratic party; men who have never been afraid that one uneducated, poor, depressed negro could put to flight and chase into degradation two educated, wealthy, thrifty white men. There never has been, nor ever will be, any negro domination in that State, and no one knows it any better than the Democratic party. It is a convenient howl, however, often resorted to in order to consummate a diabolical purpose by scaring the weak and gullible whites into support of measures and men suitable to the demagogue and the ambitious office seeker, whose crave for office overshadows and puts to flight all other considerations, fair or unfair.

As I stated on a former occasion, this young statesman has ample time to learn better and more useful knowledge than he has exhibited in many of his speeches upon this floor, and I again plead for him the statute of youth for the wild and spasmodic notions which he has endeavored to rivet upon his colleagues and this country. But I regret that Mr. Kitchin is not alone upon this floor in these peculiar notions advanced. I quote from another young member of Congress, hailing from the State of Alabama [Mr. Underwood]:

> Mr. Speaker, in five minutes the issues involved in this case can not be discussed. I was in hopes that this question would not come up at this session of Congress. When the fourteenth amendment was originally adopted it was the intention of the legislative body that enacted it and of the people who ratified it to force the Southern people to give the elective franchise to the negro. That was the real purpose of the fourteenth amendment. It failed in that purpose. The fifteenth amendment was adopted for the same purpose. That was successful for the time being. It has proved a lamentable mistake, not only to the people of the South, but to the people of the North; not only to the Democratic party, but to the Republican party.
>
> The time has now come when the bitterness of civil strife has passed. The people of the South, with fairness and justice to themselves and fairness to that race that has been forced among them—the negro race—are attempting to work away from those conditions; not to oppress or to put their foot on the neck of the negro race, but to protect their homes and their property against misgovernment and at the same time give this inferior race a chance to grow up and acquire their civilization. When you bring this resolution before this House and thrust it as a firebrand into the legislation here, you do more injury to the negro race of the South than any man has done since the fifteenth amendment was originally enacted. I tell you, sirs, there is but one way to solve this problem. You gentlemen of the North, who do not live among them and do not know the conditions, can not solve it.
>
> We of the South are trying, as God is our judge, to solve it fairly to both races. It can not be done in a day or a week; and I appeal to you, if you are in favor of the upbuilding of the negro race, if you are in favor of honest governments in the Southern States, if you are willing to let us protect our homes and our property—yes, and the investments that you have brought there among us—then I say to you, let us send this resolution to a committee where it may die and never be heard of again. When we have done that, when we have worked out the problem and put it upon a fair basis then if we are getting more representation than we are entitled to, five or six or ten years from now come to us with the proposition fairly to repeal both the fourteenth and fifteenth amendments and substitute in their place a constitutional amendment that will put representation on a basis that we can all agree is fair and equitable. Do not let us drive it along party lines.

It is an undisputed fact that the negro vote in the State of Alabama, as well as most of the other Southern States, have been effectively suppressed, either one way or the other—in some instances by constitutional amendment and State legislation, in others by cold-blooded fraud and intimidation, but whatever the method pursued, it is not denied, but frankly admitted in the speeches in this House, that the black vote has been eliminated to a large extent. Then, when some of us insist that the plain letter of the Constitution of the United States, which all of us have sworn to support, should be carried out, as expressed in the second section of the fourteenth amendment thereof, to wit:

> Representatives shall be apportioned among the several States according to their respective numbers, counting the whole number of persons in each State, excluding Indians not taxed. But when the right to vote at any election for the choice of electors for President and Vice-President of the United States, Representatives in Congress, the executive and judicial officers of a State, or the members of a legislature thereof, is denied to any of the male inhabitants of such State, being twenty-one years of age, and citizens of the United States, or in any way abridged, except for participation in rebellion, or other crime, the basis of representation therein shall be reduced in proportion which the number of such male citizens shall bear to the whole number of male citizens twenty-one years of age in such State.

That section makes the duty of every member of Congress plain, and yet the gentleman from Alabama [Mr. Underwood] says that the attempt to enforce this section of the organic law is the throwing down of firebrands, and notifies the world that this attempt to execute the highest law of the land will be retaliated by the South, and the inference is that the negro will be even more severely punished than the horrors through which he has already come.

Let me make it plain: The divine law, as well as most of the State laws, says, in substance: "He that sheddeth man's blood, by man shall his blood be shed." A highwayman commits murder, and when the officers of the law undertake to arrest, try, and punish him commensurate with the enormity of his crime, he straightens himself up to his full height and defiantly says to them: "Let me alone; I will not be arrested, I will not be tried, I'll have none of the execution of your laws, and in the event you attempt to execute your laws upon me, I will see to it that many more men, women, or children are murdered."

Here's the plain letter of the Constitution, the plain, simple, sworn duty of every member of Congress; yet these gentlemen from the South say "Yes, we have violated your Constitution of the nation; we regarded it as a local necessity; and now, if you undertake to punish us as the Constitution prescribes, we will see to it that our former deeds of disloyalty to that instrument, our former acts of disfranchisement and opposition to the highest law of the land will be repeated many fold."

Not content with all that has been done to the black man, not because of any deeds that he has done, Mr. Underwood advances the startling information that these people have been thrust upon the whites of the South, forgetting, perhaps, the horrors of the slave trade, the unspeakable horrors of the transit from the shores of Africa by means of the middle passage to the

American clime; the enforced bondage of the blacks and their descendants for two and a half centuries in the United States, now, for the first time perhaps in the history of our lives, the information comes that these poor, helpless, and in the main inoffensive people were thrust upon our Southern brethren.

Individually, and so far as my race is concerned, I care but little about the reduction of Southern representation, except in so far as it becomes my duty to aid in the proper execution of all the laws of the land in whatever sphere in which I may be placed. Such reduction in representation, it is true, would make more secure the installment of the great Republican party in power for many years to come in all of its branches, and at the same time enable that great party to be able to dispense with the further support of the loyal negro vote; and I might here parenthetically state that there are some members of the Republican party to-day—"lily whites," if you please— who, after receiving the unalloyed support of the negro vote for over thirty years, now feel that they have grown a little too good for association with him politically, and are disposed to dump him overboard. I am glad to observe, however, that this class constitutes a very small percentage of those to whom we have always looked for friendship and protection.

I wish to quote from another Southern gentleman, not so young as my other friends, and who always commands attention in this House by his wit and humor, even though his speeches may not be edifying and instructive. I refer to Mr. Otey, of Virginia, and quote from him in a recent speech on this floor, as follows:

> Justice is merely relative. It can exist between equals. It can exist among homogeneous people. Among equals—among heterogeneous people—it never has and, in the very nature of things, it never will obtain. It can exist among lions but between lions and lambs, never. If justice were absolute, lions must of necessity perish. Open his ponderous jaws and find the strong teeth which God has made expressly to chew lamb's flesh! When the Society for the Prevention of Cruelty to Animals shall overcome this difficulty, men may hope to settle the race question along sentimental lines, not sooner.
>
> These thoughts on the negro are from the pen, in the main, of one who has studied the negro question, and it was after I heard the gentleman from North Carolina, and after the introduction of the Crumpacker bill, that they occurred to me peculiarly appropriate.

I am wholly at sea as to just what Mr. Otey had in view in advancing the thoughts contained in the above quotation, unless he wishes to extend the simile and apply the lion as a white man and the negro as a lamb. In that case we will gladly accept the comparison, for of all animals known in God's creation the lamb is the most inoffensive, and has been in all ages held up as a badge of innocence. But what will my good friend of Virginia do with the Bible, for God says that He created all men of one flesh and blood? Again, we insist on having one race—the lion clothed with great strength, vicious, and with destructive propensities, while the other is weak, good natured, inoffensive, and useful—what will he do with all the heterogeneous intermediate animals, ranging all the way from the pure lion to the pure lamb, found on the plantations of every Southern State in the Union?

I regard his borrowed thoughts, as he admits they are, as very inaptly applied. However, it has perhaps served the purpose for which he intended it—the attempt to show the inferiority of the one and the superiority of the other. I fear I am giving too much time in the consideration of these personal comments of members of Congress, but I trust I will be pardoned for making a passing reference to one more gentleman—Mr. Wilson of South Carolina—who, in the early part of this month, made a speech some parts of which did great credit to him, showing, as it did, capacity for collating, arranging, and advancing thoughts of others and of making a pretty strong argument out of a very poor case.

If he had stopped there, while not agreeing with him, many of us would have been forced to admit that he had done well. But his purpose was incomplete until he dragged in the reconstruction days and held up to scorn and ridicule the few ignorant, gullible, and perhaps purchasable negroes who served in the State legislature of South Carolina over thirty years ago. Not a word did he say about the unscrupulous white men, in the main bummers who followed in the wake of the Federal Army and settled themselves in the Southern States, and preyed upon the ignorant and unskilled minds of the colored people, looted the States of their wealth, brought into lowest disrepute the ignorant colored people, then hied away to their Northern homes for ease and comfort the balance of their lives, or joined the Democratic party to obtain social recognition, and have greatly aided in depressing and further degrading those whom they had used as easy tools to accomplish a diabolical purpose.

These few ignorant men who chanced at that time to hold office are given as a reason why the black man should not be permitted to participate in the affairs of the Government which he is forced to pay taxes to support. He insists that they, the Southern whites, are the black man's best friend, and that they are taking him by the hand and trying to lift him up; that they are educating him. For all that he and all Southern people have done in this regard, I wish in behalf of the colored people of the South to extend our thanks. We are not ungrateful to friends, but feel that our toil has made our friends able to contribute the stinty pittance which we have received at their hands.

I read in a Democratic paper a few days ago, the Washington Times, an extract taken from a South Carolina paper, which was intended to exhibit the eagerness with which the negro is grasping every opportunity for educating himself. The clipping showed that the money for each white child in the State ranged from three to five times as much per capita as was given to each colored child. This is helping us some, but not to the extent that one would infer from the gentleman's speech.

If the gentleman to whom I have referred will pardon me, I would like to advance the statement that the musty records of 1868, filed away in the archives of Southern capitols, as to what the negro was thirty-two years ago, is not a proper standard by which the negro living on the threshold of the twentieth century should be measured. Since that time we have reduced the illiteracy of the race at least 45 per cent. We have written and published near 500 books. We have nearly 300 newspapers, 3 of which are dailies. We have now in practice over 2,000 lawyers and a corresponding number of doctors. We have accumulated over $12,000,000 worth of school property and about $40,000,000 worth of church property. We have about 140,000 farms and homes, valued at in the neighborhood of $750,000,000, and personal property valued at about $170,000,000. We have raised about $11,000,000 for educational purposes, and the property per capita for every colored man, woman, and child in the United States is estimated at $75.

We are operating successfully several banks, commercial enterprises among our people in the Southland, including 1 silk mill and 1 cotton factory. We have 32,000 teachers in the schools of the country; we have built, with the aid of our friends, about 2,000 churches, and support 7 colleges, 17 academies, 50 high schools, 5 law schools, 5 medical schools, and 25 theological seminaries. We have over 600,000 acres of land in the South alone. The cotton produced, mainly by black labor, has increased from 4,669,770 bales in 1860 to 11,235,000 in 1899. All this we have done under the most adverse circumstances. We have done it in the face of lynching, burning at the stake, with the humiliation of "Jim Crow" cars, the disfranchisement of our male citizens, slander and degradation of our women, with the factories closed against us, no negro permitted to be conductor on the railway cars, whether run through the streets of our cities or across the prairies of our great country, no negro permitted to run as engineer on a locomotive, most of the mines closed against us. Labor unions—carpenters, painters, brick masons, machinists, hackmen, and those supplying nearly every conceivable avocation for livelihood have banded themselves together to better their condition, but, with few exceptions, the black face has been left out. The negroes are seldom employed in our mercantile stores. At this we do not wonder. Some day we hope to have them employed in our own stores. With all these odds against us, we are forging our way ahead, slowly, perhaps, but surely. You may tie us and then taunt us for a lack of bravery, but one day we will break the bonds. You may use our labor for two and a half centuries and then taunt us for our poverty, but let me remind you we will not always remain poor. You may withhold even the knowledge of how to read God's word and learn the way from earth to glory and then taunt us for our ignorance, but we would remind you that there is plenty of room at the top, and we are climbing.

After enforced debauchery, with the many kindred horrors incident to slavery, it comes with ill grace from the perpetrators of these deeds to hold up the shortcomings of some of our race to ridicule and scorn.

"The new man, the slave who has grown out of the ashes of thirty-five years ago, is inducted into the political and social system, cast into the arena of manhood, where he constitutes a new element and becomes a competitor for all its emoluments. He is put upon trial to test his ability to be counted worthy of freedom, worthy of the elective franchise; and after thirty-five years of struggling against almost insurmountable odds, under conditions but little removed from slavery itself, he asks a fair and just judgment, not of those whose prejudice has endeavored to forestall, to frustrate his every forward movement, rather those who have lent a helping hand, that he might demonstrate the truth of 'the fatherhood of God and the brotherhood of man.' "

Mr. Chairman, permit me to digress for a few moments for the purpose of calling the attention of the House to two bills which I regard as important, introduced by me in the early part of the first session of this Congress. The first was to give the United States control and entire jurisdiction over all cases of lynching and death by mob violence. During the last session of this Congress I took occasion to address myself in detail to this particular measure, but with all my efforts the bill still sweetly sleeps in the room of the committee to which it was referred. The necessity of legislation along this line is daily being demonstrated. The arena of the lyncher no longer is confined to Southern climes, but is stretching its hydra head over all parts of the Union.

> Sow the seed of a tarnished name—
> You sow the seed of eternal shame.

It is needless to ask what the harvest will be. You may dodge this question now; you may defer it to a more seasonable day; you may, as the gentleman from Maine, Mr. Littlefield, puts it—

> Waddle in and waddle out,
> Until the mind was left in doubt,
> Whether the snake that made the track
> Was going south or coming back.

This evil peculiar to America, yes, to the United States, must be met somehow, some day.

The other bill to which I wish to call attention is one introduced by me to appropriate $1,000,000 to reimburse depositors of the late Freedman's Savings and Trust Company.

A bill making appropriation for a similar purpose passed the Senate in the first session of the Fiftieth Congress. It was recommended by President Cleveland, and was urged by the Comptroller of the Currency, Mr. Trenholm, in 1886. I can not press home to your minds this matter more strongly than by reproducing the report of the Committee on Banking and Currency, made by Mr. Wilkins on the Senate bill above referred to, as follows:

In March, 1865, the Freedman's Savings and Trust Company was incorporated by the Congress of the United States to meet the economic and commercial necessities of 7,000,000 of colored people recently emancipated.

Its incorporators, 50 in number, were named in the act authorizing its erection, and embraced the names of leading philanthropic citizens of the United States, whose names, as was intended, commended the institution to those inexperienced, simple-minded people, who are to-day its principal creditors.

The Freedman's Bank, as it is popularly called, was designed originally to perform for this trustful people the functions, as its name implies, of a savings bank, and none other than those hitherto held in slavery or their descendants were to become its depositors.

Its purpose was (to quote the paragraph in the original law)—

To receive on deposit such sums of money as may from time to time be offered therefor, by or in behalf of persons hitherto held in slavery in the United States, or their descendants, and investing the same in the stocks, bonds, and Treasury notes, or other securities of the United States.

The distinction provided in the bill in favor of the payment of "such persons in whole or in part of African descent" rests upon the foregoing paragraph of the original law, and no persons other than those named have the right to make use of this institution in any manner; neither have they the right to acquire by any means any interest in its assets.

For four years after the organization of the Freedman's Savings and Trust Company the laws seemed to have been honestly observed by its officers and the provisions in its charter faithfully recognized. Congress itself, however, seems to have been derelict in its duty. One section of the original grant provided that the books of the institution were to be open at all times to inspection and examination of officers appointed by Congress to conduct the same, yet it does not appear that Congress ever appointed an officer for this purpose, nor has an examination of the charter contemplated by Congress ever been made. The officers of the bank were to give bonds. There is nothing in the records to show that any bond was ever executed. Any proper examination would have developed this fact, and probably great loss would have been prevented thereby. In 1870 Congress changed or amended the charter without the knowledge or consent of those who had intrusted their savings to its custody.

This amendment embodied a radical change in the investment of these deposits by providing that instead of the safe, conservative, and prudent provision in the original charter "that two-thirds of all the deposits should be invested exclusively in Government securities," the dangerous privilege of allowing the irresponsible officers to loan one-half of its assets in bonds and mortgages and other securities, invest in and improve real estate without inspection, without examination, or responsibility on the part of its officers. The institution could only go on to a certain bankruptcy. In May, 1870, Congress amended the charter, and from that date began the speculative, dishonest transactions upon the part of those controlling the institution until resulting in ultimate suspension and failure, with consequent disastrous loss to this innocent and trustful people.

It is contended by your committee that there was a moral responsibility, at least, if not an equitable responsibility, assumed by the Government when Congress changed the original charter of the company as to the nature of its loans and investments, when it failed to have the consent of the depositors, because of which change most of its losses were incurred. This ought to be regarded a very strong argument in favor of this bill.

Then, again, Congress undertook the supervision of the trust and failed, so far as your committee can ascertain, to carry out their undertaking.

. . . .

May I hope that the Committee on Banking and Currency who has charge of this measure will yet see its way clear to do tardy justice, long deferred, to this much wronged and unsuspecting people. If individual sections of the country, individual political parties can afford to commit deeds of wrong against us, certainly a great nation like ours will see to it that a people so loyal to its flag as the black man has shown himself in every war from the birth of the Union to this day, will not permit this obligation to go longer uncanceled.

Now, Mr. Chairman, before concluding my remarks I want to submit a brief recipe for the solution of the so-called American negro problem. He asks no special favors, but simply demands that he be given the same chance for existence, for earning a livelihood, for raising himself in the scales of manhood and womanhood that are accorded to kindred nationalities. Treat him as a man; go into his home and learn of his social conditions; learn of his cares, his troubles, and his hopes for the future; gain his confidence; open the doors of industry to him; let the word "negro," "colored," and "black" be stricken from all the organizations enumerated in the federation of labor.

Help him to overcome his weaknesses, punish the crime-committing class by the courts of the land, measure the standard of the race by its best material, cease to mold prejudicial and unjust public sentiment against him, and my word for it, he will learn to support, hold up the hands of, and join in with that political party, that institution, whether secular or religious, in every community where he lives, which is destined to do the greatest good for the greatest number. Obliterate race hatred, party prejudice, and help us to achieve nobler ends, greater results, and become more satisfactory citizens to our brother in white.

This, Mr. Chairman, is perhaps the negroes' temporary farewell to the American Congress; but let me say, Phœnix-like he will rise up some day and come again. These parting words are in behalf of an outraged, heart-broken, bruised, and bleeding, but God-fearing people, faithful, industrious, loyal people—rising people, full of potential force.

Mr. Chairman, in the trial of Lord Bacon, when the court disturbed the counsel for the defendant, Sir Walter Raleigh raised himself up to his full height and, addressing the court, said:

Sir, I am pleading for the life of a human being.

The only apology that I have to make for the earnestness with which I have spoken is that I am pleading for the life, the liberty, the future happiness, and manhood suffrage for one-eighth of the entire population of the United States. [Loud applause.]

6

SUGGESTIONS FOR FURTHER READING

Rayford W. Logan calls the last quarter of the nineteenth century the "nadir of Afro-American history" in his book *The Negro in American Life and Thought: The Nadir, 1877–1901* (Dial, 1954), published in paperback under the title *The Betrayal of the Negro**. The development of legal segregation is described in C. Vann Woodward, *The Strange Career of Jim Crow** (rev. ed., Oxford University Press, 1955). Charles E. Wynes has edited a collection of essays dealing with various aspects of black life during this period, under the deceptive title *The Negro in the South Since 1865** (University of Alabama Press, 1965).

Works describing the condition of the black man in particular states are Charles E. Wynes, *Race Relations in Virginia, 1870–1902* (University of Virginia Press, 1961); George B. Tindall, *South Carolina Negroes, 1877–1900** (University of South Carolina Press, 1952); and Frenise A. Logan, *The Negro in North Carolina, 1876–1894* (University of North Carolina Press, 1964). The relationship between the black man and Populism is explored by Helen G. Edmonds in *The Negro and Fusion Politics in North Carolina, 1894–1901* (University of North Carolina Press, 1951). Paul Lewinson treats the disfranchisement of blacks in *Race, Class and Party: A History of Negro Suffrage and White Politics in the South** (Oxford University Press, 1932). W. E. B. Du Bois presents a study in depth of one urban black community in *The Philadelphia Negro: A Social Study** (University of Pennsylvania Press, 1899).

Afro-American thought during the last quarter of the century is represented by the relevant selections of Howard Brotz (ed.), *Negro Social and Political Thought, 1850–1920** (Basic Books, 1966), and a work by the leading black journalist of the time, T. Thomas Fortune, *Black and White: Land, Labor and Politics in the South* (Fords, Howard, and Hulbert, 1884).

7 THE ORGANIZATION OF PROTEST

Out of the despair of the 1890's emerged the most powerful black man ever to operate on the American scene, Booker T. Washington. Born into slavery about 1856, he was a man of driving ambition and obvious ability. By 1895, when he made his famous Atlanta Exposition address, he had achieved national prominence. Washington decided to concentrate on the traits that "decent" whites were prepared to allow black men to develop. He emphasized thrift, hard work, self-help, and industrial education and played down political and social rights. From his base as principal of Tuskegee Normal and Industrial Institute in Alabama, Washington tried to direct the affairs of black men in America.

Because of his policy of apparent accommodation to the racial policies of the dominant society, Washington became the conduit through which white financial support and federal political appointments flowed to the black community. Washington seemed to hold the average ignorant rural black to blame for his condition and encouraged him to better himself through thrift and accumulation—the gospel of wealth philosophy. What he failed to realize was that the rural black would gladly have been thrifty had there been anything for him to save. Washington never really came to grips with the rural South. He was more interested in organizing the growing black middle class, and to that end he founded, with the financial backing of Andrew Carnegie, the National Negro Business League to preach the virtues of black business development in black communities. Washington seemed convinced that if black people could accumulate enough wealth, they could win the acceptance of white society.

It must be pointed out that, though Washington's public posture was accommodative, privately he was actively engaged in trying to reduce the discrimination suffered by blacks. He spent a great deal of money and effort behind the scenes trying to halt disfranchisement and segregation. In retrospect, it appears that his greatest failing was his desire for personal power and prestige. He made every effort possible to stifle criticism of himself and his policies by other black men, who often felt that other voices should be heard even while they supported his policies.

By 1903, it was clear that Washington's greatest competition for the leadership of the black community would come from the brilliant and aggressive William Edward Burghardt Du Bois. Du Bois, the first black to receive a Ph.D. from Harvard, had as his original ambition to make a complete study of the history and the present condition of black people in America. Although he had worked with Washington on several projects in the first years of the century, Du Bois found Washington's inflexibility and lack of receptivity to criticism a barrier to their further cooperation.

In 1905, with the support of other black intellectuals, Du Bois founded the Niagara Movement to protest against the increasing discrimination met by blacks in the United States and to work for the reestablishment of the black man's right to vote and the elimination of race or color distinctions wherever they occurred. Although the concrete gains of the Movement were few, its manner of operation was the prototype for that of many future organizations.

Washington strongly opposed the Niagara group and used every method at his disposal to hinder its development. He bribed newspaper editors to ignore or attack the Movement and its leaders, placed undercover agents in its midst to warn him of impending programs, prevented members of the group from receiving political office, and had funds cut off from schools where the leaders of the Movement taught. Not surprisingly, this opposition was seriously detrimental to the growth of the Movement.

As the Niagara Movement was beginning to lose strength, a new organization was coming into being as a result of the desire of certain Northern white philanthropists and social workers to offer an alternative to Washington's program for racial uplift. Some of these whites had previously supported Washington but had come to feel that his monopoly in the field of race relations was not best for black people. In 1909, a call went out for a National Negro Conference, to be held in New York City. Many members of the Niagara Movement attended, along with a number of liberal whites who were political Progressives. The next year, the National Association for the Advancement of Colored People (NAACP) was founded to carry out the program formulated at the National Negro Conference. Du Bois was the only officer of the original NAACP who was black.

Although Du Bois would have preferred to work primarily with an all-black organization, it became clear to him that the financial support necessary for such a group would not be forthcoming as long as Washington dominated the philanthropic scene. Thus, he agreed to serve as director of research for the fledgling NAACP. When he left Atlanta, where he had been doing scholarly work at Atlanta University, it is said that the city administration gave a sigh of relief, for he had earned a reputation for being troublesome.

Once in New York, against the advice of some of the NAACP board members, Du Bois began to publish a monthly journal, *The Crisis*. This publication was his major interest until he broke with the Association in 1934. Fortunately for Du Bois, *The Crisis* quickly became self-supporting. This freed him from the need for financial support from the Association, which had initially sought to limit his control over the journal and the views presented in it. During the Depression, when the circulation of *The Crisis* dropped rapidly, the NAACP had to subsidize its production once again, and the leadership of the Association seized the opportunity to reassert its control over the journal and attacked Du Bois for his growing separatism.

Du Bois responded with a vigorous attack on the leadership, which he considered to be more interested in keeping the support of whites than in advancing the cause of blacks. Finally convinced that the black people had to take charge of their own liberation, Du Bois left the Association and returned to his work at Atlanta University, from which issued some of his most important writings, notably *Black Reconstruction in America* and the autobiographical *Dusk of Dawn*.

By 1915, the year of the death of Booker T. Washington and the year of the Association's first major court victory, in which the Oklahoma "grandfather" clause was declared unconstitutional by the Supreme Court, the NAACP was clearly embarked on its course as the most important contemporary defense organization for blacks.

In recent years, the NAACP has come under increasing criticism from militant blacks because of its middleclass values and its public posture of moderation. But it must be remembered that as recently as the 1950's several Southern states attempted to ban the Association because of its radicalism.

EDUCATION BEFORE EQUALITY

Booker T. Washington   /   The Atlanta Exposition Address, 1895

When called upon to make one of the opening addresses at the
Cotton States and International Exposition in Atlanta in the fall
of 1895, Booker T. Washington took the opportunity to express
his solution to the "Negro problem." Correctly sensing the mood
of the white world, both North and South, as well as that of many
blacks, he made the proposal known as the Atlanta Compromise.
Appealing to the nativist tendencies of his audience, he reminded
them of what he called the familiarity and fidelity of the Southern
black man, and, rejecting social equality as an immediate goal, he
spoke of building a new South on agricultural and industrial cooperation between the races. A firm believer in inevitable progress,
Washington rejected forced equality in favor of an equality that he
thought the black man could earn through education and hard
work.

The following selection, taken from Washington's autobiography,
includes the address as originally delivered as well as comments
about the response it drew.

The Atlanta Exposition, at which I had been asked to make an address as a
representative of the Negro race, . . . was opened with a short address
from Governor Bullock. After other interesting exercises, including an invo-
cation from Bishop Nelson, of Georgia, a dedicatory ode by Albert Howell,
Jr., and addresses by the President of the Exposition and Mrs. Joseph
Thompson, the President of the Woman's Board, Governor Bullock introduced me with the words, "We have with us to-day a representative of
Negro enterprise and Negro civilization."

When I arose to speak, there was considerable cheering, especially from
the coloured people. As I remember it now, the thing that was uppermost in
my mind was the desire to say something that would cement the friendship
of the races and bring about hearty coöperation between them. So far as my
outward surroundings were concerned, the only thing that I recall distinctly
now is that when I got up, I saw thousands of eyes looking intently into my
face. The following is the address which I delivered:—

Mr. President and Gentlemen of the Board of Directors and Citizens:

One-third of the population of the South is of the Negro race.
No enterprise seeking the material, civil, or moral welfare of this

---

FROM Booker T. Washington, *Up From Slavery* (Boston, 1901), pp. 217–27.

section can disregard this element of our population and reach the highest success. I but convey to you, Mr. President and Directors, the sentiment of the masses of my race when I say that in no way have the value and manhood of the American Negro been more fittingly and generously recognized than by the managers of this magnificent Exposition at every stage of its progress. It is a recognition that will do more to cement the friendship of the two races than any occurrence since the dawn of our freedom.

Not only this, but the opportunity here afforded will awaken among us a new era of industrial progress. Ignorant and inexperienced, it is not strange that in the first years of our new life we began at the top instead of at the bottom; that a seat in Congress or the state legislature was more sought than real estate or industrial skill; that the political convention of stump speaking had more attractions than starting a dairy farm or truck garden.

A ship lost at sea for many days suddenly sighted a friendly vessel. From the mast of the unfortunate vessel was seen a signal, "Water, water; we die of thirst!" The answer from the friendly vessel at once came back, "Cast down your bucket where you are." A second time the signal, "Water, water; send us water!" ran up from the distressed vessel, and was answered, "Cast down your bucket where you are." And a third and fourth signal for water was answered, "Cast down your bucket where you are." The captain of the distressed vessel, at last heeding the injunction, cast down his bucket, and it came up full of fresh, sparkling water from the mouth of the Amazon River. To those of my race who depend on bettering their condition in a foreign land or who underestimate the importance of cultivating friendly relations with the Southern white man, who is their next-door neighbour, I would say: "Cast down your bucket where you are"—cast it down in making friends in every manly way of the people of all races by whom we are surrounded.

Cast it down in agriculture, mechanics, in commerce, in domestic service, and in the professions. And in this connection it is well to bear in mind that whatever other sins the South may be called to bear, when it comes to business, pure and simple, it is in the South that the Negro is given a man's chance in the commercial world, and in nothing is this Exposition more eloquent than in emphasizing this chance. Our greatest danger is that in the great leap from slavery to freedom we may overlook the fact that the masses of us are to live by the productions of our hands, and fail to keep in mind that we shall prosper in proportion as we learn to dignify and glorify common labour and put brains and skill into the common occupations of life; shall prosper in proportion as we learn to draw the line between the superficial and the substantial, the ornamental gewgaws of life and the useful. No race can prosper till it learns that there is as much dignity in tilling a field as in writing a poem. It is at the bottom of life we must begin, and not at the top. Nor should we permit our grievances to overshadow our opportunities.

To those of the white race who look to the incoming of those of foreign birth and strange tongue and habits for the prosperity of the South, were I permitted I would repeat what I say to my own race, "Cast down your bucket where you are." Cast it down among the eight millions of Negroes whose habits you know, whose fidelity and love you have tested in days when to have proved treacherous meant the ruin of your firesides. Cast down your bucket among these people who have, without strikes and labour wars, tilled your fields, cleared your forests, builded your railroads and cities, and brought forth treasures from the bowels of the earth, and helped make possible this magnificent representation of the progress of the South. Casting down your bucket among my people, helping and encouraging them as you are doing on these grounds, and to education of head, hand, and heart, you will find that they will buy your surplus land, make blossom the waste places in your fields, and run your factories. While doing this, you can be sure in the future, as in the past, that you and your families will be surrounded by the most patient, faithful, law-abiding, and unresentful people that the world has seen. As we have proved our loyalty to you in the past, in nursing your children, watching by the sickbed of your mothers and fathers, and often following them with tear-dimmed eyes to their graves, so in the future, in our humble way, we shall stand by you with a devotion that no foreigner can approach, ready to lay down our lives, if need be, in defence of yours, interlacing our industrial, commercial, civil, and religious life with yours in a way that shall make the interests of both races one. In all things that are purely social we can be as separate as the fingers, yet one as the hand in all things essential to mutual progress.

There is no defence or security for any of us except in the highest intelligence and development of all. If anywhere there are efforts tending to curtail the fullest growth of the Negro, let these efforts be turned into stimulating, encouraging, and making him the most useful and intelligent citizen. Effort or means so invested will pay a thousand per cent interest. These efforts will be twice blessed—"blessing him that gives and him that takes."

There is no escape through law of man or God from the inevitable:—

> The laws of changeless justice bind
> Oppressor with oppressed;

> And close as sin and suffering joined
> We march to fate abreast.

Nearly sixteen millions of hands will aid you in pulling the load upward, or they will pull against you the load downward. We shall constitute one-third and more of the ignorance and crime of the South, or one-third its intelligence and progress; we shall contribute one-third to the business and industrial prosperity of the South, or we shall prove a veritable body of death, stagnating, depressing, retarding every effort to advance the body politic.

Gentlemen of the Exposition, as we present to you our humble effort at an exhibition of our progress, you must not expect over-much. Starting thirty years ago with ownership here and there in a few quilts and pumpkins and chickens (gathered from miscellaneous sources), remember the path that has led from these to the inventions and production of agricultural implements, buggies, steam-engines, newspapers, books, statuary, carving, paintings, the management of drug-stores and banks, has not been trodden without contact with thorns and thistles. While we take pride in what we exhibit as a result of our independent efforts, we do not for a moment forget that our part in this exhibition would fall far short of your expectations but for the constant help that has come to our educational life, not only from the Southern states, but especially from Northern philanthropists, who have made their gifts a constant stream of blessing and encouragement.

The wisest among my race understand that the agitation of questions of social equality is the extremest folly, and that progress in the enjoyment of all the privileges that will come to us must be the result of severe and constant struggle rather than an artificial forcing. No race that has anything to contribute to the markets of the world is long in any degree ostracized. It is important and right that all privileges of the law be ours, but it is vastly more important that we be prepared for the exercises of these privileges. The opportunity to earn a dollar in a factory just now is worth infinitely more than the opportunity to spend a dollar in an opera-house.

In conclusion, may I repeat that nothing in thirty years has given us more hope and encouragement, and drawn us so near to you of the white race, as this opportunity offered by the Exposition; and here bending, as it were, over the altar that represents the results of the struggles of your race and mine, both starting practically empty-handed three decades ago, I pledge that in your effort to work out the great and intricate problem which God has laid at the doors of the South, you shall have at all times the patient, sympathetic help of my race; only let this be constantly in mind, that, while from representations in these buildings of the product of field, of forest, of mine, of factory, letters, and art, much good will come, yet far above and beyond material benefits will be that higher good, that, let us pray God, will come, in a blotting out of sectional differences and racial animosities and suspicions, in a determination to administer absolute justice, in a willing obedience among all classes to the mandates of law. This, then, coupled with our material prosperity, will bring into our beloved South a new heaven and a new earth.

The first thing that I remember, after I had finished speaking, was that Governor Bullock rushed across the platform and took me by the hand, and that others did the same. I received so many and such hearty congratulations that I found it difficult to get out of the building. I did not appreciate to any degree, however, the impression which my address seemed to have made, until the next morning, when I went into the business part of the city. As soon as I was recognized, I was surprised to find myself pointed out and surrounded by a crowd of men who wished to shake hands with me. This was kept up on every street on to which I went, to an extent which embarrassed me so much that I went back to my boarding-place. The next morning I returned to Tuskegee. At the station in Atlanta, and at almost all of the stations at which the train stopped between that city and Tuskegee, I found a crowd of people anxious to shake hands with me.

The papers in all parts of the United States published the address in full, and for months afterward there were complimentary editorial references to it. Mr. Clark Howell, the editor of the Atlanta *Constitution*, telegraphed to a New York paper, among other words, the following, "I do not exaggerate when I say that Professor Booker T. Washington's address yesterday was one of the most notable speeches, both as to character and as to the warmth of its reception, ever delivered to a Southern audience. The address was a revelation. The whole speech is a platform upon which blacks and whites can stand with full justice to each other."

The Boston *Transcript* said editorially: "The speech of Booker T. Washington at the Atlanta Exposition, this week, seems to have dwarfed all the other proceedings and the Exposition itself. The sensation that it has caused in the press has never been equalled."

I very soon began receiving all kinds of propositions from lecture bureaus, and editors of magazines and papers, to take the lecture platform, and to write articles. One lecture bureau offered me fifty thousand dollars, or two hundred dollars a night and expenses, if I would place my services at its disposal for a given period. To all these communications I replied that my life-work was at Tuskegee; and that whenever I spoke it must be in the interests of the Tuskegee school and my race, and that I would enter into no arrangements that seemed to place a mere commercial value upon my services.

Some days after its delivery I sent a copy of my address to the President of the United States, the Hon. Grover Cleveland. I received from him the following autographed reply:—

Gray Gables, Buzzard's Bay, Mass.,
October 6, 1895

Booker T. Washington, Esq.:

My Dear Sir:

I thank you for sending me a copy of your address delivered at the Atlanta Exposition.

I thank you with much enthusiasm for making the address. I have read it with intense interest, and I think the Exposition would be fully justified if it did not do more than furnish the opportunity for its delivery. Your words cannot fail to delight and encourage all who wish well for your race; and if our coloured fellow-citizens do not from your utterances gather new hope and form new determinations to gain every valuable advantage offered them by their citizenship, it will be strange indeed.

Yours very truly,
GROVER CLEVELAND

EQUALITY AND EDUCATION

W. E. B. Du Bois / Of Mr. Booker T. Washington and Others

In 1903, W. E. B. Du Bois, the new contender for the position of spokesman for the black community, published the following essay under the title "Of Mr. Booker T. Washington and Others." It was the first public sign of Du Bois' growing disenchantment with Washington, with whom he had worked earlier on various projects.

Du Bois had become increasingly suspicious of the power enjoyed by Washington as a result of the financial support of the white community. He noted that, though Washington had spoken in 1895 of increased cooperation between the races, the end of the century had brought the disfranchisement of blacks and increased color discrimination. Du Bois called for criticism by blacks of Washington's program of accommodation. According to him, it was stifling the development of the "talented tenth" of black youth capable of competing on equal terms with whites and discouraging black men from insisting on the natural and civil rights necessary to their advancement.

From birth till death enslaved; in word, in deed, unmanned!

. . . .

Hereditary bondsmen! Know ye not
Who would be free themselves must strike the blow?

BYRON

Easily the most striking thing in the history of the American Negro since 1876 is the ascendancy of Mr. Booker T. Washington. It began at the time when war memories and ideals were rapidly passing; a day of astonishing commercial development was dawning; a sense of doubt and hesitation overtook the freedmen's sons,—then it was that his leading began. Mr. Washington came, with a single definite programme, at the psychological moment when the nation was a little ashamed of having bestowed so much sentiment on Negroes, and was concentrating its energies on Dollars. His programme of industrial education, conciliation of the South, and submission and silence as to civil and political rights, was not wholly original; the Free Negroes from 1830 up to wartime had striven to build industrial schools, and the American Missionary Association had from the first taught various trades; and Price and others had sought a way of honorable alliance with the best of the Southerners. But Mr. Washington first indissolubly linked these things; he put enthusiasm, unlimited energy, and perfect faith into this programme, and changed it from a by-path into a veritable Way of Life. And the tale of the methods by which he did this is a fascinating study of human life.

It startled the nation to hear a Negro advocating such a programme after many decades of bitter complaint; it startled and won the applause of the South, it interested and won the admiration of the North; and after a confused murmur of protest, it silenced if it did not convert the Negroes themselves.

To gain the sympathy and coöperation of the various elements comprising the white South was Mr. Washington's first task; and this, at the time Tuskegee was founded, seemed, for a black man, well-nigh impossible. And yet ten years later it was done in the word spoken at Atlanta: "In all things purely social we can be as separate as the five fingers, and yet one as the hand in all things essential to mutual progress." This "Atlanta Compromise" is by all odds the most notable thing in Mr. Washington's career. The South interpreted it in different ways: the radicals received it as a complete surrender of the demand for civil and political equality; the conservatives, as a generously conceived working basis for mutual understanding. So both approved it, and to-day its author is certainly the most distinguished Southerner since Jefferson Davis, and the one with the largest personal following.

Next to this achievement comes Mr. Washington's work in gaining place and consideration in the North. Others less shrewd and tactful had formerly essayed to sit on these two stools and had fallen between them; but as Mr.

FROM W. E. B. Du Bois, "Of Mr. Booker T. Washington and Others," *Souls of Black Folk* (Chicago, 1903).

Washington knew the heart of the South from birth and training, so by singular insight he intuitively grasped the spirit of the age which was dominating the North. And so thoroughly did he learn the speech and thought of triumphant commercialism, and the ideals of material prosperity, that the picture of a lone black boy poring over a French grammar amid the weeds and dirt of a neglected home soon seemed to him the acme of absurdities. One wonders what Socrates and St. Francis of Assisi would say to this.

And yet this very singleness of vision and thorough oneness with his age is a mark of the successful man. It is as though Nature must needs make men narrow in order to give them force. So Mr. Washington's cult has gained unquestioning followers, his work has wonderfully prospered, his friends are legion, and his enemies are confounded. To-day he stands as the one recognized spokesman of his ten million fellows, and one of the most notable figures in a nation of seventy millions. One hesitates, therefore, to criticise a life which, beginning with so little, has done so much. And yet the time is come when one may speak in all sincerity and utter courtesy of the mistakes and shortcomings of Mr. Washington's career, as well as of his triumphs, without being thought captious or envious, and without forgetting that it is easier to do ill than well in the world.

The criticism that has hitherto met Mr. Washington has not always been of this broad character. In the South especially has he had to walk warily to avoid the harsh judgments,—and naturally so, for he is dealing with the one subject of deepest sensitiveness to that section. Twice—once when at the Chicago celebration of the Spanish-American War he alluded to the color-prejudice that is "eating away the vitals of the South," and once when he dined with President Roosevelt—has the resulting Southern criticism been violent enough to threaten seriously his popularity. In the North the feeling has several times forced itself into words, that Mr. Washington's counsels of submission overlooked certain elements of true manhood, and that his educational programme was unnecessarily narrow. Usually, however, such criticism has not found open expression, although, too, the spiritual sons of the Abolitionists have not been prepared to acknowledge that the schools founded before Tuskegee, by men of broad ideals and self-sacrificing spirit, were wholly failures or worthy of ridicule. While, then, criticism has not failed to follow Mr. Washington, yet the prevailing public opinion of the land has been but too willing to deliver the solution of a wearisome problem into his hands, and say, "If that is all you and your race ask, take it."

Among his own people, however, Mr. Washington has encountered the strongest and most lasting opposition, amounting at times to bitterness, and even to-day continuing strong and insistent even though largely silenced in outward expression by the public opinion of the nation. Some of this opposition is, of course, mere envy; the disappointment of displaced demagogues and the spite of narrow minds. But aside from this, there is among educated and thoughtful colored men in all parts of the land a feeling of deep regret, sorrow, and apprehension at the wide currency and ascendancy which some of Mr. Washington's theories have gained. These same men admire his sincerity of purpose, and are willing to forgive much to honest endeavor which is doing something worth the doing. They coöperate with Mr. Washington as far as they conscientiously can; and, indeed, it is no ordinary tribute to this man's tact and power that, steering as he must between so many diverse interests and opinions, he so largely retains the respect of all.

But the hushing of the criticism of honest opponents is a dangerous thing. It leads some of the best of the critics to unfortunate silence and paralysis of effort, and others to burst into speech so passionately and intemperately as to lose listeners. Honest and earnest criticism from those whose interests are most nearly touched,—criticism of writers by readers, of government by those governed, of leaders by those led,—this is the soul of democracy and the safeguard of modern society. If the best of the American Negroes receive by outer pressure a leader whom they had not recognized before, manifestly there is here a certain palpable gain. Yet there is also irreparable loss,—a loss of that peculiarly valuable education which a group receives when by search and criticism it finds and commissions its own leaders. The way in which this is done is at once the most elementary and the nicest problem of social growth. History is but the record of such group-leadership; and yet how infinitely changeful is its type and character! And of all types and kinds, what can be more instructive than the leadership of a group within a group?—that curious double movement where real progress may be negative and actual advance be relative retrogression. All this is the social student's inspiration and despair.

Now in the past the American Negro has had instructive experience in the choosing of group leaders, founding thus a peculiar dynasty which in the light of present conditions is worth while studying. When sticks and stones and beasts form the sole environment of a people, their attitude is largely one of determined opposition to and conquest of natural forces. But when to earth and brute is added an environment of men and ideas, then the attitude of the imprisoned group may take three main forms,—a feeling of revolt and revenge; an attempt to adjust all thought and action to the will of the greater group; or, finally, a determined effort at self-realization and self-development despite environing opinion. The influence of all of these attitudes at various times can be traced in the history of the American Negro, and in the evolution of his successive leaders.

Before 1750, while the fire of African freedom still burned in the veins of the slaves, there was in all leadership or attempted leadership but the one motive of revolt and revenge,—typified in the terrible Maroons, the Danish blacks, and Cato of Stono, and veiling all the Americas in fear of insurrection. The liberalizing tendencies of the latter half of the eighteenth century brought, along with kindlier relations between black and white, thoughts of ultimate adjustment and assimilation. Such aspiration was especially voiced in the earnest songs of Phyllis, in the martyrdom of Attucks, the fighting of

Salem and Poor, the intellectual accomplishments of Banneker and Derham, and the political demands of the Cuffes.

Stern financial and social stress after the war cooled much of the previous humanitarian ardor. The disappointment and impatience of the Negroes at the persistence of slavery and serfdom voiced itself in two movements. The slaves in the South, aroused undoubtedly by vague rumors of the Haitian revolt, made three fierce attempts at insurrection,—in 1800 under Gabriel in Virginia, in 1822 under Vesey in Carolina, and in 1831 again in Virginia under the terrible Nat Turner. In the Free States, on the other hand, a new and curious attempt at self-development was made. In Philadelphia and New York color-prescription led to a withdrawal of Negro communicants from white churches and the formation of a peculiar socio-religious institution among the Negroes known as the African Church,—an organization still living and controlling in its various branches over a million of men.

Walker's wild appeal against the trend of the times showed how the world was changing after the coming of the cotton-gin. By 1830 slavery seemed hopelessly fastened on the South, and the slaves thoroughly cowed into submission. The free Negroes of the North, inspired by the mulatto immigrants from the West Indies, began to change the basis of their demands; they recognized the slavery of slaves, but insisted that they themselves were freemen, and sought assimilation and amalgamation with the nation on the same terms with other men. Thus, Forten and Purvis of Philadelphia, Shad of Wilmington, Du Bois of New Haven, Barbadoes of Boston, and others, strove strongly and together as men, they said, not as slaves; as "people of color," not as "Negroes." The trend of the times, however, refused them recognition save in individual and exceptional cases, considered them as one with all the despised blacks, and they soon found themselves striving to keep even the rights they formerly had of voting and working and moving as freemen. Schemers of migration and colonization arose among them; but these they refused to entertain, and they eventually turned to the Abolition movement as a final refuge.

Here, led by Remond, Nell, Wells-Brown, and Douglass, a new period of self-assertion and self-development dawned. To be sure, ultimate freedom and assimilation was the ideal before the leaders, but the assertion of the manhood rights of the Negro by himself was the main reliance, and John Brown's raid was the extreme of its logic. After the war and emancipation, the great form of Frederick Douglass, the greatest of American Negro leaders, still led the host. Self-assertion, especially in political lines, was the main programme, and behind Douglass came Elliot, Bruce, and Langston, and the Reconstruction politicians, and, less conspicuous but of greater social significance, Alexander Crummell and Bishop Daniel Payne.

Then came the Revolution of 1876, the suppression of the Negro votes, the changing and shifting of ideals, and the seeking of new lights in the great night. Douglass, in his old age, still bravely stood for the ideals of his early manhood,—ultimate assimilation *through* self-assertion, and on no other terms. For a time Price arose as a new leader, destined, it seemed, not to give up, but to re-state the old ideals in a form less repugnant to the white South. But he passed away in his prime. Then came the new leader. Nearly all the former ones had become leaders by the silent suffrage of their fellows, had sought to lead their own people alone, and were usually, save Douglass, little known outside their race. But Booker T. Washington arose as essentially the leader not of one race but of two,—a compromiser between the South, the North, and the Negro. Naturally the Negroes resented, at first bitterly, signs of compromise which surrendered their civil and political rights, even though this was to be exchanged for larger chances of economic development. The rich and dominating North, however, was not only weary of the race problem, but was investing largely in Southern enterprises, and welcomed any method of peaceful coöperation. Thus, by national opinion, the Negroes began to recognize Mr. Washington's leadership; and the voice of criticism was hushed.

Mr. Washington represents in Negro thought the old attitude of adjustment and submission; but adjustment at such a peculiar time as to make his programme unique. This is an age of unusual economic development, and Mr. Washington's programme naturally takes an economic cast, becoming a gospel of Work and Money to such an extent as apparently almost completely to overshadow the higher aims of life. Moreover, this is an age when the more advanced races are coming in closer contact with the less developed races, and the race-feeling is therefore intensified; and Mr. Washington's programme practically accepts the alleged inferiority of the Negro races. Again, in our own land, the reaction from the sentiment of war time has given impetus to race-prejudice against Negroes, and Mr. Washington withdraws many of the high demands of Negroes as men and American citizens. In other periods of intensified prejudice all the Negro's tendency to self-assertion has been called forth; at this period a policy of submission is advocated. In the history of nearly all other races and peoples the doctrine preached at such crises has been that manly self-respect is worth more than lands and houses, and that a people who voluntarily surrender such respect, or cease striving for it, are not worth civilizing.

In answer to this, it has been claimed that the Negro can survive only through submission. Mr. Washington distinctly asks that black people give up, at least for the present, three things,—

First, political power,
Second, insistence on civil rights,
Third, higher education of Negro youth,—

and concentrate all their energies on industrial education, the accumulation of wealth, and the conciliation of the South. This policy has been courageously and insistently advocated for over fifteen years, and has been triumphant for perhaps ten years. As a result of this tender of the palm-branch, what has been the return? In these years there have occurred:

1. The disfranchisement of the Negro.
2. The legal creation of a distant status of civil inferiority for the Negro.
3. The steady withdrawal of aid from institutions for the higher training of the Negro.

These movements are not, to be sure, direct results of Mr. Washington's teachings; but his propaganda has, without a shadow of doubt, helped their speedier accomplishment. The question then comes: Is it possible, and probable, that nine millions of men can make effective progress in economic lines if they are deprived of political rights, made a servile caste, and allowed only the most meagre chance for developing their exceptional men? If history and reason give any distinct answer to these questions, it is an emphatic *No*. And Mr. Washington thus faces the triple paradox of his career:

1. He is striving nobly to make Negro artisans business men and property-owners; but it is utterly impossible, under modern competitive methods, for workingmen and property-owners to defend their rights and exist without the right of suffrage.
2. He insists on thrift and self-respect, but at the same time counsels a silent submission to civic inferiority such as is bound to sap the manhood of any race in the long run.
3. He advocates common-school and industrial training, and depreciates institutions of higher learning; but neither the Negro common-schools, nor Tuskegee itself, could remain open a day were it not for teachers trained in Negro colleges, or trained by their graduates.

This triple paradox in Mr. Washington's position is the object of criticism by two classes of colored Americans. One class is spiritually descended from Toussaint the Savior, through Gabriel, Vesey, and Turner, and they represent the attitude of revolt and revenge; they hate the white South blindly and distrust the white race generally, and so far as they agree on definite action, think that the Negro's only hope lies in emigration beyond the borders of the United States. And yet, by the irony of fate, nothing has more effectually made this programme seem hopeless than the recent course of the United States toward weaker and darker peoples in the West Indies, Hawaii, and the Philippines,—for where in the world may we go and be safe from lying and brute force?

The other class of Negroes who cannot agree with Mr. Washington has hitherto said little aloud. They deprecate the sight of scattered counsels, of internal disagreement; and especially they dislike making their just criticism of a useful and earnest man an excuse for a general discharge of venom from small-minded opponents. Nevertheless, the questions involved are so fundamental and serious that it is difficult to see how men like the Grimkes, Kelly

Miller, J. W. E. Bowen, and other representatives of this group, can much longer be silent. Such men feel in conscience bound to ask of this nation three things:

1. The right to vote.
2. Civic equality.
3. The education of youth according to ability.

They acknowledge Mr. Washington's invaluable service in counselling patience and courtesy in such demands; they do not ask that ignorant black men vote when ignorant whites are debarred, or that any reasonable restrictions in the suffrage should not be applied; they know that the low social level of the mass of the race is responsible for much discrimination against it, but they also know, and the nation knows, that relentless color-prejudice is more often a cause than a result of the Negro's degradation; they seek the abatement of this relic of barbarism, and not its systematic encouragement and pampering by all agencies of social power from the Associated Press to the Church of Christ. They advocate, with Mr. Washington, a broad system of Negro common schools supplemented by thorough industrial training; but they are surprised that a man of Mr. Washington's insight cannot see that no such educational system ever has rested or can rest on any other basis than that of the well-equipped college and university, and they insist that there is a demand for a few such institutions throughout the South to train the best of the Negro youth as teachers, professional men, and leaders.

This group of men honor Mr. Washington for his attitude of conciliation toward the white South; they accept the "Atlanta Compromise" in its broadest interpretation; they recognize, with him, many signs of promise, many men of high purpose and fair judgment, in this section; they know that no easy task has been laid upon a region already tottering under heavy burdens. But, nevertheless, they insist that the way to truth and right lies in straightforward honesty, not in indiscriminate flattery; in praising those of the South who do well and criticising uncompromisingly those who do ill; in taking advantage of the opportunities at hand and urging their fellows to do the same, but at the same time in remembering that only a firm adherence to their higher ideals and aspirations will ever keep those ideals within the realm of possibility. They do not expect that the free right to vote, to enjoy civic rights, and to be educated, will come in a moment; they do not expect to see the bias and prejudices of years disappear at the blast of a trumpet; but they are absolutely certain that the way for a people to gain their reasonable rights is not by voluntarily throwing them away and insisting that they do not want them; that the way for a people to gain respect is not by continually belittling and ridiculing themselves; that, on the contrary, Negroes must insist continually, in season and out of season, that voting is necessary to modern manhood, that color discrimination is barbarism, and that black boys need education as well as white boys.

In failing thus to state plainly and unequivocally the legitimate demands of their people, even at the cost of opposing an honored leader, the thinking classes of American Negroes would shirk a heavy responsibility,—a responsibility to themselves, a responsibility to the struggling masses, a responsibility to the darker races of men whose future depends so largely on this American experiment, but especially a responsibility to this nation,—this common Fatherland. It is wrong to encourage a man or a people in evil-doing; it is wrong to aid and abet a national crime simply because it is unpopular not to do so. The growing spirit of kindliness and reconciliation between the North and South after the frightful difference of a generation ago ought to be a source of deep congratulation to all, and especially to those whose mistreatment caused the war; but if that reconciliation is to be marked by the industrial slavery and civic death of those same black men, with permanent legislation into a position of inferiority, then those black men, if they are really men, are called upon by every consideration of patriotism and loyalty to oppose such a course by all civilized methods, even though such opposition involves disagreement with Mr. Booker T. Washington. We have no right to sit silently by while the inevitable seeds are sown for a harvest of disaster to our children, black and white.

First, it is the duty of black men to judge the South discriminatingly. The present generation of Southerners are not responsible for the past, and they should not be blindly hated or blamed for it. Furthermore, to no class is the indiscriminate endorsement of the recent course of the South toward Negroes more nauseating than to the best thought of the South. The South is not "solid"; it is a land in the ferment of social change, wherein forces of all kinds are fighting for supremacy; and to praise the ill the South is to-day perpetrating is just as wrong as to condemn the good. Discriminating and broad-minded criticism is what the South needs,—needs it for the sake of her own white sons and daughters, and for the insurance of robust, healthy mental and moral development.

To-day even the attitude of the Southern whites toward the blacks is not, as so many assume, in all cases the same; the ignorant Southerner hates the Negro, the workingmen fear his competition, the money-makers wish to use him as a laborer, some of the educated see a menace in his upward development, while others—usually the sons of the masters—wish to help him to rise. National opinion has enabled this last class to maintain the Negro common schools, and to protect the Negro partially in property, life, and limb. Through the pressure of the money-makers, the Negro is in danger of being reduced to semi-slavery, especially in the country districts; the workingmen, and those of the educated who fear the Negro, have united to disfranchise him, and some have urged his deportation; while the passions of the ignorant are easily aroused to lynch and abuse any black man. To praise this intricate whirl of thought and prejudice is nonsense; to inveigh indiscriminately against "the South" is unjust; but to use the same breath in praising Governor Aycock, exposing Senator Morgan, arguing with Mr. Thomas Nelson Page, and denouncing Senator Ben Tillman, is not only sane, but the imperative duty of thinking black men.

It would be unjust to Mr. Washington not to acknowledge that in several instances he has opposed movements in the South which were unjust to the Negro; he sent memorials to the Louisiana and Alabama constitutional conventions, he has spoken against lynching, and in other ways has openly or silently set his influence against sinister schemes and unfortunate happenings. Notwithstanding this, it is equally true to assert that on the whole the distinct impression left by Mr. Washington's propaganda is, first, that the South is justified in its present attitude toward the Negro because of the Negro's degradation; secondly, that the prime cause of the Negro's failure to rise more quickly is his wrong education in the past; and, thirdly, that his future rise depends primarily on his own efforts. Each of these propositions is a dangerous half-truth. The supplementary truths must never be lost sight of: first, slavery and race-prejudice are potent if not sufficient causes of the Negro's position; second, industrial and common-school training were necessarily slow in planting because they had to await the black teachers trained by higher institutions,—it being extremely doubtful if any essentially different development was possible, and certainly a Tuskegee was unthinkable before 1880; and, third, while it is a great truth to say that the Negro must strive and strive mightily to help himself, it is equally true that unless his striving be not simply seconded, but rather aroused and encouraged, by the initiative of the richer and wiser environing group, he cannot hope for great success.

In his failure to realize and impress this last point, Mr. Washington is especially to be criticised. His doctrine has tended to make the whites, North and South, shift the burden of the Negro problem to the Negro's shoulders and stand aside as critical and rather pessimistic spectators; when in fact the burden belongs to the nation, and the hands of none of us are clean if we bend not our energies to righting these great wrongs.

The South ought to be led, by candid and honest criticism, to assert her better self and do her full duty to the race she has cruelly wronged and is still wronging. The North—her co-partner in guilt—cannot salve her conscience by plastering it with gold. We cannot settle this problem by diplomacy and suaveness, by "policy" alone. If worse comes to worst, can the moral fibre of this country survive the slow throttling and murder of nine millions of men?

The black men of America have a duty to perform, a duty stern and delicate,—a forward movement to oppose a part of the work of their greatest leader. So far as Mr. Washington preaches Thrift, Patience, and Industrial Training for the masses, we must hold up his hands and strive with him, rejoicing in his honors and glorying in the strength of this Joshua called of God and of man to lead the headless host. But so far as Mr. Washington apologizes for injustice, North or South, does not rightly value the privilege and duty of voting, belittles the emasculating effects of caste distinctions, and opposes the higher training and ambition of our brighter minds,—so far as he, the South, or the Nation, does this,—we must unceasingly and firmly oppose them. By every civilized and peaceful method we must strive for the right which the world accords to men, clinging unwaveringly to those great words which the sons of the Fathers would fain forget: "We hold these truths to be self-evident: That all men are created equal; that they are endowed by their Creator with certain unalienable rights; that among these are life, liberty, and the pursuit of happiness."

BLACK MEN ORGANIZE

The Niagara Movement Declaration of Principles, 1905

In 1905 Du Bois, following his own advice, brought together a group of black intellectuals and professionals with the clear, though unstated, purpose of opposing the Tuskegee Machine. The Niagara Movement, which held its first meeting in Canada because of discrimination met by its members in Buffalo, New York, where the meeting first assembled, put forth a demand for racial equality in all areas of American life.

Although the black movement had little influence and all but the most radical of its members joined with whites to form the National Association for the Advancement of Colored People in 1910, its program was important because it provided a comprehensive alternative to the politics of conciliation advocated by Washington.

With minor changes, the "Declaration of Principles" of the Niagara Movement, reprinted in the pages that follow, could be released again today as a summary of the demands of black men. Although the name of its author is not given, the document was almost certainly written by Du Bois.

Progress: The members of the conference, known as the Niagara Movement, assembled in annual meeting at Buffalo, July 11th, 12th and 13th, 1905, congratulate the Negro-Americans on certain undoubted evidences of progress in the last decade, particularly the increase of intelligence, the buying of property, the checking of crime, the uplift in home life, the advance in

FROM *The Niagara Movement Declaration of Principles* (1905).

literature and art, and the demonstration of constructive and executive ability in the conduct of great religious, economic and educational institutions.

Suffrage: At the same time, we believe that this class of American citizens should protest emphatically and continually against the curtailment of their political rights. We believe in manhood suffrage; we believe that no man is so good, intelligent or wealthy as to be entrusted wholly with the welfare of his neighbor.

Civil Liberty: We believe also in protest against the curtailment of our civil rights. All American citizens have the right to equal treatment in places of public entertainment according to their behavior and deserts.

Economic Opportunity: We especially complain against the denial of equal opportunities to us in economic life; in the rural districts of the South this amounts to peonage and virtual slavery; all over the South it tends to crush labor and small business enterprises; and everywhere American prejudice, helped often by iniquitous laws, is making it more difficult for Negro-Americans to earn a decent living.

Education: Common school education should be free to all American children and compulsory. High school training should be adequately provided for all, and college training should be the monopoly of no class or race in any section of our common country. We believe that, in defense of our own institutions, the United States should aid common school education, particularly in the South, and we especially recommend concerted agitation to this end. We urge an increase in public high school facilities in the South, where the Negro-Americans are almost wholly without such provisions. We favor well-equipped trade and technical schools for the training of artisans, and the need of adequate and liberal endowment for a few institutions of higher education must be patent to sincere well-wishers of the race.

Courts: We demand upright judges in courts, juries selected without discrimination on account of color and the same measure of punishment and the same efforts at reformation for black as for white offenders. We need orphanages and farm schools for dependent children, juvenile reformatories for delinquents, and the abolition of the dehumanizing convict-lease system.

Public Opinion: We note with alarm the evident retrogression in this land of sound public opinion on the subject of manhood rights, republican government and human brotherhood, and we pray God that this nation will not degenerate into a mob of boasters and oppressors, but rather will return to the faith of the fathers, that all men were created free and equal, with certain unalienable rights.

Health: We plead for health—for an opportunity to live in decent houses and localities, for a chance to rear our children in physical and moral cleanliness.

Employers and Labor Unions: We hold up for public execration the conduct of two opposite classes of men: The practice among employers of importing ignorant Negro-American laborers in emergencies, and then affording them neither protection nor permanent employment; and the practice of labor unions in proscribing and boycotting and oppressing thousands of their fellow-toilers, simply because they are black. These methods have accentuated and will accentuate the war of labor and capital, and they are disgraceful to both sides.

Protest: We refuse to allow the impression to remain that the Negro-American assents to inferiority, is submissive under oppression and apologetic before insults. Through helplessness we may submit, but the voice of protest of ten million Americans must never cease to assail the ears of their fellows, so long as America is unjust.

Color-Line: Any discrimination based simply on race or color is barbarous, we care not how hallowed it be by custom, expediency or prejudice. Differences made on account of ignorance, immorality, or disease are legitimate methods of fighting evil, and against them we have no word of protest; but discriminations based simply and solely on physical peculiarities, place of birth, color of skin, are relics of that unreasoning human savagery of which the world is and ought to be thoroughly ashamed.

"Jim Crow" Cars: We protest against the "Jim Crow" car, since its effect is and must be to make us pay first-class fare for third-class accommodations, render us open to insults and discomfort and to crucify wantonly our manhood, womanhood and self-respect.

Soldiers: We regret that this nation has never seen fit adequately to reward the black soldiers who, in its five wars, have defended their country with their blood, and yet have been systematically denied the promotions which their abilities deserve. And we regard as unjust, the exclusion of black boys from the military and naval training schools.

War Amendments: We urge upon Congress the enactment of appropriate legislation for securing the proper enforcement of those articles of freedom, the thirteenth, fourteenth and fifteenth amendments of the Constitution of the United States.

Oppression: We repudiate the monstrous doctrine that the oppressor should be the sole authority as to the rights of the oppressed. The negro race in America stolen, ravished and degraded, struggling up through difficulties and oppression, needs sympathy and receives criticism, needs help and is given hindrance, needs protection and is given mob-violence, needs justice and is given charity, needs leadership and is given cowardice and apology, needs bread and is given a stone. This nation will never stand justified before God until these things are changed.

The Church: Especially are we surprised and astonished at the recent attitude of the church of Christ—of an increase of a desire to bow to racial prejudice, to narrow the bounds of human brotherhood, and to segregate black men to some outer sanctuary. This is wrong, unchristian and disgraceful to the twentieth century civilization.

Agitation: Of the above grievances we do not hesitate to complain, and to complain loudly and insistently. To ignore, overlook, or apologize for these wrongs is to prove ourselves unworthy of freedom. Persistent manly agitation is the way to liberty, and toward this goal the Niagara Movement has started and asks the cooperation of all men of all races.

Help: At the same time we want to acknowledge with deep thankfulness the help of our fellowmen from the Abolitionist down to those who today still stand for equal opportunity and who have given and still give of their wealth and of their poverty for our advancement.

Duties: And while we are demanding, and ought to demand, and will continue to demand the rights enumerated above, God forbid that we should ever forget to urge corresponding duties upon our people:

The duty to vote.
The duty to respect the rights of others.
The duty to work.
The duty to obey the laws.
The duty to be clean and orderly.
The duty to send our children to school.
The duty to respect ourselves, even as we respect others.

This statement, complaint and prayer we submit to the American people, and Almighty God.

THE NAACP PROGRAM FOR CHANGE

NAACP / The Task for the Future—A Program for 1919

> After its conception in 1910, the NAACP very quickly clarified its task. It would concern itself with the problem of achieving first-class **citizenship** for black people. Rather than bogging down in questions of "social equality," it would work for what it called "public equality." Though it was concerned with the problem of racial prejudice, the Association thought itself best equipped to try to provide equal protection for blacks under the Constitution.
>
> Some critics have suggested that this policy was the result of the domination of the organization in the early years by Northern whites. Because it worked primarily in the area of legal rights, the NAACP never became an organization of the black masses, most of whom were never in a position to demand legal redress. There is no question, however, of the importance of this legal-rights struggle, which has indicated in our own times that the United States Constitution is only as good as its enforcement.
>
> The document that follows states the program of the NAACP on the eve of its first decade of existence. This policy has remained virtually unchanged to the present day.

F irst and foremost among the objectives for 1919 must be the strengthening of the Association's organization and resources. Its general program must be adapted to specific ends. Its chief aims have many times been stated:

1. A vote for every Negro man and woman on the same terms as for white men and women.

2. An equal chance to acquire the kind of an education that will enable the Negro everywhere wisely to use this vote.

3. A fair trial in the courts for all crimes of which he is accused, by judges in whose election he has participated without discrimination because of race.

4. A right to sit upon the jury which passes judgment upon him.

5. Defense against lynching and burning at the hands of mobs.

6. Equal service on railroad and other public carriers. This to mean sleeping car service, dining car service, Pullman service, at the same cost and upon the same terms as other passengers.

7. Equal right to the use of public parks, libraries and other community services for which he is taxed.

8. An equal chance for a livelihood in public and private employment.

9. The abolition of color-hyphenation and the substitution of "straight Americanism."

If it were not a painful fact that more than four-fifths of the colored people of the country are denied the above named elementary rights, it would seem an absurdity that an organization is necessary to demand for American citizens the exercise of such rights. One would think, if he were from Mars, or if he knew America only by reading the speeches of her leading statesmen, that all that would be needful would be to apply to the courts of the land and to the legislatures. Has not slavery been abolished? Are not all men equal before the law? Were not the Fourteenth and Fifteenth Amendments passed by the Congress of the United States and adopted by the states? Is not the Negro a man and a citizen?

When the fundamental rights of citizens are so wantonly denied and that denial justified and defended as it is by the lawmakers and dominant forces of so large a number of our states, it can be realized that the fight for the Negro's citizenship rights means a fundamental battle for real things, for life and liberty.

This fight is the Negro's fight. "Who would be free, himself must strike the blow." But, it is no less the white man's fight. The common citizenship rights of no group of people, to say nothing of nearly 12,000,000 of them, can be denied with impunity to the State and the social order which denies

---

FROM "The Task for the Future—A Program for 1919," *Report of the National Association for the Advancement of Colored People for the Years 1917 and 1918* (New York, 1919), pp. 76–80.

them. This fact should be plain to the dullest mind among us, with the upheavals of Europe before our very eyes. Whoso loves America and cherishes her institutions, owes it to himself and his country to join hands with the members of the National Association for the Advancement of Colored People to "Americanize" America and make the kind of democracy we Americans believe in to be the kind of democracy we shall have in *fact*, as well as in theory.

The Association seeks to overthrow race prejudice but its objective may better be described as a fight against *caste*. Those who seek to separate the Negro from the rest of Americans are intent upon establishing a caste system in America and making of all black men an *inferior caste*. As America could not exist "half slave and half free" so it cannot exist with an upper caste of whites and a lower caste of Negroes. Let no one be deceived by those who would contend that they strive only to maintain "the purity of the white race" and that they wish to separate the races but to do no injustice to the black man. The appeal is to history which affords no example of any group or element of the population of any nation which was separated from the rest and at the same time treated with justice and consideration. Ask the Jew who was compelled to live in the proscribed Ghetto whether being held separate he was afforded the common rights of citizenship and the "equal protection of the laws?" To raise the question is to find the answer "leaping to the eyes," as the French say.

Nor should any one be led astray by the tiresome talk about "social equality." Social equality is a private question which may well be left to individual decision. But, the prejudices of individuals cannot be accepted as the controlling policy of a state. The National Association for the Advancement of Colored People is concerned primarily with *public equality*. America is a nation—not a private club. The privileges no less than the duties of citizenship belong of right to no *separate class* of the people but to *all* the people, and to them as *individuals*. The constitution and the laws are for the protection of the minority and of the unpopular, no less than for the favorites of fortune, or they are of no meaning as American instruments of government.

Such a fight as has been outlined is worthy of the support of all Americans. The forces which seek to deny, and do deny, to the Negro his citizenship birthright, are powerful and intrenched. They hold the public offices. They administer the law. They say who may, and who may not vote, in large measure. They control and edit, in many sections, the influential organs of public opinion. They dominate. To dislodge them by legal and constitutional means as the N.A.A.C.P. proposes to endeavor to dislodge them, requires a strong organization and ample funds. These two things attained, victory is but a question of time, since justice will not forever be denied.

The lines along which the Association can best work are fairly clear. Its fight is of the brain and the soul and to the brain and the soul of America. *It seeks to reach the conscience of America.* America is a large and busy nation. It has many things to think of besides the Negro's welfare. In Congress and state legislatures and before the bar of public opinion, the Association must energetically and adequately defend the Negro's right to fair and equal treatment. To command the interest and hold the attention of the American people for *justice to the Negro* requires money to print and circulate literature which states the facts of the situation. And the appeal must be on the basis of the facts. It is easy to talk in general terms and abstractly. The presentation of concrete data necessitates ample funds.

Lynching must be stopped.   Many Americans do not believe that such horrible things happen as do happen when Negroes are lynched and burned at the stake. Lynching can be stopped when we can reach the hearts and consciences of the American people. Again, money is needed.

Legal work must be done.   Defenseless Negroes are every day denied the "equal protection of the laws" because there is not money enough in the Association's treasury to defend them, either as individuals or as a race.

Legislation must be watched.   Good laws must be promoted wherever that be possible and bad laws opposed and defeated, wherever possible. Once more, money is essential.

The public must be kept informed.   This means a regular press service under the supervision of a trained newspaper man who knows the difference between news and gossip, on the one hand, and mere opinion on the other. That colored people are contributing their fair share to the well-being of America must be made known. The war has made familiar the heroic deeds of the colored soldier. The colored civilian has been, and is now, contributing equally to America's welfare. If men have proven to be heroes in warfare, they must have had virtues in peace time. That law-abiding colored people are denied the commonest citizenship rights, must be brought home to all Americans who love fair play. Once again, money is needed.

The facts must be gathered and assembled.   This requires effort. Facts are not gotten out of one's imagination. Their gathering and interpretation is skilled work. Research workers of a practical experience are needed. Field investigations, in which domain the Association has already made some notable contributions, are essential to good work. More money.

The country must be thoroughly organized.   The Association's nearly 200 branches are a good beginning. A field staff is essential to the upbuilding of this important branch development. A very large percentage of the branch members are colored people. As a race they have less means, and less experience in public organization, than white people. But, they are developing rapidly habits of efficiency in organization. Money, again is needed.

But, not money alone is needed.   Men and women are vital to success. Public opinion is the main force upon which the Association relies for a *victory of justice.*

WHY BLACKS MUST ORGANIZE FOR LEGAL RIGHTS

The Waco Horror: A Report on a Lynching

Du Bois, in his capacity as research director of the NAACP, edited **The Crisis**, a monthly magazine that he launched in 1910 as a vehicle for Association propaganda, news, and his own personal views. Within ten years of its founding it had a circulation of over 100,000 and it had been denounced by the Joint Committee Investigating Seditious Activity for the New York state legislature for contributing to "revolutionary radicalism."

The magazine gave wide coverage to incidents involving color discrimination, particularly those of a violent nature. Vivid descriptions of lynchings, riots, chain gangs, and the like filled its pages. Early issues of the journal stand today as documentation of the helpless condition of black people when confronted by whites whose concern for "law and order" did not extend to the black community.

The following report on a lynching, in all its gory detail, is characteristic of the kind of article Du Bois printed in hopes of awakening the conscience of the larger community.

1. THE CITY

The city of Waco, Tex., is the county seat of McLennan county. It is situated on the Brazos river, about half way between Dallas and Austin. It is the junction point of seven railways. The city is in a fertile agricultural region with grain and cotton as the chief products, and with nearly two hundred manufacturing establishments, representing some seventy different industries.

It had a population of 14,445 in 1890 which increased to 20,686 in 1900, and to 26,425 in 1910. The white population in these twenty years has almost exactly doubled. The colored population has increased from 4,069 to 6,067, forming thus 23% of the population. The bulk of the population is native white of native parentage, there being only about 1,000 foreigners in the city.

The whole of McLennan county contained in 1910 a population of 73,250 of whom 17,234 were Negroes. This total population has nearly doubled in the last twenty years.

Waco is well laid out. The streets are broad, over sixty miles of them being paved. The sewer system of one hundred miles is excellent. There is a fine city-owned water system, and parks on the surrounding prairies.

There are thirty-nine white and twenty-four colored churches in Waco. By denominations the white churches are: Baptist, 14; Methodist, 9; Chris-

FROM "The Waco Horror," *The Crisis*, Vol. XII (July 1916), supplement, pp. 1–8.

tian, 4; Presbyterian, 3; Jewish, 2; Episcopal, 2; Evangelistic, 1; Lutheran, 1; Catholic, 1; Christian Science, 1; Salvation Army, 1.

The colleges are: Baylor University, Baylor Academy, the Catholic College, the Independent Biblical and Industrial School, all white; and the Central Texas College and Paul Quinn, colored colleges. There are also the A. & M. College, the Gurley School, the Waco Business College, Toby's Practical Business College, the Provident Sanitarium, and the Training School.

Baylor University was founded in 1854 and has between 1,200 and 1,300 students. It is co-educational. The president is running for the United States Senate.

Two high schools serve white and colored population, and there are seven banks, including four national banks.

In other words, Waco is a typical southern town, alert, pushing and rich.

2. THE CRIME

Near the country town of Robinson. some six miles from Waco, lived a white family of four, named Fryar, who owned a small farm. This they cultivated themselves with the help of one hired man, a colored boy of seventeen, named Jesse Washington.

Jesse was a big, well-developed fellow, but ignorant, being unable either to read or write. He seemed to have been sullen, and perhaps mentally deficient, with a strong, and even daring temper. It is said that on Saturday night before the crime he had had a fight with a neighboring white man, and the man had threatened to kill him.

On Monday, May 8, while Mr. Fryar, his son of fourteen, and his daughter of twenty-three, were hoeing cotton in one part of their farm, the boy, Jesse, was plowing with his mules and sowing cotton seed near the house where Mrs. Fryar was alone. He went to the house for more cotton seed. As Mrs. Fryar was scooping it up for him into the bag which he held, she scolded him for beating the mules. He knocked her down with a blacksmith's hammer, and, as he confessed, criminally assaulted her; finally he killed her with the hammer. The boy then returned to the field, finished his work, and went home to the cabin, where he lived with his father and mother and several brothers and sisters.

When the murdered woman was discovered suspicion pointed to Jesse Washington, and he was found sitting in his yard whittling a stick. He was arrested and immediately taken to jail in Waco. Tuesday a mob visited the jail. They came in with about thirty automobiles, each holding as many as could be crowded in. There was no noise, no tooting of horns, the lights were dim, and some had no lights at all. These were all Robinson people. They looked for the boy, but could not find him, for he had been taken to a neighboring county where the sheriff obtained a confession from him. Another mob went to this county seat to get the boy, but he was again removed to Dallas. Finally, the Robinson people pledged themselves not to lynch the boy if the authorities acted promptly, and if the boy would waive his legal rights.

A second confession in which the boy waived all his legal rights was obtained in the Dallas jail. The Grand Jury indicted him on Thursday, and the case was set for trial Monday, May 15.

Sunday night, at midnight, Jesse Washington was brought from Dallas to Waco, and secreted in the office of the judge. There was not the slightest doubt but that he would be tried and hanged the next day, if the law took its course.

There was some, but not much doubt of his guilt. The confessions were obtained, of course, under duress, and were, perhaps, suspiciously clear, and not entirely in the boy's own words. It seems, however, probable that the boy was guilty of murder, and possibly of premeditated rape.

3. WACO POLITICS

Meantime, the exigencies of Waco politics are said to have demanded a lynching. Our investigator says:

"They brought the boy back to Waco because a lynching was of political value to the county officials who are running for office. Every man I talked with said that politics was at the bottom of the whole business. All that element who took part in the lynching will vote for the Sheriff. The Judge is of value to his party because he appoints the three commissioners of the jury, and these commissioners pick the Grand Jury."

The District Judge of the Criminal Court is R. I. Munroe, appointed by Governor Campbell. He is a low order of politician, and a product of a local machine. His reputation for morality is bad, and his practice at the Bar has been largely on behalf of the vicious interests.

The Sheriff of the county, S. S. Fleming, is a candidate for re-election, and has made much political capital out of the lynching. He says, in an advertisement in the Waco *Semi-Weekly Tribune:*

"Mr. Fleming is diseased with a broad philanthropy. He believes in the equality of man. He carries with him in the daily walk of his officialdom none of the 'boast of heraldry or the pomp of power.' He is just as courteous, just as obliging, just as accommodating as Sheriff as he was when selling buggies and cultivators for the hardware company. He presents to the voters for their endorsement the record made by him and his corps of splendid deputies."

Our investigator says:

"When I saw the Sheriff (Fleming) he had a beautiful story to tell. He had his story fixed up so that the entire responsibility was shifted on the Judge. The Judge admitted he could have had a change of venue, but said the mob anywhere would have done the same thing."

Meantime, the tip went out:

"The crowd began pouring into the town the day before and continued early Monday morning. The court room was packed full and a crowd of 2,000 was on the outside. The jurors could scarcely get in and out from their seats. I asked the Judge if he could not have cleared the court room, and he answered that I did not know the South. I said, 'If a person is big enough, he can get up and stop the biggest mob.' He asked, 'Do you want to spill innocent blood for a nigger?'

"Some one had arranged it so that it would be easy to get the boy out of the courtroom. A door which opened by a peculiar device had been fixed so that it would open. One of the jurors was a convicted murderer with a suspended sentence over him.

"Lee Jenkins is the best deputy sheriff, but he is under Fleming. Barney Goldberg, the other deputy sheriff, said, 'If Lee Jenkins had had it, it would never have been, but we are working for the man higher up and must take our orders from him.' Barney Goldberg knows perfectly well that if Fleming is not re-elected, and the other candidate gets in, he will be out of a job. The other nominee for sheriff, Buchanan, is reported to be unable to read and write, but is said to have three dead 'niggers' to his 'credit.'

"The boy, Jesse Washington, was asked what he thought about the mob coming after him. He said, 'They promised they would not if I would tell them about it.' He seemed not to care, but was thoroughly indifferent."

The trial was hurried through. The Waco *Semi-Weekly Tribune,* May 17, says: "The jury returned into court at 11:22 A.M., and presented a verdict: 'We, the jury, find the defendant guilty of murder as charged in the indictment and assess his punishment at death.' This was signed by W. B. Brazelton, foreman.

" 'Is that your verdict, gentlemen?' asked Judge Munroe.

"They answered 'yes.'

"Judge Munroe began writing in his docket. He had written: 'May 15, 1916: Jury verdict of guilty,' and as he wrote there was a hush over the entire court room. It was a moment of hesitation, but just a moment. Then the tall man started over the heads of the crowd. Fred H. Kingsbury, who was standing alongside of Judge Munroe, said, 'They are coming after him,' and as the Judge looked up, the wave of people surged forward." The court room accommodates 500 persons, but the Judge had allowed 1,500 persons to crowd in.

Our investigator continues:

"The stenographer told me that there was a pause of a full minute. He said the people crowded around him and he knew what was coming, so he slipped out of the door back of the Sheriff, with his records; and Sheriff Fleming slipped out also.

"Fleming claims that all he was called upon to do in the way of protecting the boy was to get him to court.

"A big fellow in the back of the court room yelled, 'Get the Nigger!'

Barney Goldberg, one of the deputy sheriffs, told me that he did not know that Fleming had dropped orders to let them get the Negro, and pulled his revolver. Afterwards he got his friends to swear to an affidavit that he was not present. Fleming said he had sworn in fifty deputies. I asked him where they were. He asked, 'Would you want to protect the nigger?' The judge made no effort to stop the mob, although he had firearms in his desk."

4. THE BURNING

"They dragged the boy down the stairs, put a chain around his body and hitched it to an automobile. The chain broke. The big fellow took the chain off the Negro under the cover of the crowd and wound it around his own wrist, so that the crowd jerking at the chain was jerking at the man's wrist and he was holding the boy. The boy shrieked and struggled.

"The mob ripped the boy's clothes off, cut them in bits and even cut the boy. Someone cut his ear off; someone else unsexed him. A little girl working for the firm of Goldstein and Mingle told me that she saw this done.

"I went over the route the boy had been taken and saw that they dragged him between a quarter and a half a mile from the Court House to the bridge and then dragged him up two blocks and another block over to the City Hall. After they had gotten him up to the bridge, someone said that a fire was already going up at City Hall, and they turned around and went back. Several people denied that this fire was going, but the photograph shows that it was. They got a little boy to light the fire.

"While a fire was being prepared of boxes, the naked boy was stabbed and the chain put over the tree. He tried to get away, but could not. He reached up to grab the chain and they cut off his fingers. The big man struck the boy on the back of the neck with a knife just as they were pulling him up on the tree. Mr. Lester thought that was practically the death blow. He was lowered into the fire several times by means of the chain around his neck. Someone said they would estimate the boy had about twenty-five stab wounds, none of them death-dealing.

"About a quarter past one a fiend got the torso, lassoed it, hung a rope over the pummel of a saddle, and dragged it around through the streets of Waco.

"Very little drinking was done.

"The tree where the lynching occurred was right under the Mayor's window. Mayor Dollins was standing in the window, not concerned about what they were doing to the boy, but that the tree would be destroyed. The Chief of Police also witnessed the lynching. The names of five of the leaders of the mob are known to this Association, and can be had on application by responsible parties.

"Women and children saw the lynching. One man held up his little boy above the heads of the crowd so that he could see, and a little boy was in the top of the very tree to which the colored boy was hung, where he stayed until the fire became too hot."

Another account, in the Waco *Times Herald*, Monday night, says:

"Great masses of humanity flew as swiftly as possible through the streets of the city in order to be present at the bridge when the hanging took place, but when it was learned that the Negro was being taken to the City Hall lawn, crowds of men, women and children turned and hastened to the lawn.

"On the way to the scene of the burning people on every hand took a hand in showing their feelings in the matter by striking the Negro with anything obtainable, some struck him with shovels, bricks, clubs, and others stabbed him and cut him until when he was strung up his body was a solid color of red, the blood of the many wounds inflicted covered him from head to foot.

"Dry goods boxes and all kinds of inflammable material were gathered, and it required but an instant to convert this into seething flames. When the Negro was first hoisted into the air his tongue protruded from his mouth and his face was besmeared with blood.

"Life was not extinct within the Negro's body, although nearly so, when another chain was placed around his neck and thrown over the limb of a tree on the lawn, everybody trying to get to the Negro and have some part in his death. The infuriated mob then leaned the Negro, who was half alive and half dead, against the tree, he having just strength enough within his limbs to support him. As rapidly as possible the Negro was then jerked into the air at which a shout from thousands of throats went up on the morning air and dry goods boxes, excelsior, wood and every other article that would burn was then in evidence, appearing as if by magic. A huge dry goods box was then produced and filled to the top with all of the material that had been secured. The Negro's body was swaying in the air, and all of the time a noise as of thousands was heard and the Negro's body was lowered into the box.

"No sooner had his body touched the box than people pressed forward, each eager to be the first to light the fire, matches were touched to the inflammable material and as smoke rapidly rose in the air, such a demonstration as of people gone mad was never heard before. Everybody pressed closer to get souvenirs of the affair. When they had finished with the Negro his body was mutilated.

"Fingers, ears, pieces of clothing, toes and other parts of the Negro's body were cut off by members of the mob that had crowded to the scene as if by magic when the word that the Negro had been taken in charge by the mob was heralded over the city. As the smoke rose to the heavens, the mass of people, numbering in the neighborhood of 10,000, crowding the City Hall lawn and overflowing the square, hanging from the windows of buildings, viewing the scene from the tops of buildings and trees, set up a shout that was heard blocks away.

"Onlookers were hanging from the windows of the City Hall and every other building that commanded a sight of the burning, and as the Negro's body commenced to burn, shouts of delight went up from the thousands of throats and apparently everybody demonstrated in some way their satisfaction at the retribution that was being visited upon the perpetrator of such a horrible crime, the worst in the annals of McLennan county's history.

"The body of the Negro was burned to a crisp, and was left for some time in the smoldering remains of the fire. Women and children who desired to view the scene were allowed to do so, the crowds parting to let them look on the scene. After some time the body of the Negro was jerked into the air where everybody could view the remains, and a mighty shout rose on the air. Photographer Gildersleeve made several pictures of the body as well as the large crowd which surrounded the scene as spectators."

The photographer knew where the lynching was to take place, and had his camera and paraphernalia in the City Hall. He was called by telephone at the proper moment. He writes us:

"We have quit selling the mob photos, this step was taken because our 'City dads' objected on the grounds of 'bad publicity,' as we wanted to be boosters and not knockers, we agreed to stop all sale.

"F. A. GILDERSLEEVE."

Our agent continues:

"While the torso of the boy was being dragged through the streets behind the horse, the limbs dropped off and the head was put on the stoop of a disreputable woman in the reservation district. Some little boys pulled out the teeth and sold them to some men for five dollars apiece. The chain was sold for twenty-five cents a link.

"From the pictures, the boy was apparently a wonderfully built boy. The torso was taken to Robinson, hung to a tree, and shown off for a while, then they took it down again and dragged it back to town and put it on the fire again at five o'clock."

5. THE AFTERMATH

"I tried to talk to the Judge. I met him on the street and said, 'I want to talk with you about something very important.' He asked, 'What is the nature of it?' I said, 'I want to get your opinion of that lynching.' He said, 'No, I refuse to talk with you about that. What do you want it for?' I said, 'If you refuse to talk with me, there is no use of telling you what I want it for.'

"When I met him the second time, with different clothes on, he did not recognize me. I put on a strong English accent and said I was interested in clippings from New York papers which showed that Waco had made for itself an awful name, and I wanted to go back and make the northerners feel that Waco was not so bad as the papers had represented. Then he gave me the Court records."

Our investigator continues: "I went to the newspaper offices. They were all of the opinion that the best thing to do was to hush it up. They used it as a news item, and that finished it. The Dallas *News* did not cite anything editorially because not long ago they had done something quite as bad and the boy was not guilty.

"With the exception of the *Tribune*, all the papers had simply used it as a news item and let it drop. The *Tribune* is owned by Judge McCullum, who says anything he pleases. He is nearly blind. When I read the article to him I said, 'I would like to ask you, if that had been a colored woman and a white boy, would you have protected that woman?' He answered, 'No.' 'If it had been a colored boy and a colored woman? No.' 'We would not have the niggers doing anything they wanted to.' 'Do you think they would?' 'No.' 'Then, they prove their superior civilization.' Then he began to tell me how he knew all about the niggers and we northerners do not. He said that as an old southerner he knew perfectly well how to handle the colored population. He told me how he was raised with them, had a colored mammy, nursed at her breast, etc.

"There is a bunch of people in Waco who are dying to see someone go forward and make a protest, but no one in Waco would do it. Ex-Mayor Mackaye and Colonel Hamilton both said, 'We do not know what to do. We are not organized to do it. It is a case of race and politics.'

"I put out a lot of wires for a lawyer to take up the case, but no human being in Waco would take it up. I wrote to a friend in Austin and one in Houston, and the Austin friend telegraphed me that he would send me word as soon as he had found someone. I had a letter from the Houston friend who gave me the names of three lawyers, but am not sure whether they would take up a case of this kind. All have their doubts of ever getting the case into court.

"I did not dare ask much about lawyers.

"As a result of the lynching a Sunday School Convention which was to have met there, with 15,000 delegates, has been stopped.

"W. A. Brazelton, the foreman of the Jury, was very outspoken against the whole affair and blames the officials for it. He felt that as foreman of the Jury he could not lead in a protest but *thought* some protest ought to be made.

"Mr. Ainsworth, one of the newspaper men, seemed the only one who wanted to start a protest.

"Colonel Hamilton, a man of high standing, a northerner, and at one time a big railroad man, was outspoken against the whole affair, but said that if he led in a protest they would do the same thing to him. He said he would never register in any hotel that he came from Waco. Two Waco men who did not register from Waco.

"Allan Stanford, ex-Mayor of Waco, saw the Sheriff and the Judge before the trial and received assurances that the lynching would not take place. They shut the mouths of the better element of Waco by telling them that the Robinson people had promised not to do it. They had gotten the promise of the Robinson people that they would not touch the boy during the trial, but they did not get the pledge of the disreputable bunch of Waco that they would not start the affair.

"Judge Spell said the affair was deplorable, but the best thing was to forget it.

"When representing myself as a news reporter, I asked, 'What shall I tell the people up North?' Ex-Mayor Mackaye said, 'Fix it up as well as you can for Waco, and make them understand that the better thinking men and women of Waco were not in it.' I said. 'But some of your better men were down there.' The whole thing savors so rotten because the better men have not tried to protest against it. Your churches have not said a word. Dr. Caldwell was the only man who made any protest at all."

6. THE LYNCHING INDUSTRY

This is an account of one lynching. It is horrible, but it is matched in horror by scores of others in the last thirty years, and in its illegal, law-defying, race-hating aspect, it is matched by 2842 other lynchings which have taken place between January 1, 1885, and June 1, 1916. These lynchings are as follows:

COLORED MEN LYNCHED BY YEARS, 1885–1916

Year	Count	Year	Count
1885	78	1901	107
1886	71	1902	86
1887	80	1903	86
1888	95	1904	83
1889	95	1905	61
1890	90	1906	64
1891	121	1907	60
1892	155	1908	93
1893	154	1909	73
1894	134	1910	65
1895	112	1911	63
1896	80	1912	63
1897	122	1913	79
1898	102	1914	69
1899	84	1915	80
1900	107	1916 (5 mos.)	31
		TOTAL	2843

What are we going to do about this record? The civilization of America is at stake. The sincerity of Christianity is challenged. The National Association for the Advancement of Colored People proposes immediately to raise a fund of at least $10,000 to start a crusade against this modern barbarism. Already $2,000 is promised, conditional on our raising the whole amount.

Interested persons may write to Roy Nash, secretary, 70 Fifth Avenue, New York City.

7
SUGGESTIONS FOR FURTHER READING

A survey of the attitudes of black leaders in the late nineteenth century and early twentieth is found in August Meier, *Negro Thought in America, 1880–1915** (University of Michigan Press, 1963). For the ideas of Booker T. Washington, see his *Future of the American Negro* (Small, Maynard, 1899) and his autobiography *Up From Slavery** (Doubleday, Page, 1901). Surprisingly, no good biography of Washington is available, but two good studies involving him are Samuel R. Spencer, *Booker T. Washington and the Negro's Place in American Life** (Little, Brown, 1955), and Hugh Hawkins (ed.) *Booker T. Washington and His Critics** (Heath, 1962). Of the many works of W. E. B. Du Bois, the ones to read first are *The Souls of Black Folk** (McClurg, 1903) and the autobiographical *Dusk of Dawn** (Harcourt, Brace & World, 1940). Two excellent studies of Du Bois are Francis L. Broderick, *W. E. B. Du Bois: Negro Leader in a Time of Crisis** (Stanford University Press, 1959), and Elliott M. Rudwick, *W. E. B. Du Bois, A Study in Minority Group Leadership** (University of Pennsylvania, 1960).

Two books dealing with the development of the NAACP are the popular *Fight for Freedom: The Story of the NAACP** (Norton, 1962), a rather unstructured and disjointed treatment by Langston Hughes, and the more scholarly *NAACP: The History of the National Association for the Advancement of Colored People*, Vol. 1, 1909–1920 (Johns Hopkins Press, 1967), by C. F. Kellogg.

The muckraking reporter Ray Stannard Baker surveyed the condition of black people in America in *Following the Color Line: American Negro Citizenship in the Progressive Era** (Doubleday, Page, 1908). Mary White Ovington, one of the white founders of the NAACP, wrote *Half a Man, The Status of the Negro in New York* (Longmans, Green, 1911). Kelly Miller, a leading black moderate and a professor at Howard University, published his views on the leadership of Booker T. Washington and other contemporary issues in a collection of essays called *Race Adjustment* (Neale, 1908), published in paperback under the title *Radicals and Conservatives**.

Special studies of aspects of black life early in the twentieth century are Sterling D. Spero and Abram Harris, *The Black Worker** (Columbia University Press, 1931), and Louis R. Harlan, *Separate and Unequal: Public School Campaigns and Racism in Southern Seaboard States, 1901–1915** (University of North Carolina Press, 1958).

James Weldon Johnson's novel about a black man "passing" into white society, *The Autobiography of an Ex-Colored Man** (Sherman, French, 1912), contains some interesting insights. The excellent collection of documents edited by Francis L. Broderick and August Meier, *Negro Protest Thought in the Twentieth Century** (Bobbs-Merrill, 1965), gives a many-sided view of the development of Afro-American intellectual and political life from the late nineteenth century up to 1964.

8 THE GREAT MIGRATION BRINGS A NEW MOOD

The mass movement of Southern blacks to the North in the second decade of the twentieth century is one of the most important migrations in American history. Most of it was the result of economic changes brought about by the First World War. Many of the burgeoning industries of the North made a practice of staffing their factories with immigrants from Europe, but the war halted this tide. And many of those already at work marched off to war, leaving empty factory jobs in Northern cities. Between the years 1910 and 1920, the black population increased in Detroit by 611.3 per cent, in Cleveland by 307.8 per cent, in Gary (Indiana) by 1,283.6 per cent, in Chicago by 148.2 per cent.

It was not only the pull of industry that drew blacks from the South during this period. Southern agriculture was undergoing severe difficulties as the boll weevil moved up from Mexico and ravaged cotton crop after cotton crop. The tenant-farmer and sharecropper systems were driving rural blacks deeper and deeper into despair. When a black newspaper, the Chicago *Defender*, began to encourage blacks to migrate northward and Northern industry began to send labor recruiters to the South, the response was overwhelming.

At first, the white South sighed with relief; it was finally to be rid of the troublesome blacks. But as the migration grew, the whites realized the threat it posed to the Southern system and began to strike out at the migrants and those who encouraged them. In many places the Chicago *Defender* was banned, and to be caught with it in one's possession became an offense punishable by imprisonment. Jacksonville, Florida, required labor recruiters from the North to buy a license for $1,000 or go to jail for sixty days. Macon, Georgia, upped the license fee to $25,000 and insisted that the recruiter have recommendations from ten local ministers, ten local manufacturers, and twenty-five local businessmen. In Alabama, fines and jail sentences awaited anyone who was found guilty of encouraging labor to leave. In Mississippi, recruiters were arrested, trains were stopped, and ticket agents were threatened by whites. Yet the movement north gathered momentum.

When the war ended and the soldiers returned to find their jobs taken over by blacks, the inevitable racial clashes occurred. Whites, anxious to reaffirm the old caste lines, acted in ways intended to negate the economic and psychological gains made by blacks during the war, but the newly settled black laborers and the many black men returning from military service in Europe were in no mood to be pushed around. Sporadic violence broke out throughout the nation. Several black men were lynched in the uniform of the United States Army—one, simply because he wore the uniform. In 1918, in Chicago, the homes of many blacks who had bought property on the edges of white communities were bombed. All this served as a prelude to the summer of 1919, when there were twenty-two race riots in United States cities, both North and South.

The first of the riots to attract national attention was in Washington, D.C., in the middle of July. The conflict began when two hundred white servicemen invaded a black neighborhood to avenge an alleged "jostling" incident involving two black men and the wife of a white sailor. Little was done by law-enforcement authorities to control the whites until blacks began to arm themselves and fight back. The four days of rioting left several dead and many wounded.

The most violent outbreak of the summer occurred in Chicago in late July, when whites caused the drowning of a black swimmer who had crossed the invisible line dividing the black from the white area at a local bathing beach. When a white policeman refused to arrest those who had caused the drowning but instead arrested a black on a minor charge, incensed blacks attacked the policeman. The outbreak that followed lasted for a week, during which white and black mobs fought all over Chicago. At the end of the week, fifteen whites and twenty-three blacks lay dead, and countless blacks and whites were wounded.

The year 1919 marked a turning point in American history as far as racial violence is concerned. Blacks fought back openly against white attacks in greater numbers and to greater effect than ever before. In this sense, the "new Negro" spoken about so widely in the 1920's emerged from the bloody street fights of the summer of 1919.

The Great Migration created more than white reaction in Northern cities. It also created the first mass nationalist movement among American blacks—that of Marcus Garvey, a West Indian who had come to the United States during the First World War. The Garvey movement based its program on the conviction that blacks must create their own independent nation because they would never receive justice in a white man's country. Though his organization attracted mainly West Indian immigrants at first, Garvey was ready to appeal to the black migrant from the South who found that the Northern Promised Land offered neither promise nor land. Garvey proposed to set up his "Zion" in Africa, the ancestral homeland of black people. Opposed by both white authorities and black intellectuals, Garvey was convicted on a questionable charge of mail fraud, sent to prison, then released and deported, but the black nationalist political consciousness he aroused is a force still much in evidence in certain black movements.

A different, ironically antithetical response of blacks to the Great Migration emerged in the 1920's in the cultural nationalist movement called the Harlem Renaissance. Whereas political nationalism of the Garvey type anticipates the formation of an all-black society, cultural nationalism asserts the values of the past in an attempt to develop a cultural identity that can support a self-conscious racial elite and, so far as it reaches the black masses, develop in them racial pride and self-assurance. The black writers and artists of the Harlem Renaissance used the folk materials of the rural black past and the ghetto black present to assert the values of the black experience. Needless to say, there was considerable disagreement as to what these values were. From the ambivalence of works such as Jean Toomer's *Cane* to the certainties of those like James Weldon Johnson's *God's Trombones*, the creations of black artists and intellectuals strove with one another to express the complex meaning of blackness.

WHY BLACKS CHOSE TO LEAVE THE SOUTH

Letters of Negro Migrants of 1916–1918

Perhaps the most valuable sources of information about why black people left the South for Northern cities are the letters they wrote to the Chicago **Defender** asking for help. Many of the letters written between 1916 and 1918 were collected by Emmett J. Scott, for a time Booker T. Washington's secretary, and were published in 1919 in the fledgling **Journal of Negro History.**

The letters, reprinted here as they were written, speak for themselves. Futility, frustration, rage, and despair can be seen in every line. Not only were individuals anxious to leave their old lives in the South, but whole groups were prepared to drop everything and migrate in the hope of finding something better. The **Defender** certainly exaggerated the promise of the North, but thousands responded to its enticements and, following the route of the old Underground Railroad, caught the Illinois Central to the Promised Land.

JACKSONVILLE, FLA., 4–25–17.

Dear Sir: in reading a copy of the Chicago defender note that if i get in touch with you you would assist me in getting imployment. i am now imployed in Florida East coast R R service road way department any thing in working line myself and friends would be very glad to get in touch with as labors. We would be more than glad to do so and would highly appreciate it the very best we can advise where we can get work to do, fairly good wages also is it possible that we could get transportation to the destination. We are working men with familys. Please answer at once. i am your of esteem. We are not particular about the electric lights and all i want is fairly good wages and steady work.

MARCEL, MISS., 10/4/17.

Dear Sir: Although I am a stranger to you but I am a man of the so called colored race and can give you the very best or reference as to my character and ability by prominent citizens of my community by both white and colored people that knows me although am native of Ohio whiles I am a northern desent were reared in this state of Mississippi. Now I am a reader of your paper the Chicago Defender. After reading your writing ever wek

FROM Emmett J. Scott (ed.), "Letters of Negro Migrants of 1916–1918," *Journal of Negro History*, Vol. IV (July and October 1919), pp. 292, 293, 302, 304, 317, 320, 325, 329, 333, 413, 419, 420, 424, 434, 435, 437, 438, 442, 443, 450, 451, 452. Reprinted by permission of the Association for the Study of Negro Life and History, Inc.

I am compell & persuade to say that I know you are a real man of my color you have I know heard of the south land & I need not tell you any thing about it. I am going to ask you a favor and at the same time beg you for your kind and best advice. I wants to come to Chicago to live. I am a man of a family wife and 1 child I can do just any kind of work in the line of common labor & I have for the present sufficient means to support us till I can obtain a position. Now should I come to your town, would you please to assist me in getting a position I am willing to pay whatever you charge I dont want you to loan me not 1 cent but *help* me to find an occupation there in your town now I has a present position that will keep me employed till the first of Dec. 1917. now please give me your best advice on this subject. I enclose stamp for reply.

FAYETTE, GA., JANUARY 17, 1917.

Dear Sir: I have learned of the splendid work which you are doing in placing colored men in touch with industrial opportunities. I therefore write you to ask if you have an opening anywhere for me. I am a college graduate and understand Bookkeeping. But I am not above doing hard labor in a foundry or other industrial establishment. Please let me know if you can place me.

LEXINGTON, MISS., MAY 12–17.

My dear Mr. H——: —I am writing to you for some information and assistance if you can give it.

I am a young man and am disable, in a very great degree, to do hard manual labor. I was educated at Alcorn College and have been teaching a few years: but ah: me the Superintendent under whom we poor colored teachers have to teach cares less for a colored man than he does for the vilest beast. I am compelled to teach 150 children without any assistance and receives only $27.00 a month, the white with 30 get $100.

I am so sick I am so tired of such conditions that I sometime think that life for me is not worth while and most eminently believe with Patrick Henry "Give me liberty or give me death." If I was a strong able bodied man I would have gone from here long ago, but this handicaps me and, I must make inquiries before I leap.

Mr. H——, do you think you can assist me to a position I am good at stenography typewriting and bookkeeping or any kind of work not to rough or heavy. I am 4 feet 6 in high and weigh 105 pounds.

I will gladly give any other information you may desire and will greatly appreciate any assistance you may render me.

SELMA, ALA., MAY 19, 1917.

Dear Sir: I am a reader of the Chicago Defender I think it is one of the Most Wonderful Papers of our race printed. Sirs I am writeing to see if

You all will please get me a job. And Sir I can wash dishes, wash iron nursing work in groceries and dry good stores. Just any of these I can do. Sir, who so ever you get the job from please tell them to send me a ticket and I will pay them. When I get their as I have not got enough money to pay my way. I am a girl of 17 years old and in the 8 grade at Knox Academy School. But on account of not having money enough I had to stop school. Sir I will thank you all with all my heart. May God Bless you all. Please answer in return mail.

MOBILE, ALA., APRIL 21, 1917.

Dear Sirs: We have a club of 108 good men wants work we are willing to go north or west but we are not abel to pay rail road fare now if you can help us get work and get to it please answer at once. Hope to hear from you.

MOBILE, ALA., MAY 11, 1917.

Dear sir and brother: on last Sunday I addressed you a letter asking you for information and I have received no answer. but we would like to know could 300 or 500 men and women get employment? and will the company or thoes that needs help send them a ticket or a pass and let them pay it back in weekly payments? We have men and women here in all lines of work we have organized a association to help them through you.

We are anxiously awaiting your reply.

GRAHAM, LA., MAY 18, 1917.

Dear sir: a word of infermation and a ancer from you please there are about 12 or 15 of us with our famlys leaving the south and we can hear of collored peples leaving the south but we are not luckey enough to leave hear. Dr. —— clame to be an agent to sind peples off and we has bin to him so minnie times and has fail to get off untill we dont no what to do so if you will place us about 15 tickets or get some one else to do so we are honest enough to come at once and labor for you or the one that sind them until we pay you if so requir. If we war able we wood sur leave this torminting place but the job we as got and what we get it we do well to feed our family so please let me here from you at once giveing full detale of my requess.

MOBILE, ALA., 4–26–17.

Dear Sir Bro.: I take great pane in droping you a few lines hopeing that this will find you enjoying the best of health as it leave me at this time present. Dear sir I seen in the Defender where you was helping us a long in securing a posission as brickmason plaster cementers stone mason. I am writing to you for advice about comeing north. I am a brickmason an I can do cement work an stone work. I written to a firm in Birmingham an they sent me a blank stateing $2.00 would get me a ticket an pay 10 per ct of my salary for the 1st month and $24.92c would be paid after I reach Detorit and went to work where they sent me to work. I had to stay there until I pay them the sum of $24.92c so I want to leave Mobile for there. if there nothing there for me to make a support for my self and family. My wife is seamstress. We want to get away the 15 or 20 of May so please give this matter your earnest consideration an let me hear from you by return mail as my bro. in law want to get away to. He is a carpenter by trade, so please help us as we are in need of your help as we wanted to go to Detroit but if you says no we go where ever you sends us until we can get to Detroit. We expect to do whatever you says. There is nothing here for the colored man but a hard time wich these southern crackers gives us. We has not had any work to do in 4 wks. and every thing is high to the colored man so please let me hear from you by return mail. Please do this for your brother.

NEW ORLEANS, LA., 4–23–17.

Dear Editor: I am a reader of the Defender and I am askeso much about the great Northern drive on the 15th of May. We want more understanding about it for there is a great many wants to get ready for that day & the depot agents never gives us any satisfaction when we ask for they dont want us to leave here, I want to ask you to please publish in your next Saturdays paper just what the fair will be on that day so we all will know & can be ready. So many women here are wanting to go that day. They are all working women and we cant get work here so much now, the white women tell us we just want to make money to go North and we do so please kindly ans. this in your next paper if you do I will read it every word in the Defender, had rather read it then to eat when Saturday comes, it is my hearts delight & hope your paper will continue on in the south until every one reads it for it is a God sent blessing to the Race. Will close with best wishes.

ALEXANDRIA, LA., JUNE 6, 1917.

Dear Sirs: I am writeing to you all asking a favor of you all. I am a girl of seventeen. School has just closed I have been going to school for nine months and I now feel like I aught to go to work. And I would like very very well for you all to please forward me to a good job. but there isnt a thing here for me to do, the wages here is from a dollar and a half a week. What could I earn Nothing. I have a mother and father my father do all he can for me but it is so hard. A child with any respect about her self or his self wouldnt like to see there mother and father work so hard and earn nothing I feel it my duty to help. I would like for you all to get me a good job and as I havent any money to come on please send me a pass and I would work and pay every cent of it back and get me a good quite place to stay.

My father have been getting the defender for three or four months but for the last two weeks we have failed to get it. I dont know why. I am tired of down hear in this ——/ I am afraid to say. Father seem to care and then again dont seem to but Mother and I am tired tired of all of this I wrote to you all because I believe you will help I need your help hopeing to here from you all very soon.

NEWBERN, ALA., 4/7/1917.

Dear Sir: I am in receipt of a letter from —— of ——, ——, in regards to placing two young women of our community in positions in the North or West, as he was unable to give the above assistance he enclosed your address. We desire to know if you are in a position to put us in touch with any reliable firm or private family that desire to employ two young women; one is a teacher in the public school of this county, and has been for the past six years having duties of a mother and sister to care for she is forced to seek employment else where as labor is very cheap here. The other is a high school pupil, is capable of during the work of a private family with much credit.

Doubtless you have learned of the great exodus of our people to the north and west from this and other southern states. I wish to say that we are forced to go when one things of a grown man wages is only fifty to seventy five cents per day for all grades of work. He is compelled to go where there is better wages and sociable conditions, believe me. When I say that many places here in this state the only thing that the black man gets is a peck of meal and from three to four lbs. of bacon per week, and he is treated as a slave. As leaders we are powerless for we dare not resent such or to show even the slightest disapproval. Only a few days ago more than 1000 people left here for the north and west. They cannot stay here. The white man is saying that you must not go but they are not doing anything by way of assisting the black man to stay. As a minister of the Methodist Episcopal Church (north) I am on the verge of starvation simply because of the above conditions. I shall be glad to know if there is any possible way by which I could be of real service to you as director of your society. Thanking you in advance for an early reply, and for any suggestions that you may be able to offer.

With best wishes for your success, I remain,
very sincerely yours.

TROY, ALA., 3–24–17.

Dear Sir: I received you of Feb. 17 and was very delighted to hear from you in regards of the matter in which I writen you about. I am very anxious to get to Chicago and realy believe that if I was there I would very soom be working on the position in which I writen you about. Now you can just imagine how it is with the colored man in the south. I am more than anxious to go to Chicago but have not got the necessary fund in which to pay my way and these southern white peoples are not paying a man enough for his work down here to save up enough money to leave here with. Now I am asking you for a helping hand in which to assist me in getting to Chicago. I know you can do so if you only will.

Hoping to hear from you at an early date and looking for a helping hand and also any information you choose to inform me of,

I remain as ever yours truly.

HAWKINSVILLE, GA., APR. 16, 1917.

My dear friends: I writen you some time ago and never received any answer at all. I just was thinking why that I have not. I writen you for employ on a farm or any kind of work that you can give me to do I am willing to do most any thing that you want me to so dear friends if you just pleas send ticket for me I will come up thear just as soon as I receives it I want to come to the north so bad tell I really dont no what to do. I am a good worker a young boy age of .23. The reason why I want to come north is why that the people dont pay enough for the labor that a man can do down here so please let me no what can you do for me just as soon as you can I will pay you for the ticket and all so enything on your money that you put in the ticket for me, and send any kind of contrak that you send me.

ALEXANDRIA, LA., 4/23/11.

Gentlemens: Just a word of information I am planning to leave this place on about May 11th for Chicago and wants ask you assistence in getting a job. My job for the past 8 years has been in the Armour Packing Co. of this place and I cand do anything to be done in a branch house and are now doing the smoking here I am 36 years old have a wife and 2 children. I has been here all my life but would be glad to go wher I can educate my children where they can be of service to themselves, and this will never be here.

Now if you can get a job with eny of the packers I will just as soon as I arrive in your city come to your pace and pay you for your troubel. And if I cant get on with packers I will try enything that you have to effer.

CRESCENT, OKLA., APRIL 30, 1917.

Sir: I am looking for a place to locate this fall as a farmer. Do you think you could place me on a farm to work on shares. I am a poor farmer and have not the money to buy but would be glad to work a mans farm for him. I am desirous of leaving here because of the school accommodations for children as I have five and want to educate them the best I can. Prehaps you can find me a position of some kind if so kindly let me know I will be ready to leave here this fall after the harvest is layed by. I am planting cotton.

Sir: Being a constant reader of your paper, I thought of no one better than you to write for information.

I'm desirous of leaving the south but before so doing I want to be sure of a job before pulling out. I'm a member of the race, a normal and colloege school graduate, a man of a family and can give reference. Confidentially this communication between you and me is to be kept a secret.

My children I wished to be educated in a different community than here. Where the school facilities are better and less prejudice shown and in fact where advantages are better for our people in all respect. At present I have a good position but I desire to leave the south. A good position even tho' its a laborer's job paying $4.50 or $5.00 a day will suit me till I can do better. Let it be a job there or any where else in the country, just is it is east or west. I'm quite sure you can put me in touch with some one. I'm a letter carrier now and am also a druggist by profession. Perhaps I may through your influence get a transfer to some eastern or western city.

Nevada or California as western states, I prefer, and I must say that I have nothing against Detroit, Mich.

I shall expect an early reply. Remember keep this a secret please until I can perfect some arrangements.

Dear Sir: I am writing you for information I want to come north east but I have not sufficient funds and I am writing you to see if there is any way that you can help me by giving me the names of some of the firms that will send me a transportation as we are down here where we have to be shot down here like rabbits for every little orfence as I seen an orcurince hapen down here this after noon when three depties from the shrief office an one Negro spotter come out and found some of our raice mens in a crap game and it makes me want to leave the south worse than I ever did when such things hapen right at my door. hopeing to have a reply soon and will in close a stamp from the same.

Dear Sir: I hereby enclose you a few lines to find out some few things if you will be so kind to word them to me. I am a southerner lad and has never ben in the north no further than Texas and I has heard so much talk about the north and how much better the colard people are treated up there than they are down here and I has ben striveing so hard in my coming up and now I see that I cannot get up there without the ade of some one and I wants to ask you Dear Sir to please direct me in your best manner the stept that I shall take to get there and if there are any way that you can help me to get there I am kindly asking you for your ade. And if you will ade me please notify me by return mail because I am sure ancious to make it in the north because these southern white people ar so mean and they seems to be getting worse and I wants to get away and they wont pay enough for work for a man to save up enough to get away and live to. If you will not ade me in getting up there please give me some information how I can get there I would like to get there in the early spring, if I can get there if possible. Our Southern white people are so cruel we collord people are almost afraid to walke the streets after night. So please let me hear from you by return mail. I will not say very much in this letter I will tell you more about it when I hear from you please ans. soon to Yours truly.

NEW ORLEANS, LA., MAY 21, 1917.

Dear Sir: As it is my desire to leave the south for some portion of the north to make my future home I desided to write to you as one who is able to furnish proper information for such a move. I am a cook of plain meals and I have knowledge of industrial training. I recieved such training at Tuskegee Inst. some years ago and I have a letter from Mrs. Booker T. Washington bearing out such statement and letters from other responsible corporations and individuals and since I know that I can come up to such recommendations, I want to come north where it is said such individuals are wanted. Therefore will you please furnish me with names and addresses of railroad officials to whom I might write for such employment as it is my desire to work only for railroads, if possible. I have reference to officials who are over extra gangs, bridge gangs, paint gangs and pile drivers over any boarding department which takes in plain meals. I have 25 years experience in this line of work and understand the method of saving the company money.

You will please dig into this in every way that is necessary and whatever charges you want for your trouble make your bill to me, and I will mail same to you.

Wishing you much success in your papers throughout the country, especially in the south as it is the greatest help to the southern negro that has ever been read.

DAPNE, ALA., 4/20/17.

Sir: I am writing you to let you know that there is 15 or 20 familys wants to come up there at once but cant come on account of money to come with and we cant phone you here we will be killed they dont want us to leave here & say if we dont go to war and fight for our country they are going to kill us and wants to get away if we can if you send 20 passes there is no doubt that every one of us will com at once. we are not doing any thing here we cant get a living out of what we do now some of these people are farmers and som are cooks barbers and black smiths but the greater part are farmers & good worker & honest people & up to date the trash pile dont want to go no where. These are nice people and respectable find a place like that & send passes & we all will come at once we all wants to leave here out of this hard luck place if you cant use us find some place that does need this kind of people we are called Negroes here. I am a reader of the Defender and am delighted to know how times are there & was to glad to, know if we could get some one to pass us away from here to a better land. We work but cant get scarcely any thing for it & they dont want us to go away & there is not much of anything here to do & nothing for it Please find some one that need this kind of a people & send at once for us. We dont want anything but our wareing and bed clothes & have not got no money to get away from here with & beging to get away before we are killed and hope to here from you at once. We cant talk to you over the phone here we are afraid to they dont want to hear one say that he or she wants to leave here if we do we are apt to be killed. They say if we dont go to war they are not going to let us stay here with their folks and it is not any thing that we have done to them. We are law abiding people want to treat every bordy right. these people wants to leave here but we cant we are here and have nothing to go with if you will send us some way to get away from here we will work till we pay it all if it takes that for us to go or get away. Now get busy for the south race. The conditions are horrible here with us. they wont give us anything to do & say that we wont need anything but something to eat & wont give us anything for what we do & wants us to stay here. Write me at once that you will do for us we want & opertunity that all we wants is to show you what we can do and will do if we can find some place. we wants to leave here for a north drive somewhere. We see starvation ahead of us here. We want to imigrate to the farmers who need our labor. We have not had no chance to have anything here thats why we plead to you for help to leave here to the North. We are humane but we are not treated such we are treated like brute by our whites here we dont have no privilige no where in the south. We must take anything they put on us. Its hard if its fair. We have not got no cotegous diseases here. We are looking to here from you soon.

A BLOODY SMEAR IN THE PROMISED LAND

Views of a Negro During the Red Summer of 1919:
A Letter from Stanley B. Norvell

In the midst of the Great Migration and after the First World War came what James Weldon Johnson called the Red Summer of 1919. During the Red Summer—so called because of the blood that flowed in the streets—there were race riots in at least twenty-two United States cities, and seventy-four blacks were lynched.

After the Chicago riot of July 1919, the governor of Illinois created the Chicago Commission of Race Relations, composed of six blacks and six whites, to study the causes of the riot and make suggestions for avoiding future disturbances. The Commission's report, published as **The Negro in Chicago,** was a telling indictment of Chicago whites. Unfortunately, its suggestions for the most part were ignored.

Victor F. Lawson, the white editor and publisher of the **Chicago Daily News,** received the following letter shortly after being appointed to the Commission. The black author of the letter, Stanley B. Norvell, wrote to inform Mr. Lawson and the Commission that there was a "new Negro" in Chicago. No longer were blacks going to sit back and be acted upon. They were going to take the initiative and strive actively for the justice due them.

My dear Mr. Lawson:

As the cause of the Negro in America is one that is nearer and dearer to my heart than any other, it has become an obsession with me, and for that reason I am taking the liberty of inflicting upon you this unsolicited treatise on the subject. It is my fond hope that these unlettered lines—which are intended to throw a little light upon the controversy from the dark side—may be of some little service to you and your worthy commission, as data. . . .

I take it that the object of this commission is to obtain by investigation and by conference the cause or causes of the friction between the two races that started the molecules of race hatred into such violent motion as to cause the heterogeneous mixture to boil over in the recent race riots.

Few white men know the cause, for the simple reason that few white men know the Negro as an entity. On the other hand, I daresay that almost any Negro that you might meet on the street could tell you the cause, if he

FROM William Tuttle (ed.), "Views of a Negro During the Red Summer of 1919," *Journal of Negro History*, Vol. LI (July 1966), pp. 211–18. Reprinted by permission of the Association for the Study of Negro Life and History, Inc.

would, for it is doubtful—aye, very doubtful—if he would tell you, because Negroes have become highly suspicious of white men, even such white men as they deem their friends ordinarily. The Negro has always been and is now largely a menial dependent upon the white man's generosity and charity for his livelihood, and for this reason he has become an expert cajoler of the white man and a veritable artist at appearing to be that which he is not. To resort to the vernacular, "conning" the white man has become his profession, his stock in trade. Take for example the Negro in Chicago—and Chicago is fairly representative—sixty per cent of the male Negro population is engaged in menial and servile occupations such as hotel waiters, dining car waiters, sleeping car porters, barbershop porters, billiard room attendants, etc., where "tips" form the greater part of their remuneration. Thirty per cent are laborers and artisans, skilled and unskilled, governmental and municipal employees; while the remaining ten per cent are business and professional men.

Unfortunately it is always by the larger class—the menial, servitor and flunky class—that the race is judged. Even at that, we would not object to being judged by this class of our race, if those who did the judging had a thorough knowledge of the individuals who make up this class. Unfortunately they have not this knowledge nor can they get it except through the instrumentality of just such a commission as that to which you gentlemen have been assigned. The white man of America knows just about as much about the mental and moral calibre, the home life and social activities of this class of colored citizens as he does about the same things concerning the inhabitants of the thus far unexplored planet of Mars. If any white man were to be asked what he thought of George the porter on the Golden State Limited; or of James the waiter on the Twentieth Century diner; or of Shorty who gives him his billiard cue at Mussey's; or of Snowball who polishes his boots at the Palmer House; or of that old gray-haired relic of by-gone days . . . who withholds his hat and menaces him with a long-handled whisk broom until he capitulates with a nickel; I say were you to ask any white man concerning these dusky servitors he would tell you that he was either honest or dishonest, that he was either industrious or lazy, that he was smart or stupid as the case might be. He will discuss him in a general superficial sort of way and if you press him further you will be surprised to know that in spite of his years of acquaintance with the subject he knows absolutely nothing about intellect, ability, ambitions [,] the home life and environment of one with whom he has come into daily contact for years. He is just a "nigger" and he takes him for granted, as a matter of course. . . .

In hotels, barber shops and billiard rooms where the patrons come in regularly, Sambo has a chance to get well acquainted with them. . . . He knows just what each one's business is and where it is located. He knows just where each one lives and in what circumstances. . . . He knows just how much each one is going to give him. There are some that never give him anything but still he likes them immensely because they treat him with kindness and consideration. There are some who tip him most liberally whom he despises because they are always making some aspersion about his race or because they always want him to clown and demean himself in order to get their money. . . . He knows that if he says, "Yas sah, Boss," and grins that you will vote him a "good nigger" and give him something; but were he to say, "Very good, sir," you would not only not give him anything but would probably take a dislike to him and consider him supercilious. . . .

I can walk down the "Boul Mich" and be surveyed by the most critical of Sherlock Holmeses and I will wager that none of them can accurately deduce what I am or what I represent. They cannot tell whether I am well off or hard up; whether I am educated or illiterate; whether I am a northerner or a southerner; whether I am a native born Negro or a foreigner; whether I live among beautiful surroundings or in the squalor of the "black belt." I defy the shrewdest of your pseudo detectives to know whether I am a reputable citizen or whether I am a newly arrived crook. They cannot tell by looking at me what my income is. . . . The point is that I am only an ordinary, average Negro and that the white man is constantly making the mistake of discounting us and rating us too cheaply. He should wake up to the fact that brain is not peculiar to any race or nationality but is merely a matter of development.

This in a measure explains how the American white man knows less about the American Negro than the latter does about the former. . . .

The further causes of the apparent increased friction between the two races, in my opinion is due to the gradual, and inevitable evolution—metamorphosis, if you please—of the Negro. The Negro has also progressed in knowledge by his study of the white man, while the white man blinded by either his prejudice or by his indifference has failed to study the Negro judiciously, and as a consequence, he knows no more about him than he did fifty years ago and still continues to judge him and to formulate opinions about him by his erstwhile standards. Today we have with us a new Negro. A brand new Negro, if you please. What opportunities have you better class white people for getting into and observing the homes of the better class of colored people[?] Yet the duties of the colored man in his menial capacities gives him an insight of your home life. As a suggestion, if I may be permitted to make one, I suggest that the white members of this commission make it their business to try to obtain an opportunity through some of the colored members of the commission to visit the homes of some of our better class people. You will find that "Uncle Tom" that charming old figure of literature contemporary with the war of the rebellion is quite dead now and that his prototypes are almost as extinct as is the great auk, the dodo bird, old Dobbin and the chaise, and the man who refused to shave until William Jennings Bryan was elected. You will have committed an unpardonable faux pas if you should happen to call any eminently respectable old colored lady "mammy" or "auntie," and yet there still remain many misguided and well-intentioned folks of the white race who still persist in so doing. This was all brought about by education. . . . When a young colored boy of Chicago goes through the eight grades of grammar school and wins the cherished Victor F. Lawson diploma; then through a four year high school course and wins a university scholarship; and then goes to college and wins a degree . . . and is highly popular and well received among his fellow classmates, it is a very difficult thing for him to get it into his head that he is inferior to anybody that has no more knowledge, ability nor money than himself. Regardless of what the eminent sociologists may say, and the fiery and usually groundless claims of the southern negrophile [negrophobe] to the contrary notwithstanding, there is no amount of logic, nor philosophy, nor ethnology, nor anthropology, nor sociology that can convince him to his own satisfaction that he is not the possessor of all the lesser and major attributes that go to make up a good citizen by all of the standards which our republican conventions hold near and dear.

Take the late war for example, and consider the effect that it has had upon the Negro, by and large. I believe that the mental attitude of the Negro that went to war is comparable in a certain degree to the mental attitude of most of the Negroes throughout the country; so far as the awakenings are concerned. The Negro of this country has gone through the same evolution that the white man has, in his own way; and in a large percentage of the total, that way is not far removed from the way the white man's mind thought out the matter or is thinking it out, especially the soldier mind. The Negro of our country . . . the Negro of the mass I mean, is comparable in his awakening and in his manner of thought after that awakening, to these white boys who went to war. The white soldiers—being young—had but little thought of anything but their immediate concerns, and the Negro, until lately, had but little thought of anything but his immediate concerns—being segregated. How I loathe that word.

Since the war the Negro has been jolted into thinking by circumstances. . . . [Negroes] have learned that there were treaties and boundaries and Leagues of Nations and mandatories, and Balkan states, and a dismembered Poland, a ravished Belgium, a stricken France, a soviet Russia and a republic in Ireland and so on, and they have . . . for the first time in their lives taken a peep of their own volition and purely because they wanted to know, into the workings of governmental things of those other countries, and have tried to reason out the possible real cause of all of this bloodshed and woe and misery along such international, allied and foreign government and other vague lines.

Now then, this has logically—and we are nebulously logical, despite what the southern white says about us—brought us round to a sort of realization of how our government was made and is conducted. I venture to claim that any average Negro of some education, if closely questioned, and the questions were put to him in simple understandable form, will tell you that he finally has come to know that he counts as a part of his government, that he is a unit in it. It took a world war to get that idea into general Negro acceptance, but it is there now. Centuries of the dictum, which heretofore not many of us disputed, that, "This was a white man's country and that we were destined to always be hewers of wood and carriers of water," was set aside by circumstances and conditions and reactions and reflexes and direct contacts of this war. Negroes were pulled out of their ordinary pursuits all over the country and called upon to do things that they had to do because there was nobody at hand to do them, and those circumstances induced an awakening that must inevitably continue for all time.

The five hundred thousand Negroes who were sent overseas to serve their country were brought into contacts that widened both their perceptions and their perspectives, broadened them, gave them new angles on life, on government, and on what both mean. They are now new men and world men, if you please. . . .

What the Negro wants and what the Negro will not be satisfied with until he gets is that treatment and that recognition that accords him not one jot or tittle less than that which any other citizen of the United States is satisfied with. He has become tired of equal rights. He wants the same rights. He is tired of equal accommodations. He wants [the] same accommodations. He is tired of equal opportunity. He wants the same opportunity. He must and will have industrial, commercial, civil and political equality. America has already given him these inalienable rights, but she has not always seen to it that he has received them. America must see that the Negro is not deprived of any right that she has given him otherwise the gift is bare, and in view of her recent international exploits she will stand in grave danger of losing her national integrity in the eyes of Europe and she will be forced to admit to her European adversaries that her constitution is but a scrap of paper.

Social equality—that ancient skeleton in the closet of the southern negrophile [negrophobe], whose bones are always brought out and rattled ominously whenever the Negro question is discussed—is in no way a factor in the solution of the problem, but is a condition that will quite naturally exist when the problem is eventually solved—just a little prior to the millennium. Leastwise considering the unsettled condition of the world at large, the white man of this country has a great deal more to be sensibly alarmed about than the coming of social equality. Looking into the future I can see more ominous clouds on the horizon of this country's destiny than the coming of social equality.

When the Negro ponders the situation—and now he is beginning to seriously do that—it is with a feeling of poignant resentment that he sees his alleged inferiority constantly and blatantly advertised at every hand, by the press, the pulpit, the stage and by the glaring and hideous sign-boards of segregation. Try to imagine, if you can, the feelings of a Negro army officer, who clothed in the full panoply of his profession and wearing the decorations for valor of three governments, is forced to the indignity of a jim-crow car and who is refused a seat in a theatre and a bed in a hotel. Think of the feelings of a colored officer, who after having been graduated from West Point and having worked up step by step to the rank of colonel to be retired on account of blood pressure—and other pressure—in order that he might not automatically succeed to the rank of general officer. Try to imagine the smouldering hatred within the breast of an overseas veteran who is set upon and mercilessly beaten by a gang of young hoodlums simply because he is colored. Think of the feelings in the hearts of boys and girls of my race who are clean, intelligent and industrious who apply for positions only to meet with the polite reply that, "We don't hire niggers." Think how it must feel to pass at the top of the list and get notice of appointment to some nice civil service position that is paid for out of the taxes of the commonwealth, and upon reporting to assume the duties thereof, to be told that there has been a mistake made in the appointment.

When you think of these things, and consider them seriously it is easy to see the underlying, contributory causes of the friction that led up to the recent racial troubles. It is a well known fact that civilization is but a veneer which lightly covers the surface of mankind; that if slightly scratched, with the right kind of tool, a man will turn into a bloodthirsty savage in the twinkling of an eye. The overt act that is alleged to have started the recent conflagration, would not have in itself been sufficient to have ignited and exploded such vials of wrath had not the structure of society been long soaked in the inflammable gasolene of smouldering resentment.

As soon as the white man is willing to inform himself about the true status of the Negro as he finds him today, and is willing to take off the goggles of race prejudice and to study the Negro with the naked eye of fairness, and to treat him with justice and equity, he will come to the conclusion that the Negro has "arrived" and then voila, you have the solution to the problem.

We ask not charity but justice. We no longer want perquisites but wages, salary and commissions. Much has been said anent the white man's burden. We admit to having been a burden, just as an infant that cannot walk is at one time a burden. But in the natural order of things the infant soon ceases to be a burden and eventually grows up to be a crutch for the arm that once carried him. We feel that now we are able to take our first, feeble diffident steps, and we implore the white man to set his burden down and let us try to walk. Put us in your counting rooms, your factories and in your banks. The young people who went to school with us and who learned the three R's from the same black-board as ourselves will surely not object to working with us after we have graduated. If they do, it will only be because they are not yet accustomed to the new conditions. That is nothing. People soon become accustomed to new things and things that seem at first preposterous soon become commonplace. We have surely proven by years of unrequited toil and by constant and unfaltering loyalty and fealty that we are worthy of the justice that we ask. For God's sake give it to us!

STANLEY B. NORVELL

BLACK POETS SING

The literary output of the Harlem Renaissance of the 1920's was prodigious. Whether this was the result of a new burst of black talent or merely the result of the downtown publishers' "discovery" of talent that had always existed is impossible to determine. The fact remains that much of the writing of this movement has stood the test of time and entered the canon of American literature.

Selections from four poets have been chosen to illustrate some of the issues dealt with by the Renaissance.

Countee Cullen

Countee Cullen (1903–1946) was publishing poetry before his graduation from De Witt Clinton High School in New York City. He was perhaps the most distinguished black poet of the period of the Harlem Renaissance. The first poem given here is a moving statement about the anomaly of being a black poet. The second reflects the ambivalence of the black intellectual who is caught between his African past and his American present.

Yet Do I Marvel

I doubt not God is good, well-meaning, kind,
And did He stoop to quibble could tell why
The little buried mole continues blind,
Why flesh that mirrors Him must someday die,

FROM *On These I Stand* by Countee Cullen: "Yet Do I Marvel"—Copyright 1925 by Harper & Brothers; renewed 1953 by Ida M. Cullen. By permission of Harper & Row, Publishers, Incorporated.

Make plain the reason tortured Tantalus
Is baited by the fickle fruit, declare
If merely brute caprice dooms Sisyphus
To struggle up a never-ending stair.
Inscrutable His ways are, and immune
To catechism by a mind too strewn
With petty cares to slightly understand
What awful brain compels His awful hand.
Yet do I marvel at this curious thing:
To make a poet black, and bid him sing!

Heritage (*For Harold Jackman*)

What is Africa to me:
Copper sun or scarlet sea,
Jungle star or jungle track,
Strong bronzed men, or regal black
Women from whose loins I sprang
When the birds of Eden sang?
One three centuries removed
From the scenes his fathers loved,
Spicy grove, cinnamon tree,
What is Africa to me?

So I lie, who all day long
Want no sound except the song
Sung by wild barbaric birds
Goading massive jungle herds,
Juggernauts of flesh that pass
Trampling tall defiant grass
Where young forest lovers lie,
Plighting troth beneath the sky.
So I lie, who always hear,
Though I cram against my ear
Both my thumbs, and keep them there,
Great drums throbbing through the air.
So I lie, whose fount of pride,
Dear distress, and joy allied,
Is my somber flesh and skin,
With the dark blood dammed within

Like great pulsing tides of wine
That, I fear, must burst the fine
Channels of the chafing net
Where they surge and foam and fret.

Africa? A book one thumbs
Listlessly, till slumber comes.
Unremembered are her bats
Circling through the night, her cats
Crouching in the river reeds,
Stalking gentle flesh that feeds
By the river brink; no more
Does the bugle-throated roar
Cry that monarch claws have leapt
From the scabbards where they slept.
Silver snakes that once a year
Doff the lovely coats you wear,
Seek no covert in your fear
Lest a mortal eye should see;
What's your nakedness to me?
Here no leprous flowers rear
Fierce corollas in the air;
Here no bodies sleek and wet,
Dripping mingled rain and sweat,
Tread the savage measures of
Jungle boys and girls in love.
What is last year's snow to me,
Last year's anything? The tree
Budding yearly must forget
How its past arose or set—
Bough and blossom, flower, fruit,
Even what shy bird with mute
Wonder at her travail there,
Meekly labored in its hair.
One three centuries removed
From the scenes his fathers loved,
Spicy grove, cinnamon tree,
What is Africa to me?

So I lie, who find no peace
Night or day, no slight release
From the unremittant beat
Made by cruel padded feet
Walking through my body's street.
Up and down they go, and back,

Treading out a jungle track.
So I lie, who never quite
Safely sleep from rain at night—
I can never rest at all
When the rain begins to fall;
Like a soul gone mad with pain
I must match its weird refrain;
Ever must I twist and squirm,
Writhing like a baited worm,
While its primal measures drip
Through my body, crying, "Strip!
Doff this new exuberance.
Come and dance the Lover's Dance!"
In an old remembered way
Rain works on me night and day.

Quaint, outlandish heathen gods
Black men fashion out of rods,
Clay, and brittle bits of stone,
In a likeness like their own,
My conversion came high-priced;
I belong to Jesus Christ,
Preacher of humility,
Heathen gods are naught to me.

Father, Son, and Holy Ghost,
So I make an idle boast;
Jesus of the twice-turned cheek,
Lamb of God, although I speak
With my mouth thus, in my heart
Do I play a double part.
Ever at Thy glowing altar
Must my heart grow sick and falter,
Wishing He I served were black,
Thinking then it would not lack
Precedent of pain to guide it,
Let who would or might deride it;
Surely then this flesh would know
Yours had borne a kindred woe.
Lord, I fashion dark gods, too,
Daring even to give You
Dark despairing features where,
Crowned with dark rebellious hair,
Patience wavers just so much as
Mortal grief compels, while touches

Quick and hot, of anger, rise
To smitten cheek and weary eyes.
Lord, forgive me if my need
Sometimes shapes a human creed.
All day long and all night through,
One thing only must I do:
Quench my pride and cool my blood,
Lest I perish in the flood,
Lest a hidden ember set
Timber that I thought was wet
Burning like the dryest flax,
Melting like the merest wax,
Lest the grave restore its dead.
Not yet has my heart or head
In the least way realized
They and I are civilized.

Langston Hughes

Langston Hughes (1902–1967) is represented here by two short lyrics that express
the longing of the black man for his rightful place in the world. The first deals with
what Hughes considered the inevitable acceptance of the black man and the shame
white America would feel when that acceptance finally came. The second reflects
on the charms of blackness. Hughes' remarkable literary output included poetry,
essays, novels, newspaper articles, and works of history.

I, Too

I, too, sing America.

I am the darker brother.
They send me to eat in the kitchen
When company comes,
But I laugh,
And eat well,
And grow strong.

Tomorrow,
I'll be at the table
When company comes.

FROM *Selected Poems*, by Langston Hughes: "I, Too"—Copyright 1926 by Alfred A.
Knopf, Inc. and renewed 1954 by Langston Hughes. Reprinted by permission of the
publisher.

Nobody'll dare
Say to me,
"Eat in the kitchen,"
Then.

Besides,
They'll see how beautiful I am
And be ashamed—

I, too, am America.

Dream Variation

To fling my arms wide
In some place of the sun,
To whirl and to dance
Till the white day is done.
Then rest at cool evening
Beneath a tall tree
While night comes on gently,
    Dark like me—
That is my dream!

To fling my arms wide
In the face of the sun,
Dance! Whirl! Whirl!
Till the quick day is done.
Rest at pale evening . . .
A tall, slim tree . . .
Night coming tenderly
    Black like me.

James Weldon Johnson

James Weldon Johnson (1871–1938) had a varied career as a teacher, poet, diplo-
mat, and the executive secretary of the NAACP. In his poetic work **God's Trombones,**
Johnson tried to capture the imagery and the cadences of the old-time black preachers. The following is a section from this work dealing with the promise of ultimate
deliverance that played such a large part in black Christianity.

FROM *Selected Poems*, by Langston Hughes: "Dream Variation"—Copyright 1926 by
Alfred A. Knopf, Inc. and renewed 1954 by Langston Hughes. Reprinted by permission
of the publisher.

Go Down Death (*A Funeral Sermon*)

Weep not, weep not,
She is not dead;
She's resting in the bosom of Jesus.
Heart-broken husband—weep no more;
Grief-stricken son—weep no more;
She's only just gone home.

Day before yesterday morning,
God was looking down from his great, high heaven,
Looking down on all his children,
And his eye fell on Sister Caroline,
Tossing on her bed of pain.
And God's big heart was touched with pity,
With the everlasting pity.

And God sat back on his throne,
And he commanded that tall, bright angel standing at his right hand:
Call me Death!
And that tall, bright angel cried in a voice
That broke like a clap of thunder:
Call Death!—Call Death!
And the echo sounded down the streets of heaven
Till it reached away back to that shadowy place,
Where Death waits with his pale, white horses.

And Death heard the summons,
And he leaped on his fastest horse,
Pale as a sheet in the moonlight.
Up the golden street Death galloped,
And the hoof of his horse struck fire from the gold,
But they didn't make no sound.
Up Death rode to the Great White Throne,
And waited for God's command.

And God said: Go down, Death, go down,
Go down to Savannah, Georgia,
Down in Yamacraw,
And find Sister Caroline.
She's borne the burden and heat of the day,

FROM *God's Trombones* by James Weldon Johnson: "Go Down Death (A Funeral Sermon)"—Copyright 1927 by The Viking Press, Inc., renewed 1955 by Grace Nail Johnson. Reprinted by permission of The Viking Press, Inc.

She's labored long in my vineyard,
And she's tired—
She's weary—
Go down, Death, and bring her to me.

And Death didn't say a word,
But he loosed the reins on his pale, white horse,
And he clamped the spurs to his bloodless sides,
And out and down he rode,
Through heaven's pearly gates,
Past suns and moons and stars;
On Death rode,
And the foam from his horse was like a comet in the sky;
On Death rode,
Leaving the lightning's flash behind;
Straight on down he came.

While we were watching round her bed,
She turned her eyes and looked away,
She saw what we couldn't see;
She saw Old Death. She saw Old Death.
Coming like a falling star.
But Death didn't frighten Sister Caroline;
He looked to her like a welcome friend.
And she whispered to us: I'm going home,
And she smiled and closed her eyes.

And Death took her up like a baby,
And she lay in his icy arms,
But she didn't feel no chill.
And Death began to ride again—
Up beyond the evening star,
Out beyond the morning star,
Into the glittering light of glory,
On to the Great White Throne.
And there he laid Sister Caroline
On the loving breast of Jesus.

And Jesus took his own hand and wiped away her tears,
And he smoothed the furrows from her face,
And the angels sang a little song,
And Jesus rocked her in his arms,
And kept a-saying: Take your rest,
Take your rest, take your rest.

Weep not—weep not,
She is not dead;
She's resting in the bosom of Jesus.

Claude McKay

Claude McKay (1890–1948) first published in his native Jamaica. He came to the United States in his early twenties to attend Tuskegee Institute and Kansas State University. Soon he moved to New York City, where he became an important novelist and journalist. He also wrote poetry, however, and the angry poem that follows was composed during the Red Summer of 1919 as blacks fought the white mobs.

If We Must Die

If we must die—let it not be like hogs
Hunted and penned in an inglorious spot,
While round us bark the mad and hungry dogs,
Making their mock at our accursed lot.
If we must die—oh, let us nobly die,
So that our precious blood may not be shed
In vain; then even the monsters we defy
Shall be constrained to honor us though dead!
Oh, Kinsmen! We must meet the common foe;
Though far outnumbered, let us show us brave,
And for their thousand blows deal one deathblow!
What though before us lies the open grave?
Like men we'll face the murderous, cowardly pack,
Pressed to the wall, dying, but fighting back!

FREE AFRICA FOR AFRICANS

Marcus Garvey / The Negro's Greatest Enemy

Marcus Garvey organized the Universal Negro Improvement Association (UNIA) in Jamaica in 1914 to prepare for the time when all the world's black men would live together in freedom from white domination. In 1916, Garvey went to New York City, where

FROM *Selected Poems of Claude McKay:* "If We Must Die." Reprinted by permission of Twayne Publishers, Inc.

his ideas drew an enthusiastic response from rural blacks lately come to the city. After the First World War, increasingly frustrated returning servicemen and masses of unemployed urban blacks swelled the ranks of Garvey supporters. By 1919, the UNIA had thirty branches in the United States and several abroad. In 1920, an African government-in-exile was established by the UNIA with Garvey as provisional president. Through his appeal to black pride and a future black state, Garvey attracted millions of black sympathizers to his cause.

In the autobiographical article reprinted here, Garvey tells about the growing race consciousness that led him to found the UNIA. He also recounts the opposition he received from other black men in the United States—opposition that ultimately led to his imprisonment.

Garvey died in London in 1940 without ever having visited Africa, the land that held his dream.

I was born in the Island of Jamaica, British West Indies, on Aug. 17, 1887. My parents were black negroes. My father was a man of brilliant intellect and dashing courage. He was unafraid of consequences. He took human chances in the course of life, as most bold men do, and he failed at the close of his career. He once had a fortune; he died poor. My mother was a sober and conscientious Christian, too soft and good for the time in which she lived. She was the direct opposite of my father. He was severe, firm, determined, bold and strong, refusing to yield even to superior forces if he believed he was right. My mother, on the other hand, was always willing to return a smile for a blow, and ever ready to bestow charity upon her enemy. Of this strange combination I was born thirty-six years ago, and ushered into a world of sin, the flesh and the devil.

I grew up with other black and white boys. I was never whipped by any, but made them all respect the strength of my arms. I got my education from many sources—through private tutors, two public schools, two grammar or high schools and two colleges. My teachers were men and women of varied experiences and abilities; four of them were eminent preachers. They studied me and I studied them. With some I became friendly in after years, others and I drifted apart, because as a boy they wanted to whip me, and I simply refused to be whipped. I was not made to be whipped. It annoys me to be defeated; hence to me, to be once defeated is to find cause for an everlasting struggle to reach the top.

I became a printer's apprentice at an early age, while still attending school. My apprentice master was a highly educated and alert man. In the affairs of business and the world he had no peer. He taught me many things

FROM Marcus Garvey, "The Negro's Greatest Enemy," *Current History* (Old Series), Vol. XVIII (September 1923), pp. 951–57.

before I reached twelve, and at fourteen I had enough intelligence and experience to manage men. I was strong and manly, and I made them respect me. I developed a strong and forceful character, and have maintained it still.

To me, at home in my early days, there was no difference between white and black. One of my father's properties, the place where I lived most of the time, was adjoining that of a white man. He had three girls and two boys; the Wesleyan minister, another white man whose church my parents attended, also had property adjoining ours. He had three girls and one boy. All of us were playmates. We romped and were happy children playmates together. The little white girl whom I liked most knew no better than I did myself. We were two innocent fools who never dreamed of a race feeling and problem. As a child, I went to school with white boys and girls, like all other negroes. We were not called negroes then. I never heard the term negro used once until I was about fourteen.

At fourteen my little white playmate and I parted. Her parents thought the time had come to separate us and draw the color line. They sent her and another sister to Edinburgh, Scotland, and told her that she was never to write or try to get in touch with me, for I was a "nigger." It was then that I found for the first time that there was some difference in humanity, and that there were different races, each having its own separate and distinct social life. I did not care about the separation after I was told about it, because I never thought all during our childhood association that the girl and the rest of the children of her race were better than I was; in fact, they used to look up to me. So I simply had no regrets. I only thought them "fresh."

After my first lesson in race distinction, I never thought of playing with white girls any more, even if they might be next door neighbors. At home my sister's company was good enough for me, and at school I made friends with the colored girls next to me. White boys and I used to frolic together. We played cricket and baseball, ran races and rode bicycles together, took each other to the river and to the sea beach to learn to swim, and made boyish efforts while out in deep water to drown each other, making a sprint for shore crying out "shark, shark, shark." In all our experiences, however, only one black boy was drowned. He went under on a Friday afternoon after school hours, and his parents found him afloat half eaten by sharks on the following Sunday afternoon. Since then we boys never went back to sea.

"YOU ARE BLACK"

At maturity the black and white boys separated, and took different courses in life. I grew up then to see the difference between the races more and more. My schoolmates as young men did not know or remember me any more. Then I realized that I had to make a fight for a place in the world, that it was not so easy to pass on to office and position. Personally, however, I had not much difficulty in finding and holding a place for myself, for I was aggressive. At eighteen I had an excellent position as manager of a large printing establishment, having under my control several men old enough to be my grandfathers. But I got mixed up with public life. I started to take an interest in the politics of my country, and then I saw the injustice done to my race because it was black, and I became dissatisfied on that account. I went traveling to South and Central America and parts of the West Indies to find out if it was so elsewhere, and I found the same situation. I set sail for Europe to find out if it was different there, and again I found the same stumbling-block—"You are black." I read of the conditions in America. I read "Up From Slavery," by Booker T. Washington, and then my doom—if I may so call it—of being a race leader dawned upon me in London after I had traveled through almost half of Europe.

I asked, "Where is the black man's Government?" "Where is his King and his kingdom?" "Where is his President, his country, and his ambassador, his army, his navy, his men of big affairs?" I could not find them, and then I declared, "I will help to make them."

Becoming naturally restless for the opportunity of doing something for the advancement of my race, I was determined that the black man would not continue to be kicked about by all the other races and nations of the world, as I saw it in the West Indies, South and Central America and Europe, and as I read of it in America. My young and ambitious mind led me into flights of great imagination. I saw before me then, even as I do now, a new world of black men, not peons, serfs, dogs and slaves, but a nation of sturdy men making their impress upon civilization and causing a new light to dawn upon the human race. I could not remain in London any more. My brain was afire. There was a world of thought to conquer. I had to start ere it became too late and the work be not done. Immediately I boarded a ship at Southampton for Jamaica, where I arrived on July 15, 1914. The Universal Negro Improvement Association and African Communities (Imperial) League was founded and organized five days after my arrival, with the program of uniting all the negro peoples of the world into one great body to establish a country and Government absolutely their own.

Where did the name of the organization come from? It was while speaking to a West Indian negro who was a passenger on the ship with me from Southampton, who was returning home to the West Indies from Basutoland with his Basuto wife, that I further learned of the horrors of native life in Africa. He related to me in conversation such horrible and pitiable tales that my heart bled within me. Retiring from the conversation to my cabin, all day and the following night I pondered over the subject matter of that conversation, and at midnight, lying flat on my back, the vision and thought came to me that I should name the organization the Universal Negro Improvement Association and African Communities (Imperial) League. Such a name I thought would embrace the purpose of all black humanity. Thus to the world a name was born, a movement created, and a man became known.

I really never knew there was so much color prejudice in Jamaica, my own native home, until I started the work of the Universal Negro Improvement Association. We started immediately before the war. I had just returned from a successful trip to Europe, which was an exceptional achievement for a black man. The daily papers wrote me up with big headlines and told of my movement. But nobody wanted to be a negro. "Garvey is crazy; he has lost his head," "Is that the use he is going to make of his experience and intelligence?"—such were the criticisms passed upon me. Men and women as black as I, and even more so, had believed themselves white under the West Indian order of society. I was simply an impossible man to use openly the term "negro;" yet every one beneath his breath was calling the black man a negro.

I had to decide whether to please my friends and be one of the "black-whites" of Jamaica, and be reasonably prosperous, or come out openly and defend and help improve and protect the integrity of the black millions and suffer. I decided to do the latter, hence my offence against "colored-black-white" society in the colonies and America. I was openly hated and persecuted by some of these colored men of the island who did not want to be classified as negroes, but as white. They hated me worse than poison. They opposed me at every step, but I had a large number of white friends, who encouraged and helped me. Notable among them were the then Governor of the Colony, the Colonial Secretary and several other prominent men. But they were afraid of offending the "colored gentry" that were passing for white. Hence my fight had to be made alone. I spent hundreds of pounds (sterling) helping the organization to gain a footing. I also gave up all my time to the promulgation of its ideals. I became a marked man, but I was determined that the work should be done.

The war helped a great deal in arousing the consciousness of the colored people to the reasonableness of our program, especially after the British at home had rejected a large number of West Indian colored men who wanted to be officers in the British army. When they were told that negroes could not be officers in the British army they started their own propaganda, which supplemented the program of the Universal Negro Improvement Association. With this and other contributing agencies a few of the stiff-necked colored people began to see the reasonableness of my program, but they were firm in refusing to be known as negroes. Furthermore, I was a black man and therefore had absolutely no right to lead; in the opinion of the "colored" element, leadership should have been in the hands of a yellow or a very light man. On such flimsy prejudices our race has been retarded. There is more bitterness among us negroes because of the caste of color than there is between any other peoples, not excluding the people of India.

I succeeded to a great extent in establishing the association in Jamaica with the assistance of a Catholic Bishop, the Governor, Sir John Pringle, the Rev. William Graham, a Scottish clergyman, and several other white friends. I got in touch with Booker Washington and told him what I wanted to do. He invited me to America and promised to speak with me in the Southern and other States to help my work. Although he died in the Fall of 1915, I made my arrangements and arrived in the United States on March 23, 1916.

Here I found a new and different problem. I immediately visited some of the then so-called negro leaders, only to discover, after a close study of them, that they had no program, but were mere opportunists who were living off their so-called leadership while the poor people were groping in the dark. I traveled through thirty-eight States and everywhere found the same condition. I visited Tuskegee and paid my respects to the dead hero, Booker Washington, and then returned to New York, where I organized the New York division of the Universal Negro Improvement Association. After instructing the people in the aims and objects of the association, I intended returning to Jamaica to perfect the Jamaica organization, but when we had enrolled about 800 or 1,000 members in the Harlem district and had elected the officers, a few negro politicans began trying to turn the movement into a political club.

POLITICAL FACTION FIGHT

Seeing that these politicians were about to destroy my ideals, I had to fight to get them out of the organization. There it was that I made my first political enemies in Harlem. They fought me until they smashed the first organization and reduced its membership to about fifty. I started again, and in two months built up a new organization of about 1,500 members. Again the politicians came and divided us into two factions. They took away all the books of the organization, its treasury and all its belongings. At that time I was only an organizer, for it was not then my intention to remain in America, but to return to Jamaica. The organization had its proper officers elected, and I was not an officer of the New York division, but President of the Jamaica branch.

On the second split in Harlem thirteen of the members conferred with me and requested me to become President for a time of the New York organization so as to save them from the politicians. I consented and was elected President. There then sprung up two factions, one led by the politicians with the books and the money, and the other led by me. My faction had no money. I placed at their disposal what money I had, opened an office for them, rented a meeting place, employed two women secretaries, went on the streets of Harlem at night to speak for the movement. In three weeks more than 2,000 new members joined. By this time I had the association incorporated so as to prevent the other faction using the name, but in two weeks the politicians had stolen all the people's money and had smashed up their faction.

The organization under my Presidency grew by leaps and bounds. I started The Negro World. Being a journalist, I edited this paper free of cost for the association, and worked for them without pay until November, 1920. I traveled all over the country for the association at my own expense, and established branches until in 1919 we had about thirty branches in different cities. By my writings and speeches we were able to build up a large organization of over 2,000,000 by June, 1919, at which time we launched the program of the Black Star Line.

To have built up a new organization, which was not purely political, among negroes in America was a wonderful feat, for the negro politician does not allow any other kind of organization within his race to thrive. We succeeded, however, in making the Universal Negro Improvement Association so formidable in 1919 that we encountered more trouble from our political brethren. They sought the influence of the District Attorney's office of the County of New York to put us out of business. Edwin P. Kilroe, at that time an Assistant District Attorney, on the complaint of the negro politicians, started to investigate us and the association. Mr. Kilroe would constantly and continuously call me to his office for investigation on extraneous matters without coming to the point. The result was that after the eighth or ninth time I wrote an article in our newspaper, The Negro World, against him. This was interpreted as criminal libel, for which I was indicted and arrested, but subsequently dismissed on retracting what I had written.

During my many tilts with Mr. Kilroe, the question of the Black Star Line was discussed. He did not want us to have a line of ships. I told him that even as there was a White Star Line, we would have, irrespective of his wishes, a Black Star Line. On June 27, 1919, we incorporated the Black Star Line of Delaware, and in September we obtained a ship.

The following month (October) a man by the name of Tyler came to my office at 56 West 135th Street, New York City, and told me that Mr. Kilroe had sent him to "get me," and at once fired four shots at me from a .38-calibre revolver. He wounded me in the right leg and the right side of my scalp. I was taken to the Harlem Hospital, and he was arrested. The next day it was reported that he committed suicide in jail just before he was to be taken before a City Magistrate.

RECORD-BREAKING CONVENTION

The first year of our activities for the Black Star Line added prestige to the Universal Negro Improvement Association. Several hundred thousand dollars worth of shares were sold. Our first ship, the steamship Yarmouth, had made two voyages to the West Indies and Central America. The white press had flashed the news all over the world. I, a young negro, as President of the corporation, had become famous. My name was discussed on five continents. The Universal Negro Improvement Association gained millions of followers all over the world. By August, 1920, over 4,000,000 persons had joined the movement. A convention of all the negro peoples of the world was called to meet in New York that month. Delegates came from all parts of the known world. Over 25,000 persons packed the Madison Square Garden on Aug. 1 to hear me speak to the first International Convention of Negroes. It was a record-breaking meeting, the first and the biggest of its kind. The name of Garvey had become known as a leader of his race.

Such fame among negroes was too much for other race leaders and politicians to tolerate. My downfall was planned by my enemies. They laid all kinds of traps for me. They scattered their spies among the employes of the Black Star Line and the Universal Negro Improvement Association. Our office records were stolen. Employes started to be openly dishonest; we could get no convictions against them; even if on complaint they were held by a Magistrate, they were dismissed by the Grand Jury. The ships' officers started to pile up thousands of dollars of debts against the company without the knowledge of the officers of the corporation. Our ships were damaged at sea, and there was a general riot of wreck and ruin. Officials of the Universal Negro Improvement Association also began to steal and be openly dishonest. I had to dismiss them. They joined my enemies, and thus I had an endless fight on my hands to save the ideals of the association and carry out our program for the race. My negro enemies, finding that they alone could not destroy me, resorted to misrepresenting me to the leaders of the white race, several of whom, without proper investigation, also opposed me.

With robberies from within and from without, the Black Star Line was forced to suspend active business in December, 1921. While I was on a business trip to the West Indies in the Spring of 1921, the Black Star Line received the blow from which it was unable to recover. A sum of $25,000 was paid by one of the officers of the corporation to a man to purchase a ship, but the ship was never obtained and the money was never returned. The company was defrauded of a further sum of $11,000. Through such actions on the part of dishonest men in the shipping business, the Black Star Line received its first setback. This resulted in my being indicted for using the United States mails to defraud investors in the company. I was subsequently convicted and sentenced to five years in a Federal penitentiary. My trial is a matter of history. I know I was not given a square deal, because my indictment was the result of a "frame-up" among my political and business enemies. I had to conduct my own case in court because of the peculiar position in which I found myself. I had millions of friends and a large number of enemies. I wanted a colored attorney to handle my case, but there was none I could trust. I feel that I have been denied justice because of prejudice. Yet I have an abundance of faith in the courts of America, and I hope yet to obtain justice on my appeal.

ASSOCIATION'S 6,000,000 MEMBERSHIP

The temporary ruin of the Black Star Line has in no way affected the larger work of the Universal Negro Improvement Association, which now has 900 branches with an approximate membership of 6,000,000. This organization has succeeded in organizing the negroes all over the world and we now look forward to a renaissance that will create a new people and bring about the restoration of Ethiopia's ancient glory.

Being black, I have committed an unpardonable offense against the very light colored negroes in America and the West Indies by making myself famous as a negro leader of millions. In their view, no black man must rise above them, but I still forge ahead determined to give to the world the truth about the new negro who is determined to make and hold for himself a place in the affairs of men. The Universal Negro Improvement Association has been misrepresented by my enemies. They have tried to make it appear that we are hostile to other races. This is absolutely false. We love all humanity. We are working for the peace of the world which we believe can only come about when all races are given their due.

We feel that there is absolutely no reason why there should be any differences between the black and white races, if each stop to adjust and steady itself. We believe in the purity of both races. We do not believe the black man should be encouraged in the idea that his highest purpose in life is to marry a white woman, but we do believe that the white man should be taught to respect the black woman in the same way as he wants the black man to respect the white woman. It is a vicious and dangerous doctrine of social equality to urge, as certain colored leaders do, that black and white should get together, for that would destroy the racial purity of both.

We believe that the black people should have a country of their own where they should be given the fullest opportunity to develop politically, socially and industrially. The black people should not be encouraged to remain in white people's countries and expect to be Presidents, Governors, Mayors, Senators, Congressmen, Judges and social and industrial leaders. We believe that with the rising ambition of the negro, if a country is not provided for him in another 50 or 100 years, there will be a terrible clash that will end disastrously to him and disgrace our civilization. We desire to prevent such a clash by pointing the negro to a home of his own. We feel that all well disposed and broad minded white men will aid in this direction. It is because of this belief no doubt that my negro enemies, so as to prejudice me further in the opinion of the public, wickedly state that I am a member of the Ku Klux Klan, even though I am a black man.

I have been deprived of the opportunity of properly explaining my work to the white people of America through the prejudice worked up against me by jealous and wicked members of my own race. My success as an organizer was much more than rival negro leaders could tolerate. They, regardless of consequences, either to me or to the race, had to destroy me by fair means or foul. The thousands of anonymous and other hostile letters written to the editors and publishers of the white press by negro rivals to prejudice me in the eyes of public opinion are sufficient evidence of the wicked and vicious opposition I have had to meet from among my own people, especially among the very lightly colored. But they went further than the press in their attempts to discredit me. They organized clubs all over the United States and the West Indies, and wrote both open and anonymous letters to city, State and Federal officials of this and other Governments to induce them to use their influence to hamper and destroy me. No wonder, therefore, that several Judges, District Attorneys and other high officials have been against me without knowing me. No wonder, therefore, that the great white population of this country and of the world has a wrong impression of the aims and objects of the Universal Negro Improvement Association and of the work of Marcus Garvey.

THE STRUGGLE OF THE FUTURE

Having had the wrong education as a start in his racial career, the negro has become his own greatest enemy. Most of the trouble I have had in advancing the cause of the race has come from negroes. Booker Washington aptly described the race in one of his lectures by stating that we were like crabs in a barrel, that none would allow the other to climb over, but on any such attempt all would continue to pull back into the barrel the one crab that would make the effort to climb out. Yet, those of us with vision cannot desert the race, leaving it to suffer and die.

Looking forward a century or two, we can see an economic and political death struggle for the survival of the different race groups. Many of our present-day national centres will have become over-crowded with vast surplus populations. The fight for bread and position will be keen and severe. The weaker and unprepared group is bound to go under. That is why, visionaries as we are in the Universal Negro Improvement Association, we are fighting for the founding of a negro nation in Africa, so that there will be no clash between black and white and that each race will have a separate existence and civilization all its own without courting suspicion and hatred or eyeing each other with jealousy and rivalry within the borders of the same country.

White men who have struggled for and built up their countries and their own civilizations are not disposed to hand them over to the negro or any other race without let or hindrance. It would be unreasonable to expect this. Hence any vain assumption on the part of the negro to imagine that he will one day become President of the Nation, Governor of the State, or Mayor of the city in the countries of white men, is like waiting on the devil and his angels to take up their residence in the Realm on High and direct there the affairs of Paradise.

8 SUGGESTIONS FOR FURTHER READING

For a general survey of black migration to the cities, see Arna Bontemps and Jack Conroy, *They Seek a City* (Doubleday, 1945), expanded and published in paperback under the title *Anyplace But Here**. The best contemporary treatment of the Great Migration is Emmett J. Scott, *Negro Migration During the War* (Oxford University Press, 1920).

The Chicago area has received a great deal of attention by scholars of black migration. Some of the most valuable studies of this area are St. Clair Drake and Horace Cayton, *Black Metropolis** (Harcourt, Brace & World, 1945); Allan H. Spear, *Black Chicago: The Making of a Negro Ghetto, 1890–1920** (University of Chicago Press, 1967); Harold F. Gosnell, *Negro Politicians: The Rise of Negro Politics in Chicago** (University of Chicago Press, 1935); and the 1919 Riot Commission Report, *The Negro in Chicago* (University of Chicago Press, 1922). For the development of the black community in New York City, see Gilbert Osofsky, *Harlem: The Making of a Ghetto** (Harper & Row, 1966), and Ira De A. Reid, *The Negro Immigrant, His Background, Characteristics, and Social Adjustment, 1899–1937* (Columbia University Press, 1949).

Special studies of racial violence during the Great Migration include Elliott M. Rudwick, *Race Riot at East St. Louis, July 2, 1917** (Southern Illinois University Press, 1964); Arthur Waskow, *From Race Riot to Sit In: 1919 and the 1960's** (Doubleday, 1966); and portions of Walter White, *Rope and Faggot, a Biography of Judge Lynch* (Knopf, 1929).

Many of the works dealing with the black community in New York City were written by writers active in the Harlem Renaissance. Among these are Claude McKay's *Harlem: Negro Metropolis* (Dutton, 1940) and James Weldon Johnson's *Black Manhattan** (Knopf, 1930). Two edited volumes of black writing that stand as the symbols of the Renaissance are Alain Locke (ed.), *The New Negro** (Boni, 1925), and Charles S. Johnson (ed.), *Ebony and Topaz* (Urban League, 1927). Other important works of the Renaissance are Jean Toomer, *Cane* (Boni and Liveright, 1923), and the poetic works of James Weldon Johnson, Countee Cullen, Langston Hughes, and Claude McKay. Particularly valuable autobiographies of two Renaissance figures are Langston Hughes' *The Big Sea** (Knopf, 1940) and James Weldon Johnson's *Along This Way** (Viking, 1933).

Information about the Garvey movement can be found in Edmund D. Cronon, *Black Moses: The Story of Marcus Garvey and the Universal Negro Improvement Association** (University of Wisconsin Press, 1955), and in Amy Jacques-Garvey (ed.), *Philosophy and Opinions of Marcus Garvey**, 2 vols. (Universal, 1923, 1925).

9 THE DEPRESSION: UNEMPLOYMENT AND RADICALISM

The Harlem Renaissance left the masses of American blacks virtually untouched. The same could not be said, of course, of the Great Depression of the 1930's. As a matter of fact, many of the leaders of the Renaissance found themselves on the relief rolls a decade after their heyday. The black masses were those hardest hit by the unemployment that swept America. The maxim "last hired, first fired" was applied to blacks with a vengeance. In Detroit, for example, 60 per cent of the black workers were unemployed in 1931, as compared with 32 per cent of the whites. In 1937, the figures for unemployed workers throughout the North were 38.9 per cent for blacks and 18.1 per cent for whites.

Two new political options opened up for black people in this period. The first was the Democratic party, to which black Republicans shifted in massive numbers. The shift was really to the Roosevelt administration, but organized Democrats all over the country shared in the new power afforded them by the black vote. Although the Great Migration had brought many black people under the influence of Democratic urban political organizations, it was the failure of the Hoover administration to make an appeal for black support that finally drove blacks into the Democratic camp on the national level. When the New Deal went into effect and black people found they were to be included in its benefits, they swung into the Democratic column in overwhelming numbers. In the 1936 presidential election, Roosevelt received from 70 to 80 per cent of all ballots cast by blacks.

Black people were aided by all three areas of New Deal policy—relief, recovery, and reform. The decentralized operation of many of the programs worked to the blacks' disadvantage in the South, however, where the administration of federal aid often fell into the hands of people with traditionally racist ideas. Although there was a higher level of unemployment among blacks than among whites, in the Southern states in 1935 proportionately more white families were on relief. In all the Southern states except Kentucky, the relief rate for black families was less than 10 per cent. In urban areas, both South and North, blacks fared much better than they did in rural areas. In Northern cities, 52.2 per cent of all black families received relief.

When the New Deal recovery programs got under way, blacks were allowed to participate in most of them. Often, however, they participated in a lower proportion than whites and sometimes at lower wages, though this came to be against government policy. There was also wide-spread discrimination against the rise of black administrative personnel. In 1940 in fourteen Southern states, there were only eleven black supervisors in the projects of the Works Progress Administration (WPA), as compared with 10,333 white supervisors. This was the case even though 26 per cent of the WPA work force was black.

Black people faced the most discriminatory aspects of New Deal policies in the areas of housing and agriculture. The Federal Housing Administration refused to guarantee mortgages on homes that blacks sought to buy if the houses were in white communities. In this way the federal government contributed to the rise of segregated housing. The Agricultural Adjustment Administration, in paying farmers to reduce their cotton acreage, did not see to it that black tenants and sharecroppers received a fair share of the payments. When the amount of land under cultivation decreased, many of the poor blacks who worked for white farmers were thrown out of work. A great many of them ended up in the black ghettos of cities throughout America.

The most important legislation of the New Deal period for blacks was the Wagner Labor Relations Act of 1935. This act, by guaranteeing the right of workers to organize for collective bargaining, gave support to the growing campaign to organize industrial workers. The Congress of Industrial Organizations (CIO), which grew out of this campaign, had the enlightened policy of enrolling blacks alongside whites in the mass-production industries that were beginning to dominate the American labor market. It seems that the leadership of the CIO genuinely favored interracial unions, but it was also to their advantage to include blacks in their organizations, for in this way it was possible to eliminate the traditional use of black workers as strikebreakers. By 1940, there were 210,000 black members of CIO unions, whereas most of the craft unions of the American Federation of Labor (AFL) still barred blacks from membership.

The second political option of blacks during the Depression was Communism. No disinterested study of the black man in the Communist party of the United States has yet been made, so it is difficult to evaluate this aspect of black political life. The repudiation of the party by certain disgruntled intellectuals has been widely noted, but the hopes and plans of blacks who remained within the party have not been adequately dealt with.

The fact that blacks were the most oppressed group in America made them seem ripe for enlistment to Communist organizers. What was overlooked was that most blacks, even those in urban centers, were not in the working class yet, but were still virtual peasants. Organizers had some success among Southern sharecroppers, but the presence in the party of these powerless individuals was of little political value.

With blacks, as with whites, the vagaries of the Moscow line hindered the development of any consistent program for liberation among the party faithful. In the 1920's, the appeal was to separatism and the formation of a forty-ninth state for black Americans. This shifted in 1935 to the popular-front policy to oppose Nazism. The most significant development of this period was the formation of the National Negro Congress, a militant group of black intellectuals that included such "respectable" radicals as A. Philip Randolph and Ralph Bunche, as well as many members of the Communist party. The Congress was critical of the "moderate" race leadership of the NAACP and the Urban League and sought to bring about change through publicizing racial indignities. In 1940, as a result of a shift in Moscow policy, the Communists drove the non-Communists out of the convention of the Congress, and, bereft of constructive leadership, the group declined into irrelevancy.

The liberation movement of the black man had to wait until the Second World War to make its next great leap forward—a leap that cast the black man of post-war America in a new role altogether.

A NEW DEAL FOR THE BLACK MAN

Robert C. Weaver / The New Deal and the Negro

Three facets of the Roosevelt administration held strong attraction for the black people—the President's wife, Eleanor; the Secretary of the Interior, Harold Ickes; and relief. It was unquestionably the last of these that drew the greatest number of blacks to the Democratic voting column. Though the New Deal by no means guaranteed them equal treatment, black people took hope from the fact that they were allowed to participate in it at all.

There was much criticism by the NAACP of the failure of the New Deal to make equal rights a legislative concern of first importance, but certain steps taken in this direction suggested that a new day was coming, at least in the field of government service. Ickes, for example, hired several young black intellectuals to assist him in the Department of the Interior. One of these, Robert C. Weaver, answered the charges of administration critics by pointing out, in the article reprinted in the following pages, that regardless of the discrimination met on the local level by blacks, the federal government was determined to include them in the programs of the New Deal. Weaver continued in government service and eventually became the first black man to be a member of the Cabinet. He was appointed Secretary of the newly created Department of Housing and Urban Development by Lyndon Johnson in 1966.

It is impossible to discuss intelligently the New Deal and the Negro without considering the status of the Negro prior to the advent of the Recovery Program. The present economic position of the colored citizen was not created by recent legislation alone. Rather, it is the result of the impact of a new program upon an economic and social situation.

Much has been said recently about the occupational distribution of Negroes. Over a half of the gainfully employed colored Americans are concentrated in domestic service and farming. The workers in these two pursuits are the most casual and unstable in the modern economic world. This follows from the fact that neither of them requires any great capital outlay to buy necessary equipment. Thus when there is a decline in trade, the unemployment of workers in these fields does not necessitate idle plants, large depreciation costs, or mounting overhead charges. In such a situation, the employer has every incentive to dismiss his workers; thus, these two classes are fired early in a depression.

FROM Robert C. Weaver, "The New Deal and the Negro. A Look at the Facts," *Opportunity, A Journal of Negro Life*, Vol. XIII (July 1935), pp. 200–03. Reprinted by permission of the National Urban League, Inc., and the author.

The domestic worker has loomed large among the unemployed since the beginning of the current trade decline. This situation has persisted throughout the depression and is reflected in the relief figures for urban communities where 20 percent of the employables on relief were formerly attached to personal and domestic service. Among Negroes the relative number of domestics and servants on relief is even greater. The data for 30 typical cities will be found in table [below].

RELIEF DATA—SOUTHERN CITIES
AND OTHER IMPORTANT URBAN CENTERS
(May, 1934)

Cities	Total Negroes on Relief	Negroes in Domestic Service on Relief	Percentage Domestic Service
1. Bowling Green, Ky.	130	80	61.5
2. Biloxi, Miss.	360	217	60.2
3. Wheeling, W. Va.	438	200	45.6
4. Lake Charles, La.	886	328	37.0
5. Houston, Texas	6,839	3,829	56.2
6. Jackson, Miss.	1,714	964	56.2
7. Evansville, Ind.	1,647	810	49.2
8. Lexington, Ky.	1,491	644	43.2
9. Charlotte, N.C.	3,153	1,778	56.3
10. Norfolk, Va.	4,943	2,461	49.7
11. Cincinnati, Ohio	11,669	4,900	43.7
12. New Orleans, La.	14,749	5,600	38.0
13. Washington, D.C.	21,315	10,213	48.3
14. Kansas City, Mo.	4,935	2,807	56.8
15. Indianapolis, Ind.	8,477	4,263	50.2
16. St. Louis, Mo.	18,440	7,950	43.1
17. Wilmington, Del.	2,426	1,090	32.5
18. Atlanta, Ga.	16,541	10,248	61.9
19. Gastonia N.C.	140	69	49.2
20. Birmingham, Ala.	15,806	7,742	48.9
21. Oakland, Calif.	735	375	51.0
22. New York City	58,950	27,330	46.3
23. Boston, Mass.	2,534	1,232	48.6
24. Reading, Pa.	483	158	32.8
25. Rochester, N.Y.	462	203	43.9
26. Detroit, Mich.	15,070	3,380	22.4
27. Pittsburgh, Pa.	13,930	5,544	39.8
28. Akron, Ohio	2,365	995	42.0
29. Duluth, Minn.	59	15	25.4
30. Milwaukee, Wis.	1,575	495	31.4
TOTAL	278,388	121,044	43.4

In these cities, 43.4 percent of the Negroes on relief May 1, 1934, were usually employed as domestics. The demand for servants is a derived one; it is dependent upon the income and employment of other persons in the community. Thus, domestics are among the last rehired in a period of recovery.

The new works program of the Federal Government will attack this problem of the domestic worker from two angles. Insofar as it accelerates recovery by restoring incomes, it will tend to increase the demand for servants. More important, however, will be its creation of direct employment opportunities for all occupational classes of those on relief.

Although it is regrettable that the economic depression has led to the unemployment of so many Negroes and has threatened the creation of a large segment of the Negro population as a chronic relief load, one is forced to admit that Federal relief has been a godsend to the unemployed. The number of unemployed in this country was growing in 1933. According to the statistics of the American Federation of Labor, the number of unemployed increased from 3,216,000 in January, 1930, to 13,689,000 in March 1933. In November, 1934, the number was about 10,500,000 and although there are no comparable current data available, estimates indicate that current unemployment is less than that of last November. Local relief monies were shrinking; and need and starvation were facing those unable to find an opportunity to work. A Federal relief program was the only possible aid in this situation. Insofar as the Negro was greatly victimized by the economic developments, he was in a position to benefit from a program which provided adequate funds for relief.

It is admitted that there were many abuses under the relief set-up. Such situations should be brought to light and fought. In the case of Negroes, these abuses undoubtedly existed and do exist. We should extend every effort to uncover and correct them. We can admit that we have gained from the relief program and still fight to receive greater and more equitable benefits from it.

The recent depression has been extremely severe in its effects upon the South. The rural Negro—poor before the period of trade decline—was rendered even more needy after 1929. Many tenants found it impossible to obtain a contract for a crop, and scores of Negro farm owners lost their properties. The displacement of Negro tenants (as was the case for whites) began before, and grew throughout the depression. Thus, at the time of the announcement of the New Deal, there were many families without arrangements for a crop—an appreciable number without shelter. The following summary of conditions in one county of a southern state will serve as an illustration. In Greene County, North Carolina (where the population in 1930 was 18,656 divided almost equally between whites and Negroes) the FERA survey reported data as of January 1934 relative to the period of displacement of families. This material shows that for this county, displacement of tenants was most severe in 1931–1932. The figures are as follows:

Length of Time Without Tenant Status	Colored	White	Total
Less than a year	14	13	27
One year	18	8	26
Two years	21	19	40
More than two years	42	13	55
Always farmed as day laborers	5	5	10
TOTAL	100	58	158

The problems facing the Negro farmer of the South are not new. They have been accentuated by the crop reduction program. They are, for the most part, problems of a system and their resistance to reform is as old as the system. This was well illustrated by the abuses in the administration of the Federal feed, seed, and fertilizer laws in 1928–1929. These abuses were of the same nature as those which confront the AAA in its dealings with Negro tenants.

The southern farm tenant is in such a position that he cannot receive any appreciable gains from a program until steps are taken to change his position of absolute economic dependence upon the landlord. Until some effective measure for rehabilitating him is discovered, there is no hope. The new program for land utilization, rural re-habilitation, and spreading land owner-ship may be able to effect such a change. Insofar as it takes a step in that direction, it will be advantageous to the Negro farmer. The degree to which it aids him will depend upon the temper of its administration and the extent to which it is able to break away from the *status quo*.

In listing some of the gains which have accrued to Negroes under the New Deal, there will be a discussion of three lines of activity: housing, employment, and emergency education. These are chosen for discussion because each is significant in itself, and all represent a definite break from the *status quo* in governmental activity, method, and policy. They do not give a complete picture; but rather, supply interesting examples of what is, and can be, done for Negroes.

PWA HOUSING DIVISION

The Housing Division of the Federal Emergency Administration of Public Works has planned 60 Federal housing projects to be under construction by December 31, 1935. Of these, 28 are to be developed in Negro slum areas and will be tenanted predominantly or wholly by Negroes. Eight additional projects will provide for an appreciable degree of Negro occupancy. These 36 projects will afford approximately 74,664 rooms and should offer accom-modations for about 23,000 low income colored families. The estimated total cost of these housing developments will be $64,428,000, and they represent about 29 per cent of the funds devoted to Federal slum clearance develop-ments under the present allotments.

Projects in Negro areas have been announced in seven cities: Atlanta, Cleveland, Detroit, Indianapolis, Montgomery, Chicago, and Nashville. These will cost about $33,232,000 and will contain about 20,000 rooms. Two of these projects, the University development at Atlanta, and the Thurman Street development in Montgomery, are under construction. These are among the earliest Federal housing projects to be initiated by the PWA.

After a series of conferences and a period of experience under the PWA, it was decided to include a clause in PWA housing contracts requiring the payment to Negro mechanics of a given percentage of the payroll going to skilled workers. The first project to be affected by such a contractual clause was the Techwood development in Atlanta, Georgia. On this project, most of the labor employed on demolition was composed of unskilled Negro workers. About 90 per cent of the unskilled workers employed laying the foundation for the Techwood project were Negroes, and, for the first two-month construction period, February and March, 12.7 per cent of the wages paid skilled workers was earned by Negro artisans. The payroll figures for the monthly period, March 29 to April 24 inclusive, are as follows:

	White	Negro	Percentage Negro Wage
Skilled	$7,338.30	$1,185.50	13.9
Intermediate	430.20	25.50	5.6
Unskilled	2,779.45	3,356.00	54.7
TOTAL	$10,547.95	$4,567.00	30.0

FEDERAL EMERGENCY RELIEF ADMINISTRATION, EDUCATIONAL PROGRAM

Under the educational program of the FERA, out of a total of 17,879 teachers employed in 13 southern states, 5,476 or 30.6 per cent were Negro. Out of a total of 570,794 enrolled in emergency classes, 217,000 or 38 per cent were Negro. Out of a total of $886,300 expended in a month (either February or March, 1935) for the program, Negroes received $231,320 or 26.1 per cent. These southern states in which 26.1 per cent of all emergency salaries were paid to Negro teachers, ordinarily allot only 11.7 per cent of all public school salaries to Negro teachers. The situation may be summarized as follows: Six of the 13 states are spending for Negro salaries a proportion of their emergency education funds larger than the percentage of Negroes in those states. The area as a whole is spending for Negro salaries a proportion of its funds slightly in excess of the percentage of Negroes in the population. This development is an example of Government activity breaking away from the *status quo* in race relations.

There is one Government expenditure in education in reference to which there has been general agreement that equity has been established. That is the FERA college scholarship program. Each college or university not operated for profit, received $20 monthly per student as aid for 12 per cent of its college enrollment. Negro and white institutions have benefited alike under this program.

In the execution of some phases of the Recovery Program, there have been difficulties, and the maximum results have not been received by the Negroes. But, given the economic situation of 1932, the New Deal has been more helpful than harmful to Negroes. We had unemployment in 1932. Jobs were being lost by Negroes, and they were in need. Many would have starved had there been no Federal relief program. As undesirable as is the large relief load among Negroes, the FERA has meant much to them. In most of the New Deal setups, there has been some Negro representation by competent Negroes. The Department of the Interior and the PWA have appointed some fifteen Negroes to jobs of responsibility which pay good salaries. These persons have secretarial and clerical staffs attached to their offices. In addition to these new jobs, there are the colored messengers, who number around 100, and the elevator operators for the Government buildings, of whom there are several hundred. This is not, of course, adequate representation; but it represents a step in the desired direction and is greater recognition than has been given Negroes in the Federal Government during the last 20 years. Or again, in the Nashville housing project, a Negro architectural firm is a consultant; for the Southwest side housing project in Chicago, a Negro is an associate architect. One of the proposed projects will have two Negro principal architects, a Negro consultant architect, and a technical staff of about six Negro technicians. In other cities competent colored architects will be used to design housing projects.

This analysis is intended to indicate some advantages accruing to the Negro under the Recovery Program, and to point out that the New Deal, insofar as it represents an extension of governmental activity into the economic sphere, is a departure which can do much to reach the Negro citizens. In many instances it has availed itself of these opportunities. An intelligent appraisal of its operation is necessary to assure greater benefits to colored citizens.

DOMESTIC SLAVERY

Ella Baker and Marvel Cooke / The Bronx Slave Market

As Robert Weaver points out in the previous selection, the situation of the black domestic worker grew desperate during the Depression. Yet as unemployment in other unskilled areas rose, more and more black people were forced to seek domestic service.

The inhuman conditions under which some were hired received publicity through **The Crisis,** which, after Du Bois' departure, was edited by Roy Wilkins, later to become the executive director of the NAACP.

The following article was written by two black women who were investigating the so-called "slave markets" that operated at certain subway stops in New York City. They describe the degrading spectacle of women selling themselves into domestic slavery. Reflected in the article is the ethnic prejudice of the black women who found themselves working in families with unfamiliar customs and usages. This hostility to "different" customs is, regrettably, deeply ingrained in American life.

T he Bronx Slave Market! What is it? Who are its dealers? Who are its victims? What are its causes? How far does its stench spread? What forces are at work to counteract it?

Any corner in the congested sections of New York City's Bronx is fertile soil for mushroom "slave marts." The two where the traffic is heaviest and the bidding is highest are located at 167th street and Jerome avenue and at Simpson and Westchester avenues.

Symbolic of the more humane slave block is the Jerome avenue "market." There, on benches surrounding a green square, the victims wait, grateful, at least, for some place to sit. In direct contrast is the Simpson avenue "mart," where they pose wearily against buildings and lamp posts, or scuttle about in an attempt to retrieve discarded boxes upon which to rest.

Again, the Simpson avenue block exudes the stench of the slave market at its worst. Not only is human labor bartered and sold for slave wage, but human love also is a marketable commodity. But whether it is labor or love that is sold, economic necessity compels the sale. As early as 8 A.M. they come; as late as 1 P.M. they remain.

Rain or shine, cold or hot, you will find them there—Negro women, old and young—sometimes bedraggled, sometimes neatly dressed—but with the invariable paper bundle, waiting expectantly for Bronx housewives to buy their strength and energy for an hour, two hours, or even for a day at the munificent rate of fifteen, twenty, twenty-five, or, if luck be with them, thirty cents an hour. If not the wives themselves, maybe their husbands, their sons, or their brothers, under the subterfuge of work, offer worldly-wise girls higher bids for their time.

Who are these women? What brings them here? Why do they stay? In the boom days before the onslaught of the depression in 1929, many of these women who are now forced to bargain for day's work on street corners, were employed in grand homes in the rich Eighties, or in wealthier

FROM Ella Baker and Marvel Cooke, "The Bronx Slave Market," *The Crisis*, Vol. XLII (November 1935), pp. 330–31, 340.

homes in Long Island and Westchester, at more than adequate wages. Some are former marginal industrial workers, forced by the slack in industry to seek other means of sustenance. In many instances there had been no necessity for work at all. But whatever their standing prior to the depression, none sought employment where they now seek it. They come to the Bronx, not because of what it promises, but largely in desperation.

Paradoxically, the crash of 1929 brought to the domestic labor market a new employer class. The lower middle-class housewife, who, having dreamed of the luxury of a maid, found opportunity staring her in the face in the form of Negro women pressed to the wall by poverty, starvation and discrimination.

Where once color was the "gilt edged" security for obtaining domestic and personal service jobs, here, even, Negro women found themselves being displaced by whites. Hours of futile waiting in employment agencies, the fee that must be paid despite the lack of income, fraudulent agencies that sprung up during the depression, all forced the day worker to fend for herself or try the dubious and circuitous road to public relief.

As inadequate as emergency relief has been, it has proved somewhat of a boon to many of these women, for with its advent, actual starvation is no longer their ever-present slave driver and they have been able to demand twenty-five and even thirty cents an hour as against the old fifteen and twenty cent rate. In an effort to supplement the inadequate relief received, many seek this open market.

And what a market! She who is fortunate (?) enough to please Mrs. Simon Legree's scrutinizing eye is led away to perform hours of multifarious household drudgeries. Under a rigid watch, she is permitted to scrub floors on her bended knees, to hang precariously from window sills, cleaning window after window, or to strain and sweat over steaming tubs of heavy blankets, spreads and furniture covers.

Fortunate, indeed, is she who gets the full hourly rate promised. Often, her day's slavery is rewarded with a single dollar bill or whatever her unscrupulous employer pleases to pay. More often, the clock is set back for an hour or more. Too often she is sent away without any pay at all.

HOW IT WORKS

We invaded the "market" early on the morning of September 14. Disreputable bags under arm and conscientiously forlorn, we trailed the work entourage on the West side "slave train," disembarking with it at Simpson and Westchester avenues. Taking up our stand outside the corner flower shop whose show window offered gardenias, roses and the season's first chrysanthemums at moderate prices, we waited patiently to be "bought."

We got results in almost nothing flat. A squatty Jewish housewife, patently lower middle class, approached us, carefully taking stock of our "wares."

"You girls want work?"

"Yes." We were expectantly noncommittal.

"How much you work for?"

We begged the question, noting that she was already convinced that we were not the "right sort." "How much do you pay?"

She was walking away from us. "I can't pay your price," she said and immediately started bargaining with a strong, seasoned girl leaning against the corner lamp post. After a few moments of animated conversation, she led the girl off with her. Curious, we followed them two short blocks to a dingy apartment house on a side street.

We returned to our post. We didn't seem to be very popular with the other "slaves." They eyed us suspiciously. But, one by one, as they became convinced that we were one with them, they warmed up to friendly sallies and answered our discreet questions about the possibilities of employment in the neighborhood.

Suddenly it began to rain, and we, with a dozen or so others, scurried to shelter under the five-and-ten doorway midway the block. Enforced close communion brought about further sympathy and conversation from the others. We asked the brawny, neatly dressed girl pressed close to us about the extent of trade in the "oldest profession" among women.

"Well," she said, "there is quite a bit of it up here. Most of 'those' girls congregate at the other corner." She indicated the location with a jerk of her head.

"Do they get much work?" we queried.

"Oh, quite a bit," she answered with a finality which was probably designed to close the conversation. But we were curious and asked her how the other girls felt about it. She looked at us a moment doubtfully, probably wondering if we weren't seeking advice to go into the "trade" ourselves.

"Well, that's their own business. If they can do it and get away with it, it's all right with the others." Or probably she would welcome some "work" of that kind herself.

"Sh-h-h." The wizened West Indian woman whom we had noticed, prior to the rain, patroling the street quite belligerently as if she were daring someone not to hire her, was cautioning us. She explained that if we kept up such a racket the store's manager would kick all of us out in the rain. And so we continued our conversation in whispered undertone.

"Gosh. I don't like this sort of thing at all." The slender brown girl whom we had seen turn down two jobs earlier in the morning, seemed anxious to talk. "This is my first time up here—and believe me, it is going to be my last. I don't like New York nohow. If I don't get a good job soon, I'm going back home to Kansas City." So she had enough money to travel, did she?

CUT RATE COMPETITION

The rain stopped quite as suddenly as it started. We had decided to make a careful survey of the district to see whether or not there were any employment agencies in the section. Up one block and down another we tramped, but not one such institution did we encounter. Somehow the man who gave us a sly "Hello, babies" as he passed was strangely familiar. We realized two things about him—that he had been trailing us for some time and that he was manifestly, plain clothes notwithstanding, one of "New York's finest."

Trying to catch us to run us in for soliciting, was he? From that moment on, it was a three-cornered game. When we separated he was at sea. When we were together, he grinned and winked at us quite boldly. . . .

We sidled up to a friendly soul seated comfortably on an upturned soap-box. Soon an old couple approached her and offered a day's work with their daughter way up on Jerome avenue. They were not in agreement as to how much the daughter would pay—the old man said twenty-five cents an hour—the old lady scowled and said twenty. The car fare, they agreed, would be paid after she reached her destination. The friendly soul refused the job. She could afford independence, for she had already sucessfully bargained for a job for the following day. She said to us, after the couple started negotiations with another woman, that she wouldn't go way up on Jerome avenue on a wild goose chase for Mrs. Roosevelt, herself. We noted, with satisfaction, that the old couple had no luck with any of the five or six they contacted.

It struck us as singularly strange, since it was already 10:30, that the women still lingered, seemingly unabashed that they had not yet found employment for a day. We were debating whether or not we should leave the "mart" and try again another day, probably during the approaching Jewish holidays at which time business is particularly flourishing, when, suddenly, things looked up again. A new batch of "slaves" flowed down the elevated steps and took up their stands at advantageous points.

The friendly soul turned to us, a sneer marring the smooth roundness of her features. "Them's the girls who makes it bad for us. They get more jobs than us because they will work for anything. We runned them off the corner last week." One of the newcomers was quite near us and we couldn't help but overhear the following conversation with a neighborhood housewife.

"You looking for work?"

"Yes ma'am."

"How much you charge?"

"I'll take what you will give me." . . . What was this? Could the girl have needed work that badly? Probably. She did look run down at the heels. . . .

"All right. Come on. I'll give you a dollar." Cupidity drove beauty from the arrogant features. The woman literally dragged her "spoil" to her den. . . . But what of the girl? Could she possibly have known what she was letting herself in for? Did she know how long she would have to work for that dollar or what she would have to do? Did she know whether or not she would get lunch or car fare? Not any more than we did. Yet, there she was, trailing down the street behind her "mistress."

"You see," philosophized the friendly soul. "That's what makes it bad for the rest of us. We got to do something about those girls. Organize them or something." The friendly soul remained complacent on her up-turned box. Our guess was that if the girls were organized, the incentive would come from some place else.

Business in the "market" took on new life. Eight or ten girls made satisfactory contacts. Several women—and men approached us, but our price was too high or we refused to wash windows or scrub floors. We were beginning to have a rollicking good time when rain again dampened our heads and ardor. We again sought the friendly five-and-ten doorway.

"FOR FIVE BUCKS A WEEK"

We became particularly friendly with a girl whose intelligent replies to our queries intrigued us. When we were finally convinced that there would be no more "slave" barter that day, we invited her to lunch with us at a near-by restaurant. After a little persuasion, there we were, Millie Jones between us, refreshing our spirits and appetites with hamburgers, fragrant with onions, and coffee. We found Millie an articulate person. It seems that, until recently, she had had a regular job in the neighborhood. But let her tell you about it.

"Did I have to work? And how! For five bucks and car fare a week. Mrs. Eisenstein had a six-room apartment lighted by fifteen windows. Each and every week, believe it or not, I had to wash every one of those windows. If that old hag found as much as the teeniest speck on any one of 'em, she'd make me do it over. I guess I would do anything rather than wash windows. On Mondays I washed and did as much of the ironing as I could. The rest waited over for Tuesday. There were two grown sons in the family and her husband. That meant that I would have at least twenty-one shirts to do every week. Yeah, and ten sheets and at least two blankets, besides. They all had to be done just so, too. Gosh, she was a particular woman.

"There wasn't a week, either, that I didn't have to wash up every floor in the place and wax it on my hands and knees. And two or three times a week I'd have to beat the mattresses and take all the furniture covers off and shake 'em out. Why, when I finally went home nights, I could hardly move. One of the sons had "hand trouble" too, and I was just as tired fighting him off, I guess, as I was with the work.

"Say, did you ever wash dishes for an Orthodox Jewish family?" Millie took a long, sibilant breath. "Well, you've never really washed dishes, then. You know, they use a different dishcloth for everything they cook. For instance, they have one for 'milk' pots in which dairy dishes are cooked, another for glasses, another for vegetable pots, another for meat pots, and so on. My memory wasn't very good and I was always getting the darn things mixed up. I used to make Mrs. Eisenstein just as mad. But I was the one who suffered. She would get other cloths and make me do the dishes all over again.

"How did I happen to leave her? Well, after I had been working about five weeks, I asked for a Sunday off. My boy friend from Washington was coming up on an excursion to spend the day with me. She told me if I didn't come in on Sunday, I needn't come back at all. Well, I didn't go back. Ever since then I have been trying to find a job. The employment agencies are no good. All the white girls get the good jobs.

"My cousin told me about up here. The other day I didn't have a cent in my pocket and I just had to find work in order to get back home and so I took the first thing that turned up. I went to work about 11 o'clock and I stayed until 5:00—washing windows, scrubbing floors and washing out stinking baby things. I was surprised when she gave me lunch. You know, some of 'em don't even do that. When I got through, she gave me thirty-five cents. Said she took a quarter out for lunch. Figure it out for yourself. Ten cents an hour!

MINIATURE ECONOMIC BATTLEFRONT

The real significance of the Bronx Slave Market lies not in a factual presentation of its activities; but in focusing attention upon its involved implications. The "mart" is but a miniature mirror of our economic battlefront.

To many, the women who sell their labor thus cheaply have but themselves to blame. A head of a leading employment agency bemoans the fact that these women have not "chosen the decent course" and declares: "The well-meaning employment agencies endeavoring to obtain respectable salaries and suitable working conditions for deserving domestics are finding it increasingly difficult due to the menace and obstacles presented by the slavish performances of the lower types of domestics themselves, who, unlike the original slaves who recoiled from meeting their masters, rush to meet their mistresses."

The exploiters, judged from the districts where this abominable traffic flourishes, are the wives and mothers of artisans and tradesmen who militantly battle against being exploited themselves, but who apparently have no scruples against exploiting others.

The general public, though aroused by stories of these domestics, too often think of the problems of these women as something separate and apart and readily dismisses them with a sigh and a shrug of the shoulders.

The women, themselves present a study in contradictions. Largely unaware of their organized power, yet ready to band together for some immediate and personal gain either consciously or unconsciously, they still cling to the American illusion that any one who is determined and persistent can get ahead.

The roots, then of the Bronx Slave Market spring from: (1) the general ignorance of and apathy towards organized labor action; (2) the artificial barriers that separate the interest of the relief administrators and investigators from that of their "case loads," the white collar and professional worker from the laborer and the domestic; and (3) organized labor's limited concept of exploitation, which permits it to fight vigorously to secure itself against evil, yet passively or actively aids and abets the ruthless destruction of Negroes.

To abolish the market once and for all, these roots must be torn away from their sustaining soil. Certain palliative and corrective measures are not without benefit. Already the seeds of discontent are being sown.

The Women's Day Workers and Industrial League, organized sixteen years ago by Fannie Austin, has been, and still is, a force to abolish the existing evils in day labor. Legitimate employment agencies have banded together to curb the activities of the racketeer agencies and are demanding fixed minimum and maximum wages for all workers sent out. Articles and editorials recently carried by the New York Negro press have focused attention on the existing evils in the "slave market."

An embryonic labor union now exists in the Simpson avenue "mart." Girls who persist in working for less than thirty cents an hour have been literally run off the corner. For the recent Jewish holiday, habitues of the "mart" actually demanded and refused to work for less than thirty-five cents an hour.

A BLACK WORKINGMAN IN THE COMMUNIST PARTY

Angelo Herndon   /   You Cannot Kill the Working Class

In trying to attract support from blacks for its program, the Communist party organized the International Labor Defense (ILD) in the late 1920's. The purpose of this organization was to dramatize the injustice suffered by blacks at the hands of the courts. The two most celebrated cases it handled were the Scottsboro case and that of Angelo Herndon. The former involved nine black Alabama youths who were convicted and sentenced to death for allegedly raping two white prostitutes. After many years of litigation and appeal, they were freed.

The case of Angelo Herndon is of particular interest because Herndon, a party member arrested on the vague charge of "inciting to insurrection," remained an unrepentant Communist throughout his imprisonment. The brief autobiographical statement that follows was published by the ILD and the League of Struggle for Negro Rights to gain support for his case. Herndon was finally freed by Supreme Court action.

Herndon presents a persuasive argument for the appeal of the Communist party to the black workingman, and one wonders why more blacks did not enlist in the cause. Perhaps the fear of what happened to Herndon deterred many.

M y great-grandmother was ever such a tiny girl when some white plantation owners rode up to the Big House and arranged to carry her off.
They bargained for a bit and then came down to the Negro quarters and
grabbed her away from her mother. They could do that because my great-
grandmother's folks were slaves in Virginia.

My great-grandmother lived to be very old. She often told me about
those times.

There is one story of hers that keeps coming back to me. She was still
a young girl, and mighty pretty, and some rich young white men decided
they wanted her. She resisted, so they threw her down on the floor of the
barn, and tied her up with ropes, and beat her until the blood ran. Then
they sent to the house for pepper and salt to rub in the wounds.

Her daughter—my grandmother—couldn't remember much about slave
days. While she was still a child, the Civil War was fought out and chattel-
slavery was ended. One childhood scene, though, was scarred on her mind.
It was during the Civil War. Some white men burst into her cabin. They
seized her sister and strung her to a tree, and riddled her body with bullets.
My grandmother herself stayed hidden, and managed to get away alive.

I remember these stories, not because they were so different from life in
my own day, but for the opposite reason. They were exactly like some of
the things that happened to me when I went South.

My father, Paul Herndon, and my mother, Hattie Herndon, lived for
many years in Birmingham, and then came North. They settled down in
Wyoming, Ohio, a little steel and mining town just outside of Cincinnati.

I AM BORN INTO A MINER'S FAMILY

I was born there on May 6, 1913. My name was put down in the big family
Bible as Eugene Angelo Braxton Herndon.

They say that once a miner, always a miner. I don't know if that's so,
but I do know that my father never followed any other trade. His sons
never doubted that they would go down into the mines as soon as they got
old enough. The wail of the mine whistle morning and night, and the sight
of my father coming home with his lunch-pail, grimy from the day's coat-
ing of coal-dust, seemed a natural and eternal part of our lives.

Almost every working-class family, especially in those days, nursed the

FROM Angelo Herndon, *You Cannot Kill the Working Class* (New York, n.d.). Probably published in 1934.

idea that one of its members, anyway, would get out of the factory and wear clean clothes all the time and sit at a desk. My family was no exception. They hoped that I would be the one to leave the working-class. They were ready to make almost any sacrifices to send me through high-school and college. They were sure that if a fellow worked hard and had intelligence and grit, he wouldn't have to be a worker all his life.

I haven't seen my mother or most of my family for a long time—but I wonder what they think of that idea now!

My father died of miner's pneumonia when I was very small, and left my mother with a big family to care for. Besides myself, there were six other boys and two girls. We all did what we could. Mother went out to do housework for rich white folks. An older brother got a job in the steel mills. I did odd jobs, working in stores, running errands, for $2 and $3 a week. They still had the idea they could scrimp and save and send me through college. But when I was 13, we saw it wouldn't work.

I GO TO WORK

So one fine morning in 1926, my brother Leo and I started off for Lexington, Ky. It was just across the border, and it had mines, and we were miner's kids.

A few miles outside of Lexington, we were taken on at a small mine owned by the powerful DeBardeleben Coal Corporation. There didn't seem to be any question in anyone's mind about a kid of 13 going to work, and I was given a job helping to load coal.

We worked under the contracting system. One worker contracts to get a certain amount of work done, and a number of workers are put under him. The contractor's pay depends on how much the men under him load. It's a clever way of getting one worker to speed the others up. It divides the workers against each other, and saves a good deal of management expenses for the operators.

On my job we were paired off in twos, shovelling coal into the cars. We got about $35 per estimate. An estimate is two weeks. Remember, that was in 1926, before the crash, and we averaged 10 or 11 hours a day, and sometimes worked 14. Besides this, we had to walk three or four miles from the surface of the mine to our work, for there was no mantrip. We didn't get any pay for this time.

They deducted about $10 or $15 every estimate for bath, school, doctor, hospital, insurance, and supplies. We had to buy all our mining supplies, like carbide, lamps, dynamite, fuses, picks and so on, at the company store. The company store soaked us.

They weighed our coal and charged us for the slate in it. They cheated awfully on the slate. Then after they skinned us that way, they skinned us again on the weight. The checkweighman had been hired by the company. He had the scales all fixed beforehand, and the cars just slid over the scales. Everybody could see it was a gyp, but we weren't organized, and though we grumbled we couldn't get any satisfaction.

THE COMPANY TOWN

We lived in the company town. It was pretty bad. The houses were just shacks on unpaved streets. We seldom had anything to eat that was right. We had to buy everything from the company store, or we'd have lost our jobs. They kept our pay low and paid only every two weeks, so we had to have credit between times. We got advances in the form of clackers, which could be used only in the company store. Their prices were very high. I remember paying 30 cents a pound for pork-chops in the company store and then noticing that the butcher in town was selling them for 20 cents. The company store prices were just robbery without a pistol.

The safety conditions in the mine were rotten. The escapeways were far from where we worked, and there was never enough timbering to keep the rocks from falling. There were some bad accidents while I was there. I took all the skin off my right hand pushing a car up into the facing. The cars didn't have enough grease and there were no cross-ties just behind me to brace my feet against. That was a bit of the company's economy. The car slipped, the track turned over, and the next thing I knew I had lost all the skin and a lot of the flesh off my right hand. The scars are there to this day.

This DeBardeleben mine in Lexington was where the Jim-Crow system first hit me. The Negroes and whites very seldom came in contact with each other. Of course there were separate company patches for living quarters. But even in the mine the Negroes and the whites worked in different places. The Negroes worked on the North side of the mine and the whites on the South.

The Negroes never got a look-in on most of the better-paying jobs. They couldn't be section foremen, or electricians, or surveyors, or head bank boss, or checkweighmen, or steel sharpeners, or engineers. They could only load the coal, run the motors, be mule-boys, pick the coal, muck the rock. In other words, they were only allowed to do the muscle work.

Besides that, the Negro miners got the worst places to work. We worked in the low coal, only 3 or 4 feet high. We had to wear knee pads, and work stretched flat on our bellies most of the time.

A SLASHING PAY-CUT

One day the company put up a notice that due to large overhead expenses, they would have to cut our pay from 42 to 31 cents a ton. We were sore as hell. But there wasn't any union in the mine, and practically none of us had had any experience at organization, and though we grumbled plenty we didn't take any action. We were disgusted, and some of us quit. Whites and Negroes both.

I was one of those who quit. My contact with unions, and with organization, and the Communist Party, and unity between black and white miners —all that was still in the future. The pay-cut and the rotten conditions got my goat, and I walked off, because as yet I didn't know of anything else to do.

Well, my brother Leo and I set out for Birmingham, where there were relatives—and plenty more mines. I was out of work for a long time. Finally I went to an employment agency and paid down $3 for a job. They signed a lot of us on to work putting up the plant of the Goodyear Rubber Company at Gadsden, Ala. They carried us up there on trucks, promising us we would get $3 a day. When we got there they told us we would get only $1.75 a day. We started work with the concrete mixer, preparing the foundations for the place. We worked night and day, often two shifts one right after the other. We worked like dogs and slept in stifling tents and ate rotten food.

At the end of the first week we lined up to get our pay. Around the pay-office stood dozens of uniformed policemen and company guards. The foreman came out and told us that we had no pay coming, because everything we'd earned had been eaten up by transportation and flops and food.

We were wild with anger. We kept swarming up to the pay-office, but as quick as a group formed there the cops and guards drove us away. The Goodyear Company wouldn't even agree to send us back to Birmingham.

I still didn't have any idea what to do about things like this. I didn't figure we men could get together and organize and make the company come across.

Leo and I hitch-hiked back to Birmingham, and made the round of the mines. I finally got work at the Docena mine of the Tennessee Coal, Iron and Railroad Co.

THE LORDS OF ALABAMA

I want to talk a little about that. When I sat in jail this spring and read that the workers of the Tennessee Coal and Iron Company had come out on strike, I knew that a new day had come in the South. The T.C.I. just about owns Alabama. It owns steel mills and coal-mines and a railroad and all sorts of subsidiary plants. It owns company patches and houses. It certainly owns most of the Alabama officials. It dictates the political life of the state. It has made Jim-Crowism a fine art. It has stool-pigeons in every corner. The T.C.I. is like some great, greedy brute that holds a whip over the whole state. Its shadow is everywhere—on factories, schools, judges' benches, even the pulpits of churches.

The Tennessee Coal and Iron Company has always been in the forefront of the fight against unions in the South. They had—and still have—a company-union scheme, which they make a great deal out of, but which doesn't fool any of the workers. I noticed that whatever checkweighman the company put up, would always be elected.

I started surface work at the Docena mine, helping to build transformation lines, cutting the right of way for wires. I was supposed to get $2.78 a day, but there were lots of deductions.

THE POWER OF ORGANIZATION

It was while I was on this job that I first got a hint of an idea that workers could get things by organizing and sticking together.

It happened this way: one of my buddies on the job was killed by a trolley wire. The shielding on that wire had been down two weeks, and the foreman had seen it down, but hadn't bothered with it. All of us surface men quit work for the day, when we saw our buddy lying burnt and still, tangled up in that wire.

The next week we were called before the superintendent to explain the accident. Of course we were expected to whitewash the foreman and the company, so they wouldn't have to pay any insurance to the dead man's family. Something got into me, and I spoke up and said that the foreman and the whole company was to blame. The men backed me up. One of the foremen nudged me and told me to hush. He said: "Boy, you're talking too damn much." But I kept on. The foreman was removed and the dead man's family got some compensation from the T.C.I.

That was my first lesson in organization.

By this time the crisis had hit the United States. Mines and factories closed their doors, and businesses crashed, and workers who had never been out of jobs before began to tramp the streets. Those of us who still had jobs found our wages going down, down. The miners got one cut after another. Often, when we got our pay-envelopes, we'd find a blank strip. That meant that the company had taken all our wages for supplies and food advances.

I BEGIN TO QUESTION

The Jim-Crow system was in full force in the mines of the Tennessee Coal and Iron Company, and all over Birmingham. It had always burnt me up, but I didn't know how to set about fighting it. My parents and grandparents were hard-boiled Republicans, and told me very often that Lincoln had freed the slaves, and that we'd have to look to the Republican Party for everything good. I began to wonder about that. Here I was, being Jim-Crowed and cheated. Every couple of weeks I read about a lynching somewhere in the South. Yet there sat a Republican government up in Washington, and they weren't doing a thing about it.

My people told me to have faith in God, and he would make everything come right. I read a lot of religious tracts, but I got so I didn't believe them. I figured that there was no use for a Negro to go to heaven, because if he went there it would only be to shine some white man's shoes.

I wish I could remember the exact date when I first attended a meeting of the Unemployment Council, and met up with a couple of members of the

Communist Party. That date means a lot more to me than my birthday, or any other day in my life.

The workers in the South, mostly deprived of reading-matter, have developed a wonderful grapevine system for transmitting news. It was over this grapevine that we first heard that there were "reds" in town.

The foremen—when they talked about it—and the newspapers, and the big-shot Negroes in Birmingham, said that the "reds" were foreigners, and Yankees, and believed in killing people, and would get us in a lot of trouble. But out of all the talk I got a few ideas clear about the Reds. They believed in organizing and sticking together. They believed that we didn't have to have bosses on our backs. They believed that Negroes ought to have equal rights with whites. It all sounded O.K. to me. But I didn't meet any of the Reds for a long time.

I FIND THE WORKING-CLASS MOVEMENT

One day in June, 1930, walking home from work, I came across some handbills put out by the Unemployment Council in Birmingham. They said: "Would you rather fight—or starve?" They called on the workers to come to a mass meeting at 3 o'clock.

Somehow I never thought of missing that meeting. I said to myself over and over: "It's war! It's war! And I might as well get into it right now!" I got to the meeting while a white fellow was speaking. I didn't get everything he said, but this much hit me and stuck with me: that the workers could only get things by fighting for them, and that the Negro and white workers had to stick together to get results. The speaker described the conditions of the Negroes in Birmingham, and I kept saying to myself: "That's it." Then a Negro spoke from the same platform, and somehow I knew that this was what I'd been looking for all my life.

At the end of the meeting I went up and gave my name. From that day to this, every minute of my life has been tied up with the workers' movement.

I joined the Unemployment Council, and some weeks later the Communist Party. I read all the literature of the movement that I could get my hands on, and began to see my way more clearly.

I had some mighty funny ideas at first, but I guess that was only natural. For instance, I thought that we ought to start by getting all the big Negro leaders like DePriest and Du Bois and Walter White into the Communist Party, and then we would have all the support we needed. I didn't know then that DePriest and the rest of the leaders of that type are on the side of the bosses, and fight as hard as they can against the workers. They don't believe in fighting against the system that produces Jim-Crowism. They stand up for that system, and try to preserve it, and so they are really on the side of Jim-Crowism and inequality. I got rid of all these ideas after I heard Oscar Adams and others like him speak in Birmingham.

That happened this way:

Birmingham had just put on a Community Chest drive. The whites gave and the Negroes gave. Some gave willingly, thinking it was really going to help feed the unemployed, and the rest had it taken out of their wages. There was mighty little relief handed out to the workers, even when they did get on the rolls. The Negroes only got about half what the whites got. Some of the workers waiting at the relief station made up a take-off on an old prison song. I remember that the first two lines of it went:

> I've counted the beans, babe,
> I've counted the greens. . . .

The Unemployment Council opened a fight for cash relief, and aid for single men, and equal relief for Negro and white. They called for a meeting in Capitol Park, and we gathered about the Confederate Monument, about 500 of us, white and Negro, and then we marched on the Community Chest Headquarters. There were about 100 cops there. The officials of the Community Chest spoke, and said that the best thing for the Negroes to do was to go back to the farms. They tried very hard to give the white workers there the idea that if the Negroes went back to the farms, the whites would get a lot more relief.

Of course our leaders pointed out that the small farmers and share-croppers and tenants on the cotton-lands around Birmingham were starving, and losing their land and stock, and hundreds were drifting into the city in hope of getting work.

Then Oscar Adams spoke up. He was the editor of the *Birmingham Reporter*, a Negro paper. What he said opened my eyes—but not in the way he expected. He said we shouldn't be misled by the leaders of the Unemployment Council, that we should go politely to the white bosses and officials and ask them for what they wanted, and do as they said.

Adams said: "We Negroes don't want social equality." I was furious. I said inside of myself: "Oscar Adams, we Negroes want social and every other kind of equality. There's no reason on God's green earth why we should be satisfied with anything less."

TRAITORS IN THE RANKS

That was the end of any ideas I had that the big-shots among the recognised Negro leaders would fight for us, or really put up any struggle for equal rights. I knew that Oscar Adams and the people like him were among our worst enemies, especially dangerous because they work from inside our ranks and a lot of us get the idea that they are with us and of us.

I look back over what I've written about those days since I picked up the leaflet of the Unemployment Council, and wonder if I've really said what I mean. I don't know if I can get across to you the feeling that came over me whenever I went to a meeting of the Council, or of the Communist Party, and heard their speakers and read their leaflets. All my life I'd been sweated and stepped on and Jim-Crowed. I lay on my belly in the mines for a few dollars a week, and saw my pay stolen and slashed, and my buddies killed. I lived in the worst section of town, and rode behind the "Colored" signs on streetcars, as though there was something disgusting about me. I heard myself called "nigger" and "darky," and I had to say "Yes, sir" to every white man, whether he had my respect or not.

I had always detested it, but I had never known that anything could be done about it. And here, all of a sudden, I had found organizations in which Negroes and whites sat together, and worked together, and knew no difference of race or color. Here were organizations that weren't scared to come out for equality for the Negro people, and for the rights of the workers. The Jim-Crow system, the wage-slave system, weren't everlasting after all! It was like all of a sudden turning a corner on a dirty, old street and finding yourself facing a broad, shining highway.

The bosses, and the Negro misleaders like Oscar Adams, told us that these Reds were "foreigners" and "strangers" and that the Communist program wasn't acceptable to the workers in the South. I couldn't see that at all. The leaders of the Communist Party and the Unemployment Council seemed people very much like the ones I'd always been used to. They were workers, and they talked our language. Their talk sure sounded better to me than the talk of Oscar Adams, or the President of the Tennessee Coal, Iron and Railroad Co. who addressed us every once in a while. As for the program not being acceptable to us—I felt then, and I know now, that the Communist program is the only program that the Southern workers—whites and Negroes both—can possibly accept in the long run. It's the only program that does justice to the Southern worker's ideas that everybody ought to have an equal chance, and that every man has rights that must be respected.

WORK AGAINST ODDS

The Communist Party and the Unemployment Council had to work under the most difficult conditions. We tried to have a little headquarters, but it was raided and closed by the police. We collected money for leaflets, penny by penny, and mimeographed them on an old, rickety hand-machine we kept in a private home. We worked very quietly, behind drawn shades, and were always on the look-out for spies and police. We put the leaflets out at night, from door-step to door-step. Some of our members who worked in factories sneaked them in there.

Sometimes we would distribute leaflets in a neighborhood, calling for a meeting in half an hour on a certain corner. We would put up just one speaker, he would give his message in the fewest possible words, we would pass out pamphlets and leaflets, and the meeting would break up before the cops could get on the scene.

The bosses got scared, and the Ku Klux Klan got busy. The Klan would parade up and down the streets, especially in the Negro neighborhoods, in full regalia, warning the Negroes to keep away from the Communists. They passed out leaflets saying: "Communism Must Be Wiped Out. Alabama Is a Good Place for Good Negroes, but a Bad Place for Negroes Who Want Social Equality."

In June, 1930, I was elected a delegate to the National Unemployment Convention in Chicago. Up to this point I had been staying with relatives in Birmingham. They were under the influence of the Negro misleaders and preachers, and they told me that if I went to the convention I need never come to their house again. The very morning I was to leave, I found a leaflet on my doorstep, put there by the Ku Klux Klan.

I went to Chicago, riding the rods to get there.

A WORLD MOVEMENT

In Chicago, I got my first broad view of the revolutionary workers' movement. I met workers from almost every state in the union, and I heard about the work of the same kind of organizations in other countries, and it first dawned on me how strong and powerful the working-class was. There wasn't only me and a few others in Birmingham. There were hundreds, thousands, millions of us!

My family had told me not to come back. What did I care? My real family was the organization. I'd found that I had brothers and sisters in every corner of the world, I knew that we were all fighting for one thing and that they'd stick by me. I never lost that feeling, in all the hard days to come, in Fulton Tower Prison with the threat of the electric chair and the chain-gang looming over me.

I went back to Birmingham and put every ounce of my strength into the work of organization. I built groups among the miners. I read and I studied. I worked in the Young Communist League under the direction of Harry Simms, the young white boy who was later, during the strike of the Kentucky miners, to give his life for the working-class.

I helped organize an Anti-Lynching Conference in Chattanooga. This conference selected delegates to the first convention of the League of Struggle for Negro Rights, held in St. Louis in 1930.

DEATH PENALTY TO THE LYNCHERS

I myself was not a delegate to the St. Louis Conference—but the decisions of the conference impressed me. All the Negro organizations before this, and all the white liberal groups, had pussy-footed and hesitated and hemmed and hawed on the burning issue of lynching. When I read the slogan of the League of Struggle for Negro Rights—"Death Penalty to Lynchers!"—the words seemed blazed right across the page. The St. Louis conference called for a determined struggle for equality for the Negro people.

I had a number of experiences about this time, that taught me a great deal. I went into the Black Belt, and talked with the Negro and white sharecroppers and tenants. The price of cotton had crashed, and the burden was being put on the croppers and tenants, so the landlords might go on living in style. There was practically nothing to eat in the cabins. The croppers had applied for government loans, but when the loans came the landlords, with the help of the rural postmasters, stole the money. There was as yet no Share Croppers Union, which was later to challenge the landlords' system of debt-slavery.

A Negro preacher with whom I had made contact notified a Negro secret service-man that I was about, and together they tried to terrorize me. The preacher said: "I don't know anything about the conditions of the people here. I only know that I myself am happy and comfortable." Well, the upshot of it was that the preacher called the sheriff, and lynch-mob began to form, and I escaped by grabbing the first train out of town. My escape was a matter of minutes. It was a white share-cropper who supplied me with the funds to get away.

SCOTTSBORO

It was while I was in New Orleans for a few weeks as representative of the Trade Union Unity League, that I first saw the name Scottsboro. I want to go into that a bit, because the Scottsboro case marked a new stage in the life of the Negro people—and the white workers too—in the United States.

One morning I picked up a capitalist paper and saw that "nine black brutes had raped two little white girls." That was the way the paper put it. There was a dock strike on at the time in New Orleans, and the bosses would have been glad to see this issue, the Scottsboro case, used as a method of whipping up hatred of white and Negro longshoremen against each other.

I knew the South well enough to know at once that here was a vicious frame-up. I got to work right away organizing committees among the workers of New Orleans. We visited clubs, unions, churches to get support for the Scottsboro boys.

On May 31, 1931, I went as a delegate to the first All-Southern Scottsboro Conference, held in Chattanooga.

The hall where the conference was to be held was surrounded by gunmen and police, but we went through with the meeting just the same. The bosses and dicks were boiling mad because we had white and Negro meeting together—and saying plainly that the whole Scottsboro case was a rotten frame-up. I spoke at that conference.

While I was in Chattanooga that trip, I went to a meeting in a Negro church addressed by William Pickens, field secretary of the National Association for the Advancement of Colored People. Pickens made an attack on the International Labor Defense. He said we shouldn't get the governor and the courts mad. We should try to be polite to them. He said: "You people don't know how to fight. Give your money to me and to lawyers and we'll take care of this." Then he attacked the mothers of the Scottsboro boys as being a lot of ignorant fools.

Well, I was so mad I hardly knew what I was doing. I spoke up and said that the Scottsboro boys would never get out of prison until all the workers got together and brought terrific pressure on the lynchers. I said: "We've been polite to the lynchers entirely too long. As long as we O.K. what they do, as long as we crawl to them and assure them we have no wish to change their way of doing things—just so long we'll be slaves."

WHAT SCOTTSBORO MEANS

Later, while I lay in jail in Atlanta, I followed the Scottsboro case as best I could. Every time I got a paper—and that wasn't too often—I looked eagerly for news of the Scottsboro boys. I was uplifted, brimming over with joy because of the splendid fight we made at the new trial in Decatur. I could hardly contain myself when I saw how the workers were making the Scottsboro case a battering-ram against Jim-Crowism and oppression. I watched the protests in the Scottsboro case swelling to a roar that echoed from one end of the world to the other. And I'd pace that cell, aching to get out and throw myself into the fight.

If you know the South as I do, you know what the Scottsboro case means. Here were the landlords in their fine plantation homes, and the big white bosses in their city mansions, and the whole brutal force of dicks and police who do their bidding. There they sat, smug and self-satisfied, and oh, so sure that nothing could ever interfere with them and their ways. For all time they would be able to sweat and cheat the Negro people, and jail and frame and lynch and shoot them, as they pleased.

And all of a sudden someone laid a hand on their arm and said: "STOP." It was a great big hand, a powerful hand, the hand of the workers. The bosses were shocked and horrified and scared. I know that. And I know also that after the fight began for the Scottsboro boys, every Negro worker in mill or mine, every Negro cropper on the Black Belt plantations, breathed a little easier and held his head a little higher.

I'm ahead of my story now, because I got carried away by the thought of Scottsboro.

I settled down for work in Birmingham, especially among the miners. Conditions in the mines had become worse than horrible. The company had gunmen patrolling the highways, watching the miners. I was arrested several times during this period, and quizzed and bullied.

During one of these arrests the police demanded that I tell them where the white organizers lived. They said: "Where's that guy Tom? We'd like to lay our hands on the son-of-a-bitch."

I said: "I haven't seen Tom for days."

All of a sudden one of the policemen struck me across the mouth. "Mr. Tom to you, you bastard!" he roared.

THE WILLIE PETERSON FRAME-UP

But it was during the Willie Peterson frame-up that I first got a real taste of police brutality.

There was frame-up in the air for weeks before the Peterson case started. The miners were organizing against wage-cuts; the white and Negro workers were beginning to get together and demand relief and jobs and the human rights that had been taken from them. If the bosses could engineer a frame-up against some Negro, a lot of white workers would begin to think about that instead of about bread and jobs. If they could be made to think of the Negroes they worked with as rapists and murderers, they wouldn't be so anxious to organize with them in unions and Unemployment Councils. Also, such frame-ups are always the excuse for terrorizing the Negroes.

On August 3, in Birmingham, two white girls were killed. More than 70 Negroes were lynched in the fury that was whipped up around this case! One of the papers said that the man who shot these girls was a Negro, and that he had made a "Communist speech" to them before the murder.

A dragnet was thrown out, and I was one of the first to be caught.

I was lying in bed when a large white man came to our window and put a gun in my face. At the same moment there was a crash, and some other men broke in the door. My roommate and I were forced out of bed and handcuffed. We didn't know what it was all about.

I was locked up. About an hour later, police came to my cell and dragged me down the stairs and into a car. I was carried to the woods, about 20 miles out of town. On the way one of the gun-thugs kept pointing out places where he had killed "niggers."

The car stopped and we all got out. They asked me: "Who shot Nell Williams?" I said I didn't know.

THIRD DEGREE

Two of the men pulled their coats off and slipped a rubber hose from their trousers. I was still handcuffed. They began to beat me over the head. When one man got tired, another would take the hose from him and go on with the beating. They said they knew that I had shot Nell Williams. They demanded that I point out some of the white comrades. I shut my lips tight over my teeth, and said nothing.

Next morning I couldn't get my hat on my swollen head. My ears were great raw lumps of flesh.

Willie Peterson, an unemployed coal-miner, a veteran of the World War, was framed for that murder. He is as innocent as I was.

By now I was known to every stool-pigeon and policeman in Birmingham, and my work became extremely difficult. It was decided to send me to Atlanta.

I want to describe the conditions of the Atlanta workers, because that will give some idea of why the Georgia bosses find it necessary to sentence workers' organizers to the chain-gang. I couldn't say how many workers were unemployed—the officials keep this information carefully hidden. It was admitted that 25,000 families, out of 150,000 population, were on relief. Hundreds who were jobless were kept off the relief rolls.

In the factories, the wages were little higher than the amount of relief doled out to the unemployed. The conditions of the Southern textile workers is known to be extremely bad, but Atlanta has mills that even the Southern papers talk about as "sore spots." The Fulton Bag Company was one of these. There, and in the Piedmont and other textile plants, young girls worked for $6 and even less a week, slaving long hours in ancient, unsanitary buildings.

In the spring of 1930, six organizers of the workers—two white women, two white men and two Negro men—were arrested and indicted for "inciting to insurrection." The state was demanding that they be sent to the electric chair.

SPLITTING THE WORKERS

The Black Shirts—a fascist organization—held parades quite often, demanding that all jobs be taken away from Negroes and given to whites. They said that all the Negroes should go back to Africa. I smiled the first time I heard this—it amused me to see how exactly the program of Marcus Garvey fitted in with the program of the Klan.

Of course the demand of the Black Shirts to give all the jobs to the whites was an attempt to split the white workers from the Negroes and put an end to joint struggles for relief. As organizer for the Unemployment Council, I had to fight mighty hard against this poison.

From the cradle onward, the Southern white boy and girl are told that they are better than Negroes. Their birth certificates are tagged "white"; they sit in white schools, play in white parks and live on white streets. They pray in white churches, and when they die they are buried in white cemeteries. Everywhere before them are signs: "For White." "For Colored." They are taught that Negroes are thieves, and murderers, and rapists.

I remember especially one white worker, a carpenter, who was one of the first people I talked to in Atlanta. He was very friendly to me. He came to me one day and said that he agreed with the program, but something was holding him back from joining the Unemployment Council.

"What's that, Jim?" I asked. Really, though, I didn't have to ask. I knew the South, and I could guess.

"Well, I just don't figure that white folks and Negroes should mix together," he said. "It won't never do to organize them in one body."

I said: "Look here, Jim. You know that the carpenters and all the other workers get a darn sight less pay for the same work in the South than they do in other parts. Did you ever figure out why?"

He hadn't.

THE PRICE OF DIVISION

"Well," I said, "I'll tell you why. It's because the bosses have got us all split up down here. We Southern workers are as good fighters as there are anywhere, and yet we haven't been able to get equal wages with the workers in other places, and we haven't got any rights to speak of. That's because we've been divided. When the whites go out on strike, the bosses call in the Negroes to scab. When the Negroes strike, the bosses call in the whites to scab.

"Did you ever figure out why the unions here are so weak? It's because the whites don't want to organize with the Negroes, and the Negroes don't trust the whites.

"We haven't got the simplest human rights down here. We're not allowed to organize and we're not allowed to hold our meetings except in secret. We can't vote—most of us—because the bosses are so anxious to keep the Negroes from voting that they make laws that take this right away from the white workers too.

"We Southern workers are like a house that's divided against itself. We're like an army that goes out to fight the enemy and stops on the way because its men are all fighting each other.

"Take this relief business, now," I said. "The commissioners tell the whites that they can't give them any more relief because they have to feed so many Negroes, and the Negroes ought to be chased back to the farms. Then they turn around and tell the Negroes that white people have to come first on the relief, so there's nothing doing for colored folks. That way they put us off, and get us scrapping with each other.

"Now suppose the white unemployed, and the Negro unemployed, all go to the commissioners together and say: 'We're all starving. We're all in need. We've decided to get together into one strong, powerful organization to make you come across with relief.'

"Don't you think that'll bring results, Jim?" I asked him. "Don't you see how foolish it is to go into the fight with half an army when we could have a whole one? Don't you think that an empty belly is a pretty punk exchange for the honor of being called a 'superior' race? And can't you realize that as long as one foot is chained to the ground the other can't travel very far?"

WHAT HAPPENED TO JIM

Jim didn't say anything more that day. I guess he went home and thought it over. He came back about a week later and invited me to his house. It was the first time he'd ever had a Negro in the house as a friend and equal. When I got there I found two other Negro workers that Jim had brought into the Unemployment Council.

About a month later Jim beat up a rent collector who was boarding up the house of an evicted Negro worker. Then he went to work and organized a committee of whites and Negroes to see the mayor about the case. "Today it's the black worker across town; tomorrow it'll be me," Jim told the mayor.

There are a lot of Jims today, all over the South.

We organized a number of block committees of the Unemployed Councils, and got rent and relief for a large number of families. We agitated end-lessly for unemployment insurance.

In the middle of June, 1932, the state closed down all the relief stations. A drive was organized to send all the jobless to the farms.

We gave out leaflets calling for a mass demonstration at the courthouse to demand that the relief be continued. About 1000 workers came, 600 of them white. We told the commissioners we didn't intend to starve. We re-minded them that $800,000 had been collected in the Community Chest drive. The commissioners said there wasn't a cent to be had.

But the very next day the commission voted $6,000 for relief to the jobless!

On the night of July 11, I went to the Post Office to get my mail. I felt myself grabbed from behind and turned to see a police officer.

I was placed in a cell, and was shown a large electric chair, and told to spill everything I knew about the movement. I refused to talk, and was held incommunicado for eleven days. Finally I smuggled out a letter through another prisoner, and the International Labor Defense got on the job.

THE INSURRECTION LAW

Assistant Solicitor John Hudson rigged up the charge against me. It was the charge of "inciting to insurrection." It was based on an old statute passed in 1861, when the Negro people were still chattel slaves, and the white masters needed a law to crush slave insurrection and kill those found giving aid to the slaves. The statute read:

> If any person be in any manner instrumental in bringing, introducing or circulating within the state any printed or written paper, pamphlet, or circular for the purpose of exciting insurrection, revolt, conspiracy or resistance on the part of slaves, Negroes or free persons of color in this state he shall be guilty of high misdemeanor which is punishable by death.

Since the days of the Civil War that law had lain, unused and almost forgotten. Now the slaves of the new order—the white and black slaves of capitalism—were organizing. In the eyes of the Georgia masters, it was a crime punishable by death.

The trial was set for January 16, 1933. The state of Georgia displayed the literature that had been taken from my room, and read passages of it to the jury. They questioned me in great detail. Did I believe that the bosses and government ought to pay insurance to unemployed workers? That Negroes should have complete equality with white people? Did I believe in the demand for the self-determination of the Black Belt—that the Negro people should be allowed to rule the Black Belt territory, kicking out the white landlords and government officials? Did I feel that the working-class could run the mills and mines and government? That it wasn't necessary to have bosses at all?

I told them I believed all of that—and more.

The courtroom was packed to suffocation. The I.L.D. attorneys, Benjamin J. Davis, Jr., and John H. Geer, two young Negroes—and I myself—fought every step of the way. We were not really talking to that judge, nor to those prosecutors, whose questions we were answering. Over their heads we talked to the white and Negro workers who sat on the benches, watching, listening, learning. And beyond them we talked to the thousands and millions of workers all over the world to whom this case was a challenge.

We demanded that Negroes be placed on jury rolls. We demanded that the insulting terms, "nigger" and "darky," be dropped in that court. We asserted the right of the workers to organize, to strike, to make their demands, to nominate candidates of their choice. We asserted the right of the Negro people to have complete equality in every field.

The state held that my membership in the Communist Party, my possession of Communist literature, was enough to send me to the electric chair. They said to the jury: "Stamp this damnable thing out now with a conviction that will automatically carry with it a penalty of electrocution."

And the hand-picked lily-white jury responded:

"We, the jury, find the defendant guilty as charged, but recommend that mercy be shown and fix his sentence at from 18 to 20 years."

I had organized starving workers to demand bread, and I was sentenced to live out my years on the chain-gang for it. But I knew that the movement itself would not stop. I spoke to the court and said:

"They can hold this Angelo Herndon and hundreds of others, but it will never stop these demonstrations on the part of Negro and white workers who demand a decent place to live in and proper food for their kids to eat."

I said: "You may do what you will with Angelo Herndon. You may indict him. You may put him in jail. But there will come thousands of Angelo Herndons. If you really want to do anything about the case, you must go out and indict the social system. But this you will not do, for your role is to defend the system under which the toiling masses are robbed and oppressed.

"You may succeed in killing one, two, even a score of working-class organizers. But you cannot kill the working class."

FULTON TOWER PRISON

Now began the long months in Fulton Tower Prison. How can I describe those days? I was starved. I was ill. I was denied the sight of friends, denied the literature of the class struggle, which meant more than food and drink to me. I was tortured by the jailers, who taunted me, and threatened me, and searched feverishly for a thousand and one ways to make the days of a jailed man a living hell.

But worse than anything was the way time dragged, dragged, till each separate minute became an eternity of torture. Time became my personal enemy—an enemy I had to fight with all my strength. The first hours became a day, and the first days became weeks, and then began the long succession of months—six of them, a year of them, seventeen, eighteen, nineteen. I lay on my filthy bunk, and studied the patterns on walls and ceilings, and learned to know every spot and crack. I watched the shadows of the jail bars on the floor shorten and lengthen again. I saw men come and go, and now and again return. Prisoners arrived with horrible stories of torture and brutality on the chain-gang for which I was headed. I said good-bye to ten men as they left the cell to go to the death-chair.

Meanwhile, beyond the walls, the working-class movement was fighting on. Sometimes I got a newspaper, torn and dirty, and lay on the floor piecing it together. Sometimes—very rarely—a friend was allowed to see me for a moment. In this way I learned what was going on.

The crisis got worse, and the New Deal came in. The workers learned that it meant more hunger and misery, and strikes broke out. The map of the United States was dotted with strikes. The workers in the very hell-holes I had once slaved in, downed tools and fought to better their conditions. The farmers massed to stop the sale of their land. The Scottsboro fight went on ceaselessly, was carried across the world, piled up new mountains of strength.

In Germany, Hitler took over power, poured a sea of blood over the country, and yet could not drown the organizations, the fighting spirit of the working-class. The Chinese Soviets tore a fifth of China from the grip of the foreign and the native exploiters.

In the Soviet Union, the workers, all power in their hands, built vast new dams and power-stations, laid new railways, fired new blast furnaces, planted great farms and built, stone upon stone, the structure of a new society of peace and plenty.

The war danger flared and died down and flared again—the workers watching constantly to stamp out the spark.

"THE WORKERS WILL SET ME FREE"

I wanted to be out in the struggle, taking my part in it, doing my share. But not for one minute did I doubt that the workers would make me free. Even the news that the Georgia Supreme Court had denied me a new trial did not dishearten me. From the letters I received, I knew that the workers everywhere were fighting for me. I wrote letters—never knowing if they would leave the jail or not—and I read what papers and books I had, and I waited.

The day I heard that the International Labor Defense had had bail set for me, I packed up my belongings and got ready to go. The jailers laughed at me. "Bail set ain't bail raised," they said. But I knew I'd go. And I went.

One morning Joe Brodsky, the lawyer who'd also fought for the Scottsboro boys, came to my cell and said: "We're going, Angelo."

The working-class had determined on my release, and I was free. They had raised, penny by penny, the enormous sum of $15,000 to get a class brother out of jail.

I took the train for the North. All along the way I was greeted by my comrades. In Washington, in Baltimore, in Philadelphia and Newark, workers stood on the platform to watch the train come by, and they cheered me, and I cheered their spirit and their determination. I stepped out of the train at Pennsylvania Station, into the arms of 7,000 of my white and Negro class-brothers and class-sisters.

I am happy to be out. Now, for a time at least, I can take my place once more in the ranks of the working-class. Now I am back in the fight.

DEPRESSION HITS THE PROMISED LAND

E. Franklin Frazier / Some Effects of the Depression on the Negro in Northern Cities

---

During the Depression, radical intellectuals both black and white set to work to lay guidelines for a new society. Among the ideas widely discussed in radical periodicals of the time was the need for the black and white masses to join together to advance the interests of the working class in face of widespread exploitation by the capitalist system in America.

E. Franklin Frazier, perhaps the finest black sociologist America has yet produced, developed a radical critique of the black middle class that found its final statement in his **Black Bourgeoisie,** published in 1957. The article reprinted here appeared in the Marxist journal **Science and Society** in 1938 and is primarily a description of the effect of the Depression on blacks living in Northern cities. Frazier depicts the impact of the Depression on the black family and goes on to attack what he calls the "racial chauvinism" of the black middle class.

Since the migration of thousands of Negroes to the metropolitan areas of the North during and following the World War, there has been a growing tendency to view the problems of the Negro in relationship to the

FROM E. Franklin Frazier, "Some Effects of the Depression on the Negro in Northern Cities," *Science and Society*, Vol. II (Fall 1938), pp. 489–99. (Originally a paper read before the annual meeting of the Eastern Sociological Society, Vassar College, April 16, 1938.) Reprinted by permission of *Science and Society*.

dominant social and economic currents in American life. As an example of this shift in viewpoint, one might mention Professor Frank A. Ross's study of the urbanization of the Negro population which views the cityward movement of the Negro as a part of the whole process of urbanization in America.[1] Viewed from this standpoint, the Negro migrations to northern industrial centers are seen in their relation to changes in southern agriculture and the cessation of European immigration coupled with a demand for cheap unskilled labor. Consequently, it was not by accident, but because of certain fundamental economic forces in American life that New York, Chicago, Philadelphia, and Detroit became the chief goals of the migrating black masses. Within the metropolitan districts of these four cities, there were, in 1930, 1,185,530 Negroes or about a half of the entire Negro population in the North. The remainder of the Negro population in the North, excluding less than 300,000 rural dwellers, was concentrated in smaller industrial centers where there was a demand for cheap labor. The social consequences of the shift of these peasant folk to the industrial centers of the North has been the subject of a vast literature.[2] But concerning the effects of the depression on these newcomers to modern industrial society very little systematic information is available. In this paper, an attempt will be made to bring together and interpret the available information which we have been able to secure from various sources.

Concerning the volume of unemployment and relief in the Negro population in northern cities, our information is about as reliable as that for the whites. In fourteen of the sixteen northern and western cities included in the unemployment census of 1931, the percentage of Negroes unemployed was higher than that of either native or foreign-born whites. This was true for women as well as men. For example, in Chicago, 40.3 per cent of the employable Negro men and 55.4 of the women were reported unemployed, whereas only 24.6 per cent of the foreign-born white men and 12.0 per cent of the foreign-born white women; and 23.4 per cent of the native white men and 16.9 per cent of native white women were reported unemployed.[3] Klein, in his recent survey of Pittsburgh, reported that in February 1934, "48 per cent of the employable Negroes were entirely without employment . . . while only 31.1 per cent of the potential white workers were unemployed."[4] That this situation was generally true in regard to Negro women was indicated in a study of fluctuations in the employment of women from 1928 to 1931 in Bridgeport, Buffalo, Syracuse, and Philadelphia. According

[1] Frank A. Ross, "Urbanization and the Negro," *Publication of the American Sociological Society*, XXVI, 115–128.
[2] See Louise V. Kennedy, *The Negro Peasant Turns Cityward* (New York, 1930) and E. Franklin Frazier, "The Impact of Urban Civilization Upon Negro Family Life," *American Sociological Review*, II, 609–618.
[3] *Fifteenth Census of the United States: 1930, Unemployment*, II, 370–373.
[4] Phillip Klein, *A Social Study of Pittsburgh. Community Problems and Social Services of Allegheny County* (New York, 1938), p. 279.

to this study, "the proportion of Negro women unemployed ordinarily was greater than their share in the total woman population or among those in gainful employment."[5]

Although there is a rather general but uncritical acceptance of the belief that the "Negro is the last to be hired and the first to be fired," it is difficult to make any generalization concerning practices during the depression in northern cities. In a paper read before the Conference on the Economic Status of the Negro held in Washington, D.C., in May 1933, it was reported that in the meat packing industry, "Reductions in the working force due to the depression have in general left these Negro workers in relatively larger proportions than other workers."[6] On the other hand, Dr. Joseph H. Willits of the University of Pennsylvania, in a study of unemployment among several groups in Philadelphia, found the following situation during the years 1929 to 1933. "In 1929 when 9.0 per cent of all white employables were unemployed, 15.7 per cent of the Negroes were unemployed. In 1930 it was 13.8 per cent for whites and 19.4 per cent for Negroes; in 1931 it was 24.1 per cent for whites and 35.0 per cent for Negroes; and in 1932 it was 39.7 per cent for whites and 56.0 per cent for Negroes."[7] It is likely that these figures are typical of northern cities since the vast majority of Negro workers are employed on jobs which are generally susceptible to fluctuations in industry.

We are on much surer ground when we consider the incidence of relief. When the unemployment relief census was taken in 1933, there was in New York, Chicago, Philadelphia, and Detroit, a total of 78,027 Negro families on relief or 32.5 per cent of the Negro families in these four cities. Measured in terms of population, New York with 23.9 per cent and Detroit with 27.6 per cent had smaller precentages of Negroes on relief than Chicago and Philadelphia in each of which cities 34 per cent of the Negro population was on relief.[8] The situation was even worse in Pittsburgh and Cleveland each with 43 per cent and Akron, Ohio, with 67 per cent of the Negro population on relief. After the census of 1933 was taken, the situation in these cities undoubtedly became worse. For example, by February 1935, "practically three out of every five Negroes in Allegheny County," where Pittsburgh is located, were on the relief rolls.[9] A study of the situation in

---

[5] *Employment Fluctuations and Unemployment of Women.* Certain Indications from Various Sources, 1928–31. By Mary Elizabeth Pidgeon, U. S. Department of Labor, Bulletin of the Women's Bureau, Washington: 1933. p. 43.

[6] *The Economic Status of Negroes.* Summary and Analysis of the Materials Presented at the Conference on the Economic Status of the Negro, held in Washington, D. C., May 11–13, 1933, under the Sponsorship of the Julius Rosenwald Fund. Prepared by Charles S. Johnson. Fisk University Press, 1933. p. 10.

[7] *Ibid.,* p. 19.

[8] *Federal Emergency Relief Administration. Unemployment Relief Census,* October 1933. Report No. 1. Washington: 1934. p. 78, 8.

[9] Klein, *op. cit.,* p. 279.

the Harlem area of New York City in 1935 revealed that 24,293 or 43.2 per cent of 56,157 Negro families were receiving relief.[10] In addition to these relief families, 7,560 unattached Negro men had registered with the Emergency Relief Bureau over a period of four years.

There is good reason for believing that as the depression lifted momentarily, Negroes were not reabsorbed into industry to the same extent as white workers. According to a report of the F.E.R.A. on Baltimore, Bridgeport, Connecticut, Chicago, Detroit, Omaha, St. Louis, Mo., and Paterson, N.J., as late as May 1935, Negroes were "being added to the relief population in greater proportions of total intake than they existed in the general population (1930 Census)." The report ventured the explanation that it reflected in part "a tendency for employers to favor unemployed white persons as compared with Negro workers."[11] In Pittsburgh, two of the largest employers of Negroes in the steel industry who claimed that they had brought hundreds of Negroes north would not guarantee the reemployment of Negroes because, in their opinion, Negro workers had been demoralized by relief and had become radical.[12] Although there is some evidence that Negroes have been displaced by white workers in northern cities, the question has not been studied systematically. The 1930 census indicated that for the country as a whole the Negro was being pushed back into domestic and personal service. However, in an analysis of the occupational statistics for individual cities, it was found that this was true in southern rather than in northern cities. But, it appears from statistics on relief that Negro domestic workers in northern cities have become unemployed as the depression has become worse. In New York State, there were 26,359 unemployed Negro domestic workers on relief in 1935.

Negro workers who have not lost their jobs have suffered a reduction in earning power. In Kiser's study of 2,061 Negro households in a section of Harlem in New York City, it was found that the median income of skilled workers had declined from $1,955 in 1929 to $1,003 in 1932 or 48.7 per cent. The decline in the incomes of semi-skilled and unskilled workers was slightly less or 43 per cent.[13] This study also gave information on the effect of the depression on the earning power of the Negro middle class which had rapidly emerged in response to the varied demands of large Negro communities in northern cities. It was found that among the white collar workers, who comprised 16 per cent of the households studied, "the income decreases were 35 per cent in the professional class, 44 per cent in the proprietary class and 37 per cent among clerical and kindred workers." First

[10] From an unpublished *Social and Economic Survey of the Harlem Negro Community* made by the writer for The Mayor's Commission on Conditions in Harlem.

[11] *Federal Emergency Relief Administration. Research Bulletin. Current Changes in the Urban Relief Population.* May 1935. Series I, Number 12, p. 3.

[12] Klein, *op. cit.,* p. 280.

[13] Clyde V. Kiser, "Diminishing Family Income in Harlem," *Opportunity*, XIII, 173–174.

hand observations and reports of college students indicate that this was representative of the Negro middle class throughout the North. Their savings and incomes, and investments from business, which gave this class a favored position in the Negro community, were largely wiped out and even Negro doctors were forced to seek relief.

Concerning the effects of the depression upon the Negro family in the northern city, the void in our knowledge is not illumined even by one shining exception such as Cavan and Ranck have provided in their study of one hundred white families.[14] However, it appears that among Negroes, just as these authors found among white families, "well organized families met the depression with less catastrophic consequences than families that were already disorganized."[15] That this was true of upper-class Negro families was revealed in the documents furnished by college students who come from the more stabilized elements in the Negro population. Although in many cases, savings were lost or consumed, homes were mortgaged or lost, and the children had to delay their college education for one to three years, these families maintained their solidarity and by pooling their resources were able to achieve some of their major family objectives. But since family disorganization among the masses has been one of the main problems resulting from the migration of the Negro to the northern city, it is not unreasonable to assume that family disorganization increased as a result of the depression.[16] First, among the consequences of reduction or loss of income was the seeking of cheaper living quarters or the crowding of families and relatives in a single household. We have a record of a case of mass housing in Chicago, where 67 families were permitted to move into an old apartment building that had been partially destroyed by fire and was without heat and light. For heat, they used coal stoves such as are used in the rural districts, and for light, they burned kerosene lamps. The owners of the building operated the house through a committee of Negroes and collected rents from those families who were able to pay. In some cases, the men in the families made payments in terms of various services. Although thousands of Negro families in northern cities, who had constantly lived close to the margin of existence, had been crowded into slum areas, the depression made their condition worse and reduced thousands of others to their level. An analysis of deserted "under care" families of the Charity Organization Society of New York City revealed that the number of families with one or more relatives had increased significantly during the depression. Although even under normal conditions from 10 to 30 per cent of Negro families in northern cities have women heads, it is probable that the number increased during the depression. Among the relief families in Chicago, Detroit, New York, and Philadelphia,

---

[14] Ruth Shonle Cavan and Katherine Howland Ranck, *The Family and the Depression, A Study of One Hundred Chicago Families* (Chicago, 1938). See Introduction.

[15] *Ibid.*, Introduction, p. viii.

[16] See E. Franklin Frazier, *The Negro Family in Chicago* (Chicago, 1932).

we find that only from 29 per cent (in Chicago) to 50 per cent (in New York City), were normal family groups; i.e., man, wife, and children. Among the relief families in these same cities, a fifth to a fourth of the families had a woman head. Moreover, it is also significant that a relatively larger number of Negro dependents than white dependents were unattached women. It is because of this fact that the F.E.R.A. views the rehabilitation of Negroes as less a problem of the aged than a problem of female dependency often involving children.[17]

The next question to which an answer has been sought is: What effect has the depression had on the health and survival of the Negro in the northern city? The studies of Thompson and Whelpton indicate that prior to the depression Negroes in large cities, including New York and Chicago "were not maintaining their numbers on a permanent basis in either 1920 or 1928."[18] For the period subsequent to the depression, we might draw some conclusions from the preliminary data released by the National Health Survey.[19] These data indicate that illnesses disabling for one week or longer in a twelve month period occurred among families on relief at a rate 57 per cent higher than among families with annual incomes of $3,000 and over. Since Negroes were included among such families, and as a matter of fact a larger proportion of the Negro families enumerated were on relief than white families, it is reasonable to conclude that Negro relief families have been subject to disabling illnesses more than those not on relief.[20]

In this connection, we can cite the results of a statistical study, growing out of our social and economic survey of Harlem, which deals with the relation between dependency and birth and death rates.[21] In this study, a graduate student at Columbia University worked out correlations between the percentage of families on relief and the changes in the birth and death rates and infant mortality in eleven health areas, each with a population of 5,000 or more Negroes. A high positive correlation (.89 for birth rates and .83 for death rates) was found between the dependency rate and the percentage of change in birth and death rates. The author of this closely thought-out study presented cogent reasons for believing that the correlation between increases in birth rates and dependency was due to a shifting of the population, which tended to segregate the relief families, that nor-

---

[17] *Federal Emergency Relief Administration. Unemployment Relief Census*, October 1933. Report No. 3. Washington: 1934. pp. 90–91, 32–33.

[18] Warren S. Thompson and P. K. Whelpton, *Population Trends in the United States* (New York, 1933), p. 280.

[19] *Preliminary Reports. The National Health Survey Sickness and Medical Care Series*, Bulletin No. 2. United States Public Health Service, Washington, 1938.

[20] The proportion of white and Negro relief families among those enumerated in three cities was as follows: Chicago—white, 11.3 per cent; Negro, 34.9 per cent; Philadelphia —white, 12.2 per cent; Negro, 47.0 per cent; Detroit—white, 10.1 per cent; Negro, 32.8.

[21] Herbert L. Bryan, "Birth Rates and Death Rates in Relation to Dependency in Selected Health Areas in Harlem." (M.A. Thesis) Columbia University, 1936.

mally had a relatively higher birth rate in certain areas. But, he also presented good reasons for his belief that the changes in the death rates were due to the depression which resulted in a lack of adequate food, changes in habits of living, and vicious behavior often associated with idle adults on relief. On the other hand, there was a relatively high negative correlation ($-.60$) between changes in infant mortality and dependency. His explanation of the tendency of the infant mortality to decrease as the dependency rate mounted was as follows:

> The Home Relief Bureau made available medical services to the recipients of relief which they had been unable to afford previously out of their own earnings; the fact that a trained investigator visited the home periodically, was able to advise and instruct the families in the proper care of their children, refer them to the community pre and post natal clinics, arrange for their hospitalization, and distribute and explain literature on the proper care of mother and infant before and after birth proved to be a very helpful factor in overcoming some of the above mentioned things which contributed to the very high rate of infant mortality. There is also the factor that the mother, if employed prior to the family's going on relief, worked several months during pregnancy and returned to work within a minimum time after the birth of the child whereas the mother on relief remains at home and is thus able to take greater precautions in regard to her own health during pregnancy, and devote more care to her child after its birth. . . . It is much easier to get an expectant mother to visit the clinics regularly and exercise the proper precautions to insure the good health of her offspring, but the problem becomes more difficult when persuading an adult to exercise proper care about his own health, visit clinics regularly, take preventive measures, and seek medical attention and advice.[22]

If the author's explanation of these correlations may be taken as valid, and if the situation in Harlem is typical of other northern cities, then it appears that the Negro child has been afforded a better chance of survival because of relief measures than if he had been born into a family existing upon the sub-standards of living of the great body of Negro workers who make their own livelihood.

We turn, finally, to those changes in the Negro's philosophy and outlook on life which may reasonably be attributed to the depression. First, among these changes, one might mention the disillusionment of the Negro middle class. Probably no section of the middle class in America had such high hopes as the Negro middle class during the years of prosperity. Their dream of reaping the rewards of individual thrift and foresight which had had only a partial fulfillment in the South seemed to have come true in the northern city. The Negro professional and business man had prospered upon the earnings of the black masses in northern cities. Moreover, the

---

[22] *Ibid.*, pp. 39–40.

political power of the Negro had opened the way to political patronage and the civil service held out a substantial living for many educated Negroes. Then, suddenly, the purchasing power and savings of the masses began to melt. Doctors' and lawyers' fees dwindled and finally ceased, and the hot-house growth of Negro business behind the walls of segregation shriveled and died, often swallowing up the savings of the black masses. Fine homes and cars and other forms of conspicuous consumption were given up. In their disillusionment, some of the very professional men in New York who had laughed at the small group of radical intellectuals now formed a class to study Marx. But disillusionment did not breed radicalism among a very large group. It appears that more often, they turned to racial chauvinism as a way of realizing their dreams. In Chicago, those of the middle class who had laughed at Garvey's grandiose ideas of a back to Africa movement began to talk of a Forty-ninth State which according to their specifications would be a Black Utopia where the black middle class could exploit the black workers without white competition. In New York City, small Negro business men pointed to the Jewish merchant as the cause of their failures and began to demand that Harlem be reserved as their field of exploitation.

Closely associated with the chauvinistic aims of many members of the middle class have been the efforts of Negroes in a number of northern cities to organize cooperatives as a solution of the Negro's economic problems. However, little or no success has attended these efforts which tended in some instances to nurture if not encourage racial chauvinism. Another movement of greater significance so far as it reflects the growth of militancy directed toward immediate economic ends, has been the picketing and boy-cotting of stores in order to enforce the employment of Negro workers, usually as clerks. In Columbus, Ohio, the Housewives League assumed the leadership in the movement.[23] Although in some cities white storekeepers have made concessions to the demands of the Negroes, they secured relief for a time through court injunctions. But the recent ruling of the United States Supreme Court on a case in the District of Columbia has removed legal barriers against this type of picketing. Inasmuch as the demands for employment in stores where Negroes were the chief customers involved the employment of Negroes as clerks and salesmen, it implied a demand for status, which redounded also to the economic advantage of the middle class.

Although the middle class Negro intellectuals and business men tried to arouse the Negro masses to support their chauvinistic aims, the militancy of the Negro masses did not flow in a single channel. Much of the militancy was unorganized and without an ideology. There were rent strikes to force lowering of rentals. When tenants were evicted for non-payment of rent, crowds often gathered and returned the belongings of the evicted family to the house. In one of these battles in Chicago, several were killed. It has

---

[23] Richard Clyde Minor, "The Negro in Columbus, Ohio" (Ph.D. Dissertation), The Ohio State University, 1936, p. 67.

often been charged that white radicals were responsible for the militancy on the part of the Negroes. It seems nearer to the truth to say that white radicals attempted to give direction to these more or less spontaneous outbursts and to provide Negroes with the ideology of the class struggle. This was undoubtedly true of the spontaneous outburst in Harlem in March 1935. This riot, which began during a time of severe economic stress and when there was much complaint against the Home Relief Bureau, flared up when a flimsy rumor was circulated that a boy had been murdered in a five and ten cent store for stealing a pocket knife. Although the riot at first had a racial character, under the stimulation, if not the direction of white radicals, it became a riot against property rather than persons. The influence of radical white leadership was probably most effective in the various unemployed councils in which Negroes participated on a basis of equality. Perhaps, one of the chief effects of the depression in northern cities upon the thinking of the Negro has been the spread of radical ideas among working class Negroes through cooperation with white workers. Probably at no time in the past have the Negro masses had so many white allies as in their present struggle for work and relief. This newly developed sympathy and cooperation between the two races has even extended to white collar workers especially in the relief agencies.

In summing up the effects of the depression on the Negro in northern cities, one can say, first, that the depression has laid bare the general economic insecurity of the Negro masses. It has tended to destroy the high hopes that were kindled during the War period when it appeared that the Negro, though at the bottom of the industrial ladder, had secured a firm foothold in the industries of the North. From a position of increased earning power, unequalled during his career in America, the Negro has become the ward of the community with from a third to a half of his numbers dependent upon relief. His family life, which had been shattered by the impact of the modern metropolis upon his simple folk life, had scarcely had time to recover and reorganize itself before the shock of the depression shattered it once again. The struggle for survival, always precarious and in doubt, became even more uncertain, though relief has probably enabled children to survive who otherwise would have died. Naturally, the crisis produced a tremendous change in the Negro's evaluation of his position in American life. Many conflicting currents of thought were set in motion. Though the fatuous philosophy of racial chauvinism supported by a segregated black economy, advocated by many of the middle class, did not succeed in winning the masses, they, as a whole, have not accepted a radical definition of their problems. But, at least, it seems certain that the Negro in the northern city with his back to the wall and cut off from retreat because of the collapse of southern agriculture will fight rather than starve and that he has found allies among whites, especially those who find themselves in similar circumstances.

9 SUGGESTIONS FOR FURTHER READING

No book-length study of the black man during the Depression exists. However, much information about Afro-Americans in the period is contained in Gunnar Myrdal, *An American Dilemma**, 2 vols. (Harper, 1944). Constance M. Green, in *The Secret City: A History of Race Relations in the Nation's Capital** (Princeton University Press, 1967), surveys the life of Afro-Americans in Washington, D.C., and tells of the influx of blacks to federal service positions during the New Deal. Robert C. Weaver, who went to the capital during the 1930's, describes the increased growth of urban black communities of the time in *The Negro Ghetto* (Harcourt, Brace & World, 1948). A collection of essays on the black man and organized labor that includes several studies of the Depression era is Julius Jacobson (ed.), *The Negro and the American Labor Movement** (Doubleday, 1968).

The condition of the Southern black in the 1930's is described in Charles S. Johnson, *Shadow of the Plantation** (University of Chicago Press, 1934); Arthur F. Raper, *Preface to Peasantry** (University of North Carolina Press, 1936); Hortense Powdermaker, *After Freedom: A Cultural Study in the Deep South** (Viking, 1939); and Allison Davis and John Dollard, *Children of Bondage** (American Council on Education, 1940). In *Black Boy** (Harper, 1945), novelist Richard Wright describes his childhood in Southern poverty.

Two works that treat different aspects of black religious life are A. H. Fauset, *Black Gods of the Metropolis* (University of Pennsylvania Press, 1944), concerned with urban cults, and Benjamin E. Mays and Joseph W. Nicholson, *The Negro's Church* (Institute of Social and Religious Research, 1933), dealing with the more traditional black churches.

Wilson Record has written two works that overemphasize the resistance of the black man to the appeal of Communism: *The Negro and The Communist Party* (University of North Carolina Press, 1951) and *Race and Radicalism: The NAACP and the Communist Party in Conflict** (Cornell University Press, 1964). The Scottsboro case is considered by one of the accused, Haywood Patterson, in *Scottsboro Boy** (Doubleday, 1950). And Dan T. Carter has published a major study of the case, *Scottsboro: A Tragedy of the American South* (Louisiana State University Press, 1969). *The Crisis of the Negro Intellectual** (Morrow, 1967), by Harold Cruse, a black Marxist, is a polemic and controversial history of black radicalism in this country. Benjamin J. Davis, who was Angelo Herndon's lawyer, has left a memoir called *Communist Councilman from Harlem** (International, 1969).

Sterling Brown, a member of the Howard University faculty, published two important works on the black man in literature that have been printed together in paperback, *Negro Poetry and Drama and the Negro in American Fiction** (Associates in Negro Folk Education, 1937). Two outstanding novels by black men that deal with the Depression era are Richard Wright's *Native Son** (Harper, 1940) and Ralph Ellison's *Invisible Man** (Random House, 1952).

10 THE SECOND WORLD WAR AND THE DOUBLE V

Although unemployment was decreasing as the 1930's drew to a close, it took full-fledged defense and war mobilization to pull the United States out of the Great Depression. As national defense programs began to get under way in the fall of 1940, only 10 per cent of all defense contractors had black workers in their plants in other than menial capacities. The Roosevelt administration recommended that something be done to correct this condition but was told that local customs would not support a policy change. Even when a job training program for defense industry was set up by the administration, only 4,600 of its 175,000 participants were black.

When it appeared that Roosevelt planned to do nothing to improve the situation, black labor took the issue into its own hands. With support from a broad base of black leadership, A. Philip Randolph announced to the President that if he did not take action against discriminatory hiring in defense industry, 50,000 to 100,000 black people would march on the national capitol to demand fair treatment. A few days before the march was set to begin, Roosevelt, either afraid of the violence that such a march might provoke or reluctant to embarrass the United States before the Allied nations, signed an executive order calling for a nondiscriminatory policy in defense production.

Even though enforcement of Roosevelt's order was lax, a change in hiring policy gradually ensued. The Fair Employment Practice Committee was set up to investigate industry policy, and through a hearing procedure, it was instrumental in opening up job opportunities, particularly in new industries. By the end of the war, hundreds of thousands of blacks had been through job training programs and had received positions in industry.

Roosevelt also increased the number of black people in federal jobs. The number of blacks in government positions in Washington increased from 8.5 per cent to 17 per cent between 1938 and 1942. Many of the jobs opened to blacks were clerical or professional. Indeed, the civil service gains made by blacks under the Roosevelt administration have never been reversed. Black people flocked to Washington when it seemed that the opportunities for work there would be continually expanding.

As the migration of blacks to industrial jobs in Northern and Western cities increased, certain patterns that had developed during the Great Migration of the 1920's were repeated. Racial hostility reached a peak, and several major race riots exploded—one in Harlem, one in Los

Angeles, and two in Detroit. The second Detroit riot, in 1943, one of the worst outbreaks of racial violence in American history, brought about a change in the attitude of public officials throughout the North. It became apparent that something had to be done to ease the conditions that led to such outbreaks, and several commissions were set up to prepare proposals for the elimination of the threat of violent race riots. As a result of the work of these commissions, the conclusion of the Second World War was not marked by the eruptions of racial violence that had followed each earlier war involving the United States.

While the situation on the home front was changing for black people, the military was undergoing a shift in its traditional posture toward blacks. Black men had fought willingly in all previous wars of the United States, and the Second World War was no exception. But there was a change in the attitude of black fighting men toward the nature of their military service. More and more they objected to the second-class treatment traditionally accorded them.

When the war began, the policy of the War Department toward the black man was as follows: the proportion of blacks to be enlisted would be the same as the proportion of blacks in the population as a whole (approximately 10 per cent), and black and white military units would remain segregated. Soon after the war began, however, expediency dictated shifts in this policy. Black army officers were trained alongside whites in officer training schools, even in the South. The air force, however, continued to maintain separate training facilities for its black pilots—facilities located, ironically, at Tuskegee Institute in Alabama.

The policy of the navy at the beginning of the war was to allow blacks to serve only as "messmen." The need for personnel grew so rapidly, however, that within five months of Pearl Harbor the navy began to accept blacks in other jobs. Still they were prohibited from combat areas and kept in separate units. Several units of black sailors rebelled at the job restrictions, and eventually they were allowed to participate in most phases of naval work. In 1946, the navy officially ended segregation within its units. It was the first branch of the service to take this important step.

In the army, there was a reluctance to allow black soldiers into combat areas, probably due to fear that they could not be trusted to be courageous in the face of the enemy. Experimental desegregated units were sent into action, however, and proved so successful that the practice of recruiting black platoons within white companies was instituted. In 1945, a War Department report called for the grouping together of white and black units, the assignment of blacks to training camps outside the South, and the expansion of the corps of black officers.

Many of the changes brought about in military policy toward the blacks came as a result of strong and continuous pressure from the black troops themselves; others resulted from civilian and governmental action. In 1948, President Harry Truman issued an executive order that officially put an end to segregated military service. Although it took several years for the order to be thoroughly implemented, the maintenance of separate units for black and white servicemen was from then on clearly contrary to government policy.

After the Second World War, there was no going back to the old caste patterns for black and white America. Black troops had fought for what they called the "double *V*"—victory abroad and victory at home. They were on the march and were not to be turned back. White society discovered that what it had always suspected was indeed the case—if black people are given some freedom, they will begin to feel they have a right to more.

MARCH FOR A FAIR SHARE

A. Philip Randolph / The March on Washington Movement, 1941

Asa Philip Randolph has been an active agitator for the rights of black people since at least 1917, when he and a friend started publishing **The Messenger,** a socialist magazine that was radically critical of American capitalism. In 1918, Randolph was arrested for opposing the entry of the United States into the First World War. Subsequently, he was described by a congressional committee as "the most dangerous Negro in America."

In the 1920's, Randolph began organizing Pullman car porters, and in 1928 he changed the name of his magazine to **The Black Worker.** In 1937, the organization called the Brotherhood of Sleeping Car Porters was certified, and Randolph triumphantly took his place at its head.

From this position he directed over a number of years many civil rights struggles, including the March on Washington for Jobs and Freedom of August 1963, when several hundred thousand people affirmed their belief in racial equality by gathering in Washington, D.C., for a symbolic march.

The 1963 march was not without antecedents, though the most important of them never took place. In 1941, Randolph announced that he intended to lead a large number of blacks in a march on Washington to protest their exclusion from jobs in defense industry and their segregation in the armed forces. Six days before the march was to take place, Roosevelt issued an executive order barring discrimination in defense work. Randolph then canceled the march. Desegregation of the armed forces had to wait until after the war.

Following are Randolph's call for a march on Washington in 1941 and his subsequent message canceling the march. The latter originated as a radio address, broadcast on June 28, 1941. The discrepancy between the number of marchers originally called for and the number cited in the cancellation speech suggests the dimensions of the response to Randolph's appeal.

Greetings:

We call upon you to fight for jobs in National Defense.

We call upon you to struggle for the integration of Negroes in the armed forces, such as the Air Corps, Navy, Army and Marine Corps of the Nation.

FROM A. Philip Randolph, "Call to Negro America 'To March on Washington for Jobs and Equal Participation in National Defense,' July 1, 1941," *The Black Worker* (May 1941); and "The Negro March on Washington," *The Black Worker* (July 1941).

We call upon you to demonstrate for the abolition of Jim-Crowism in all Government departments and defense employment.

This is an hour of crisis. It is a crisis of democracy. It is a crisis of minority groups. It is a crisis of Negro Americans.

What is this crisis?

To American Negroes, it is the denial of jobs in Government defense projects. It is racial discrimination in Government departments. It is widespread Jim-Crowism in the armed forces of the Nation.

While billions of the taxpayers' money are being spent for war weapons, Negro workers are being turned away from the gates of factories, mines and mills—being flatly told, "NOTHING DOING." Some employers refuse to give Negroes jobs when they are without "union cards," and some unions refuse Negro workers union cards when they are "without jobs."

What shall we do?

What a dilemma!

What a runaround!

What a disgrace!

What a blow below the belt!

'Though dark, doubtful and discouraging, all is not lost, all is not hopeless. 'Though battered and bruised, we are not beaten, broken or bewildered.

Verily, the Negroes' deepest disappointments and direst defeats, their tragic trials and outrageous oppressions in these dreadful days of destruction and disaster to democracy and freedom, and the rights of minority peoples, and the dignity and independence of the human spirit, is the Negroes' greatest opportunity to rise to the highest heights of struggle for freedom and justice in Government, in industry, in labor unions, education, social service, religion and culture.

With faith and confidence of the Negro people in their own power for self-liberation, Negroes can break down the barriers of discrimination against employment in National Defense. Negroes can kill the deadly serpent of race hatred in the Army, Navy, Air and Marine Corps, and smash through and blast the Government, business and labor-union red tape to win the right to equal opportunity in vocational training and re-training in defense employment.

Most important and vital to all, Negroes, by the mobilization and co-ordination of their mass power, can cause PRESIDENT ROOSEVELT TO ISSUE AN EXECUTIVE ORDER ABOLISHING DISCRIMINATIONS IN ALL GOVERNMENT DEPARTMENTS, ARMY, NAVY, AIR CORPS AND NATIONAL DEFENSE JOBS.

Of course, the task is not easy. In very truth, it is big, tremendous and difficult.

It will cost money.

It will require sacrifice.

It will tax the Negroes' courage, determination and will to struggle. But we can, must and will triumph.

The Negroes' stake in national defense is big. It consists of jobs, thousands of jobs. It may represent millions, yes, hundreds of millions of dollars in wages. It consists of new industrial opportunities and hope. This is worth fighting for.

But to win our stakes, it will require an "all-out," bold and total effort and demonstration of colossal proportions.

Negroes can build a mammoth machine of mass action with a terrific and tremendous driving and striking power that can shatter and crush the evil fortress of race prejudice and hate, if they will only resolve to do so and never stop, until victory comes.

Dear fellow Negro Americans, be not dismayed in these terrible times. You possess power, great power. Our problem is to harness and hitch it up for action on the broadest, daring and most gigantic scale.

In this period of power politics, nothing counts but pressure, more pressure, and still more pressure, through the tactic and strategy of broad, organized, aggressive mass action behind the vital and important issues of the Negro. To this end, we propose that ten thousand Negroes MARCH ON WASHINGTON FOR JOBS IN NATIONAL DEFENSE AND EQUAL INTEGRATION IN THE FIGHTING FORCES OF THE UNITED STATES.

An "all-out" thundering march on Washington, ending in a monster and huge demonstration at Lincoln's Monument will shake up white America.

It will shake up official Washington.

It will give encouragement to our white friends to fight all the harder by our side, with us, for our righteous cause.

It will gain respect for the Negro people.

It will create a new sense of self-respect among Negroes.

But what of national unity?

We believe in national unity which recognizes equal opportunity of black and white citizens to jobs in national defense and the armed forces, and in all other institutions and endeavors in America. We condemn all dictatorships, Fascist, Nazi and Communist. We are loyal, patriotic Americans, all.

But, if American democracy will not defend its defenders; if American democracy will not protect its protectors; if American democracy will not give jobs to its toilers because of race or color; if American democracy will not insure equality of opportunity, freedom and justice to its citizens, black and white, it is a hollow mockery and belies the principles for which it is supposed to stand.

To the hard, difficult and trying problem of securing equal participation in national defense, we summon all Negro Americans to march on Washington. We summon Negro Americans to form committees in various cities to recruit and register marchers and raise funds through the sale of buttons and other legitimate means for the expenses of marchers to Washington by buses, train, private automobiles, trucks, and on foot.

We summon Negro Americans to stage marches on their City Halls and Councils in their respective cities and urge them to memorialize the President to issue an executive order to abolish discrimination in the Government and national defense.

However, we sternly counsel against violence and ill-considered and intemperate action and the abuse of power. Mass power, like physical power, when misdirected is more harmful than helpful.

We summon you to mass action that is orderly and lawful, but aggressive and militant, for justice, equality and freedom.

Crispus Attucks marched and died as a martyr for American independence. Nat Turner, Denmark Vesey, Gabriel Prosser, Harriet Tubman and Frederick Douglass fought, bled and died for the emancipation of Negro slaves and the preservation of American democracy.

Abraham Lincoln, in times of the grave emergency of the Civil War, issued the Proclamation of Emancipation for the freedom of Negro slaves and the preservation of American democracy.

Today, we call upon President Roosevelt, a great humanitarian and idealist, to follow in the footsteps of his noble and illustrious predecessor and take the second decisive step in this world and national emergency and free American Negro citizens of the stigma, humiliation and insult of discrimination and Jim-Crowism in Government departments and national defense.

The Federal Government cannot with clear conscience call upon private industry and labor unions to abolish discrimination based upon race and color as long as it practices discrimination itself against Negro Americans.

NEGROES' COMMITTEE TO MARCH ON WASHINGTON FOR EQUAL PARTICIPATION IN NATIONAL DEFENSE.

2289 7th Avenue, New York City

EDgecombe 4-4340

> Walter White
> Rev. William Lloyd Imes
> Lester B. Granger
> Frank R. Crosswaith
> Layle Lane
> Richard Parrish
> Dr. Rayford Logan
> Henry K. Craft
> A. Philip Randolph

The march of 100,000 Negroes on Washington for jobs in national defense which was scheduled for July 1st is off. The march is unnecessary at this time. This decision was reached by the National Committee for the mobilization of Negroes to march on Washington. The members of this Committee are Walter White, Rev. William Lloyd Imes, Lester B. Granger, Frank R. Crosswaith, Layle Lane, Richard Parrish, Dr. Rayford Logan, J. Finley Wilson, Rev. Adam C. Powell, Jr., Noah A. Walters and E. E. Williams. These persons are not wild-eyed crackpots. They are not Communists. They have no sympathy with Communists, Communism, its program or policies. They are upright, plain, responsible Negro citizens, who love their country and the Negro race.

The reason for this decision is the issuance of an executive order by President Roosevelt banning discriminations in defense industries on account of race, creed, color or national origin, the attainment of which was the main and vital aim of the march-on-Washington movement. This is the first executive order which has been issued by a President of the United States in behalf of Negroes since the immortal Abraham Lincoln issued the Emancipation Proclamation in 1863.

Some of my listeners may be asking the question: "Why the proposed march of 100,000 Negroes on Washington?" The answer to this question is that Negroes were being turned down whenever they applied for jobs, regardless of qualifications, in defense industries all over the country. Conferences have been held with various representatives of the Government, but to no avail. Meanwhile, a wave of bitter resentment, disillusionment and desperation was sweeping over the Negro masses throughout the country. It was apparent that in order to avoid blind, reckless and undisciplined outbursts of emotional indignation against discriminations upon defense jobs, that some unusual, bold and gigantic effort must be made to awaken the American people and the President of the Nation to the realization that the Negroes were the victims of sharp and unbearable oppression, and that the fires of resentment were flaming higher and higher. In order that this threatening condition might be met with resolute, sober, sane and constructive action, a few Negro leaders came together at the call of the speaker and set up a national committee to mobilize 100,000 Negroes to march on Washington. The proposal met with prompt and instant response throughout the Nation. The favorable reaction of the Negro masses to this plan to march on Washington for jobs was due to a sense of frustration, futility and defeatism which had come over them as they watched their own communities assume the character of dead economic areas because of the lack of jobs and purchasing power, while in the white communities, the economic life of the people was throbbing, expanding and moving with promise and hope.

It was natural and inevitable that such a violent and disturbing contrast between the Negro and white communities was due to one thing, namely, that the white section of the population was enjoying participation and integration in national defense employment opportunities, whereas the Negro section of the population was being denied employment opportunities, and yet, both black and white peoples of America are equally taxed for the development and maintenance of our great defense program.

But when this grave situation was brought to the attention of the President, he definitely expressed his deep concern about it and his desire to see discriminations on account of race, color, creed and national origin abolished. He therefore issued a statement to the country and to the Office of Production Management, calling for the recognition of the right of workers to employment in national defense industries without regard to race, creed, color, or national origin. The Negro March-on-Washington Committee viewed this statement with admiration. We considered it commendable, but not enough. We therefore called upon the President to issue an executive order that had teeth in it which would give the Negro people some concrete assurance that they would no longer be given the run-around when they sought jobs in the great defense industries of the Nation.

In a statesmanlike and forthright manner, the President issued the following executive order:

REAFFIRMIING POLICY OF FULL PARTICIPATION IN THE DEFENSE PROGRAM BY ALL PERSONS, REGARDLESS OF RACE, CREED, COLOR, OR NATIONAL ORIGIN, AND DIRECTING CERTAIN ACTION IN FURTHERANCE OF SAID POLICY.

Whereas it is the policy of the United States to encourage full participation in the national defense program by all citizens of the United States, regardless of race, creed, color, or national origin, in the firm belief that the democratic way of life within the Nation can be defended successfully only with the help and support of all groups within its borders: and

Whereas there is evidence that available and needed workers have been barred from employment in industries engaged in defense production solely because of considerations of race, creed, color, or national origin, to the detriment of workers' morale and of national unity:

Now, Therefore, by virtue of the authority vested in me by the Constitution and the statutes, and as a prerequisite to the successful conduct of our national defense production effort, I do hereby reaffirm the policy of the United States that there shall be no discrimination in the employment of workers in defense industries or government because of race, creed, color, or national origin, and I do hereby declare that it is the duty of employers and of labor organizations, in furtherance of said policy and of this order, to provide for the full and equitable participation of all workers in defense industries, without discrimination because of race, creed, color, or national origin:

And it is hereby ordered as follows:

1. All departments and agencies of the Government of the United States concerned with vocational and training programs for defense pro-

duction shall take special measures appropriate to assure that such programs are administered without discrimination because of race, creed, color, or national origin;

2. All contracting agencies of the Government of the United States shall include in all defense contracts hereafter negotiated by them a provision obligating the contractor not to discriminate against any worker because of race, creed, color, or national origin;

3. There is established in the Office of Production Management a Committee on Fair Employment Practice, which shall consist of a chairman and four other members to be appointed by the President. The chairman and members of the Committee shall serve as such without compensation but shall be entitled to actual and necessary transportation, subsistence and other expenses incidental to performance of their duties. The Committee shall receive and investigate complaints of discrimination in violation of the provisions of this order and shall take appropriate steps to redress grievances which it finds to be valid. The Committee shall also recommend to the several departments and agencies of the Government of the United States and to the President all measures which may be deemed by it necessary or proper to effectuate the provisions of this order.

FRANKLIN D. ROOSEVELT

THE WHITE HOUSE,
June 25, 1941

I know that this order is certain to stir the hopes and aspirations of Negroes throughout the Nation, who only seek opportunities to work according to their qualifications. Tersely put, Negroes seek opportunity and not alms. It is the hope of the Negro March-on-Washington Committee that this executive order will represent thousands of jobs and hundreds of millions of dollars in increased wages in Negro communities, which will reflect themselves in higher standards of living, more education and recreation for the children, a greater security and assurance of more abundant life.

While the Negro March-on-Washington Committee wishes in this connection publicly to express its appreciation and gratitude to the President for his statesmanlike action in realistically facing this grave question of discrimination in defense jobs arising out of race, color, creed and national origin, and for his promulgation of this executive order, it cannot too strongly emphasize and stress the fact that this act of the President does not meet the vital and serious issue of discrimination against persons on a basis of race, color, creed and national origin in various departments of the federal government itself. It is the firm and reasoned judgment of the Negro March-on-Washington Committee that the inexcusable practice of discrimination against persons because of race, color, creed and national origin, by the government itself serves as a cue to and pattern for private employers to commit un-American and un-democratic offenses of discrimination also.

The President has declared in this executive order that it is the policy of the government not to countenance discrimination on account of race, color, creed or national origin in government service. Therefore the Negro March-on-Washington Committee wishes to express the hope that the President may find it possible, in the interest of National Unity and National Defense, at an early date, to issue a second executive order, complementing and supplementing this one, that will strike down for all times discrimination due to race, color, creed or national origin in all departments of the federal government, and which will give reality and force to our profession concerning democracy and to the great and all-out struggle our country is making to crush and destroy all subversive forces seeking to wreck our democratic way of life.

The Negro March-on-Washington Committee feels that it has done the Nation a great service in waging this fight for the abolition of discriminations in national defense industries based upon race, color, creed and national origin and the elimination of discriminations in departments of the federal government, since it will help to cleanse the soul of America of the poisons of hatreds, antagonisms and hostilities of race, religion, color and nationality and strengthen our country's foundation for national unity and national defense and give it the moral and spiritual force to achieve the preservation of our democratic faiths, traditions, ideals, values and heritages, the battle for which is being so nobly led by the President of the United States.

I, therefore, wish to announce and advise the Negro March-on-Washington Committees throughout the country that the march on Washington July 1st is unnecessary and will not take place.

I wish also to advise and urge that the Committees remain intact and watch and check the industries in their communities to determine the extent to which they are observing the executive order of the President.

BATTLE ON THE HOME FRONT

Walter White   /   What Caused the Detroit Riots?

Walter White succeeded James Weldon Johnson as executive director of the NAACP in 1928, on the eve of the Great Depression. He served with distinction until his death in 1955. So light-skinned that he could easily pass for white, White was able to go places and do things connected with his work that would have been impossible for a darker man. Once, in fact, he was taken for a white man and was almost killed in a Harlem riot.

When the Detroit riot of June 1943 broke out, White had the governor of Michigan call out state troops to patrol the city and protect the black people from marauding whites. White and other members of the national office of the NAACP rushed to Detroit to set up relief programs for the blacks left homeless by the riot. Later White wrote an analysis of the causes of the riot, which was printed with an attack on the Detroit police prepared by Thurgood Marshall.

White's report, reprinted in the following pages, reiterates the findings of almost every other investigation of a race riot undertaken in this century. The riot was triggered by a random act of violence and then fed by long pent-up hostility; the last traces of control disappeared as blacks and whites battled in the streets. Law-enforcement authorities, instead of trying to restore order, fought on the side of the whites. In the case of the Detroit riots, White defined the primary factors contributing to the buildup of hostility as job competition under the conditions of a war-boom economy and the systematic oppression of blacks in every area of social interaction. The fires of racial prejudice were fed by professional racists active in Detroit at the time.

In 1916 there were 8,000 Negroes in Detroit's population of 536,650. In 1925 the number of Negroes in Detroit had been multiplied by ten to a total of 85,000. In 1940, the total had jumped to 149,119. In June, 1943, between 190,000 and 200,000 lived in the Motor City.

According to the War Manpower Commission, approximately 500,000 in-migrants moved to Detroit between June, 1940, and June, 1943. Because of discrimination against employment of Negroes in industry, the overwhelming majority—between 40,000 and 50,000—of the approximately 50,000 Negroes who went to Detroit in this three-year period moved there during the fifteen months prior to the race riot of June, 1943. According to Governor Harry S. Kelly, of Michigan, a total of 345,000 persons moved into Detroit during the same fifteen-month period. There was comparatively little out-migration as industry called for more and more workers in one of the tightest labor markets in the United States. The War Manpower Commission failed almost completely to enforce its edict that no in-migration be permitted into any industrial area until all available local labor was utilized. Thus a huge reservoir of Negro labor existed in Detroit, crowded into highly-congested slum areas. But they did have housing of a sort and this labor was already in Detroit. The coming of white workers recruited chiefly in the

---

FROM Walter White, "What Caused the Detroit Riots?" Part I in *What Caused the Detroit Riots?* by Walter White and Thurgood Marshall (New York, 1943), pp. 5–16. Reprinted with the permission of the National Association for the Advancement of Colored People.

South not only gravely complicated the housing, transportation, educational and recreation facilities of Detroit, but they brought with them traditional prejudices of Mississippi, Arkansas, Louisiana, and other Deep South states against the Negro.

The sudden increase in Negro in-migration was due to labor scarcity which forced employers to hire Negroes, or be unable to fill government orders. The same circumstance—plus governmental and community pressures—created the necessity for modest upgrading of competent Negroes. One of the most important factors in bringing about such promotions was the unequivocal position taken by the top leadership of the United Automobile Workers–CIO.

According to the Research and Analysis Department of the UAW-CIO, the United States Employment Service, the Detroit Bureau of Governmental Research, and the Detroit branch of the National Association for the Advancement of Colored People, the overwhelming majority of the 250,000 to 300,000 white in-migrants to Detroit during the year immediately preceding the race riot came from the South. There was no surplus labor in nearby industrial centers like Chicago, Pittsburgh, Cleveland, Toledo, Akron, and Kansas City. Recruiting, therefore, was concentrated in the Deep South with the result that the already high percentage of Detroiters with South background was enormously increased. Here and there among these Southern whites were members of the UAW-CIO and other labor unions, churchmen and others who sloughed off whatever racial prejudices they had brought with them from the South. But the overwhelming majority retained and even increased their hostility to Negroes. This was particularly noticeable when Negroes were forced by sheer necessity to purchase or rent houses outside the so-called Negro area. For years preceding the riot, there had been mob attacks dating back as far as the famous Sweet case in 1925 upon the homes of Negroes. In some instances there had been police connivance in these attacks. In practically no cases had there been arrests of whites who had stoned or bombed the houses of Negroes. During July, 1941, there had been an epidemic of riots allegedly by Polish youths which had terrorized colored residents in Detroit, Hamtramck and other sections in and about Detroit. Homes of Negroes on Horton, Chippewa, West Grand Boulevard and other streets close to but outside of the so-called Negro areas were attacked by mobs with no police interference.

Detroit's 200,000 Negroes are today largely packed into two segregated areas. The larger of these is on the East Side bounded by Jefferson on the South, John R. on the West, East Grand Boulevard on the North, and Russell on the East. This area covers approximately 60 square blocks. A somewhat smaller Negro area is on the West Side bounded by Epworth Boulevard on the West, West Warren on the South, Grand River on the East along a line running Northwest to West Grand Boulevard and Tireman —an area of approximately 30 square blocks. In addition to these two wholly

Negro areas, there are scattered locations throughout Detroit of mixed occupancy in which, significantly, there was during the riot less friction than in any other area.

The desperate scarcity of housing for whites, however, limited Negroes in finding places to live outside of the Negro areas. The Detroit newspapers have contained for months many advertisements offering rewards for housing of any nature or quality for whites. Meantime, but little public housing was created to meet the tragic need for housing of both whites and Negroes in Detroit. Even this was characterized by shameful vacillation and weakness in Washington which only added fuel to the flames of racial tension in Detroit. The notorious riots revolving about the question of who should occupy the Sojourner Truth Housing project in February, 1942, are an example of this. These riots resulted when fascist elements, emboldened by the vacillation of the National Housing Administration which reversed itself several times on Negro occupancy, joined with pressure of real estate interests to bring to a head the mob violence which led to the smashing of the furniture and beating of Negro tenants attempting to move into the project.

Previously, the Public Workers Administration had built the Brewster Project of 701 units in 1938 to which the United States Housing Authority had added the Brewster addition of 240 units completed in 1940 and 1941. All these provided housing for only about 3,000 Negroes, however.

From all other public housing projects erected in Detroit, Negroes were totally excluded, although Negroes and whites had lived together in complete amity in some of the areas on which these public housing projects, erected through the taxation of Negro as well as white Americans, were built.

Equally contributory to the explosion which was to come has been the attitude of the Detroit Real Estate Association. Mention has already been made of the opposition of the real estate interests to public housing in Detroit. Their contention was that such housing as Detroit needed should be created by private interests. But by the time private interests were ready to begin erections of homes and apartments for the greatly augmented population of wartime Detroit, priorities on building materials were put into effect. Meantime, every train, bus, or other public conveyance entering Detroit disgorged an ever increasing torrent of men, women, and children demanding places to live while they earned the war wages Detroit factories were paying. Overcrowding, lack of sanitation, a mounting disease rate resulting in absenteeism and a severe tax on the hospital and clinical facilities of Detroit were bad enough among whites. Among Negroes it resulted in a scandalous condition.

JOBS

Early, in July, 1943, 25,000 employees of the Packard Plant, which was making Rolls-Royce engines for American bombers and marine engines for the famous PT boats, ceased work in protest against the upgrading of three Negroes. Subsequent investigation indicated that only a relatively small percentage of the Packard workers actually wanted to go on strike. The UAW-CIO bitterly fought the strike. But a handful of agitators charged by R. J. Thomas, president of the UAW-CIO, with being members of the Ku Klux Klan, had whipped up sentiment particularly among the Southern whites employed by Packard against the promotion of Negro workers. During the short-lived strike, a thick Southern voice outside the plant harangued a crowd shouting, "I'd rather see Hitler and Hirohito win than work beside a nigger on the assembly line." The strike was broken by the resolute attitude of the union and of Col. George E. Strong of the United States Aircraft Procurement Division, who refused to yield to the demand that the three Negroes be down-graded. Certain officials of the Packard Company were clearly responsible in part for the strike. C. E. Weiss, Personnel Manager, George Schwartz, General Foreman, and Robert Watts of the Personnel Division, urged the strikers to hold out in their demand that Negroes not be hired or upgraded. Weiss is alleged to have told the men that they did not have to work beside Negroes. At the time this report is written, Weiss, Schwartz, and Watts are still employed by the Packard Motor Car Company. The racial hatred created, released, and crystallized by the Packard strike played a considerable role in the race riot which was soon to follow. It also was the culmination of a long and bitter fight to prevent the employment of Negroes in wartime industry. There had been innumerable instances, unpublicized, in the Detroit area of work stoppages and slow downs by white workers, chiefly from the South, and of Polish and Italian extraction. Trivial reasons for these stoppages had been given by the workers when in reality they were in protest against employment or promotion of Negroes. A vast number of man hours and of production had been irretrievably lost through these stoppages. John S. Bugas in charge of the Detroit office of the FBI, states that his investigations prove that the Ku Klux Klan at no time has had more than 3,000 members in Detroit. Other investigations by officials and private agencies corroborate this fact. But the Klan did not need to be a large organization to cause serious disruption of war production in Detroit, because of the circumstance already mentioned—the increasing percentage of Southern whites who went to Detroit to work during 1942 and 1943.

The Willow Run Bomber plant is typical in this connection. This plant employed in July 45,000 workers. An analysis of its employes revealed that 30% came from outside the Detroit area, and 20.3% were last employed outside of Michigan. Between 40% and 50% of those employed in July, 1943, at Willow Run came originally from the Deep South. In July, practically all of the new hires were Southern. The labor turnover at Willow Run has been exceedingly high. So, too, has been the number of work stoppages whose real cause is opposition to employment of Negroes. Because of wartime censorship, it was impossible to ascertain the number of such episodes or the loss of production caused by it. But it is reasonable to assume that the experience at Willow Run has been characteristic of a large number of other Detroit plants. The activities of the Ku Klux Klan under the name of the Forrest Club of which "Uncle Charlie" Spare seems to be the spokesman, has had its numbers and agents industriously organizing anti-Negro sentiment among those with racial prejudice against the Negro in several of the Detroit plants. "Strikes" against the employment or promotion of Negroes can be traced to these agitators in the Dodge Truck plant, the Hudson Arsenal, the Packard Plant, and other plants. The Klan has been active in Detroit as far back as the early 20's. Early in the 20's it almost succeeded in electing a Mayor of Detroit. It was shortly after this disaster was averted that a series of attacks upon the homes of Negroes took place, culminating in the

---

The Bureau of Labor Statistics of the U. S. Department of Labor lists the strikes in Detroit to prevent employment and upgrading of colored workers for the three-month period March 1, 1943, through May 31, 1943. This record shows that 101,955 man-days or 2,446,920 man-hours of war production were lost by these stoppages. The record is as follows:

MARCH 1, 1943 THROUGH MAY 31, 1943

Company	Beginning date	Number of workers involved	Man-days idle	Issue
1. U.S. Rubber Company	March 19	1,064	3,955	Hiring colored workers and demand for separate sanitary facilities.
2. Vickers, Inc.	March 25	40	60	Colored help placed in Production Department.
3. Hudson Motor Car Co.	April 20	15	45	Hiring of colored plant guards.
4. Hudson Naval Arsenal	May 17	750	750	Refusal to work with colored tool-maker.
5. Packard Motor Car Co.	May 26	26,883	97,145	Upgrading of colored workers.

Sweet case in 1925. Following this case tried before Judge Frank Murphy and in which the defendants were represented by the late Clarence Darrow, the Klan in Detroit dropped out of existence, along with its demise in other parts of the country. But agencies with similar methods and ideologies succeeded it. Though short-lived, a vicious successor was the notorious Black Legion which was characterized by Professor Elmer Akers, of the University of Michigan, in 1937 in his "A Social-Psychological Interpretation of the Black Legion" as a movement of "Vigilante nativism," which began as an offshot of the Ku Klux Klan.

Originally conceived to secure and insure jobs for white Southerners, the organization soon expanded its fields of activity to include putting down by violence, if necessary, all movements the Black Legion decided were "alien" or "un-American." After the conviction of its leader, Virgil F. Effinger, former Klansman, for the murder in 1936 of Charles A. Poole, a Detroit Catholic, the 4-year-old, crime-besmirched Black Legion virtually expired, but was followed quickly by others of similar purpose and method, among them The National Workers League (held chiefly responsible for the Sojourner Truth riot which saw the League's Parker Sage, Garland Alderman and Virgil Chandler indicted but never tried on charges of seditious conspiracy) which is reputedly financed in part by Nazi Bund and Silver Shirt money.

Gerald L. K. Smith, former assistant and protege of the late Huey Long, has been long active in stirring up discord and dissension in the Detroit area. His activities in America First, anti-union, and other similar groups have been greatly increased in effectiveness by his also being a Southerner trained in the art of demagogy by Huey Long, and provided with a fertile field due to the predominantly Southern white psychology of Detroit. Active also have been the followers of Father Coughlin, some Polish and Italian Catholic priests and laymen, and others who, wittingly or otherwise, have utilized anti-Negro sentiment for selfish and sometimes sinister objectives in much the same manner that the Nazis utilized anti-Semitism in Germany during the late 20's. Ingrained or stimulated prejudice against the Negro has been used as much against organized labor as it has been against the Negro. Employers and employers associations have been apathetic to the storm which was brewing. Apparently they were interested only in the size and continuation of profits. It has been frequently charged and not displayed that some of the employers have financed or contributed heavily to some of the organizations which have organized and capitalized upon race prejudice as a means of checking the organization of workers in Detroit plants.

DETROIT LABOR UNIONS AND THE NEGRO

One of the most extraordinary phenomena of the riot was the fact that while mobs attacked Negro victims outside some of the industrial plants of Detroit, there was not only no physical clash inside any plant in Detroit but not as far as could be learned even any verbal clash between white and Negro workers. This can be attributed to two factors: first, a firm stand against discrimination and segregation of Negro workers by the UAW-CIO, particularly since the Ford strike of 1941. The second factor is that when the military took over, the armed guards in the plants were ordered by the Army to maintain order at all costs and to prevent any outbreak within the plants. There is possibly a third factor, namely, that on Monday, June 21st, and to a lesser extent on succeeding days, Negroes were unable to get to the plants because of attacks upon them when they sought to return to work by roving mobs chiefly composed of boys between the ages of 17 and 25.

The Detroit riot brought into sharp focus one of the most extraordinary labor situations in the United States. Prior to the Ford strike of 1941 many Negroes in Detroit considered Ford their "great white father" because the Ford plant almost alone of Detroit industries employed Negroes. When the UAW-CIO and the UAW-AFL sought to organize Ford workers, their approach at the beginning was a surreptitious one. The unions felt that the very high percentage of Southern whites in Detroit would refuse to join the Union if Negroes were too obviously participating. But when the strike broke, far-sighted Negro leaders in Detroit took an unequivocal position in behalf of the organization of workers. A serious racial clash was averted by the intercession of thoughtful whites and Negroes. Following the winning of the NLRB election by the union, it began to take a broader and more unequivocal position that all workers and union members should share in the benefits of union agreements irrespective of race, creed, or color.

During the recent riot, R. J. Thomas, president of the UAW-CIO proposed an eight-point program which was widely published, and which helped to emphasize the basic causes of the riot. These points included: (1) creation of a special grand jury to investigate the cause of the riots and to return justifiable indictments, with a competent Negro attorney appointed as an assistant Prosecutor to work with the grand jury; (2) immediate construction and opening of adequate park and recreation facilities. Thomas called it "disgraceful that the City's normal, inadequate park space was permitted to be overtaxed further by the influx of hundreds of thousands of new war workers"; (3) immediate and practical plans for rehousing Negro slum dwellers in decent, Government-financed housing developments; (4) insistence that plant managements as well as workers recognize the right of Negroes to jobs in line with their skill and seniority; (5) a full investigation by the special grand jury of the conduct of the Police Department during the riots; (6) special care by the courts in dealing with many persons arrested. Those found guilty should be severely punished, and there must be no discrimination between white and Negro rioters; (7) the loss of homes and small businesses, as well as personal injuries, is the responsibility of the community, and the city should create a fund to make good these losses;

(8) creation by the Mayor of a special bi-racial committee of ten persons to make further recommendations looking toward elimination of racial differences and frictions, this committee to have a special job in connection with high schools "where racial hatred has been permitted to grow and thrive in recent years."

VACILLATION ON FAIR EMPLOYMENT PRACTICE COMMITTEE

A contributory factor to the breakdown of discrimination in employment in Detroit was the issuance on June 25, 1941, by President Roosevelt of Executive Order 8802 under which was established the President's Committee on Fair Employment Practice. Although limited in personnel, budget and authority, the FEPC as the affirmative expression of a moral principle had strengthened the efforts to eliminate discrimination in Detroit war plants. Members of the FEPC staff had carefully investigated charges of discrimination in Detroit areas. In a considerable number of cases negotiations with employers by FEPC representatives had resulted in the abolishing or lessening of discrimination. Employers, employes and labor unions knew that the Federal Government was opposed to denial of the right to work or to be upgraded on account of race, creed, color or national origin.

But in the summer of 1942, the FEPC was robbed of its independent status and placed under the control of the War Manpower Commission. The conviction in Detroit and other places began to grow that the FEPC was being quietly shelved and that the government no longer was insistent that discrimination in employment be abolished. This conviction grew as the FEPC became more and more inactive due to the failure to provide it with a budget for many months during the summer and fall of 1942 and during the period when it was stopped from functioning effectively.

Conviction crystallized into certainty when early in 1943, the Detroit railroad and Mexican hearings were indefinitely postponed. This certainty was fixed more definitely in the public mind by the long delay in selecting a new Chairman of the FEPC and defining its status and the nature of the sanctions with which it would be armed. As the FEPC lapsed into total inactivity fear of Federal action died among those who were guilty of discrimination. Anti-Negro organizations and individuals renewed and increased their agitation against the employment and upgrading of Negroes. Despair deepened in the Negro communities as they saw hordes of Southern whites imported into Detroit, provided with such housing as was available including tax-supported houses, apartments and dormitories, speedily upgraded to the better paid jobs while Negroes who had lived in Detroit for many years were still shut out.

Morale and morals of Negroes were affected adversely as they saw the one agency which had been created to do away with discrimination emasculated. Those Negroes who were employed found themselves with money they could not spend for decent houses or other improvements in their living standards. Some invested in War Bonds and insurance; others threw away their money in riotous living because they had been robbed of hope.

Politically minded public officials have winked at the activities of agencies like the Klan, the Black Legion, the National Workers' League, the followers of Father Coughlin and other similar groups. During the 30's especially when there was keen competition for jobs because of the depression, Southern whites sought and secured jobs on the police force of Detroit and in the courts. There was a period of years when cold-blooded killings of Negroes by policemen were a constant source of bitterness among Negroes. Eventually, protest by such organizations as the Detroit branch of the NAACP and other Negro and inter-racial groups led to a diminution and eventually a practical cessation of such killings. But a residue of distrust of the police remained. When the riot of June, 1943, broke forth, this suspicion of the police by Negroes was more than justified when 29 of the 35 killed were Negroes, 17 of them shot by police and a number of these shot in the back. The justification usually given by the police was "looting." There is no question that shameful and inexcusable looting of stores operated by whites in the East Side Negro area, particularly on Hastings and John R. Streets was perpetrated by Negroes. Part of this looting was for the sake of the loot. But part was due to bitter frenzy which had been too long bottled up in Negroes, and which was a form of vengeance both against the prejudice in Detroit from which Negroes had suffered, and against the looting of Negro homes and businesses ten days before in the Beaumont, Tex., riot of June 15–16, 1943.

Samuel Leiberman of the East Side Merchants Association reports that white policemen joined Negroes in the looting of stores on the East Side. In one instance a policeman carried two twenty-five-pound cans of lard from a store and locked it in the back of the police patrol car to be transported, apparently, to his home. There also is evidence that at least one of the 17 Negroes shot for "looting" was not looting, nor was there any evidence to substantiate such a charge.

The wilful inefficiency of the Detroit police in its handling of the riot is one of the most disgraceful episodes in American history. When the riot broke out on Sunday night, June 20, following a dispute between a white and Negro motorist on the Belle Isle Bridge, an efficient police force armed with night sticks and fire hoses could have broken up the rioting on Woodward Avenue and broken the back of the insurrection, had the police been determined to do so. Instead, the police did little or nothing, though there were a few individual instances of courage by policemen which are commendable.

More typical, however, was the following episode: An official of the Detroit educational system was riding Monday afternoon, June 21st, on a

Woodward Avenue car. According to his statement, an inspector of police boarded the car with eight patrolmen. He announced that a mob was headed in that direction and that he and the patrolmen would take charge of and protect any Negroes on the car who wished such protection. Four of the eight Negroes accepted the offer. The other four chose to remain on the car. They crouched on the floor of the car and were concealed by the skirts of sympathetic white women. These four got to their destinations safely. But the four who had entrusted themselves to the police were either taken from the police by the mob and beaten unmercifully, or were turned over to the mob by the police.

After Federal troops had restored a semblance of order to Detroit, Police Commissioner John W. Witherspoon sought to shift the blame for the total failure of the Detroit Police Department to the Federal government for not sending troops sooner to police Detroit. Commissioner Witherspoon alleged that he had not been given information by the Federal authorities that a Presidential proclamation was necessary before Federal troops could be brought in. He sought also to prove that the police had been blameless. But this assertion was negated by photographs taken by the Detroit *Free Press* and other newspapers. Most revelatory of these is one taken on Woodward Avenue during the day of June 21st. An elderly Negro's arms are pinioned by two policemen while two mounted police sit astride their horses immediately behind. In the meantime, a white rioter strikes the helpless Negro full in the face with no indication on the part of any of the four policemen of any effort to protect the Negro.

The Detroit *Free Press* also took photographs of the same man in four separate acts of mob violence. As this report is written, this easily identified rioter is unarrested. Two other photographs show another white man engaged in two separate acts of violence against Negroes. In one of them he is about to strike a fleeing Negro with an iron bar. It is stated that this man was arrested but released almost immediately "for lack of evidence."

The faces of between 800 and 1,000 white rioters engaged in assaulting, killing, kicking or otherwise violating the law against the persons of Negroes, or engaged in wilful destruction of property such as the overturning and burning of the automobiles of Negroes are clearly identifiable. But as of the date of the writing of this report, few if any, of them have even been arrested.

The anti-Negro motivation of the Detroit police department is further illustrated by these facts and figures. It has already been pointed out that the Negro population of Detroit at the time of the riot was 200,000 or less, out of a total population of more than 2,000,000. The inevitable riot was the product of anti-Negro forces which had been allowed to operate without check or hindrance by the police over a period of many years. But 29 of the 35 persons who died during the riot were Negroes. An overwhelming majority of the more than 600 injured were Negroes. Of the 1832 persons arrested for rioting, more than 85% were Negroes. And this in the face of the indisputable fact that the aggressors over a period of years were not Negroes but whites.

Commissioner Witherspoon along with Attorney General Herbert J. Rushton, State Police Commissioner Oscar C. Olander, and Wayne County Prosecutor William E. Dowling were appointed by Governor Harry S. Kelly to investigate the riot. But a few days later, the investigating committee reported that there was no necessity of a Grand Jury investigation.

YOUTH OF WHITE RIOTERS

One of the most disturbing phenomena of the riot was the extreme youth of many of the rioters. The Detroit *Free Press* quoted Bugas, head of the Detroit Office of the FBI, as stating that seventy per cent of the rioters were boys between the ages of sixteen and twenty-five. Other observers estimate a somewhat lower percentage; but most are agreed, and their opinions are borne out by newspaper photographs of the rioters, that not less than fifty per cent of the rioters were boys and young men of this age and white women. What is perhaps a new and exceedingly dangerous factor in periods of emotional strain caused by war is indicated by the youth of the rioters. A few of them are not in the army because of deferments gained by industrial skills. But most of them fall into two categories. The first is made up of those who for physical, mental or moral reasons have been rejected by the armed services. A compensatory bravado seems to have been created in some of these young men who by the physical violence of mobbing sought to convince themselves and others that they were as physically able as those who had gone into the army. The most stable young men of their age having been syphoned off into the Army, Navy and other armed services, the restraining influence of the more normal had been removed from those left behind.

The second category seems to have been made up of those between fifteen and eighteen who are emotionally unstable because they know that should the war last longer they will go into the armed services. All soldiers know that when one goes into the war he may not return. Even if he does, whatever plans he may have made for the charting of his life will be interrupted and perhaps materially changed. The stabilizing influence of plans having been removed, it appears that there is an even greater willingness to indulge in physical violence when fear of punishment is removed, such as in a race riot. It is conceivable that other riots during the war and the immediate years thereafter may be distinctly affected by this wartime phenomenon.

THE PRESS

The Hearst-owned Detroit *Times* has for years featured crime, real or alleged, by Negroes and has been distinctly unfriendly in its attitude towards the Negro and his aspirations. But it was quick to characterize the riot of June 20–21 as "the worst disaster which has befallen Detroit since Pearl Harbor." The conservative Detroit *News* has been apathetic though not unfriendly. The Detroit *Free Press*, prior to its purchase by John B. Knight, followed the same pattern. But since its acquisition by Mr. Knight and under the editorship of Douglass Martin and Malcolm Bingay, it has followed an objective and enlightened attitude on the issue of race. It has featured news about Negro achievement such as the visit of the distinguished Negro agronomist, Dr. George Washington Carver, to Detroit at the invitation of Henry Ford, and the death of Dr. Carver. Its coverage of the riot was full, fair, and complete, both in its news, editorial and pictorial treatment. The attitude of the *Free Press* did much to restore sanity to the city.

Three widely-circulated Negro newspapers, the Michigan *Chronicle*, the Detroit *Tribune*, and the Detroit edition of the Pittsburgh *Courier*, have given full coverage during recent years to the favorable and unfavorable changes in the Negro's status in Detroit. This in large measure has contributed to a very well-informed opinion by Negroes.

THE MAYOR

During his term as president of the Detroit Council of Churches, Dr. Benjamin Bush and other Protestant ministers and laymen of both races had sought action by the City of Detroit to avert the inevitable race clash which threatened the city. The Council had repeatedly urged Mayor Edward J. Jeffries to appoint an interracial committee and to give that committee sufficient authority to tackle some of the problems of housing, police efficiency, employment, recreation and education which affected both Negroes and whites in Detroit, and the relations between the races. But Mayor Jeffries refused to act giving as his reason that such recognition of the existence of the problem might conceivably accentuate it. Six days after the riot, however, Mayor Jeffries appointed an interracial commission with William J. Norton of the Children's Fund as chairman. But Mr. Norton had served as chairman of a committee of the Detroit Urban League to investigate an interracial clash in the Northwestern High School in 1941. The report of that committee, most modest in its analysis of the problems involved and its recommendations, was neither acted upon nor even made public by the Mayor.

It would be a mistake to classify Mayor Jeffries as being anti-Negro.

His failure to meet the crisis or to take action on conditions which inevitably were leading to a crisis was due to weakness, lack of vision, and to political ambition. It was known that he aspired to be Governor of Michigan or United States Senator. With such ambition, he hesitated to offend any politically important group in the city of Detroit or the State of Michigan. In the meantime, the dry grass of race hatred mounted, waiting only until a spark set off a conflagration.

The War Production Board on June 26 announced that more than one million man hours of production were lost forever during the riot. No figures are available of the man hours previously lost by work stoppages and slow down strikes to keep Negroes from being employed or upgraded. As the chief war production center of the country, the pattern of behaviour there has affected and will continue to affect other war production centers. Failure to correct conditions similar to those in Detroit, or failure by federal, state, and municipal governments to act against those who, deliberately or unwittingly, foment similar racial and industrial clashes cannot but jeopardize the winning of the war. General Dwight Eisenhower reported in the spring of 1943 that photographs of the Sojourner Truth Riot were used by Axis propagandists in North Africa to create prejudice against the United States. The same riot and the one of June, 1943, as well as stories of lynchings, attacks upon Negro soldiers, continued discrimination and segregation in the armed forces of the United States, the anti-Negro fulminations of men like Governor Talmadge of Georgia and Congressman Rankin of Mississippi are grist to the mill of the Tokyo and Berlin radios which cite these outrages to the one billion brown, yellow, and black peoples of the Pacific and Africa, and to the millions of colored peoples of the Caribbean and South America as evidence of what will happen to these colored peoples if the United Nations win. Timorousness in attacking the problem and cowardice in surrender to the divisive forces of Detroit and other cities may conceivably cause the United States to lose the war or, most certainly, to prolong it unnecessarily at the sacrifice of the lives of American soldiers who would not otherwise die. One of the few bright spots of the Detroit riot has been the almost universal condemnation of the riot by Detroit members of the armed services. Typical of many of these is the following letter written by Corporal James E. Ferriero from the Station Hospital at Camp Crowder, Mo., to the Detroit *Times*, appearing in its issue of July 6, 1943:

> Why are these race riots going on there in Detroit and in other cities in this land—supposedly the land of freedom, equality and brotherhood?
> We who are doing the fighting, and will do the fighting to preserve this country from such acts of discrimination; we who recognize no discrimination in the trenches and fox-holes; we shed the same blood—one kind of blood—red. Things like race riots and strikes make us fighters think—WHAT ARE WE FIGHTING FOR?
> Americanism means everything to us, but it is swiftly turning to be an unfounded word. Regardless, we will continue to fight, to die for our loved ones. But we want to feel and know that we are fighting for the principles that gave birth to the United States of America.
> In this hospital ward, we eat, laugh, and sleep uncomplainingly together. Jim Stanley, Negro; Joe Wakamatau, Japanese; Eng Yu, Chinese;

John Brennan, Irish; Paul Colosi, Italian; Don Holzheimer, German; Joe Wojiechowski, Polish; and Mike Cohen, Jewish.

We were all injured in the line of duty. Yes—Hitler, Mussolini, Hirohito, all rub their fists in glee that their fifth column work of under-mining our country is bearing fruit. Things like this prolong the war, and give the Axis time to strengthen their forces. They might possibly mean DEFEAT for us. Now more than ever we should pull together, and work side by side, unhampered by riots and strikes. We want to know that you are behind us 100 per cent. We want to know you want us back regardless of creed, race or color.

We want to know so that we can fight harder and, if need be, die willingly.

THE ATTITUDE OF THE BLACK FIGHTING MAN

Grant Reynolds / What the Negro Thinks of This War

The statement from a soldier at the conclusion of the preced-ing report on the Detroit riot of 1943 echoes a theme heard often during the Second World War. Black men wondered why they were fighting for freedom abroad when freedom was denied them at home. The ambivalence of the black fighting man has been noted in almost every war in which the United States has been involved.

Grant Reynolds, who served as a chaplain to black troops in the Second World War, wrote an article in **The Crisis** cataloging some of the complaints of black soldiers about the treatment they re-ceived at the hands of military authorities. Reynolds' angry article, reprinted here, warns of the possibility of a Third World uprising in which the non-white nations will seek to throw off white domination. Where then will the American black man stand, and on whose side will he fight? Reynolds pointedly asks.

For the past two years and ten months I have been a Chaplain on active duty with the United States Army. I have found Negro soldiers bitterly resentful of their lot in this war. My having served with Medical Troops in

FROM Grant Reynolds, "What the Negro Thinks of This War," *The Crisis*, Vol. LI (September 1944), pp. 289–91, 299. Reprinted with the permission of The Crisis Publish-ing Company.

Virginia, Infantry Troops in Massachusetts, raw recruits at a reception center in Michigan, sick and wounded soldiers from both Negro Divisions at a hospital in Arizona, and the troops comprising a Station Complement in California, has given me a broad picture of the conditions which affect our men from coast to coast. In each instance, regardless of the geography, the net result has been the same . . . Negro soldiers are damned tired of the treatment they are getting. This dislike cannot be attributed to the natural antipathy of the majority of soldiers, white and black, developed out of their efforts to adjust themselves to the rigors and uncertainties of war. Now the Negro soldier is as easily adaptable as any other American soldier. I'd even go as far as to say that he is more adaptable. His lifetime of adjusting himself to the whims and inconsistencies of the American white man substantiates this claim. His resentment then goes much deeper than this. It grows out of the un-American treatment which plagues his every day while at the same time having to listen to loud voices telling him what a great honor it is to die for his country.

The Negro soldier needs no one to remind him that this is his country. He knows this. But he knows also that there is a lot of unfinished business about individual human decency that he would like to see cleared up before he becomes a corpse for *any* country. To deny him food when he is hungry, dignified transportation when he has to travel, a voice in choosing those who rule him, or just the most fundamental aspects of our proclaimed method of living, and then propagandize him daily into becoming a hero for democracy, is nauseating, to say the least. As one Negro soldier asked me in this respect: "Chaplain, do the white folks who are running this war think we are fools? Or, are they a pack of damned fools themselves? Excuse me, sir, for being profane, but this mess makes a man say a lot of nasty things."

WIDE EXPERIENCE

My tour of active duty which began in Virginia and ended in California, after periods of service in Massachusetts, Michigan, Ohio, and Arizona, has provided me the opportunity not only of observing the Negro soldier under the varied JIM-CROW conditions which make life miserable for him, but because I am a Negro too I have lived under the same conditions and shared his resentment to them. Then too it must be remembered that a chaplain who tries to do a real job does more than sermonize on Sundays. His activities extend into areas concerned with the thoughts and lives of the thousands of men he serves.

How do I know what the Negro soldier thinks? Until a few days ago I was one myself. I have lived with him in his barracks because white officers in Virginia would not permit a colored officer to occupy quarters built by the War Department for its officers. Interesting, to say the least, is a personal experience which grew out of this insult. By a sudden jolt of fate I began my military career at Camp Lee, Virginia. There I immediately discovered

the South more vigorously engaged in fighting the Civil War than in training soldiers to resist Hitler. And what was obvious, though nonetheless disturbing, this war was being won . . . as far as the Negro was concerned
anyway. Because of the few officers needed with my small outfit less than
fifty percent of the available rooms in the officers' barracks were occupied.
But there was no room for me. I was therefore assigned quarters with the
enlisted men in their barracks. What did it matter that such an assignment
infringed upon the freedom of Negro soldiers during their leisure moments?
What did it matter how this personal embarrassment and humiliation impaired my morale? My job, it seemed, was to *build* morale, not to *have* it.
Anyhow, of what importance is the condition of the Negro soldier's morale
to the proper performance of his duty? But of equal importance, what did it
matter that army policy prohibiting officers and enlisted men from sharing
common quarters except under field conditions was deliberately ignored? The
Negro soldier has learned that army policy, binding upon whites, far too
often relaxes to his disadvantage. This separation of officers and enlisted
men is supported on the grounds that the familiarity involved is destructive
to proper discipline. There are other methods of maintaining discipline
among Negro soldiers, some of which make Gestapo Chief Himmler look
like a rank amateur. What *did* matter in this situation was the doctrine of
white supremacy which had to remain undefiled regardless of the cost. To
assign a Negro officer quarters in an officers' barracks which housed white
officers was unthinkable! Entirely ignored was the fact that this officer by
virtue of his military status indicated the same willingness to die for American fair play . . . for democracy.

EXCLUSIVE QUARTERS

After some weeks of this humiliation, which the Negro soldiers resented as
much as I did, I was called to meet with the Post Construction Officer. To
my utter amazement he showed me the blue prints of plans for the construction of an officers' quarters for my exclusive use. As an added favor to me
I was given the privilege of selecting the site where the quarters of the "un-
touchable" would be erected. But here I made my usual mistake, a mistake
which was to plague the remainder of my military service. I did not say:
"Thank you white folks for being so kind and generous to this nigger."
Instead I summoned the effrontery to remark that this was an unnecessary
waste of the taxpayers' money. For this I was immediately labelled as a
Negro who not only did not "know his place," but one who was also a
base ingrate.

I have been on occasion the only colored officer in the Negro soldier's
outfit and therefore the one most likely to hear both his gripes and his
legitimate complaints. I have marched with him in the heat of a southern
sun, shivered with him in the wake of a New England blizzard, and with
him I too have breathed the scorching dust of an Arizona desert. I have

laughed with him in his moments of pleasure, heard his confession of the worthlessless of his former life as he embraced the Christian religion, sorrowed with him in the loss of loved ones, and suffered with him under the heel of the dehumanizing demon of American race prejudice. I know what the Negro soldier thinks, not only because he has told me, but because I know my own thoughts.

Not long ago Secretary of War Stimson revealed in no uncertain terms what the War Department thought about the Negro soldier. I propose to relate in like manner what the Negro soldier thinks about the War Department's War. . . . But a word about Mr. Stimson's insult. Negroes throughout the nation along with other decent Americans were scandalized and they were prompt in making their protests known. But let us not be too harsh on a man who is the victim of the "logic" of his own thinking. Anyone sharing the traditional American regard for the colored citizen, and being party to that regard as it daily segregated the Negro soldier and citizen, could not have reached any other conclusion. This is especially true if he had given ear to reports of Army Intelligence on the Negro Soldier.

DIXIE SECOND FRONT

Mr. Stimson must have been told that the Negro soldier is demoralized, that he does not want to fight—unless a second front is opened in Mississippi, Texas, Georgia, South Carolina, Louisana, or just *anywhere* below the Mason and Dixon Line—that his heart is not in this war. Such a soldier cannot be depended upon to offer up his life against German or Japanese soldiers who know why they are fighting and demonstrate each day their willingness to die for their beliefs. Where are the American soldiers, of any color, who would destroy their own lives rather than fall into the hands of a hated enemy. The Japs did this on Attu. Incidentally, the record of our forces at Anzio and Cassino for 4 months showed that American white troops with only one enemy to fight were hardly super men in face of their German opposition. We might just as well realize that the Negro soldier has two enemies to fight, one foreign and the other at home. Now since public opinion forced the Secretary of War to give some reason for the War Department's refusal to allow Negro soldiers to die for America in some appreciable manner other than in labor battalions and in the "highfalutin Engineers," which is a camouflaged term meaning practically the same thing, Mr. Stimson's hand was called. Those who expected the unvarnished truth about this matter were either dreamers or drunks. Who among our military authorities would admit that the nation's indecent treatment of the Negro soldier had rendered him unfit for combat with a foreign enemy? So following the traditional point of view, since this point of view led to the creation of the dilemma in the first place, the Negro soldier was promptly discredited. Not because he could not master the technique of modern weapons of war—this was the Secretary of War's claim—but because this is the logical stand that the traditional race haters were bound to use in defense of their hypocritical and infamous conduct. Talk about impeding the war effort! What *is* treason anyway?

Out on the Pacific Coast I found young Negroes holding key positions in the industries—the airplane industry to be exact—which produce the most difficult of weapons to master, the army bomber. Other young Negroes are now flying these planes. Still other young Negroes are now prepared to be their navigators. Now it is a commonly accepted fact among honest men and women that no racial group has cornered the market on either intelligence or native ability. This is what the celebrated pamphlet *The Races of Mankind* would have told a few thousand army officers had it not been banned by stupid people who refuse to recognize the obvious. All Negro soldiers are not graduate engineers. Nor are all white soldiers. All Negro soldiers were not born in that section of the nation, which because it seeks to keep the Negro in the educational gutter, directs that white youth too must wallow in the pig sty of ignorance. But the Honorable Secretary of War has not claimed that white soldiers cannot master the techniques of modern weapons of war. His blanket statement about the Negro soldier's inability in this respect not only insults the thousands of intelligent Negro youth in our armed forces from all sections of the country, but by indirection it classifies them as morons incapable of attaining the intelligence level of the most ignorant southern cracker. What does the Negro soldier think about this? He considers it a vicious attack upon his manhood. And what is more he thinks that the Administration continues to insult him as long as such men are allowed to control his destiny in this war. The Negro soldier will not give his life for the perpetuation of this outright lynching of his ability, nor for the right of domestic nazis to make of him a military scapegoat.

WAR AIMS HOLLOW

Every factual pronouncement which falls from the lips of Anglo-Saxon war leaders in this conflict lays foundation for the Negro soldier's conviction that this is a war to maintain the white man's right to keep the colored man in social and economic bondage. The Negro soldier is not so dumb as far too many people in authority lead themselves to believe. He is asking a lot of questions. Does the Atlantic Charter apply to colored people now enslaved by the British, Dutch, Portuguese, and other imperialistic powers? Why is our ally Britain silent about the fate of Hong Kong and Singapore in the post war world? Why are the great leaders of India, especially Nehru, kept in prison at the very moment when all India should be rallied against the Japanese invader? Why does our foreign policy fail to make clear America's stand in regard to spilling the blood of its sons to dictate the destiny of people who admittedly have a right to self-determination? But most important of all, the Negro soldier is asking how he can be expected to give his last full measure of devotion for his country when each day, while he wears the uniform of his country, he is insulted, humiliated, and even murdered for attempting to be an American?

My experience with Negro soldiers has led me to oppose the idea that the majority of them consider this a "race war." One must confess, however, that at times they are given strong evidence to the contrary. To say that all Negro soldiers share this or any one point of view is to engage in deliberate falsehood. Many of them think that this is a white man's war, "lock, stock, and barrel." This conclusion is reached in spite of Hitler's treatment of the people in the occupied countries and what the Chinese have suffered at the hands of the Japanese. Like countless thousands of whites this group has listened too intently to the expressed convictions of the "white supremacy boys." Responsibility for their conclusion can be traced to the ravings of such misrepresentatives of the nation as Bilbo, Rankin, "Cotton" Ed Smith and many others of the same litter. "But what about Russia?" you ask them. The immediate answer is that there are good betting odds that Russia will have to fight Britain and the United States before peace actually comes. This group knows too well what everyone willing to face reality knows— that there are far too many people in high places who love Russia less than they hate Nazi Germany. If Russia were not killing so many German soldiers and therefore the only hope at the moment for an Allied victory, the anti-Red voices in this country would be reaching a deafening crescendo. But Russia, these soldiers will tell you, is merely a tool to be used until it can be safely cast aside. Anglo-Saxon pride and a sense of imminent danger make strange bedfellows.

CONFUSION AND BEWILDERMENT

Much more strongly entrenched in the Negro soldier's thinking is the firm conviction that Soviet Russia's expulsion of the nazi race-haters from Russian soil and the herculean struggle of the Chinese people are evidence that something far more valuable than concepts of race is involved in this struggle. The freedom of millions of men and women, and countless generations which follow them, is involved . . . possibly his freedom too. The realization of this, however, does not lessen in any great degree his state of confusion and bewilderment. What man who has worn the shackles of slavery would not gladly strike a blow for freedom? The Negro soldier is prevented from striking that blow, at least with great enthusiasm, because freedom for his race during the past eighty years has not gibed with its definition in the dictionary. The march of daily events convince the Negro soldier that his efforts in the struggle for freedom might well result in solidifying the control with which the South now directs and determines the national welfare and vigorously thwarts every effort of scientific progress in the field of human relations. A struggle for freedom which materialized in such a goal would not be worth a single drop of sweat . . . to say nothing about a single drop of blood. As a result the Negro soldier sees himself a miserable pawn in the inexorable hands of a fate which has already stacked the cards against him. He will fight if ordered in contact with the enemy. But this will be a fight for personal survival, a fight for his own life. His fight will hardly be characterized by that spark of enthusiasm which in war raises men to the heights of glory and heroism to which normally they would not dare aspire. Yet who knows but that the absence of this mysterious, though highly essential quality, in the Negro soldier may some day explain the difference between defeat and victory for a potentially great nation? The Negro soldier deplores the existence of such a probability.

One of the great soldiers which has emerged from this war is Lt. Col. Evans F. Carlson, famous for his development of that group of super-marine fighters known as *Carlson's Raiders*. This man not only built this extraordinary fighting outfit but led it in the Makin Island raid which resulted in complete destruction of all enemy military emplacements and annihilation of more than eight hundred Japanese soldiers which constituted the island garrison. Only eighteen of Carlson's Raiders lost their lives. Col. Carlson borrowed the fighting slogan, GUNG HO, from the Chinese Red Army with which he spent many months as a military observer. This experience convinced him that men, although they were hungry, nondescript, and poorly equipped could by living the full meaning of this slogan become unconquerable in the face of overwhelming odds. When he was called upon to train a group of American soldiers in the technique of guerilla warfare he not only made GUNG HO their battle cry but insisted that the deeper significance of this battle cry become the philosophy which undergirded every thought and action of every man. GUNG HO means: WORK TOGETHER . . . WORK IN HARMONY.

USA LACKS GUNG HO

The nation's utter lack of this essential spirit would seem to direct that it be made our national battle cry on both the military and home fronts. In fact GUNG HO could with great wisdom be extended to comprise the entire war effort of the United Nations. It would pay far greater dividends than the existing pattern of suspicion and dissension. Hats off then to a great soldier who was first a great man. The inspired feats of Carlson's Raiders have made military history, and with the passing of time will take on legendary dimensions. Said Col. Carlson: "My men, who are professionally competent, *know* why they are fighting."

The young Americans who followed this leader were not Negroes. How could they have been if honest answers were given to the following questions which Col. Carlson asked each man before accepting him: "Do you know why this war is being fought? What do you expect the world to be like after this war? Do you think the American dream of the post war world is worth suffering for as much as you will probably have to suffer?" Can't you hear the Negro soldier ask the Colonel: "Sir, are you all right?"

The answer contained in this contemporary colloquialism would not be a flippant answer. Negro soldiers want to be heroes just like their white comrades; they want to distinguish themselves for the land they love. But most of all they want to be given the opportunity to become *real soldiers;* they want to be able to find clarity out of the maze of confusion and contradiction from which this love for country grows.

In spite of his frustration the Negro soldier sees a New World A-Coming. But he hasn't read about it in anybody's book. He sees its light beginning to break across the dark and distant horizon of time and events. It won't dawn tomorrow, nor on any tomorrow for a long time to come. This knowledge makes him sad. But that light has begun to shine, dimly 'tis true, and the darkness of man's inhumanity will not prevail against it because it is the light of determined millions of men and women marching toward freedom. That light is burning in the hearts of Russia's intrepid millions and brightens the path of the victorious Red Army. That light has provided the spark of warm hope which has kept the valiant millions of Chinese from capitulating to a superior military power. That light is slowly penetrating the darkness of India's miserable millions, causing an unmistakable urge toward freedom that will ultimately destroy all opposition.

That light now burning weakly will on some not too far distant tomorrow burst into a consuming flame in the hearts of more than a billion darker people. Thus will be created a power for good so intense in our rapidly shrinking world that human debasement can no longer exist anywhere. The Negro soldier sees this light and it quickens his pulse . . . yes, in spite of little minds now wielding big clubs trying to hold back the dawn.

The Negro soldier thinks . . . !

10 SUGGESTIONS FOR FURTHER READING

The March on Washington movement is treated in Hubert Garfinkel, *When Negroes March: The March on Washington Movement in the Organizational Politics for FEPC** (Free Press, 1959), and the Fair Employment Practice Committee (FEPC) in Louis Ruchames, *Race, Jobs and Politics: The Story of FEPC* (Columbia University Press, 1953).

Two books dealing with aspects of black life in the United States during the Second World War are Roi Ottley, *New World A-Coming* (Houghton Mifflin, 1943), which describes the many facets of Harlem life, and the collection of essays by prominent blacks edited by Rayford Logan, *What the Negro Wants* (University of North Carolina Press, 1943).

Robert C. Weaver surveyed the labor scene at the close of the war in *Negro Labor: A National Problem* (Harcourt, Brace & World, 1946). Walter White, the head of the NAACP, anticipated changes that would take place when the black servicemen returned home in *A Rising Wind* (Doubleday, 1945). In *Black Bourgeoisie** (Free Press, 1957), E. Franklin Frazier discusses the past and, by implication, the future role of the black middle class in American life.

One aspect of the legal program of the NAACP is examined in Clement E. Vose, *Caucasians Only: The Supreme Court, the NAACP and the Restrictive Covenant Cases** (University of California Press, 1959). The black man in the military is the subject of Richard Dalfiume's *Desegregation of the U.S. Armed Forces* (University of Missouri Press, 1969) and of an interesting novel by John O. Killens, *And Then We Heard the Thunder** (Knopf, 1963), which deals with racial tensions in the Second World War.

11 SCHOOL DESEGREGATION

For a hundred years before the end of the Second World War, the black man struggled with the courts of America over the question of the education of his children. In 1849, the courts of Massachusetts ruled that black children could be excluded from white schools if a black school was available. In reaction to this decision, the Massachusetts legislature passed an act desegregating the schools in 1855. Charles Sumner, a senator from Massachusetts who had been involved on the side of the blacks in the Massachusetts court case, tried unsuccessfully to get a provision for desegregated schooling included in the federal Civil Rights Act of 1875—the act declared unconstitutional by the Supreme Court in 1883. When the principle of "separate but equal" was set up in the case *Plessy v. Ferguson* in 1896, it was of course applied to education as well as to transportation and public accommodations.

Unfortunately, there was no real attempt to make the separate schools equal. For example, in 1915 the South Carolina public school system spent an average of $23.76 per white child and only $2.91 per black child. By 1954 the entire South was spending only $115 per black pupil per year as compared to $165 per white child.

By 1945, the federal courts had eased the legal restrictions on black people in the area of voting rights and had ruled against the use of restrictive real estate covenants to bar blacks from owning property. Yet education in the South remained as segregated as it had been in 1900. The NAACP finally decided to make a frontal attack on legally segregated school systems. Under the leadership of Thurgood Marshall, who later became the first black justice on the United States Supreme Court, a campaign against segregated schools was carefully planned.

Desegregation cases were initiated in South Carolina, Kansas, Virginia, and Delaware. The cases eventually reached the Supreme Court, grouped together under the designation *Brown v. Board of Education of Topeka, Kansas*. The Court, in a unanimous decision issued in May 1954, ruled that segregated schools were unconstitutional under the Fourteenth Amendment—that they were inherently unequal and deprived black children of equal protection of the laws. In its ruling, the Court gave the following explanation: "Segregation of white and colored children in public schools has a detrimental effect upon the colored children. The impact is greater when it has the sanction of the law; for the policy of separating the races is usually interpreted as denoting the inferiority of the Negro group."

Compliance with the decision began in the fall of 1954, when a few large cities—including Wilmington, Delaware; Washington, D.C.; and Baltimore, Maryland—and scattered towns in Missouri, Arkansas, and West Virginia initiated school desegregation. By 1955, when the Court somewhat ambiguously ordered the states to proceed with desegregation with "all deliberate speed," many powerful forces opposing desegregation were being marshaled. Representative of the strength of this opposition was the Southern Manifesto of 1956, a document signed by nineteen United States senators and eighty-one members of the House of Representatives praising "those states which have declared the intention to resist forced integration by any lawful means."

As the threat of forced integration loomed large, many doctrines from the past were resurrected, notably the idea of nullification (now called interposition)—the idea that a state could interpose itself between its citizens and rulings of the federal government if it found the federal law inimical to the interests of its citizens. Needless to say, the only citizens with whom the states concerned themselves were the white citizens. A hundred years after the Civil War, the federal government found itself faced with another Great Rebellion—another deep division of opinion that would, before it was all over, again require the use of federal troops to protect the rights of black men.

In the fall of 1958, desegregation came to a virtual standstill as the South threatened to close its public schools rather than give in to the Court ruling. Public schools were actually shut down in Little Rock, Arkansas, and in certain counties in Virginia during the 1958–59 school year. By 1959, however, the South had relaxed its posture to some extent, and the number of black children in formerly white schools began to creep upward. In 1963, after nine years of school desegregation, 9.2 per cent of the black children in public schools in the South attended classes with whites on a desegregated basis. Only Alabama, Mississippi, and South Carolina had completely segregated systems at the end of the 1962–63 school year. After 1963–64, only Mississippi held out, and it was soon to give way.

Apart from the legal barriers erected to prevent black children from entering white schools, several extralegal blocking procedures were developed. Because most school desegregation plans required that black parents sue for their children's admission to white schools, the parents were vulnerable to various kinds of intimidation. They were fired from their jobs, their mortgages were foreclosed by banks, they were regularly evicted from rented quarters, and they were in many other ways physically and emotionally abused. What was remarkable was the persistence of parents and children in the face of such harassment.

In many places the organizations that aided black parents and children came under attack as well. The Urban League, for example, was cut off from Community Chest fund drives. And the NAACP was viciously attacked on many levels: it was accused of being Communist dominated and was prosecuted under the various sedition laws of the Southern states; its members were barred from state jobs (a tactic particularly effective with school teachers); it was required to submit membership lists to state investigatory authorities.

A turning point in the school desegregation controversy came when it became apparent that the *Brown* ruling applied to segregated schools in the North as well as in the South. Although segregation in the North was not *de jure* (legally sanctioned), it was nevertheless *de facto* (actually in existence), and therefore it was subject to the Supreme Court ruling. Much of the Northern school segregation was the result of gerrymandered school districts based on segregated housing patterns. Although many plans for overcoming this situation have been proposed, school segregation in the North has in fact increased since 1954. For some, the struggle has shifted away from school integration to the issue of community control of decentralized school systems.

SEPARATE SCHOOLS ARE DELIBERATELY UNEQUAL

NAACP Legal Defense and Education Fund / Summary of Argument
Presented to the Supreme Court of the United States, 1953

In 1939, the cost of legal defense activities grew too large for the regular treasury of the NAACP to bear, and a special tax-exempt corporation was set up to raise money and carry on much of the legal work of the Association. This corporation, the NAACP Legal Defense and Education Fund, Inc., was responsible for the cases leading to the landmark Supreme Court decision of May 17, 1954, declaring racially segregated schools unconstitutional.

The argument in the Court was based on the Fourteenth Amendment to the Constitution, which provides that "no State shall make or enforce any law which shall abridge the privileges or immunities of citizens of the United States; nor shall any ·State deprive any person of life, liberty, or property, without due process of law; nor deny to any person within its jurisdiction the equal protection of the laws." The Fund maintained that in 1868, when the Amendment was ratified, it was clearly understood by both its supporters and its opponents to preclude discrimination based on color or race.

The following is a portion of the brief filed by the Fund with the Supreme Court late in 1953. A summary of the full brief, this section outlines the structure of the argument and indicates its basis in both legal precedent and the Fourteenth Amendment.

These cases consolidated for argument before this Court present in different factual contexts essentially the same ultimate legal questions.

The substantive question common to all is whether a state can, consistently with the Constitution, exclude children, solely on the ground that they are Negroes, from public schools which otherwise they would be qualified to attend. It is the thesis of this brief, submitted on behalf of the excluded children, that the answer to the question is in the negative: the Fourteenth Amendment prevents states from according differential treatment to American children on the basis of their color or race. Both the legal precedents and the judicial theories, discussed in Part I hereof, and the evidence concerning the intent of the framers of the Fourteenth Amendment and the understanding of the Congress and the ratifying states, developed in Part II hereof, support this proposition.

Denying this thesis, the school authorities, relying in part on language

FROM NAACP Legal Defense and Education Fund, Inc., *In the Supreme Court of the United States,* "Summary of Argument" (October term, 1953), pp. 15–20.

originating in this Court's opinion in *Plessy v. Ferguson*, 163 U. S. 537, urge that exclusion of Negroes, *qua* Negroes, from designated public schools is permissible when the excluded children are afforded admittance to other schools especially reserved for Negroes, *qua* Negroes, if such schools are equal.

The procedural question common to all the cases is the role to be played, and the time-table to be followed, by this Court and the lower courts in directing an end to the challenged exclusion, in the event that this Court determines, with respect to the substantive question, that exclusion of Negroes, *qua* Negroes, from public schools contravenes the Constitution.

The importance to our American democracy of the substantive question can hardly be overstated. The question is whether a nation founded on the proposition that "all men are created equal" is honoring its commitments to grant "due process of law" and "the equal protection of the laws" to all within its borders when it, or one of its constituent states, confers or denies benefits on the basis of color or race.

1. Distinctions drawn by state authorities on the basis of color or race violate the Fourteenth Amendment. *Shelley v. Kraemer*, 334 U. S. 1; *Buchanan v. Warley*, 245 U. S. 60. This has been held to be true even as to the conduct of public educational institutions. *Sweatt v. Painter*, 339 U. S. 629; *McLaurin v. Oklahoma State Regents*, 339 U. S. 637. Whatever other purposes the Fourteenth Amendment may have had, it is indisputable that its primary purpose was to complete the emancipation provided by the Thirteenth Amendment by ensuring to the Negro equality before the law. The *Slaughter House Cases*, 16 Wall. 36; *Strauder v. West Virginia*, 100 U. S. 303.

2. Even if the Fourteenth Amendment did not *per se* invalidate racial distinctions as a matter of law, the racial segregation challenged in the instant cases would run afoul of the conventional test established for application of the equal protection clause because the racial classifications here have no reasonable relation to any valid legislative purpose. See *Quaker City Cab Co. v. Pennsylvania*, 277 U. S. 389; *Truax v. Raich*, 239 U. S. 33; *Smith v. Cahoon*, 283 U. S. 553; *Mayflower Farms v. Ten Eyck*, 297 U. S. 266; *Skinner v. Oklahoma*, 316 U. S. 535. See also *Tunstall v. Brotherhood of Locomotive Firemen*, 323 U. S. 210; *Steele v. Louisville & Nashville R. R. Co.*, 323 U. S. 192.

3. Appraisal of the facts requires rejection of the contention of the school authorities. The educational detriment involved in racially constricting a student's associations has already been recognized by this Court. *Sweatt v. Painter*, 339 U. S. 629; *McLaurin v. Oklahoma State Regents*, 339 U. S. 637.

4. The argument that the requirements of the Fourteenth Amendment are met by providing alternative schools rests, finally, on reiteration of the separate but equal doctrine enunciated in *Plessy v. Ferguson*.

Were these ordinary cases, it might be enough to say that the *Plessy* case can be distinguished—that it involved only segregation in transportation. But these are not ordinary cases, and in deference to their importance it seems more fitting to meet the *Plessy* doctrine head-on and to declare that doctrine erroneous.

Candor requires recognition that the plain purpose and effect of segregated education is to perpetuate an inferior status for Negroes which is America's sorry heritage from slavery. But the primary purpose of the Fourteenth Amendment was to deprive the states of *all* power to perpetuate such a caste system.

5. The first and second of the five questions propounded by this Court requested enlightenment as to whether the Congress which submitted, and the state legislatures and conventions which ratified, the Fourteenth Amendment contemplated or understood that it would prohibit segregation in public schools, either of its own force or through subsequent legislative or judicial action. The evidence, both in Congress and in the legislatures of the ratifying states, reflects the substantial intent of the Amendment's proponents and the substantial understanding of its opponents that the Fourteenth Amendment would, of its own force, proscribe all forms of state-imposed racial distinctions, thus necessarily including all racial segregation in public education.

The Fourteenth Amendment was actually the culmination of the determined efforts of the Radical Republican majority in Congress to incorporate into our fundamental law the well-defined equalitarian principle of complete equality for all without regard to race or color. The debates in the 39th Congress and succeeding Congresses clearly reveal the intention that the Fourteenth Amendment would work a revolutionary change in our state-federal relationship by denying to the states the power to distinguish on the basis of race.

The Civil Rights Bill of 1866, as originally proposed, possessed scope sufficiently broad in the opinion of many Congressmen to entirely destroy all state legislation based on race. A great majority of the Republican Radicals—who later formulated the Fourteenth Amendment—understood and intended that the Bill would prohibit segregated schools. Opponents of the measure shared this understanding. The scope of this legislation was narrowed because it was known that the Fourteenth Amendment was in process of preparation and would itself have scope exceeding that of the original draft of the Civil Rights Bill.

6. The evidence makes clear that it was the intent of the proponents of the Fourteenth Amendment, and the substantial understanding of its opponents, that it would, of its own force, prohibit all state action predicated upon race or color. The intention of the framers with respect to any specific example of caste state action—in the instant cases, segregated education— cannot be determined solely on the basis of a tabulation of contemporaneous statements mentioning the specific practice. The framers were formulating

a constitutional provision setting broad standards for determination of the relationship of the state to the individual. In the nature of things they could not list all the specific categories of existing and prospective state activity which were to come within the constitutional prohibitions. The broad general purpose of the Amendment—obliteration of race and color distinctions—is clearly established by the evidence. So far as there was consideration of the Amendment's impact upon the undeveloped educational systems then existing, both proponents and opponents of the Amendment understood that it would proscribe all racial segregation in public education.

7. While the Amendment conferred upon Congress the power to enforce its prohibitions, members of the 39th Congress and those of subsequent Congresses made it clear that the framers understood and intended that the Fourteenth Amendment was self-executing and particularly pointed out that the federal judiciary had authority to enforce its prohibitions without Congressional implementation.

8. The evidence as to the understanding of the states is equally convincing. Each of the eleven states that had seceded from the Union ratified the Amendment, and concurrently eliminated racial distinctions from its laws, and adopted a constitution free of requirement or specific authorization of segregated schools. Many rejected proposals for segregated schools, and none enacted a school segregation law until after readmission. The significance of these facts is manifest from the consideration that ten of these states, which were required, as a condition of readmission, to ratify the Amendment and to modify their constitutions and laws in conformity therewith, considered that the Amendment required them to remove all racial distinctions from their existing and prospective laws, including those pertaining to public education.

Twenty-two of the twenty-six Union states also ratified the Amendment. Although unfettered by Congressional surveillance, the overwhelming majority of the Union states acted with an understanding that it prohibited racially segregated schools and necessitated conformity of their school laws to secure consistency with that understanding.

9. In short, the historical evidence fully sustains this Court's conclusion in the *Slaughter House Cases*, 16 Wall. 36, 81, that the Fourteenth Amendment was designed to take from the states all power to enforce caste or class distinctions.

10. The Court in its fourth and fifth questions assumes that segregation is declared unconstitutional and inquires as to whether relief should be granted immediately or gradually. Appellants, recognizing the possibility of delay of a purely administrative character, do not ask for the impossible. No cogent reasons justifying further exercise of equitable discretion, however, have as yet been produced.

It has been indirectly suggested in the briefs and oral argument of appellees that some such reasons exist. Two plans were suggested by the United States in its Brief as *Amicus Curiae*. We have analyzed each of these plans as well as appellees' briefs and oral argument and find nothing there of sufficient merit on which this Court, in the exercise of its equity power, could predicate a decree permitting an effective gradual adjustment from segregated to non-segregated school systems. Nor have we been able to find any other reasons or plans sufficient to warrant the exercise of such equitable discretion in these cases. Therefore, in the present posture of these cases, appellants are unable to suggest any compelling reasons for this Court to postpone relief.

LITTLE ROCK PREPARES FOR DESEGREGATION

Daisy Bates / Governor Faubus Rouses the Mob

It first appeared that Little Rock, Arkansas, would deal with the Supreme Court decision on school desegregation as did many moderate cities outside the Deep South. Nine black students had been selected to attend the formerly all-white Central High School in the fall of 1957. Then Governor Faubus of Arkansas, previously considered a racial moderate, called out the state-controlled National Guard to prevent the black students from entering Central High, thus precipitating a clash between the federal and state powers that reached dimensions unknown since 1877. Faubus' use of armed force to prevent the carrying out of a federal court order obliged President Eisenhower to employ federal troops to force the desegregation of the Little Rock school. The black students attended the school under guard for the 1957–58 school year, but the Governor closed all the Little Rock high schools the next year rather than permit them to open on a desegregated basis.

The story of the desegregation of the Little Rock school is compellingly told in the book from which the following selection is taken. The author, Mrs. Daisy Bates, was a former newspaper editor and the president of the Arkansas State NAACP. Here she tells of the reaction of the blacks to the calling out of the National Guard and the effect of this action on the people of Little Rock the day the schools opened.

It was Labor Day, September 2, 1957. The nine pupils who had been selected by the school authorities to enter Central High School—Carlotta Walls, Jefferson Thomas, Elizabeth Eckford, Thelma Mothershed, Melba Pattillo,

---

FROM Daisy Bates, *The Long Shadow of Little Rock* (New York: McKay, 1962), pp. 59–68. Reprinted by permission of David McKay Company, Inc.

Ernest Green, Terrance Roberts, Gloria Ray, and Minnijean Brown—were enjoying the last day of their summer vacation. Some of them were picnicking, others swimming, playing tennis, or just visiting with friends and relatives. About midafternoon young Jefferson Thomas was on his way home from the pool and stopped at my house for a brief visit. While Jeff was raiding the refrigerator, a news flash came over the radio that the Governor would address the citizens of Arkansas that night.

"I wonder what he's going to talk about," said Jeff. The youngster then turned to me and asked, "Is there anything they can do—now that they lost in court? Is there any way they can stop us from entering Central tomorrow morning?"

"I don't think so," I said.

About seven o'clock that night a local newspaper reporter rang my doorbell. "Mrs. Bates, do you know that national guardsmen are surrounding Central High?"

L. C. and I stared at him incredulously for a moment. A friend who was visiting us volunteered to guard the house while we drove out to Central. L. C. gave him the shotgun. We jumped into our car and drove to Central High. We parked a half block from the school. Under the street lights stretched a long line of brown Army trucks with canvas tops. Men in full battle dress—helmets, boots, and bayonets—were piling out of the trucks and lining up in front of the school.

As we watched, L. C. switched on the car radio. A newscaster was saying, "National guardsmen are surrounding Central High School. No one is certain what this means. Governor Faubus will speak later this evening."

Ahead of us we could see reporters rushing up trying to talk to the soldiers. However, it soon became clear that the guardsmen were under orders to say nothing. They remained silent.

The whole scene was incredible. "Let's go back home and hear Faubus!" I suggested.

The phone was ringing as we pulled into our driveway. An excited friend wanted to know what it all meant, what was going to happen. All I could offer was, "Listen to Faubus." As soon as I put down the receiver, the phone rang again. This time it was the father of one of the children. "What's going on, Daisy? What's going to happen?" All I could do was to give him the same answer.

On television, Governor Faubus creates almost the same impression he does in person. He customarily wears a dark suit, white shirt, and dark tie. He is a big man physically, and affects a big man's easy congeniality. He specializes in the folksy manner, fixing his unseen audience with an "I'm-right-here-with-you-good-folks" glance.

I don't recall all the details of what Governor Faubus said that night. But his words electrified Little Rock. By morning they shocked the United States. By noon the next day his message horrified the world.

Faubus' alleged reason for calling out the troops was that he had received information that caravans of automobiles filled with white supremacists were heading toward Little Rock from all over the state. He therefore declared Central High School off limits to Negroes. For some inexplicable reason he added that Horace Mann, a Negro high school, would be off limits to whites.

Then, from the chair of the highest office of the State of Arkansas, Governor Orval Eugene Faubus delivered the infamous words, "blood will run in the streets" if Negro pupils should attempt to enter Central High School.

In a half dozen ill-chosen words, Faubus made his contribution to the mass hysteria that was to grip the city of Little Rock for several months.

The citizens of Little Rock gathered on September 3 to gaze upon the incredible spectacle of an empty school building surrounded by 250 National Guard troops. At about eight fifteen in the morning, Central students started passing through the line of national guardsmen—all but the nine Negro students.

I had been in touch with their parents throughout the day. They were confused, and they were frightened. As parents voiced their fears, they kept repeating Governor Faubus' words that "blood would run in the streets of Little Rock" should their teen-age children try to attend Central—the school to which they had been assigned by the school board.

Typical of the parents was Mrs. Birdie Eckford. "Mrs. Bates," she asked, "what do you think we should do? I am frightened. Not for myself but for the children. When I was a little girl, my mother and I saw a lynch mob dragging the body of a Negro man through the streets of Little Rock. We were told to get off the streets. We ran. And by cutting through side streets and alleys, we managed to make it to the home of a friend. But we were close enough to hear the screams of the mob, close enough to smell the sickening odor of burning flesh. And, Mrs. Bates, they took the pews from Bethel Church to make the fire. They burned the body of this Negro man right at the edge of the Negro business section.

"Mrs. Bates, do you think this will happen again?"

I reminded Mrs. Eckford that Little Rock was a different city now. Different from 1927, when the lynching and the burning had taken place. True, Governor Faubus spoke of blood. But in the next breath he had said that he called out the guardsmen to protect life and property against violence. Surely he meant the lives of the Negro students as well as white! No, it was inconceivable that troops, and responsible citizens, would stand by and let a mob attack children.

The NAACP attorneys, Wiley Branton and Thurgood Marshall, appealed to Federal Judge Ronald N. Davies for instruction. Their question was, in effect: What do we do now? The judge stated that "he was accepting the Governor's statement at face value—that his purpose in calling out the Guard was to protect 'life and property' against possible mob violence." Therefore, Judge Davies directed the school board again to put its plan for integration into operation immediately.

On the afternoon of the same day, September 3, when the school was scheduled to open, Superintendent Blossom called a meeting of leading Negro citizens and the parents of the nine children. I was not notified of the meeting, but the parents called me and asked me to be present. At the meeting Superintendent Blossom instructed the parents *not* to accompany their children the next morning when they were scheduled to enter Central. "If violence breaks out," the Superintendent told them, "it will be easier to protect the children if the adults aren't there."

During the conference Superintendent Blossom had given us little assurance that the children would be adequately protected. As we left the building, I was aware of how deeply worried the parents were, although they did not voice their fears.

About ten o'clock that night I was alone in the downstairs recreation room, my mind still occupied by the problems raised during the conference. L. C. appeared in the doorway. With him was a local reporter whom I had known for some time.

Words began pouring from the young reporter. "Look, Daisy," he said anxiously. "I know about the Superintendent's instructions. I know he said the children must go alone to Central in the morning. But let me tell you, this is murder! I heard those people today. I've never seen anything like it. People I've known all my life—they've gone mad. They're totally without reason. You must know you can't expect much protection—if any—from the city police. Besides, the city police are barred from the school grounds!"

My friend's voice took on a pleading quality, as if there were something I could do. "I swear there must have been about five hundred people at the school today," he continued. "And new recruits are pouring into the city from outlying areas. Even from other states. By morning there could be several thousand."

"What do you think we should do?" I asked him.

"I really don't know," he answered. "I really don't know."

The young reporter left. I sat huddled in my chair, dazed, trying to think, yet not knowing what to do. I don't recall how much time went by —a few minutes, an hour, or more—before some neighbors entered. One of them was the Reverend J. C. Crenchaw, President of the Little Rock branch of the NAACP.

His presence in my house immediately gave me an idea.

"Maybe," I said, "maybe we could round up a few ministers to go with the children tomorrow. Maybe then the mob wouldn't attack them. Maybe with the ministers by their side—"

Mr. Crenchaw caught on to the idea right away. "We can try, Daisy. At least we can try. Maybe this is the answer."

I called a white minister, Rev. Dunbar Ogden, Jr., President of the Inter-racial Ministerial Alliance. I did not know Mr. Ogden. I explained the situation, then asked if he thought he could get some ministers to go with the children to school the next morning.

"Well, Mrs. Bates, I don't know," he said. "I'll call some of the ministers and see what they think about it. You know, this is a new idea to me."

I said the idea was new to me, too; and that it had just occurred to me moments before. Tensely I waited for his return call. When it came, he sounded apologetic. The white ministers he had talked to had questioned whether it was the thing to do. Some of the Negro ministers had pointed out that the Superintendent of Schools had asked that no Negro adults go with the children, and that in view of this they felt they shouldn't go. Then he added gently, "I'll keep trying—and, God willing, I'll be there."

Next I called the city police. I explained to the officer in charge that we were concerned about the safety of the children and that we were trying to get ministers to accompany them to school the next morning. I said that the children would assemble at eight thirty at Twelfth Street and Park Avenue. I asked whether a police car could be stationed there to protect the children until the ministers arrived.

The police officer promised to have a squad car there at eight o'clock. "But you realize," he warned, "that our men cannot go any closer than that to the school. The school is off limits to the city police while it's 'occupied' by the Arkansas National Guardsmen."

By now it was two thirty in the morning. Still, the parents had to be called about the change in plan. At three o'clock I completed my last call, explaining to the parents where the children were to assemble and the plan about the ministers. Suddenly I remembered Elizabeth Eckford. Her family had no telephone. Should I go to the Union Station and search for her father? Someone had once told me that he had a night job there. Tired in mind and body, I decided to handle the matter early in the morning. I stumbled into bed.

A few hours later, at about eight fifteen in the morning, L. C. and I started driving to Twelfth Street and Park Avenue. On the way I checked out in my mind the possibilities that awaited us. The ministers might be there—or again they might not. Mr. Ogden, failing to find anyone to accompany him, understandably might not arrive. Would the police be there? How many? And what if—

The bulletin over the car radio interrupted. The voice announced: "A Negro girl is being mobbed at Central High. . . ."

"Oh, my God!" I cried. "It must be Elizabeth! I forgot to notify her where to meet us!"

L. C. jumped out of the car and rushed to find her. I drove on to Twelfth Street. There were the ministers—two white—Mr. Ogden and Rev. Will Campbell, of the National Council of Churches, Nashville, Tennessee

—and two colored—the Reverend Z. Z. Driver, of the African Methodist Episcopal Church, and the Reverend Harry Bass, of the Methodist Church. With them also was Mr. Ogden's twenty-one-year-old son, David. The children were already there. And, yes, the police had come as promised. All of the children were there—all except Elizabeth.

Soon L. C. rushed up with the news that Elizabeth finally was free of the mob. He had seen her on a bus as it pulled away.

The children set out, two ministers in front of them, two behind. They proceeded in that formation until they approached the beginning of the long line of guardsmen. At this point they had their first brush with the mob. They were jostled and shoved. As they made their way toward the school grounds, the ministers and their charges attempted to pass the guardsmen surrounding Central High. A National Guard captain stopped them. He told Mr. Ogden he could not allow them to pass through the guard line. When Mr. Ogden asked why, the captain said it was by order of Governor Faubus.

The ministers returned to the car with the students and Mr. Ogden reported what the captain of the guardsmen had said. I told him that in view of the school board's statement the previous evening that Central High School would be open to Negro students in the morning, it was my feeling that the students should go immediately to the office of the Superintendent for further instructions.

When we arrived at the office, the Superintendent was out. When he failed to return within an hour, I suggested that we appeal to the United States Attorney, Osro Cobb, since Federal Judge Davies had ordered the Federal Bureau of Investigation, under the direction of the United States Attorney, to conduct a thorough investigation into who was responsible for the interference with the Court's integration order.

Mr. Cobb looked surprised when we entered his office. I told him that we were there because the students had been denied admittance to Central High School by the national guardsmen and we wanted to know what action, if any, his office planned to take.

After questioning the pupils, he directed them to the office of the FBI, where they gave a detailed report of what had happened to them that morning.

I might add here that during the school year the FBI interviewed hundreds of persons. Many of those who had participated in the mob could easily have been identified from photographs taken in front of the school. Yet no action was taken against anyone by the office of the United States Attorney, Osro Cobb, or the Department of Justice.

MEREDITH CRACKS OLE MISS

James Meredith / I'll Know Victory or Defeat

James Meredith has been one of the loneliest of the heroes of the school desegregation movement. He broke the segregation barrier at the University of Mississippi in the fall of 1962, an event that led to the second massive intrusion of federal troops into the South since Reconstruction (the first was at Little Rock in 1957). President John F. Kennedy sent five thousand Army regulars and nationalized guardsmen to patrol the streets of Oxford, Mississippi, after a night-long riot sparked by opposition to Meredith's presence on the campus.

Meredith set out on a lonely path again in 1966 when he began his much publicized "march against fear." He decided to walk the two hundred miles from Memphis to Jackson, Mississippi, to demonstrate that it was possible for a black man to do so without fear and to survive. Twenty-eight miles from Memphis he was shot down in the road by a white supremacist, who was later acquitted of the assault. Meredith recovered and returned to studies at the Columbia University Law School.

One can sense from the following article, written by Meredith during the terrible autumn in Oxford, the massive pride and stubborn loneliness of a man determined to see the end of a condition he knows to be unjust.

If you asked me when it all began—what brought me to the campus in Oxford that first week in October—I guess I would say it began when I was a boy in Kosciusko, up in the hill country of Mississippi, where I was born. I used to lie in bed and dream about a city—I didn't know what city or where it was—I knew it would be different from Kosciusko, because I didn't like the way things were there.

Kosciusko isn't altogether typical of Mississippi, I would say. It is an area of small farms, and most of the farmers, Negro and white, own their own places. I think the Negroes there might be a little more progressive than in some other parts of the state. Some Negroes there—my father, for example —have been voting for as long as I know of. I think you'll find that many progressive Negroes come from an area like this, where they own their own land. Still, I certainly can't say I liked it in Kosciusko. They tell me I was always strong on the race issue when I was young. For example,

FROM James Meredith, "I'll Know Victory or Defeat," *Saturday Evening Post*, Vol. CCXXV (November 10, 1962), pp. 14–17. Reprinted with permission of *The Saturday Evening Post* © 1962.

I remember a wealthy white man who used to go around town handing out nickels and dimes to Negro children. I never would take any.

In Kosciusko I grew up between things. Part of my family was much older than I was, and part was much younger. It was like being an only child. I really only got to know my brothers and sisters later. Also, I lived in the country and went to school in town. In small towns in the South you're either a "city boy" or a "country boy," but I wasn't either. I got used to taking care of things by myself.

When I was 16 I left Kosciusko to finish my last year of high school in St. Petersburg, Florida. I had a desire to go to a better school, and I had an uncle and a sister living there. I graduated from high school in June of 1951 and enlisted in the Air Force the next month. I had a brother in the Air Force, but that wasn't the reason I joined. It was common knowledge among Negroes that the Air Force was a better branch of service for them.

INFLUENCE OF AIR FORCE DUTY

Certainly my Air Force days were the most influential time of my life. I served in nothing but integrated units. It seems to me the integration of the armed forces is one of the most important things that has happened to the Negro in the United States. For that reason, I thought it was particularly unfortunate that the Army apparently resegregated its units in Oxford after the night of campus rioting. If Negroes could fight side by side with whites around the world, they should be able to serve with them in Mississippi.

I never had any "bad" incidents when I was in the Air Force. There were occasional small things, reminders that a Negro was a Negro. I remember when I was in basic training at Sampson Air Force Base in New York State, all of us were invited to spend weekends with families in Syracuse. I spent a weekend with a white family there, and they were very nice, but they kept reminding me in subtle ways that they were being unusually nice—in other words, they didn't have to do this; it was just a favor. There is always that air of difference about being a Negro that you can never quite touch.

But life was pretty good in the Air Force. As I say, I served in nothing but integrated units, and everything was OK as far as promotions went too. I remember very well one particular hearing for promotion, when I was up for staff sergeant. I was to go before a board of three colonels. Usually they question you about your qualifications and try to decide whether or not you can take on the responsibilities of the next rank. I came up before the board just two months after the Supreme Court school-desegregation decision in 1954, and they didn't ask me anything about my qualifications. All they asked about was my opinion of the decision, what my family thought about it, and all that. Well, I told them. I'll always remember that when it was over and I had made staff sergeant, they told me they were with me in the struggle but that "the outcome will depend on you." I took that "you" to mean Negroes, all Negroes, and I guess it has been sort of a badge of responsibility ever since.

In 1955 I reenlisted. I always had it in mind to come back to Mississippi and study law, but I didn't think I was ready then for the responsibilities I would have to face, so I reenlisted. I was in Japan from 1957 till 1960, and there isn't any doubt that this was the settling-down point for me. I decided not only what I wanted to do, which I have known for a long time in a vague way, but how to go about doing it.

Being in Japan was an amazing experience. Negroes say, "When you're in Japan you have to look in a mirror to remember you're a Negro," and it's true. Japan is the only place where I have not felt the "air of difference."

I was surprised that the Japanese people were so aware of the racial situation in America. For instance, I met a boy—I don't suppose he was more than 12 or 13—and he knew more about Little Rock than most American kids that age. He was amazed when I told him I was from Mississippi and that I intended to go back. This kind of reaction further convinced me that I would go back to Mississippi and try to improve these conditions. I was discharged in July, 1960, and by the end of the month I was back in Kosciusko.

I entered Jackson State College, a Negro school in Jackson, and quickly met other students who felt as I did—that Negroes in Mississippi did not have the rights of full citizens, including the right to the best education the state offered. Someone had to seek admission to the University of Mississippi, and I decided to do it. But there were many of us involved. Although the lawsuit was mine, the others were with me, and I sought their advice on every move I made.

As soon as I filed application for admission, I contacted Medgar Evers, Mississippi field secretary for the N.A.A.C.P., and through him I asked for N.A.A.C.P. legal aid. Mrs. Constance Motley, associate counsel of the N.A.A.C.P. Legal Defense Fund, came to my assistance. The N.A.A.C.P. was prompt and efficient, and that was of prime importance. There was a great morale factor here, and every time we called them, they were there.

The court fight was long, and there were times when I wondered if it would be successful. I kept winning in court, but I didn't get any nearer to the university. Finally, after the Fifth Circuit Court of Appeals had said I should be registered, I felt the responsibility was the Federal Government's; it was out of my hands to do anything.

People have asked me if I wasn't terribly afraid the night we went to Oxford. No, my apprehensions came a long time before that. The hardest thing in human nature is to decide to act. I was doing all right in the Air Force. I got married in 1956, and my wife was able to work as a civil servant on the same bases where I was stationed. I had to give this up, this established way of things, this status, and try something new and unknown. That's where the big decision was—not here, last month, but there, a couple of years ago. Once I made that decision, things just had to happen the way they happened.

I think maybe a quote from Theodore Roosevelt that I read somewhere was more important than anything else in helping me make this decision. I think I read it around 1952, and I clipped it out, and everywhere I've gone since then—every place I've lived or everywhere I've worked—I have put that saying in front of me. I guess I must have read it two or three thousand times by now. It says, "It is not the critic who counts. . . . The credit belongs to the man who is actually in the arena, whose face is marred by dust and sweat and blood . . . who at the best knows in the end the triumph of high achievement, and who at the worst, if he fails, at least fails while daring greatly, so that his place will never be with those cold and timid souls who know neither victory nor defeat." At different times different parts of that quotation have been important to me, but when I made the decision to return to Mississippi and later to enroll at the university, the part I kept seeing was the part about "cold and timid souls who know neither victory nor defeat." I didn't want to be one of those.

FEAR IS JUST ANOTHER OBSTACLE

As far as fear of death or personal injury goes—and I consider this most important for everybody to understand—I put death or the fear of getting hurt in the same category with legal objections to my entering the university, or moral objections, or objections on grounds of custom. They are all on the same level. They are all just ways to keep me out of the university, and no one is any more important than any other. It wouldn't matter if I stumbled and fell and couldn't go to classes or whether I cut my finger and couldn't write for a month or whether I was shot and killed—they're all just things in my way. I might do quite a bit to put a stop to the act of being killed. I have done this several times already—I've taken the advice of the Federal marshals on several occasions, for instance. But this was because, if something happened to me, it would have put everything back as far as the Negroes in Mississippi are concerned. If I have lost an hour's sleep in recent weeks, it has been over some philosophical point, or through apprehension of not succeeding in entering the university, and of discouraging others from trying if I failed, but not over what might happen to me personally.

I was sure that if I were harmed or killed, somebody else would take my place one day. I would hate to think another Negro would have to go through that ordeal, but I would hate worse to think there wouldn't be another who would do it.

I had an older brother who was scary as a boy. Back home he wouldn't go certain places after dark or walk here or there. I always walked wherever I wanted. I walked four miles to Scout meetings at night, and I always went through all the hollows and the places where you were supposed to be afraid to go. I must admit my hair has stood up on my head at times, but I never ran. They used to say, "If you see a 'hant' put your hand on it." Most of the time you find it isn't there. I think it's an utter waste of time to worry about dying. It's living that matters—doing somehing to justify being here on God's green earth. I do what I do because I must. I've never felt I had a choice. There is some urge that I can't explain easily— I guess that's as close as I can come to defining it.

There is something else here, too, and it's hard to say right. People can misunderstand it. But it's this—generally at home I was always thought to be pretty smart. I wasn't particularly proud of it; it was just almost a fact of life. There was an expectation or a more or less acknowledged fact that I was one of the sharpest in the group. I was a champion in my group in Mississippi, but then, when I went to Florida to change high schools, I wasn't a champion at all. I had to fight to keep up. I hadn't been prepared. Since then, one of the biggest things in my life is that I have always felt I was never able to develop my talents. I have felt many times that, given the opportunity, I could develop into practically anything. Many times I have been angry at the world for not giving me an opportunity to develop. I am sure this has been a strong motivating force with me, and I'm sure it is with many Negroes. Since then I've always tried to see myself in relation to the whole society. Too many Negroes see themselves only in relation to other Negroes. But that's not good enough. We have to see ourselves in the whole society. If America isn't for everybody, it isn't America.

Through all that has happened I have tried to remain detached and objective. I have had all sorts of reactions to things that have happened, but mostly they have been personal reactions and realistic reactions, both at the same time. When I was in the middle of the force of marshals being gathered to take me to Oxford I thought, personally, how utterly ridiculous this was, what a terrible waste of time and money and energy, to iron out some rough spots in our civilization. But realistically I knew that these changes were necessary. I knew change was a threat to people and that they would fight it and that this was the only way it could be accomplished.

I have tried to be detached and realistic. When we were turned away the first time I tried to register at the university, and especially the second time, at the State Capitol in Jackson, I saw the mobs and heard them jeering, "Go home, nigger" and that stuff, but I never recognized them as individuals at all, even those who showed the greatest contempt for me. I felt they were not personally attacking me but that they were protesting a change and this was something they felt they must do. I thought it was impersonal. Some of them were crying, and their crying indicated to me even more the pain of change and the fear of things they did not know. I feel the people were keyed up by the actions of their leaders. With Gov. Ross Barnett taking the position he did, the people were bound to act that way, and it didn't really have anything to do with me personally. That's the way I saw it.

I might add that I thought the governor put on a pretty good performance. The first time, when he turned us away at the university, he reminded me of Charlton Heston, I believe it was, in a movie about Andrew Jackson. Very dramatic.

I don't think I have had a real low point in recent weeks. It always seemed to me it was the Government's job to carry out the court order and it would be done. The most annoying time was when there was so much talk about a possible deal between the Federal Government and Governor Barnett. But when the Federal officers told me we were going that Sunday, just a few minutes before we took off for Oxford, the annoyance disappeared.

When we landed in Oxford it was almost dark. We got in a car and I remember seeing a truckload of marshals in front of us and one behind. I went straight to the university and was taken to my rooms—an apartment, I guess you could call it. Since they knew some Government men would be staying with me, I had two bedrooms and a living room and a bathroom. The first thing I did was make my bed. When the trouble started, I couldn't see or hear very much of it. Most of it was at the other end of the campus, and besides I didn't look out the window. I think I read a newspaper and went to bed around 10 o'clock. I was awakened several times in the night by the noise and shooting outside, but it wasn't near me, and I had no way of knowing what was going on. Some of the students in my dormitory banged their doors for a while and threw some bottles in the halls, but I slept pretty well all night.

I woke up about six-thirty in the morning and looked out and saw the troops. There was a slight smell of tear gas in my room, but I still didn't know what had gone on during the night, and I didn't find out until some marshals came and told me how many people were hurt and killed. I had gotten to know these marshals pretty well in recent weeks, and I was so sorry about this. Some supposedly responsible newspapermen asked me if I thought attending the university was worth all this death and destruction. That really annoyed me. Of course I was sorry! I didn't want that sort of thing. I believe it could have been prevented by responsible political leaders. I understand the President and the attorney general were up most of the night. They had all the intelligence at their disposal, and I believe they handled it to the best of their knowledge and ability. I think it would have been much worse if we had waited any longer. Social change is a painful thing, but it depends on the people at the top. Here they were totally opposed—the state against the Federal Government. There was bound to be trouble, and there was trouble.

Monday morning at eight o'clock I registered, and at nine I went to a class in Colonial American History. I was a few minutes late, and I took a seat at the back of the room. The professor was lecturing on the background in England, conditions there at the time of the colonization of America, and he paid no special attention when I entered. I think there were about a dozen students in the class. One said hello to me, and the others were silent. I remember a girl—the only girl there, I think—and she was crying, but it might have been from the tear gas in the room. I was crying from it myself.

I had three classes scheduled that day. I went to two, and the third didn't meet because there was too much gas in the room. No marshals were in the classrooms with me, nor were they all week.

I have received hundreds of telegrams and more than 1,000 letters, most of them expressions of support. One guy sent me a piece of singed rope, and another sent a poem, I guess you'd have to call it:

> *Roses are red, violets are blue;*
> *I've killed one nigger and might as well make it two.*

But most of the letters and telegrams have supported me, and some of them have been really touching—letters from 10- and 11-year-olds who think I'm right and offer me their help and that sort of thing.

As far as my relations with the students go, I make it a practice to be courteous. I don't force myself on them, but that's not my nature anyway. Many of them—most, I'd say—have been courteous, and the faculty members certainly have been. When I hear the jeers and the catcalls—"We'll get you, nigger" and all that—I don't consider it personal. I get the idea people are just having a little fun. I think it's tragic that they have to have this kind of fun about me, but many of them are children of the men who lead Mississippi today, and I wouldn't expect them to act any other way. They have to act the way they do. I think I understand human nature enough to understand that.

It hasn't been all bad. Many students have spoken to me very pleasantly. They have stopped banging doors and throwing bottles into my dormitory now.

One day a fellow from my home town sat down at my table in the cafeteria. "If you're here to get an education, I'm for you," he said. "If you're here to cause trouble, I'm against you." That seemed fair enough to me.

MARSHALS ARE A DISTRACTION

I am taking five courses—Colonial American History; a political science course called American Political Parties, Theories and Pressure Groups; French literature; English literature; and algebra. I expect to be able to get my B.A. in history, with a minor in political science, in two semesters and one summer, if everything goes right.

I'm not sure what I will do in the future. A lot depends on how things go at the university. We are just at the beginning of a process of change in Mississippi. I would like to help that process along, and that probably would mean some kind of job in public life. Whether this will be possible in Mississippi or not we'll just have to wait to see. I do know this: If I can't live in Mississippi, I very definitely will leave the country.

If the decision is made to keep the marshals and troops on the campus until I complete my course, it is all right with me, but certainly I hope that won't be necessary. I think the marshals have been superb. They have had an image of America—that the law must be obeyed, no matter what they may think of it or what anybody else may think of it—but they are certainly a distraction on the campus. The thing that grieves me most about all this is that the students are not getting the best college results because they're spending too much time looking on at these various events involving me. I didn't get much studying done that first week, and I don't think anybody else did.

Personally the year will be a hardship for me. My wife will be in college in Jackson. Our son John Howard, who will be three in January, is living with my parents in Kosciusko. I expect to see them both very often, but I don't think families should live apart. On the other hand, this is nothing new to my wife. We spent most of our courtship discussing my plan to come back to Mississippi some day, and I guess you could say her understanding that I would try to do this sometime was almost part of the marriage contract. She has been truly marvelous through all of it. I called her three nights after the trouble, and she picked up the phone and was so calm you'd have thought we just finished a game of 500 rummy and she won. She's a remarkable woman.

I don't think this has had any effect on my family in Kosciusko. I have talked to my father. He asks me how I am, and I ask him how he is. He knows what I mean by the question, and I know what he means by the answer. That's the way it is in our family.

I don't pretend that all the problems are over. But, whatever the problems are, I don't expect them to be too much for me. Nobody really knows where his breaking point is, and I can't say I know where mine is. But I know one thing—in the past the Negro has not been allowed to receive the education he needs. If this is the way it must be accomplished, and I believe it is, then it is not too high a price to pay.

11 SUGGESTIONS FOR FURTHER READING

The story of school desegregation is told by Benjamin Muse in *Ten Years of Prelude: The Story of Integration Since the Supreme Court's 1954 Decision* (Viking, 1964) and by Anthony Lewis and *The New York Times* in *Portrait of a Decade: The Second American Revolution** (Random House, 1964). The first years of desegregation are the focus of Don Shoemaker (ed.), *With All Deliberate Speed* (Harper and Row, 1957). For background on the education of blacks in the South, see Henry Bullock, *A History of Negro Education in the South* (Harvard University Press, 1967).

The legal aspects of change in racial policy are surveyed in Jack Greenberg, *Race Relations and American Law* (Columbia University Press, 1959), and the legal aspects of the Supreme Court decision on school desegregation are discussed in Albert Blaustein and C. C. Ferguson (eds.), *Desegregation and the Law** (Rutgers University Press, 1957). Loren Miller, a black judge, has written a useful work on the relationship between the Supreme Court and the black man, *The Petitioners: The Story of the Supreme Court of the United States and the Negro** (World, 1966).

Benjamin Muse examines the opposition to desegregation in Virginia in *Virginia's Massive Resistance* (Indiana University Press, 1961). James Meredith's experience at the University of Mississippi is covered by William Lord in *The Past That Would Not Die** (Harper and Row, 1965) and by Meredith himself in *Three Years in Mississippi* (Indiana University Press, 1966).

Robert Coles has published his studies of the effects of desegregation on the children taking part in it in *Children of Crisis: A Story of Courage and Fear** (Little, Brown, 1967).

Two periodicals that reported in depth on the process of school desegregation are *New South*, a publication of the Southern Regional Council, and *Southern School News* (which later became *Southern Education Report*), a publication of the Southern Education Reporting Service.

12 THE NONVIOLENT CIVIL RIGHTS MOVEMENT

The prototypes of the nonviolent direct-action campaigns of the late 1950's and the early 1960's are found in A. Philip Randolph's March on Washington movement and the Congress of Racial Equality (CORE). The latter was organized by religious pacifists in 1942 in an attempt to apply Gandhian techniques to the racial struggle in America. Its founder, James Farmer, was black, but CORE was made up primarily of whites until the 1960's. Although CORE was not directly involved in the events that led to the nonviolent movement among Southern students in the 1960's, its skill in the analysis of and training for nonviolent protests was put at the service of the students once the movement began.

The tactic of massive nonviolent direct action appeared on the scene of American race relations with the Montgomery, Alabama, bus boycott of 1955. Rosa Parks, a black woman, decided not to stand up when ordered to give her seat to a white person on a Montgomery bus, thus breaking city law. She was arrested, and the nonviolent civil rights movement was on. For more than a year blacks refused to ride the buses in an attempt to bring about a slight modification in the seating arrangements on public transportation. As a result of the boycott they were subjected to intimidation, arrest, and economic reprisals of various sorts. On November 13, 1956, the Supreme Court ruled that bus segregation violated the Constitution, and the Montgomery boycott was declared ended. In the aftermath of the decision that finally forced a change in Southern customs, several black churches were bombed.

The churches were an appropriate target for hostile whites, for it was from them that the boycott leadership had emerged. A Montgomery church furnished the movement with the man who served as its symbolic head until his assassination in 1968, Martin Luther King, Jr. Fresh from graduate school and just beginning to act as pastor of a Baptist church in Montgomery, King was elected to serve as head of the boycott committee. From there he joined with others to found the Southern Christian Leadership Conference (SCLC), which was to be a civil rights organization of major importance in the decades to come.

As the use of the boycott technique spread, an event occurred that changed all the rules and tactics of the protest movements. On February 1, 1960, four black college students "sat in" at a lunch counter in a Woolworth store in Greensboro, North Carolina. For some reason, this act provided the spark that set off the latent dynamite of Southern race relations. Within a matter of weeks, tens of thousands of students all over the South were engaged in sit-in campaigns. The number of arrests and violent acts of retaliation by whites soared. It has been estimated that at least 20,000 persons were arrested as a result of participation in nonviolent demonstrations in the South between 1960 and 1963.

In April 1960, the SCLC decided to call a conference of college students involved in the demonstrations. From this conference emerged the Student Nonviolent Coordinating Committee (SNCC), which was henceforth to guide the fortunes of the student movement. At the beginning, SNCC's philosophy was one of religious nonviolence, patterned after the ideas of Martin Luther King. But even then, most of the students accepted nonviolence as a practical measure, not as a total philosophy of life. Later, when SNCC shifted away from the demonstration as a technique, not so much a change in philosophy as a change in tactics was required. Under the leadership of brilliant young blacks, SNCC transformed the college campus scene in America from one of passive alienation to one of militant commitment.

The most direct contribution of CORE to the nonviolent action movement came with the Freedom Rides of 1961, undertaken to test the South's submission to the Supreme Court ruling outlawing segregation in bus and train terminals. Although their buses were bombed and burned, many continued their journeys, and over three hundred persons ended up in the Jackson, Mississippi, jail. The Freedom Rides marked the begining of a shift of civil rights activity from the upper to the lower South, where most nonviolent direct-action campaigns were to meet with little or no success.

As SNCC began to be active in the rural Deep South, primarily trying to get the poor blacks to register for the vote, the students began to move away from their previous "middleclass" goals. This led to a rift between SNCC and King and the SCLC—a rift that became a complete split at the conclusion of the summer of 1964. Until this time, many whites had participated in the organizational activities of SNCC, and in the summer of 1964, often called Freedom Summer, Mississippi was invaded by hundreds of college students, black and white, from North and South, in an attempt to focus national attention on the state's denial of basic rights to its black citizens. In terms of this immediate goal, the summer was a great success, for it brought the horrors of Mississippi dramatically before the public eye.

Perhaps even more important in the long run, Freedom Summer

marked a turning point in the black student movement. When it became apparent that it was the "whiteness" of the summer that attracted the news media, the black students decided that they had to cast out their white allies and become an all-black movement. Only in that way, they felt, could they build a movement that would ensure the coming of true liberation for black people. As long as the nation cared for blacks only when they were accompanied by whites, there would be no certainty of freedom for the black man taken alone.

The disenchantment of many blacks with what they considered the "political" approach of white liberals was strengthened when, in August 1964 at the Democratic Party Convention, the Mississippi Freedom Democratic Party (MFDP), a predominantly black organization loyal to the national Democratic party, was let down by Hubert Humphrey. The MFDP had agreed to accept a compromise proposal seating all members of the regular Democratic party and of the MFDP who would sign a pledge of loyalty and dividing the vote of the Mississippi delegation between the two groups on the basis of the number of delegates seated by each. But Humphrey, working for the vice-presidential nomination, had the Credentials Committee reject the agreed-upon compromise in favor of allowing the MFDP two at-large votes. The new compromise was rejected by the MFDP over the objections of civil rights leaders like Martin Luther King, Jr.—a clear sign that the integrationist phase of the movement for black liberation was coming to a close.

In 1966, Stokely Carmichael was elected to the chairmanship of SNCC, and violence continued to erupt in the black urban ghettos of the North. It was time to admit that the nonviolent civil rights movement had either reached an end or changed so drastically that it had to be described with an altogether new terminology.

THE PHILOSOPHY OF NONVIOLENT COERCION

Martin Luther King, Jr. / Letter from Birmingham Jail

It was a happy coincidence that twenty-seven-year-old Martin Luther King, Jr., had recently accepted a pastorate in Montgomery, Alabama, when the bus boycott broke out. Since his days as a seminary student, King had been developing a nonviolent philosophy of life based on the writings of Gandhi and the New Testament. As a result, King became the philosopher of the movement for nonviolent coercion.

After King brought the movement into Birmingham, Alabama, in 1963, he was arrested and jailed, along with Ralph Abernathy and Fred Shuttlesworth, on Good Friday for leading a protest march. A group of Alabama clergymen wrote King a letter while he was in jail, accusing him of coming in from the outside to stir up trouble and even to foment violence.

From the jail, King wrote a letter of reply to their charges. The letter, reprinted in the following pages, stands as an explanation and a vindication of nonviolent direct action as well as a repudiation of the charge that organized civil rights workers coming into the South fell into the category of "outside agitators." This document, perhaps more than any other from the period, catches the flavor of the nonviolent movement that brought such significant changes in the patterns of social interaction in many towns and cities of the South.

My Dear Fellow Clergymen:

While confined here in the Birmingham city jail, I came across your recent statement calling my present activities "unwise and untimely." Seldom do I pause to answer criticism of my work and ideas. If I sought to answer all the criticisms that cross my desk, my secretaries would have little time for anything other than such correspondence in the course of the day, and I would have no time for constructive work. But since I feel that you are men of genuine good will and that your criticisms are sincerely set forth, I want to try to answer your statement in what I hope will be patient and reasonable terms.

I think I should indicate why I am here in Birmingham, since you have been influenced by the view which argues against "outsiders coming in." I have the honor of serving as president of the Southern Christian Leadership Conference, an organization operating in every southern state, with headquarters in Atlanta, Georgia. We have some eighty-five affiliated organizations across the South, and one of them is the Alabama Christian Movement for Human Rights. Frequently we share staff, educational and financial resources with our affiliates. Several months ago the affiliate here in Birmingham asked us to be on call to engage in a nonviolent direct-action program if such were deemed necessary. We readily consented, and when the hour came we lived up to our promise. So I, along with several members of my staff, am here because I was invited here. I am here because I have organizational ties here.

But more basically, I am in Birmingham because injustice is here. Just as the prophets of the eighth century B.C. left their villages and carried their "thus saith the Lord" far beyond the boundaries of their home towns, and just as the Apostle Paul left his village of Tarsus and carried the gospel of Jesus Christ to the far corners of the Greco-Roman world, so am I compelled to carry the gospel of freedom beyond my own home town. Like Paul, I must constantly respond to the Macedonian call for aid.

Moreover, I am cognizant of the interrelatedness of all communities and states. I cannot sit idly by in Atlanta and not be concerned about what happens in Birmingham. Injustice anywhere is a threat to justice everywhere. We are caught in an inescapable network of mutuality, tied in a single garment of destiny. Whatever affects one directly, affects all indirectly. Never again can we afford to live with the narrow, provincial "outside agitator" idea. Anyone who lives inside the United States can never be considered an outsider anywhere within its bounds.

You deplore the demonstrations taking place in Birmingham. But your statement, I am sorry to say, fails to express a similar concern for the conditions that brought about the demonstrations. I am sure that none of you would want to rest content with the superficial kind of social analysis that deals merely with effects and does not grapple with underlying causes. It is unfortunate that demonstrations are taking place in Birmingham, but it is even more unfortunate that the city's white power structure left the Negro community with no alternative.

In any nonviolent campaign there are four basic steps: collection of the facts to determine whether injustices exist; negotiation; self-purification; and direct action. We have gone through all these steps in Birmingham. There can be no gainsaying the fact that racial injustice engulfs this community. Birmingham is probably the most thoroughly segregated city in the United States. Its ugly record of brutality is widely known. Negroes have experienced grossly unjust treatment in the courts. There have been more unsolved bombings of Negro homes and churches in Birmingham than in any other city in the nation. These are the hard, brutal facts of the case. On the basis of these conditions, Negro leaders sought to negotiate with the city fathers. But the latter consistently refused to engage in good-faith negotiation.

Then, last September, came the opportunity to talk with leaders of Birmingham's economic community. In the course of the negotiations, certain promises were made by the merchants—for example, to remove the stores' humiliating racial signs. On the basis of these promises, the Reverend Fred Shuttlesworth and the leaders of the Alabama Christian Movement for Human Rights agreed to a moratorium on all demonstrations. As the weeks and months went by, we realized that we were the victims of a broken promise. A few signs, briefly removed, returned; the others remained.

As in so many past experiences, our hopes had been blasted, and the shadow of deep disappointment settled upon us. We had no alternative except to prepare for direct action, whereby we would present our very bodies as a means of laying our case before the conscience of the local and the national community. Mindful of the difficulties involved, we decided to undertake a process of self-purification. We began a series of workshops on nonviolence, and we repeatedly asked ourselves: "Are you able to accept blows without retaliating?" "Are you able to endure the ordeal of jail?" We decided to schedule our direct-action program for the Easter season, realizing that except for Christmas, this is the main shopping period of the year. Knowing that a strong economic-withdrawal program would be the by-product of direct action, we felt that this would be the best time to bring pressure to bear on the merchants for the needed change.

Then it occurred to us that Birmingham's mayoralty election was coming up in March, and we speedily decided to postpone action until after election day. When we discovered that the Commissioner of Public Safety, Eugene "Bull" Connor, had piled up enough votes to be in the run-off, we decided again to postpone action until the day after the run-off so that the demonstrations could not be used to cloud the issues. Like many others, we waited to see Mr. Connor defeated, and to this end we endured postponement after postponement. Having aided in this community need, we felt that our direct-action program could be delayed no longer.

You may well ask: "Why direct action? Why sit-ins, marches and so forth? Isn't negotiation a better path?" You are quite right in calling for negotiation. Indeed, this is the very purpose of direct action. Nonviolent direct action seeks to create such a crisis and foster such a tension that a community which has constantly refused to negotiate is forced to confront the issue. It seeks so to dramatize the issue that it can no longer be ignored. My citing the creation of tension as part of the work of the nonviolent-resister may sound rather shocking. But I must confess that I am not afraid of the word "tension." I have earnestly opposed violent tension, but there is a type of constructive, nonviolent tension which is necessary for growth. Just as Socrates felt that it was necessary to create a tension in the mind so that individuals could rise from the bondage of myths and half-truths to the unfettered realm of creative analysis and objective appraisal, so must we see the need for nonviolent gadflies to create the kind of tension in society that will help men rise from the dark depths of prejudice and racism to the majestic heights of understanding and brotherhood.

The purpose of our direct-action program is to create a situation so crisis-packed that it will inevitably open the door to negotiation. I therefore concur with you in your call for negotiation. Too long has our beloved Southland been bogged down in a tragic effort to live in monologue rather than dialogue.

One of the basic points in your statement is that the action that I and my associates have taken in Birmingham is untimely. Some have asked: "Why didn't you give the new city administration time to act?" The only answer that I can give to this query is that the new Birmingham administration must be prodded about as much as the outgoing one, before it will act. We are sadly mistaken if we feel that the election of Albert Boutwell as mayor will bring the millennium to Birmingham. While Mr. Boutwell is a much more gentle person than Mr. Connor, they are both segregationists, dedicated to maintenance of the status quo. I have hope that Mr. Boutwell will be reasonable enough to see the futility of massive resistance to desegregation. But he will not see this without pressure from devotees of civil rights. My friends, I must say to you that we have not made a single gain in civil rights without determined legal and nonviolent pressure. Lamentably, it is an historical fact that privileged groups seldom give up their privileges voluntarily. Individuals may see the moral light and voluntarily give up their unjust posture; but, as Reinhold Niebuhr has reminded us, groups tend to be more immoral than individuals.

We know through painful experience that freedom is never voluntarily given by the oppressor; it must be demanded by the oppressed. Frankly, I have yet to engage in a direct-action campaign that was "well timed" in the view of those who have not suffered unduly from the disease of segregation. For years now I have heard the word "Wait!" It rings in the ear of every Negro with piercing familiarity. This "Wait" has almost always meant "Never." We must come to see, with one of our distinguished jurists, that "justice too long delayed is justice denied."

We have waited for more than 340 years for our constitutional and God-given rights. The nations of Asia and Africa are moving with jetlike speed toward gaining political independence, but we still creep at horse-and-buggy pace toward gaining a cup of coffee at a lunch counter. Perhaps it is easy for those who have never felt the stinging darts of segregation to say, "Wait." But when you have seen vicious mobs lynch your mothers and fathers at will and drown your sisters and brothers at whim; when you have seen hate-filled policemen curse, kick and even kill your black brothers and sisters; when you see the vast majority of your twenty million Negro brothers smothering in an airtight cage of poverty in the midst of an affluent society; when you suddenly find your tongue twisted and your speech stammering as you seek to explain to your six-year-old daughter why she can't go to the public amusement park that has just been advertised on television, and see tears welling up in her eyes when she is told that Funtown is closed to colored children, and see ominous clouds of inferiority beginning to form in her little mental sky, and see her beginning to distort her personality by developing an unconscious bitterness toward white people; when you have to concoct an answer for a five-year-old son who is asking: "Daddy, why do white people treat colored people so mean?"; when you take a cross-country drive and find it necessary to sleep night after night in the uncomfortable corners of your automobile because no motel will accept you; when you are humiliated day in and day out by nagging signs reading "white" and "colored"; when your first name becomes "nigger," your middle name becomes "boy" (however old you are) and your last name becomes "John," and your wife and mother are never given the respected title "Mrs."; when you are harried by day and haunted by night by the fact that you are a Negro, living constantly at tiptoe stance, never quite knowing what to expect next, and are plagued with inner fears and outer resentments; when you are forever fighting a degenerating sense of "nobodiness"—then you will understand why we find it difficult to wait. There comes a time when the cup of endurance runs over, and men are no longer willing to be plunged into the abyss of despair. I hope, sirs, you can understand our legitimate and unavoidable impatience.

You express a great deal of anxiety over our willingness to break laws. This is certainly a legitimate concern. Since we so diligently urge people to obey the Supreme Court's decision of 1954 outlawing segregation in the public schools, at first glance it may seem rather paradoxical for us consciously to break laws. One may well ask: "How can you advocate breaking some laws and obeying others?" The answer lies in the fact that there are two types of laws: just and unjust. I would be the first to advocate obeying just laws. One has not only a legal but a moral responsibility to obey just laws. Conversely, one has a moral responsibility to disobey unjust laws. I would agree with St. Augustine that "an unjust law is no law at all."

Now, what is the difference between the two? How does one determine whether a law is just or unjust? A just law is a man-made code that squares with the moral law or the law of God. An unjust law is a code that is out of harmony with the moral law. To put it in the terms of St. Thomas Aquinas: An unjust law is a human law that is not rooted in eternal law and natural law. Any law that uplifts human personality is just. Any law that degrades human personality is unjust. All segregation statutes are unjust because segregation distorts the soul and damages the personality. It gives the segregator a false sense of superiority and the segregated a false sense of inferiority. Segregation, to use the terminology of the Jewish philosopher Martin Buber, substitutes an "I-it" relationship for an "I-thou" relationship and ends up relegating persons to the status of things. Hence segregation is not only politically, economically and sociologically unsound, it is morally wrong and sinful. Paul Tillich has said that sin is separation. Is not segregation an existential expression of man's tragic separation, his awful estrangement, his terrible sinfulness? Thus it is that I can urge men to obey the 1954 decision of the Supreme Court, for it is morally right; and I can urge them to disobey segregation ordinances, for they are morally wrong.

Let us consider a more concrete example of just and unjust laws. An unjust law is a code that a numerical or power majority group compels a minority group to obey but does not make binding on itself. This is *difference* made legal. By the same token, a just law is a code that a majority compels a minority to follow and that it is willing to follow itself. This is *sameness* made legal.

Let me give another explanation. A law is unjust if it is inflicted on a minority that, as a result of being denied the right to vote, had no part in enacting or devising the law. Who can say that the legislature of Alabama which set up that state's segregation laws was democratically elected? Throughout Alabama all sorts of devious methods are used to prevent Negroes from becoming registered voters, and there are some counties in which, even though Negroes constitute a majority of the population, not a single Negro is registered. Can any law enacted under such circumstances be considered democratically structured?

Sometimes a law is just on its face and unjust in its application. For instance, I have been arrested on a charge of parading without a permit. Now, there is nothing wrong in having an ordinance which requires a permit for a parade. But such an ordinance becomes unjust when it is used to maintain segregation and to deny citizens the First-Amendment privilege of peaceful assembly and protest.

I hope you are able to see the distinction I am trying to point out. In no sense do I advocate evading or defying the law, as would the rabid segregationist. That would lead to anarchy. One who breaks an unjust law must do so openly, lovingly, and with a willingness to accept the penalty. I submit that an individual who breaks a law that conscience tells him is unjust, and who willingly accepts the penalty of imprisonment in order to arouse the conscience of the community over its injustice, is in reality expressing the highest respect for law.

Of course, there is nothing new about this kind of civil disobedience. It was evidenced sublimely in the refusal of Shadrach, Meshach and Abednego to obey the laws of Nebuchadnezzar, on the ground that a higher moral law was at stake. It was practiced superbly by the early Christians, who were willing to face hungry lions and the excruciating pain of chopping blocks rather than submit to certain unjust laws of the Roman Empire. To a degree, academic freedom is a reality today because Socrates practiced civil disobedience. In our own nation, the Boston Tea Party represented a massive act of civil disobedience.

We should never forget that everything Adolf Hitler did in Germany was "legal" and everything the Hungarian freedom fighters did in Hungary was "illegal." It was "illegal" to aid and comfort a Jew in Hitler's Germany. Even so, I am sure that, had I lived in Germany at the time, I would have aided and comforted my Jewish brothers. If today I lived in a Communist country where certain principles dear to the Christian faith are suppressed, I would openly advocate disobeying that country's antireligious laws.

I must make two honest confessions to you, my Christian and Jewish brothers. First, I must confess that over the past few years I have been gravely disappointed with the white moderate. I have almost reached the regrettable conclusion that the Negro's great stumbling block in his stride toward freedom is not the White Citizen's Counciler or the Ku Klux Klanner, but the white moderate, who is more devoted to "order" than to justice; who prefers a negative peace which is the absence of tension to a positive peace which is the presence of justice; who constantly says: "I agree with you in the goal you seek, but I cannot agree with your methods of direct action"; who paternalistically believes he can set the timetable for another man's freedom; who lives by a mythical concept of time and who constantly advises the Negro to wait for a "more convenient season." Shallow understanding from people of good will is more frustrating than absolute misunderstanding from people of ill will. Lukewarm acceptance is much more bewildering than outright rejection.

I had hoped that the white moderate would understand that law and order exist for the purpose of establishing justice and that when they fail in this purpose they become the dangerously structured dams that block the flow of social progress. I had hoped that the white moderate would understand that the present tension in the South is a necessary phase of the transition from an obnoxious negative peace, in which the Negro passively accepted his unjust plight, to a substantive and positive peace, in which all men will respect the dignity and worth of human personality. Actually, we who engage in nonviolent direct action are not the creators of tension. We merely bring to the surface the hidden tension that is already alive. We bring it out in the open, where it can be seen and dealt with. Like a boil that can never be cured so long as it is covered up but must be opened with all its ugliness to the natural medicines of air and light, injustice must be exposed, with all the tension its exposure creates, to the light of human conscience and the air of national opinion before it can be cured.

In your statement you assert that our actions, even though peaceful, must be condemned because they precipitate violence. But is this a logical assertion? Isn't this like condemning a robbed man because his possession of money precipitated the evil act of robbery? Isn't this like condemning Socrates because his unswerving commitment to truth and his philosophical inquiries precipitated the act by the misguided populace in which they made him drink hemlock? Isn't this like condemning Jesus because his unique God-consciousness and never-ceasing devotion to God's will precipitated the evil act of crucifixion? We must come to see that, as the federal courts have consistently affirmed, it is wrong to urge an individual to cease his efforts to gain his basic constitutional rights because the quest may precipitate violence. Society must protect the robbed and punish the robber.

I had also hoped that the white moderate would reject the myth concerning time in relation to the struggle for freedom. I have just received a letter from a white brother in Texas. He writes: "All Christians know that the colored people will receive equal rights eventually, but it is possible that you are in too great a religious hurry. It has taken Christianity almost two thousand years to accomplish what it has. The teachings of Christ take time to come to earth." Such an attitude stems from a tragic misconception of time, from the strangely irrational notion that there is something in the very flow of time that will inevitably cure all ills. Actually, time itself is neutral; it can be used either destructively or constructively. More and more I feel that the people of ill will have used time much more effectively than have the people of good will. We will have to repent in this generation not merely for the hateful words and actions of the bad people but for the appalling silence of the good people. Human progress never rolls in on wheels of inevitability; it comes through the tireless efforts of men willing to be co-workers with God, and without this hard work, time itself becomes an ally of the forces of social stagnation. We must use time creatively, in the knowledge that the time is always ripe to do right. Now is the time to make real the promise of democracy and transform our pending national elegy into a creative psalm of brotherhood. Now is the time to lift our national policy from the quicksand of racial injustice to the solid rock of human dignity.

You speak of our activity in Birmingham as extreme. At first I was rather disappointed that fellow clergymen would see my nonviolent efforts as those of an extremist. I began thinking about the fact that I stand in the middle of two opposing forces in the Negro community. One is a force of complacency, made up in part of Negroes who, as a result of long years of oppression, are so drained of self-respect and a sense of "somebodiness" that they have adjusted to segregation; and in part of a few middle-class Negroes who, because of a degree of academic and economic security and because in some ways they profit by segregation, have become insensitive to the problems of the masses. The other force is one of bitterness and hatred, and it comes perilously close to advocating violence. It is expressed in the various black nationalist groups that are springing up across the nation, the largest and best-known being Elijah Muhammad's Muslim movement. Nourished by the Negro's frustration over the continued existence of racial discrimination, this movement is made up of people who have lost faith in America, who have absolutely repudiated Christianity, and who have concluded that the white man is an incorrigible "devil."

I have tried to stand between these two forces, saying that we need emulate neither the "do-nothingism" of the complacent nor the hatred and despair of the black nationalist. For there is the more excellent way of love and nonviolent protest. I am grateful to God that, through the influence of the Negro church, the way of nonviolence became an integral part of our struggle.

If this philosophy had not emerged, by now many streets of the South would, I am convinced, be flowing with blood. And I am further convinced that if our white brothers dismiss as "rabble-rousers" and "outside agitators" those of us who employ nonviolent direct action, and if they refuse to support our nonviolent efforts, millions of Negroes will, out of frustration and despair, seek solace and security in black-nationalist ideologies—a development that would inevitably lead to a frightening racial nightmare.

Oppressed people cannot remain oppressed forever. The yearning for freedom eventually manifests itself, and that is what has happened to the American Negro. Something within has reminded him of his birthright of freedom, and something without has reminded him that it can be gained. Consciously or unconsciously, he has been caught up by the *Zeitgeist,* and with his black brothers of Africa and his brown and yellow brothers of Asia, South America and the Caribbean, the United States Negro is moving with a sense of great urgency toward the promised land of racial justice. If one recognizes this vital urge that has engulfed the Negro community, one should readily understand why public demonstrations are taking place. The Negro has many pent-up resentments and latent frustrations, and he must release them. So let him march; let him make prayer pilgrimages to the city hall; let him go on freedom rides—and try to understand why he must do so. If his repressed emotions are not released in nonviolent ways, they will seek expression through violence; this is not a threat but a fact of history. So I have not said to my people: "Get rid of your discontent." Rather, I have tried to say that this normal and healthy discontent can be channeled into the creative outlet of nonviolent direct action. And now this approach is being termed extremist.

But though I was initially disappointed at being categorized as an extremist, as I continued to think about the matter I gradually gained a measure of satisfaction from the label. Was not Jesus an extremist for love: "Love your enemies, bless them that curse you, do good to them that hate you, and pray for them which despitefully use you, and persecute you." Was not Amos an extremist for justice: "Let justice roll down like waters and righteousness like an ever-flowing stream." Was not Paul an extremist for the Christian gospel: "I bear in my body the marks of the Lord Jesus." Was not Martin Luther an extremist: "Here I stand; I cannot do otherwise, so help me God." And John Bunyan: "I will stay in jail to the end of my days before I make a butchery of my conscience." And Abraham Lincoln: "This nation cannot survive half slave and half free." And Thomas Jefferson: "We hold these truths to be self-evident, that all men are created equal . . ." So the question is not whether we will be extremists, but what kind of extremists we will be. Will we be extremists for hate or for love? Will we be extremists for the preservation of injustice or for the extension of justice? In that dramatic scene on Calvary's hill three men were crucified. We must never forget that all three were crucified for the same crime—the crime of extremism. Two were extremists for immorality, and thus fell below their environment. The other, Jesus Christ, was an extremist for love, truth and goodness, and thereby rose above his environment. Perhaps the South, the nation and the world are in dire need of creative extremists.

I had hoped that the white moderate would see this need. Perhaps I was too optimistic; perhaps I expected too much. I suppose I should have realized that few members of the oppressor race can understand the deep groans and passionate yearnings of the oppressed race, and still fewer have the vision to see that injustice must be rooted out by strong, persistent and determined action. I am thankful, however, that some of our white brothers in the South have grasped the meaning of this social revolution and committed themselves to it. They are still all too few in quantity, but they are big in quality. Some—such as Ralph McGill, Lillian Smith, Harry Golden, James McBride Dabbs, Ann Braden and Sarah Patton Boyle—have written about our struggle in eloquent and prophetic terms. Others have marched with us down nameless streets of the South. They have languished in filthy, roach-infested jails, suffering the abuse and brutality of policemen who view them as "dirty nigger-lovers." Unlike so many of their moderate brothers and sisters, they have recognized the urgency of the moment and sensed the need for powerful "action" antidotes to combat the disease of segregation.

Let me take note of my other major disappointment. I have been so greatly disappointed with the white church and its leadership. Of course, there are some notable exceptions. I am not unmindful of the fact that each of you has taken some significant stands on this issue. I commend you, Reverend Stallings, for your Christian stand on this past Sunday, in welcoming Negroes to your worship service on a nonsegregated basis. I commend the Catholic leaders of this state for integrating Spring Hill College several years ago.

But despite these notable exceptions, I must honestly reiterate that I have been disappointed with the church. I do not say this as one of those negative critics who can always find something wrong with the church. I say this as a minister of the gospel, who loves the church; who was nurtured in its bosom; who has been sustained by its spiritual blessings and who will remain true to it as long as the cord of life shall lengthen.

When I was suddenly catapulted into the leadership of the bus protest in Montgomery, Alabama, a few years ago, I felt we would be supported by the white church. I felt that the white ministers, priests and rabbis of the South would be among our strongest allies. Instead, some have been outright opponents, refusing to understand the freedom movement and misrepresenting its leaders; all too many others have been more cautious than courageous and have remained silent behind the anesthetizing security of stained-glass windows.

In spite of my shattered dreams, I came to Birmingham with the hope that the white religious leadership of this community would see the justice of our cause and, with deep moral concern, would serve as the channel through which our just grievances could reach the power structure. I had hoped that each of you would understand. But again I have been disappointed.

I have heard numerous southern religious leaders admonish their worshipers to comply with a desegregation decision because it is the law, but I have longed to hear white ministers declare: "Follow this decree because integration is morally right and because the Negro is your brother." In the midst of blatant injustices inflicted upon the Negro, I have watched white churchmen stand on the sideline and mouth pious irrelevancies and sanctimonious trivialities. In the midst of a mighty struggle to rid our nation of racial and economic injustice, I have heard many ministers say: "Those are social issues, with which the gospel has no real concern." And I have watched many churches commit themselves to a completely otherworldly religion which makes a strange, un-Biblical distinction between body and soul, between the sacred and the secular.

I have traveled the length and breadth of Alabama, Mississippi and all the other southern states. On sweltering summer days and crisp autumn mornings I have looked at the South's beautiful churches with their lofty spires pointing heavenward. I have beheld the impressive outlines of her massive religious-education buildings. Over and over I have found myself asking: "What kind of people worship here? Who is their God? Where were their voices when the lips of Governor Barnett dripped with words of interposition and nullification? Where were they when Governor Wallace gave a clarion call for defiance and hatred? Where were their voices of support when bruised and weary Negro men and women decided to rise from the dark dungeons of complacency to the bright hills of creative protest?"

Yes, these questions are still in my mind. In deep disappointment I have wept over the laxity of the church. But be assured that my tears have been tears of love. There can be no deep disappointment where there is not deep love. Yes, I love the church. How could I do otherwise? I am in the rather unique position of being the son, the grandson and the great-grandson of preachers. Yes, I see the church as the body of Christ. But, oh! How we have blemished and scarred that body through social neglect and through fear of being nonconformists.

There was a time when the church was very powerful—in the time when the early Christians rejoiced at being deemed worthy to suffer for what they believed. In those days the church was not merely a thermometer that recorded the ideas and principles of popular opinion; it was a thermostat that transformed the mores of society. Whenever the early Christians entered a town, the people in power became disturbed and immediately sought to convict the Christians for being "disturbers of the peace" and "outside agitators." But the Christians pressed on, in the conviction that they were "a colony of heaven," called to obey God rather than man. Small in number, they were big in commitment. They were too God-intoxicated to be "astronomically intimidated." By their effort and example they brought an end to such ancient evils as infanticide and gladiatorial contests.

Things are different now. So often the contemporary church is a weak, ineffecual voice with an uncertain sound. So often it is an archdefender of the status quo. Far from being disturbed by the presence of the church, the power structure of the average community is consoled by the church's silent—and often even vocal—sanction of things as they are.

But the judgment of God is upon the church as never before. If today's church does not recapture the sacrificial spirit of the early church, it will lose its authenticity, forfeit the loyalty of millions, and be dismissed as an irrelevant social club with no meaning for the twentieth century. Every day I meet young people whose disappointment with the church has turned into outright disgust.

Perhaps I have once again been too optimistic. Is organized religion too inextricably bound to the status quo to save our nation and the world? Perhaps I must turn my faith to the inner spiritual church, the church within the church, as the true *ekklesia* and the hope of the world. But again I am thankful to God that some noble souls from the ranks of organized religion have broken loose from the paralyzing chains of conformity and joined us as active partners in the struggle for freedom. They have left their secure congregations and walked the streets of Albany, Georgia, with us. They have gone down the highways of the South on tortuous rides for freedom. Yes, they have gone to jail with us. Some have been dismissed from their churches, have lost the support of their bishops and fellow ministers. But they have acted in the faith that right defeated is stronger than evil triumphant. Their witness has been the spiritual salt that has preserved the true meaning of the gospel in these troubled times. They have carved a tunnel of hope through the dark mountain of disappointment.

I hope the church as a whole will meet the challenge of this decisive hour. But even if the church does not come to the aid of justice, I have no despair about the future. I have no fear about the outcome of our struggle in Birmingham, even if our motives are at present misunderstood. We will reach the goal of freedom in Birmingham and all over the nation, because the goal of America is freedom. Abused and scorned though we may be, our destiny is tied up with America's destiny. Before the pilgrims landed at Plymouth, we were here. Before the pen of Jefferson etched the majestic words of the Declaration of Independence across the pages of history, we were here. For more than two centuries our forebears labored in this country without wages; they made cotton king; they built the homes of their masters while suffering gross injustice and shameful humiliation—and yet out of a bottomless vitality they continued to thrive and develop. If the inexpressible cruelties of slavery could not stop us, the opposition we now face will surely fail. We will win our freedom because the sacred heritage of our nation and the eternal will of God are embodied in our echoing demands.

Before closing I feel impelled to mention one other point in your statement that has troubled me profoundly. You warmly commended the Birmingham police force for keeping "order" and "preventing violence." I doubt that you would have so warmly commended the police force if you had seen its dogs sinking their teeth into unarmed, nonviolent Negroes. I doubt that you would so quickly commend the policemen if you were to observe their ugly and inhumane treatment of Negroes here in the city jail; if you were to watch them push and curse old Negro women and young Negro girls; if you were to see them slap and kick old Negro men and young boys; if you were to observe them, as they did on two occasions, refuse to give us food because we wanted to sing our grace together. I cannot join you in your praise of the Birmingham police department.

It is true that the police have exercised a degree of discipline in handling the demonstrators. In this sense they have conducted themselves rather "nonviolently" in public. But for what purpose? To preserve the evil system of segregation. Over the past few years I have consistently preached that nonviolence demands that the means we use must be as pure as the ends we seek. I have tried to make clear that it is wrong to use immoral means to attain moral ends. But now I must affirm that it is just as wrong, or perhaps even more so, to use moral means to preserve immoral ends. Perhaps Mr. Connor and his policemen have been rather nonviolent in public, as was Chief Pritchett in Albany, Georgia, but they have used the moral means of nonviolence to maintain the immoral end of racial injustice. As T. S. Eliot has said: "The last temptation is the greatest treason: To do the right deed for the wrong reason."

I wish you had commended the Negro sit-inners and demonstrators of Birmingham for their sublime courage, their willingness to suffer and their amazing discipline in the midst of great provocation. One day the South will recognize its real heroes. They will be the James Merediths, with the noble sense of purpose that enables them to face jeering and hostile mobs, and with the agonizing loneliness that characterizes the life of the pioneer. They will be old, oppressed, battered Negro women, symbolized in a seventy-two-year-old woman in Montgomery, Alabama, who rose up with a sense of dignity and with her people decided not to ride segregated buses, and who responded with ungrammatical profundity to one who inquired about her weariness: "My feets is tired, but my soul is at rest." They will be the young high school and college students, the young ministers of the gospel and a host of their elders, courageously and nonviolently sitting in at lunch counters and willingly going to jail for conscience' sake. One day the South will know that when these disinherited children of God sat down at lunch counters, they were in reality standing up for what is best in the American dream and for the most sacred values in our Judaeo-Christian heritage, thereby bringing our nation back to those great wells of democracy which were dug deep by the founding fathers in their formulation of the Constitution and the Declaration of Independence.

Never before have I written so long a letter. I'm afraid it is much too long to take your precious time. I can assure you that it would have been much shorter if I had been writing from a comfortable desk, but what else can one do when he is alone in a narrow jail cell, other than write long letters, think long thoughts and pray long prayers?

If I have said anything in this letter that overstates the truth and indicates an unreasonable impatience, I beg you to forgive me. If I have said anything that understates the truth and indicates my having a patience that allows me to settle for anything less than brotherhood, I beg God to forgive me.

I hope this letter finds you strong in the faith. I also hope that circumstances will soon make it possible for me to meet each of you, not as an integrationist or a civil-rights leader but as a fellow clergyman and a Christian brother. Let us all hope that the dark clouds of racial prejudice will soon pass away and the deep fog of misunderstanding will be lifted from our fear-drenched communities, and in some not too distant tomorrow the radiant stars of love and brotherhood will shine over our great nation with all their scintillating beauty.

Yours for the cause of Peace and Brotherhood,
MARTIN LUTHER KING, JR.

JAIL, NOT BAIL

Thomas Gaither   /   Jailed-In

Early in 1961, SNCC recommended that in order to draw more attention to the segregation laws in Southern communities, demonstrators refuse bail and serve jail sentences in case of arrest. The campaign, marked by the slogan "Jail, Not Bail," began in

Rock Hill, South Carolina, on February 1, 1961, the anniversary of the first student sit-in. Along with Thomas Gaither, a field secretary of CORE, several members of SNCC were arrested and sentenced to the road gang. Before the month was over, eighty students from black colleges were serving jail sentences for their participation in the sit-ins.

Gaither wrote the following account of the Rock Hill episode, in which he explains the role played by CORE in many of the student sit-ins. The rude treatment the students received from legal authorities served initially to give solidarity and purpose to the movement for nonviolent action. But it was clear to some even then that there would come a time when the students would have enough of official violence and jail and the freedom movement would take a new turn.

E ight Friendship Junior College students and I served 30 days on the York County road gang for the "crime" of sitting-in at McCrory's lunch counter in Rock Hill, South Carolina. While hundreds of students have been jailed since the start of the sit-in movement, we were the first to be committed to a road gang, which is the present-day version of the dreaded southern chain gang.

We could have paid $100 fines, or we could have posted $200 bail each and gone out pending appeal. Instead, we chose to be jailed-in. All nine of us felt that this would strengthen the impact of our protest. Furthermore, instead of the city being $900 richer for the injustice it had committed, it would have to pay the expense of boarding and feeding us for 30 days.

WHAT HAPPENED BEFORE

The story behind our case opens on Lincoln's Birthday, 1960. This was the date of the first sit-ins at Rock Hill, which were also the first in the state of South Carolina. Immediately following the original sit-in at Greensboro, North Carolina, on February 1, students at Friendship Junior College in Rock Hill expressed interest in joining the south-wide protest movement. Under the very able leadership of Abe Plummer and Arthur Hamm, they sought advice from Rev. C. A. Ivory and other local civil rights leaders. CORE Field Secretary James T. McCain, who has worked for civil rights in South Carolina for most of his life, was dispatched to Rock Hill to help train the students in sit-ins and other nonviolent techniques. A Student Civic Committee was established for the purpose of planning and coordination. By Lincoln's Birthday, preparations for the first sit-in were complete.

On that date groups of students entered the Woolworth and McCrory

---

FROM Thomas Gaither, *Jailed-In* (New York, 1961). Reprinted by permission of the publisher, the League for Industrial Democracy, and of the Congress of Racial Equality.

stores and sat down at the lunch counters. A gang of whites rapidly gathered, some of them armed with homemade ammonia bombs, which were hurled at the sit-inners. A counterman kept wiping the surfaces with an ammonia-soaked rag. The students remained quietly in their seats.

Violence by whites continued in the days that ensued. Negro adults, who were not involved in sit-ins in any way, were assaulted on the streets. Rev. Ivory received repeated threatening phone calls.

On March 15, Friendship Junior College students joined a mass protest demonstration in Orangeburg in which 350 were arrested and herded into an open-air stockade. Being a student at Claflin College, I was among those jailed on that day. It was on this occasion that Governor Hollings asserted that no such demonstration would be tolerated, adding: *"They think they can violate any law, especially if they have a Bible in their hands."*

In Rock Hill, sit-ins and picketing continued throughout the school year. After the college students left for summer vacation, a number of high school students became involved. Arthur Hamm, one of the college student leaders, remained in town to give them direction. On June 7, Hamm was arrested while sitting-in at McCrory's. Arrested with him was Rev. Ivory, who had the courage to engage in this type of action even though he is crippled and confined to a wheelchair. The gross indignity of arresting a crippled minister in a wheelchair gave this incident nationwide publicity. Wheeling Rev. Ivory out the rear entrance and across the street to the jail, was an awkward task for Police Captain Honeysucker. Shaking-down the minister in his wheelchair for concealed weapons and taking him downstairs for fingerprinting also presented a problem. Finally, after going through all the procedures of being booked, Rev. Ivory was rolled into a cell where he stayed until his attorney got him out on bail. Hamm, too, was released. Next day he was back at his sit-ins and picketing with a group of high school students. Before the end of June, Hamm had to leave Rock Hill for a summer job with the American Friends Service Committee.

During July and August the campaign slowed down. But with September and the reopening of college, sit-ins were resumed. At about this same time, I went to work as a CORE field secretary and one of the first places to which I was dispatched was Rock Hill.

THE TOWN OF ROCK HILL

This textile manufacturing town of 33,000 people was not new to me. Both my father and mother had attended Friendship Junior College. As a child, I used to come into town often. I even recall visiting the McCrory and Woolworth stores, now the focal points of the struggle for lunch counter integration in Rock Hill. I never bought more than a bag of popcorn or some cashews but it occurred to me even then to wonder why we couldn't ever sit down and get something to eat at the counter. Of course, I didn't realize why.

By the time of the memorable Montgomery bus boycott, I was 17 and I well remember the sympathy action taken by Negroes in Rock Hill. Following the lead of Montgomery, they too decided to stop riding the buses until they were free to sit where they chose. Within a few months the bus company went out of business. The job of furnishing transportation for Negroes was undertaken by a special committee, initiated by Rev. Ivory. The committee eventually bought two buses, one of which is still running today.

As I walked up the street upon arrival in Rock Hill last fall, a little Negro boy suddenly rushed out in front of me. He was dirty, ragged and suffering from a severe cold. We got to talking. His mother is a domestic worker who in addition brings home wash. His father has worked for years in the bleachery. He has never been promoted and never will be. His wage scale is low: unions have somehow not been able to make inroads at Rock Hill. The total weekly income of both he and his wife is less than $45. I describe this family because it seems to me so typical of the Negro's lot in a town like Rock Hill.

It is a town of many churches, but the worship of God is on a strictly segregated basis. Rock Hill's first kneel-ins occurred only recently, on the Sunday of the big supporting demonstration on our behalf when we were on the road gang. The Negro kneel-inners were admitted at three of the white churches but barred at two others. Even the Christian so-called liberals in Rock Hill feel that Negroes should be satisfied with second class citizenship. One exception is the Catholic school in town, which desegregated without incident—and without any outcry from the segregationists. In addition to Friendship, the town has another small Negro church-run college, Clinton, and a state-operated white girls' college, Winthrop. The heads of the two Negro colleges were at first fairly neutral in regard to the local sit-ins. They did not come out in public support, but neither did they pressure students against participation, as was the case in Baton Rouge and in some other Negro college communities. However, as the situation developed, James Goudlock, president of Friendship College took a strong position in support of the sit-ins.

As for the public officials, they have been blatantly pro-segregation and opposed to any compromise. Rock Hill's mayor has flatly refused to set up a bi-racial committee of the type which has been established in some southern communities as an outcome of the student protests. Much of the ill-will evidenced by whites when the Rock Hill sit-ins started, was brought on by the segregationist agitation of local and state political leaders.

My familiarity with Rock Hill, coupled with my experience in the student movement in South Carolina, were factors in CORE's dispatching me there soon after I took the field secretary's job. Upon arrival, it didn't take me long to conclude that the most urgent need was for training student leaders. The Friendship students who had become involved in sit-ins and picketing at the start of the 1960–61 school year were mostly freshmen. I suggested that CORE hold an action workshop. This took place on the weekend of Dec. 9–11 at the college from which I had graduated the previous year: Claflin, in Orangeburg. One outcome was a full understanding by the students of the effectiveness of jail-ins, as opposed to accepting bail or paying fines. Immediately after the workshop a really intensified program of sit-ins and picketing got under way in Rock Hill.

As Robert McCullough, one of our jail-inners, later told the press regarding the month of January preceding our arrest: *"City officials pointed out that we had staged 19 demonstrations during January and suddenly we felt sort of ashamed of ourselves that we hadn't staged 31. After all, there are 31 days in January, so what had we been doing the other 12 days?"*

HOUR OF DECISION

The 26th day of January had been selected as the date for the sit-in, which inevitably would lead to the jail-in. Rev. Diggs, the college chaplain had suggested that the students involved should first register for the spring term to make sure of being able to return to classes following release from jail. To facilitate this the sit-in date was changed to the 31st. From Sumter, where I had been working with students at Morris College, I returned to Rock Hill on January 25.

On the 29th we held a meeting in an attempt to enroll more students in the action. Two members of the basketball team, Mack Workman and David "Scoop" Williamson signed up. The way some of the original members of our group felt was summarized by John Gaines when he said: *"I will go to jail and stay there, even if no one else does."*

Making a decision to go to jail for the first time was not easy. In some cases, it meant leaving a girl friend; in others, antagonizing parents who had little understanding of nonviolent action and much fear for their children's safety. There was also the danger that parents might be fired from their jobs as a result of their children's action.

On the night before the scheduled sit-in . . . in fact at about one in the morning . . . Clarence Graham, who had been considering the matter for some days, reached his final decision and got out of bed to write a letter of explanation to his mother and father.

"Try to understand that what I'm doing is right," the letter said. *"It isn't like going to jail for a crime like stealing or killing, but we are going for the betterment of all Negroes."*

Came January 31, the nine of us committed to be jailed-in and one who was to come out on appeal as a legal test, assembled in the college lounge. Willie McCleod was prepared to the extent of carrying his toothbrush in his pocket. Surprised to see Willy Massey, a student with a goatee and dressed like a typical cool cat, I asked why he had come to the meeting. *"Man, I'm going to jail!"* was his reply. An atmosphere of parting sorrow filled the room. Girlfriends were there to say goodbye and, in some cases, to ask their boyfriends to reconsider.

At the end of the meeting we headed uptown for McCrory's and Woolworth's. Woolworth's lunch counter had been discontinued in the course of the month-long intensive campaign and had been replaced with a flower counter, but picketing continued. McCrory's lunch counter was still open. It closed down the day after our demonstration. As we walked uptown, some of us wondered whether any of our group would change his decision on the way and withdraw. None did.

As we approached the stores we were stopped briefly by Police Captain Honeysucker and an official of the South Carolina Law Enforcement Division, who advised us to return to the campus, and avoid *"getting in trouble."* Instead, we established picket lines at the two stores. Fifteen minutes later, our group entered McCrory's and took seats at the lunch counter.

ARREST AND TRIAL

The manager, who was perspiring and obviously jittery, told us *"We can't serve you here."* Hardly were the words out of his mouth when city and state police who were standing by roughly pushed us off our stools and hauled us out the back door onto a parking lot area and across the street to jail. We were first searched and then locked in cells. We started singing freedom songs and spirituals. An hour or so later we were joined by another Negro prisoner named NuNu, who had been picked up for being drunk. At 5:30 we were fed a piece of cold barbecued chicken and cold coffee without sugar. Then we received a visit from Rev. Ivory and Rev. Diggs. We slept on bare steel bunks, which bruised our bones but not our morale. At dawn we were awakened by a prisoner on the white side asking for a cigaret. He kept yelling and banging on the walls.

It was February 1 and, as I noted mentally, the first anniversary of the south-wide sit-in movement. We were taken into the courtroom for trial. The charge was trespassing.

On direct examination, Lieutenant Thomas admitted that he had given us only between 3 and 15 *seconds* to leave the store. However, he changed this to between 3 and 15 *minutes* when cross-examined by our attorney, Ernest A. Finney, Jr. So confused did the lieutenant become with his two stories, that he requested and obtained permission to rest a little before proceeding. Finally, even Judge Billy Hayes stated that according to the evidence, we had not been given sufficient time to leave the store, even if we had wanted to take the opportunity of doing so. Police Captain Honeysucker, who was seated to the judge's right, looked dejected. An atmosphere of indecision prevailed. Were we finally going to win a legal case in a lower court in the deep south? We were called upon to enter our pleas. We pleaded not guilty. Hardly were the words out of our mouths, when the judge pronounced us guilty and sentenced us to 30 days hard labor on the road gang or $100 fines. Surprise and shock filled the courtroom when it became known that we had chosen to be jailed-in. The only thing they had to beat us over the head with was a threat of sending us to jail. So we disarmed them by using the only weapon we had left . . . jail without bail. It was the only practical thing we could do. It upset them considerably.

"YOU'RE ON THE CHAIN GANG NOW"

From the courtroom we were taken to the York County road gang stockade. We got there about four in the afternoon. It consisted of two large dormitories, one for whites the other for Negroes. It was like a barracks except for the bars and mesh-wire which made it unmistakably like a jail.

First, we were taken to the clothing room to get our prison clothes. In charge was Captain Dagler, who, as we learned later, was one of the toughest guards in the camp. *"Boy, cut that thing from under your chin and pull off that jitterbug hat,"* he said to Willy Massey. *"You're on the chain gang now!"* Meanwhile, "Scoop" Williamson was trying to scoop a pair of shoes out of the huge pile on the middle of the floor. He finally found a pair that fitted.

Inside the prison, our initial feeling was one of uncertainty. As we entered the Negro dormitory, we were met with curious stares from the other prisoners. Some already knew, via the grapevine, why we were there; others didn't.

"THE STUFF IS ON"

One prisoner commented *"The stuff is on, now!"* Others echoed the slogan. By the *"stuff"* they meant anti-Negro hatred. They explained that the *"stuff"* had been *"on"* only recently in the white dormitory, following the much-publicized marriage of the Negro singer-actor, Sammy Davis, Jr. and the white screen star, May Britt.

"If anybody bothers you, let us know; we can handle them," volunteered one of the prisoners in talking to James Wells. The latter explained that all in our group believe in nonviolence. Our would-be protector seemed surprised.

As it turned out, the Negro prisoners' fears regarding our effect on the white prisoners, proved unfounded. Most of us worked in integrated gangs (until after we were put in solitary) without incident. In fact, when we were in solitary, a white prisoner took the initiative of writing the FBI that he considered this unjust. Another white prisoner volunteered to assert that it was wrong to single-out Negro prisoners only—including us students—to go out on Lincoln's Birthday, a Sunday, and erect a barbed wire fence in anticipation of the crowds expected to visit us on that occasion. By the end of our stretch, some of the white prisoners would actually request us to sing one of the freedom hymns which we had sung at our morning devotional services.

The only *"stuff"* which did occur was a single incident in which a white prisoner serving life, upon coming in from work one day, started cursing at Clarence Graham and Robert McCullough and finally drew a knife on them. The two simply looked at him and walked on. When the Negro prisoners heard about it, some of them were ready to fight. Again, we had to try to explain our adherence to nonviolence.

"A PRISON—NOT A DAMNED SCHOOL"

As to the Negro prisoners, they held us in high esteem. We were called upon repeatedly to serve as final authorities in arguments. Our presence prompted frequent discussions of world problems. We conducted classes in English and Current Events.

But we were barred from keeping up with our studies. On our sixth day in jail, Captain Dagler ordered me to gather up all the college textbooks which the students had brought along and carry them up-front. He said that the books were being taken away from us because the prison did not want to be responsible for them. I assured him that each of us was willing to assume responsibility for his own books. He retorted that he was simply carrying out orders. I then inquired who had given the orders, to which he answered:

"Quit asking questions. This is a prison—not a damned school. If this was a school, we'd have teachers here."

Obviously, it was a prison. We got up at 5:30 in the morning, ate a breakfast of grits, fatback with flour gravy and black coffee. Then, we went out for the day's labor. On our first day, the temperature was 24°.

My first job was loading sand onto a truck. There was one white prisoner on my gang; the rest were Negroes. Among them was NuNu, who had been thrown into our cell at the city jail the day we were arrested. NuNu was always the center of attention. He had apparently been involved in numerous petty difficulties with the law.

The guards' attitudes toward us ranged from indifference to hostility. Captain Jim, the guard bossing my work gang, was a fat, jovial type who seemed to me surprisingly broad-minded. I discovered he had been raised among Negroes. He frequently recalled how, when he was a youth, he used to play baseball with Negro kids on Sundays and whenever there was spare time. He usually referred to Negroes as "darkies," not seeming to realize that the term is derogatory.

On February 7 we were joined by a student from Charlotte, North Carolina and one from Petersburg, Virginia. Along with two female students from Nashville and Atlanta, Diane Nash and Ruby Smith, they had sat-in at a Rock Hill lunch counter. Like us, all four had been sentenced to 30 days and had refused to pay fines. There being no road gang for women, the two girls were confined to the women's county jail.

With the addition of the two new students—Charles Jones and Charles

Sherrod—the jail-inners on our road gang totaled 11. Our original group included John Gaines, Clarence Graham, Willie McCleod, Robert McCullough, Willy Massey, James Wells, David Williamson, Mack Workman and myself.

SOLITARY

February 7 was memorable for us because we spent the entire morning in solitary confinement. The periodic shouting, cursing and other loud noises which emanated from the prisoners' quarters apparently did not bother the officials. However, for several days they had objected to our singing hymns at the morning devotional services which we had initiated.

One line that particularly irritated them was *"Before I'll be a slave, I'll be buried in my grave."* No sooner would we start to sing, than a guard would order us to *"cut out that damned fuss!"* Of course, we refused and simply kept on singing. When this happened on February 7, Captain Maloney, the prison superintendent, put us in solitary.

He accused us of *"trying to run the prison."* I tried to explain that we were simply exercising our right of religious freedom. He replied: *"If y'all are that religious, why ain't y'all preachers?"* I explained that two of us were actually studying for the ministry.

At this point, Charles Jones, as a goodwill gesture, stepped forward and presented the prison superintendent with a box of chocolates which he had received as a present. Maloney slammed it down on a table outside the solitary cell door and proceeded to lock us in.

We found ourselves in a 12-by-12 foot, dark room furnished with a commode, a small sink and one lone drinking cup. Obscuring the window was a metal sheet and steel bars. Lights went on at mealtimes only and meals consisted of bread and water.

But on this occasion we never got a chance to taste this sumptuous food. Shortly after noon, Captain Maloney unlocked our door and asked if we were ready to go back to work. He fully realized that we had no intention of ceasing our morning hymn-singing, but in order to save face, he did not raise the issue.

We were given a meal of beans, cornbread, milk and a peach, and were driven under heavy guard to the city dump, where the county maintains a topsoil pit. We eleven students were now on a separate work gang. It soon became clear that in putting us back to work, rather than keeping us in solitary, the prison officials' strategy was to *"work-the-hell"* out of us. By quitting time we had shoveled 14 loads of topsoil onto the 7-ton dump trucks. It was backbreaking work.

VISITING

The parents' difficulty at grasping what we were trying to accomplish did not deter them from coming to the camp on visiting days. I mentioned earlier how Clarence Graham, had been so worried about his parents' reactions, that he drafted an explanatory letter to them at 1 A.M. of the day we were to be arrested. Both his father and mother came to visit. So did John Gaines's 95-year-old great-grandmother, who is in a wheelchair. She brought $200 cash just in case John should want to change his mind and accept bail.

"*I don't think I ever got it explained completely to my great-grandmother,*" Gaines explained. "*She was afraid they'd work me too hard and that I couldn't stand it. She was still puzzled when I told her that it was a privilege for a Negro to go to jail for his rights.*"

Regarding his grandmother, who is a cook at the college, Gaines said: "*She told me I was disobedient when I said I had to go to jail. But once I got locked up, she was quite changed. She came to jail and asked me if I was all right or needed anything.*"

Gaines's grandmother's attitude was typical of many of the parents who came to visit. In addition to relatives, friends and supporters came from many parts of the country. This gave us great encouragement. On our first Sunday, a caravan of 60 cars and a bus brought more than 300 Negro and white visitors to the isolated road camp.

The following Sunday, Lincoln's Birthday, over 1,000 local citizens and students from other states participated in a pilgrimage to Rock Hill on behalf of our cause. It was early that morning that we were ordered to erect a barbed-wire fence around the compound. From the dormitory window, I could see an endless line of highway patrol cars. Some residents in the vicinity had posted their property in such a way that if Negroes should step on it, they could be accused of trespassing. A few white hoodlums speeded their cars up and down the road in an attempt at intimidation. But the pilgrimage was not deterred. Guards, posted between us and our visitors, started to take notes on what was being said. They failed to dampen our enthusiasm over this significant demonstration of support for our efforts. We were additionally encouraged to learn that since our arrest, the jail-ins had spread to Atlanta and Lynchburg bringing the total number of students involved—including us—to almost 100.

SPEED-UP

As the days went by, following our return to work from solitary, it became increasingly clear that we were the victims of a speed-up. Starting the second day, we were expected to load 36 trucks of topsoil, or double the workload of other prisoners. I was cited by the captain as an experienced chain gang man—possibly because I was the oldest in the group—and singled-out to lead the pace. In a kidding vein, Massey kept yelling at me to shovel faster. "*Come on Moses!*" he would say.

We decided to refuse to go along with the speedup. Two of our gang, Jones and Sherrod had gotten sick, the former with an injured shoulder muscle. On February 13 our work output decreased considerably. The following morning, the prison superintendent warned us that unless we worked faster we would be transferred to the state penitentiary. When we reached the topsoil pit, we found an additional truck had been dispatched for us to load. We worked at a moderate pace and after about an hour and a half, a group of prison officials arrived to inspect us. As they departed, John Gaines waved to them in a joking manner. His wave was misinterpreted as a threatening gesture, and Gaines was ordered into the officials' car.

The rest of us stopped work and planted our shovels in the topsoil. We started toward the officials to inquire where they were taking Gaines. They told us to resume work—or join Gaines. We chose the latter, as a move of solidarity. We were then loaded onto one of the dump trucks, and driven back to camp.

BACK INTO SOLITARY

Upon arrival at the stockade, we found ourselves back in solitary confinement for a second time. But before locking us in, a guard came and took Gaines away. Our attempts to inquire where he was being taken proved fruitless. Aware of what might happen to a lone Negro "agitator" in the hands of white southern prison guards, we feared for Gaines's safety. We decided to go on a hunger strike until we learned his whereabouts. This did not constitute too much of a sacrifice, since the only food in solitary was bread—three times a day. But it was at least some demonstration of our concern.

Furthermore it had an impact on the guards. They seemed quite disturbed at the end of the first day to discover there were 24 pieces of corn bread to be removed from our cell. Lying on the floor in this cramped space, with only our jackets on or under us—and with Mack Workman's snoring—we didn't get too much sleep during our first night in solitary. The lack of sleep added to the gnawing of the hunger strike on our stomachs made us feel miserable on the second day. Some of us had stomach aches; others felt as if our bellies had shrunk. Graham described it as "*a turbulent dispute between my backbone and my stomach.*" We kidded ourselves with graphic descriptions of our favorite things to eat.

In the course of the third day, we were finally told what had happened to Gaines. He had been transferred to the county jail and was unharmed. Upon learning this, we decided to end our hunger strike. The superintendent and the guards had become so worried over the hunger strike that when we resumed eating, they were happier than we were. They brought us seconds on everything. We were ordered back to work.

JAIL TERM ENDS—STRUGGLE GOES ON

The labor was not easy, but the speed-up plan described for us earlier was no longer in evidence. During our last few days on the road gang, we worked laying drainage pipes under rural roads. Prison officials were anxious to avoid any publicity or supporting demonstrations on the day of our release. Captain Dagler made this known to us on our final day, March 2. After only a half day's work, he took us back to the stockade. We were given lunch, ordered to change into our regular clothes and loaded aboard a caged truck. The prison superintendent and his assistant escorted us to the Rock Hill city limits.

There we were set free and walked in a group to the Friendship campus. Our 30 days on the road gang were over, but not our struggle to end lunch counter discrimination in Rock Hill.

As Clarence Graham expressed it at our first major press conference after getting out: "*If requesting first class citizenship in the south is to be regarded as a crime, then I will gladly go back to jail again.*"

One of our group, Willy Massey, *was* back in jail again less than two weeks later. He and four other students were arrested March 14 while picketing a drug store with a segregated lunch counter. Like our group, they refused to pay fines. The day before, two other members of our group —John Gaines and Robert McCullough—were assaulted on the picket line by white hoodlums. Gaines was clubbed unconscious and taken to York County hospital. Two hours later, he and McCullough resumed picketing accompanied with three others of our group—Clarence Graham, James Wells and me.

These students are determined to carry on the nonviolent action campaign until Rock Hill's lunch counters desegregate. Our jail-in has strengthened—not weakened—that determination. Unfortunately, I cannot stay with them. CORE field secretaries have to cover considerable territory and I will be dispatched elsewhere. For me, Rock Hill was my second jail-in. My first was in Miami, Florida, in August when seven of us at CORE's Interracial Action Institute remained 10 days in jail rather than accept bail. The Rock Hill experience has fortified my conviction in the effectiveness of jail-ins in cases of unjust arrests.

BLACK POLITICAL ACTION IN THE SOUTH

Life in Mississippi: An Interview with Fannie Lou Hamer

The Mississippi Freedom Democratic Party was organized in the spring of 1964 in order to provide a political voice for blacks in the state who were deprived of a voice in the regular party. The MFDP elected delegates to the Democratic National Convention in August and demanded that they be seated. Though it was disappointed in its attempt to gain seats for its delegates and real representation at the convention for the black Democrats of Mississippi, the incident brought useful publicity to the struggle for civil rights in the Deep South.

Fannie Lou Hamer was one of the delegates of the MFDP to the National Convention, and her speech before the Credentials Committee in August was carried over national television. When she described how Mississippi policemen had beaten her as she tried to register to vote, the entire nation heard.

Following is an interview with Mrs. Hamer conducted by J. H. O'Dell, an editor of **Freedomways**. In it, she describes the dangers involved in threatening the status quo in her home state and indicates her intention to plunge ahead with the work for change.

O'DELL. Mrs. Hamer, it's good to see you again. I understand you have been to Africa since we last talked? I would like for you to talk about your African trip today.

HAMER. It was one of the proudest moments in my life.

O'DELL. That is a marvelous experience for any black American particularly for anyone who has lived here all of his life. Then, too, we want to talk about some of your early childhood experiences which helped to make you the kind of person you are and provided the basis for your becoming so active in the Freedom Movement.

HAMER. I would like to talk about some of the things that happened that made me know that there was something wrong in the south from a child. My parents moved to Sunflower County when I was two years old. I remember, and I will never forget, one day—I was six years old and I was playing beside the road and this plantation owner drove up to me and stopped and asked me "could I pick cotton." I told him I didn't know and he said, "Yes, you can. I will give you things that you want from the commissary store," and he named things like crackerjacks and sardines—and it was a huge list that he called off. So I picked the 30 pounds of cotton that week, but I found out what actually happened was he was trapping me into beginning the work I was to keep doing and I never did get out of his debt again. My parents tried so hard to do what they could to keep us in school, but school didn't last but four months out of the year and most of the time we didn't have clothes to wear. My parents would make huge crops of sometimes 55 to 60 bales of cotton. Being from a big family where there were 20 children, it wasn't too hard to pick that much cotton.

FROM "Life in Mississippi: An Interview with Fannie Lou Hamer," by permission of *Freedomways* magazine, 799 Broadway, New York, N.Y. 10003. From Vol. 5, No. 2 (Spring 1965), pp. 231–42.

But my father, year after year, didn't get too much money and I remember he just kept going. Later on he did get enough money to buy mules. We didn't have tractors, but he bought mules, wagons, cultivators and some farming equipment. As soon as he bought that and decided to rent some land, because it was always better if you rent the land, but as soon as he got the mules and wagons and everything, somebody went to our trough —a white man who didn't live very far from us—and he fed the mules Paris Green, put it in their food and it killed the mules and our cows. That knocked us right back down. And things got so tough then I began to wish I was white. We worked all the time, just worked and then we would be hungry and my mother was clearing up a new ground trying to help to feed us for $1.25 a day. She was using an axe, just like a man, and something flew up and hit her in the eye. It eventually caused her to lose both her eyes and I began to get sicker and sicker of the system there. I used to see my mother wear clothes that would have so many patches on them, they had been done over and over and over again. She would do that but she would try to keep us decent. She still would be ragged and I always said if I lived to get grown and had a chance, I was going to try to get something for my mother and I was going to do something for the black man of the south if it would cost my life; I was determined to see that things were changed. My mother got down sick in '53 and she lived with me, an invalid, until she passed away in 1961. And during the time she was staying with me sometime I would be worked so hard I couldn't sleep at night. . . .

o'DELL. What kind of work were you doing?

HAMER. I was a timekeeper and sharecropper on the same plantation I was fired from. During the time she was with me, if there was something I had to do without, I was determined to see that she did have something in her last few years. I went almost naked to see that my mother was kept decent and treated as a human being for the first time in all of her life. My mother was a great woman. To look at her from the suffering she had gone through to bring us up—20 children: 6 girls and 14 boys, but still she taught us to be decent and to respect ourselves, and that is one of the things that has kept me going, even after she passed. She tried so hard to make life easy for us. Those are the things that forced me to try to do something different and when this Movement came to Mississippi I still feel it is one of the greatest things that ever happened because only a person living in the State of Mississippi knows what it is like to suffer; knows what it is like to be hungry; knows what it is like to have no clothing to wear. And these people in Mississippi State, they are not "down"; all they need is a chance. And I am determined to give my part not for what the Movement can do for me, but what I can do for the Movement to bring about a change in the State of Mississippi. Actually, some of the things I experienced as a child still linger on; what the white man has done to the black people in the south!

One of the things I remember as a child: There was a man named Joe Pulliam. He was a great Christian man; but one time, he was living with a white family and this white family robbed him of what he earned. They didn't pay him anything. This white man gave him $150 to go to the hill, (you see, I lived in the Black Belt of Mississippi) . . . to get another Negro family. Joe Pulliam knew what this white man had been doing to him so he kept the $150 and didn't go. This white man talked with him then shot him in the shoulder and Joe Pulliam went back into the house and got a Winchester and killed this white man. The other white fellow that was with him he "outrun the word of God" back to town. That gave this Negro a chance to go down on the bayou that was called Powers Bayou and he got in a hollowed-out stump where there was enough room for a person. He got in there and he stayed and was tracked there, but they couldn't see him and every time a white man would peep out, he busted him. He killed 13 white men and wounded 26 and Mississippi was a quiet place for a long time. I remember that until this day and I won't forget it. After they couldn't get him, they took gas—one man from Clarksdale used a machine gun—(Bud Doggins)—they used a machine gun and they tried to get him like that and then they took gas and poured it on Powers Bayou. Thousands of gallons of gas and they lit it and when it burned up to the hollowed-out stump, he crawled out. When they found him, he was unconscious and he was lying with his head on his gun but the last bullet in the gun had been snapped twice. They dragged him by his heels on the back of a car and they paraded about with that man and they cut his ears off and put them in a showcase and it stayed there a long, long time—in Drew, Mississippi. All of those things, when they would happen, would make me sick in the pit of my stomach and year after year, everytime something would happen it would make me more and more aware of what would have to be done in the State of Mississippi.

O'DELL. What do you think will have to be done?

HAMER. The only thing I really feel is necessary is that the black people, not only in Mississippi, will have to actually upset this applecart. What I mean by that is, so many things are under the cover that will have to be swept out and shown to this whole world, not just to America. There is so much hypocrisy in America. This thing they say of "the land of the free and the home of the brave" is all on paper. It doesn't mean anything to us. The only way we can make this thing a reality in America is to do all we can to destroy this system and bring this thing out to the light that has been under the cover all these years. That's why I believe in Christianity because the Scriptures said: "The things that have been done in the dark will be known on the house tops."

Now many things are beginning to come out and it was truly a reality to me when I went to Africa, to Guinea. The little things that had been taught to me about the African people, that they were "heathens," "savages," and they were just downright stupid people. But when I got to Guinea, we were greeted by the Government of Guinea, which is *Black People*—and we stayed at a place that was the government building, because we were the guests of the Government. You don't know what that meant to me when I got to Guinea on the 12th of September. The President of Guinea, Sekou Touré, came to see us on the 13th. Now you know, I don't know how you can compare this by me being able to see a President of a country, when I have just been there two days; and here I have been in America, born in America, and I am 46 years pleading with the President for the last two to three years to just give us a chance—and this President in Guinea recognized us enough to talk to us.

O'DELL. How many were in your delegation?

HAMER. It was eleven of us during that time, and I could get a clear picture of actually what had happened to the black people of America. Our foreparents were mostly brought from West Africa, the same place that we visited in Africa. We were brought to America and our foreparents were sold; white people bought them; white people changed their names . . . and actually . . . here, my maiden name is supposed to be Townsend; but really, what is my maiden name . . . ? What is my name? This white man who is saying "it takes time." For three hundred and more years they have had "time," and now it is time for them to listen. We have been listening year after year to them and what have we got? We are not even allowed to *think* for ourselves. "I know what is best for you," but they *don't* know what is best for us! It is time now to let them know what they owe us, and they owe us a great deal. Not only have we paid the price with our names in ink, but we have also paid in blood. And they can't say that black people can't be intelligent, because going back to Africa, in Guinea, there are almost 4 million people there and what he, President Touré, is doing to educate the people: as long as the French people had it they weren't doing a thing that is being done now. I met one child there eleven years old, speaking three languages. He could speak English, French and Malinke. Speaking my language actually better than I could. And this hypocrisy—they tell us here in America. People should go there and see. It would bring tears in your eyes to make you think of all those years, the type of brain-washing that this man will use in America to keep us separated from our own people. When I got on that plane, it was *loaded* with *white* people going to Africa for the Peace Corps. I got there and met a lot of them, and actually they had more peace there in Guinea than I have here. I talked to some of them. I told them before they would be able to clean up somebody else's house you would have to clean up yours; before they can tell somebody else how to run their country, why don't they do something here. This problem is not only in Mississippi. During the time I was in the Convention in Atlantic City, I didn't get any threats from Mississippi. The threatening letters were from Philadelphia, Chicago and other big cities.

o'DELL. You received threatening letters while you were at the Convention?

HAMER. Yes. I got pictures of us and they would draw big red rings around us and tell what they thought of us. I got a letter said, "I have been shot three times through the heart. I hope I see your second act." But this white man who wants to stay *white*, and to think for the Negro, he is not only destroying the Negro, he is destroying himself, because a house divided against itself cannot stand and that same thing applies to America. America that is divided against itself cannot stand, and we cannot say we have all this unity they say we have when black people are being discriminated against in every city in America I have visited.

I was in jail when Medgar Evers was murdered and *nothing*, I mean *nothing* has been done about that. You know what really made me sick? I was in Washington, D.C. at another time reading in a paper where the U.S. gives Byron de la Beckwith—the man who is charged with murdering Medgar Evers—they were giving him so much money for some land and I ask "Is this America?" We can no longer ignore the fact that America is NOT the "land of the free and the home of the brave." I used to question this for years—what did our kids actually fight for? They would go in the service and go through all of that and come right out to be drowned in a river in Mississippi. I found this hypocrisy is all over America.

The 20th of March in 1964, I went before the Secretary of State to qualify to run as an official candidate for Congress from the 2nd Congressional District, and it was easier for me to qualify to run than it was for me to pass the literacy test to be a registered voter. And we had four people to qualify and run in the June primary election but we didn't have enough Negroes registered in Mississippi. The 2nd Congressional District where I ran, against Jamie Whitten, is made up of 24 counties. Sixty-eight per cent of the people are Negroes, only 6–8 per cent are registered. And it is not because Negroes don't want to register. They try and they try and they try. That's why it was important for us to set up the "Freedom Registration" to help us in the Freedom Democratic Party.

o'DELL. This was a registration drive organized by the Movement?

HAMER. Yes. The only thing we took out was the Constitution of the State of Mississippi and the interpretation of the Constitution. We had 63,000 people registered on the Freedom Registration form. And we tried from every level to go into the regular Democratic Party medium. We tried from the precinct level. The 16th of June when they were holding precinct meetings all across the state, I was there and there was eight of us there to attend the meeting, and they had the door locked at 10 o'clock in the morning. So we had our own meeting and elected our permanent chairman and secretary and regulars and alternates and we passed a resolution as the law requires and then mailed it to Oscar Townsend, our permanent chairman. This is what's happening in the State of Mississippi. We had hoped for a change, but these people (Congressmen) go to Washington and stay there 25 and 30 years and more without representing the people of Mississippi. We have never been represented in Washington. You can tell this by the program the federal government had to train 2,400 tractor drivers. They would have trained Negro and white together, but this man, Congressman Jamie Whitten, voted against it and everything that was decent. So, we've got to have somebody in Washington who is concerned about the people of Mississippi.

After we testified before the Credentials Committee in Atlantic City, their Mississippi representative testified also. He said I got 600 votes but when they made the count in Mississippi, I was told I had 388 votes. So actually it is no telling how many votes I actually got.

O'DELL. In other words, a Mr. Collins came before the Credentials Committee of the Democratic National Convention and actually gave away the secret in a sense, because the figure he gave was not the same figure he gave to you as an official candidate?

HAMER. That's right. He also said I had been allowed to attend the precinct meeting which was true. But he didn't say we were locked out of the polling place there and had to hold our meeting on the lawn.

O'DELL. So now you have a situation where you had the basis for a Freedom Democratic Party. You have had four candidates to run for Congress. You had a community election where 63,000 of our folk showed their interest in the election. How do you size up the situation coming out of Atlantic City? What impressions did you get from your effort in Atlantic City to be seated, and how do you feel the people back home are going to react to this next period you are going into?

HAMER. The people at home will work hard and actually all of them think it was important that we made the decision that we did make *not to compromise;* because we didn't have anything to *compromise* for. Some things I found out in the National Convention I wasn't too glad I did find out. But we will work hard, and it was important to actually really bring this out to the open, the things I will say some people knew about and some people didn't; this stuff that has been kept under the cover for so many years. Actually, the world and America is upset and the only way to bring about a change is to upset it more.

O'DELL. What was done about the beating you and Miss Annelle Ponder, your colleague in the citizenship school program, experienced while in jail? Was any action taken at all?

HAMER. The Justice Department filed a suit against the brutality of the five law officials and they had this trial. The trial began the 2nd of December 1963 and they had white jurors from the State of Mississippi, and the Federal Judge Clayton made it plain to the jurors that they were dealing with "nigras" and that "who would actually accuse such upstanding people like those law officials"—be careful what they was doing because they are law-abiding citizens and were dealing with agitators and niggers. It was as simple as that. And those police were cleared. They were on the loose for about a week before I left for Atlantic City. One of those men was driving a truck from the State Penitentiary. One night he passed my house and pointed me out to one of the other men in the State Penitentiary truck and that same night I got a threat: "We got you located Fannie Lou and we going to put you in the Mississippi River." A lot of people say why do they let the *hoodlums* do that? But it is those people supposed to have *class* that are doing the damage in Mississippi. You know there was a time, in different places, when people felt safe going to a law official. But I called them that day and got the answer back, "You know you don't look to us for help."

O'DELL. This threat: the man called you up and said "we've got you spotted"; I gather from that that the river has some special meaning to us living there in Mississippi?

HAMER. Yes. So many people have been killed and put in the Mississippi River. Like when they began to drag the river for Mickey and Chaney and Andy.[1] Before he was to go to Oxford, Ohio, Mickey was telling me his life had been threatened and a taxi driver had told him to be careful because they was out to get him.

When they (the sailors) began to drag the river they found other people and I actually feel like they stopped because they would have been shook up to find so many if they had just been fishing for bodies. The Mississippi is not the only river. There's the Tallahatchie and the Big Black. People have been put in the river year after year, these things *been* happening.

O'DELL. The general policy of striking fear in people's hearts. In other words, it is like lynching used to be. They used to night ride. . . .

HAMER. They still night ride. The exact count was 32 churches they had burned in the State of Mississippi and they still ride at night and throw bombs at night. You would think they would cut down with Mrs. Chaney. But since they murdered James Chaney, they have shot buckshot at his mother's house. And hate won't only destroy us. It will destroy these people that's hating as well. And one of the things is, they are afraid of getting back what they have been putting out all of these years. You know the Scripture says "be not deceived for God is not mocked; whatsoever a man sow that shall he also reap." And *one day*, I don't know how they're going to get it, but they're going to get some of it back. They are scared to death and are more afraid now than we are.

O'DELL. How active is the White Citizen's Council? Has it the kind of outlet through TV and radio and so forth that Negroes are aware of its presence?

---

[1] Michael Schwerner, James Chaney and Andrew Goodman.

HAMER. They announce their programs. In fact, one day I was going to Jackson and I saw a huge sign that U.S. Senator John Stennis was speaking that night for the White Citizens Council in Yazoo City and they also have a State Charter that they may set up for "private schools." It is no secret.

O'DELL. Does it seem to be growing? Is the white community undergoing any change as a result of all the pressure that has been put now with the Mississippi Summer Project and the killing of the three civil rights workers? What effect is it having on the white community?

HAMER. You can't ever tell. I have talked to two or three whites that's decent in the State of Mississippi, but you know, just two or three speaking out. I do remember, one time, a man came to me after the students began to work in Mississippi and he said the white people were getting tired and they were getting tense and anything might happen. Well, I asked him "how long he thinks *we* had been getting tired"? I have been *tired* for 46 years and my parents was *tired* before me and their parents were *tired;* and I have always wanted to do something that would help some of the things I would see going on among Negroes that I didn't like and I don't like now.

O'DELL. Getting back just for a minute to Atlantic City. You all were in the national spotlight because there was nothing else happening in the Democratic National Convention other than your challenge to the Mississippi delegation and I would like to go back to that and pull together some of the conclusions you might have drawn from that experience.

HAMER. In coming to Atlantic City, we believed strongly that we were right. In fact, it was just right for us to come to challenge the seating of the regular Democratic Party from Mississippi. But we didn't think when we got there that we would meet people, that actually the other leaders of the Movement would differ with what we felt was right. We would have accepted the Green proposal. But, when we couldn't get that, it didn't make any sense for us to take "two votes at large." What would that mean to Mississippi? What would it have meant to us to go back and tell the Mississippi people? And actually, I think there will be great leaders emerging from the State of Mississippi. The people that have the experience to know and the people not interested in letting somebody pat you on the back and tell us "I think it is right." And it was very important for us not to accept a compromise and after I got back to Mississippi, people there said it was the most important step that had been taken. We figured it was right and it *was* right, and if we had accepted that compromise, then we would have been letting the people down in Mississippi. Regardless of leadership, *we have to think for ourselves!*

O'DELL. In other words, you had *two* battles on your hands when you went to Atlantic City?

HAMER. Yes. I was in one of the meetings when they spoke about accepting two votes and I said I wouldn't dare think about anything like this. So, I wasn't allowed to attend the other meetings. It was *quite* an experience.

O'DELL. There will be other elections and other conventions and the people in Mississippi should be a little stronger.

HAMER. I think so.

O'DELL. Well, it's good to know that the people you have to work with every day are with *you.*

HAMER. Yes, they are with us one hundred per cent.

O'DELL. That's encouraging because it makes the work that much easier. Is there any final thing you want to say that is part of this historic statement of life in Mississippi for yourself as a person who lives there?

HAMER. Nothing other than we will be working. When I go back to Mississippi we will be working as hard or harder to bring about a change, but things are not always pleasant there.

O'DELL. You will probably have the support of more people than you have ever had, all around the country.

HAMER. Yes, actually since the Convention I have gotten so many letters that I have tried to answer but every letter said they thought this decision, not to accept the compromise, was so important. There wasn't one letter I have gotten so far that said we should have accepted the compromise—not one.

O'DELL. So, those are the people who are interested in your work, and as you get back into the main swing of things you will be keeping in touch with those people so that they should be asked to help in any way they can regardless of where they live. It is national and international public pressure that is needed.

Are you aware that there has been any coverage of the African trip by the Mississippi press? Have they made any comments on it?

HAMER. I don't know about the press, but I know in the town where I live everybody was aware that I was in Africa, because I remember after I got back some of the people told me that Mayor Durr of our town said he just wished they would boil me in tar. But, that just shows how ignorant he is, I didn't see any tar over there. But I was treated much better in Africa than I was treated in America. And you see, often I get letters like this: "Go back to Africa."

Now I have just as much right to stay in America—in fact, the black people have contributed more to America than any other race, because our kids have fought here for what was called "democracy"; our mothers and fathers were sold and bought here for a price. So all I can say when they say "go back to Africa," I say "when you send the Chinese back to China, the Italians back to Italy, etc., and you get on that Mayflower from whence you came, and give the Indians their land back, who really would be here at home?" It is our right to stay here and we will stay and stand up for what belongs to us as American citizens, because they can't say that we haven't had patience.

O'DELL. Was there a lot of interest in your trip among the African people that you met?

HAMER. Yes. I saw how the Government was run there and I saw where black people were running the banks. I saw, for the first time in my life, a black stewardess walking through a plane and that was quite an inspiration for me. It shows what black people can do if we only get the chance in America. It is there within us. We can do things if we only get the chance. I see so many ways America uses to rob Negroes and it is sinful and America can't keep holding on, and doing these things. I saw in Chicago, on the street where I was visiting my sister-in-law, this "Urban Renewal" and it means one thing: "Negro removal." But they want to tear the homes down and put a parking lot there. Where are those people going? Where will they go? And as soon as Negroes take to the street demonstrating, one hears people say, "they shouldn't have done it." The *world* is looking at America and it is really beginning to show up for what it is really like. "Go Tell It on the Mountain." We can no longer ignore this, that America is not "the land of the free and the home of the brave."

O'DELL. Thank you, Mrs. Fannie Lou Hamer, Vice-Chairman of the Freedom Democratic Party of Mississippi; courageous fighter for human rights.

WE SHALL OVERCOME: FREEDOM SONGS

The nonviolent civil rights movement was a singing movement. Every aspect of its development was marked by song. Some of the songs were traditional songs of protest; others were adaptations of Spirituals or labor union songs; still others were composed on the spot by participants in the movement. The songs that follow are typical of the hundreds that strengthened the will of the marchers and protesters.

We Shall Overcome

"We Shall Overcome" was the unofficial theme song of the freedom movement. Adapted from a union version of an old Spiritual by the staff of the Highlander Folk School in Tennessee, it was sung wherever the movement went.

> We shall overcome, we shall overcome,
> We shall overcome someday.
> Oh, deep in my heart, I do believe,
> We shall overcome someday.

We are not afraid, we are not afraid,
We are not afraid today.
Oh, deep in my heart, I do believe,
We shall overcome someday.

We are not alone, we are not alone,
We are not alone today.
Oh, deep in my heart, I do believe,
We are not alone today.

The truth will make us free, the truth will make us free,
The truth will make us free someday.
Oh, deep in my heart, I do believe,
We shall overcome someday.

We'll walk hand in hand, we'll walk hand in hand,
We'll walk hand in hand someday.
Oh, deep in my heart, I do believe,
We shall overcome someday.

The Lord will see us through, the Lord will see us through,
The Lord will see us through someday.
Oh, deep in my heart, I do believe,
We shall overcome someday.

Black and white together, black and white together,
Black and white together now.
Oh, deep in my heart, I do believe,
We shall overcome someday.

We shall all be free, we shall all be free,
We shall all be free someday.
Oh, deep in my heart, I do believe,
We shall overcome someday.

NEW words and new music arrangement by Zilphia Horton, Frank Hamilton, Guy Carawan, and Pete Seeger. TRO Copyright © 1960 and 1963 by Ludlow Music, Inc., New York, N.Y. Used by permission. Royalties derived from this composition are being contributed to The Freedom Movement under the trusteeship of the writers.

If You Miss Me from the Back of the Bus

"If You Miss Me from the Back of the Bus" is an example of the kind of song that won great popularity in the movement—a song with a simple melody and lyrics that could be adapted to a variety of situations. This version, sung by the members of SNCC, centers around the areas of protest in which the students were most involved.

If you miss me from the back of the bus,
 and you can't find me nowhere,
Come on up to the front of the bus,
 I'll be ridin' up there.
I'll be ridin' up there, I'll be ridin' up there,
Come on up to the front of the bus,
 I'll be ridin' up there.

If you miss me from the front of the bus,
 and you can't find me nowhere,
Come on up to the driver's seat,
 I'll be drivin' up there.
I'll be drivin' up there, I'll be drivin' up there,
Come on up to the front of the bus,
 I'll be drivin' up there.

If you miss me from Jackson State,
 and you can't find me nowhere,
Come on over to Ole Miss,
 I'll be studyin' over there.
I'll be studyin' over there, I'll be studyin' over there,
Come on over to Ole Miss,
 I'll be studyin' over there.

If you miss me from knockin' on doors,
 and you can't find me nowhere,
Come on down to the registrar's room,
 I'll be the registrar there.
I'll be the registrar there, I'll be the registrar there,
Come on down to the registrar's room,
 I'll be the registrar there.

If you miss me from the cotton field,
 and you can't find me nowhere,

WORDS adapted by members of SNCC. From *We Shall Overcome!*, compiled by Guy and Candie Carawan. Copyright © 1963 Oak Publications, A Division of Embassy Music Corporation. Used by permission.

Come on down to the court house,
  I'll be votin' right there.
I'll be votin' right there, I'll be votin' right there,
Come on down to the court house,
  I'll be votin' right there.

If you miss me from the picket line,
  and you can't find me nowhere,
Come on down to the jail house,
  I'll be roomin' down there.
I'll be roomin' down there, I'll be roomin' down there,
Come on down to the jail house,
  I'll be roomin' down there.

If you miss me from the Mississippi River,
  and you can't find me nowhere,
Come on down to the city pool,
  I'll be swimmin' in there.
I'll be swimmin' in there, I'll be swimmin' in there,
Come on down to the city pool,
  I'll be swimmin' in there.

Ain't Gonna Let Nobody Turn Me 'Round

"Ain't Gonna Let Nobody Turn Me 'Round" was introduced to the movement in Albany, Georgia, by Ralph Abernathy during the summer of 1962. Because of its adaptability, it was subsequently used widely in the movement. The proper names that appear in this version are those of public officials in Albany and Terrell counties, Georgia.

Ain't gonna let nobody turn me 'round,
  turn me 'round, turn me 'round,
Ain't gonna let nobody turn me 'round,
I'm gonna keep on a walkin', keep on a talkin',
Marching up to freedom land.

Ain't gonna let Nervous Nelly turn me 'round,
  turn me 'round, turn me 'round,
Ain't gonna let Nervous Nelly turn me 'round,

ADAPTATION by members of the Albany Movement. From *We Shall Overcome!*, compiled by Guy and Candie Carawan. Copyright © 1963 Oak Publications, A Division of Embassy Music Corporation. Used by permission.

I'm gonna keep on a walkin', keep on a talkin',
Marching up to freedom land.

Ain't gonna let Chief Pritchett turn me 'round,
   turn me 'round, turn me 'round,
Ain't gonna let Chief Pritchett turn me 'round,
I'm gonna keep on a walkin', keep on a talkin',
Marching up to freedom land.

Ain't gonna let Mayor Kelly turn me 'round,
   turn me 'round, turn me 'round,
Ain't gonna let Mayor Kelly turn me 'round,
I'm gonna keep on a walkin', keep on a talkin',
Marching up to freedom land.

Ain't gonna let segregation turn me 'round,
   turn me 'round, turn me 'round,
Ain't gonna let segregation turn me 'round,
I'm gonna keep on a walkin', keep on a talkin',
Marching up to freedom land.

Ain't gonna let Z. T. turn me 'round,
   turn me 'round, turn me 'round,
Ain't gonna let Z. T. turn me 'round,
I'm gonna keep on a walkin', keep on a talkin',
Marching up to freedom land.

Ain't gonna let no jailhouse turn me 'round,
   turn me 'round, turn me 'round,
Ain't gonna let no jailhouse turn me 'round,
I'm gonna keep on a walkin', keep on a talkin',
Marching up to freedom land.

Ain't gonna let no injunction turn me 'round,
   turn me 'round, turn me 'round,
Ain't gonna let no injunction turn me 'round,
I'm gonna keep on a walkin', keep on a talkin',
Marching up to freedom land.

Freedom Is a Constant Struggle

"Freedom Is a Constant Struggle" was composed by the Freedom Singers, members of SNCC who traveled around the country singing freedom songs and trying to build up support for the students. When the deaths of the civil rights workers James Chaney, Michael Schwerner, and Andrew Goodman in Mississippi were announced to a mass meeting of students during Freedom Summer, the group responded with this passionate and compassionate song.

They say that freedom is a constant struggle,
They say that freedom is a constant struggle,
They say that freedom is a constant struggle,
Oh Lord, we've struggled so long,
We must be free, we must be free.

They say that freedom is a constant crying,
They say that freedom is a constant crying,
They say that freedom is a constant crying,
Oh Lord, we've cried so long,
We must be free, we must be free.

They say that freedom is a constant sorrow,
They say that freedom is a constant sorrow,
They say that freedom is a constant sorrow,
Oh Lord, we've sorrowed so long,
We must be free, we must be free.

They say that freedom is a constant moaning,
They say that freedom is a constant moaning,
They say that freedom is a constant moaning,
Oh Lord, we've moaned so long,
We must be free, we must be free.

They say that freedom is a constant dying,
They say that freedom is a constant dying,
They say that freedom is a constant dying,
Oh Lord, we've died so long,
We must be free, we must be free.

FROM *Freedom Is a Constant Struggle*, compiled by Guy and Candie Carawan (New York: Oak, 1968). Copyright © by the Freedom Singers.

12 SUGGESTIONS FOR FURTHER READING

Martin Luther King, Jr., tells the story of the Montgomery bus boycott in *Stride Toward Freedom: The Montgomery Story** (Harper and Row, 1958). The ideas and the influence of King are discussed in Lerone Bennett, Jr., *What Manner of Man** (Johnson, 1964), and in William Robert Miller, *Martin Luther King, Jr., His Life, Martyrdom, and Meaning for the World** (Weybright and Talley, 1968).

The student nonviolent movement is described in Howard Zinn, *SNCC: The New Abolitionists** (Beacon, 1964), and in a moving autobiography by a member of the movement, Anne Moody, called *Coming of Age in Mississippi: An Autobiography* (Dial, 1968).

James Farmer, former director of CORE, presented his analysis of the movement in *Freedom—When?* (Random House, 1966). One aspect of CORE's work is treated in James Peck, *Freedom Ride* (Simon and Schuster, 1962).

Freedom Summer of 1964 has been the subject of many books. Among the most valuable of these are William McCord, *Mississippi: The Long Hot Summer* (Norton, 1965); Len Holt, *The Summer That Didn't End* (Morrow, 1965); Sally Belfrage, *Freedom Summer** (Viking, 1965); Tracy Sugarman, *Stranger at the Gates: A Summer in Mississippi** (Hill and Wang, 1966); Elizabeth Sutherland, *Letters from Mississippi** (McGraw-Hill, 1965); and William Bradford Huie, *Three Lives for Mississippi** (Trident, 1965).

Robert Penn Warren interviewed many of the leaders of the civil rights movement and presented their views in *Who Speaks for the Negro** (Random House, 1965). The difficulties met by blacks in Southern courtrooms are described in Leon Friedman (ed.), *Southern Justice** (Pantheon, 1965). Friedman has also edited a useful collection of documents from the period of the nonviolent action movement, *The Civil Rights Reader** (Walker, 1967). The growing importance of the black vote in the South is considered by Pat Watters and Reece Cleghorn in *Climbing Jacob's Ladder: The Arrival of Negroes in Southern Politics* (Harcourt, Brace & World, 1967).

Josh Dunson has analyzed the songs of the movement in *Freedom in the Air: Song Movements of the 60's** (International, 1965). And Guy Carawan and Candie Carawan have edited two excellent collections of freedom songs: *We Shall Overcome: Songs of the Southern Freedom Movement** (Oak, 1963) and *Freedom Is a Constant Struggle: Songs of the Freedom Movement** (Oak, 1968).

13 THE MILITANT BLACK LIBERATION MOVEMENT

After Freedom Summer of 1964, the focus of the movement for the liberation of black people began to shift from the South to the urban ghettos of the North and the West. As more and more legal battles were won, it became apparent that these victories had little relevance to the masses of black people, most of whom remained mired in poverty and the fear generated by helplessness before the economic and political power of the white community. After the nonviolent direct-action campaigns had desegregated lunch counters and public facilities, these gains, compared to the demands of real freedom, began to seem inconsequential to many blacks—especially to the militant young. The murderers of black and white civil rights workers throughout the South went free, even those who had publicly boasted of their crimes. Racism was revealed to be not merely the sum of individual whites' hostility to blacks but an attitude insidiously built into the institutions of American society—a more elusive target than had been imagined.

A harbinger of the change that was to transform the civil rights crusade came in 1959 when Robert F. Williams, of Monroe, North Carolina, advocated that black people buy arms and undertake to protect themselves since they could not depend on the established law-enforcement authorities for protection. Later, an organization that called itself the Deacons for Defense was started in Louisiana to protect civil rights workers and local black people from violence.

As the popular press, along with racial liberals and moderates, applauded the gains black people had made in the South through legal defense and nonviolent direct action, there occurred a series of explosions—variously called riots, insurrections, and civil disorders—that turned the attention of the nation to the black ghettos of Northern and Western cities. Black people living in poverty and despair were venting their long-suppressed hostility through attacks on the things that most directly oppressed them, their slum dwellings and the ghetto merchants. Most of the disturbances were triggered by incidents involving the visible symbol of white oppression, the policeman. Built on the frustrations of the black ghetto dweller and the student activists, black nationalism again became an openly advocated alternative.

The new nationalism drew much of its inspiration from the successful struggles for liberation carried on by formerly colonized peoples of Africa and Asia. The key concept was "self-determination." Black people must be free to decide for themselves what they will do, where they will live, how and what they will study, and how they will carry out the plans for their general liberation from the oppressors.

At first it seemed that leadership for the new nationalism would come from the Lost-Found Nation of Islam (the Black Muslims), led by Elijah Muhammad. This movement had attracted a considerable number of members and many sympathizers among urban ghetto dwellers through its clear-cut descriptions of the crimes committed against black people by the "white devils." When it became apparent that the Muslims were essentially a conservative group, more interested in the salvation of black souls and the building up of its own organization than in making a frontal attack on racist institutions and seeking the liberation of all black men, a split occurred in the Muslim movement. The dissidents, led by Malcolm X, minister of the New York City Muslims, formed the Muslim Mosque, Inc., and Malcolm X founded the Organization of Afro-American Unity to carry out his plans for racial liberation. Contrary to Elijah Muhammad's posture of withdrawal and disengagement from white America, Malcolm X prepared for an ongoing struggle against the forces of white racism. Although Malcolm remained a black nationalist, he realized that black people alone could not free themselves in America and was prepared to seek support in the white community.

As a result of the hostility created by the split in the Muslim forces, Malcolm was killed by a black assassin in February 1965. His death was a profound tragedy for both black and white America, for it seems that he might have been the leader who could mold a movement out of the frustrated ghetto dwellers whose anger so often led to self-destruction. Almost every segment of the black liberation movement of the late 1960's claims Malcolm X as one of its martyrs.

Meanwhile, in the South, after the ambiguous success of Freedom Summer, in which the attention of the nation had indeed been focused on Mississippi but little progress had been made in terms of real social change, SNCC virtually went into seclusion. For a year it worked quietly, organizing voters in rural communities and rethinking its philosophy. It found itself agreeing with the aggressive-defensive policies enunciated by Malcolm X. SNCC made its new posture public in May 1966 with the election of Stokely Carmichael as its chairman and the announcement that it intended to call upon black Americans to build and maintain control of independent institutions through which they could implement social change. Black men of North and South thus joined together in nationalism. In 1969 the new position of SNCC was given even more formal recognition when the name of the organization was officially changed to Student *National* Coordinating Committee.

Carmichael gave the new philosophy a watchword in June 1966 during James Meredith's bold "march against fear" (see p. 378). When Meredith was shot and wounded from ambush after completing only a fraction of his journey, the leaders of SCLC, CORE, and SNCC continued the march. It was the new leader of SNCC who dominated the situation. After being arrested and briefly jailed, Carmichael announced that he was not going to jail again. Then he shouted the words that sent a wave of shock through the ranks of the civil rights organizations and chills down the spine of white America—"Black Power." Why this particular phrase set off such an uproar is a subject for study by the social pathologist. But it is clear that the two words conjured up a host of devils in the minds of whites and a host of possibilities in the minds of blacks. Henceforth, "Black Power" became the focus of racial ideology and program.

THE SINGING IS OVER

Julius Lester   /   The Angry Children of Malcolm X

No one caught the fury that swept over the young blacks of SNCC after Freedom Summer of 1964 better than Julius Lester, a song-writer, folk singer, essayist, and journalist who was himself a member of the movement. In the following article, which first appeared in 1966 in **Sing Out!,** a folk song magazine on which he served as an editor, Lester comments on the increasing disillusionment of blacks with the interracial civil rights movement.

The brutality of the law-enforcement authorities toward blacks and the tokenism of the "liberal" federal government finally led SNCC to decide that black people must take charge of their own liberation, leaving whites the responsibility of eliminating racism among their own people. Violence had been used by whites through the years to subjugate blacks, and, Lester warned, it might be necessary for blacks to use the same tactic to free themselves. In so doing, they would find themselves a part of the revolutionary Third World, and thereby they would stand a chance of gaining self-determination and freedom from white domination.

The world of the black American is different from that of the white American. This difference comes not only from the segregation imposed on the black, but it also comes from the way of life he has evolved for himself under these conditions. Yet, America has always been uneasy with the separate world in its midst. Feeling most comfortable when the black man emulates the ways and manners of white Americans, America has, at the same time, been stolidly unwilling to let the black man be assimilated into the mainstream.

With its goal of assimilation on the basis of equality, the civil rights movement was once the great hope of black men and liberal whites. In 1960 and 1961 Negroes felt that if only Americans knew the wrongs and sufferings they had to endure, these wrongs would be righted and all would be well. If Americans saw well-dressed, well-mannered, clean Negroes on their television screen not retaliating to being beaten by white Southerners, they would not sit back and do nothing. *Amor vincit omnia!* and the Reverend Dr. Martin Luther King, Jr., was the knight going forth to prove to the father that he was worthy of becoming a member of the family. But there was something wrong with this attitude and young Negroes began to feel

FROM Julius Lester, "The Angry Children of Malcolm X," *Sing Out!*, XVI (October–November 1966), pp. 21–25. Copyright © by Julius Lester 1966. Used with permission of the author and Ronald Hobbs Literary Agency.

uneasy. Was this not another form of the bowing and scraping their grand-parents had had to do to get what they wanted? Were they not acting once again as the white man wanted and expected them to? And why should they have to be brutalized, physically and spiritually, for what every other American had at birth? But these were only timid questions in the mind for which no answer was waited. You simply put your body in the struggle and that meant entering the church in Albany, Danville, Birmingham, Greenwood, Nashville, or wherever you were, entering the church and listening to prayers, short sermons on your courage and the cause you were fighting, singing freedom songs—Ain't Gon' Let Nobody Turn Me Round, Turn Me Round, Turn Me Round and you would name names, the sheriff's, the Mayor's, the Governor's and whoever else you held responsible for the conditions and—always at the end—We Shall Over-come with arms crossed, holding the hands of the persons next to you and swaying gently from side to side, We Shall Overcome Someday someday but not today because you knew as you walked out of the church, two abreast, and started marching toward town that no matter how many times you sang about not letting anybody turn you around red-necks and po' white trash from four counties and some from across the state line were waiting with guns, tire chains, baseball bats, rocks, sticks, clubs and bottles, waiting as you turned the corner singing about This Little Light of Mine and how you were going to let it shine as that cop's billy club went upside your head shine shine shining as you fell to the pavement with someone's knee crashing into your stomach and someone's foot into your back until a cop dragged you away, threw you into the paddy wagon and off to the jail you and the others went, singing I Ain't Scared of Your Jail 'Cause I Want My Freedom. Freedom! Freedom! Was it a place some-where between Atlanta and Birmingham and you kept on missing it every-time you drove that way? It was a street in Itta Bena, Mississippi. Ain't that a bitch? Freedom Street! Ran right by the railroad tracks in the Negro part of town and Love Street ran right into it. Freedom and Love. It would be nice to have a house right on that corner. Freedom and Love. But from what you'd heard it was just a street in Itta Bena. Maybe it was a person—Freedom. Somebody sitting on a porch somewhere. You wondered what he looked like as you sat in the jail cell with ten, twenty, thirty others and one toilet that wouldn't flush and one useless window stopped up with bars. If it was summer the jailer would turn the heat on and if it was winter he'd turn it off and take the mattresses and you'd sing Freedom Songs (your brother sent you a note and said you looked real good on the six o'clock news on TV walking down the street singing) until the guard came and said Shut Up All That Damn Noise and you'd sing louder and he'd take one of you out at a time and everybody'd get quiet and listen to the screams and cries from the floor above and then that one would come back, bleeding, and you'd sing again because if one went to jail, all went; if one got a beating, all got beatings and then that night or the next day or the day after the people would've got up enough money to bail you out and you'd go back to the church and march again and your brother would see you on the six o'clock news for thirty seconds between the stock market report and Jackie Kennedy flying to Switzerland with her children for skiing lessons.

But a response did begin to come from the nation. All across the North young white kids held sympathy demonstrations and then with the Freedom Rides in 1961 whites came South to go to jail with Negroes—for Freedom. Those who came said integration was their fight, too, because they could never be whole men, either, in a segregated society. Some whites stayed after the Freedom Rides and moved into Negro communities to live and to work.

At that time there was a split between activists in The Movement. Some felt that more and more demonstrations were needed, while others felt that the effect of demonstrations was limited. Power was what was needed and power came through having a say in the system. That came through the ballot. Once you had some say in government, you could have a say about jobs. After all, what was the point of desegregating a lunch counter if you didn't have the money to buy a hamburger?

So began the slow tedious work of going into a town, finding someone who wouldn't be afraid to have a civil rights worker living in his house and would help the worker become known in the community. The civil rights worker had to find a minister courageous enough to let his church be used for a mass meeting and then he had to go around the community asking people to come out to the meeting. At the mass meeting there was usually hymn singing and a prayer service first. Then the minister would make a few remarks before introducing the civil rights worker, who by that time, if he were a veteran, would've been through the sit-ins, the Freedom Rides, five or six different jails and a lot of hungry days. He had dropped out of college, or quit his job if he had never been to college to become a full-time organizer for SNCC. His job was simple: organize the community to march down to the courthouse to register to vote. In small Mississippi towns, though, he didn't even think of organizing the community. He would feel good if he could convince five people to go. If five went and if the inevitable happened (violence, arrests), he had a good chance of organizing the community. It was not important at that time if one name was put on the voter registration rolls. The most important thing was to get the people organized.

It was out of Mississippi that one of the most important concepts of "the movement" came. Let the people lead themselves. SNCC field workers provided the impetus to a community, but let the community choose its leaders from its own ranks. To symbolize their new feeling, they began wearing denim work overalls, saying that they, too, were one of the community, that community of the poor. They rejected the idea of the "talented tenth," who would come out of the colleges to lead. There would be no "talented tenth." Only the community.

There were still demonstrations, but now they were not aimed as much at public accommodations, the most obvious symbols of oppression. The picket line around the courthouse, the symbol of the seat of power, was the new target. The immediate result was the same. Heads that had been beaten before were beaten again. Heads that had never been beaten were beaten. New bloody heads were on the six o'clock news alongside ones that still had scabs from the last head-whipping session. If you were a civil rights worker in Mississippi you learned many things quickly. Don't sleep by windows if possible. Don't answer a knock at the door in the middle of the night unless your caller showed you nothing less than his birth certificate. If you're on the highway at night you learned to drive as if you were training to be an astronaut. If a car was following you while you were doing ninety and it didn't sound a siren, it was safe to assume that the people in that car were not delivering a telegram. One SNCC worker, an ex-stock car driver, learned how to make a U-turn while doing ninety. (Take your hands off the wheel and pull the hand-brake. The car will spin around. Release the hand-brake and accelerate.) Each organizer had his own little techniques for staying alive. Non-violence might do something to the moral conscience of a nation, but a bullet didn't have morals and it was beginning to occur to more and more organizers that white folks had plenty more bullets than they did conscience.

How naive, how idealistic they were then. They had honestly believed that once white people knew what segregation did, it would be abolished. But why shouldn't they have believed it? They had been fed the American Dream, too. They believed in Coca Cola and the American Government. "I dreamed I got my Freedom in a Maidenform bra." They were in the Pepsi Generation, believing that the F.B.I. was God's personal emissary to uphold good and punish evil.

That was before the countless demonstrations where the F.B.I. took notes standing next to cracker cops while they were wiping nigger blood off their billy clubs and checking the batteries on their cattle-prods. That was before the promises of the Justice Department began to sound like the teasing of a virgin who never gets down to where it's at. Sure, it was nice to see that picture of Bobby Kennedy up all night at his desk during the Freedom Rides. He looked almost like a civil rights worker drinking coffee with his shoes off, but it took those Freedom Rides to make the ICC rule out segregated seating on interstate bus travel. It was Birmingham, '63 that finally forced the Image of Youth and Liberality, John Kennedy, into proposing a Civil Rights Bill, which was then almost immediately compromised into ineffectiveness when the Brother of the Image, Bobby the K, appeared before the Senate Judiciary Committee. They didn't like the idea of the March on Washington, but managed to turn it into a Kennedy victory by finally endorsing it as being in the American tradition, whatever that means. After the march the American Monarch had the Big Six Negro Leaders over to the White House for tea and cookies and to chat with Jackie about the Riviera in the winter (it's a whole lot better than the Delta I hear). The Monarch, his face rugged from the spray of the windswept Atlantic, as thousands of eulogies have proclaimed since his swift demise, stood there smiling, feeling pretty good because all the liquor stores and bars in Washington had been closed for the day so there was no danger of a bunch of niggers getting a hold of some fire-water and forgetting that they weren't in Harlem, Buttermilk Bottom and all those other weird-named places niggers pick to live in. (The order forbidding the sale of alcoholic beverages is one of the biggest insults Negroes have ever had hurled at them. It would've been much easier to take if it had simply been said The Great White Father can't trust his pickaninnies if the bars and liquor stores are left open.) Jack could also stand there and smile because John Lewis of SNCC had had his speech censored by the more "responsible" leaders, who threatened to withdraw from the March. Even censored, Lewis' speech raised pertinent questions—questions that had been on the minds of many, those not leaders, those not responsible. "The party of Kennedy is also the party of Eastland. The party of Javits is also the party of Goldwater. *Where is our party?*" But Jack could smile, because John Lewis had deleted from his speech the most pertinent question of all "I want to know— which side is the Federal Government on?"

A lot of people wanted to know that, particularly after Lyndon Baines Johnson became President of the United States in a split second one Friday afternoon. When he asked for the nation's help and God's in that cracker drawl Negroes began pulling out road maps, train schedules and brushing up on their Spanish. A lot of them had always wanted to see what Mexico was like anyway and it looked as if the time to do that thing was near.

But Big Lyndon, despite his beagle hounds and daughters, fooled everybody. Not only did he strengthen the civil rights bill and support it fully, he started giving Martin Luther King competition as to who was going to lead "the movement." King lost.

With the push for the civil rights bill in Congress there began talk of a white blacklash in the '64 elections. It seemed that whites were getting a little tired of picking up the papers and seeing niggers all over the front page. Even if they were getting their heads kicked in half the time, four years of seeing that was about enough. The average white person didn't know what niggers wanted and didn't much care. By now they should've gotten whatever the hell it was they said they didn't have and if they hadn't got it by now, they either didn't deserve it or didn't need it.

What was really bothering northern whites, however, was the fact that The Movement had come North. De Facto Segregation and De Facto

Housing were new phrases, meaning No Niggers Allowed in This School and You Damn Well Better Believe No Niggers Allowed in This Neighborhood. If you believed the liberal press, though, it wasn't as serious a problem as the one down South, because in the North segregation wasn't deliberate. It just sorta happened that way. Many Negroes never found out exactly what De Facto meant, but they assumed it was the De Facto and not segregation they ran up against when they couldn't find an apartment to rent outside of Harlem. Soon, though, the mask fell from the North's face. In New York it happened when CORE threatened a stall-in on all of the city's expressways the morning of the World's Fair opening. The threat alone was enough to make over three-fourths of the people who drove to work leave their cars in the garage and take the train or simply call in sick. The threat alone was enough to make New York's liberal newspapers read as if they had come out of the editorial room of the Birmingham News and the radio and television commentators sounded as if they had acquired southern accents over night. A few months later an organization arose in New York which called itself SPONGE—Society for the Prevention of Negroes Getting Everything. It was difficult to speak any longer of a North and a South. As Malcolm X once said, everything south of the Canadian border was South. There was only up South and down South now, and you found "crackers" both places.

While the North was being shocked into realizing that there were Negroes in its midst, the South was sympathizing with the assault that Mississippi was about to suffer. Almost a thousand white students were going into the state in June, 1964, to work in Freedom schools, community centers and to register people in the Mississippi Freedom Democratic Party, a political party organized that winter which was going to challenge the state Democratic organization at the Democratic Convention in August.

The Mississippi Summer Project was the apex of white participation in The Movement and marked the end of that participation. Within SNCC there had been widespread opposition to the idea. Many felt that it was admitting that Negroes couldn't do the job alone. Others felt that it would destroy everything which they had accomplished. Whites, no matter how well-meaning, could not relate to the Negro community. A Negro would follow a white person to the courthouse, not because he'd been convinced he should register to vote, but simply because he had been trained to say Yes to whatever a white person wanted. Others felt, however, that if they were to ever expose Mississippi's racism to America, it would only be through using whites.. After all, SNCC had repeatedly informed the press of the five Negroes killed that year in Mississippi because of their involvement with The Movement. The press had refused to print or investigate the information. Put a thousand white kids in Mississippi and the press would watch everything and print it. And who could tell? Maybe one of them white boys would get himself killed and really bring some publicity. A few said it. Most thought it. It happened.

The murders of Goodman, Schwerner and Chaney stunned the nation. Whites were shocked. Negroes were hurt and angry. Rita Schwerner, wife of one of the murdered men, reflected the feelings of Negroes when she commented that if James Chaney had been killed alone, no one would've cared. This was made even more evident the following year when Jimmie Lee Jackson's murder in Alabama evoked little reaction from whites, but the murder of Rev. James Reeb brought thousands of whites to Harlem on a march protesting his slaying.

The Mississippi Summer Project accomplished its purpose; the press came to Mississippi. The feature stories it wrote usually went something like, "Blop-blop is a blue-eyed blond from Diamond Junction-on-the-Hudson, New York. She's a twenty-year-old junior at Radcliffe majoring in Oriental metaphysics and its relationship to the quantum theory when the sun is in Sagittarius. This summer she's living with a Negro family in Fatback, Mississippi who has never heard of the quantum theory, etc., etc., etc." All summer the articles came about white boys and white girls living with poor Negroes in Mississippi. It didn't escape the attention of Negroes that seemingly no one cared about the Negro civil rights workers who had been living and working in Mississippi for the previous three years. Didn't anyone care about Willie Peacock, born and raised on a Mississippi plantation, who couldn't go back to his home town because he was an organizer for SNCC and the white people would kill him if he went to see his mother? Apparently not.

Mississippi was taken out of the headlines in July, however, when Harlem held its own Summer Project to protest the murder of a 13-year-old boy by a policeman. Summer Projects, northern style, usually involve filling a Coke bottle with gasoline, stuffing a rag down the neck and lighting it. *Things Go Better with Coke!* Harlem, Bedford-Stuyvesant, Rochester and Chicago sent Coke after Coke after Coke that summer with the grandaddy of them all, Watts, to come the following summer.

If the press had ever screamed as loudly for an end to segregation and discrimination as it screamed for law and order, segregation would be a vague memory today. Somehow, though, law and order becomes all important only when Negroes take to the streets and burn down a few of the white man's stores. Law and order is never so important to the press when police are whuppin' nigger's heads on the week-end. It slowly began to dawn on Negroes that whites didn't care as much about helping them get their freedom as they did about law and order. "Law and order must prevail" has become the cliché of the sixties. Law and order has always prevailed—upside the black man's head at every available opportunity.

The system was breaking down, but it was breaking in ways few had foreseen and fewer understood. The walls of segregation and discrimination were not crumbling and giving way to flowers of love and brotherhood. The walls were crumbling, but only to reveal a gigantic castle with walls ten times thicker than the walls of segregation. The castle was painted a brilliant white and lettered in bright red were the words Racism. What it meant to the Negro was simple. The white man only wanted you to have what he wanted you to have and you couldn't get it any other way except the way he said you could get it. Racism. It was the attitude that closed the bars and liquor stores on the day of the March. It was the attitude which made newspapers and Government officials, even Big Lyndon Himself, say, "that if Negroes went about things in the wrong way they would lose the friends they already had." It was the attitude that made the press continue to call Muhhamud Ali, Cassius Clay even though that was no longer his name. But the movement was moving. It was no longer a Friendship Contest. It was becoming a War of Liberation.

More than any other person Malcolm X was responsible for the new militancy that entered The Movement in 1965. Malcolm X said aloud those things which Negroes had been saying among themselves. He even said those things Negroes had been afraid to say to each other. His clear, uncomplicated words cut through the chains on black minds like a giant blowtorch. His words were not spoken for the benefit of the press. He was not concerned with stirring the moral conscience of America, because he knew —America had no moral conscience. He spoke directly and eloquently to black men, analyzing their situation, their predicament, events as they happened, explaining what it all meant for a black man in America.

America's reaction to what the Negro considered just demands was a disillusioning experience. Where whites could try to attain the American Dream, Negroes always had had to dream themselves attaining The Dream. But The Dream was beginning to look like a nightmare and Negroes didn't have to dream themselves a nightmare. They'd been living one a long time. They had hopes that America would respond to their needs and America had equivocated. Integration had once been an unquestioned goal that would be the proudest moment for Negro America. Now it was beginning to be questioned.

The New York school boycotts of 1964 pointed this up. Integration to the New York City Board of Education meant busing Negro children to white schools. This merely said to Negroes that whites were saying Negroes had nothing to offer. Integration has always been presented as a Godsend for Negroes and something to be endured for whites. When the Board of Ed decided to bus white children to Negro schools the following year, the reaction was strangely similar to that of New Orleans and Little Rock. Today, whites in Chicago and New York chant at Negro demonstrators, "I wish I was an Alabama deputy, so I could kill a nigger legally."

When it became more and more apparent that integration was only designed to uplift Negroes and improve their lot, Negroes began wondering whose lot actually needed improving. Maybe the white folks weren't as well-educated and cultured as they thought they were. Thus, Negroes began cutting a path toward learning who they were.

Of the minority groups in this country, the Negro is the only one lacking a language of his own. This is significant in that this has made it difficult for him to have a clear concept of himself as a Negro. It has made him more susceptible to the American lie of assimilation than the Puerto Rican, Italian or Jew who can remove himself from America with one sentence in his native language. Despite the assimilation lie, America is not a melting pot. It is a nation of national minorities, each living in a well-defined geographical area and retaining enough of the customs of the native land to maintain an identity other than that of an American. The Negro has two native lands: America and Africa. Both have deliberately been denied him.

Identity has always been the key problem for Negroes. Many avoid their blackness as much as possible by trying to become assimilated. They remove all traces of blackness from their lives. Their gestures, speech, habits, cuisine, walk, everything becomes as American Dream as possible. Generally, they are the "responsible leaders," the middle class, the undercover, button-down collar Uncle Toms, who front for the white man at a time of racial crisis, reassuring the nation that "responsible Negroes deplore the violence and looting and we ask that law and order be allowed to prevail." A small minority avoid the crux of their blackness by going to another extreme. They identify completely with Africa. Some go to the extent of wearing African clothes and speaking Swahili. They, however, are only unconsciously admitting that the white man is right when he says, Negroes don't have a thing of their own.

For other Negroes the question of identity is only now being solved by the realization of those things that are theirs. Negroes do have a language of their own. The words may be English, but the way a Negro puts them together and the meaning that he gives them creates a new language. He has another language, too, and that language is rhythm. It is obvious in music, but it is also expressed in the way he walks and the way he talks. There is a music and rhythm to the way he dresses and the way he cooks. This has been recognized by Negroes for some time now. "Soul" is how these things peculiarly black are recognized by black men in America. In Africa they speak Negritude. It is the same. The recognition of those things uniquely theirs which separate them from the white man. "Soul" and Negritude become even more precious when it is remembered that the white man in America systematically tried to destroy every vestige of racial identity through slavery and slavery's little brother, segregation. It is a testament to the power of "Soul" that it not only survived, but thrived.

Now the Negro is beginning to study his past, to learn those things that have been lost, to recreate what the white man destroyed in him and to destroy that which the white man put in its stead. He has stopped being a Negro and has become a black man in recognition of his new identity, his real identity. "Negro" is an American invention which cut him off from those of the same color in Africa. He recognizes now that part of himself is in Africa. Some feel this in a deeply personal way, as did Mrs.

Fannie Lou Hamer who cried when she was in Africa, because she knew she had relatives there and she would never be able to know them. Her past would always be partially closed.

Many things that have happened in the past six years have had little or no meaning for most whites, but have had vital meaning for Negroes. Wasn't it only a month after the March on Washington that four children were killed in a church bombing in Birmingham? Whites could feel morally outraged, but they couldn't know the futility, despair and anger that swept through The Nation within a nation—Black America. There were limits to how much one people could endure and Birmingham Sunday possibly marked that limit. The enemy was not a system. It was an inhuman fiend who never slept, who never rested and no one would stop him. Those Northern protest rallies where Freedom Songs were sung and speeches speeched and applause applauded and afterwards telegrams and letters sent to the President and Congress—they began to look more and more like moral exercises. See, my hands are clean. I do not condone such a foul deed, they said, going back to their magazine and newspapers, feeling purged because they had made their moral witness.

What was needed that Sunday was ol' John Brown to come riding into Birmingham as he had ridden into Lawrence, Kansas, burning every building that stood and killing every man, woman and child that ran from his onslaught. Killing, killing, killing, turning men into fountains of blood, spouting spouting spouting until Heaven itself drew back before the frothing red ocean.

But the Liberal and his Negro sycophants would've cried, Vengeance accomplishes nothing. You are only acting like your oppressor and such an act makes you no better than him. John Brown, his hands and wrists slick with blood, would've said, oh so softly and so quietly, Mere Vengeance is folly. Purgation is necessity.

Now it is over. America has had chance after chance to show that it really meant "that all men are endowed with certain inalienable rights." America has had precious chances in this decade to make it come true. Now it is over. The days of singing freedom songs and the days of combating bullets and billy clubs with Love. We Shall Overcome (and we have overcome our blindness) sounds old, out-dated and can enter the pantheon of the greats along with the IWW songs and the union songs. As one SNCC veteran put it after the Mississippi March, "Man, the people are too busy getting ready to fight to bother with singing anymore." And as for Love? That's always been better done in bed than on the picket line and marches. Love is fragile and gentle and seeks a like response. They used to sing "I Love Everybody" as they ducked bricks and bottles. Now they sing

> Too much love,
> Too much love,
> Nothing kills a nigger like
> Too much love.

They know, because they still get headaches from the beatings they took while love, love, loving. They know, because they died on those highways and in those jail cells, died from trying to change the hearts of men who had none. They know, the ones who have bleeding ulcers when they're twenty-three and the ones who have to have the eye operations. They know that nothing kills a nigger like too much love.

At one time black people desperately wanted to be American, to communicate with whites, to live in the Beloved Community. Now that is irrelevant. They know that it can't be until whites want it to be and it is obvious now that whites don't want it.

Does all of this mean that every American white is now a potential victim for some young Nat Turner? Does it mean the time is imminent when the red blood of blue-eyed, blonde-haired beauties will glisten on black arms and hands?

For many black people, the time is imminent. For others it simply means the white man no longer exists. He is not to be lived with and he is not to be destroyed. He is simply to be ignored, because the time has come for the black man to control the things which effect his life. Like the Irish control Boston, the black man will control Harlem. For so long the black man lived his life in reaction to whites. Now he will live it only within the framework of his own blackness and his blackness links him with the Indians of Peru, the miner in Bolivia, the African and the freedom fighters of Vietnam. What they fight for is what the American black man fights for— the right to govern his own life. If the white man interprets that to mean hatred, it is only a reflection of his own fears and anxieties and black people leave him to deal with it. There is too much to do to waste time and energy hating white people.

The old order passes away. Like the black riderless horse, boots turned the wrong way in the stirrups, following the coffin down the boulevard, it passes away. But there are no crowds to watch as it passes. There are no crowds, to mourn, to weep. No eulogies to read and no eternal flame is lit over the grave. There is no time for there are streets to be cleaned, houses painted and clothes washed. Everything must be scoured clean. Trash has to be thrown out. Garbage dumped and everything unfit, burned.

> The new order is coming, child.
> The old is passing away.

CONDITIONS IN THE URBAN GHETTO

HARYOU–ACT / Cries of Harlem

The gains of the nonviolent civil rights movement and the legal programs of the NAACP had little relevance to the ghetto dweller, for whom the conditions of life steadily worsened as more and more people were crushed together and confined in the "black" sections of the nation's cities. In 1964 and 1965, the black urban ghettos exploded, and the cities of the North and the West replaced the South as the focus of protest activity. Since that time the urban black has dominated the racial scene.

Harlem Youth Opportunities Unlimited, Inc. (HARYOU) was established in 1962 to try to bring some order to the urban chaos. Its magnificent study of 1964, **Youth in the Ghetto: A Study of the Consequences of Powerlessness,** provided an analysis of the problems of ghetto youth that has not been surpassed. The following statements, taken from that work, give insight into the conditions of the ghetto and the state of mind of the ghetto dweller.

— No, you have to survive. You have to survive, if you don't . . . Well, I'll say if you don't have the proper education that you should have, and you go *downtown* and work, they don't pay you any money worthwhile. You can work all your life and never have anything, and you will always be in debt. So you take to the streets, you understand? You take to the streets and try to make it in the street, you know what you have; out here in the street you try to make it. All right. Being out in the street takes your mind off all these problems. You have no time to think about things because you're trying to make some money. So this is why I'm not up to par on different organizations. I don't belong to any, but perhaps I should. But I haven't taken the time to see or to try to figure it out. I've been trying to make it so hard and trying to keep a piece of money. I'm trying not to work like a dog to get it, and being treated any sort of way to get it. How to make another buck enters your mind. As far as bettering the community, this never enters your mind because it seems to me, well, I'm using my opinions—to me the white man has it locked up. The black man is progressing, but slowly. The only solution I see to it, I mean, if you are actually going to be here awhile, you have to stay healthy and not die, for one thing. The other thing is while you're here you want to live the

---

FROM "Cries of Harlem," *Youth in the Ghetto*, by HARYOU-ACT (New York, 1964), pp. 314, 315–18, 319–20, 323, 334, 336–37, 341. Reprinted with permission of HARYOU-ACT.

best that you can. And since Whitey has all the luxuries, I mean, he has it all locked up, you want to get a piece of it, so you have to make some kind of money so you can get it. You can't get what he's got, definitely, but you can get enough to make you feel comfortable. So you're always scheming how to, you know, how to make some money. —

DRUG ADDICT, MALE,
AGE ABOUT 37.

— Now, they had been complaining to the Department of Health about conditions in the building, about all the violations; no lights in the hall, the rats and roaches literally moving the tenants out of the building, and about six months ago the plumbing in the basement got jammed up somehow or other and there has been standing water in the basement, and the flies and maggots and everything else have been breeding there. Now, yesterday, I understand something happened in one apartment; rats forced the woman out of her apartment. She couldn't at all control the rats; they were running all over the kitchen and all throughout the house and everything. So, last night, the picket line was decided on. —

— Where is the apartment? —

— Where is the apartment? I think it's apartment 2W in —— West 117th Street. So, during the picket line, four tenants who live in this building were out and most of the members of the Leadership Training Program here at HARYOU. There was a meeting with the Deputy Commissioner and in this meeting, all of the violations were pointed out to this man and he said that he would send inspectors to the building today. He suggested that the tenants organize their own council and pool their rents and have repairs made themselves. Now, up until this point, the tenants have been trying to keep the halls clean and you know, keep roaches down, and put down rat poisoning, but the situation got completely out of hand and the health conditions there are so bad that it is really what could break out to be a real health epidemic in that whole block because in ——, the building next to it has been vacated completely and, on occasions, workmen with their trucks have been dumping refuse into this building and other people in the neighborhood throw their garbage down to this building and there is a great accumulation of rats and roaches and everything there. At —— you have maggots and mosquitoes and flies breeding in the basement and rats running all over the building. This naturally spreads on to ——, and then on down the whole block.

As far as press coverage of the whole situation, I don't know about that. The Deputy Commissioner did send out inspectors and I understand that they have just left the building and have gone back down to the Health Department to make a report. Now the thing is that this could, as actually happened before, be tied up in a whole lot of red tape, you know. The

Commissioner said that he would try and find the landlord. The tenants have been complaining for months about conditions. He said that they had tried to find the landlord and they believe that the landlord has just disappeared because the city can't find him. Mr. Gray and some of the tenants say that they know where the landlord is and, in fact, they said that Mr. Gray had spoken to the landlord on the phone. And they have been in contact with the landlord's lawyers, but the city still says that they can't serve a summons on him until they find him. So this could mean being tied up in red tape for a few months more and the fact is that these people can't live under these conditions for a few months more. —

— Yeah, well, one woman said that the rats had chewed the clothes off her baby. That was one thing that was brought out this morning. I don't know about any others. —

— From what I understand, most of the tenants there have children and need from five to six rooms. Now in the past, when they were paying rent, they were only paying around $40 to $45 a month rent and I don't think I know of any place, and I don't think that anybody else does really, where they can get six rooms for $40, you know. —

— I think since this building has been jammed up down there in the basement, if there are large puddles of water down in the basement, I think that's a situation where the tenants should move out immediately; water can get under the building and the whole building can collapse. So I think they should move out immediately. —

— The Deputy Commissioner mentioned that today but the thing is finding places large enough and at rents that they can afford.

They have been filing complaints at the Health Department I know. Then, today the Commissioner came down after the complaints that the people had filed and he had sent inspectors to the building and obviously that's all that's been done.

The tenants said, "We have rats running all over the building!" and he said, "Yes, in May, you reported that. You reported that there was a lot of garbage and there were conditions that could breed rats." Then they said, like the stairs were broken down or something, and he said, "Yes, in February, you know, you reported that and we sent out an inspector," blah, blah, blah. This is all he has been doing is sending out inspectors. —

— What is the next step? —

— A live-in! It is a very nice office. That would be the step for tomorrow morning if nothing constructive is done today. No, this is for tomorrow because they are waiting for the word of what's going to be done from the Health Department because the inspectors just left the building to report back to the Health Department. —

GIRL, AGE 15.

— There's only one teacher that can control them and that was our lady teacher. She was a lady, a big fat lady. Her name was Miss P. and she always argues, and she hits you sometimes, but she was strict. She had big "buns," she was a lady about forty, you know. And the other teachers they used to fool with you, you know, but nobody never could do nothing to her. The whole school respected her; she was the only one that could keep a class organized. And then what happened, when the men teachers—you know, the young men teachers—they come to school and want to show off, you know, so they caught it more.

You know what happened, when I came to this class, my first class; I went to class, and you couldn't do no kind of work. The teacher was so scared to turn his back on the boys, real scared, and they throw a book at him, and the teacher is so scared, they tell him come on and fight, and they all sit down and laugh. They don't care, they like that, so they fight.

Then you'd be sitting down in front and they'd say "Hey, Moe." They call him names. "Hey, Moe, come here, you crazy thing." So he walks out to get the principal and they lock the door, and he can't get back in and the principal can't get in the door. And the next thing you know they take a book, throw it out the window—breaks the class up and then they can't do nothing.

Then we have the lady teachers. They get behind the lady teachers, they feel her ass, they feel her whole body, and the teacher don't say nothing because she's scared.

One class they was able to control was typewriting, because everybody like typewriting, so they controlled it. She was a young teacher. She was kind of skinny, you know, but I tell you, she going to be fighting them, so nobody ain't going to touch her. You go to school, find typewriters broken; you're lucky if you find one typewriter that's good, so everybody's fighting all the time for that, you know.

You have four classes of gym; say four times thirty, that's a lot of people. What happens you can't play basketball 'cause they are so crowded. So you got to do exercise, line up and do exercise; nobody ever do exercise. So what happens, everybody keeps on their nice clean clothes, nobody puts on gym clothes, so they make you get on the floor—everybody with nice clean pants on—they get mad, so one guy says, "I'm not getting on the floor," so the teacher goes on over there; he fight with him a little while, then he tell everybody go in the back and stand there, go in the back and just stand up, or else you gonna get hit. So you go back and you stand up.

Everybody wants to play basketball, that's one of the main things in life, so people get a basketball and they go out in the yard and play basketball. Then the Dean runs out in the yard and catches them and write them up, and every time it's the same thing. The same ones playing basketball, 'cause that's what they like.

Sometimes the school would be crowded, you know, 'cause it's cold outside, so you go to school that day. —

BOY, AGE 15.

— Now when a white kid gets to be 17 or 18, he's ready to go into business. Any subject that you choose to take, or any place that you choose to go, he's qualified because this is his education, he's been taught this. And when he goes to college and comes out, I mean he's ready to master anything that he chooses to take up. But here, I should get the same education, but I can't do it. Even though I'm willing to work and sweat for it, I mean I can't do it. They don't want me to do it! Why? This is what I can't understand. If I'm willing to get out—okay, so I'm willing to take the shovel and go out to dig a ditch. All right, so they're paying $6 an hour for digging this ditch. I'm willing to take a shovel and go dig it; why won't they let me? But the white boys. . . . Take years ago, I mean all you could find on the shovel was black men. —

— So you're saying that they are taking the jobs away from the black man? —

— That's what they're doing because the unions have it in. They organize and run the prices so high that, I mean, it's too much money for the black man, they figure, to be making. —

MAN, AGE ABOUT 30.

— Now we have sense enough to know, the majority of us out here, that to say, for example, the NAACP, when they find work for the members, they think the masses out here should be satisfied because they gave one NAACP member a six thousand a year job. Here are fifteen million hungry people and they should be happy over it? No, it won't last. And I see many things that are going to happen because I am one of the masses. I live with them each and every day, I sleep with them, and I am on the corners with them. When I find work, I will work. And I think that as far as radio and television, I think I am qualified to stand on my own there. They say the old thing is "The first to be fired and the last to be hired." Well, as long as you are black you will get this. You can walk down here and go into the employment office, and before you get up to the desk the head is being shaken—no work. Anything, other than black, behind you, come behind you—"Oh, yes, sit down. Stand over there. We have something for you. Maybe we can find something for you." And two to one, when they leave they have employment. We don't have it. Right here in Harlem, thirty to forty million dollars a year leaves here, and we don't get any of it. —

MAN, AGE 35.

— The white merchants you see in Harlem, that have kids, we send them to college. But how many Negroes do you know in this community send their kids to college? We pay for all the white merchants' kids, for all their schooling. *We* do this, understand what I mean, through dealing with these people. But the rate of colored kids in comparison to the white is very few.

I think we should be trying to do—what we actually should be trying to do is take the money we have, instead of spending it in bars, building churches, as this fellow said, I think we should be trying to take the money and invest it in some worthy business for Whitey! They work for Whitey, and definitely Whitey is not going to have anyone working for him that is not qualified to make him a dollar, or to save him one. If we can do it for him, we can do it for ourselves. That's what we need, the buck! Get that, and you have everything! —

MAN, AGE 30.

— Last night, for instance, the officer stopped some fellows on 125th Street, Car No. ——, that was the number of the car, and because this fellow spoke so nicely for his protection and his rights, the officer said, "All right, everybody get off the street or inside!" Now, it's very hot. We don't have air-conditioned apartments in most of these houses up here, so where are we going if we get off the streets? We can't go back in the house because we almost suffocate. So we sit down on the curb, or stand on the sidewalk, or on the steps, things like that, till the wee hours of the morning, especially in the summer when it's too hot to go up. Now where were we going? But he came out with his nightstick and wants to beat people on the head, and wanted to—he arrested one fellow. The other fellow said, "Well, I'll move, but you don't have to talk to me like a dog."

— I think we should all get together—everybody—all get together and every time one draws back his stick to do something to us, or hits one of us on the head, take the stick and hit *him* on *his* head, so he'll know how it feels to be hit on the head, or kill him, if necessary. Yes, kill him, if necessary. That's how I feel. There is no other way to deal with this man. The only way you can deal with him is the way he has been dealing with us.

MAN, AGE ABOUT 35.

— Churches don't mean us no good. We've been having churches all our lives under the same conditions, and look at the condition we're still in. The church must not have meant anything. See, when you go to church you don't learn how to read and write, and count, at church. You learn that in school. See what I mean? So what good the churches doing us? They are not doing us any good! You could build some factories or something in Harlem and give our people some work near home. That would do us more good than a church. —

MAN, AGE ABOUT 45.

LIBERATION BY ANY MEANS NECESSARY

Malcolm X / Address to a Meeting in New York, 1964

Malcolm X (formerly Malcolm Little) was born in Nebraska in 1925. His father was a militant Baptist clergyman who was also an organizer for Garvey's UNIA. When Malcolm was a child, the family was threatened by the Ku Klux Klan and other racist groups. Eventually, his father was murdered "by person or persons unknown," in the words of the law-enforcement officials who investigated the case.

In his late teens, Malcolm drifted into a life of petty crime and then into a career as a successful hustler. He was caught, arrested, and jailed, and it was while in jail that he was converted to Elijah Muhammad's Nation of Islam. After his release, his remarkable talents led him straight to the number-two spot in the Muslim organization. In 1964, he withdrew from the Nation of Islam and set up an orthodox Muslim mosque as well as a black protest organization, the Association of Afro-American Unity. The last year of his life was spent trying to develop a comprehensive program for black liberation.

The speech reprinted here was given by Malcolm X at a meeting sponsored by the Militant Labor Forum, a socialist organization in New York City, on April 8, 1964, less than a month after his break with Elijah Muhammad. In the speech can be seen the growing internationalism of Malcolm's outlook as well as his critical view of the various civil rights organizations active at the time.

According to Malcolm X, a revolution is necessary to free the black man in America, and though it is possible that this can be accomplished without bloodshed, it is unlikely that it will happen so. Less than a year after he delivered this speech, Malcolm himself was dead, felled by an assassin's bullet.

Friends and enemies, tonight I hope that we can have a little fireside chat with as few sparks as possible being tossed around. Especially because of the very explosive condition that the world is in today. Sometimes, when a person's house is on fire and someone comes in yelling fire, instead of the person who is awakened by the yell being thankful, he makes the mistake of charging the one who awakened him with having set the fire. I hope that this little conversation tonight about the black revolution won't cause many of you to accuse us of igniting it when you find it at your doorstep.

FROM Malcolm X, "The Black Revolution," *Two Speeches by Malcolm X* (New York: Merit, 1965). Reprinted by permission of Merit Publishers and Betty Shabazz.

I'm still a Muslim, that is, my religion is still Islam. I still believe that there is no god but Allah and that Mohammad is the apostle of Allah. That just happens to be my personal religion. But in the capacity which I am functioning in today, I have no intention of mixing my religion with the problems of 22,000,000 black people in this country. Just as it's possible for a great man whom I greatly respect, Ben Bella, to be a Muslim and still be a nationalist, and another one whom I greatly respect, Gamal Nasser, to be a Muslim and still be a nationalist, and Sukarno of Indonesia to be a Muslim and still be a nationalist, it was nationalism which enabled them to gain freedom for their people.

I'm still a Muslim but I'm also a nationalist, meaning that my political philosophy is black nationalism, my economic philosophy is black nationalism, my social philosophy is black nationalism. And when I say that this philosophy is black nationalism, to me this means that the political philosophy of black nationalism is that which is designed to encourage our people, the black people, to gain complete control over the politics and the politicians of our own community.

Our economic philosophy is that we should gain economic control over the economy of our own community, the businesses and the other things which create employment so that we can provide jobs for our own people instead of having to picket and boycott and beg someone else for a job.

And, in short, our social philosophy means that we feel that it is time to get together among our own kind and eliminate the evils that are destroying the moral fiber of our society, like drug addiction, drunkenness, adultery that leads to an abundance of bastard children, welfare problems. We believe that we should lift the level or the standard of our own society to a higher level wherein we will be satisfied and then not inclined toward pushing ourselves into other societies where we are not wanted.

All of that aside, tonight we are dealing with the black revolution. During recent years there has been much talk about a population explosion and whenever they are speaking of the population explosion, in my opinion they are referring primarily to the people in Asia or in Africa—the black, brown, red, and yellow people. It is seen by people of the West that as soon as the standard of living is raised in Africa and Asia, automatically the people begin to reproduce abundantly. And there has been a great deal of fear engendered by this in the minds of the people of the West, who happen to be, on this earth, a very small minority.

In fact, in most of the thinking and planning of whites in the West today it's easy to see the fear in their minds, conscious minds and subconscious minds, that the masses of dark people in the West, in the East rather, who already outnumber them, will continue to increase and multiply and grow until they eventually overrun the people of the West like a human sea, a human tide, a human flood. And the fear of this can be seen in the minds, in the actions, of most of the people here in the West in practically everything that they do. It governs political views and it governs their economic views and it governs most of their attitudes toward the present society.

REASON FOR FILIBUSTER

I was listening to Dirksen, the Senator from Illinois, in Washington, D.C., filibustering the civil-rights bill and one thing that he kept stressing over and over and over was that if this bill is passed it will change the social structure of America. Well, I know what he's getting at, and I think that most other people today, and especially our people, know what is meant when these whites who filibuster these bills, and express fears of changes in the social structure, our people are beginning to realize what they mean.

Just as we can see that all over the world one of the main problems facing the West is race, likewise here in America today, most of your Negro leaders as well as the whites agree that 1964 itself appears to be one of the most explosive years yet in the history of America on the racial front, on the racial scene. Not only is this racial explosion probably to take place in America, but all of the ingredients for this racial explosion in America to blossom into a world-wide racial explosion present themselves right here in front of us. America's racial powder keg, in short, can actually fuse or ignite a world-wide powder keg.

And whites in this country who are still complacent when they see the possibilities of racial strife getting out of hand and you are complacent simply because you think you outnumber the racial minority in this country, what you have to bear in mind is wherein you might outnumber us in this country, you don't outnumber us all over the earth.

And any kind of racial explosion that takes place in this country today, in 1964, is not a racial explosion that can be confined to the shores of America. It is a racial explosion that can ignite the racial powder keg that exists all over the planet that we call earth. Now I think that nobody would disagree that the dark masses of Africa and Asia and Latin America are already seething with bitterness, animosity, hostility, unrest, and impatience with the racial intolerance that they themselves have experienced at the hands of the white West.

And just as they themselves have the ingredients of hostility toward the West in general, here we also have 22,000,000 African-Americans, black, brown, red, and yellow people in this country who are also seething with bitterness and impatience and hostility and animosity at the racial intolerance not only of the white West but of white America in particular.

BLACK NATIONALIST PARTY

And by the hundreds of thousands today we find our own people have become impatient, turning away from your white nationalism, which you call democracy, toward the militant uncompromising policy of black nationalism. I point out right here that as soon as we announced we were going to start a black nationalist party in this country we received mail from coast to coast, especially from young people at the college level, the university level, who expressed complete sympathy and support and a desire to take an active part in any kind of political action based on black nationalism, designed to correct or eliminate immediately evils that our people have suffered here for 400 years.

The black nationalists to many of you may represent only a minority in the community. And therefore you might have a tendency to classify them as something insignificant. But just as the fuse is the smallest part or the smallest piece in the powder keg it is yet that little fuse that ignites the entire powder keg. The black nationalists to you may represent a small minority in the so-called Negro community. But they just happen to be composed of the type of ingredient necessary to fuse or ignite the entire black community. And this is one thing that whites—whether you call yourselves liberals or conservatives or racists or whatever else you might choose to be—one thing that you have to realize is, where the black community is concerned, although there the large majority you come in contact with may impress you as being moderate and patient and loving and long-suffering and all that kind of stuff, the minority who you consider to be Muslims or nationalists happen to be made of the type of ingredient that can easily spark the black community. This should be understood. Because to me a powder keg is nothing without a fuse.

1964 will be America's hottest year; her hottest year yet; a year of much racial violence and much racial bloodshed. But it won't be blood that's going to flow only on one side. The new generation of black people that have grown up in this country during recent years are already forming the opinion, and it's a just opinion, that if there is to be bleeding, it should be reciprocal—bleeding on both sides.

It should also be understood that the racial sparks that are ignited here in America today could easily turn into a flaming fire abroad which only means it could engulf all the people of this earth into a giant race war. You cannot confine it to one little neighborhood, or one little community, or one little country. What happens to a black man in America today happens to the black man in Africa. What happens to a black man in America and Africa happens to the black man in Asia and to the man down in Latin America. What happens to one of us today happens to all of us. And when this is realized I think that the whites—who are intelligent even if they aren't moral or aren't just or aren't impressed by legalities—those who are intelligent will realize that when they touch this one, they are touching all of them, and this in itself will have a tendency to be a checking factor.

The seriousness of this situation must be faced up to. I was in Cleveland last night, Cleveland, Ohio. In fact I was there Friday, Saturday and yesterday. Last Friday the warning was given that this is a year of bloodshed, that the black man has ceased to turn the other cheek, that he has ceased to be non-violent, that he has ceased to feel that he must be confined to all these restraints that are put upon him by white society in struggling for what white society says he was supposed to have had a hundred years ago.

So today, when the black man starts reaching out for what America says are his rights, the black man feels that he is within his rights—when he becomes the victim of brutality by those who are depriving him of his rights —to do whatever is necessary to protect himself. And an example of this was taking place last night at this same time in Cleveland, where the police were putting water hoses on our people there and also throwing tear gas at them and they met a hail of stones, a hail of rocks, a hail of bricks. Couple weeks ago in Jacksonville, Florida, a young teenage Negro was throwing Molotov cocktails.

Well Negroes didn't do this ten years ago. But what you should learn from this is that they are waking up. It was stones yesterday, Molotov cocktails today; it will be hand grenades tomorrow and whatever else is available the next day. The seriousness of this situation must be faced up to. You should not feel that I am inciting someone to violence. I'm only warning of a powder-keg situation. You can take it or leave it. If you take the warning perhaps you can still save yourself. But if you ignore it or ridicule it, well death is already at your doorstep. There are 22,000,000 African-Americans who are ready to fight for independence right here. When I say fight for independence right here, I don't mean any non-violent fight, or turn-the-other-cheek fight. Those days are gone. Those days are over.

If George Washington didn't get independence for this country non-violently, and if Patrick Henry didn't come up with a non-violent statement, and you taught me to look upon them as patriots and heroes, then it's time for you to realize that I have studied your books well.

POWER OF MINORITY

Our people, 22,000,000 African-Americans, are fed up with America's hypocritical democracy and today we care nothing about the odds that are against us. Every time a black man gets ready to defend himself some Uncle Tom tries to tell us, how can you win? That's Tom talking. Don't listen to him. This is the first thing we hear: the odds are against you. You're dealing with black people who don't care anything about odds. We care nothing about odds.

Again I go right back to the people who founded and secured the independence of this country from the colonial power of England. When George Washington and the others got ready to declare or come up with the Declaration of Independence, they didn't care anything about the odds of the British Empire. They were fed up with taxation without representation. And you've got 22,000,000 black people in this country today, 1964, who are fed up with taxation without representation, and will do the same thing. Who are ready, willing and justified to do the same thing today to bring about independence for our people that your forefathers did to bring about independence for your people.

And I say your people because I certainly couldn't include myself among those for whom independence was fought in 1776. How in the world can a Negro talk about the Declaration of Independence when he is still singing "We Shall Overcome." Our people are increasingly developing the opinion that we just have nothing to lose but the chains of segregation and the chains of second-class citizenship.

STRUGGLES WILL MERGE

So 1964 will see the Negro revolt evolve and merge into the world-wide black revolution that has been taking place on this earth since 1945. The so-called revolt will become a real black revolution. Now the black revolution has been taking place in Africa and Asia and in Latin America. Now when I say black, I mean non-white. Black, brown, red or yellow. Our brothers and sisters in Asia, who were colonized by the Europeans, our brothers and sisters in Africa, who were colonized by the Europeans, and in Latin America, the peasants, who were colonized by the Europeans, have been involved in a struggle since 1945 to get the colonialists, or the colonizing powers, the Europeans, off their land, out of their country.

This is a real revolution. Revolution is always based on land. Revolution is never based on begging somebody for an integrated cup of coffee. Revolutions are never fought by turning the other cheek. Revolutions are never based upon love your enemy, and pray for those who spitefully use you. And revolutions are never waged singing, "We Shall Overcome." Revolutions are based upon bloodshed. Revolutions are never compromising. Revolutions are never based upon negotiations. Revolutions are never based upon any kind of tokenism whatsoever. Revolutions are never even based upon that which is begging a corrupt society or a corrupt system to accept us into it. Revolutions overturn systems, and there is no system on this earth which has proven itself more corrupt, more criminal than this system, that in 1964 still colonizes 22,000,000 African-Americans, still enslaves 22,000,000 Afro-Americans.

There is no system more corrupt than a system that represents itself as the example of freedom, the example of democracy and can go all over this earth telling other people how to straighten out their house, and you have citizens of this country who have to use bullets if they want to cast a ballot. The greatest weapon the colonial powers have used in the past against our people has always been divide and conquer.

America is a colonial power. She has colonized 22,000,000 Afro-Americans by depriving us of first-class citizenship, by depriving us of civil rights, actually by depriving us of human rights. She has not only deprived us of the right to be a citizen, she has deprived us of the right to be human beings, the right to be recognized and respected as men and women. And in this country the black can be 50 years old and he is still a "boy."

I grew up with white people. I was integrated before they even invented the word and I have never met white people yet—if you are around them long enough—who won't refer to you as a "boy" or a "gal," no matter how old you are or what school you came out of, no matter what your intellectual or professional level is. In this society we remain "boys."

AMERICA'S STRATEGY

So America's strategy is the same strategy as that which was used in the past by the colonial powers: divide and conquer. She plays one Negro leader against the other. She plays one Negro organization against the other. She makes us think we have different objectives, different goals. As soon as one Negro says something, she runs to this Negro and asks him what do you think about what he said. Why anybody can see through that today—except some of the Negro leaders.

All of our people have the same goals. The same objective. That objective is freedom, justice, equality. All of us want recognition and respect as human beings. We don't want to be integrationists. Nor do we want to be separationists. We want to be human beings. Integration is only a method that is used by some groups to obtain freedom, justice, equality and respect as human beings. Separation is only a method that is used by other groups to obtain freedom, justice, equality or human dignity.

So our people have made the mistake of confusing the methods with the objectives. As long as we agree on objectives, we should never fall out with each other just because we believe in different methods or tactics or strategy to reach a common objective.

We have to keep in mind at all times that we are not fighting for integration, nor are we fighting for separation. We are fighting for recognition as human beings. We are fighting for the right to live as free humans in this society. In fact, we are actually fighting for rights that are even greater than civil rights and that is human rights.

We are fighting for human rights in 1964. This is a shame. The civil-rights struggle has failed to produce concrete results because it has kept us barking up the wrong tree. It has made us put the cart ahead of the horse. We must have human rights before we can secure civil rights. We must be respected as humans before we can be recognized as citizens.

Among the so-called Negroes in this country, as a rule the civil-rights groups, those who believe in civil rights, they spend most of their time trying to prove they are Americans. Their thinking is usually domestic, confined to the boundaries of America, and they always look upon themselves as a minority. When they look upon themselves upon the American stage, the American stage is a white stage. So a black man standing on that stage in America automatically is in the minority. He is the underdog, and in his struggle he always uses an approach that is a begging, hat-in-hand, compromising approach.

Whereas the other segment or section in America, known as the nationalist, black nationalists, are more interested in human rights than they are in civil rights. And they place more stress on human rights than they do on civil rights. The difference between the thinking and the scope of the Negroes who are involved in the human-rights struggle and those who are involved in the civil-rights struggle—those so-called Negroes involved in the human-rights struggle don't look upon themselves as Americans.

They look upon themselves as a part of dark mankind. They see the whole struggle not within the confines of the American stage, but they look upon the struggle on the world stage. And, in the world context, they see that the dark man outnumbers the white man. On the world stage the white man is just a microscopic minority.

So in this country you find two different types of Afro-Americans, the type who looks upon himself as a minority and you as the majority, because his scope is limited to the American scene; and then you have the type who looks upon himself as part of the majority and you as part of a microscopic minority. And this one uses a different approach in trying to struggle for his rights. He doesn't beg. He doesn't thank you for what you give him, because you are only giving him what he should have had a hundred years ago. He doesn't think you are doing him any favors.

NO PROGRESS

He doesn't see any progress that he has made since the Civil War. He sees not one iota of progress because, number one, if the Civil War had freed him, he wouldn't need civil-rights legislation today. If the Emancipation Proclamation, issued by that great shining liberal called Lincoln, had freed him, he wouldn't be singing "We Shall Overcome" today. If the amendments to the Constitution had solved his problem, still his problem wouldn't be here today. And even if the Supreme Court desegregation decision of 1954 was genuinely and sincerely designed to solve his problem, his problem wouldn't be with us today.

So this kind of black man is thinking, he can see where every maneuver that America has made—supposedly to solve this problem—has been nothing but political trickery and treachery of the worst order. So today he doesn't have any confidence in these so-called liberals. Now I know that you—all that have come in here tonight don't call yourselves liberals. Because that's a nasty name today. It represents hypocrisy. So these two different types of black people exist in the so-called Negro community and they are beginning to wake up and their awakening is producing a very dangerous situation.

So you have whites in the community who express sincerity when they say they want to help. Well how can they help? How can a white person help the black man solve his problem? Number one: you can't solve it for him. You can help him solve it, but you can't solve it for him today. One of the best ways that you can solve it—or to help him solve it—is to let the so-called Negro, who has been involved in the civil-rights struggle, see that the civil-rights struggle must be expanded beyond the level of civil rights to human rights. Once it is expanded beyond the level of civil rights to the level of human rights, it opens the door for all of our brothers and sisters in Africa and Asia, who have their independence, to come to our rescue.

CRIMINAL SITUATION

Why, when you go to Washington, D.C., expecting those crooks down there to pass some kind—and that's what they are—to pass some kind of civil-rights legislation to correct a very criminal situation, what you are doing is encouraging the black man, who is the victim, to take his case into the court that's controlled by the criminal that made him the victim. It will never be solved in that way. Just like running from the wolf to the fox. The civil-rights struggle involves the black man taking his case to the white man's court. But when he fights it at the human-rights level, it is a different situation. It opens the door to take Uncle Sam to the world court. The black man doesn't have to go to court to be free. Uncle Sam should be taken to court and made to tell why the black man is not free in a so-called free society. Uncle Sam should be taken into the United Nations and charged with violating the UN charter on human rights.

You can forget civil rights. How are you going to get civil rights with men like Eastland and men like Dirksen and men like Johnson? It has to be taken out of their hands and taken into the hands of those whose power and authority exceed theirs. Washington has become too corrupt. Uncle Sam's conscience—Uncle Sam has become bankrupt when it comes to a conscience—it is impossible for Uncle Sam to solve the problem of 22,000,000 black people in this country. It is absolutely impossible to do it in Uncle Sam's courts—whether it is the Supreme Court or any other kind of court that comes under Uncle Sam's jurisdiction.

The only alternative that the black man has in America today is to take it out of Senator Dirksen's and Senator Eastland's and President Johnson's jurisdiction and take it downtown on the East River and place it before that body of men who represent international law and let them know that the human rights of black people are being violated in the country that professes to be the moral leader of the free world.

Any time you have a filibuster in America, in the Senate, in 1964 over the rights of 22,000,000 black people, over the citizenship of 22,000,000 black people or that will effect the freedom and justice and equality of 22,000,000 black people, it's time for that government itself to be taken before a world court. How can you condemn South Africa? There are only 11,000,000 of our people in South Africa, there are 22,000,000 of them here. And we are receiving an injustice which is just as criminal as that which is being done to the black people of South Africa.

So today those whites who profess to be liberals—and as far as I am concerned it's just lip profession—you understand why our people don't have civil rights. You're white. You can go and hang out with another white liberal and see how hypocritical they are. While a lot of you sitting right here, know that you've seen whites up in a Negro's face with flowery words and as soon as that Negro walks away you listen to how your white friend talks. We have black people who can pass as white. We know how you talk.

We can see that it is nothing but a governmental conspiracy to continue to deprive the black people in this country of their rights. And the only way we will get these rights restored is by taking it out of Uncle Sam's hands. Take him to court and charge him with genocide, the mass murder of millions of black people in this country—political murder, economic murder, social murder, mental murder. This is the crime that this government has committed and, if you yourself don't do something about it in time, you are going to open the doors for something to be done about it from outside forces.

I read in the paper yesterday where one of the Supreme Court Justices, Goldberg, was crying about the violation of human rights of 3,000,000 Jews in the Soviet Union. Imagine this. I haven't got anything against Jews, but that's their problem. How in the world are you going to cry about problems on the other side of the world when you haven't got the problems straightened out here? How can the plight of 3,000,000 Jews in Russia be qualified to be taken to the United Nations by a man who is a Justice in this Supreme Court, and is supposed to be a liberal, supposed to be a friend of black people and hasn't opened up his mouth one time about taking the plight of black people down here to the United Nations?

POLITICALLY MATURE

Our people are becoming more politically mature. Their eyes are coming open. They are beginning to see the trend in all of the American politics today. They notice that every time there is an election it is so close among whites that they have to count the votes over again. This happened in Massachusetts when they were running for governor, this happened in Rhode Island, it happened in Minnesota, and many other places, and it happened in the election between Kennedy and Nixon. Things are so close that any minority that has a bloc vote can swing it either way.

And I think that most students of political science agree that it was the 80 per cent support that Kennedy got from the black man in this country that enabled him to sit in the White House. Sat down there four years and the Negro was still in the doghouse. The same ones that we put in the White House have continued to keep us in the doghouse. The Negro can see that he holds the balance of power in this country politically.

It is he who puts in office the one who gets in office. Yet when the Negro helps that person get in office the Negro gets nothing in return. All he gets is a few appointments. A few handpicked Uncle Tom handkerchief-head Negroes are given big jobs in Washington, D.C. And then those Negroes come back and try and make us think that that administration is going to lead us to the promised land of integration. And the only ones whose problems have been solved have been those handpicked Negroes. A few big Negroes got jobs who didn't even need the jobs. They already were working. But the masses of black people are still unemployed.

The present administration, the Democratic administration, has been there for four years. Yet no meaningful legislation has been passed by them that proposes to benefit black people in this country, despite the fact that in the House they have 267 Democrats and only 177 are Republicans. They control two thirds of the House. In the Senate there are 67 Democrats and only 33 Republicans. The Democrats control two thirds of the government and it is the Negroes who put them in a position to control the government. Yet they give the Negroes nothing in return but a few handouts in the form of appointments that are only used as window-dressing to make it appear that the problem is being solved.

TRICKERY AND TREACHERY

No, something is wrong. And when these black people wake up and find out for real the trickery and the treachery that has been heaped upon us you are going to have revolution. And when I say revolution I don't mean that stuff they were talking about last year about "We Shall Overcome." The Democrats get Negro support, yet the Negroes get nothing in return. The Negroes put the Democrats first, yet the Democrats put the Negroes last. And the alibi that the Democrats use—they blame the Dixiecrats.

A Dixiecrat is nothing but a Democrat in disguise. You show me a Dixiecrat and I'll show a Democrat. And chances are, you show me a Democrat and I'll show you a Dixiecrat. Because Dixie in reality means all that territory south of the Canadian border. There are 16 Senatorial committees that run this government. Of the 16 Senatorial committees that run the government, ten of them are controlled by chairmen that are from the South. Of the 20 Congressional committees that help run the government, 12 of them are controlled by Southern segregationists.

Think of this: ten of the Senatorial committees are in the hands of the Dixiecrats, 12 of the 20 Congressional committees are in the hands of the Dixiecrats. These committees control the government. And you're going to tell us that the South lost the Civil War? The South controls the government. And they control it because they have seniority. And they have seniority because in the states that they come from, they deny Negroes the right to vote.

If Negroes could vote south of the—yes, if Negroes could vote South of the Canadian border—south South, if Negroes could vote in the southern part of the South, Ellender wouldn't be the head of the Agricultural and Forestry Committee, Richard Russell wouldn't be head of the Armed Services Committee, Robertson of Virginia wouldn't be head of the Banking and Currency Committee. Imagine that, all of the banking and currency of the government is in the hands of a cracker.

In fact, when you see how many of these committee men are from the South you can see that we have nothing but a cracker government in Washington, D.C. And their head is a cracker President. I said a cracker President. Texas is just as much a cracker state as Mississippi—and even more so. In Texas they lynch you with a Texas accent and in Mississippi they lynch you with a Mississippi accent.

And the first thing this man did when he came in office was invite all the big Negroes down for coffee. James Farmer was one of the first ones —the head of CORE. I have nothing against him. He's all right—Farmer, that is. But could that same President have invited James Farmer to Texas for coffee? And if James Farmer went to Texas, could he have taken his white wife with him to have coffee with the President? Any time you have a man who can't straighten out Texas, how can he straighten out the country? No, you're barking up the wrong tree.

If Negroes in the South could vote, the Dixiecrats would lose power. When the Dixiecrats lost power, the Democrats would lose power. A Dixiecrat lost is a Democrat lost. Therefore the two of them have to conspire with each other to stay in power. The Northern Dixiecrat puts all the blame on the Southern Dixiecrat. It's a con game, a giant political con game. The job of the Northern Democrat is to make the Negro think that he is our friend. He is always smiling and wagging his tail and telling us how much he can do for us if we vote for him. But, at the same time he's out in front telling us what he's going to do, behind the door he's in cahoots with the Southern Democrat setting up the machinery to make sure he'll never have to keep his promise.

This is the conspiracy that our people have faced in this country for the past 100 years. And today you have a new generation of black people who have come on the scene who have become disenchanted with the entire system, who have become disillusioned over the system and who are ready now and willing to do something about it. So in my conclusion in speaking about the black revolution, America today is at a time or in a day or at an hour where she is the first country on this earth that can actually have a bloodless revolution. In the past revolutions have been bloody. Historically you just don't have a peaceful revolution. Revolutions are bloody, revolutions are violent, revolutions cause bloodshed and death follows in their paths. America is the only country in history in a position to bring about a revolution without violence and bloodshed. But America is not morally equipped to do so.

Why is America in a position to bring about a bloodless revolution? Because the Negro in this country holds the balance of power and if the Negro in this country were given what the Constitution says he is supposed to have, the added power of the Negro in this country would sweep all of the racists and the segregationists out of office. It would change the entire political structure of the country. It would wipe out the Southern segregationism that now controls America's foreign policy, as well as America's domestic policy.

And the only way without bloodshed that this can be brought about is that the black man has to be given full use of the ballot in every one of the 50 states. But if the black man doesn't get the ballot, then you are going to be faced with another man who forgets the ballot and starts using the bullet.

Revolutions are fought to get control of land, to remove the absentee landlord and gain control of the land and the institutions that flow from that land. The black man has been in a very low condition because he has had no control whatsoever over any land. He has been a beggar economically, a beggar politically, a beggar socially, a beggar even when it comes to trying to get some education. So that in the past the type of mentality that was developed in this colonial system among our people, today is being overcome. And as the young ones come up they know what they want. And as they listen to your beautiful preaching about democracy and all those other flowery words, they know what they're supposed to have.

So you have a people today who not only know what they want, but also know what they are supposed to have. And they themselves are clearing another generation that is coming up that not only will know what it wants and know what it should have, but also will be ready and willing to do whatever is necessary to see that what they should have materializes immediately. Thank you.

ALL POWER TO THE PEOPLE—BLACK POWER TO BLACK PEOPLE

The Black Panther Party / What We Want, What We Believe

A new organization of militant young blacks appeared on the West Coast in 1966. Borrowing the emblem of a black political party in Lowndes County, Alabama, they called themselves the Black Panther Party for Self Defense. The panther was an apt symbol, for though it is not an aggressive animal, it fiercely defends itself when cornered. The purpose of the Black Panthers was to defend the black people in the Oakland, California, ghetto.

Founded by Huey Newton and Bobby Seale, the Panther Party has attracted many young blacks because of its uncompromising position on racial liberation and its affirmation of black strength and black pride. Needless to say, it has also attracted the hostility of the law-enforcement authorities, who have systematically tried to suppress the party since its inception and have put most Panther leaders across the country in jail on one charge or another.

The following is the platform and program of the Black Panther Party, drawn up in October 1966. It is based on the theory of self-determination typical of the nationalists and contains specific criticisms of some of the policies that have led to the oppression of black people. The document concludes with some familiar words about the justice, even the necessity, of revolution when a government loses the consent of the governed.

---

1. We want freedom. We want power to determine the destiny of our Black Community.

We believe that black people will not be free until we are able to determine our destiny.

2. We want full employment for our people.

We believe that the federal government is responsible and obligated to give every man employment or a guaranteed income. We believe that if the white American businessmen will not give full employment, then the means of production should be taken from the businessmen and placed in the community so that the people of the community can organize and employ all of its people and give a high standard of living.

3. We want an end to the robbery by the white man of our Black Community.

We believe that this racist government has robbed us and now we are demanding the overdue debt of forty acres and two mules. Forty acres and two mules was promised 100 years ago as restitution for slave labor and mass murder of black people. We will accept the payment in currency which will be distributed to our many communities. The Germans are now aiding the Jews in Israel for the genocide of the Jewish people. The Germans murdered six million Jews. The American racist has taken part in the slaughter of over fifty million black people; therefore, we feel that this is a modest demand that we make.

4. We want decent housing, fit for shelter of human beings.

We believe that if the white landlords will not give decent housing to our black community, then the housing and the land should be made into cooperatives so that our community, with government aid, can build and make decent housing for its people.

FROM the Black Panther Party, "Platform and Program of the Black Panther Party" (October 1966). Reprinted with permission.

5. We want education for our people that exposes the true nature of this decadent American society. We want education that teaches us our true history and our role in the present-day society.

We believe in an educational system that will give to our people a knowledge of self. If a man does not have knowledge of himself and his position in society and the world, then he has little chance to relate to anything else.

6. We want all black men to be exempt from military service.

We believe that Black people should not be forced to fight in the military service to defend a racist government that does not protect us. We will not fight and kill other people of color in the world who, like black people, are being victimized by the white racist government of America. We will protect ourselves from the force and violence of the racist police and the racist military, by whatever means necessary.

7. We want an immediate end to POLICE BRUTALITY and MURDER of black people.

We believe we can end police brutality in our black community by organizing black self-defense groups that are dedicated to defending our black community from racist police oppression and brutality. The Second Amendment to the Constitution of the United States gives a right to bear arms. We therefore believe that all black people should arm themselves for self-defense.

8. We want freedom for all black men held in federal, state, county and city prisons and jails.

We believe that all black people should be released from the many jails and prisons because they have not received a fair and impartial trial.

9. We want all black people when brought to trial to be tried in court by a jury of their peer group or people from their black communities, as defined by the Constitution of the United States.

We believe that the courts should follow the United States Constitution so that black people will receive fair trials. The 14th Amendment of the U.S. Constitution gives a man a right to be tried by his peer group. A peer is a person from a similar economic, social, religious, geographical, environmental, historical and racial background. To do this the court will be forced to select a jury from the black community from which the black defendant came. We have been, and are being tried by all-white juries that have no understanding of the "average reasoning man" of the black community.

10. We want land, bread, housing, education, clothing, justice and peace. And as our major political objective, a United Nations–supervised plebiscite to be held throughout the black colony in which only black colonial subjects will be allowed to participate, for the purpose of determining the will of black people as to their national destiny.

When, in the course of human events, it becomes necessary for one people to dissolve the political bands which have connected them with another, and to assume, among the powers of the earth, the separate and equal station to which the laws of nature and nature's God entitle them, a decent respect to the opinions of mankind requires that they should declare the causes which impel them to the separation.

We hold these truths to be self-evident, that all men are created equal; that they are endowed by their Creator with certain unalienable rights; that among these are life, liberty, and the pursuit of happiness. That, to secure these rights, governments are instituted among men, deriving their just powers from the consent of the governed; that, whenever any form of government becomes destructive of these ends, it is the right of the people to alter or to abolish it, and to institute a new government, laying its foundation on such principles, and organizing its powers in such form, as to them shall seem most likely to effect their safety and happiness. Prudence, indeed, will dictate that governments long established should not be changed for light and transient causes; and, accordingly, all experience hath shown, that mankind are more disposed to suffer, while evils are sufferable, than to right themselves by abolishing the forms to which they are accustomed. But, when a long train of abuses and usurpations, pursuing invariably the same object, evinces a design to reduce them under absolute despotism, it is their right, it is their duty, to throw off such government, and to provide new guards for their future security.

13

SUGGESTIONS FOR FURTHER READING

Benjamin Muse, *The American Negro Revolution: From Nonviolence to Black Power, 1963–1967* (Indiana University Press, 1968), though highly opinionated, is useful because it contains a wealth of detail. The beginnings of the shift from nonviolence to militancy can be seen in Robert F. Williams' *Negroes With Guns* (Marzani and Munsell, 1964) and in James Baldwin's ambivalent *The Fire Next Time** (Dial, 1963). Harold Isaacs, in *The New World of Negro Americans** (Day, 1963), describes the growing international perspective of American blacks during the early 1960's. The increasing militancy of blacks is perceptively treated in Charles E. Silberman, *Crisis in Black and White** (Random House, 1964).

The conditions of life in the ghetto are compellingly revealed in two auto-biographies, Claude Brown's *Manchild in the Promised Land** (Macmillan, 1965) and Piri Thomas' *Down These Mean Streets** (Knopf, 1967). Kenneth Clark, in *Dark Ghetto: Dilemmas of Social Power** (Harper and Row, 1965), analyzes the destructive elements of black ghetto existence.

The Kerner Riot Commission Report, officially titled *Report of the National Advisory Commission on Civil Disorders** (U.S. Government Printing Office, 1968), is a good starting place for a study of urban violence. Two books dealing with specific outbreaks are Robert Conot's excellent *Rivers of Blood, Years of Darkness** (Bantam, 1967), the story of the Watts riot of 1965, and John Hersey's *The Algiers Motel Incident* (Knopf, 1968), a treatment of one aspect of the Detroit riot of 1967.

The best available book on black nationalism in America is by the Nigerian political scientist E. U. Essien-Udom. This work, *Black Nationalism: The Search for an Identity in America** (University of Chicago Press, 1962), is primarily a study of the Black Muslims, but its implications are far-reaching. C. Eric Lincoln, *The Black Muslims in America** (Beacon, 1961), is weak on analysis but contains much valuable information about the Muslims. For Muslim thought, see Elijah Muhammad, *The Supreme Wisdom: The Solution to the So-called Negroes' Problem* (University of Islam, 1957).

A basic source for a study of recent black nationalist thought is *The Wretched of the Earth** (Grove, 1963), by Frantz Fanon, a French West Indian black who was active in the war for Algerian independence. The most important American black nationalist leader was Malcolm X, who was assassinated in 1964. His literary legacy includes *The Autobiography of Malcolm X** (Grove, 1964) and *Malcolm X Speaks** (Merit, 1965). The latter was edited by George Breitman, who also wrote *The Last Year of Malcolm X** (Merit, 1967). A collection of essays dealing with the influence of Malcolm X on subsequent developments in the black community is John Henrik Clarke (ed.), *Malcolm X: The Man and His Times** (Macmillan 1969).

Other works of interest are Thomas F. Pettigrew, *A Profile of the Negro*

*American** (Van Nostrand, 1964), an excellent social-psychological study of the black American, and Lee Rainwater and William Yancy (eds.), *The Moynihan Report and the Politics of Controversy** (M.I.T. Press, 1967), which contains the controversial Moynihan report on the black family and the responses to that report. The first work to appear on the Black Panther Party is Gene Marine, *The Black Panthers** (New American Library, 1969).

14 BLACK POWER EXPLAINED

Once the singing was over, what was to be done? The cry of "Black Power" had been raised, and new ranks were forming to carry on the struggle for civil rights. It was ironic that the first lines drawn in the new black movement were between the young militant groups and the older, more moderate organizations such as the NAACP and the Urban League. Many lost sight of the fact that the older groups were the ones that had brought about the change in the legal atmosphere that permitted such a cry to be raised. If Carmichael had shouted "Black Power" a generation earlier, he would have been jailed for a long period of time or, even more likely, shot down in the road by the law-enforcement authorities. The gains of the movement for equal rights had led to what is often called a "revolution of rising expectations": demands rose in intensity as they grew closer to being fulfilled.

Although "Black Power" was first raised merely as a battle cry in the field, it soon began to take on a broader meaning, much of it derived from black nationalist thought of the distant as well as the immediate past. In the fall of 1966, Carmichael himself wrote several articles in liberal journals in which he attempted to give substance to the notion of black power. When he had finished. it sounded very much like the black nationalism of which Malcolm X had spoken before his death—self-determination for black people in communities of their own. Carmichael followed Malcolm X in emphasizing human rights rather than civil rights. This stress on human rights was intended to point out that even if civil rights were obtained in the United States, many people would continue to lead oppressed lives because of the basic capitalist structure of American society.

While the NAACP continued to work in its traditional patterns, providing aid and counsel to those deprived of civil rights, other organizations were visibly shifting their line of attack. Beginning in January 1966, CORE, under the leadership of Floyd McKissick, assumed a more aggressive posture on the civil rights scene. During its convention in July of that year, CORE adopted resolutions calling for United States disengagement from the war in Vietnam, rejecting the technique of nonviolence in the fight for black liberation, and adopting black power as a goal for the organization. Since that time, white participation in CORE has been discouraged by the leadership, and the originally nonviolent organization has become increasingly militant and nationalist in outlook. In 1969, under the leadership of Roy Innis,

CORE became the primary advocate among black organizations of the Nixon administration's avowed policy of developing black capitalism—that is, the policy of strengthening the economic resources of the black community.

The Urban League, on the other hand, has not sought to divest itself of the support of interested whites. But it has focused its attention on the urban ghetto as the place where massive aid is needed. It has provided supplemental education in store-front schools and academies and has concentrated even more than previously on bringing help to the urban poor. In the past, the League has been responsible for many a breakthrough for blacks in the urban labor market, but now it is attempting to make an even greater impact by beginning its work earlier, with job-training and apprenticeship programs of all kinds.

The potency of the slogan "Black Power" was revealed as almost every old civil rights organization and several new ones took positions explaining what the words meant to them. In July 1966, a group that called itself the National Committee of Negro (later Black) Churchmen issued a statement explaining that black power was merely the demand that black Americans get what whites already had, the sense of worth that can only be gained when men have power over their own lives.

In Newark in 1967, at a Black Power Conference from which whites were generally barred, the idea of establishing a separate, all-black nation within the current borders of the United States was revived. The Black Muslims had spoken before of such a nation, but always in such vague terms that the notion of partition never really took roots in the black community. After the Newark Conference, however, separatist ideology began to flourish among some groups of militant blacks. Rejecting the struggle for equality or even group self-determination within an integrated United States, radical separatists called for the establishment of an independent "homeland" for black Americans.

Perhaps the most important development within black America since the Newark meeting has been the increasing visibility and militancy of the black student movement on both predominantly black and predominantly white campuses. One reason for the change has undoubtedly been the enrollment of large numbers of ghetto youths in the colleges. As they encountered what seemed to them to be the irrelevancies of higher education, they began to insist on courses of study that would help them establish their identities and aid them in reconstructing the ghettos from which they came. Many of these young blacks reject the normal route of upward economic mobility—the customary reward for receiving academic credentials. Instead, often deriving their ideology from the black revolutionary writings of such men as Frantz Fanon, the black supporter of the Algerian Revolution, and Eldridge Cleaver and Huey Newton of the California Black Panthers, they seek to transform the capitalist system by reorganizing it from the bottom up. They see American blacks as a colonized people searching for liberation. New forms of economic and political organization will be needed in this process. To this end, black student groups are experimenting with power and community development.

In the face of increasing student militancy, the established authorities of the larger society have begun to try to put down the incipient rebellion. This has led to several violent clashes between police and young black militants, many of whom are students. But the current student generation. both black and white, is not likely to be turned around as it struggles to build a more humane society. Freedom is still indivisible; as long as one man is a slave, no one is truly free.

THE MEANING OF BLACK POWER

Stokely Carmichael / Toward Black Liberation

Carmichael undertook to explain the meaning of black power in the fall of 1966. Speaking often and writing much about the subject, he developed a theory that closely resembled the black nationalism enunciated by Malcolm X.

In the article that follows, Carmichael attacks the unjustified sensationalism with which the press approached the notion of black power. He goes on to point out how the press tended to divide the civil rights movement into "responsible" and "irresponsible" groups, thus diminishing the possibility of cooperation among all black people.

In his analysis of powerlessness, which he considered to be the heart of the race problem, Carmichael distinguished between individual and institutional racism and suggested that the same tactics would not work to eliminate both. What was needed was for black people to gain control over their lives, economically, socially, and politically, so that they would no longer have to submit to the institutions of a racist white world. The practical working out of this plan Carmichael left to others.

One of the most pointed illustrations of the need for Black Power, as a positive and redemptive force in a society degenerating into a form of totalitarianism, is to be made by examining the history of distortion that the concept has received in national media of publicity. In this "debate," as in everything else that affects our lives, Negroes are dependent on, and at the discretion of, forces and institutions within the white society which have little interest in representing us honestly. Our experience with the national press has been that where they have managed to escape a meretricious special interest in "Git Whitey" sensationalism and race-war mongering, individual reporters and commentators have been conditioned by the enveloping racism of the society to the point where they are incapable even of objective observation and reporting of racial *incidents*, much less the analysis of *ideas*. But this limitation of vision and perceptions is an inevitable consequence of the dictatorship of definition, interpretation, and consciousness, along with the censorship of history that the society has inflicted upon the Negro—and itself.

Our concern for black power addresses itself directly to this problem,

FROM Stokely Carmichael, "Toward Black Liberation," *The Massachusetts Review*, Vol. VII (Autumn 1966), pp. 639–51. Copyright © 1966, The Student Nonviolent Coordinating Committee. Reprinted with permission.

the necessity to reclaim our history and our identity from the cultural terrorism and depredation of self-justifying white guilt.

To do this we shall have to struggle for the right to create our own terms through which to define ourselves and our relationship to the society, and to have these terms recognized. This is the first necessity of a free people, and the first right that any oppressor must suspend. The white fathers of American racism knew this—instinctively it seems—as is indicated by the continuous record of the distortion and omission in their dealings with the red and black men. In the same way that southern apologists for the "Jim Crow" society have so obscured, muddied and misrepresented the record of the reconstruction period, until it is almost impossible to tell what really happened, their contemporary counterparts are busy doing the same thing with the recent history of the civil rights movement.

In 1964, for example, the National Democratic Party, led by L. B. Johnson and Hubert H. Humphrey, cynically undermined the efforts of Mississippi's Black population to achieve some degree of political representation. Yet, whenever the events of that convention are recalled by the press, one sees only that version fabricated by the press agents of the Democratic Party. A year later the House of Representatives in an even more vulgar display of political racism made a mockery of the political rights of Mississippi's Negroes when it failed to unseat the Mississippi Delegation to the House which had been elected through a process which methodically and systematically excluded over 450,000 voting-age Negroes, almost one half of the total electorate of the state. Whenever this event is mentioned in print it is in terms which leaves one with the rather curious impression that somehow the oppressed Negro people of Mississippi are at fault for confronting the Congress with a situation in which they had no alternative but to endorse Mississippi's racist political practices.

I mention these two examples because, having been directly involved in them, I can see very clearly the discrepancies between what happened, and the versions that are finding their way into general acceptance as a kind of popular mythology. Thus the victimization of the Negro takes place in two phases—first it occurs in fact and deed, then, and this is equally sinister, in the official recording of those facts.

The "Black Power" program and concept which is being articulated by SNCC, CORE, and a host of community organizations in the ghettoes of the North and South has not escaped that process. The white press has been busy articulating their own analyses, their own interpretations, and criticisms of their own creations. For example, while the press had given wide and sensational dissemination to attacks made by figures in the Civil Rights movement—foremost among which are Roy Wilkins of the NAACP and Whitney Young of the Urban League—and to the hysterical ranting about black racism made by the political chameleon that now serves as Vice-President, it has generally failed to give accounts of the reasonable and productive dialogue which is taking place in the Negro community, and in certain important areas in the white religious and intellectual community. A national committee of influential Negro Churchmen affiliated with the National Council of Churches, despite their obvious respectability and responsibility, had to resort to a paid advertisement to articulate their position, while anyone shouting the hysterical yappings of "Black Racism" got ample space. Thus the American people have gotten at best a superficial and misleading account of the very terms and tenor of this debate. I wish to quote briefly from the statement by the national committee of Churchmen which I suspect that the majority of Americans will not have seen. This statement appeared in the *New York Times* of July 31, 1966.

> *We an informal group of Negro Churchmen in America are deeply disturbed about the crisis brought upon our country by historic distortions of important human realities in the controversy about "black power." What we see shining through the variety of rhetoric is not anything new but the same old problem of power and race which has faced our beloved country since 1619.*
>
> *. . . The conscience of black men is corrupted because, having no power to implement the demands of conscience, the concern for justice in the absence of justice becomes a chaotic self-surrender. Powerlessness breeds a race of beggars. We are faced now with a situation where powerless conscience meets conscience-less power, threatening the very foundations of our Nation.*
>
> *. . .* We deplore the overt violence of riots, but we feel it is more important to focus on the real sources of these eruptions. These sources may be abetted inside the Ghetto, but their basic cause lies in the silent and covert violence which white middleclass America inflicts upon the victims of the inner city.
>
> *. . .* In short; the failure of American leaders to use American power to create equal opportunity *in life* as well as *law*, this is the real problem and not the anguished cry for black power.
>
> *. . .* Without the capacity to *participate with power, i.e.,* to have some organized political and economic strength to really influence people with whom one interacts—integration is not meaningful.
>
> *. . .* America has asked its Negro citizens to fight for opportunity as *individuals,* whereas at certain points in our history what we have needed most has been opportunity for the *whole group,* not just for selected and approved Negroes.
>
> *. . .* We must not apologize for the existence of this form of group power, for we have been oppressed as a group and not as individuals. We will not find our way out of that oppression until both we and America accept the need for Negro Americans, as well as for Jews, Italians, Poles, and white Anglosaxon Protestants, among others, to have and to wield group power.[1]

Traditionally, for each new ethnic group, the route to social and political integration into America's pluralistic society, has been through the organ-

---

[1] [© 1966 by The New York Times Company. Reprinted by permission. Ed.]

ization of their own institutions with which to represent their communal needs within the larger society. This is simply stating what the advocates of black power are saying. The strident outcry, *particularly* from the liberal community, that has been evoked by this proposal can only be understood by examining the historic relationship between Negro and White power in this country.

Negroes are defined by two forces, their blackness and their powerlessness. There have been traditionally two communities in America. The White community, which controlled and defined the forms that all institutions within the society would take, and the Negro community which has been excluded from participation in the power decisions that shaped the society, and has traditionally been dependent upon, and subservient to the White community.

This has not been accidental. The history of every institution of this society indicates that a major concern in the ordering and structuring of the society has been the maintaining of the Negro community in its condition of dependence and oppression. This has not been on the level of individual acts of discrimination between individual whites against individual Negroes, but as total acts by the White community against the Negro community. This fact cannot be too strongly emphasized—that racist assumptions of white superiority have been so deeply ingrained in the structure of the society that it infuses its entire functioning, and is so much a part of the national subconscious that it is taken for granted and is frequently not even recognized.

Let me give an example of the difference between individual racism and institutionalized racism, and the society's response to both. When unidentified white terrorists bomb a Negro Church and kill five children, that is an act of individual racism, widely deplored by most segments of the society. But when in that same city, Birmingham, Alabama, not five but 500 Negro babies die each year because of a lack of proper food, shelter and medical facilities, and thousands more are destroyed and maimed physically, emotionally and intellectually because of conditions of poverty and deprivation in the ghetto, that is a function of institutionalized racism. But the society either pretends it doesn't know of this situation, or is incapable of doing anything meaningful about it. And this resistance to doing anything meaningful about conditions in that ghetto comes from the fact that the ghetto is itself a product of a combination of forces and special interests in the white community, and the groups that have access to the resources and power to change that situation benefit, politically and economically, from the existence of that ghetto.

It is more than a figure of speech to say that the Negro community in America is the victim of white imperialism and colonial exploitation. This is in practical economic and political terms true. There are over 20 million black people comprising ten percent of this nation. They for the most part live in well-defined areas of the country—in the shanty-towns and rural black belt areas of the South, and increasingly in the slums of northern and western industrial cities. If one goes into any Negro community, whether it be in Jackson, Miss., Cambridge, Md., or Harlem, N.Y., one will find that the same combination of political, economic, and social forces are at work. The people in the Negro community do not control the resources of that community, its political decisions, its law enforcement, its housing standards; and even the physical ownership of the land, houses, and stores *lie outside that community*.

It is white power that makes the laws, and it is violent white power in the form of armed white cops that enforces those laws with guns and nightsticks. The vast majority of Negroes in this country live in these captive communities and must endure these conditions of oppression because, and only because, *they are black and powerless*. I do not suppose that at any point the men who control the power and resources of this country ever sat down and designed these black enclaves, and formally articulated the terms of their colonial and dependent status, as was done, for example, by the Apartheid government of South Africa. Yet, one can not distinguish between one ghetto and another. As one moves from city to city it is as though some malignant racist planning-unit had done precisely this—designed each one from the same master blueprint. And indeed, if the ghetto had been formally and deliberately planned, instead of growing spontaneously and inevitably from the racist functioning of the various institutions that combine to make the society, it would be somehow less frightening. The situation would be less frightening because, if these ghettoes were the result of design and conspiracy, one could understand their similarity as being artificial and consciously imposed, rather than the result of identical patterns of white racism which repeat themselves in cities as distant as Boston and Birmingham. Without bothering to list the historic factors which contribute to this pattern—economic exploitation, political impotence, discrimination in employment and education—one can see that to correct this pattern will require far-reaching changes in the basic power-relationships and the ingrained social patterns within the society. The question is, of course, what kinds of changes are necessary, and how is it possible to bring them about?

In recent years the answer to these questions which has been given by most articulate groups of Negroes and their white allies, the "liberals" of all stripes, has been in terms of something called "integration." According to the advocates of integration, social justice will be accomplished by "integrating the Negro into the mainstream institutions of the society from which he has been traditionally excluded." It is very significant that each time I have heard this formulation it has been in terms of "the Negro," the individual Negro, rather than in terms of the community.

This concept of integration had to be based on the assumption that there was nothing of value in the Negro community and that little of value could be created among Negroes, so the thing to do was to siphon off the "acceptable" Negroes into the surrounding middle-class white community. Thus the goal of the movement for integration was simply to loosen up the restrictions barring the entry of Negroes into the white community. Goals around which the struggle took place, such as public accommodation, open housing, job opportunity on the executive level (which is easier to deal with than the problem of semi-skilled and blue collar jobs which involve more far-reaching economic adjustments), are quite simply middle-class goals, articulated by a tiny group of Negroes who had middle-class aspirations. It is true that the student demonstrations in the South during the early sixties, out of which SNCC came, had a similar orientation. But while it is hardly a concern of a black sharecropper, dishwasher, or welfare recipient whether a certain fifteen-dollar-a-day motel offers accommodations to Negroes, the overt symbols of white superiority and the imposed limitations on the Negro community had to be destroyed. Now, black people must look beyond these goals, to the issue of collective power.

Such a limited class orientation was reflected not only in the program and goals of the civil rights movement, but in its tactics and organization. It is very significant that the two oldest and most "respectable" civil rights organizations have constitutions which *specifically* prohibit partisan political activity. CORE once did, but changed that clause when it changed its orientation toward black power. But this is perfectly understandable in terms of the strategy and goals of the older organizations. The civil rights movement saw its role as a kind of liaison between the powerful white community and the dependent Negro one. The dependent status of the black community apparently was unimportant since—if the movement were successful—it was going to blend into the white community anyway. We made no pretense of organizing and developing institutions of community power in the Negro community, but appealed to the conscience of white institutions of power. The posture of the civil rights movement was that of the dependent, the suppliant. The theory was that without attempting to create any organized base of political strength itself, the civil rights movement could, by forming coalitions with various "liberal" pressure organizations in the white community—liberal reform clubs, labor unions, church groups, progressive civic groups—and at times one or other of the major political parties—influence national legislation and national social patterns.

I think we all have seen the limitations of this approach. We have repeatedly seen that political alliances based on appeals to conscience and decency are chancy things, simply because institutions and political organizations have no consciences outside their own special interests. The political and social rights of Negroes have been and always will be negotiable and expendable the moment they conflict with the interests of our "allies." If we do not learn from history, we are doomed to repeat it, and that is precisely the lesson of the Reconstruction. Black people were allowed to register, vote and participate in politics because it was to the advantage of powerful white allies to promote this. But this was the result of white decision, and it was ended by other white men's decision before any political base powerful enough to challenge that decision could be established in the southern Negro community. (Thus at this point in the struggle Negroes have no assurance—save a kind of idiot optimism and faith in a society whose history is one of racism—that if it were to become necessary, even the painfully limited gains thrown to the civil rights movement by the Congress will not be revoked as soon as a shift in political sentiments should occur.)

The major limitation of this approach was that it tended to maintain the traditional dependence of Negroes, and of the movement. We depended upon the good-will and support of various groups within the white community whose interests were not always compatible with ours. To the extent that we depended on the financial support of other groups, we were vulnerable to their influence and domination.

Also the program that evolved out of this coalition was really limited and inadequate in the long term and one which affected only a small select group of Negroes. Its goal was to make the white community accessible to "qualified" Negroes and presumably each year a few more Negroes armed with their passport—a couple of university degrees—would escape into middle-class America and adopt the attitudes and life styles of that group; and one day the Harlems and the Watts would stand empty, a tribute to the success of integration. This is simply neither realistic nor particularly desirable. You can integrate communities, but you assimilate individuals. Even if such a program were possible its result would be, not to develop the black community as a functional and honorable segment of the total society, with its own cultural identity, life patterns, and institutions, but to abolish it—the final solution to the Negro problem. Marx said that the working class is the first class in history that ever wanted to abolish itself. If one listens to some of our "moderate" Negro leaders it appears that the American Negro is the first race that ever wished to abolish itself. The fact is that what must be abolished is not the black community, but the dependent colonial status that has been inflicted upon it. The racial and cultural personality of the black community must be preserved and the community must win its freedom while preserving its cultural integrity. This is the essential difference between integration as it is currently practiced and the concept of black power.

What has the movement for integration accomplished to date? The Negro graduating from M.I.T. with a doctorate will have better job opportunities available to him than to Lynda Bird Johnson. But the rate of unemployment in the Negro community is steadily increasing, while that in the white community decreases. More educated Negroes hold executive jobs in major corporations and federal agencies than ever before, but the gap between white income and Negro income has almost doubled in the last twenty years. More suburban housing is available to Negroes, but housing conditions in the ghetto are steadily declining. While the infant mortality rate of New York City is at its lowest rate ever in the city's history, the infant mortality rate of Harlem is steadily climbing. There has been an organized national resistance to the Supreme Court's order to integrate the schools, and the federal government has not acted to enforce that order. Less than fifteen percent of black children in the South attend integrated schools; and Negro schools, which the vast majority of black children still attend, are increasingly decrepit, over-crowded, under-staffed, inadequately equipped and funded.

This explains why the rate of school dropouts is increasing among Negro teenagers, who then express their bitterness, hopelessness, and alienation by the only means they have—rebellion. As long as people in the ghettoes of our large cities feel that they are victims of the misuse of white power without any way to have their needs represented—and these are frequently simple needs: to get the welfare inspectors to stop kicking down your doors in the middle of the night, the cops from beating your children, the landlord to exterminate the vermin in your home, the city to collect your garbage—we will continue to have riots. These are not the products of "black power," but of the absence of any organization capable of giving the community the power, the black power, to deal with its problems.

SNCC proposes that it is now time for the black freedom movement to stop pandering to the fears and anxieties of the white middle class in the attempt to earn its "good-will," and to return to the ghetto to organize these communities to control themselves. This organization must be attempted in northern and southern urban areas as well as in the rural black belt counties of the South. The chief antagonist to this organization is, in the South, the overtly racist Democratic party, and in the North the equally corrupt big city machines.

The standard argument presented against independent political organization is "But you are only 10%." I cannot see the relevance of this observation, since no one is talking about taking over the country, but taking control over our own communities.

The fact is that the Negro population, 10% or not, is very strategically placed because—ironically—of segregation. What is also true is that Negroes have never been able to utilize the full voting potential of our numbers. Where we could vote, the case has always been that the white political machine stacks and gerrymanders the political subdivisions in Negro neighborhoods so the true voting strength is never reflected in political strength. Would anyone looking at the distribution of political power in Manhattan, ever think that Negroes represented 60% of the population there?

Just as often the effective political organization in Negro communities is absorbed by tokenism and patronage—the time honored practice of "giving" certain offices to selected Negroes. The machine thus creates a "little machine," which is subordinate and responsive to it, in the Negro community. These Negro political "leaders" are really vote deliverers, more responsible to the white machine and the white power structure, than to the community they allegedly represent. Thus the white community is able to substitute patronage control for audacious black power in the Negro community. This is precisely what Johnson tried to do even before the Voting Rights Act of 1966 was passed. The National Democrats made it very clear that the measure was intended to register Democrats, not Negroes. The President and top officials of the Democratic Party called in almost 100 selected Negro "leaders" from the Deep South. Nothing was said about changing the policies of the racist state parties, nothing was said about repudiating such leadership figures as Eastland and Ross Barnett in Mississippi or George Wallace in Alabama. What was said was simply "Go home and organize your people into the local Democratic Party—*then* we'll see about poverty money and appointments." (Incidentally, for the most part the War on Poverty in the South is controlled by local Democratic ward heelers—and outspoken racists who have used the program to change the form of the Negroes' dependence. People who were afraid to register for fear of being thrown off the farm are now afraid to register for fear of losing their Head-Start jobs.)

We must organize black community power to end these abuses, and to give the Negro community a chance to have its needs expressed. A leadership which is truly "responsible"—not to the white press and power structure, but to the community—must be developed. Such leadership will recognize that its power lies in the unified and collective strength of that community. This will make it difficult for the white leadership group to conduct its dialogue with individuals in terms of patronage and prestige, and will force them to talk to the community's representatives in terms of real power.

The single aspect of the black power program that has encountered most criticism is this concept of independent organization. This is presented as third-partyism which has never worked, or a withdrawal into black nationalism and isolationism. If such a program is developed it will not have the effect of isolating the Negro community but the reverse. When the Negro community is able to control local office, and negotiate with other groups from a position of organized strength, the possibility of meaningful political alliances on specific issues will be increased. That is a rule of politics and there is no reason why it should not operate here. The only difference is that we will have the power to define the terms of these alliances.

The next question usually is, "So—can it work, can the ghettoes in fact be organized?" The answer is that this organization must be successful, because there are no viable alternatives—not the War on Poverty, which was at its inception limited to dealing with effects rather than causes, and has become simply another source of machine patronage. And "Integration" is meaningful only to a small chosen class within the community.

The revolution in agricultural technology in the South is displacing the rural Negro community into northern urban areas. Both Washington, D.C. and Newark, N.J. have Negro majorities. One third of Philadelphia's population of two million people is black. "Inner city" in most major urban areas is already predominantly Negro, and with the white rush to suburbia, Negroes will in the next three decades control the heart of our great cities. These areas can become either concentration camps with a bitter and volatile population whose only power is the power to destroy, or organized and powerful communities able to make constructive contributions to the total society. Without the power to control their lives and their communities, without effective political institutions through which to relate to the total society, these communities will exist in a constant state of insurrection. This is a choice that the country will have to make.

THE URBAN LEAGUE INTERPRETS BLACK POWER

Whitney Young, Jr. / Address to a CORE Convention in
Columbus, Ohio, 1968

The National Urban League is one of the oldest organizations for racial uplift in America. Organized in 1911 to assist the migrants to the cities to find jobs and housing, it has been more a social-work organization than one of protest. In recent years, however, under the leadership of Whitney Young, Jr., the League has begun more aggressive campaigns to aid the urban poor, attempting to do far more than merely break down job discrimination.

When the slogan "Black Power" was first raised, Young was cautious in his criticisms. He was determined to get a clear idea of the meaning of the term before he took a position. Then, at the CORE convention in July 1968, Young made the following statement on black power. In effect, he said that he was for it if it meant self-determination but against it if it meant withdrawal from the mainstream of American life. Young's address was a thoughtful and judicious restatement of his belief in the necessity of racial interdependence in America.

Brothers and Sisters:

Your invitation to address this luncheon was given high priority for several reasons. First, my long time friendship and respect for Floyd McKissick. We have on most issues agreed, but when we in rare instances

FROM Whitney Young, Jr., address to a CORE Convention in Columbus, Ohio, July 6, 1968. Used by permission of the author and the National Urban League, Inc.

did not, we never questioned the motives or the personal honesty of each other. Our entire families have warm affection for each other. Second, the tragic events of recent months involving those who sought change and the crucial issues and challenges before us in this election year make necessary the highest possible degree of unity which can be achieved among those seeking equal opportunity and equal results for all Americans.

One cannot help but view with dismay that, for the most part in America, it is only the good men seeking reform and change who are assassinated—Abraham Lincoln, Malcolm X, the two Kennedys, Martin Luther King, Jr. The reactionaries, the racists, the klansmen, all seeking to reverse progress in human relations are apparently safe in the U.S.A.

As to unity, I come to this convention believing that the goals and objectives we have in common are far greater than those on which we may differ, and unity does not require uniformity. In fact, in a war, and we are in a war against racism and injustice, it would be the height of folly to have only a single method of attack—only one branch of the service and all doing the same thing. What is important is that each do his thing well, understanding fully his dependence on the other. It has often been a CORE frontal direct attack on a problem that has made a negotiable or a legislative solution by the Urban League or the NAACP possible. Here we have much to learn from the labor movement, for timing is important and when to use what method by whom is crucial. To negotiate across the table, or to engage in political activity is sometimes more militant and effective than continuing to picket. But the important thing to remember is that no war is ever won unless there is an intelligent division of labor with each respecting the other.

Of equal importance to unity and effectiveness during this period is the necessity to distinguish rhetoric from relevance or symbols from substance. Too many people believe we can shout, sing or shoot our way into power. Let me assure you now that the real enemy of the black man in America is not remotely concerned about our lung power or our fire power. In fact he welcomes it as a justification for further suppression and indiscriminate use of his superior fire power. Net results—mainly black people killed and black communities damaged or destroyed. What is feared most is our brain power, our political power, our economic power. This comes from what we continue to develop, namely, a new sense of pride, of dignity, of destiny as well as roots. And most of all a new sense of unity of community. No longer can we afford the luxury of blacks fighting and killing blacks. Neither can we fall in the same trick bag as white people have done in generalizing about all black people. You and I must know that no race has a monopoly on vice or virtue. Most black people have been beautiful, but some black men killed Malcolm X, your Associate Director Roy Innis' son, and daily exploit their people either as employers, landlords, or merchants. Most white people, as the Kerner Commission Report pointed out, are racist, but some are not. Particularly among young people do we witness an attempt to rid themselves of the disease of prejudice and a willingness to challenge the institutions and the systems which have perpetuated racism. Significantly, an increasing number of top corporate leaders and public officials have demonstrated a flexibility and a desire for change. These must not be ignored, and we and our children must be prepared to capitalize on these breakthroughs and relationships. We must continue to fight and reject those white racists and ideological revolutionists who would send us back to Africa or establish a more formal American apartheid.

The Urban League does not apologize for its past contribution to our black brothers. We were for many years the only resource to which black citizens could turn for jobs, welfare, housing, education, recreation. Given the limits of law, public attitude, and our small resources, we achieved miracles. But what we did yesterday and the way we did it is not good enough for today so we have changed some of our focus and are continuing even more.

Recently we announced a new thrust which included a shift from our role as honest power broker to that of providing technical assistance to the ghetto to help it organize, document its needs, select its own leadership and arrange for creative confrontation with appropriate officials. In addition, we have or are planning programs for middle-class black people; programs to reduce white racism; expand leadership development and black ownership of businesses; ICBO, program for black campus leaders; programs for ghetto youth groups, which involve the Mission Rebels, Real Great Society, Thugs, Inc., Blackstone Rangers, Pride, Inc.

This does not mean we will not continue our present programs of job development, placement, and training nor our work to improve the quantity and quality of housing, education, health, and welfare resources. But the reality of today's situation demands that our major thrust be in the ghetto, developing what we call ghetto power which the system must be responsive to.

Brothers and sisters, let me make it clear. The Urban League believes strongly in that interpretation of Black Power which emphasizes self-determination, pride, self-respect, participation, and control of one's destiny and community affairs. We support as legitimate and historically consistent a minority's mobilization of its economic and political power to reward its friends and punish its enemies (others have done this but did not chant). We do not believe in cultural absorption but rather cultural exchange. We believe black people have in the past given much to America which we insist all our educational systems must record and teach for both blacks and whites. We believe blacks are giving much to the present society and will contribute even more to the future if there is to be a future for America or mankind.

We believe, therefore, that black Americans should have the same options and choices as white Americans when it comes to choosing a job, a home, educational institutions, or a religion. We are, therefore, opposed to enforced segregation as historically advocated by white southern racists or practiced in South Africa. On the other hand, we believe that those who choose segregated living (as other ethnic groups have done for a period) should not suffer inferior services or facilities. We must have black capitalists, black economic stability, black doctors, biologists, etc. But there is not and never can be in America black capitalism, a black community, black medicine, black biology. Our seeking of power must assure us of a more major role in the responsibilities and rewards of the mainstream, not a way to escape it with the token handouts granted always to those on the reservations.

Finally, may I repeat my pleasure at the receipt of your invitation and commend CORE and its leadership for its effort through this conference to establish not only the symbol of black unity but also the substance. Whatever our differences, and this conference has proved they are small compared to our similarities, may we never forget we are black brothers who carry on our shoulders the responsibility, as did our forefathers, for thousands of our brothers who still exist in the midnight of poverty and despair, and, more important, for yet unborn generations of black children who will have reason, I hope, to bless rather than curse us.

BLACK REVOLUTIONARY NATIONALISM

Huey Newton Speaks from Jail: An Interview

The most revolutionary proposals for solving the racial problem in America have come, not from the separatists, but from the Black Panthers. There is no reason to assume that a separate black state would not be capitalist, with both the exploited and the exploiter being black. So the Panthers, taking the demand for change a step further, reject the capitalist system altogether and propose socialism as a system under which racial tensions could be alleviated.

The following interview, conducted by Liberation News Service with Huey Newton, Defense Minister of the Panthers, in 1968, presents the ideas that have made the Panthers such a threat to the established order. Basing his theories partly on the analysis of colonial peoples made by Frantz Fanon in **The Wretched of the Earth,** Newton speaks of the need for revolution and discusses the possibility of cooperation between white and black radicals. At the time of the interview, Newton was in jail, having been arrested in a police-Panther shootout and accused of killing a policeman. He was subsequently found guilty of involuntary manslaughter and committed to prison, where it is not likely that his ideas will become less revolutionary.

QUESTION. The question of nationalism is a vital one in the black movement today. Some have made a distinction between cultural nationalism and revolutionary nationalism. Would you comment on the differences and give us your views?

HUEY P. NEWTON. Revolutionary nationalism first is dependent upon a people's revolution with the end goal being the people in power. Therefore, to be a revolutionary nationalist you would by necessity have to be a socialist. If you are a reactionary nationalist your end goal is the oppression of the people.

Cultural nationalism, or pork chop nationalism, as I sometimes call it, is basically a problem of having the wrong political perspective. It seems to be a reaction instead of a response to political oppression. The cultural nationalists are concerned with returning to the old African culture and thereby regaining their identity and freedom. In other words, they feel that the African culture automatically will bring political freedom.

The Black Panther Party, which is a revolutionary group of black people, realizes that we have to have an identity. We have to realize our black heritage in order to give us strength to move on and progress. But as far as returning to the old African culture, it's unnecessary and not advantageous in many respects. We believe that culture itself will not liberate us. We're going to need some stronger stuff.

A good example of revolutionary nationalism was the revolution in Algeria when Ben Bella took over. The French were kicked out, but it was a people's revolution because the people ended up in power. The leaders that took over were not interested in the profit motive where they could exploit the people and keep them in a state of slavery. They nationalized the industry and plowed the would-be profits into the community. That's what socialism is all about in a nutshell. The people's representatives are in office strictly on the leave of the people. The wealth of the country is controlled by the people and they are considered whenever modifications in the industries are made.

The Black Panther Party is a revolutionary Nationalist group and we see a major contradiction between capitalism in this country and our

FROM Huey Newton, "Huey Newton Speaks from Jail," *motive*, Vol. XXIX (October 1968), pp. 8–16. Reprinted by permission.

interests. We realize that this country became very rich upon slavery and that slavery is capitalism in the extreme. We have two evils to fight, capitalism and racism. We must destroy both racism and capitalism.

QUESTION. Directly related to the question of nationalism is the question of unity within the black community. There has been some question about this since the Black Panther Party has run candidates against other black candidates in recent California elections. What is your position on this matter?

HUEY. A very peculiar thing has happened. Historically, you have what Malcolm X calls the field nigger and the house nigger. The house nigger had some privileges. He got the worn-out clothes of the master and he didn't have to work as hard as the field black. He came to respect the master to such an extent that he identified with the master, because he got a few of the leftovers that the field blacks did not get. And through this identity with him, he saw the slavemaster's interest as being his interest. Sometimes he would even protect the slavemaster more than the slavemaster would protect himself. Malcolm makes the point that if the master's house happened to catch on fire, the house Negro would work harder than the master to put the fire out and save the master's house, while the field black was praying that the house burned down. The house black identified with the master so much that, when the master would get sick, the house Negro would say, "Master, we's sick!"

Members of the Black Panther Party are the field blacks; we're hoping the master dies if he gets sick. The Black bourgeoisie seem to be acting in the role of the house Negro. They are pro-administration. They would like a few concessions made, but as far as the overall setup, they have more material goods, a little more advantage, a few more privileges than the black have-nots, the lower class, and so they identify with the power structure and they see their interest as the power structure's interest. In fact, it's against their interest.

The Black Panther Party was forced to draw a line of demarcation. We are for all of those who are for the promotion of the interests of the black have-nots, which represents about 98 percent of blacks here in America. We're not controlled by the white mother country radicals nor are we controlled by the black bourgeoisie. We have a mind of our own and if the black bourgeoisie cannot align itself with our complete program, then the black bourgeoisie sets itself up as our enemy.

QUESTION. The Black Panther Party has had considerable contact with white radicals since its earliest days. What do you see as the role of these white radicals?

HUEY. The white mother country radical is the offspring of the children of the beast that has plundered the world exploiting all people, concentrating on the people of color. These are children of the beast that seek now to be redeemed because they realize that their former heroes, who were slavemasters and murderers, put forth ideas that were only façades to hide the treachery they inflicted upon the world. They are turning their backs on their fathers.

The white mother country radical, in resisting the system, becomes a somewhat abstract thing because he's not oppressed as much as black people are. As a matter of fact, his oppression is somewhat abstract simply because he doesn't have to live in a reality of oppression.

Black people in America, and colored people throughout the world, suffer not only from exploitation, but they suffer from racism. Black people here in America, in the black colony, are oppressed because we're black and we're exploited. The whites are rebels, many of them from the middle class and as far as any overt oppression this is not the case. Therefore, I call their rejection of the system a somewhat abstract thing. They're looking for new heroes. They're looking to wash away the hypocrisy that their fathers have presented to the world. In doing this, they see the people who are really fighting for freedom. They see the people who are really standing for justice and equality and peace throughout the world. They are the people of Vietnam, the people of Latin America, the people of Asia, the people of Africa, and the black people in the black colony here in America.

This presents something of a problem in many ways to the black revolutionary, especially to the cultural nationalist. The cultural nationalist doesn't understand the white revolutionaries because he can't see why anyone white would turn on the system. He thinks that maybe this is some more hypocrisy being planted by white people.

I personally think that there are many young white revolutionaries who are sincere in attempting to realign themselves with mankind, and to make a reality out of the high moral standards that their fathers and forefathers only expressed. In pressing for new heroes, the young white revolutionaries found these heroes in the black colony at home and in the colonies throughout the world.

The young white revolutionaries raised the cry for the troops to withdraw from Vietnam, to keep hands off Latin America, to withdraw from the Dominican Republic and also to withdraw from the black community or the black colony. So we have a situation in which the young white revolutionaries are attempting to identify with the oppressed people of the colonies against the exploiter.

The problem arises, then, in what part they can play. How can they aid the colony? How can they aid the Black Panther Party or any other black revolutionary group? They can aid the black revolutionaries first, by simply turning away from the establishment, and secondly, by choosing their friends. For instance, they have a choice between whether they will be a friend of Lyndon Baines Johnson or a friend of Fidel Castro. A friend of mine or a friend of Johnson's. These are direct opposites. After they make this choice, then the white revolutionaries have a duty and a responsibility to act.

The imperialistic or capitalistic system occupies areas. It occupies Vietnam now. It occupies areas by sending soldiers there, by sending policemen there. The policemen or soldiers are only a gun in the establishment's hand, making the racist secure in his racism, the establishment secure in its exploitation. The first problem, it seems, is to remove the gun from the establishment's hand. Until lately, the white radical has seen no reason to come into conflict with the policeman in his own community. I said "until recently," because there is friction now in the mother country between the young revolutionaries and the police; because now the white revolutionaries are attempting to put some of their ideas into action, and there's the rub. We say that it should be a permanent thing.

Black people are being oppressed in the colony by white policemen, by white racists. We are saying they must withdraw.

As far as I'm concerned, the only reasonable conclusion would be to first realize the enemy, realize the plan, and then when something happens in the black colony—when we're attacked and ambushed in the black colony —then the white revolutionary students and intellectuals and all the other whites who support the colony should respond by defending us, by attacking the enemy in their community.

The Black Panther Party is an all black party, because we feel, as Malcolm X felt, that there can be no black-white unity until there first is black unity. We have a problem in the black colony that is particular to the colony, but we're willing to accept aid from the mother country as long as the mother country radicals realize that we have, as Eldridge Cleaver says in *Soul on Ice*, a mind of our own. We've regained our mind that was taken away from us and we will decide the political, as well as the practical, stand that we'll take. We'll make the theory and we'll carry out the practice. It's the duty of the white revolutionary to aid us in this.

QUESTION. You have spoken a lot about dealing with the protectors of the system, the armed forces. Would you like to elaborate on why you place so much emphasis on this?

HUEY. The reason that I feel so strongly is simply because without this protection from the army, the police and the military, the institutions could not go on in their racism and exploitation. For instance, as the Vietnamese are driving the American imperialist troops out of Vietnam, it automatically stops the racist imperialist institutions of America from oppressing that particular country. The country cannot implement its racist program without guns. The guns are the military and the police. If the military were disarmed in Vietnam, then the Vietnamese would be victorious.

We are in the same situation here in America. Whenever we attack the system, the first thing the administrators do is to send out their strong-arm men. If it's a rent strike, because of the indecent housing we have, they will send out the police to throw the furniture out the window. They don't come themselves. They send their protectors. To deal with the corrupt exploiter, we are going to have to deal with his protector, which is the police who take orders from him. This is a must.

QUESTION. Would you like to be more specific on the conditions which must exist before an alliance or coalition can be formed with the predominantly white groups? Would you comment specifically on your alliance with the California Peace and Freedom Party?

HUEY. We have an alliance with the Peace and Freedom Party because it has supported our program in full, and this is the criterion for a coalition with the black revolutionary group. If it had not supported our program in full, then we would not have seen any reason to make an alliance with them, because we are the reality of the oppression. They are not. They are only oppressed in an abstract way; we are oppressed in the real way. We are the real slaves! So it's a problem that we suffer from more than anyone else and it's our problem of liberation. Therefore we should decide what measures and what tools and what programs to use to become liberated. Many of the young white revolutionaries realize this and I see no reason not to have a coalition with them.

QUESTION. Other black groups seem to feel that from past experience it is impossible for them to work with whites and impossible for them to form alliances. What do you see as the reasons for this and do you think that the history of the Black Panther makes this less of a problem?

HUEY. There was a somewhat unhealthy relationship in the past with the white liberals supporting the black people who were trying to gain their freedom. I think that a good example of this would be the relationship that SNCC had with its white liberals. I call them white liberals because they differ strictly from the white radicals. The relationship was that the whites controlled SNCC for a very long time. From the very start of SNCC until recently, whites were the mind of SNCC. They controlled the program of SNCC with money and they controlled the ideology, or the stands SNCC would take. The blacks in SNCC were completely controlled program-wise; they couldn't do any more than the white liberals wanted them to do, which wasn't very much. So the white liberals were not working for self-determination for the black community. They were interested in a few concessions from the power structure. They undermined SNCC's program.

Stokely Carmichael came along, and realizing this, started Malcolm X's program of Black Power. Whites were afraid when Stokely said that black people have a mind of their own and that SNCC would seek self-determination for the black community. The white liberals withdrew their support, leaving the organization financially bankrupt. The blacks who were in the organization, Stokely and H. Rap Brown, were left angry and bewildered with the white liberals who had been aiding them under the guise of being sincere.

As a result, the leadership of SNCC turned away from the white liberal, which was good. I don't think they distinguished between the white liberal and the white revolutionary; because the revolutionary is white also, and they are very much afraid to have any contact with white people—even to the point of denying that the white revolutionaries could help by supporting programs of SNCC in the mother country. Not by making programs, not by being a member of the organization, but simply by resisting.

I think that one of SNCC's great problems is that they were controlled by the traditional administrator: the omnipotent administrator, the white person. He was the mind of SNCC. SNCC regained its mind, but I believe that it lost its political perspective. I think that this was a reaction rather than a response. The Black Panther Party has NEVER been controlled by white people. We have always had an integration of mind and body. We have never been controlled by whites and therefore we don't fear the white mother country radicals. Our alliance is one of organized black groups with organized white groups. As soon as the organized white groups do not do the things that would benefit us in our struggle for liberation, that will be the point of our departure. So we don't suffer in the hang-up of a skin color. We don't hate white people; we hate the oppressor.

QUESTION. You indicate that there is a psychological process that has historically existed in white-black relations in the U.S. that must change in the course of revolutionary struggle. Would you like to comment on this?

HUEY. Yes. The historical relationship between black and white here in America has been the relationship between the slave and the master; the master being the mind and the slave the body. The slave would carry out the orders that the mind demanded him to carry out. By doing this, the master took the manhood from the slave because he stripped him of a mind. In the process, the slave-master stripped himself of a body. As Eldridge Cleaver puts it, the slave-master became the omnipotent administrator and the slave became the super-masculine menial. This puts the omnipotent administrator into the controlling position or the front office and the super-masculine menial into the field.

The whole relationship developed so that the omnipotent administrator and the super-masculine menial became opposites. The slave being a very strong body doing all the practical things, all of the work becomes very masculine. The omnipotent administrator in the process of removing himself from all body functions realizes later that he has emasculated himself. And this is very disturbing to him. So the slave lost his mind and the slave-master his body.

This caused the slave-master to become very envious of the slave because he pictured the slave as being more of a man, being superior sexually, because the penis is part of the body. The omnipotent administrator laid down a decree when he realized that in his plan to enslave the black man, he had emasculated himself. He attempted to bind the penis of the slave. He attempted to show that his penis could reach further than the super-masculine menial's penis. He said "I, the omnipotent administrator, can have access to the black woman." The super-masculine menial then had a psychological attraction to the white female (the ultra-feminine freak) for the simple reason that it was forbidden fruit. The omnipotent administrator decreed that this kind of contact would be punished by death.

At the same time, in order to reinforce his sexual desire, to confirm, to assert his manhood, he would go into the slave quarters and have sexual relations with the black women (the self-reliant Amazon), not to be satisfied but simply to confirm his manhood. If he could only satisfy the self-reliant Amazon then he would be sure that he was a man. Because he didn't have a body, he didn't have a penis, but psychologically wanted to castrate the black man. The slave was constantly seeking unity within himself: a mind and a body. He always wanted to be able to decide, to gain respect from his woman, because women want one who can control.

I give this outline to fit into a framework of what is happening now. The white power structure today in America defines itself as the mind. They want to control the world. They go off and plunder the world. They are the policemen of the world exercising control especially over people of color.

The white man cannot gain his manhood, cannot unite with the body, because the body is black. The body is symbolic of slavery and strength. It's a biological thing as he views it. The slave is in a much better situation because his not being a full man has always been viewed psychologically. And it's always easier to make a psychological transition than a biological one. If he can only recapture his mind, then he will lose all fear and will be free to determine his destiny. This is what is happening today with the rebellion of the world's oppressed people against the controller. They are regaining their mind and they're saying that we have a mind of our own. They're saying that we want freedom to determine the destiny of our people, thereby uniting the mind with their bodies. They are taking the mind back from the omnipotent administrator, the controller, the exploiter.

QUESTION. You have mentioned that the guerilla was the perfect man and this kind of formulation seems to fit directly with the guerilla as a political man. Would you comment on this?

HUEY. The guerilla is a very unique man. This is in contrast to Marxist-Leninist orthodox theories where the party controls the military. The guerilla is not only the warrior, the military fighter; he is also the military commander as well as the political theoretician. Regis Debray says "poor the pen without the guns, poor the gun without the pen." The pen being just an extension of the mind, a tool to write down concepts, ideas. The gun is only an extension of the body, the extension of our fanged teeth that we lost through evolution. It's the weapon, it's the claws that we lost, it's the body. The guerilla is the military commander and the political theoretician all in one.

What we have to do as a vanguard of the revolution is to correct this through activity. The large majority of black people are either illiterate or semi-literate. They don't read. They need activity to follow. This is true of any colonized people. The same thing happened in Cuba where it was necessary for twelve men with the leadership of Che and Fidel to take to the hills and then attack the corrupt administration, to attack the army who were the protectors of the exploiters in Cuba. They would have leafleted the community and they could have written books, but the people would not respond. They had to act and the people could see and hear about it and therefore become educated on how to respond to oppression.

In this country black revolutionaries have to set an example. We can't do the same things that were done in Cuba because Cuba is Cuba and the U.S. is the U.S. Cuba had many terrains to protect the guerilla. This country is mainly urban. We have to work out new solutions to offset the power of the country's technology and communication. We do have solutions to these problems and they will be put into effect. I wouldn't want to go into the ways and means of this, but we will educate through action. We have to engage in action to make the people want to read our literature. They are not attracted to all the writing in this country; there's too much writing. Many books make one weary.

QUESTION.   Kennedy before his death, and to a lesser extent Rockefeller and Lindsay and other establishment liberals, have been talking about making reforms to give black people a greater share of the pie and thus stop any developing revolutionary movement. Would you comment on this?

HUEY.   I would say this: If a Kennedy or a Lindsay or anyone else can give decent housing to all of our people; if they can give full employment to our people with a high standard; if they can give full control to the black people to determine the destiny of their community; if they can give fair trials in the court system by turning the structure over to the community; if they can end their exploitation of people throughout the world; if they can do all these things, they will have solved the problems. But I don't believe under this present system, under capitalism, that they will be able to solve these problems.

I don't think black people should be fooled by their come-ons because everyone who gets in office promises the same thing. They promise full employment and decent housing; the Great Society, the New Frontier. All of these names, but no real benefits. No effects are felt in the black community, and black people are tired of being deceived and duped. The people must have full control of the means of production. Small black businesses cannot compete with General Motors. That's just out of the question. General Motors robbed us and worked us for nothing for a couple hundred years and took our money and set up factories and became fat and rich and then talks about giving us some of the crumbs. We want full control. We're not interested in anyone promising that the private owners are going to all of a sudden become human beings and give these things to our community. It hasn't ever happened and, based on empirical evidence, we don't expect them to become Buddhists overnight.

QUESTION. The Panthers' organizing efforts have been very open. Would you like to comment about the question of an underground political organization versus an open organization at this point in the struggle?

HUEY. Some of the black nationalist groups feel that they have to be underground because they'll be attacked, but we don't feel that you can romanticize being underground. They say we're romantic because we're trying to live revolutionary lives, and we are not taking precautions. But we say that the only way we would go underground is if we're driven underground. All real revolutionary movements are driven underground.

This is a pre-revolutionary period and we feel it is very necessary to educate the people while we can. So we're very open about this education. We have been attacked and we will be attacked even more in the future, but we're not going to go underground until we get ready to go underground because we have a mind of our own. We're not going to let anyone force us to do anything. We're going to go underground after we educate all of the black people and not before that time. Then it won't really be necessary for us to go underground because you can see black anywhere. We will just have the stuff to protect ourselves and the strategy to offset the great power that the strong-arm men of the establishment have and are planning to use against us.

QUESTION. Do you see the possibility of organizing a white Panther Party in opposition to the establishment, possibly among poor and working whites?

HUEY. As I said before, Black Power is people's power and as far as organizing white people we give white people the privilege of having a mind and we want them to get a body. They can organize themselves. We can tell them what they should do, but their responsibility, if they're going to claim to be white revolutionaries or white mother country radicals, is to arm themselves and support the colonies around the world in their just struggle against imperialism. Anything more than that they will have to do on their own.

QUESTION. What do you mean by Black Power?

HUEY. Black Power is really people's power. The Black Panther Program, Panther Power as we call it, will implement this people's power. We have respect for all of humanity and we realize that the people should rule and determine their destiny. Wipe out the controller. To have Black Power doesn't humble or subjugate anyone to slavery or oppression. Black Power is giving power to people who have not had power to determine their destiny. We advocate and we aid any people who are struggling to determine their destiny. This is regardless of color. The Vietnamese say Vietnam should be able to determine its own destiny. Power of the Vietnamese people. We also chant power of the Vietnamese people. The Latins are talking about Latin America for the Latin Americans. Cuba, si and Yanqui, no. It's not that they don't want the Yankees to have any power; they just don't want them to have power over them. They can have power over themselves. We in the black colony in America want to be able to have power over our destiny, and that's black power.

QUESTION. How would you characterize the mood of black people in America today? Are they disenchanted, wanting a larger slice of the pie, or alienated, not wanting to integrate into Babylon? What do you think it will take for them to become alienated and revolutionary?

HUEY. I was going to say disillusioned, but I don't think that we were ever under the illusion that we had freedom in this country. This society definitely is a decadent one and we realize it. Black people cannot gain their freedom under the present system, the system that is carrying out its plans to institutionalize racism. Your question is what will have to be done to stimulate them to revolution. I think it's already being done. It's a matter of time now for us to educate them to a program and show them the way to liberation. The Black Panther Party is the beacon light to show black people the way to liberation.

You notice the insurrections that have been going on throughout the country; in Watts, in Newark, in Detroit. They were all responses of the people demanding that they have freedom to determine their destiny, rejecting exploitation. The Black Panther Party does not think that the traditional riots, or insurrections, that have taken place are the answer. It is true that they have been against the Establishment, they have been against authority and oppression within their community; but they have been unorganized. However, black people have learned from each of these insurrections.

They learned from Watts. I'm sure that the people in Detroit were educated by what happened in Watts. Perhaps this was wrong education. It sort of missed the mark. It wasn't quite the correct activity, but the people were educated through the activity. The people of Detroit followed the example of the people in Watts, only they added a little scrutiny to it. The people in Detroit learned that the way to put a hurt on the administration is to make Molotov cocktails and to go into the streets in mass numbers. So this was a matter of learning. The slogan went up, "burn, baby, burn." People were educated through the activity and it spread throughout the country. The people were educated on how to resist, but perhaps incorrectly.

THE BLACK MANIFESTO

James Forman / Address to the National Black Economic
Development Conference, 1969

The idea of paying reparations to the black people of the United
States is not a new one. During Reconstruction a proposal to provide each freedman with "forty acres and a mule" gained some support, indicating a desire to repair some of the economic damage
done to the slaves. As recently as 1966, the "freedom budget" proposed by Bayard Rustin and A. Philip Randolph called upon the
United States government to devote at least $185 billion to the
fight against poverty and racism.

A new approach to the issue of reparations was announced on
May 4, 1969, when James Forman, who preceded Stokely Carmichael as chairman of SNCC, disrupted the Sunday worship
service of the Riverside Church of New York City to read the
Black Manifesto. Forman's Manifesto had been adopted on April
26, 1969, by the National Black Economic Development Conference, which met in Detroit. The Conference was called by the
Interreligious Foundation for Community Organization, a coalition
of representatives of ten Protestant denominations and some
Jewish and Catholic groups that was recently formed to channel
funds from the various denominations into poverty projects.

Reprinted here is Forman's entire presentation to the Conference. First, Forman explains the purpose behind the Manifesto:
in his view, black people must now aim at gaining total control
of all the institutions in which they are involved. Following is the
text of the Manifesto, in which white Christians and Jews are
called upon to contribute $500 million (a figure since raised to
$3 billion) to establish the economic independence of black peo-
ple. Though many church groups have responded favorably to the
idea of reparations, few have so far endorsed either the Black
Economic Development Conference (BEDC) or Forman's revolutionary ideology.

Brothers and Sisters:

We have come from all over the country, burning with anger and despair
not only with the miserable economic plight of our people, but fully
aware that the racism on which the Western world was built dominates
our lives. There can be no separation of the problems of racism from the

FROM James Forman, "Black Manifesto," a speech delivered at the National Black
Economic Development Conference in Detroit, Michigan, April 26, 1969. Reprinted
from *Renewal* magazine, Vol. IX, No. 6 (June 1969), pp. 9–13, with permission.

problems of our economic, political, and cultural degradation. To any black man, this is clear.

But there are still some of our people who are clinging to the rhetoric of the Negro and we must separate ourselves from those Negroes who go around the country promoting all types of schemes for Black Capitalism.

Ironically, some of the most militant Black Nationalists, as they call themselves, have been the first to jump on the bandwagon of black capitalism. They are pimps; Black Power Pimps and fraudulent leaders and the people must be educated to understand that any black man or Negro who is advocating a perpetuation of capitalism inside the United States is in fact seeking not only his ultimate destruction and death, but is contributing to the continuous exploitation of black people all around the world. For it is the power of the United States Government, this racist, imperialist government, that is choking the life of all people around the world.

We are an African people. We sit back and watch the Jews in this country make Israel a powerful conservative state in the Middle East, but we are not concerned actively about the plight of our brothers in Africa. We are the most advanced technological group of black people in the world, and there are many skills that could be offered to Africa. At the same time, it must be publicly stated that many African leaders are in disarray themselves, having been duped into following the lines as laid out by the Western Imperialist governments.

Africans themselves succumbed to and are victims of the power of the United States. For instance, during the summer of 1967, as the representatives of SNCC, Howard Moore and I traveled extensively in Tanzania and Zambia. We talked to high, very high, governmental officials. We told them there were many black people in the United States who were willing to come and work in Africa. All these government officials who were part of the leadership in their respective governments, said they wanted us to send as many skilled people that we could contact. But this program never came into fruition and we do not know the exact reasons, for I assure you that we talked and were committed to making this a successful program. It is our guess that the United States put the squeeze on these countries, for such a program directed by SNCC would have been too dangerous to the international prestige of the U.S. It is also possible that some of the wild statements by some black leader frightened the Africans.

In Africa today, there is a great suspicion of black people in this country. This is a correct suspicion since most of the Negroes who have left the States for work in Africa usually work for the Central Intelligence Agency (CIA) or the State Department. But the respect for us as a people continues to mount and the day will come when we can return to our homeland as brothers and sisters. But we should not think of going back to Africa today, for we are located in a strategic position. We live inside the U.S. which is the most barbaric country in the world and we have a chance to help bring this government down.

Time is short and we do not have much time and it is time we stop mincing words. Caution is fine, but no oppressed people ever gained their liberation until they were ready to fight, to use whatever means necessary, including the use of force and power of the gun to bring down the colonizer.

We have heard the rhetoric, but we have not heard the rhetoric which says that black people in this country must understand that we are the Vanguard Force. We shall liberate all the people in the U.S. and we will be instrumental in the liberation of colored people the world around. We must understand this point very clearly so that we are not trapped into diversionary and reactionary movements. Any class analysis of the U.S. shows very clearly that black people are the most oppressed group of people inside the United States. We have suffered the most from racism and exploitation, cultural degradation and lack of political power. It follows from the laws of revolution that the most oppressed will make the revolution, but we are not talking about just making the revolution. All the parties on the left who consider themselves revolutionary will say that blacks are the Vanguard, but we are saying that not only are we the Vanguard, but we must assume leadership, total control, and we must exercise the humanity which is inherent in us. We are the most humane people within the U.S. We have suffered and we understand suffering. Our hearts go out to the Vietnamese for we know what it is to suffer under the domination of racist America. Our hearts, our soul and all the compassion we can mount go out to our brothers in Africa, Santo Domingo, Latin America and Asia who are being tricked by the power structure of the U.S. which is dominating the world today. These ruthless, barbaric men have systematically tried to kill all people and organizations opposed to its imperialism. We no longer can just get by with the use of the word capitalism to describe the U.S., for it is an imperial power, sending money, missionaries and the army throughout the world to protect this government and the few rich whites who control it. General Motors and all the major auto industries are operating in South Africa, yet the white-dominated leadership of the United Auto Workers sees no relationship to the exploitation of black people in South Africa and the exploitation of black people in the U.S. If they understand it, they certainly do not put it into practice which is the actual test. We as black people must be concerned with the total conditions of all black people in the world.

But while we talk of revolution which will be an armed confrontation and long years of sustained guerilla warfare inside this country, we must also talk of the type of world we want to live in. We must commit ourselves to a society where the total means of production are taken from the rich and placed into the hands of the state for the welfare of all the people. This is what we mean when we say total control. And we mean that black people who have suffered the most from exploitation and racism must move to protect their black interest by assuming leadership inside of the United States of everything that exists. The time has passed when we are second in command and the white boy stands on top. This is especially true of the Welfare Agencies in this country, but it is not enough to say that a black man is on top. He must be committed to building the new society, to taking the wealth away from the rich people such as General Motors, Ford, Chrysler, the DuPonts, the Rockefellers, the Mellons, and all the other rich white exploiters and racists who run this world.

Where do we begin? We have already started. We started the moment we were brought to this country. In fact, we started on the shores of Africa, for we have always resisted attempts to make us slaves and now we must resist the attempts to make us capitalists. It is the financial interest of the U.S. to make us capitalists, for this will be the same line as that of integration into the mainstream of American life. Therefore, brothers and sisters, there is no need to fall into the trap that we have to get an ideology. We *HAVE* an ideology. Our fight is against racism, capitalism and imperialism and we are dedicated to building a socialist society inside the United States where the total means of production and distribution are in the hands of the State and that must be led by black people, by revolutionary blacks who are concerned about the total humanity of this world. And, therefore, we obviously are different from some of those who seek a black nation in the United States, for there is no way for that nation to be viable if in fact the United States remains in the hands of white racists. Then too, let us deal with some arguments that we should share power with whites. We say that there must be a revolutionary black Vanguard and that white people in this country must be willing to accept black leadership, for that is the only protection that black people have to protect ourselves from racism rising again in this country.

Racism in the U.S. is so pervasive in the mentality of whites that only an armed, well-disciplined, black-controlled government can insure the stamping out of racism in this country. And that is why we plead with black people not to be talking about a few crumbs, a few thousand dollars for this cooperative, or a thousand dollars which splits black people into fighting over the dollar. That is the intention of the government. We say . . . think in terms of total control of the U.S. Prepare ourselves to seize state power. Do not hedge, for time is short and all around the world, the forces of liberation are directing their attacks against the U.S. It is a powerful country, but that power is not greater than that of black people. We work the chief industries in this country and we could cripple the economy while the brothers fought guerilla warfare in the streets. This will take some long-range planning, but whether it happens in a thousand years is of no consequence. It cannot happen unless we start. How then is all of this related to this conference?

First of all, this conference is called by a set of religious people, Christians, who have been involved in the exploitation and rape of black people since the country was founded. The missionary goes hand in hand with the power of the states. We must begin seizing power wherever we are and we must say to the planners of this conference that you are no longer in charge. We the people who have assembled here thank you for getting us here, but we are going to assume power over the conference and determine from this moment on the direction in which we want it to go. We are not saying that the conference was planned badly. The staff of the conference have worked hard and have done a magnificent job in bringing all of us together and we must include them in the new membership which must surface from this point on. The conference is now the property of the people who are assembled here. This we proclaim as fact and not rhetoric and there are demands that we are going to make and we insist that the planners of this conference help us implement them.

We maintain we have the revolutionary right to do this. We have the same rights, if you will, as the Christians had in going into Africa and raping our Motherland and bringing us away from our continent of peace and into this hostile and alien environment where we have been living in perpetual warfare since 1619.

Our seizure of power at this conference is based on a program and our program is contained in the following *Manifesto:*

TO THE WHITE CHRISTIAN CHURCHES AND THE JEWISH SYNAGOGUES
IN THE UNITED STATES OF AMERICA AND ALL OTHER RACIST INSTITUTIONS

Black Manifesto

We the black people assembled in Detroit, Michigan, for the National Black Economic Development Conference are fully aware that we have been forced to come together because racist white America has exploited our resources, our minds, our bodies, our labor. For centuries we have been forced to live as colonized people inside the United States, victimized by the most vicious, racist system in the world. We have helped to build the most industrial country in the world.

We are therefore demanding of the white Christian churches and Jewish synagogues which are part and parcel of the system of capitalism, that they begin to pay reparations to black people in this country. We are demanding $500,000,000 from the Christian white churches and the Jewish synagogues. This total comes to 15 dollars per nigger. This is a low estimate for we maintain there are probably more than 30,000,000 black people in this country. $15 a nigger is not a large sum of money and we know that the churches and synagogues have a tremendous wealth and its membership, white America, has profited from and still exploits black people. We are also not unaware that the exploitation of colored peoples around the world is aided and abetted by the white Christian churches and synagogues. This demand for $500,000,000 is not an idle resolution or empty words. Fifteen dollars for every black brother and sister in the United States is only a beginning of the reparations due us as people who have been exploited and degraded, brutalized, killed and persecuted. Underneath all of this exploitation, the racism of this country has produced a psychological effect upon us that we are beginning to shake off. We are no longer afraid to demand our full rights as a people in this decadent society.

We are demanding $500,000,000 to be spent in the following way:

1. We call for the establishment of a Southern Land Bank to help our brothers and sisters who have to leave their land because of racist pressure for people who want to establish cooperative farms, but who have no funds. We have seen too many farmers evicted from their homes because they have dared to defy the white racism of this country. We need money for land. We must fight for massive sums of money for this Southern Land Bank. We call for $200,000,000 to implement this program.

2. We call for the establishment of four major publishing and printing industries in the United States to be funded with ten million dollars each. These publishing houses are to be located in Detroit, Atlanta, Los Angeles, and New York. They will help to generate capital for further cooperative investments in the black community, provide jobs and an alternative to the white-dominated and controlled printing field.

3. We call for the establishment of four of the most advanced scientific and futuristic audio-visual networks to be located in Detroit, Chicago, Cleveland and Washington, D.C. These TV networks will provide an alternative to the racist propaganda that fills the current television networks. Each of these TV networks will be funded by ten million dollars each.

4. We call for a research skills center which will provide research on the problems of black people. This center must be funded with no less than 30 million dollars.

5. We call for the establishment of a training center for the teaching of skills in community organization, photography, movie making, television making and repair, radio building and repair and all other skills needed in communication. This training center shall be funded with no less than ten million dollars.

6. We recognize the role of the National Welfare Rights Organization and we intend to work with them. We call for ten million dollars to assist in the organization of welfare recipients. We want to organize the welfare workers in this country so that they may demand more money from the government and better administration of the welfare system of this country.

7. We call for $20,000,000 to establish a National Black Labor Strike and Defense Fund. This is necessary for the protection of black workers and their families who are fighting racist working conditions in this country.

*8. We call for the establishment of the International Black Appeal (IBA). This International Black Appeal will be funded with no less than $20,000,000. The IBA is charged with producing more capital for the establishment of cooperative businesses in the United States and in Africa, our Motherland. The International Black Appeal is one of the most important demands that we are making for we know that it can generate and raise funds throughout the United States and help our African brothers. The IBA is charged with three functions and shall be headed by James Forman:

(a) Raising money for the program of the National Black Economic Development Conference.

(b) The development of cooperatives in African countries and support of African Liberation movements.

(c) Establishment of a Black Anti-Defamation League which will protect our African image.

9. We call for the establishment of a Black University to be funded with $130,000,000 to be located in the South. Negotiations are presently under way with a Southern University.

10. We demand that IFCO allocate all unused funds in the planning budget to implement the demands of this conference.

In order to win our demands we are aware that we will have to have massive support, therefore:

(1) We call upon all black people throughout the United States to consider themselves as members of the National Black Economic Development Conference and to act in unity to help force the racist white Christian churches and Jewish synagogues to implement these demands.

(2) We call upon all the concerned black people across the country to contact black workers, black women, black students and the black unemployed, community groups, welfare organizations, teacher organizations, church leaders and organizations, explaining how these demands are vital to the black community of the U.S. Pressure by whatever means necessary should be applied to the white power structure of the racist white Christian churches and Jewish synagogues. All black people should act boldly in confronting our white oppressors and demanding this modest reparation of 15 dollars per black man.

(3) Delegates and members of the National Black Economic

---

* (Revised and approved by Steering Committee.)

Development Conference are urged to call press conferences in the cities and to attempt to get as many black organizations as possible to support the demands of the conference. The quick use of the press in the local areas will heighten the tension and these demands must be attempted to be won in a short period of time, although we are prepared for protracted and long-range struggle.

(4) We call for the total disruption of selected church-sponsored agencies operating anywhere in the U.S. and the world. Black workers, black women, black students and the black unemployed are encouraged to seize the offices, telephones, and printing apparatus of all church-sponsored agencies and to hold these in trusteeship until our demands are met.

(5) We call upon all delegates and members of the National Black Economic Development Conference to stage sit-in demonstrations at selected black and white churches. This is not to be interpreted as a continuation of the sit-in movement of the early sixties but we know that active confrontation inside white churches is possible and will strengthen the possibility of meeting our demands. Such confrontation can take the form of reading the Black Manifesto instead of a sermon or passing it out to church members. The principle of self-defense should be applied if attacked.

(6) On May 4, 1969, or a date thereafter, depending upon local conditions, we call upon black people to commence the disruption of the racist churches and synagogues throughout the United States.

(7) We call upon IFCO to serve as a central staff to coordinate the mandate of the conference and to reproduce and distribute en masse literature, leaflets, news items, press releases and other material.

(8) We call upon all delegates to find within the white community those forces which will work under the leadership of blacks to implement these demands by whatever means necessary. By takings such actions, white Americans will demonstrate concretely that they are willing to fight the white skin privilege and the white supremacy and racism which has forced us as black people to make these demands.

(9) We call upon all white Christians and Jews to practice patience, tolerance, understanding and nonviolence as they have encouraged, advised and demanded that we as black people should do throughout our entire enforced slavery in the United States. The true test of their faith and belief in the Cross and the words of the prophets will certainly be put to a test as we seek legitimate and extremely modest reparations for our role in developing the industrial base of the Western world through our slave labor. But we are no longer slaves, we are men and women, proud of our African heritage, determined to have our dignity.

(10) We are so proud of our African heritage and realize concretely that our struggle is not only to make revolution in the United States, but to protect our brothers and sisters in Africa and to help them rid themselves of racism, capitalism, and imperialism by whatever means necessary, including armed struggle. We are and must be willing to fight the defamation of our African image wherever it rears its ugly head. We are therefore charging the Steering Committee to create a Black Anti-Defamation League to be funded by money raised from the International Black Appeal.

(11) We fully recognize that revolution in the United States and Africa, our Motherland, is more than a one-dimensional operation. It will require the total integration of the political, economic, and military components and therefore, we call upon all our brothers and sisters who have acquired training and expertise in the fieldings of engineering, electronics, research, community organization, physics, biology, chemistry, mathematics, medicine, military science and warfare to assist the National Black Economic Development Conference in the implementation of its program.

(12) To implement these demands we must have a fearless leadership. We must have a leadership which is willing to battle the church establishment to implement these demands. To win our demands we will have to declare war on the white Christian churches and synagogues and this means we may have to fight the total government structure of this country. Let no one here think that these demands will be met by our mere stating them. For the sake of the churches and synagogues, we hope that they have the wisdom to understand that these demands are modest and reasonable. But if the white Christians and Jews are not willing to meet our demands through peace and good will, then we declare war and we are prepared to fight by whatever means necessary. We are, therefore, proposing the election of the following Steering Committee:

Lucious Walker	Mark Comfort
Renny Freeman	Earl Allen
Luke Tripp	Robert Browne
Howard Fuller	Vincent Harding
James Forman	Mike Hamlin
John Watson	Len Holt
Dan Aldridge	Peter Bernard
John Williams	Michael Wright
Ken Cockrel	Muhammed Kenyatta
Chuck Wooten	Mel Jackson
Fannie Lou Hamer	Howard Moore
Julian Bond	Harold Holmes

Brothers and sisters, we no longer are shuffling our feet and scratching our heads. We are tall, black and proud.

And we say to the white Christian churches and Jewish synagogues, to the government of this country and to all the white racist imperialists who compose it, there is only one thing left that you can do to further degrade black people and that is to kill us. But we have been dying too long for this country. We have died in every war. We are dying in Vietnam today fighting the wrong enemy.

The new black man wants to live and to live means that we must not become static or merely believe in self-defense. We must boldly go out and attack the white Western world at its power centers. The white Christian churches are another form of government in this country and they are used by the government of this country to exploit the people of Latin America, Asia and Africa, but the day is soon coming to an end. Therefore, brothers and sisters, the demands we make upon the white Christian churches and the Jewish synagogues are small demands. They represent 15 dollars per black person in these United States. We can legitimately demand this from the church power structure. We must demand more from the United States Government.

But to win our demands from the church which is linked up with the United States Government, we must not forget that it will ultimately be by force and power that we will win.

We are not threatening the churches. We are saying that we know the churches came with the military might of the colonizers and have been sustained by the military might of the colonizers. Hence, if the churches in colonial territories were established by military might, we know deep within our hearts that we must be prepared to use force to get our demands. We are not saying that this is the road we want to take. It is not, but let us be very clear that we are not opposed to force and we are not opposed to violence. We were captured in Africa by violence. We were kept in bondage and political servitude and forced to work as slaves by the military machinery and the Christian church working hand in hand.

We recognize that in issuing this Manifesto we must prepare for a long-range educational campaign in all communities of this country, but we know that the Christian churches have contributed to our oppression in white America. We do not intend to abuse our black brothers and sisters in black churches who have uncritically accepted Christianity. We want them to understand how the racist white Christian church with its hypocritical declarations and doctrines of brotherhood has abused our trust and faith. An attack on the religious beliefs of black people is not our major objective, even though we know that we were not Christians when we were brought to this country, but that Christianity was used to help enslave us. Our objective in issuing this Manifesto is to force the racist white Christian church to begin the payment of reparations which are due to all black people, not only by the church but also by private business and the U.S. government. We see this focus on the Christian church as an effort around which all black people can unite.

Our demands are negotiable, but they cannot be minimized, they can only be increased and the church is asked to come up with larger sums of money than we are asking. Our slogans are:

ALL ROADS MUST LEAD TO REVOLUTION

UNITE WITH WHOMEVER YOU CAN UNITE

NEUTRALIZE WHEREVER POSSIBLE

FIGHT OUR ENEMIES RELENTLESSLY

VICTORY TO THE PEOPLE

LIFE AND GOOD HEALTH TO MANKIND

RESISTANCE TO DOMINATION BY THE WHITE CHRISTIAN CHURCHES
  AND THE JEWISH SYNAGOGUES

REVOLUTIONARY BLACK POWER

WE SHALL WIN WITHOUT A DOUBT

14 SUGGESTIONS FOR FURTHER READING

A book that gives a feeling for the anger that has swept over the black community is *Black Rage** (Basic Books, 1968), written by two black psychiatrists, William H. Grier and Price Cobbs. Julius Lester has described the background of the burst of emphasis on black power in *Look Out Whitey! Black Power Gon' Get Your Mama!** (Dial, 1968). Stokely Carmichael and Charles V. Hamilton, in *Black Power: The Politics of Liberation in America** (Random House, 1967), explore the various meanings of the slogan "Black Power." Floyd Barbour has edited a collection of pertinent historical and contemporary documents in *The Black Power Revolt** (Porter Sargent, 1968). Political possibilities of the past and the present are explored in Chuck Stone, *Black Political Power in America* (Bobbs-Merrill, 1968).

Black leaders of the times present their ideas in several books: H. Rap Brown, in *Die Nigger Die!* (Dial, 1969); Whitney Young, Jr., in *Beyond Racism: Building an Open Society* (McGraw-Hill, 1969); Eldridge Cleaver, in *Soul on Ice** (McGraw-Hill, 1968) and *Post-Prison Writings and Speeches** (Random House, 1969); and Albert B. Cleage, Jr., in *The Black Messiah* (Sheed and Ward, 1968).

An important reflection of black militant thought is the work of current black literary artists. See, for example, LeRoi Jones and Larry Neal (ed.), *Black Fire: An Anthology of Afro-American Writing* (Morrow, 1968); William Couch, Jr. (ed.), *New Black Playwrights: An Anthology* (Louisiana State University Press, 1968); and the novels of such writers as John A. Williams and William Melvin Kelley.

The possibility of building a politically revolutionary black movement is considered regularly in the columns of the newspapers *The Guardian* and *The Black Panther*. This topic also dominates the collected essays of Julius Lester, published under the title *Revolutionary Notes* (Richard Baron, 1969).

GENERAL READING SUGGESTIONS

There are several available surveys of black American history. The best of these are John Hope Franklin, *From Slavery to Freedom: A History of American Negroes** (Knopf, 1947); E. Franklin Frazier, *The Negro in the United States* (Macmillan, 1949); August Meier and Elliott P. Rudwick, *From Plantation to Ghetto: An Interpretive History of American Negroes** (Hill and Wang, 1966); Benjamin Quarles, *The Negro in the Making of America** (Macmillan, 1964); Lerone Bennett, Jr., *Before the Mayflower: A History of the Negro in America, 1619–1964** (Johnson, 1962); and Carter G. Woodson and Charles H. Wesley, *The Negro in Our History* (Associated, 1922). Also useful as surveys are some recent collections of articles and excerpts from scholarly works: Melvin Drimmer (ed.), *Black History: A Reappraisal* (Doubleday, 1968); Dwight Hoover (ed.), *Understanding Negro History** (Quadrangle, 1968); and the excellent August Meier and Elliott P. Rudwick (eds.), *The Making of Black America: Essays in Negro Life and History**, 2 vols. (Atheneum, 1969).

Of the many documentary histories now available, Herbert Aptheker (ed.), *A Documentary History of the Negro People in the United States**, 2 vols. (Citadel, 1951), is by far the best for the period before 1910, which is as far as it goes. A third volume, which will bring the collection up to the present, is said to be near completion. Other collections of documents that may prove useful are Joanne Grant (ed.), *Black Protest** (Fawcett, 1968), particularly strong on the period of the student nonviolent protest movements; William L. Katz (ed.), *Eyewitness: The Negro in American History** (Pitman, 1967); Albert Blaustein and Robert Zangrando (eds.), *Civil Rights and the American Negro** (Washington Square Press, 1968), strong on legal documents; Leslie H. Fishel, Jr., and Benjamin Quarles (eds.), *The Negro American: A Documentary History** (Scott, Foresman, 1967); and Gilbert Osofsky (ed.), *The Burden of Race** (Harper and Row, 1967).

General works on specific aspects of black history that the student might want to consult are E. Franklin Frazier, *The Negro Family in the United States** (University of Chicago Press, 1939) and *The Negro Church in America** (Schocken, 1963), and Richard Bardolph, *The Negro Vanguard** (Rinehart, 1959), a study of black leaders of historical significance. A work intended for general reference is John A. Davis (ed.), *The American Negro Reference Book* (Prentice-Hall, 1966).

For an introduction to black writing, see the following: James A. Emanual and Theodore L. Gross (eds.), *Dark Symphony: Negro Literature in America** (Free Press, 1968); Abraham Chapman (ed.), *Black Voices: An Anthology of Afro-American Literature** (New American Library, 1968); John Henrik Clarke (ed.), *American Negro Short Stories** (Hill and Wang, 1966); Arna Bontemps (ed.), *American Negro Poetry** (Hill and Wang, 1963); Langston Hughes and Arna Bontemps (eds.), *The Poetry of the Negro, 1746–1949: An Anthology* (Doubleday, 1949); and Addison Gayle, Jr., *Black Expression** (Weybright and Talley, 1969).

Periodicals dealing with matters of interest in black history include *The Journal of Negro History*, *Phylon: Atlanta University Review of Race and Culture*, *Freedomways*, *Negro Digest*, *The Crisis*, and *Journal of Negro Education*.

A 9
B 0
C 1
D 2
E 3
F 4
G 5
H 6
I 7
J 8